Government Alive!®
Power, Politics, and You

NATIONAL CONSTITUTION CENTER

TCi™

Chief Executive Officer
Bert Bower

Chief Operating Officer
Amy Larson

Director of Product Development
Maria Favata

Director of Outreach
Natasha Martin

Strategic Product Manager
Nathan Wellborne

Project Manager
Marsha Ifurung

Production Manager
Jodi Forrest

Editorial Associates
Mikaila Garfinkel
Ginger Wu

Teachers' Curriculum Institute
P.O. Box 1327
Rancho Cordova, CA 95741

Customer Service: 800-497-6138
www.teachtci.com

ISBN 978-1-934534-23-6
4 5 6 7 8 9 10 -WC- 20 19 18

Manufactured by Webcrafters, Inc., Madison, WI
United States of America, July, 2018, Job # 135378

Program Director
Bert Bower

Program Author

Diane Hart is a nationally recognized author and assessment consultant. She has written textbooks on U.S. history, world history, geography, American government, and economics, most of which are still used in elementary, middle, and high schools across the country. She also authored the first civics text for Palau, a newly emerging nation in the South Pacific. Ms. Hart has consulted with a wide range of clients on curriculum and instructional design issues. She had also worked with the departments of education in several states on the development of standards-based social studies assessments.

Her most recent project has been the development of cross-cultural competency training programs to prepare military service personnel to work effectively with people from cultures very different from their own. She is also an active member of the National Council for the Social Studies, serving on the board of directors and contributing to Social Education. As a writer, Ms. Hart is passionate about engaging all students in the compelling drama of human development across time and space. As an educator, she is equally passionate about preparing young people to deal successfully with life in an increasingly complex world.

Senior Writer
Brent Goff

Contributing Writers
Melissa Biegert
David Fasulo
Linda Scher

Creative Development Manager
Kelly Shafsky

Curriculum Developers
Nicole Boylan
Julie Cremin
Erin Fry
Amy George
Steve Seely

Program Consultant
Sharon Pope
Houston, Texas

Teacher and Content Consultants
Karl Grubaugh
Granite Bay High School
Granite Bay, California

Cathy Hix
Swanson Middle School
Arlington, Virginia

Deidre Jackson
Taylor High School
Houston, Texas

Eli Lesser
National Constitution Center
Constitution High School
Philadelphia, Pennsylvania

Greg Nakata
Glendora High School
Glendora, California

Ron Pike
Lincoln High School
San Jose, California

Ken Shears
Ponderosa High School
Shingle Springs, California

Steve Watts
Davidson High School
Hilliard, Ohio

Nathan Wellborne
Taylor High School
Houston, Texas

Scholars
Dr. Paul Barresi
Southern New Hampshire University

Dr. Dave Campbell
Notre Dame University, Indiana

Dr. Jim Gimpel
University of Maryland

Dr. George Gordon
Illinois State University
Illinois Wesleyan University

Dr. Darla Mallein
Emporia State University, Kansas

Dr. Patrice McMahon
University of Nebraska-Lincoln

Dr. Richard Niemi
University of Rochester, New York

Dr. Tari Renner
Illinois Wesleyan University

Dr. Michael Smith
Emporia State University, Kansas

Dr. Beth Theiss-Morse
University of Nebraska-Lincoln

Music Consultant
Melanie Pinkert
Music Faculty
Montgomery College, Maryland

Cartographer
Mapping Specialists
Madison, Wisconsin

Internet Consultant
Clinton Couse
Cedar Valley Community School
Edmonds School District
Edmonds, Washington

Researcher
Carla Valetich
Pittsboro, North Carolina

NATIONAL CONSTITUTION CENTER

525 Arch Street Independence Mall
Philadelphia | PA 19106 | T 215 409 6600 | F 215 409 6650
www.constitutioncenter.org

Dear Student,

We are pleased to introduce Government Alive! Power, Politics, and You. This textbook is the result of a wonderful collaboration between TCI and the National Constitution Center, and every page reflects our shared mission: to teach you how American government works and inspire you to participate in the political process as an active citizen. Since 1787, when the Framers signed the U.S. Constitution, our government has been sustained by the day-to-day actions of "We the People." This textbook provides the tools you need to continue the Constitution's legacy of civic engagement and freedom.

The National Constitution Center is an interactive museum, a national town hall, and a civic education headquarters. Our innovative, dynamic resources about the Constitution, American history, and democracy are available to you 24 hours a day, 7 days a week on our website, constitutioncenter.org. In addition, you can access an engaging and informative series on the Constitution and how it affects you and your life called Constitution Hall Pass at constitutioncenter.org/hallpass. I encourage you to use these valuable online resources to further examine issues addressed in the Government Alive! program.

We also hope you take the opportunity to visit our state-of-the-art museum in Philadelphia, just steps from where the Constitution was signed. At the National Constitution Center, you can explore hundreds of hands-on exhibits, films, and rare artifacts. You can watch the powerful, 360-degree theatrical performance Freedom Rising, called "the best 17-minute civics lesson in the country" by retired Supreme Court Justice Sandra Day O'Connor. You can sign the Constitution alongside 42 bronze statues of the Founding Fathers. The Center also houses the Annenberg Center for Education and Outreach, the national hub for constitutional education, which offers cutting-edge learning programs and materials to enhance your experience.

We trust that Government Alive! Power, Politics, and You will equip you with the knowledge and skills essential to becoming an active, informed citizen. Your participation in our democracy helps ensure a bright future for our country and citizenry.

Sincerely,

Vince Stango

Chief Operating Officer

Power, Authority, and Government

Foundations of American Government

Political Participation and Behavior

The Legislative Branch

The Executive Branch

The Judicial Branch

The United States and the World

U.S. Supreme Court Cases

U.S. Supreme Court Cases: You Make the Call

Find additional cases online in your Student Subscription. You will learn the key facts of each case and the question before the Supreme Court. Then, you "make the call" on how the court should decide the case and why before reading the actual Supreme Court decision.

Graphs, Diagrams, and Tables

Graphs, Diagrams, and Tables (continued)

Graphs, Diagrams, and Tables (continued)

Political Cartoons

Maps

Chapter 1

The Nature of Power, Politics, and Government

Why should you care about power, politics, and government?

◼ 1.1 Introduction

The United States of America was born in an explosion of rebellion against **authority**. The Declaration of Independence, defending that rebellion, spit forth a list of all the British monarch's crimes against the American colonies. Clearly, many colonists had lost faith in the British **government**—if not in government in general. In his widely read pamphlet *Common Sense*, the colonial firebrand Thomas Paine expressed a viewpoint held by many colonial Americans:

> *Society in every state [condition] is a blessing, but Government, even in its best state, is but a necessary evil; in its worst state, an intolerable one.*
> —Thomas Paine, *Common Sense*, 1776

This general mistrust of government did not end with the American victory in the Revolutionary War. It continues to this day. In 2011, more than a thousand Americans were asked this question in an opinion poll sponsored by two news organizations, CNN and ORC International: *How much of the time do you think you can trust the government in Washington to do what is right: just about always, most of the time, or only some of the time?*

Only 2 percent, or 1 person in 50, answered, "just about always." 13 percent responded, "most of the

The U.S. Capitol Building, located in Washington D.C.

By permission of John L. Hart F. L. P. and Creators Syndicate, Inc.

Americans may distrust government, but as this cartoon suggests, it is something people can't live without. Most groups of people, large and small, develop some form of government to help order their lives. The term government comes from a Greek word that means "to steer" or "to control."

time." About three fourths answered, "only some of the time." And a disgruntled 8 percent said, "never."

This distrust of government also shows up in popular movies and television dramas. Corrupt or power-hungry politicians are often the villains in action movies. The plot lines of some television shows center on conspiracies hatched by public officials at the highest levels of government. Conspiracy theories about government involvement in the assassinations of President John F. Kennedy and civil rights leader Martin Luther King Jr. continue to generate books and magazine articles even today.

Is this attitude that politicians and government in general cannot be trusted justified? Is government at its best, in the words of Thomas Paine, "a necessary evil"? Or is it necessary at all? To answer these questions, we must first figure out what government is and what it does. One way to begin is to examine the central concern of all governments: **power**.

■ 1.2 The Power to Rule

The power to rule can be gained—or lost—in many ways. In the 1100s B.C.E., the Shang dynasty ruled north central China. However, tough military campaigns against other nearby kingdoms eventually exhausted the Shang's fighting forces. In time, the neighboring Zhou, under a leader named Wu, took advantage of this weakness. From their lands to the west, the Zhou attacked and quickly overwhelmed the Shang defenses. The Shang ruler reportedly committed suicide, and Wu became his people's new ruler.

The history of China, like that of many countries, is filled with tales of the violent overthrow of one government after another. The history of the United States, on the other hand, reveals mostly peaceful transfers of power. Whether one looks at an ancient Chinese ruler or a modern American president, what they have in common is the power to rule. How they use that power, however, can vary greatly.

What Is Power, and How Is It Exercised?

Power is a difficult concept to define. People seem to know it when they see it, but they have a hard time pinning down exactly what it is. The sociologist Max Weber defined power as "the possibility of imposing one's will upon the behavior of other persons." In his book *Three Faces of Power*, economist Kenneth E. Boulding refers to power as "our capacity to get other people to do things that contribute to what we want."

That's about as simple as the concept gets. When scholars dig deeper into the sources, uses, and effects of power, the subject seems to expand in many different directions. There are five sources of power, ranging from persuasion to **coercion,** or the use of force. Governments throughout the ages have relied on each of these types of powers, often in combination.

Whatever its source, the power to rule can be used for positive or negative ends, or purposes. Through the centuries, some rulers have used their power to build cities, promote the arts, or feed the poor. Others have abused their power by looting their subjects' wealth, turning captives into slaves, and even committing mass murder.

In *Common Sense,* Thomas Paine characterized British rule of the colonies as "a long and violent abuse of power." In his view, "a thirst for absolute power is the natural disease of monarchy." A century later, British historian Lord Acton echoed Paine's observations on the **abuse of power** when he wrote, "Power tends to corrupt, and absolute power corrupts absolutely."

How Does Power Relate to Authority?

People with the right to use power are said to have authority. But how do they get that authority? Sometimes it comes through tradition. For example, parents have authority over their children. Religious leaders have authority over their congregations.

In the field of government, political scientists speak of **formal authority,** or power that has been defined in some legal or other official way. People with formal authority have the legal right to use power. The source of their authority might be a constitution, a contract, or another legal document. School principals have formal authority, as do police officers and presidents.

What Gives a Ruler Legitimacy?

Leaders whose power and authority are accepted as valid by the people they govern are said to have **legitimacy**. Legitimacy rises and falls depending on the willingness of those being led to follow those doing the leading. A military leader can seize power by force,

Five Sources of Power

This diagram shows five sources of power exercised by people in a variety of roles. Political leaders often combine these sources of power to get citizens to act in a certain way. For example, a president might speak to the nation (combining formal authority and persuasion) about offering tax breaks (a reward) to people who buy fuel-efficient cars.

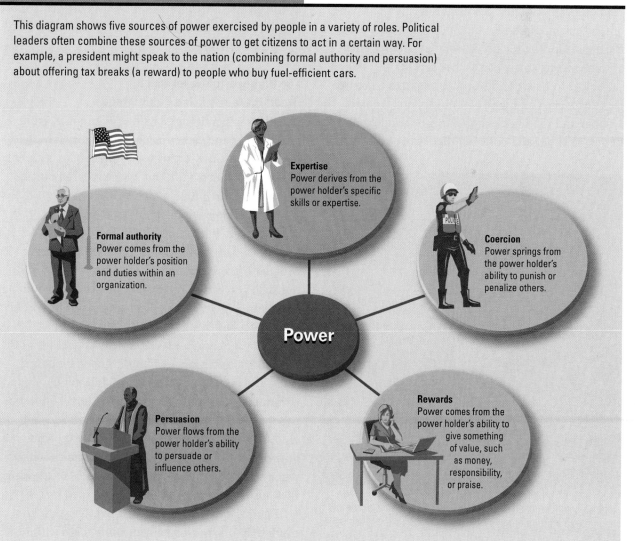

Expertise
Power derives from the power holder's specific skills or expertise.

Formal authority
Power comes from the power holder's position and duties within an organization.

Coercion
Power springs from the power holder's ability to punish or penalize others.

Power

Persuasion
Power flows from the power holder's ability to persuade or influence others.

Rewards
Power comes from the power holder's ability to give something of value, such as money, responsibility, or praise.

as in the example of the Zhou leader, Wu. But to be considered a legitimate ruler, Wu had to convince the people he conquered of his right to govern them.

To enhance Wu's standing among the Shang, the Zhou introduced the **mandate of heaven**—a doctrine of legitimacy that would endure for more than 2,000 years. According to this doctrine, the Chinese ruler was the "son of heaven" and thus had authority over "all under heaven." The ruler retained this right only so long as he ruled his subjects in a moral manner. If he failed to rule well, the mandate of heaven would pass to someone else. The Shang leader, they argued, had lost the mandate of heaven to Wu, who had been sent by heaven to unseat him.

In the 1500s, powerful European monarchs proclaimed a similar doctrine of legitimacy, known as the **divine right of kings**. This doctrine, like the mandate of heaven, held that monarchs represented God on Earth. Because their right to rule was divine, or God-given, monarchs did not have to answer to the people for their actions. God had granted them absolute power to govern as they saw fit.

Before long, some Europeans began to challenge this doctrine. The English philosophers Thomas Hobbes and John Locke popularized what became known as the **social-contract theory** of government.

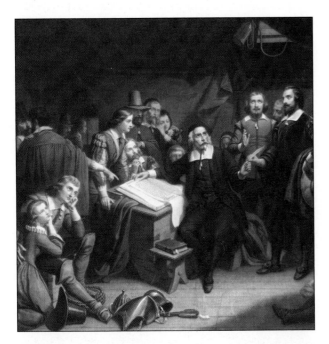

The Mayflower Compact is an example of how a central government can stabilize a group of people. In addition to quelling revolts, the Mayflower Compact also became the foundation of the colonists' government once they landed at Plymouth.

According to this theory, the legitimacy of a government stems from an unwritten contract between the ruler and the ruled. Under the terms of this contract, the people agree to obey a ruler in exchange for the ruler's promise to protect their rights. A ruler who breaks this contract by abusing power loses legitimacy and should be removed from power.

■ 1.3 The Foundations of Government

In 1620, a group of English colonists arrived off the shore of Plymouth, Massachusetts. They hoped to settle there as a community. However, before their ship landed, some colonists threatened to split off from the others. To quell this revolt, the group's leaders demanded that all adult males sign a document promising to obey the rules and laws enacted by the group. This agreement, the Mayflower Compact, organized the signers into a "civil body politic," or a government.

The Purposes of Government: Order, Protection, and Public Goods

Like the signers of the Mayflower Compact, groups of all shapes and sizes throughout history have felt the need for some sort of government. Government serves many purposes. Among the most important are maintaining public order, protecting life and property, and providing **public goods**.

Living in violent times, both Hobbes and Locke emphasized the need for government to preserve order and protect people's lives and property. Without such protection, wrote Hobbes, people would be condemned to live in "continual fear and danger of violent death."

Today, governments are equally concerned with providing a wide range of public goods to their citizens. You benefit directly from public goods. Your community's schools, the roads you travel on to get to school, and the fire and police protection you enjoy are all public goods that you receive from your government. You also benefit from public goods when you visit a national park or feel safer knowing that our nation is protected by the armed forces.

Public goods have two key characteristics. First, more than one person can consume them without reducing the amount available to others. Consider

Public goods, such as Millennium Park in Chicago, Illinois, belong to all citizens. Government creates public goods, and citizens pay for them with their tax dollars. Unlike private goods, public goods are available to everyone. Once they are established, even people who pay no taxes are free to use them.

streetlamps. If you walk under a streetlamp, you do not reduce the ability of others to use its light. Second, once a public good is made available, all people have the right to use it. After being installed, a streetlamp shines its light on everyone.

Neither of these characteristics is true of private goods. Consider an apple that you buy at a grocery store. Once you take a bite of the apple, you have reduced the amount available to others. And since you own the apple, nobody else has a right to consume it. Your apple is a private good.

The Building Blocks of Government: Coercion and Revenue Collection

Governments throughout history have had two key powers that are essential for providing protection and public goods. These two building blocks of government are (1) a means of coercion and (2) a means of collecting revenue.

Coercion refers to the various ways in which government can use its power to force citizens to behave in certain ways. The most obvious means of coercion include the police, the courts, and the prison system. Governments use the threat of arrest and punishment to maintain public order and keep people secure in their homes and in public spaces.

Other means of coercion relate to involuntary services required of citizens. One example is conscription, or a military draft, in which government compels young men and women to serve in the armed forces. Another involuntary service is jury duty, in which a panel of citizens decides an accused person's guilt or innocence.

The second building block of government is a means of collecting **revenue**. All governments need money to provide security and pay for public goods. They generally get that money from the people they govern or control.

The ways that governments collect revenue have varied historically. Ancient empires extracted **tribute,** or payments, from the smaller states they controlled. Such "gifts" of goods or money were a sign of submission from the smaller states. For much of its history, China received tribute from peoples on its borders. China also levied taxes on its citizens. Through taxation, the Qin dynasty acquired the resources it needed to build one of history's early public goods: the Great Wall.

Who Should Rule: The One, the Few, or the Many?

Governments take many forms. In the past, most governments, like that of China, were headed by a single, powerful ruler. In contrast, the ancient Greeks experimented with forms of government ranging from rule by the rich and powerful to rule by all male citizens.

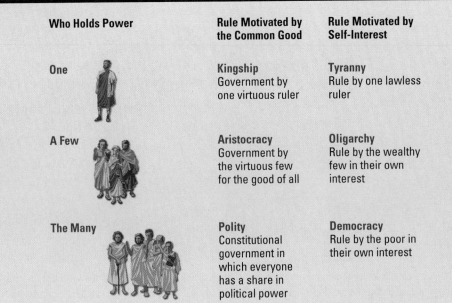

The ancient Greek philosopher Aristotle sought to determine the best form of government. He considered the number of people who might take part in governing and the moral character of those who held power. He concluded that power spread out over a large number of people lessened the chances of tyranny—whether by a single, selfish leader or a thoughtless mob.

Who Holds Power		Rule Motivated by the Common Good	Rule Motivated by Self-Interest
One		**Kingship** Government by one virtuous ruler	**Tyranny** Rule by one lawless ruler
A Few		**Aristocracy** Government by the virtuous few for the good of all	**Oligarchy** Rule by the wealthy few in their own interest
The Many		**Polity** Constitutional government in which everyone has a share in political power	**Democracy** Rule by the poor in their own interest

The ancient Greek philosopher Aristotle, who is revered as the father of political science, thought deeply about who should have the power to rule. Aristotle was motivated by an interest in ethics, or proper conduct. This led him to an examination of many possible forms of government.

Aristotle categorized governments along two lines. One was how many people are involved in governing—one powerful ruler, a few upper-class aristocrats, or the mass of common people. The second was their motivation in making decisions. Ideal rulers, he said, cared about the common good. Corrupt rulers, in contrast, cared only about advancing their own selfish interests.

As a philosopher, Aristotle liked to consider ideal forms. The ideal form of government, he reasoned, was a monarchy led by a single, virtuous ruler. But Aristotle also prided himself on being a realist. Rule by a single person, he knew from experience, could easily lead to the abuse of power. He admitted that

Political writers, although they have excellent ideas, are often unpractical. We should consider, not only what form of government is best, but also what is possible and what is easily attainable by all.

—Aristotle, *The Politics*, Book IV

In the real world, Aristotle wrote, rule by the well-intentioned many would suit most societies. He called this kind of government a **polity**. In a polity, he argued, the best-qualified citizens, whether rich or poor, would dominate government.

Two thousand years after Aristotle wrote about government, the founders of the United States faced some of the same questions he had explored. Although they ended up creating a different kind of government than imagined by Aristotle, his writings strongly influenced their thinking.

The Governments of Modern Nation-States

When political scientists study government today, they are usually concerned with the larger and complicated governments of **nation-states**. All nation-states share these four characteristics:

Territorial integrity. A nation-state occupies a specific geographic territory, with internationally recognized boundaries.

Stable population. A nation-state has people living permanently within its boundaries.

Code of laws. The people of a nation-state agree to live under a common legal system.

National **sovereignty**. A nation-state is independent and self-governing.

The nation-state is a fairly modern political phenomenon. It merges two concepts: the nation and the state. A nation is a group of people who share a common ethnic origin, culture, and language. A state is a geographical area controlled by a single government.

The governments of modern nation-states are quite varied. In some, power is concentrated in the hands of one or a very few powerful leaders. In others, like the United States, power comes from the people and is broadly distributed throughout the government.

■ 1.4 Politics and Political Activity

The idea that governments should provide public goods is not new. In the early American republic, federal and state governments supported the building of ports, roads, and canals to facilitate travel and commerce. These projects did not come together overnight. The idea for the Erie Canal, for example, was first proposed in 1724, when New York was still a colony. The first bill supporting the building of the canal reached the state legislature in 1787 but failed

Rule by the Many in the United States

In the United States, the people govern by participating in elections and politics. These graphs show the percentage of American adults who participated in political activities during the presidential election year of 2008. Can you see yourself doing all of these things or just a few?

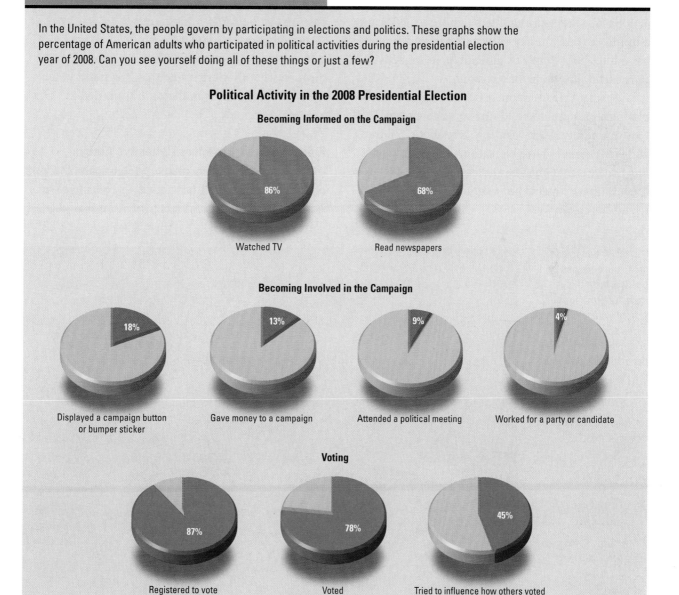

Political Activity in the 2008 Presidential Election

Becoming Informed on the Campaign

86% Watched TV

68% Read newspapers

Becoming Involved in the Campaign

18% Displayed a campaign button or bumper sticker

13% Gave money to a campaign

9% Attended a political meeting

4% Worked for a party or candidate

Voting

87% Registered to vote

78% Voted

45% Tried to influence how others voted

Source: *The ANES Guide to Public Opinion and Electoral Behavior*, American National Election Studies, www.electionstudies.org.

to win passage. Construction finally began in 1817, but only after extensive debate, planning, report writing, compromising, and arm-twisting—in short, **politics**.

The political process that results in projects such as the Erie Canal is extremely complex. Yet political scientist Harold Lasswell was able to boil it down to just a few words. He famously described politics as the process of determining "who gets what, when, how." People who participate in that process engage in many forms of political activity. But all political activity has a few common characteristics.

Political Activity Has a Purpose

Political activity can range from looking at a political cartoon to running for public office. Some political actions take little effort. Others require a significant amount of time, money, effort, and even courage. No matter how simple or difficult, political activity is purposeful. It is done for a reason.

Consider this situation. A city council is contemplating a proposal to build a new skateboard park in the community. Most residents care about children and want them to have recreational opportunities. For that reason alone, they at least follow the issue in the local newspaper. They might also discuss it with friends or co-workers.

Some citizens, however, are motivated to look more deeply into the proposal. One group, concerned that construction and insurance costs might cause their taxes to go up, speaks out against the proposal at city council meetings. Another group, believing that the skateboard park will make the town more attractive for young families, speaks up in support.

Prompted by their enthusiasm for the park proposal, a group of skaters and their parents become more actively involved. Some seek appointment to a study group that is reviewing the proposal. One parent even decides to run for a seat on the city council in the next election. For these citizens, the possible benefits of becoming politically active outweigh the costs in time, effort, and resources.

As this example suggests, political activity is intentional, not random. That is, people think through what they are trying to achieve and weigh the costs and benefits of the actions needed to achieve their goals.

Political Activity Involves Collective Action

Individuals can achieve many of their goals by acting on their own. But political activity is collective—it involves working with others to achieve shared goals.

Formal written rules guide the activities of political institutions, from Congress to your school's student council. Some scholars even argue that the rules *are* the institution. Without the structure these rules provide, they say, an institution could not function and might even cease to exist.

As the late American anthropologist Margaret Mead once wrote,

> *Never doubt that a small group of thoughtful, committed citizens can change the world. Indeed, it is the only thing that ever has.*
> —Margaret Mead

Even when people share a common goal, acting collectively can be challenging. Once again, consider the proposed skateboard park. Skateboarding enthusiasts from around the city come together to plan how best to make their case. They all want the park to be built, but they do not agree on where it should be located.

Conflicts within a small group like this one can often be resolved through face-to-face negotiation, or informal bargaining. In large groups, bargaining sessions may follow more formal rules. In either case, for collective action to work, the people involved need to be prepared to seek and accept compromise.

Institutions Shape Political Activity

The **institutions** we live with also influence political activity. Institutions are organizations or sets of rules that shape the behavior of groups. They have a social purpose and permanence in human affairs. The family is an ancient institution. Its purpose now, as long ago, is to provide for the physical and emotional well-being of its members. Schools, hospitals, and governments are other old and familiar institutions.

Institutions establish routines for dealing with recurring problems. For example, when students misbehave in class, schools have standard procedures for dealing with the problem. In this way, institutions tend to limit conflict while encouraging the kind of cooperation that can lead to the solution of a problem.

Institutions also establish the rules, both written and unwritten, that shape political activity. These rules tell us who has the authority to make decisions, how decisions get made, and how we can influence those decisions.

In the scenario involving a proposed skateboard park, the community's political institutions shape how residents participate in the decision-making process. Some residents share their views in meetings. Others send e-mails to the city council. A few join a study group looking at alternative sites. But once a decision is finally made, most people accept the result, believing that their voices have been heard in the process of determining "who gets what, when, how."

■ 1.5 Political Games People Play

Politics is serious business. Decisions made by governments can have a profound impact on people's health, wealth, and happiness. Yet politics is also a form of competition. Politicians and citizens who engage in political activity are all players in the "game of politics." Following are the goals and strategies of five political "games."

Horse Trading: Winning by Giving to Get

Horse trading is a classic American business. In the old days, traders brought their horses to a local market where interested buyers would examine them to determine their value. Horse traders were shrewd bargainers. Hearing the low bid, the trader might walk away in disgust only to suddenly turn on his heel and make a counteroffer—one much higher than the horse was worth. The buyer and seller would go back and forth until they reached a price they both agreed on.

Kentucky politician Henry Clay was a master player in the horse-trading game. He is shown here addressing the Senate in 1850 at a crisis point over the expansion of slavery. Clay, called the "Great Compromiser," worked out a win-win solution known as the Compromise of 1850. This compromise had something for both pro- and antislavery lawmakers to like.

Today, horse trading is another name for the kind of hard bargaining that goes on in politics. The key players are often politicians who want something that they cannot get without help from their political opponents. Often this "something" is a proposed law.

The objective of the horse-trading game is to achieve a "win-win situation," in which both players walk away satisfied. The basic strategy involves giving up something one's opponent wants in exchange for something of equal—or greater—value.

The famous Missouri Compromise was the result of horse trading in Congress. After much debate, the Northern states, which had abolished slavery, agreed to allow Missouri to enter the Union as a slave state. In exchange, the Southern states accepted a ban on slavery in much of Louisiana Territory and admission of Maine as a free state. This win-win compromise helped postpone the Civil War for several decades.

The horse-trading game is familiar to many children and parents. A teenager, for example, might negotiate to stay out an hour beyond normal curfew on a Saturday night in exchange for a pledge to help clean out the garage the next day. In this game, each side has given up something to get something else it wants.

Walkout: Winning by Refusing to Play

The walkout game is similar to horse trading in some ways. But instead of giving something to the opposition, players take something away—usually themselves. They walk out of the game and refuse to return until the opposition agrees to give them something they want.

The classic example of this strategy occurs in a pickup basketball or football game when the owner of the ball gets upset, perhaps about a disputed rule or a foul. The offended player picks up the ball and threatens to go home. This puts pressure on the other players to give in. They know that without the ball, the game cannot continue.

On a larger scale, the walkout game is commonly played by labor unions to back up demands for better pay and working conditions. If employers refuse those demands, union workers may choose to strike, or walk off their jobs. Without workers, businesses find it difficult to function. This puts pressure on the employer to come to terms with the union.

César Chávez successfully used walkout tactics in his struggle to improve the lives of California farmworkers. In 1962, Chávez, along with Dolores Huerta, founded the National Farm Workers

César Chávez played the walkout game with great effectiveness. His United Farm Workers strike against California grape growers quickly gained support from organized labor, religious groups, minorities, and students across the country. Chávez died in 1993, but his influence remains strong. In 1994, President Bill Clinton presented Chávez's widow with the Presidential Medal of Freedom, the nation's highest civilian award. Chávez, the president said, "faced formidable, often violent opposition with dignity and nonviolence. And he was victorious. César Chávez left our world better than he found it, and his legacy inspires us still."

Association, later to become the United Farm Workers. Their goal was to convince growers to treat their workers fairly, with dignity and respect.

When growers refused to bargain with the new union, Chávez organized a strike of California grape pickers. In addition to the strike, he encouraged all Americans to boycott table grapes as a show of support. The strike and boycott lasted five years and brought national attention to the struggle of farmworkers for decent pay and working conditions. It also led to the first major labor victory for farm-workers in the United States.

Power Struggle: Winning by Being Smarter and Stronger than the Opposition

Politics often involves power struggles between people with very different goals. When engaged in such a struggle, clever politicians try to win by outfoxing or overpowering their opponents.

The strategies needed to win the power struggle game were first described by a 16th-century political philosopher named Niccolò Machiavelli. Machiavelli was born in Florence, Italy, and rose to a high position in the city's government. In that role, he faced the question of how wealthy Florence could best defend itself against enemy attacks.

After leaving government, Machiavelli studied this question more deeply. He examined the behavior of leaders, good and bad. From this, he developed ideas about how best to win the power struggle game.

In his most famous book, *The Prince,* Machiavelli described strategies that a prince, or ruler, could use to acquire power, create a strong state, and keep it safe from attack. In it he urged rulers to take a hard look at the world as it is, not as it ought to be. Italy at that time was plagued by political corruption, merce-nary armies, and backstabbing politicians. Given this reality, a prince could not afford to look to Christian morality as his guide to action. As Machiavelli put it,

> *How we live is so far removed from how we ought to live, that he who abandons what is done for what ought to be done, will rather bring about his own ruin than his preservation.*
> —Niccolò Machiavelli, *The Prince,* 1532

To play the power struggle game, Machiavelli wrote, a ruler needed to be as smart as a fox and as strong as a lion. He explained in *The Prince* that

> *The lion cannot defend himself against snares and the fox cannot defend himself against wolves. Therefore, it is necessary to be a fox to discover the snares and a lion to terrify the wolves.*

As a player in this game, a prince had to be pre-pared to do whatever was necessary for the survival of his state. "In the actions of men, and especially of Princes," Machiavelli wrote, "the end justifies the means." He wrote that a prince must not hesitate to "destroy those who can and will injure him" and instill fear in others, even if this costs him the love of the people. "If we must choose between them," he advised, "it is far safer to be feared than loved."

So great was Machiavelli's influence on the study of politics that *The Prince* is still widely read today. Moreover, we often describe politicians who use cunning tricks and amoral tactics in the power struggle game as **Machiavellian**.

Niccolò Machiavelli's *The Prince* was an early how-to book for rulers engaged in power struggles with other states. While he is often credited with the phrase "the ends justify the means," many students of his work don't believe he was literally advocating an "anything goes as long as it is for a good purpose" philosophy. The end he had in mind was "maintaining the state." A prince who did this, he wrote, "will always be judged honourable and praised by every one."

Here, President John F. Kennedy meets with his top military advisers during the 1962 Cuban missile crisis. At times during this crisis, Kennedy behaved like a lion as he readied the military to attack Cuba. At other times, he behaved like a fox as he looked for ways to end the crisis peacefully.

President John F. Kennedy played the power struggle game with the Soviet Union during the Cuban missile crisis. The president viewed Soviet construction of missile bases in Cuba as a threat to the security of the United States. To end that threat, he employed both force and cunning.

On October 22, 1962, Kennedy ordered a naval quarantine, or blockade, of Cuba. The U.S. Navy prepared to forcibly board Soviet ships heading to Cuba and search them for missiles. The president also made plans to invade the island, if necessary, to remove the missiles.

Meanwhile, the president began negotiating with the Soviet Union. After several tense days, the Soviets agreed to remove the missiles on two conditions. First, the United States would promise not to invade Cuba. Second, it would remove its missiles from Turkey, a U.S. ally bordering the Soviet Union. Kennedy agreed publicly to the first condition and secretly to the second, thereby ending the crisis. By keeping the second condition secret, however, the president left the impression that he had forced the Soviets to back down simply by threatening war.

Demolition Derby: Winning by Wiping Out the Opposition

While the goal of the power struggle game is survival in a sea of enemies, the aim of demolition derby is the complete destruction of one's opponents. The game takes its name from car-crashing contests in which drivers use their vehicles as weapons to demolish the

other cars. The winner is the last car running at the end of the contest. In the political version of this game, players try to eliminate all real and perceived enemies.

The key players in demolition derby are those who command the means of force. They include military leaders, dictators, and monarchs. Players use a variety of strategies, ranging from fear and intimidation to murder and massacres, to wipe out the opposition.

The demolition derby game often ends in a bloodbath. This was the case in the century-long struggle for control of the Mediterranean region between ancient Rome and the North African city-state of Carthage. By the end of the first two Punic Wars, Rome had stripped Carthage of much of its military power. Yet Roman politicians continued to argue that "Carthage must be destroyed."

In the Third Punic War, Rome did just that. Its army totally demolished Carthage, burning the city to the ground. The 50,000 Carthaginians who survived this destruction were sold into slavery. According to legend, the Romans then plowed salt into the ground surrounding Carthage so that nothing would ever grow there again.

Civil Disobedience: Winning by Shaming the Opposition

At the opposite end of the spectrum from demolition derby players are those who forsake violence for the moral high road. The key players in the political game of **civil disobedience** are people of conscience, moral crusaders whose goal is to end some social or political evil. Their strategy involves publicly shaming the opposition. They accomplish this by deliberately disobeying what they consider an unjust law.

The word **civil** in this game's name means having to do with citizens. As the name suggests, the players in this game are usually ordinary citizens protesting an injustice. In this game, the protest typically involves an "in-your-face" but peaceful confrontation with authorities. By remaining nonviolent, the protesters hope to contrast their high moral vision with the unjust laws and actions of the government.

One of the most revered players of this game was Mohandas Gandhi, one leader of the struggle to free India from British colonial rule after World War I. Gandhi organized massive civil disobedience campaigns to protest the injustices of colonialism. His followers refused to work for the government,

Inspired by Mohandas Gandhi, Martin Luther King Jr. brought the philosophy and tactics of the civil disobedience game to the U.S. civil rights movement. Civil rights demonstrators held marches without parade permits, sat at lunch counters reserved for "whites only," and refused to sit at the back of the bus. This photograph shows how civil rights activists communicated their powerful messages through organized, peaceful protest.

pulled their children out of government schools, and blocked city streets so that nothing could move.

Gandhi was arrested many times and spent seven years in prison altogether. Each time he used his imprisonment to remind the world that taking action against an unjust government was the highest duty of a citizen. In 1947, he finally won his great struggle when Britain granted India its independence.

The political game of civil disobedience is difficult to play. As Gandhi's story shows, it takes courage, patience, and strength of character. But played well, it can produce amazing results.

Summary

Throughout our history, Americans have tended to be distrustful of power, government, and politics. Nonetheless, we look to our government to provide goods and services that we all want and need.

Power The term power is often defined as the ability to make people act in ways they might not otherwise choose to act. The power to influence others comes from many sources, from formal authority to coercion. Historically, rulers have used power for both good and ill.

Government Groups of people organize government to maintain order and provide public goods, such as roads and national defense. To fulfill these functions, governments must have the means to coerce the population and to extract revenue from it.

Politics When people work to influence the decisions made by groups, they are engaging in politics. Political activity is purposeful and involves collective action. Because politics involves competition, it is often described as a game. While most political competition is peaceful, it can turn deadly.

What is high-quality power— and how can you get it?

No one likes to feel powerless. But few of us think all that much about what power is and how to get it. This is not true, however, of the American writer and futurist Alvin Toffler. Toffler has spent much of his career studying how people have gained and used power throughout human history. In his book *PowerShift,* Toffler argues that there are three kinds of power—but only one is high-quality power for the 21st century.

As you read the excerpt, think about your own experiences with different kinds of power. Also ask yourself, If Toffler is right, how can I gain more high-quality power for myself?

From *PowerShift: Knowledge, Wealth, and Violence at the Edge of the 21st Century*

by Alvin Toffler

High-Quality Power

Most conventional assumptions about power, in Western culture at least, imply that power is a matter of quantity. But, while some of us clearly have less power than others, this approach ignores what may now be the most important factor of all: the *quality* of power . . .

No one doubts that violence—embodied in a mugger's switchblade or a nuclear missile—can yield awesome results. The shadow of violence or force, embedded in the law, stands behind every act of government, and in the end every government relies on soldiers and police to en*force* its will . . .

But violence in general suffers from important drawbacks. To begin with, it encourages us to carry a can of Mace, or to crank up an arms race that increases risks to everyone. Even when it "works," violence produces resistance. Its victims or their survivors look for the first chance to strike back.

The main weakness of brute force or violence, however, is its sheer inflexibility. It can only be used to punish. It is, in short, low-quality power.

Wealth, by contrast, is a far better tool of power. A fat wallet is much more versatile. Instead of just threatening or delivering punishment, it can also offer finely graded rewards—payments and payoffs, in cash or kind. Wealth can be used in either a positive or a negative way. It is, therefore, much more flexible than force. Wealth yields medium-quality power.

The highest-quality power, however, comes from the application of knowledge . . .

High-quality power is not simply clout . . . High quality implies much more. It implies efficiency—using up the fewest power resources to achieve a goal. Knowledge can often be used to make the other party *like* your agenda for action. It can even persuade the person that she or he originated it.

Of the three root sources of social control, therefore, it is knowledge, the most versatile, that produces what Pentagon brass like to call "the biggest bang for the buck." It can be

used to punish, reward, persuade, and even transform. It can transform enemy into ally. Best of all, with the right knowledge one can circumvent nasty situations in the first place, so as to avoid wasting force or wealth altogether . . .

The Democratic Difference
Besides its great flexibility, knowledge has other important characteristics that make it fundamentally different from lesser sources of power in tomorrow's world.

Thus force, for all practical concerns, is finite. There is a limit to how much force can be employed before we destroy what we wish to capture or defend. The same is true for

wealth. Money cannot buy everything, and at some point even the fattest wallet empties out.

By contrast, knowledge does not. We can always generate more . . . Knowledge, in principle at least, is infinitely expandable.

Knowledge is also inherently different from both muscle and money, because, as a rule, if I use a gun, you cannot simultaneously use the same gun. If you use a dollar, I can't use the same dollar at the same time.

By contrast, both of us can use the same knowledge either for or against each other—and in that very process we may even produce still more knowledge. Unlike bullets or budgets, knowledge itself doesn't get

used up. This alone tells us that the rules of the knowledge-power game are sharply different from the precepts relied on by those who use force or money to accomplish their will.

But a last, even more crucial difference sets violence and wealth apart from knowledge as we race into what has been called an information age: By definition, both force and wealth are the property of the strong and the rich. It is the truly revolutionary characteristic of knowledge that it can be grasped by the weak and the poor as well.

Knowledge is the most democratic source of power.

Which makes it a continuing threat to the powerful, even as they use it to enhance their own power. It also explains why every power-holder—from the patriarch of a family to the president of a company or the Prime Minister of a nation—wants to control the quantity, quality, and distribution of knowledge within his or her domain . . .

The control of knowledge is the crux of tomorrow's worldwide struggle for power in every human institution.

Alvin Toffler has written several influential books, including Future Shock, The Third Wave, *and* PowerShift.

Chapter 2

Comparing Forms of Government

How should political and economic power be distributed in a society?

■ 2.1 Introduction

In September 2012, delegates representing the 193 members of the United Nations met in New York City for the 67th session of the UN General Assembly. The majority of these nations' governments are categorized as **democracies**. The governments of a few nations are **monarchies**. Fewer yet are **dictatorships**.

Among the members of the United Nations are countries with vastly different populations, forms of government, and economic systems. Consider, for example, the differences between two of the newest members: Switzerland and South Sudan. Switzerland joined the United Nations in 2002, and South Sudan joined in 2011. However, other than UN membership, Switzerland and South Sudan have little in common.

Switzerland existed as an independent nation in Central Europe for more than 350 years before joining the United Nations. Eight million Swiss live in a prosperous nation with a thriving **market economy**. With a literacy rate of 99 percent, the Swiss are among the world's best-educated people. They also enjoy one of the world's highest standards of living.

In contrast, South Sudan became an independent state several days before joining the United Nations in 2011. Prior to its independence, South Sudan was part of Sudan, a landlocked African country with a history of political instability and civil wars. Since

Flags of countries with different forms of government fly outside the United Nations headquarters in New York City

Speaking of Politics

democracy
A system of government in which citizens exercise supreme power, acting either directly on their own or through elected representatives.

monarchy
A system of government in which a single ruler exercises supreme power based on heredity or divine right. In a monarchy, the right to rule passes from one generation of the ruling family to the next.

dictatorship
A system of government in which a single person or group exercises supreme power by controlling the military and police.

market economy
An economic system that relies mainly on markets to determine what goods and services to produce and how to produce them.

traditional economy
An economic system in which decisions about what to produce and how are made on the basis of customs, beliefs, and tradition.

republic
A nation in which supreme power rests with the citizens and is exercised by their elected representatives.

parliament
A legislative assembly in which elected representatives debate and vote on proposed laws. The name comes from the French term *parler*, meaning "to talk."

command economy
An economic system that relies mainly on the central government to determine what goods and services to produce and how to produce them.

Two democratic elections led to the independence of South Sudan. As a result of the general election in 2010, Salva Kiir became the acting president of southern Sudan. In a referendum that took place in January 2011, the people of southern Sudan voted for independence. Here, Kiir speaks to the public after casting his ballot for the referendum.

Sudan gained independence from British rule in 1956, the people of southern Sudan sparsely won positions in their government. After years of war and discontent, South Sudan finally gained independence. Today, South Sudan is an impoverished nation with a **traditional economy**. About a quarter of adults in South Sudan can read, and living standards are low.

The people of Switzerland and South Sudan do have one thing in common. When facing the question of who should have power to rule their nations, both answered, "the people." For the Swiss, this decision was made in 1848, when they adopted a constitution that created a democratic government. The South Sudanese, however, only recently decided to build a democracy. Whether this endeavor will be successful in this troubled country remains to be seen.

◼ 2.2 The Origins and Evolution of Government

All societies, large and small, develop some form of government. During prehistoric times, when small bands of hunter-gatherers wandered Earth in search of food and game, government might have been as simple as a few elders making decisions for the group. The invention of farming triggered the evolution of more formal systems of governments. Once people learned how to raise food, they settled down into permanent villages. This new way of life created

a host of novel problems and conflicts. Governments had to evolve to meet the needs of the more complex societies they ruled.

The Ancient World: From City-States to Empires

Over time, some farming villages grew into cities and **city-states**. A city-state is a sovereign state consisting of a city and its surrounding territory.

Around 3000 B.C.E., the first city-states arose in Sumer, a region located in what is today southern Iraq. There, between the Tigris and Euphrates rivers, the Sumerians grew crops of barley, wheat, dates, apples, and plums.

Then, as now, the land between the Tigris and Euphrates was largely desert. Farming in this region depended on irrigation. Governments arose to resolve issues pertaining to the fair and orderly distribution of water. They also provided protection by building walls around their cities and organizing armies to ward off invasions by nomadic tribes. A similar evolution occurred in ancient Egypt, India, and China.

Gradually, power in many city-states became concentrated in the hands of a single ruler. The strongest of these rulers conquered neighboring city-states to create the world's first empires. Sargon of Akkad was one of Sumer's early conquerors. Sargon, whose name is thought to mean "the true king," carried out more than 30 battles against the Sumerian city-states to consolidate his empire. To legitimize their power, empire-builders like Sargon often declared that the gods had given them the right to rule. Some rulers even claimed to be gods themselves. As power passed from father to son in these early empires, monarchy became the most common form of government in the ancient world.

Greece and Rome: Early Forms of People Power

In the fifth century B.C.E., the Greek city-state of Athens made a radical change in its form of government. The Athenians reorganized their city-state as a **direct democracy**. In a direct democracy, public decisions are made directly by citizens meeting together in an assembly or voting by ballot. The Athenian leader Pericles explained the new form of government this way:

> *Our constitution is called a democracy because power is in the hands not of a minority but of the whole people. When it is a question of settling private disputes, everyone is equal before the law; when it is a question of putting one person before another in positions of public responsibility, what counts is not membership of a particular class, but the actual ability which the man possesses.*
> —Pericles, *Funeral Oration*, 431 B.C.E.

"The Athenians are here, Sire, with an offer to back us with ships, money, arms, and men—and, of course, their usual lectures about democracy."

The Athenians established an early form of direct democracy in the fifth century B.C.E. This cartoon pokes fun at the belief held by most people living in a democracy that their form of government is superior to all other forms.

When Pericles spoke of government being in the hands of "the whole people," he meant in the hands of male citizens of Athens. Women, slaves, and foreign-born people living in Athens were not allowed to participate in government affairs. For those who did qualify, however, they participated on a scale that was unique in the ancient world. Never before had so many people dedicated so much of their time to the business of governing themselves.

Elsewhere, the Italian city-state of Rome was developing a different form of people power. In 509 B.C.E., the Roman people overthrew their monarchy and turned Rome into a **republic**. Over time, the Romans set up a **representative democracy** to govern their republic. In a representative democracy, public decisions are made by leaders who are elected by the citizens to represent their interests.

The Roman Republic lasted nearly 500 years. During that time, officials elected by Rome's citizens headed the government. Then, in 31 B.C.E., after 20 years of civil war, the Roman Empire was established. Power passed from elected leaders to emperors who held absolute power for life.

The Middle Ages: From Feudalism to Nation-States

For a time, Rome's emperors ruled an empire that included most of Europe, as well as North Africa and western Asia. In 476 C.E., Rome fell to invading tribes from the east. In parts of Europe once ruled by mighty Rome, the empire broke into tiny districts, each ruled by a duke, lord, king, or other noble.

With no strong central government to provide security, each district had to look out for itself. It often made sense for weak nobles to look to a nearby, more powerful neighbor for protection. However, protection had a price. Because money was scarce, the powerful lord or local king usually took his payment in land. In this way, some lords gained control of very large areas.

By the 700s, many lords acquired more land than they could manage. They began granting parcels of land, called *fiefs*, to tenants. In return, the tenant became the lord's vassal. A vassal took an oath of loyalty to the lord and promised to provide him with military service in time of war. This system of exchanging the use of land for military and other services became known as **feudalism**.

In addition to serving as warriors, the vassals also had political obligations. For example, they all sat together at the lord's court to help settle disputes. The lord was also expected to seek the advice and consent of his vassals before making new laws. Europe's **parliaments** developed from meetings of vassals summoned by a lord or king.

During the 1200s, the feudal system of lords and vassals entered a period of decline. The 1300s saw the rise of **absolute monarchies,** or governments headed by hereditary rulers who claimed unlimited powers. These powerful monarchs consolidated the patchwork of feudal districts in their kingdoms into the world's first nation-states.

By the 1700s, several European countries had become nation-states headed by absolute monarchs. These all-powerful rulers based their legitimacy on the divine right of kings theory. So important was the role of the monarch in France that Louis XIV is reported to have said of himself, *"L'état c'est moi"* ("I am the state").

The Age of Revolutions:
Democracies and Dictatorships

Some monarchs ruled with the best interests of their people in mind. Others ruled as **despots,** or tyrants, who used their power for selfish ends. Growing dissatisfaction with this form of government triggered a series of world-altering revolutions, first in Europe and then in the American colonies.

The first of these revolutions against tyranny occurred in England in 1688. The Glorious Revolution, also known as the Bloodless Revolution, led to the establishment of Europe's first **constitutional monarchy**—a system of government in which the powers of the monarch are limited by a constitution, either written or unwritten.

The second of these revolutions began in 1775 when American colonists rebelled against what they saw as British tyranny. The American Revolution led to the creation of the first modern **constitutional democracy**—a democratic government based on a written constitution. Abraham Lincoln would later describe this form of democracy as "government of the people, by the people, for the people."

A third revolution broke out in 1789, when the French people took up arms against their king. At first the French Revolution seemed likely to produce another constitutional democracy. Instead it took a radical turn and eventually collapsed into chaos. In time Napoleon Bonaparte restored order, but only by establishing an **authoritarian regime**—a system of government in which the state exercises broad control over the lives of its citizens. Napoleon, for example, used secret police forces to spy on French citizens. To stifle opposition, he censored the press while mounting his own propaganda campaigns.

Some historians argue that Napoleon's approach to governing set the stage for rise of **totalitarianism**

The American and French revolutions both rejected monarchy in favor of democracy. In both revolutions, a military hero played a large role in the formation of a new regime. In the United States, George Washington helped forge a constitutional democracy that still endures. In France, Napoleon Bonaparte established a short-lived dictatorship. Washington died a hero while Napoleon died in disgrace. After his fall from power, Napoleon reportedly lamented, "They wanted me to be another Washington."

in the 20th century. A totalitarian government is an extreme form of an authoritarian regime that seeks to control almost every aspect of its citizens' lives.

Twentieth-century totalitarianism dates back to the Russian Revolution of 1917. That revolution overthrew the Russian monarchy. In its place, revolutionaries established the Soviet Union as the world's first state based on **communism.**

The term communism has several meanings. It can mean a system of government in which a single political party controls the government and the economy. It can also mean the theories developed by German philosopher Karl Marx about the ideal society. Marx's goal was the creation of a society that provides equality and economic security for all. To accomplish that end, he called for government ownership of land, factories, and other resources.

The theory of communism appealed to many people in the 1900s. In practice, however, it led to the creation of totalitarian states, first in the Soviet Union and later in other countries, such as China, Vietnam, and Cuba. In these states, dictators like Joseph Stalin used spies, secret police, and government censors to suppress all opposition.

Three Forms of Totalitarianism

Communism

Joseph Stalin ruled the Soviet Union from 1922 to 1953. Historians hold him responsible for the deaths of millions of Russians. The hammer in this communist symbol represents industrial workers, while the sickle represents agricultural workers.

Key Characteristics

- The Communist Party holds supreme power
- Belief that the state should control the economy
- Brutal suppression of opposition
- Hostility to religion and human rights

Fascism

Benito Mussolini was dictator of Italy from 1922 to 1943. He used his power to control every aspect of the government and the press. This symbol of fascism suggests that while a single stick may be easily broken, a bundle of sticks bound together is too strong to break.

Key Characteristics

- Dictator holds supreme power
- Belief that everyone should serve the state
- Extreme nationalism
- Glorification of the military
- Use of censorship and terror to suppress opposition

Nazism

While ruling Germany from 1933 to 1945, Adolf Hitler tried to rid Europe of Jews, Gypsies, and others he deemed "undesirable." The swastika is an ancient Hindu symbol of well-being. The Nazis adopted it as a symbol of the German master race.

Key Characteristics

- The Nazi Party holds supreme power
- Belief in racial superiority
- Aggressive territorial expansion
- Elimination of "inferior" minorities
- Rejection of democracy and civil liberties

A form of totalitarianism known as **fascism** first appeared in Italy during the 1920s. Fascism resembles communism in terms of its control of citizens' lives. Unlike communism, however, fascism allows businesses to remain in private ownership, though under government control. Benito Mussolini, the fascist dictator of Italy, used his power to turn his country into a police state.

A third type of totalitarianism, **Nazism,** took root in Germany. Nazism is a variety of fascism built in part on the myth of racial superiority. After taking power in Germany in 1933, Nazi leader Adolf Hitler launched an extermination campaign against Jews, Gypsies, and other groups he defined as "undesirable."

2.3 Forms of Government in Today's World

With the exception of Antarctica, the landmasses on Earth are divided into nation-states. Some of these countries, such as Switzerland, have existed for hundreds of years. Others, like South Sudan, are new. Almost all have some form of functioning government. As Aristotle observed more than 2,000 years ago, these governments fall into three broad groups: rule by the one (monarchies and dictatorships), rule by the few (theocracies and single-party states), and rule by the many (parliamentary and presidential democracies).

Monarchy: Rule by the One Hereditary Ruler

Monarchies are one of the oldest forms of government still found in the world today. For monarchal government to have survived for thousands of years, it must have enduring attractions.

One of those attractions is efficiency. Traditionally, a ruling monarch has been able to make decisions and have them carried out on his or her word alone. As a result, new policies can be carried out without a lot of political bickering. A second advantage is a clear line of succession. Citizens living in a monarchy know who is next in line for the throne. A third is the unifying power of monarchy. Loyalty to a ruling family can be a strong bond holding a nation together.

At the same time, monarchal government has its drawbacks. One is the varying quality of hereditary leaders. An exemplary monarch in one generation

may be followed by an incompetent one in the next. Also, the job of running a modern nation-state has become too big for any but the most exceptional monarchs to do well.

Today's monarchs go by many names, including king, queen, sultan, emperor, and emir. Most have inherited their power and expect to rule for life. But the modern monarch's power is rarely as great as in the days of Louis XIV and other absolute monarchs.

Most monarchs today face rigid legal restrictions on their power, often imposed by a constitution. The British monarch, for example, has the formal authority to call elections and appoint a new prime minister. These functions, however, are strictly ceremonial. Real power rests with Great Britain's democratically elected leaders.

In contrast, Saudi Arabia's king exercises broad powers. He inherits his position and has legislative, executive, and judicial powers. There are no recognized political parties or national elections in Saudi Arabia. The king may seek support from the royal family, religious leaders, and other important members of Saudi society. However, in theory, only Islamic law and Saudi traditions limit his powers.

In 2011, a series of uprisings known as the Arab Spring challenged monarchies in Southwest Asian countries. Several protests erupted in Saudi Arabia, but King Abdullah maintained his power.

In Saudi Arabia, the monarch has real power. King Abdullah acts as the ceremonial chief of state and as the head of government of Saudi Arabia. Here, King Abdullah (right) meets with Emir Sheikh Hamad bin Khalifa Al Thani, the hereditary ruler and head of state of Qatar, who also has real power.

NHIỆT LIỆT CHÀO MỪNG KỶ NIỆM 57 NĂM GIẢI PHÓNG THỦ ĐÔ

Vietnam has been a single-party state since the end of the Vietnam War in 1975. In 2011, this propaganda poster called on Vietnamese to celebrate Vietnam's independence from French rule and to recognize the communist party's continuous political dominance.

Dictatorships: Rule by the One Powerful Leader

Whereas monarchs inherit their power, dictators take and hold power by force. Muammar al-Gaddafi, for example, took control of Libya in a military **coup d'etat,** or coup, in 1969. The term coup d'etat means "blow to the state" in French. A coup is the sudden overthrow of a government by a small group of military officers or political leaders. This often happens during a time of political unrest or a national emergency.

Dictatorships share some of the advantages of absolute monarchies. Power is centralized in the hands of a single military or political leader who can get things done efficiently. With control of the military and police, the leader can put an end to political unrest and maintain peace and order. That same power, however, can easily be used to abuse citizens who oppose the dictator's authoritarian regime.

Dictatorships face serious legitimacy problems. Over time, pressure often builds to return the government to control by elected leaders. When this happens, ruling becomes increasingly difficult. For example, in February 2011, growing discontent led to a wave of protests in Libya, calling for an end to Gaddafi's rule. Months later, he was overthrown.

Theocracy: Rule by the Few Religious Leaders

A **theocracy** is a government headed by religious leaders. In ancient city-states, theocracies were common, with government officials serving as religious leaders as well. Having a government based on one set of religious beliefs had clear benefits. A single, state-supported religion encouraged political and social unity. It also ensured that political decisions were in line with the people's moral values and beliefs.

As states grew larger, however, enforcing religious unity became increasingly difficult. Religious minorities were often marginalized or even persecuted. Religious warfare broke out as groups with differing beliefs fought for control of their governments.

By 2007, only two theocracies existed in the world: Vatican City and Iran. Vatican City is the governmental and spiritual center of the Catholic Church. Although located in the heart of Rome, Italy, it is an independent state headed by the Catholic pope.

Iran changed from a monarchy to a theocracy in 1979. That year, Iranians expelled their hereditary ruler and formed an Islamic republic headed by a religious leader known as the Ayatollah Khomeini. As Iran's supreme leader, the Ayatollah put into practice his belief that "in Islam, the legislative power and competence to establish laws belong exclusively to God Almighty." The most influential body in Iran's theocracy is the 12-person Council of Guardians. Their job is to make sure that the laws of the country conform to Islamic religious law.

Single-Party State: Rule by the Political Elite

In a **single-party state,** the constitution allows only one political party to govern. Power is exercised by the leading members of the party, who form the nation's political **elite,** or a small group of people within a larger group who have more power, wealth, or talent than the others. The party elite nominate candidates for public office and make most policy decisions for the country.

As this map clearly shows, the governments of the vast majority of nation-states are some form of democracy. Not all of these democratic states, however, are equally open and free.

Form of Government

Monarchy
Governments in which a monarch exercises considerable power are no longer common. They are usually found in parts of the world where tradition outweighs the forces of modernity.

Theocracy
Governments headed by religious leaders are rare. With the rise of Islamic fundamentalism, however, theocracies may increase in number.

Dictatorship
Dictatorships often arise out of a national crisis, such as riots or civil war. The dictator who seizes power promises to restore order. Such governments rarely outlast their leaders.

Single-Party State
Most single-party governments today are dominated by the Communist Party. Elections may be held, but only for candidates chosen by the party. Real power rests with party leaders.

Parliamentary Democracy
In a parliamentary democracy, elected members of parliament choose the prime minister. The prime minister then serves as both head of the executive branch and leader of the legislature.

Presidential Democracy
In some presidential democracies, the president is the sole head of the government. In others, the president shares power with a prime minister. In a few counties, the president, while elected, presides over an authoritarian regime.

Transitional or Unstable
In 2012, a handful of countries had governments that were in transition from one form to another or that were so unstable that their governments were not able to function effectively.

Ideally, a single-party system avoids much of the political wrangling that is common in multiparty states, making it easier to pass laws and implement government policies. This party unity comes at a cost, however. The views of the party elite may be very different from the interests of the people as a whole, leading to social unrest. Also, people with differing political views or solutions to problems are often completely shut out of the political process.

The handful of single-party states today are mainly socialist republics, in which the Communist Party rules. In China, for example, the Communist Party is the only legal political party, and it has controlled the government since 1949. The legislature in China usually approves all legislation proposed by the Communist Party.

Direct Democracy: Rule by All Citizens

In the direct democracy of ancient Athens, several thousand citizens met regularly as an assembly to make decisions for their city-state. Each citizen had an equal voice in public affairs, and decisions, once made, had widespread support. Nonetheless, this form of government was time-consuming for citizens. That may be one reason why Athenian-style democracy was not widely copied in the ancient world.

In the modern world, no country is governed as a pure direct democracy. The country that comes closest is Switzerland. Swiss citizens regularly vote to approve laws passed by their legislature. This form of direct democracy is known as the **referendum process**. Citizens may also propose laws and submit them directly to voters in what is known as the **initiative process**. As much as the Swiss value their form of democracy, voter turnout is often low, because people tire of frequent elections.

Limited forms of direct democracy exist in the United States. One is the New England town meeting, where townspeople meet to discuss and solve local problems. In several states, voters help shape public policy through the initiative and referendum processes. They may also be able to vote an elected official out of office by means of a **recall election**. In 2012, the governor of Wisconsin, Scott Walker, faced a recall election. However, the recall failed, and he retained his position.

Parliamentary Democracy: Rule by a Legislative Majority

Most nations today have adopted one of two forms of representative democracy: parliamentary or presidential. Both forms use elections to choose national leaders. But they differ in other ways.

The United Kingdom, India, and Australia are examples of **parliamentary democracies**. In a parliamentary democracy, voters elect lawmakers to represent them in the nation's parliament. The party that wins a legislative majority forms a new administration. If no single party wins a majority, several parties join together to form a ruling coalition.

The legislative majority then selects a member of parliament to serve as the nation's **prime minister,** or chief executive. Usually the person chosen is the leader of the party with the most seats. The prime minister then chooses other members of parliament to head key government **ministries,** or executive branch departments.

The Folketing, the Danish national parliament, has legislative power in Denmark. Like in most parliamentary democracies, the party that wins the most seats in parliament selects a member to serve as the prime minister of Denmark.

In a presidential democracy, such as the United States, citizens vote for their legislators and also for a president. Legislative and executive powers are thus separated. In a parliamentary democracy, voters elect only their legislators. The majority party in the parliament then chooses one of its own to be prime minister. Legislative and executive powers are thus joined.

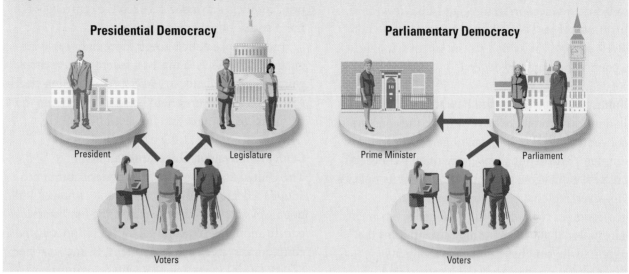

Presidential Democracy

President — Legislature — Voters

Parliamentary Democracy

Prime Minister — Parliament — Voters

In a parliamentary democracy, there is no clear-cut separation between the executive and legislative branches of government. Members of the legislative majority usually vote with the prime minister on key issues. This may make it easier to get legislation passed than in a presidential system. However, the lack of separation means there is no real check on the prime minister's power. Also, the prime minister may lack the legitimacy and public support of an elected president.

Prime ministers remain in power only so long as they have the support of parliament. Should parliament approve a **vote of no confidence,** the prime minister must resign. At that point, an election may be held to choose a new legislative majority. Although forcing an unpopular prime minister out of office in this way may seem democratic, it can also make parliamentary governments unstable.

Presidential Democracy: Rule by Representatives of the People

The United States, Russia, and most countries in Latin America are **presidential democracies.** Voters in these countries choose a president to lead the government as the head of the executive branch. They also elect lawmakers to represent them in a national legislature. Both the president and the legislators serve fixed terms of office.

This system has some advantages over a parliamentary democracy. Because presidents are directly elected by the people, they may be more responsive to the public than to their party. They may also enjoy more legitimacy and public support than does a prime minister chosen by a parliament. The presidential system also separates executive and legislative powers, which allows each branch to watch over the other to prevent abuses of power. Also, with fixed terms, a presidential system may be more stable than one in which the prime minister can be dismissed at any time.

This system does have several disadvantages when compared with a parliamentary one. First, it is almost impossible to remove presidents from power before their terms end, no matter how unpopular they might be. Also, when presidents are not from the political party that controls the legislature, the result can be gridlock—a situation in which little or no progress is made on pressing issues. Finally, in some countries, presidents have used their power to establish authoritarian regimes.

2.4 The Distribution of Power in Governments Today

In almost all nation-states, government power is exercised at a minimum of two levels: national and regional. In the United States, each region is called a state. In other countries, regions have names such as canton, province, prefecture, land, and *département*. Just how power is distributed between these two levels depends on which system of government a country has: unitary, federal, or confederal.

Unitary Systems Centralize Power

In a **unitary system of government,** the constitution concentrates power in the national, or central, government. The national government may choose to create regional governments to carry out its policies. However, regional governments exercise only those powers given to them by the national government. The national government may also appoint the officials who run the regional governments.

Most nation-states have unitary systems. The main advantage of this system is that it promotes national unity by having all parts of a country follow the same laws and policies. However, most unitary nations have discovered that too much centralization is not good in practice. Policies that fit one region of the country may not work as well in another. Also, officials working at the national level cannot know the needs of every town and village. As a result, most unitary states have decentralized to a certain degree, allowing regions some powers of their own.

In Japan, for example, the central government has the constitutional power to control its 47 regions, which are called prefectures. It makes national laws that the regional governments must carry out. It also provides funds without which the prefectures could not operate. Yet the prefectures—along with Japan's cities, towns, and villages—have a significant amount of control over local affairs.

Federal Systems Divide Power

In a **federal system of government,** the constitution divides power between the national government and the regional governments. The national government has some fixed responsibilities, such as protecting the nation. The regional government has other responsibilities, such as setting up schools.

A federal system of government is most likely to be adopted in large countries with diverse populations. The main advantage of such a system is the flexibility it gives regional governments in meeting the needs of different language and ethnic groups. The downside of this flexibility can be a patchwork of competing laws from region to region. In addition, conflicts may arise between the central government and regional governments.

India, whose people speak more than 1,000 languages and dialects, adopted a federal system after gaining independence in 1947. Its constitution clearly specifies how powers are to be divided between the national government and the 28 Indian states.

Confederal Systems Decentralize Power

The United States was the first modern country to adopt a federal system of government. However, it did not always have a federal system. The first American constitution, the Articles of Confederation, created a **confederal system of government.** In such a system, power resides in the regions, which are independent states. The regions grant only as much power to the national government as needed to maintain security and to coordinate activities among the regions.

The American states first chose a confederal system because it offered two important advantages. It allowed the states to unite for some purposes without giving up the power to run their own affairs. This allowed for greater flexibility in meeting local needs. And, by limiting the powers of the central government, a confederal system reduced the likelihood that it would become an authoritarian regime.

Within a few years, however, the states reconsidered their choice. The central government, they realized, was too weak to meet the needs of the nation as a whole. It also lacked the power to end quarreling among the states. The result was an unworkable system that threatened the very survival of the nation.

No nation-state is organized as a confederation today. However, some **supranational organizations,** such as the European Union (EU), are modeled on confederal systems. The member nations of the EU give some power to the EU government, such as control over cross-border trade. But they remain sovereign nations and can leave the EU at any time. Thus far, its members have found the benefits of union worth the cost of sharing some power with the EU.

Power is highly centralized in a unitary system, divided in a federal system, and decentralized in a confederal system. Most nations today have a unitary system. None has a confederal system. Federal systems are more likely to be found in large nations with diverse populations.

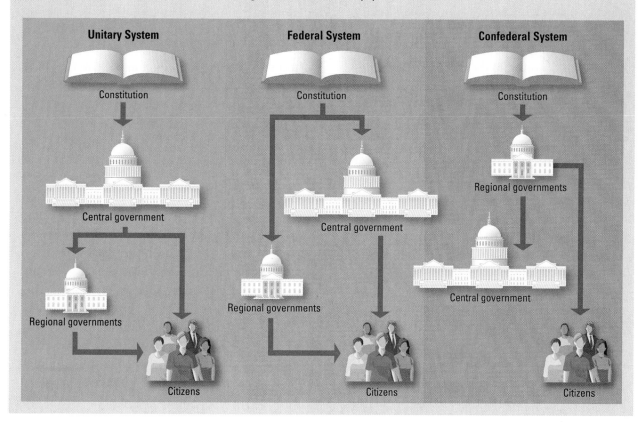

Unitary System

Constitution

Central government

Regional governments

Citizens

Federal System

Constitution

Central government

Regional governments

Citizens

Confederal System

Constitution

Regional governments

Central government

Citizens

2.5 Economic Systems Around the World

Just as forms of government vary from one nation to the next, so do **economic systems**. An economic system is a way of organizing the production and consumption of goods and services. Economic systems exist because people must meet certain needs to survive. These survival needs include food, clothing, and shelter. In addition, people have endless wants. Such wants may include things that make life more comfortable, more entertaining, or more satisfying in some way.

Three Fundamental Economic Questions: What to Produce, How, and for Whom?

If a nation's resources were unlimited, it might be possible to meet all of these wants and needs. But such is never the case. Resources are always limited.

As a result, every economic system must answer three fundamental economic questions:

What goods and services should be produced? For example, should a nation's limited resources be used mainly to provide public goods, such as clean air and water, or to produce private goods, such as homes?

How should these goods and services be produced? Should corn and wheat be raised mainly on giant factory farms? Or is farming better done on smaller family farms?

How should the people share goods and services? Who should get what? Only those who can afford whatever they want? Or should goods and services go to the people who need them the most?

Economic systems differ from one country to another because each society answers these questions in its own way.

The Four Factors of Production: Land, Labor, Capital, and Entrepreneurship

Countries also differ in how they use what economists call the **factors of production**. These factors are the resources required to produce most goods and services. They include the following:

Land. By land, economists mean the natural resources of a nation. These raw materials include fertile soil, water, plants, and minerals.

Labor. Labor refers to the effort—both mental and physical—that people put into producing goods and services.

Capital. The term *capital* has multiple meanings. It can mean the money needed to start a business. It can mean the machinery, buildings, tools, and equipment used to produce goods and services. It can also mean human capital—the knowledge and skills that workers bring to their jobs.

Entrepreneurship. This last factor is the human effort that goes into organizing land, labor, and capital to produce and sell goods and services. Entrepreneurs risk their money and time to turn an idea into something that people will want or need.

The way a society uses these factors of production is determined by its economic system. Three basic types of economic systems exist in the world today: traditional, market, and command.

Traditional Economies: Decision Making by Custom

In a society with a traditional economy, people rely on time-tested customs to answer the three fundamental economic questions. What worked for their ancestors still works today.

People in traditional economies provide for themselves. Some are hunters and gatherers, as they have been for thousands of years. The majority are farmers. Most people in a traditional economy live at a subsistence level, producing just enough goods to feed, clothe, and house their families. If they have any goods left over, they trade them for other things they need or want.

Many of the Inuit of Alaska and northern Canada still maintain a traditional economy based on hunting and fishing. They rely on skills and strategies that have helped their people survive since prehistoric times. Likewise, many African farmers and herders follow the same economic patterns as their ancestors.

In a traditional society, the production and distribution of food, clothing, and shelter is woven into the fabric of society. Economic activities do not need to be coordinated or regulated in any way by the government. Tradition and community values serve to keep the economy running smoothly. However, the standard of living of most people in traditional economies is very low. Families do not earn enough

This Maasai family of herders in Africa works in a traditional economy. Traditionally, the Maasai measure wealth in terms of cattle and children, not money. The more of both, the richer a Maasai is.

to do more than meet their most basic needs. They have only limited access to goods such as cars or services like medical care.

Market Economies: Decision Making by Individuals

In a country with a market economy, individual producers and consumers answer the three basic economic questions. In a pure free-market economy, the government plays little or no role in economic affairs. Producers are free to decide what goods and services to produce and how much to charge for them. Consumers are free to decide what to buy. Prices are determined by the **market**. In economic terms, a market is any place or situation in which people buy and sell goods and services.

You have probably heard other names for a market economy. Some people refer to it as a **free enterprise system**. A free enterprise system relies on the profit motive, economic competition, and the forces of supply and demand to direct the production and distribution of goods and services.

Others use the term **capitalism** to describe a market system. Under capitalism, individual investors, or capitalists, privately own the means of production, such as farmland or factories. Workers provide labor in exchange for wages or a salary.

One advantage of a market system is its efficiency at meeting peoples' needs. When demand for a product rises, its price in the market goes up. This signals businesses to produce more. Meanwhile, competition among producers of similar goods usually keeps prices from rising too high. Efficiency also leads to economic growth. Businesses invest in factories and equipment, as well as in research and technology, to stay competitive. This helps the economy grow.

One disadvantage of a market economy, some would argue, is its instability. Periods of growth and prosperity in market economies usually alternate with recessions, or slowdowns, in business and employment. During these downturns, people who lose their jobs suffer from a loss of income.

Another disadvantage of a market economy is its unequal distribution of wealth. The market divides wealth to people according to how society values what they do. For example, a quarterback whose team wins the Superbowl earns more than a public school teacher. This may seem unfair, but there are more teachers than Superbowl-winning quarterbacks.

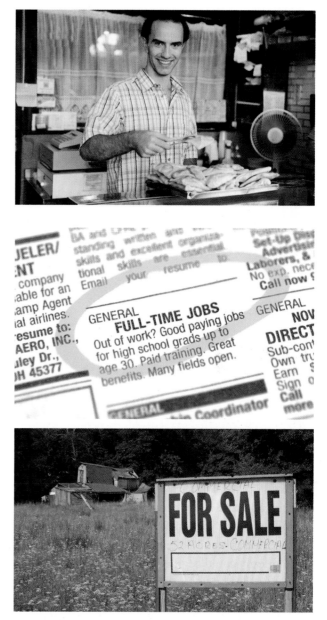

In a capitalist economy, like that of the United States, people enjoy many freedoms. They are free to start a business, to choose jobs and change jobs, and to own private property. Some political scientists believe that free markets and democracy go hand in hand.

Command Economies: Decision Making by Government Planners

In a **command economy,** the government answers the three basic economic questions. In a pure command economy, the means of production are publicly owned. Government planners decide what goods and services should be produced and how. They also determine how goods and services should be distributed to consumers and at what cost.

A Market Economy Versus a Command Economy

	Market Economy	Command Economy
Key Features	• Private ownership of the means of production • Economic decisions made by market forces • Fierce competition among producers for customers	• Public ownership of the means of production • Economic decisions made by government planners • Little or no competition among producers for customers
Advantages	• Efficient use of factors of production • Faster economic growth • High-quality goods and services • Higher standards of living	• Full employment • No economic recessions • Greater income equality • Greater economic security
Disadvantages	• Greater unemployment • Frequent economic recessions • Greater income inequality • Greater economic insecurity	• Inefficient use of factors of production • Slower or stagnant economic growth • Low-quality goods and services • Lower standards of living

Command economies are based on political theories that arose in Europe during the late 1800s. Known both as **socialism** and communism, these theories addressed the inequalities of capitalism by calling for public ownership of farms and factories. Once the people controlled the means of production, the economy could be operated on such principles as equality and fairness to all. Karl Marx, the originator of communism, summed up how such an economy would work in this slogan: "From each according to his ability, to each according to his needs."

In theory, a command economy has distinct advantages over a market economy. Central planners can ensure full employment by devising enough projects to absorb all members of the workforce. This ability, along with controls on prices, can bring stability to the economy. A command economy can also distribute income more equally than a market economy, because everyone shares in the nation's wealth.

In practice, however, the performance of command economies has been disappointing. Because the government controls wages and prices, workers have little incentive to work hard or to produce high-quality goods. The goods they do produce are usually inferior to similar goods produced in a market economy.

The core problem in a command economy is that government planners, no matter how well intentioned, are less efficient at making economic decisions than the market is. By harnessing the intelligence of millions of buyers and sellers, the market is far better at providing people with what they want and need than government officials will ever be.

Mixed Economies: Shared Decision Making

Pure forms of traditional, market, and command economic systems do not exist today. They are theoretical extremes. In the real world, most countries have **mixed economies** that fall somewhere in between those extremes. A mixed economy blends reliance on market forces with some government involvement in the marketplace. The degree of that involvement varies from country to country.

The United States has historically had a free-market economy. Yet the government plays a vital role in economic affairs. The government, for example, protects private property rights. It regulates

Since China reformed its command economy in the late 1970s, it has enjoyed rapid economic growth. No city has benefited more than Shanghai, a booming center of trade and finance. Shanghai's skyline, with its soaring skyscrapers, has become a symbol of China's new prosperity.

the marketplace to protect both consumers and producers from unfair business practices. It also redistributes wealth to those in need through its social welfare policies.

In contrast, China has had a command economy since the Communist Party took control of its government in 1949. For many years, the communist government controlled every aspect of the Chinese economy. The result was economic stagnation.

In the late 1970s, the Chinese government moved from a strict command economy to a system called market socialism. This system mixes public and private ownership of businesses. It also encourages competition in the marketplace. At the same time, the Communist Party has remained in overall control of the economy. As Deng Xiaoping, the leader of this change, explained, "Planning and market forces are both ways of controlling economic activity."

Summary

Governments have existed since the rise of city-states in ancient times. Over time, governments have evolved in size, complexity, and form. Even today, who rules and for what purpose varies from one country to the next.

Forms of government Modern governments can be classified according to who holds power. Monarchies and dictatorships ruled by one person are relatively rare. So are theocracies and single-party states in which leaders of a religion or political party run the government. Most of the world's governments today are either parliamentary or presidential democracies.

Distribution of power Modern governments can be defined according to how power is distributed between the national and regional governments. In a unitary system, power is centralized at the national level. In a federal system, the national and regional governments share power. In a confederal system, it is decentralized to regional governments.

Economic systems All economic systems must answer three basic economic questions: What should be produced? How should it be produced? How should it be distributed? In today's market economies, the government plays a minor role in answering those questions. In command economies, the government plays a major role in economic decision making.

Is freedom on the march around the world?

Between 1976 and 2012, the number of countries that could be considered "free" more than doubled, from 42 to 87. Freedom, it seemed, was on the march worldwide. But do elections translate into freedom? An NGO (nongovernmental organization) called Freedom House tries to answer such questions with hard facts. Every year, Freedom House rates how well each country protects the rights and liberties of its people.

The information in this article is based on Freedom House's ratings for 2011. In this study, Freedom House evaluated the impact of the Arab Spring on freedom and the influence of these uprisings on countries around the world. As you study the map and article, ask yourself these questions: Is freedom on the march around the world? Or are we entering a new age of authoritarian regimes?

The Arab Uprisings and Their Global Repercussions

by Arch Puddington

The political uprisings that swept across the Arab world over the past year represent the most significant challenge to authoritarian rule since the collapse of Soviet communism. In a region that had seemed immune to democratic change, coalitions of activist reformers and ordinary citizens succeeded in removing dictators who had spent decades entrenching themselves in power. In some cases, protest and upheaval was followed by the beginnings of democratic institution building. At year's end, two countries with unbroken histories of fraudulent polling, Tunisia and Egypt, had conducted elections that observers deemed competitive and credible, and freedom of expression had gained momentum in many Middle Eastern societies.

Unfortunately, the gains that were recorded in Tunisia, and to a considerably lesser extent in Egypt and Libya, were offset by more dubious trends elsewhere in the region. Indeed, the overthrow of autocrats in these countries provoked determined and often violent responses in many others, most notably in Syria, where by year's end the Assad dictatorship had killed over 5,000 people in its efforts to crush widespread antigovernment protests. Similar if less bloody crackdowns took place in Bahrain and Yemen.

This pattern of protest and repression—with an emphasis on the latter—was echoed elsewhere in the world as news of the Arab uprisings spread beyond the Middle East and North Africa. In China, the authorities responded to events in Cairo's Tahrir Square with a near-hysterical campaign of arrests, incommunicado detentions, press censorship, and stepped-up control over the internet. The Chinese Communist Party's pushback, which aimed to quash potential prodemocracy demonstrations before they even emerged, reached a crescendo in December with the sentencing of a number of dissident writers to long terms in prison. In Russia, the state-controlled media bombarded domestic audiences with predictions of chaos and instability as a consequence of the Arab

Freedom Around the World, 2011

This map shows how well each country protects the rights and liberties of its people. Democratic nations are not necessarily considered "free." Some countries, such as Tunisia and Egypt, technically have been democratic for years, but due to fraudulent elections, Freedom House classifies them as "not free." In 2011, however, uprisings in a regional event known as the Arab Spring led to political reforms in Tunisia and Egypt. After Tunisia held its first truly free election, its status improved to "partly free." Egypt also made gains in 2011, though it remains "not free." Even with these improvements, Tunisia and Egypt need to overcome many obstacles in order to continue on this path toward freedom.

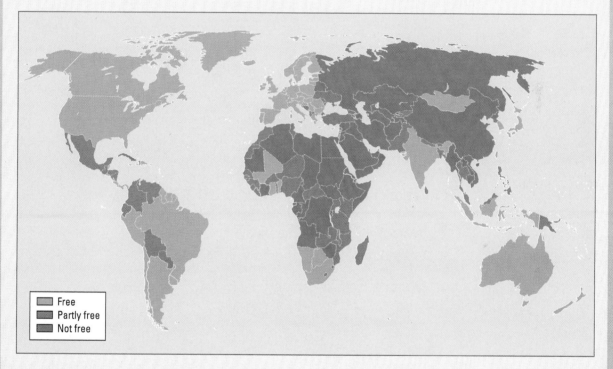

Free
Partly free
Not free

Source: Freedom House, www.freedomhouse.org.

protests, with a clear message that demands for political reform in Russia would have similarly catastrophic results. In other Eurasian countries and in parts of Africa, the authorities went to considerable lengths to suppress demonstrations and isolate the democratic opposition.

The authoritarian response to change in the Middle East had a significant impact on the state of global freedom at year's end. The findings of *Freedom in the World 2012* . . . showed that slightly more countries registered declines than exhibited gains over the course of 2011.

This marks the sixth consecutive year in which countries with declines outnumbered those with improvements.

Arch Puddington is Vice President of Research for Freedom House.

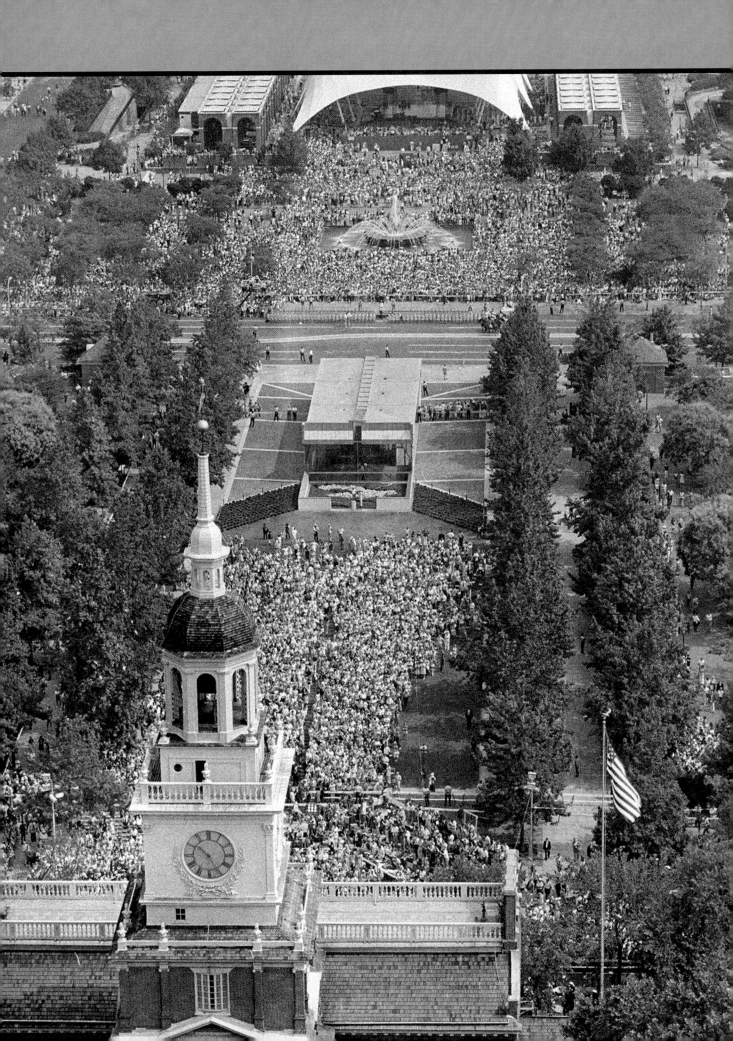

Chapter 3

The Roots of American Democracy

What ideas gave birth to the world's first modern democratic nation?

■ 3.1 Introduction

On July 4, 1976, Americans celebrated their nation's 200th birthday. Two centuries earlier, the United States of America had come into being with the signing of the Declaration of Independence. In 1776, no one had been more pleased than John Adams, who had worked tirelessly for independence. The anniversary of that first Independence Day would, he hoped, "be commemorated as the day of deliverance." He added,

> *It ought to be solemnized with pomp and parade, with shows, games, sports, guns, bells, bonfires, and illuminations, from one end of this continent to the other, from this time forward forevermore.*

In 1976, President Gerald Ford marked the bicentennial with a speech in Philadelphia, where the Declaration was signed. "The American adventure is a continuing process," he said. "As one milestone is passed, another is sighted . . . As we begin our third century, there is still so much to be done." Across the nation that evening, magnificent fireworks displays lit the skies, just as Adams had hoped.

Eleven years later, on September 17, 1987, Americans celebrated another bicentennial—this time to commemorate the signing of the U.S. Constitution. In Philadelphia, where the Constitution had been written during a long hot summer, a quarter of a million people turned out for a grand celebration.

Americans gather around Independence Hall in Philadelphia, Pennsylvania, to celebrate the bicentennial in 1976

At 4:00 P.M., the hour in which the Constitution was signed in 1787, former U.S. chief justice Warren Burger rang a replica of the Liberty Bell. At that moment, other bells rang out in communities across the nation and at U.S. embassies and military bases around the world.

These two bicentennial events reminded Americans that they live in a country that is held together not by blood or history, but by ideas. Those ideas, first put forth in the Declaration and then given shape in the Constitution, were not new. Some had roots extending into ancient times. But never before had anyone tried to build a nation on something so powerful, yet intangible, as ideas.

◼ 3.2 Ideas That Shaped Colonial Views on Government

The Declaration of Independence and the U.S. Constitution are among the most important political documents ever written. Their authors—men like Thomas Jefferson, John Adams, Benjamin Franklin, and James Madison—were among the most creative political thinkers of their time. But these men did not operate in an ideological vacuum. They were influenced by political ideas and ethical teachings that had roots in ancient times. These ideas and beliefs helped shape political views in the colonies and eventually gave rise to the American system of government.

The Religious and Classical Roots of Colonial Ideas About Government

Colonial thinkers were strongly influenced by the ethical ideas shared by the Judeo-Christian religious traditions. Their notion of justice, for example, was rooted in the principles of ancient Judaism, which stressed that people should seek to create a just society based on respect for the law.

They were also influenced by the concept of **natural law**. This was the belief that there exists, beyond the framework of human laws, a universal set of moral principles that can be applied to any culture or system of justice. According to the Christian philosopher Thomas Aquinas, people could discover these natural laws using both reason and their inborn sense of right and wrong. A human law that violated natural law, many colonists believed, was unjust and should be changed.

The creators of the Declaration of Independence used natural law to explain why the 13 colonies needed to rebel against the British. The Declaration states that "the Laws of Nature and of Nature's God" empowered the colonies to seek a "separate and equal station" from an oppressive government.

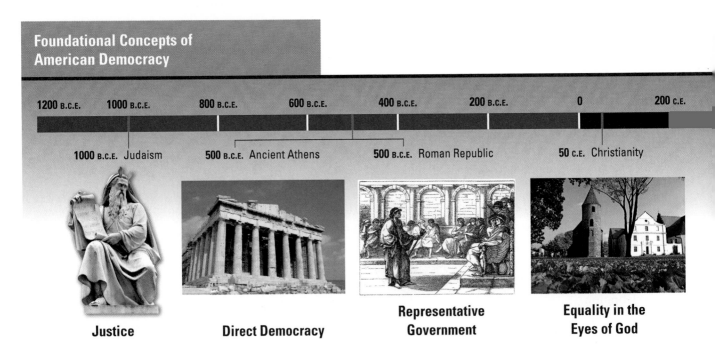

Foundational Concepts of American Democracy

| 1200 B.C.E. | 1000 B.C.E. | 800 B.C.E. | 600 B.C.E. | 400 B.C.E. | 200 B.C.E. | 0 | 200 C.E. |

1000 B.C.E. Judaism — 500 B.C.E. Ancient Athens — 500 B.C.E. Roman Republic — 50 C.E. Christianity

Justice   **Direct Democracy**   **Representative Government**   **Equality in the Eyes of God**

Colonial leaders also looked to the past for ideas about how to govern a society. From the Greek city-state of Athens came the tradition of direct democracy, or decision making by all citizens. Direct democracy took root in New England's town meetings, where citizens gathered to discuss and solve their local problems.

From the Roman Republic came the idea of republicanism, or **representative government,** which refers to decision making by officials elected from the citizenry. Many colonists also admired the Roman idea of **civic virtue**. They understood this to mean a willingness to serve one's country.

The English Roots of American Government

The traditions and principles of English government also had a great influence on political views in the colonies. Although the colonists eventually rebelled against British rule, they had great respect for English common law and Britain's constitutional system. This system was based on a set of laws, customs, and practices that limited the powers of government and guaranteed the people certain basic rights. In fact, one reason the colonists rebelled was to secure the "rights of Englishmen" that they believed had been denied to them.

This tradition of English rights was based on three key documents: the Magna Carta, the Petition of Right, and the English Bill of Rights. The first—the Magna Carta, or "Great Charter"—was signed by King John in 1215. A **charter** is a written grant of authority. The Magna Carta was forced on the king by English nobles, who were angered by the heavy taxes and arbitrary rules imposed by their monarch.

The Magna Carta defined the rights and duties of English nobles and set limits on the monarch's power. For example, the charter stated that the monarch could not make special demands for money from his nobles without their consent. In time, this provision was used to support the argument that no tax should be levied by a monarch without Parliament's consent.

In addition, the Magna Carta established the principle of the **rule of law**. One article of the charter says that the king cannot sell, deny, or delay justice. Another states that "no free man shall be seized or imprisoned . . . except by the lawful judgment of his equals or by the law of the land." The Magna Carta made it clear that all people, including the monarch, were subject to the rule of law.

Over the next few centuries, English monarchs often ignored or defied the principles set down in the Magna Carta. Royal taxation and abuse of power sparked ongoing struggles with Parliament. In 1628, Parliament tried to limit the power of King Charles I by passing a law called the Petition of Right. This

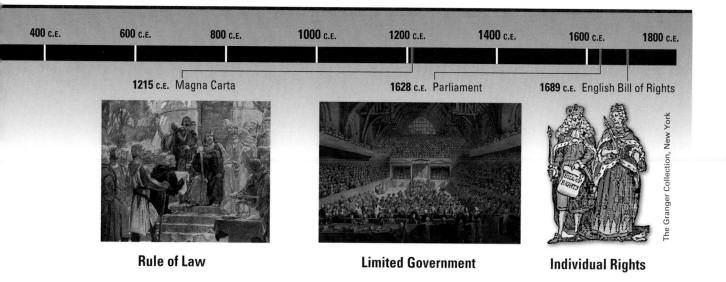

| 400 c.e. | 600 c.e. | 800 c.e. | 1000 c.e. | 1200 c.e. | 1400 c.e. | 1600 c.e. | 1800 c.e. |

1215 c.e. Magna Carta

1628 c.e. Parliament

1689 c.e. English Bill of Rights

The Granger Collection, New York

Rule of Law

Limited Government

Individual Rights

second key document prohibited arbitrary arrests and the quartering of troops in private homes without the owners' consent. The Petition of Right underscored the principle of **limited government** by affirming that the king's power was not absolute.

The third key document, the English Bill of Rights, was passed by Parliament in 1689. At the time, Britain was just emerging from years of political turmoil and civil war. Parliament offered the throne to a new king and queen, William and Mary of Orange, but insisted that they accept the Bill of Rights as a condition of their rule.

The English Bill of Rights reaffirmed the principle of **individual rights** established in the Magna Carta and the Petition of Right. New individual rights guaranteed to British subjects included the right to petition the king, the right to bear arms, and freedom from cruel and unusual punishments. Other provisions included the right to trial by jury and to hold elections without royal interference. The English Bill of Rights also finally established the power of Parliament over the monarchy. The king could not levy taxes or maintain an army during peacetime, for example, without Parliament's consent.

The Contributions of English Enlightenment Thinkers
Colonial leaders were also strongly influenced by the ideas of the Enlightenment, an intellectual movement of the 1600s and 1700s. Enlightenment thinkers stressed the value of science and reason, not only for studying the natural world, but also for improving human society and government.

Two key figures of the early Enlightenment were the English philosophers Thomas Hobbes and John Locke. Both men helped develop the social-contract theory, which stated that people in society agreed to give up some of their freedom to governments in exchange for security and order.

Hobbes first introduced the idea that government was the result of a social contract between people and their rulers. In his book *Leviathan,* published in 1651, Hobbes theorized that people had once lived in a state of nature. This state was an imaginary time before any governments had been formed. People living in this mythical time were free to do as they pleased, without laws or other restraints. Because some people used their freedom to prey on others, however, the result was a war of "every man against

every man." For most people, Hobbes wrote, life in this time was "solitary, poor, nasty, brutish, and short."

To escape from this misery, Hobbes argued, people entered into a social contract. This contract obliged the people to give up some of their freedom by agreeing to obey an absolute ruler. In exchange for this pledge of obedience, the ruler agreed to bring peace and order to society. Hobbes was obviously not promoting democracy in his writing, but his social-contract theory did lay the groundwork for the idea that government was formed by the consent of the people.

Locke took the idea of a social contract between the people and their rulers a step further. In his *Second Treatise on Government,* published in 1689, Locke argued that in the state of nature, all people were equal and enjoyed certain **natural rights,** or rights that all people have by virtue of being human. These rights include the right to life itself, to liberty, and to the ownership of property produced or gained through one's own labors.

Locke agreed with Hobbes that it was in people's self-interest to enter into a social contract that exchanged some of their freedom for the protection of government. He went on to argue that this social contract was provisional. If a ruler failed to protect the people's life, liberty, and property, then the people had a right to overthrow that ruler and establish a new government.

The idea that the purpose of government was to protect the rights of the people exerted a powerful influence on colonial thinkers. Eventually this idea would be used to help justify the American Revolution.

Influences of French Enlightenment Thinkers
Two French thinkers also made major contributions to political thought during the Enlightenment. One was Charles-Louis de Secondat, more commonly known as Baron de Montesquieu. The other was Jean-Jacques Rousseau.

Montesquieu is most famous for his book *The Spirit of Laws,* published in 1748. In this book, Montesquieu argued that governments should be organized in a way that prevents any one person or group from dominating or oppressing others. This argument led him to propose a three-branch system of government—executive, legislative, and judicial— with separate functions for each branch. In this

Thomas Hobbes (1588–1679) was an English philosopher who developed the notion of a social contract between rulers and their subjects. He thought that people were too selfish to govern themselves and needed the protection of a strong ruler. He wrote, "All mankind [has] a perpetual and restless desire of power . . . that ceaseth only in death."

John Locke (1632–1704) was an English political theorist and philosopher whose ideas helped lay the foundations for democratic government. Unlike Hobbes, Locke believed that people formed governments to protect their rights, not to save them from themselves. "The end [purpose] of law is not to abolish or restrain," he wrote, "but to preserve and enlarge freedom."

Baron de Montesquieu (1689–1755) was a French aristocrat and political philosopher. He believed that democracy was the best form of government. But he said that power must be divided among different groups for democracy to work. "When the [lawmaking] and [law enforcement] powers are united in the same person," he wrote, "there can be no liberty."

Jean-Jacques Rousseau (1712–1778), a French philosopher, believed that people were naturally good but were corrupted and enslaved by society. "Man is born free," he observed, but "everywhere he is in chains." Rousseau said that governments had a duty to secure freedom for their people. If they did not, they had no right to exist. "Force does not create right," he wrote. "Obedience is due only to legitimate powers."

system, each branch would act to limit the power of the other branches. This principle of **separation of powers** was so admired by Americans that they applied it to their colonial governments.

Rousseau was a Swiss-born philosopher who spent much of his life in France. In his book *The Social Contract,* Rousseau extended the social contract still further. He added the idea that for a government formed by a social contract to have legitimacy, it must be based on **popular sovereignty,** or the general will of the people. He wrote,

> *The heart of the idea of the social contract may be stated simply: Each of us places his person and authority under the supreme direction of the general will, and the group receives each individual as an indivisible part of the whole.*
> —Jean-Jacques Rousseau,
> *The Social Contract,* 1762

Rousseau further argued that if a government acted contrary to the general will, it had broken the social contract and should be dissolved. Many colonial leaders agreed with Rousseau that government should be based on the will of the people. Thomas Paine, whose book *Common Sense* helped push the colonies toward independence, was particularly influenced by Rousseau's writings.

■ 3.3 From Ideas to Independence: The American Revolution

The colonists gathered ideas about government from many sources and traditions. But these ideas did not all come from the study of ancient history or European philosophy. They were also shaped by the colonists' everyday experiences of life in colonial America.

Colonial Experience with Self-Government

Most of the 13 colonies were established under royal charters issued by the king. These charters gave ultimate power to the king and his appointed officials. But because the colonies were so far from Britain, the charters left a significant amount of local control in the hands of the colonists themselves.

In several colonies, the settlers modified their royal charters or added other agreements. One example of an early agreement was the Mayflower Compact. This historic document was named after the *Mayflower,* the small ship that brought English colonists to Massachusetts in 1620.

Before the settlers landed, they drew up a **compact,** or agreement, for the governing of the new colony. In this compact, they agreed to live in a "Civil Body Politic." They also agreed to obey "just and equal Laws" enacted by representatives of their choosing "for the general good of the Colony." This was the first written framework for self-government in the American colonies.

New England colonists soon developed their own form of local government, a version of direct democracy known as the town meeting. At these meetings, residents could discuss issues and make decisions that affected their community.

Later, in 1641, colonists in Massachusetts created New England's first code of laws, called the Massachusetts Body of Liberties. Following in the tradition of English government, this code guaranteed certain basic rights to the colonists.

By the early 1700s, most colonies had developed a governing structure of executive, legislative, and judicial branches. The executive was a governor, usually appointed by the king. Royal governors had substantial power, although that power could be partly limited by colonial legislatures.

The legislatures typically consisted of two houses. The upper house was a council appointed by the governor. The lower house was an elected assembly with members chosen by voters in the colony.

The first elected assembly in the colonies was Virginia's House of Burgesses, established in 1619. Later, the other colonies formed elected assemblies. Like Parliament, these assemblies held the "power of the purse"—the power to approve new taxes or spending—which meant they could exercise some control over the governor.

The colonial assemblies were hardly models of democracy, because in most cases only white, male landowners were allowed to vote. Nevertheless, the assemblies reflected a belief in self-government. They also affirmed the principle that the colonists could not be taxed except by their elected representatives. Over time, the assemblies would play an increasingly important role in colonial government.

The first representative assembly in colonial America, Virginia's House of Burgesses, was founded in Jamestown in 1619 but later moved to the new capital of Williamsburg. Today, a restored version of the Capitol, where the assembly met, is one of the prime attractions of Colonial Williamsburg.

From "Benign Neglect" to Armed Rebellion

By the mid-1700s, the colonies were accustomed to managing their own affairs. Although Britain provided defense and a market for products grown or produced in the colonies, it rarely interfered with the day-to-day business of government.

In the 1760s, however, Britain reversed this policy of "benign neglect" by enforcing taxes and restrictions on the colonies. This change came about after the French and Indian War, a war fought against France and its Indian allies on North American soil.

Britain won the French and Indian War in 1763. As a result, it gained control of Canada and the Ohio Valley, areas formerly claimed by France. To defend that territory, Britain had to station more troops in the colonies. The British government argued that the colonies should pay some of the cost of this added defense. To achieve that end, Parliament enacted the Stamp Act in 1765, which said Americans must buy stamps to place on their deeds, mortgages, liquor licenses, playing cards, almanacs, and newspapers.

The colonists were outraged. In their eyes, the stamps were a form of taxation. As British citizens, only their elected representatives could tax them.

Therefore, because the colonies had no representation in Parliament, the taxes were illegal.

Raising the cry of "no taxation without representation," the colonists united in protest against the Stamp Act. In response, the British government repealed the hated act. But it continued trying to control the colonies through taxes and other measures. Protests continued and violence flared. On March 5, 1770, British troops shot and killed five agitators in Boston, an incident known as the Boston Massacre.

In 1773, Parliament tried again to force the colonies to accept its authority, this time by placing a tax on imported tea. Late that year, three ships arrived in Boston Harbor with the first load of taxed tea. Colonists dressed as Indians emptied 342 chests of tea into the harbor in defiance of British authority.

In a belated effort to crack down on such protests, Parliament imposed sanctions known in the colonies as the Intolerable Acts. These harsh penalties further inflamed colonial resistance to British rule. Hoping to defuse the escalating conflict, colonial leaders gathered in Philadelphia in 1774. This assembly, called the First Continental Congress, called for peaceful opposition to British policies.

A series of actions and events starting in the 1760s set the American colonies on a course toward armed revolution and independence.

1760

affix the STAMP.

This is the Place to

1765 Stamp Act
A tax levied by Parliament on all paper goods in the colonies raises cries of "no taxation without representation."

1767 Townshend Acts
These acts place duties on goods imported into the colonies. The colonists resist by boycotting all British goods.

1765

1770 Boston Massacre
Protesters in Boston provoke British soldiers, causing them to fire into the crowd, killing five people. Paul Revere's famous engraving of the event helps spark further protests.

1770

1773–1774 Boston Tea Party and the Intolerable Acts
Colonists protesting the Tea Act dump taxed tea into Boston Harbor. Britain responds by imposing the Intolerable Acts on the colonies. George Washington calls the acts "repugnant to every principle of natural justice."

1775

1775 Fighting begins
Militia troops skirmish with British soldiers at Lexington and Concord, beginning the American Revolution.

1776 Declaration of Independence
The Continental Congress adopts a resolution declaring the colonies to be "Free and Independent States."

1780

Thomas Jefferson, shown here with Benjamin Franklin and John Adams, drafted the Declaration of Independence. In many ways, Jefferson, a Virginia slaveholder, was an odd choice for this task. For all his fine words about liberty and equality, he was unwilling to apply his "self-evident" truths to the men and women he held in bondage.

By this time, however, colonial patriots were already forming **militias,** or groups of armed citizens, to defend their rights. On April 19, 1775, militia troops from Massachusetts clashed with British soldiers in battles at Lexington and Concord. These skirmishes marked the beginning of the American Revolution.

The Decision to Declare Independence

Shortly after fighting broke out in Massachusetts, the Continental Congress met again. The delegates quickly voted to form a Continental Army made up of volunteers from all the colonies. They chose George Washington, a leading officer in the Virginia militia, to be the new army's commanding officer.

Still, the Congress hesitated to call for a final break with Britain. Many delegates hoped instead that a peaceful resolution could be found. John Adams of Massachusetts, however, was not among them. Over the next year, Adams worked tirelessly to convince his fellow delegates that independence should be their goal.

Finally, in June 1776, the Congress formed a committee to draft a declaration of independence. This committee consisted of five men: Thomas Jefferson of Virginia, John Adams of Massachusetts, Benjamin Franklin of Pennsylvania, Roger Sherman of Connecticut, and Robert R. Livingston of New York. The task of crafting the first draft went to Jefferson. A gifted writer steeped in Enlightenment ideas, Jefferson wrote,

> We hold these truths to be self-evident, that all men are created equal, that they are endowed by their Creator with certain unalienable Rights, that among these are Life, Liberty and the pursuit of Happiness.—That to secure these rights, Governments are instituted among Men, deriving their just powers from the consent of the governed.

—Declaration of Independence, 1776

In these two sentences, Jefferson set forth a vision of a new kind of nation. Unlike old nations based on blood ties or conquest, this new nation was born of two key ideas. The first is that governments are formed to protect people's **unalienable rights**. In a slight twist on Locke, Jefferson defined those basic individual rights as the rights to life, liberty, and the pursuit of happiness. The second key idea is that governments derive "their just powers from the consent of the governed."

The Declaration goes on to say that if a government fails to protect people's rights, the people should abolish it and form a new one. To bolster the case for doing just that, the Declaration details "a long train of abuses" that violated the colonists' rights. The document concludes with the bold declaration that

> These United Colonies are, and of Right ought to be Free and Independent States; . . . they are Absolved from all Allegiance to the British Crown, and . . . all political connection between them and the State of Great Britain, is and ought to be totally dissolved . . . And for the support of this Declaration, with a firm reliance on the protection of divine Providence, we mutually pledge to each other our Lives, our Fortunes and our sacred Honor.
> —Declaration of Independence, 1776

On July 4, 1776, the members of Congress formally approved the Declaration of Independence. The Declaration was later written on parchment for delegates to sign. By signing the Declaration, the delegates were making a formal declaration of war against what was then the most powerful nation on Earth.

Creating a New Government During Wartime

The fighting with Great Britain dragged on for five more years, finally ending in 1781 with the surrender of the British army at Yorktown, Virginia. During this time, the Continental Congress served as the new nation's government. It raised troops and supplies for the war effort, borrowed large sums of money, and negotiated treaties with foreign countries. Most of this was done without the backing of a constitution, but not for lack of trying on the part of Congress.

After declaring independence, Congress appointed a committee to prepare a plan of government known as the Articles of Confederation. This plan was approved by Congress in 1777 and sent to the states for **ratification,** or formal approval. The states did not get around to approving the Articles until 1781, just months before the fighting ended.

With or without a constitution, Congress had a hard time managing the war effort. It depended on the states for funding and was often short of money.

This statue in the Virginia State Capitol shows George Washington as an American "Cincinnatus." The name comes from a legendary citizen-soldier in ancient Rome named Cincinnatus. Like Washington, Cincinnatus led an army to victory in a time of crisis. Also like Washington, he retired to his farm after the war ended rather than trying to seize power. In honor of this display of civic virtue, officers in the Continental Army formed the Society of the Cincinnati, with Washington as its first president. The society's motto is, "He gave up everything to serve the republic."

As a result, it had difficulty supplying the troops with arms and provisions. Many soldiers had to fight without adequate weapons, uniforms, or food to sustain them.

By the war's end, many Americans were skeptical of Congress's ability to govern the new nation. Some believed that the country needed a strong ruler to ensure stability. The obvious choice was George Washington, commander of the army and hero of the revolution.

In 1782, an army officer who longed for such a strong ruler wrote a letter to Washington. In it, he expressed his hope, shared by many of his fellow officers, that the independent American states would be joined into "a kingdom with Washington as the head." The general was appalled. He had fought for too long to sever ties with a monarchy to aspire to becoming a new king. He responded to his admirer,

> *Be assured Sir, no occurrence in the course of the War, has given me more painful sensations than your information of there being such ideas existing in the Army . . . banish these thoughts from your mind.*
> —George Washington, 1782

Although Washington rejected the idea of an American monarchy, this incident hinted at some of the difficulties facing the new American government.

■ 3.4 Putting Ideas to Work: Framing New Constitutions

The Articles of Confederation was only one of many new plans of government drafted during the war. Each of the 13 states also needed a constitution. As leaders in each state set about this task, they found few models to guide them. England did not have a written constitution. Its system of government was based on an assortment of laws, policies, and customs developed over the centuries. When it came to writing formal constitutions, the Americans were on their own.

State Constitutions: Giving Power to the People
In framing their new plans of government, state lawmakers demonstrated their commitment to **constitutionalism,** or the idea that government should be based on an established set of principles. These principles included popular sovereignty, limited government, the rule of law, and **majority rule**. The lawmakers also separated the powers of government by creating executive, legislative, and judicial branches, just as Montesquieu had described.

In addition, all state constitutions began with a statement of individual rights. The first of these, the Virginia Declaration of Rights, was adopted in June 1776 as part of Virginia's constitution. It served as a model for other state constitutions and later for the U.S. Bill of Rights.

The governments created under the new state constitutions derived their power from the people. However, they were not completely democratic. The states typically limited voting rights to white men who paid taxes or owned a certain amount of property. None of the original 13 state constitutions specifically outlawed slavery, and all states south of Pennsylvania denied slaves equal rights as human beings.

Governing Under the Articles of Confederation
The national government created under the Articles of Confederation was much weaker than the governments established in the states. Although some members of Congress wanted a strong central government, the majority preferred a loose confederation, with most powers remaining at the state level. The Articles emphasized that each state would retain its "sovereignty, freedom, and independence." Any power not specifically given to Congress was reserved for the states.

The government created under the Articles consisted only of a congress, with members chosen by the states. It had neither an executive to carry out laws nor a judicial branch to settle legal questions. On paper, at least, Congress did have several key powers. It could declare war, negotiate with foreign countries, and establish a postal system. It could also settle disputes between states. But it had no power to impose taxes, which meant it was often starved for funds.

Despite these limitations, Congress held the nation together through years of war. It also enacted at least one landmark piece of legislation, the Northwest Ordinance of 1787. This law established procedures for the creation of new states in the Northwest Territory, a region bounded by the Ohio and Mississippi rivers. The Northwest Ordinance served as a model for all territories that later entered the Union as states.

For the most part, however, the government created by the Articles of Confederation was a failure. Lacking the power to levy taxes, Congress could not raise the funds needed to support the Continental Army. It had to borrow heavily to fund the revolution. After the war, it had no way to raise funds to repay those debts.

Equally troubling, Congress lacked power to control trade among the states. After the war, states began setting up trade barriers and quarreling among themselves. Matters came to a head when farmers, led by Daniel Shays, attacked a federal arsenal in Springfield, Massachusetts. Although Shays' Rebellion was finally put down by state troops, it revealed how little Congress could do to hold together the increasingly unstable country.

By 1786, it was clear to many of the nation's leaders that the government formed under the Articles was not working. That fall, representatives from various states met at Annapolis, Maryland, to discuss trade issues. While there, they issued a call for a constitutional convention to meet the following year in Philadelphia.

In theory, the purpose of the convention was to revise the Articles of Confederation. Once the delegates met, however, they decided to scrap the Articles and create an entirely new constitution. The table below lists some of the weaknesses of the Articles and explains how they were eventually fixed under the new plan of government.

Mending the Articles of Confederation

Weaknesses of the Articles of Confederation	Weaknesses Fixed Under the Constitution
Congress could not levy or collect taxes, leaving the government starved for funds.	Congress has the power to levy taxes to support the government.
Congress could not regulate trade among the states or with other countries.	Congress has the power to regulate interstate trade and trade with foreign countries.
Congress had only one house, and each state had only one vote in Congress, regardless of population.	Congress has two houses, and representation in the House of Representatives is based on population.
Nine out of 13 states in Congress had to agree to pass a major law.	Laws are passed by a simple majority of members of Congress.
All 13 states had to agree to amend the Articles.	Amendments can be ratified by three-fourths of the states.
The government lacked an executive branch to enforce laws and a court system to settle legal disputes.	The government has a legislative branch, an executive branch, and a judicial branch.
Congress could not create a uniform currency. Money was issued by states.	Congress has the sole power to issue money.
The states could and did ignore laws passed by Congress.	The Constitution and laws passed by Congress are the "supreme Law of the Land."
The states were loosely joined in a "league of friendship."	The states are bound together in a permanent union.

Convening the Constitutional Convention

On May 25, 1787, the Constitutional Convention began. Delegates from all the states except Rhode Island came together at the Pennsylvania State House in Philadelphia, later known as Independence Hall. They met in the same room where the Declaration of Independence had been signed 11 years before.

The 55 delegates were prominent in American political life. All were white men. Among them were former soldiers, governors, members of Congress, and men who had drafted state constitutions. Their average age was 42.

The delegates represented a wide range of personalities and experience. At 81, Benjamin Franklin was the senior member. The wisdom and wit of this writer, inventor, and diplomat enlivened the proceedings. George Washington lent dignity to the gathering, while his former military aide Alexander Hamilton brought intellectual brilliance. Other delegates, like Roger Sherman of Connecticut, contributed legal and business experience. James Madison of Virginia was perhaps the most profound political thinker and the best prepared of all the delegates.

Several key figures were not at the convention. Both Thomas Jefferson and John Adams were in Europe, serving as U.S. diplomats. On reading over the delegates' names, Jefferson described the convention as "an assembly of demigods."

Other leaders, like Samuel Adams of Massachusetts and Patrick Henry of Virginia, were suspicious of efforts to strengthen the central government. They, too, did not attend.

During the convention, no one played a greater role than Madison. Although he was just 36 years old, he had already served in Congress and the Virginia legislature. He was a serious student of politics and democratic theory. As the meetings got underway, he took detailed notes of the discussions and worked tirelessly to promote the new plan. For his role in shaping the new framework, he is rightly called the Father of the Constitution.

Reaching a Compromise on Representation

The first thing the delegates did was elect George Washington as the convention's presiding officer. They also adopted rules of procedure, including a vow of secrecy. Although it was stiflingly hot and humid in Philadelphia that summer, they shut the doors and windows of their meeting room to keep the proceedings private. They knew that the public was intensely curious about their discussions, and they did not want public pressure to affect their decisions.

Next, the Virginia delegates, who favored a strong national government, put forth a plan for a new constitution. The Virginia Plan, written mainly by James Madison, was clearly designed to replace the Articles, not to revise them. It called for a government of three branches. The legislative branch would make the laws, the executive branch would carry out the laws, and the judicial branch would interpret the laws.

Under the Virginia Plan, the new government would have a **bicameral,** or two-house, legislature. The Virginia Plan proposed that representation in both houses should be based on the population of each state. This would give the more populous states more representatives, and thus more influence, than states with smaller populations.

For about two weeks, the delegates discussed the details of the Virginia Plan. Some thought it gave too much power to the national government. Some opposed a bicameral legislature. Moreover, the smaller states did not like their representation in Congress being tied to population.

On June 13, William Patterson of New Jersey introduced an alternative approach. The New Jersey Plan proposed a series of amendments to the Articles of Confederation. These changes would have created a somewhat more powerful national government with a **unicameral,** or one-house, legislature in which all states had equal representation.

Delegates from the smaller states welcomed the New Jersey Plan. But after several days of debate, the convention voted to reject this proposal and return to discussion of the Virginia Plan.

For the next month, the delegates debated the Virginia Plan point by point. They continued to argue about the critical issue of representation in Congress. The debate grew so heated at times that some delegates threatened to walk out.

Finally, Roger Sherman of Connecticut proposed a compromise designed to satisfy both sides. His plan called for a bicameral legislature with a different form of representation in each house. In the Senate, states would have equal representation. In the House of Representatives, states would have representation

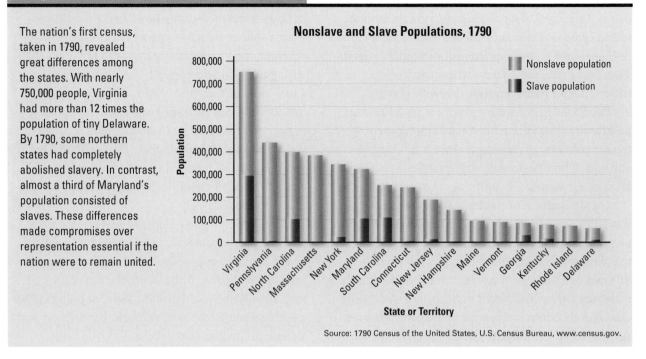

The nation's first census, taken in 1790, revealed great differences among the states. With nearly 750,000 people, Virginia had more than 12 times the population of tiny Delaware. By 1790, some northern states had completely abolished slavery. In contrast, almost a third of Maryland's population consisted of slaves. These differences made compromises over representation essential if the nation were to remain united.

Nonslave and Slave Populations, 1790

Nonslave population
Slave population

Population

State or Territory

Virginia, Pennsylvania, North Carolina, Massachusetts, New York, Maryland, South Carolina, Connecticut, New Jersey, New Hampshire, Maine, Vermont, Georgia, Kentucky, Rhode Island, Delaware

Source: 1790 Census of the United States, U.S. Census Bureau, www.census.gov.

based on their populations. Sherman's plan, known as the Great Compromise, resolved the thorny issue of representation in Congress and allowed the convention to move forward.

Compromises on Slavery and Commerce

Other issues also divided the delegates. Those from northern states differed sharply with those from southern states on questions of slavery and commerce. Many northern delegates wanted the constitution to include a provision for abolishing slavery. But most southerners opposed ending a system of labor on which their agricultural economy depended.

These differences over slavery spilled into debates on representation and taxes. Since most slaves lived in the South, delegates from the South wanted slaves to be counted when determining representation in the House of Representatives. Yet they did not want slaves counted when determining each state's share of taxes to support the national government. The graph above shows which states had large slave populations at that time.

In contrast, delegates from the North wanted slaves to be counted for taxation, but not when determining representation. After much debate, the delegates reached another important compromise. For purposes of both representation and taxation, a slave was to be counted as three-fifths of all "free persons."

The Three-Fifths Compromise helped hold the new nation together. However, by treating a slave as less than a free person, this provision contradicted the basic ideal of equality set forth in the Declaration of Independence. This contradiction between democratic ideals and the cruel inequality of slavery would haunt the nation for decades to come and would eventually result in the Civil War.

Delegates from the North and South also argued over commerce. Northerners favored giving Congress broad powers to control trade. Southerners worried that Congress might outlaw the slave trade and place heavy taxes on southern exports of crops, such as cotton and tobacco. Again the delegates reached a compromise. Congress would have the power to regulate foreign and interstate commerce, but it could not tax exports, and it could not outlaw the slave trade until 1808.

Creating the Executive Branch: One Head or Many?

Another major issue concerned the formation of the executive branch. Some delegates wanted a single executive to head the government. Others were concerned that giving power to a single leader might give rise to a monarchy or tyranny. Instead they favored an executive committee made up of at least two members. In the end, however, the delegates voted for a single president.

The next question was how to choose the president. Some delegates thought Congress should do it, while others favored popular elections. They finally decided to set up a special body called the **Electoral College**. This body would be made up of electors from each state who would cast votes to elect the president and vice president. Each state would have as many electors as the number of senators and representatives it sent to Congress. Adding the two senators to the number of electors from each state boosted the influence of small states and of those with large slave populations.

On September 17, 1787, after months of hard work, the Constitution was signed by 39 of the 42 delegates present. The document they signed that day began with these ringing words:

> *We the People of the United States, in Order to form a more perfect Union, establish Justice, insure domestic Tranquility, provide for the common defence, promote the general Welfare, and secure the Blessings of Liberty to ourselves and our Posterity, do ordain and establish this Constitution for the United States of America.*
> —Preamble to the Constitution, 1787

After that, it was up to the states to decide whether this plan of government would indeed establish "a more perfect Union."

■ 3.5 Ratifying the Constitution

The Constitution included a provision for ratification. To go into effect, the new plan of government would need to be ratified by at least 9 of the 13 states. Ratification was to take place at state conventions made up of delegates elected for this purpose. Success was by no means assured.

The pro-ratification effort was led by supporters of the Constitution who called themselves **Federalists**. They favored the creation of a strong federal government that shared power with the states. Their opponents were known as **Anti-Federalists**. These were people who preferred the loose association of states established under the Articles of Confederation. The battle between these two groups was played out in the press, in state legislatures, and at the state ratifying conventions.

Anti-Federalists Speak Out Against the Constitution

Anti-Federalists opposed the Constitution for various reasons. Some worried about the increased powers of taxation granted to the national government.

THE FOUNDATION OF AMERICAN GOVERNMENT

Only 39 of the original 55 delegates signed the Constitution on September 17, 1787. Thirteen delegates had returned home before the conclusion of the convention, and three others refused to sign.

Others were concerned that the government would create a large standing army or that a federal court system would overrule state courts.

Anti-Federalists, however, had two chief complaints about the proposed Constitution. The first was, as Virginia delegate, George Mason, pointed out, "There is no Declaration of Rights," or a bill of rights. The second was that the Constitution would make the national government too powerful. Mason worried that "the laws of the general government" would be "paramount to the laws and constitutions of the several states."

The Anti-Federalists feared that a strong national government would lead to tyranny. They believed that the states, being smaller, were more able to represent the people's rights and preserve democracy. For that reason, they argued that the states, not the national government, should hold most of the power.

The Anti-Federalist camp initially included some of the leading figures of the American Revolution, including Samuel Adams, Patrick Henry, and John Hancock. In their minds, the Constitution represented a betrayal of the democratic ideals that had motivated the American Revolution.

Federalists Defend the Constitution

In the face of such criticism, the Federalists mounted a spirited defense of the Constitution. Three men led this campaign: Alexander Hamilton, James Madison, and John Jay. Hamilton and Madison had helped frame the Constitution. Jay was a prominent New York lawyer, diplomat, and political leader who had played a key role in the revolution.

Together, these men wrote a series of 85 essays known as *The Federalist Papers*. These essays were published over the course of several months and made a strong case for the new plan of government. Some historians have called the publication of these papers one of the most powerful public relations campaigns in history.

The Federalist Papers authors explained the key features of the Constitution and tried to undercut the claims of their opponents. In *The Federalist* No. 10, for example, Madison addressed the Anti-Federalists' charge that it would be impossible to make representative government work over a large territory like the United States. Madison countered

that the size of the United States was actually an advantage in establishing a representative government. Because such a government would represent so many people, it would be less likely to fall under the sway of factions, or groups that want power for selfish ends. The governments of small nations, he argued, were more prone to being taken over by factions, because factions find it easier to win over a small population than a large one. As Madison wrote,

The fewer the distinct parties and interests, the more frequently will a majority be found of the same party; and the smaller the number of individuals composing a majority, . . . the more easily will they . . . execute their plans of oppression. Extend the sphere [to a larger government], and you take in a greater variety of parties and interests; you make it less probable that a majority of the whole will have a common motive to invade the rights of other citizens.
—James Madison,
The Federalist No. 10, 1787

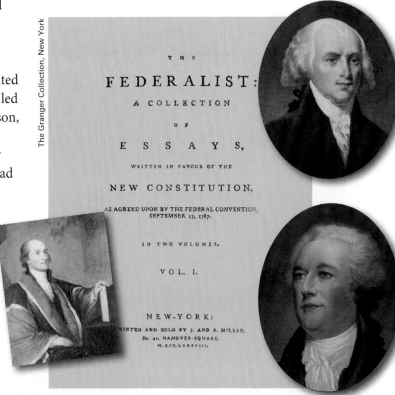

The Granger Collection, New York

The Federalist Papers, first published in 1787, made a strong case for ratification of the Constitution. These essays, written by John Jay (lower left), James Madison (upper right), and Alexander Hamilton (lower right), provide valuable insight into the political thinking behind the Constitution.

In *The Federalist* No. 51, Madison addressed the concern that a strong national government would lead to tyranny. He explained how the checks and balances built into the Constitution were designed to keep this from happening. "If men were angels," he wrote, "no government would be necessary. If angels were to govern," he continued, "neither external nor internal controls on government would be necessary." In a government of men, he argued, "ambition must be made to counteract ambition."

It is impossible to know how many minds were changed by these essays. But over more than two centuries, these have proved to be invaluable insights to the thinking and intentions of the Constitution's framers.

The Constitution Goes into Effect

By January 1788, Delaware, Pennsylvania, and New Jersey had ratified the Constitution. Georgia and Connecticut soon followed. In Massachusetts, however, the ratifying convention deadlocked over a key issue: the lack of a bill of rights. After much debate, the Massachusetts delegates agreed to ratify after receiving assurance that such a list of rights would be added after ratification.

A number of other states ratified with the same understanding. By the summer of 1788, all but two states had ratified. The Constitution was now in effect. North Carolina would join the new union in 1789, and Rhode Island in 1790.

Meanwhile, Congress prepared to make way for the new government. Elections were held for the Senate and House of Representatives. A date was also set in February 1789 for the first presidential election.

The winner of that election, by unanimous vote in the Electoral College, was George Washington. The former general had previously retired to his home, Mount Vernon, in Virginia. But he answered

On April 30, 1789, George Washington was inaugurated as the nation's first president in New York City. In his inaugural speech, he spoke of "the republican model of government" as an "experiment entrusted to the hands of the American people."

the call to duty and made his way to New York City, the seat of the first federal government. There, in Federal Hall on April 30, 1789, Washington placed his hand on a Bible, and like every president since that day, repeated this solemn oath:

> *I do solemnly swear [or affirm] that I will faithfully execute the office of President of the United States, and will to the best of my ability, preserve, protect and defend the Constitution of the United States.*

■ 3.6 Adding the Bill of Rights

In his inaugural speech, President Washington urged Congress to move quickly to draft a bill of rights for the Constitution. Those amendments, he said, should show "a reverence for the characteristic rights of freemen and a regard for public harmony." In urging Congress to take on this task, Washington was acting on promises made during the ratification process. He knew that without the pledge of a bill of rights, the Constitution would not have been ratified.

Proposing a List of Rights

No one was more aware of that pledge than James Madison. He had made just such a promise while lobbying for ratification in his home state of Virginia. As a new member of the House of Representatives, Madison immediately set out to draft a bill of rights.

Like most Federalists, Madison had initially opposed a bill of rights, arguing that the democratic principles embedded in the Constitution made such protections unnecessary. Even if one branch of the new national government tried to curtail the individual rights of citizens, he argued, the other branches would act to prevent such abuses.

Thomas Jefferson persuaded Madison to change his mind. In a letter to Madison, Jefferson wrote, "a bill of rights is what the people are entitled to against every government on earth . . . and what no just government should refuse." Another reason for adding a bill of rights to the Constitution, he observed in a later letter to Madison, was "the legal check which it puts into the hands of the judiciary."

In 1789, Madison introduced to Congress a series of proposed amendments. His list of rights drew from the many different proposals made at the state ratifying conventions. Madison also pulled ideas from other documents, including the Virginia Declaration of Rights, adopted in 1776. Another was the Virginia Statute for Religious Freedom, written by Thomas Jefferson in 1779. The English Bill of Rights was a key influence, as well.

Madison also drew from the writings of William Blackstone, a prominent English lawyer and judge. In his famous work *Commentaries on the Laws of England,* Blackstone wrote extensively about the "personal liberty" and the "rights of persons." Among those rights, Blackstone argued, was "liberty of the press," which he saw as "essential to the nature of a free state."

Having introduced his bill of rights, Madison faced an uphill battle getting the amendments

The Bill of Rights is on display at the National Archives in Washington, D.C. This exhibit also houses the Declaration of Independence and the Constitution. These three important documents that established the foundation for the U.S. government are collectively known as the Charters of Freedom.

approved by Congress. Some legislators wanted to postpone them in favor of more pressing matters. Others wanted to wait until flaws in the new government became more apparent. But Madison insisted on quick action, saying that the public might otherwise think "we are not sincere in our desire to . . . secure those rights."

Once Congress finally agreed to debate Madison's proposed amendments, lawmakers were merciless in their criticisms. After months of debate, Madison wrote to a friend that getting a bill of rights through Congress had become "a nauseous project." In the end, however, Congress approved 12 amendments and passed them on to the states for ratification.

Ratifying the Bill of Rights

Most states quickly ratified the Bill of Rights. By the summer of 1790, nine states had approved at least ten of the amendments. Shortly afterward, Vermont became the 14th state in the Union, which raised the number of states necessary for ratification to 11. On December 15, 1791, Virginia became the 11th state to ratify the Bill of Rights.

Two of the proposed amendments, however, failed to win ratification in 1791. The first, dealing with the number of members of the House of Representatives, was never adopted. The other, limiting the ability of Congress to increase the salaries of its members, was finally ratified two centuries later as the Twenty-seventh Amendment.

Three of the original 13 states—Georgia, Massachusetts, and Connecticut—failed to ratify in 1791. All three finally voted for ratification in 1939, on the 150th anniversary of the Bill of Rights. By then, the Bill of Rights had become an integral part of the framework of American government.

Summary

The United States was founded on a set of ideas and principles developed over many centuries. Those ideas helped give rise to a system of representative government based on the rule of law and a respect for individual rights and liberties.

Ideas on government American colonists drew their ideas about government from various sources, including classical civilizations, English law, and Enlightenment philosophy. They combined those ideas with their own experiences in colonial self-government.

Declaring independence Accustomed to self-rule, colonists were quick to react when Great Britain tried to impose taxes on the colonies. In 1776, the colonies declared themselves to be "Free and Independent States."

Framing constitutions While fighting for independence, Americans wrote state constitutions and a national plan of government called the Articles of Confederation. Weaknesses in the Articles led to the framing of a new constitution that gave more power to the national government.

Ratifying the Constitution By 1788, enough states had ratified the Constitution to make it the law of the land. A new government, with George Washington as president, was installed in 1789.

Adding the Bill of Rights To satisfy critics of the Constitution, James Madison drafted a series of amendments to protect individual rights. The Bill of Rights was ratified by the states in 1791 and became the first ten amendments to the Constitution.

What can you do to keep our republic alive and well?

After the Constitutional Convention, people asked Benjamin Franklin what kind of government the new Constitution would create. "A republic, if you can keep it," he replied.

In this article, a scholar with the National Constitution Center looks at the challenges our nation has faced over two centuries to make the Constitution work. You will also find results from a survey on what Americans think about the Constitution. As you read this information, think about Franklin's warning: "if you can keep it." What can you do to keep our republic healthy for the century to come?

A Republic, If You Can Keep It

by Robert R. Beeman, PhD

While today we marvel at the extraordinary accomplishment of our Founding Fathers, their own reaction to the US Constitution . . . was considerably less enthusiastic . . .

Nearly all of the delegates harbored objections . . . Their over-riding concern was the tendency in nearly all parts of the young country toward disorder and disintegration. Americans had used the doctrine of popular sovereignty—"democracy"—as the rationale for their successful rebellion against English authority in 1776.

But they had not yet worked out fully the question that has plagued all nations aspiring to democratic government ever since: how to implement principles of popular majority rule while at the same time preserving stable governments that protect the rights and liberties of all citizens . . .

The American statesmen who succeeded those of the founding generation served their country with a self-conscious sense that the challenges of maintaining a democratic union were every bit as great after 1787 as they were before. Some aspects of their nation-building program—their continuing toleration of slavery and genocidal policies toward American Indians—are fit objects of national shame, not honor. But statesmen of succeeding generations—Lincoln foremost among them—would continue the quest for a "more perfect union" . . .

As we look at the state of our federal union . . . [two centuries] after the Founders completed their work, there is cause for satisfaction that we have avoided many of the plagues afflicting so many other societies, but this is hardly cause for complacency. To be sure, the US Constitution itself has not only survived the crises confronting it in the past, but in so doing, it has in itself become our nation's most powerful symbol of unity . . .

Moreover, our Constitution is a stronger, better document than it was when it initially emerged from the Philadelphia Convention. Through the amendment process (in particular, through the 13th, 14th, 15th and 19th Amendments), it has become the protector of the rights of all the people, not just some of the people.

On the other hand, the challenges to national unity under our Constitution are, if anything, far greater than those confronting the infant nation in 1787.

Public Opinion on the Constitution

In 2011, the Pew Research Center conducted a survey on how the Constitution should be interpreted. Americans were asked whether the Supreme Court should base its rulings on what the Constitution means in current times or what it meant when it was originally written. These graphs show how different groups of Americans believe the Constitution should be interpreted. How do their views differ?

Should the Supreme Court base its rulings on what the Constitution means in current times or meant as originally written?

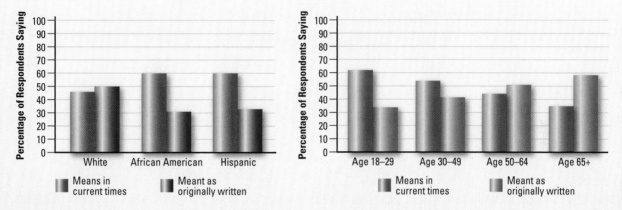

Source: Pew Research Center for the People and the Press, "Ideological Chasm Over Interpreting Constitution," June 20, 2011.

Although the new nation was a pluralistic one by the standards of the 18th century, the face of America in 1998 looks very different from the original: we are no longer a people united by a common language, religion or culture; and while our overall level of material prosperity is staggering by the standards of any age, the widening gulf between rich and poor is perhaps the most serious threat to a common definition of the "pursuit of happiness."

The conditions that threaten to undermine our sense of nationhood . . . are today both more complex and diffuse. Some of today's conditions are part of the tragic legacy of slavery—a racial climate marked too often by mutual mistrust and misunderstanding and a condition of desperate poverty within our inner cities that has left many young people so alienated that any standard definition of citizenship becomes meaningless.

More commonly, but in the long run perhaps just as alarming, tens of millions of Americans have been turned-off by the corrupting effects of money on the political system. Bombarded with negative advertising about their candidates, they express their feelings of alienation by staying home on election day.

If there is a lesson in all of this it is that our Constitution is neither a self-actuating nor a self-correcting document. It requires the constant attention and devotion of all citizens . . . Democratic republics are not merely founded upon the consent of the people, they are also absolutely dependent upon the active and informed involvement of the people for their continued good health.

Dr. Beeman is a professor of history at the University of Pennsylvania and a scholar at the National Constitution Center.

Reprinted with permission of the National Constitution Center. Originally published online at www.constitutioncenter.org.

DO ORDAIN AND ESTABLISH THIS CONSTITUTION
FOR THE UNITED STATES OF AMERICA

The people made the Constitution and they can unmake it.
It is the Creature of their will, and lives only by their will.

Chief Justice John Marshall, 1821

Chapter 4

The United States Constitution

How and why did the framers distribute power in the Constitution?

4.1 Introduction

One February morning in 1971, Dwight Lopez headed off to his classes at Central High School in Columbus, Ohio. Things had been tense at school lately. Students were in shock over the recent shooting of two African American students by whites. Many were also upset about the school's cancellation of Black History Week celebrations. These events would help to provoke a major disturbance at school that day.

Like many American cities in the early 1970s, Columbus was experiencing social upheaval. Growing opposition to the Vietnam War was fueling large anti-war demonstrations. At the same time, racial tensions were high. Despite the gains made by the civil rights movement in the 1960s, most African Americans had yet to experience any real social or economic progress. Many blacks blamed racism for their lack of advancement. In the Columbus public schools, racial conflict was increasing.

On that day in February, tensions boiled over and violence erupted in the school cafeteria. School property was destroyed, and 75 students were given ten-day suspensions from school. One of those students was Dwight Lopez. He claimed that he was an innocent bystander who just happened to be in the cafeteria when the incident occurred. But the school refused to hear his appeal.

Bronze statues of the Founding Fathers at the National Constitution Center in Philadelphia, Pennsylvania

The Constitution guarantees Americans accused of a crime due process of law, or a fair trial. Most trials take place before a judge and jury in courtrooms like the one pictured here.

In response, Lopez took the school district to court, claiming his constitutional right to due process of law had been violated. **Due process,** guaranteed by the Fifth and Fourteenth amendments to the Constitution, requires that those accused of a crime be given a fair hearing and the chance to defend themselves. But this right had never been applied in schools.

The Ohio courts decided in favor of Lopez and eight other students who joined in the case. But the school district appealed the decision to the U.S. Supreme Court. This case, now called *Goss v. Lopez,* would help to define the rights of students—and therefore *your* rights—under the Constitution.

■ **4.2 Elements of the Constitution**

The Constitution provides the basic framework for American government. It also guarantees the rights and freedoms that we, as Americans, sometimes take for granted. Cases like *Goss v. Lopez* help to clarify those rights. They also underscore the role played by the Constitution in our democratic system.

The Constitution is a three-part document, consisting of the Preamble, the articles, and the amendments. Although it may seem complicated, the Constitution is actually a relatively brief and straightforward document. It consists of just over 7,000 words, making it shorter than the sports section in most newspapers. Adopted as the "law of the land" in 1788, it is the oldest written constitution still in use anywhere in the world.

For more than two centuries, we have relied on the Constitution as the basis for our political system. It serves as both a practical outline for government and a symbol of our national way of life. Learning about the Constitution not only helps us understand the rights and freedoms we enjoy as Americans, but also gives us tools to defend those freedoms.

The Preamble Sets the Purpose

The opening paragraph, the Preamble, is a single, long sentence that defines the broad purposes of the **republican government** created by the Constitution. It begins with the phrase "We the people," signifying that power and authority in our system of government come from the people, not the states.

The Preamble goes on to set various goals for the nation under the Constitution. These goals are expressed in a series of key phrases.

Form a more perfect union. The framers of the Constitution wanted to ensure cooperation among the states, and between the states and the national government.

Establish justice. The framers hoped to create a system of government based on fair laws that apply equally to all people.

Ensure domestic tranquility. The framers wanted government to ensure peace and order.

Provide for the common defense. The framers wanted the government to protect the nation against foreign enemies.

Promote the general welfare. The framers hoped the government would ensure the well-being of the citizens.

Secure the blessings of liberty to ourselves and our posterity. The framers hoped to guarantee freedom for Americans, then and in the future.

The Articles Establish Our National Government

The main body of the Constitution consists of seven articles. These seven articles are further divided into sections and clauses. The first three articles establish the three branches of government—legislative, executive, and judicial—and define their powers. These articles lay out the basic structure of the national government.

The four remaining articles of the Constitution cover various subjects, including relations among the states, the supremacy of national law, and the amendment process.

Article I Establishes the Legislative Branch

The first article sets up Congress as the lawmaking body in government. It describes the two chambers of Congress, the Senate and the House of Representatives, as well as the election, terms, and qualifications of their members. It also sets guidelines for rules and procedures in each chamber. This is the longest article in the Constitution, reflecting the founders' belief in the importance of the legislature in a representative democracy.

Section 8 of Article I lays out some of the main powers granted to Congress. These powers are both enumerated and implied. **Enumerated powers** are those that are specifically listed in the Constitution, such as the power to collect taxes, coin money, and declare war.

Implied powers are those that the legislature can claim as part of its lawmaking responsibility. This claim to implied power stems from Clause 18 of Section 8, which says that Congress can "make all laws which shall be necessary and proper" for carrying out its duties. This **Necessary and Proper Clause** is also known as the **Elastic Clause,** since it can be "stretched" to cover a variety of issues and circumstances.

Section 9 of Article I lists powers denied to Congress. Among these denied powers are the suspension of **habeas corpus** and the granting of titles of nobility.

The Structure of the Constitution

The Constitution has a three-part structure. The Preamble is the introduction to the document. The articles make up the body. The amendments are additions and changes made over time.

Preamble	Articles	Amendments
Purpose of government	I: Legislative branch	Formal changes to the Constitution
	II: Executive branch	
	III: Judicial branch	
	IV: Relations among the states	
	V: Amendment process	
	VI: Payment of debts; Supremacy Clause; oaths of office	
	VII: Ratification	

Habeas corpus is the right of accused persons to be brought before a judge to hear the charges against them. The ban on titles of nobility reflects the principle that "all men are created equal," as expressed in the Declaration of Independence.

Article II Establishes the Executive Branch

The executive branch is led by the president and vice president. As it does for members of Congress, the Constitution describes the election, terms of office, and qualifications of these executive officers. It also defines the powers of the president, which include the power to command the armed forces, to make treaties, and to appoint other executive officials.

Article III Establishes the Judicial Branch

Article III creates the Supreme Court, the highest court in the land, while leaving Congress to create the lower courts. It defines the **jurisdiction** of the federal courts, specifying the types of cases that can be tried. It also guarantees the right to trial by jury in criminal cases and defines the crime of treason.

Article IV Concerns Relations Among the States

Article IV has four sections, which make the following key points:

Full faith and credit. Each state must honor the laws and court decisions of other states.

Treatment of citizens. No state may discriminate against the residents of another state. It must treat them as it treats its own residents. States must return suspected criminals to the states in which they are wanted.

New states and territories. Only Congress can authorize the creation of new states. It also has power over territories and other jurisdictions of the United States.

Protection of states. The national government guarantees each state a republican form of government. It also promises to protect states from outside attack and, if requested, to help states put down internal rebellions.

Article V Describes the Amendment Process

The framers understood that it might be necessary to make changes to the Constitution from time to time. Article V spells out the ways such amendments can be proposed and ratified.

Article VI Makes the Constitution the Supreme Law of the Land

Article VI covers several topics. It states that the national government agrees to repay all of the debts that were incurred under the Articles of Confederation. This was critical to ensure support for the new government.

Powers of the Three Branches of Government

The Constitution establishes a government of three branches, with separate powers for each branch. By dividing power, the framers hoped to ensure that no single branch would become too powerful.

Legislative

- Makes the laws
- Appropriates funds for laws and programs
- Approves treaties and executive appointments
- Establishes federal courts

Executive

- Enforces the laws
- Acts as commander in chief of military
- Negotiates treaties
- Appoints federal judges and other top officials

Judicial

- Interprets the laws
- Reviews lower-court decisions
- Judges whether laws and executive actions are constitutional
- Rules on cases between states

The Constitution spells out four methods of approving amendments. All amendments except one have been proposed by Congress and ratified by the state legislatures. The one exception was the Twenty-first Amendment, which repealed the Eighteenth Amendment and ended the national ban on alcohol, known as prohibition.

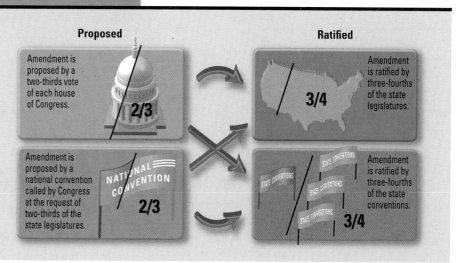

It also states that the Constitution is the "supreme Law of the Land." This section, known as the **Supremacy Clause,** means that federal law supersedes all state and local laws. When the laws conflict, federal law reigns supreme.

In addition, it stipulates that all federal and state officials must take an oath swearing their allegiance to the Constitution. Also, no religious standard can be imposed on any official as a qualification for holding office.

Article VII Explains the Ratification Process

Article VII stipulates that the Constitution would not take effect until ratified by at least nine states. Although the Constitution was signed by the framers on September 17, 1787, ratification did not occur until the following year.

▪ 4.3 Amending the Constitution

The framers never meant for the Constitution to provide a complete and detailed blueprint for government. As Alexander Hamilton noted in 1788, "Constitutions should consist only of general provisions: The reason is, that they must necessarily be permanent, and that they cannot calculate for the possible changes of things."

In general, the framers made broad statements and left it to political leaders to work out many of the specific details of governing. They also built in an amendment process, in Article V, that would allow for formal changes to the Constitution. They hoped that this flexibility would allow the Constitution and the government to endure.

The Amendment Process Is Not Easy

Although the framers understood that amendments might be necessary, they did not want such changes to be taken lightly. For that reason, they made the amendment process difficult. More than 11,000 amendments have been introduced in Congress over the years, but only 33 have been sent on to the states for ratification, and of these, only 27 have been ratified.

Article V lays out a two-step amendment process. Amendments can be proposed and ratified in four ways, as shown in this diagram. However, one method has been used almost exclusively over the years.

In this typical method, an amendment is first proposed by a two-thirds vote in both houses of Congress. The proposed amendment is then sent to the states, where it must be ratified by the legislatures of at least three-fourths of the states.

Only one amendment, the Twenty-first, which ended prohibition, was ratified in a different way. It was approved not by state legislatures, but by special conventions in three-fourths of the states.

The president has no formal role in the amendment process. The chief executive can support or oppose a proposed amendment, but has no power to approve or block its passage. That power lies exclusively with Congress and the states.

"The way I see it, the Constitution cuts both ways. The First Amendment gives you the right to say what you want, but the Second Amendment gives me the right to shoot you for it."

In this cartoon, a man broadly interprets the freedoms guaranteed by the First and Second amendments. However, in reality, these freedoms are limited. Americans disagree on what each amendment in the Bill of Rights was meant to protect.

Only one provision of the Constitution—the equal representation of states in the Senate—is not open to amendment. This point is made explicit in Article V: "no State, without its Consent, shall be deprived of its equal Suffrage in the Senate." This prohibition was meant to ensure that all states—even the smallest and least populated—would always have two seats in the Senate. This was a key compromise worked out during the writing of the Constitution.

Some critics contend that the equal-representation provision is undemocratic. They point out that today over half the U.S. population lives in just nine states: California, Texas, New York, Florida, Illinois, Pennsylvania, Ohio, Michigan, and Georgia. Yet just 18 out of 100 senators represent this half of the population.

The First Ten Amendments: The Bill of Rights

The first ten amendments to the Constitution—also known as the Bill of Rights—were proposed by Congress in 1789 and ratified by the states in 1791. The rights listed in the Bill of Rights outline the freedoms guaranteed to the people and the states.

First Amendment: Basic freedoms. Guarantees five basic freedoms: religion, speech, press, assembly, and petition.

Second Amendment: Right to bear arms. Protects the right to bear arms and form state militias. The national and state governments, however, claim the right to regulate firearms.

Third Amendment: Quartering of soldiers. Bans quartering of troops in private homes during peacetime. This was a key concern in the 1700s but has little relevance today.

Fourth Amendment: Search and seizure. Prevents unreasonable search and seizure. Police and other authorities have no right to search or seize property or people without just cause.

Fifth Amendment: Rights of the accused. Outlines the right to due process of law and other legal protections. This amendment covers various rights of people accused of crimes. It also covers **eminent domain,** which prevents the government from taking over private property without just or fair compensation.

Sixth Amendment: Right to a fair trial. Guarantees the right to public and speedy trial by a jury in criminal cases. The accused also has other rights such as to call witnesses and to be represented by an attorney.

Seventh Amendment: Civil trials. Guarantees the right to jury trial in civil cases. A **civil case,** such as a lawsuit, is one that does not involve criminal conduct.

Eighth Amendment: Bail and punishment. Bans excessive bail and punishment. The courts may not impose unreasonable bail, fines, or cruel and unusual punishment.

Ninth Amendment: Rights retained by the people. Guarantees other rights not listed in the Constitution or Bill of Rights.

Tenth Amendment: States' rights. Reserves powers for the states and the people that are not specifically given to the national government.

Two Early Amendments Strengthened the New Federal Government

The remaining amendments came about because of a widely recognized problem, or as the result of a reform movement, or both. The first of these, the Eleventh Amendment, adopted in 1795, protected states from lawsuits by citizens of other states or

Amendments Defining the Powers of Government

Eleventh Amendment (1795)
Limited federal court jurisdiction over lawsuits involving states

Fourteenth Amendment (1868)
Defined citizenship and prohibited states from denying due process, equal protection, and other basic rights to citizens

Sixteenth Amendment (1913)
Gave Congress the power to levy and collect taxes on incomes

Twenty-seventh Amendment (1992)
Limited the power of Congress to raise members' pay

Amendments Affecting the Election or Tenure of Officeholders

Twelfth Amendment (1804)
Required separate electoral college ballots for president and vice president

Seventeenth Amendment (1913)
Called for the direct election of senators by voters

Twentieth Amendment (1933)
Changed the date when the president, vice president, and members of Congress take office

Twenty-second Amendment (1951)
Limited the president to two full terms or no more than ten years in office

Twenty-fifth Amendment (1967)
Provided for succession in case of the president's death or disability

Amendments Reflecting Changing Social Values

Thirteenth Amendment (1865)
Banned slavery and involuntary servitude

Eighteenth Amendment (1919)
Empowered the federal government to prohibit the sale of alcohol

Twenty-first Amendment (1933)
Repealed the highly unpopular 18th Amendment (prohibition)

Amendments Expanding Voting Rights

Fifteenth Amendment (1870)
Extended voting rights to male citizens of all races

Nineteenth Amendment (1920)
Extended the right to vote to women

Twenty-third Amendment (1961)
Granted voting rights in presidential elections to the residents of the District of Columbia

Twenty-fourth Amendment (1964)
Banned poll taxes, or fees imposed on voters

Twenty-sixth Amendment (1971)
Lowered the voting age from 21 to 18

---

foreign countries. It was adopted after Georgia lost a Supreme Court case involving a suit brought by a South Carolina resident.

The Twelfth Amendment, ratified in 1804, changed voting procedures in the Electoral College to separate the vote for president and vice president. This became necessary after the 1800 election resulted in an Electoral College tie.

Three Civil War–Era Amendments Extended Rights to African Americans
The Thirteenth Amendment made President Lincoln's emancipation of slaves the law of the land. The

Fourteenth Amendment overturned the Supreme Court's Dred Scott decision—which had denied citizenship to African Americans—by making all people born in the United States citizens with equal rights and protections. The Fifteenth Amendment was passed to protect the voting rights of freedmen during Reconstruction.

Four Progressive-Era Amendments Dealt with Social and Political Reforms
The Progressive period of the early 1900s saw the ratification of four amendments, all designed to promote social and political reform. The Sixteenth

Amendment allowed Congress to establish an income tax. Today the income tax is the main source of revenue for the federal government.

The Seventeenth Amendment provided for the direct election of senators. Previously, senators were elected by state legislatures. The Nineteenth Amendment extended voting rights to women.

The Eighteenth Amendment instituted prohibition, banning the sale of alcohol. The Twenty-first Amendment later repealed prohibition.

Four Twentieth-Century Amendments Addressed Governance

The Twentieth Amendment changed the start date of presidential and congressional terms. Known as the "lame duck" amendment, it shortened the period in which officeholders who had not been reelected remained in office.

The Twenty-second Amendment limited presidents to two terms. This amendment was prompted by the election of Franklin D. Roosevelt to four terms. The Twenty-fifth Amendment provided for succession to the presidency in case of a president's death or disability and the filling of a vacancy in the office of vice president.

The Twenty-seventh Amendment—the last to be ratified, in 1992—was first proposed 203 years earlier, along with the Bill of Rights. It states that any pay raise Congress votes for itself cannot go into effect until after the next congressional election.

Three Civil Rights–Era Amendments Extended Voting Rights

Between 1961 and 1971, three amendments expanded suffrage for different groups. The Twenty-third Amendment allowed residents of the District of Columbia to vote in presidential elections. As a result, district voters now elect three members of the Electoral College.

The Twenty-fourth Amendment banned poll taxes, which had been used to keep African Americans from voting in some states.

The Twenty-sixth Amendment lowered the voting age from 21 to 18. Ratified during the Vietnam War, it was prompted by arguments that anyone who is old enough to go to war—that is, an 18-year-old—is old enough to vote.

Of all the amendments proposed by Congress but never ratified by the states, perhaps the most famous is the equal rights amendment. The ERA, first introduced in 1923, was intended to guarantee equal rights for women. It was proposed by Congress again in 1972, but did not win ratification in the necessary three-fourths of the states.

■ 4.4 Guiding Principles of the Constitution

Over the years, the Constitution has acquired an almost sacred status for Americans. Part of the reason for that is its durability: the Constitution has survived, with relatively few changes, for more than two centuries. It ensures stability and continuity in American political life. Furthermore, it has come to represent who we are as a people and a nation. It symbolizes our collective values in a way that most Americans—no matter what their political views—are able to embrace.

Establishing a Limited Government

The framers' main goal in crafting the Constitution was to create a system of limited government. They knew that absolute power often leads to the abuse of rights. On the other hand, they also knew that a lack of governmental power could result in chaos and instability.

The framers tried to make sure that the Constitution gave the government enough power to ensure peace and order, but not so much that its power went unchecked. As James Madison wrote in *The Federalist* No. 51, "You must first enable the government to control the governed; and in the next place to oblige it to control itself."

The limited government envisioned in the Constitution is based on six guiding principles: (1) popular sovereignty, (2) the rule of law, (3) separation of powers and checks and balances, (4) federalism, (5) an independent judiciary, and (6) individual rights.

Popular Sovereignty

This principle means that power resides in the will of the people. The framers understood that making people the source of power is the best assurance that government will act in the people's interest.

In *The Federalist* No. 39, Madison defined a republic as "a government which derives all its powers directly or indirectly from the great body of

Lampposts in front of the Supreme Court Building in Washington, D.C., are decorated with this carving of a female figure popularly known as Lady Justice or Blind Justice. Portraying Justice as a female figure dates back to ancient times. Today Justice is usually shown with a set of scales, representing the impartiality of the law. She carries a sword symbolizing the power of those who make decisions based on the law. She wears a blindfold to indicate that justice is blind to considerations such as wealth and social status.

the people." The Constitution supports popular sovereignty through **republicanism,** or the idea that people elect leaders to a governing body of citizens. One section that upholds this idea is the following:

The House of Representatives shall be composed of Members chosen every second Year by the People of the several States.
— Article I, Section 2, Clause 1

In other words, the people elect members of the House, the more representative body of Congress. Another section ensures republicanism in the states:

The United States shall guarantee to every State in this Union a Republican Form of Government.
— Article IV, Section 4

By guaranteeing republican government in the states, the Constitution extends the principle of popular sovereignty to the states.

The Rule of Law

This principle requires that the American people and their government abide by a system of laws. This is another way to ensure that power is limited and not used in an arbitrary manner. Examples in the Constitution include these:

The Citizens of each State shall be entitled to all Privileges and Immunities of Citizens in the several States.
— Article IV, Section 2, Clause 1

In other words, no state may discriminate against the residents of another state. The law must be applied in the same way to all. Another section says,

The Constitution . . . shall be the supreme Law of the Land.
— Article VI, Section 2

This section asserts the authority of the Constitution and federal law over state and local law. When there is a conflict, the Constitution prevails.

The system of checks and balances is a guiding principle of the Constitution and a key component of limited government. This system works to prevent any one branch from wielding too much power.

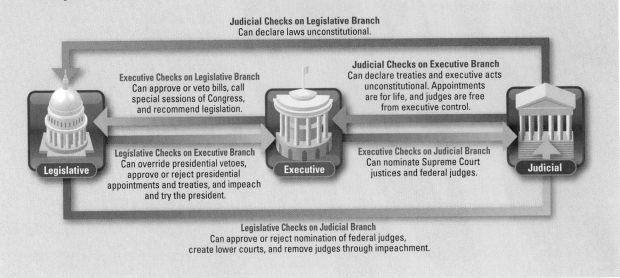

Judicial Checks on Legislative Branch
Can declare laws unconstitutional.

Executive Checks on Legislative Branch
Can approve or veto bills, call special sessions of Congress, and recommend legislation.

Judicial Checks on Executive Branch
Can declare treaties and executive acts unconstitutional. Appointments are for life, and judges are free from executive control.

Legislative Checks on Executive Branch
Can override presidential vetoes, approve or reject presidential appointments and treaties, and impeach and try the president.

Executive Checks on Judicial Branch
Can nominate Supreme Court justices and federal judges.

Legislative

Executive

Judicial

Legislative Checks on Judicial Branch
Can approve or reject nomination of federal judges, create lower courts, and remove judges through impeachment.

Separation of Powers—Checks and Balances

The Constitution divides power in the national government among the three separate branches. This separation of powers was a key component in the framers' vision of limited government. In *The Federalist* No. 47, James Madison wrote, "The accumulation of all powers, legislative, executive, and judiciary, in the same hands . . . may justly be pronounced the very definition of tyranny."

In the framers' view, separating the powers of government among the three branches would ensure that no one branch could dominate. The framers took this principle a step further by inserting provisions in the Constitution that would allow each branch to check, or limit, the power of each of the other branches. This system of **checks and balances** can be seen in many parts of the Constitution, including the following provision:

> *He [the president] shall have Power, by and with the Advice and Consent of the Senate, to make Treaties, provided two thirds of the Senators present concur.*
> —Article II, Section 2, Clause 2

Although the president has the power to make treaties, such treaties must be approved by a two-thirds vote of the Senate to take effect. In this way, the Senate can check the power of the president. This clause goes on to say that the Senate can also block the president's appointment of ambassadors, Supreme Court justices, and executive officers.

Another clause establishes the president's **veto power** over bills passed by Congress. It says that the president can refuse to sign a bill into law and instead send it back to Congress:

> *Every Bill which shall have passed the House of Representatives and the Senate, shall, before it become a Law, be presented to the President of the United States; If he approve he shall sign it, but if not he shall return it, with his Objections to the House in which it shall have originated.*
> —Article I, Section 7, Clause 2

The clause goes on to say, however, that if Congress passes the bill again with a two-thirds majority, it becomes law without the president's signature, thus checking the president's veto power.

Other sections of Article I address the removal of top officials:

> *The House of Representatives shall . . . have the sole Power of Impeachment.*
> —Article I, Section 2, Clause 5

The only way to remove a president, other members of the executive branch, or federal judges from office is by **impeachment**. This process requires that a simple majority of House members vote to impeach, or formally charge, the official with wrongdoing. A trial then takes place in the Senate:

The Senate shall have the sole Power to try all Impeachments . . . And no Person shall be convicted without the Concurrence of two thirds of the Members present.
—Article I, Section 3, Clause 6

Conviction in a Senate trial requires a two-thirds vote of guilty. The power of impeachment gives Congress a check on the other two branches of government.

Federalism

The fourth guiding principle, **federalism,** divides power between the central government and the various state governments. In creating a federal system of government, the Constitution also established three types of powers: delegated, reserved, and concurrent.

Delegated powers are those powers granted to the national government. Delegated powers may be either enumerated or implied in the Constitution. The delegated powers of the federal government include regulating immigration, making treaties, and declaring war.

Reserved powers are those powers kept by the states. Reserved powers allow states to set marriage and divorce laws, issue driver's licenses, and establish public schools, among many other things. Under the Constitution, much of the exercise of day-to-day power affecting citizens is carried out by the states.

Concurrent powers are those that are shared by the federal government and state governments. Examples of concurrent powers include taxation and law enforcement.

The federalist principle in the Constitution is most evident in articles and amendments that refer to delegated, reserved, and concurrent powers, such as these:

The Congress shall have Power . . . To regulate Commerce with foreign Nations, and among the several States, and with the Indian Tribes.
—Article I, Section 8, Clause 3

This clause, known as the **Commerce Clause,** gives the federal government the power to regulate trade across state lines within the United States and to both regulate and tax foreign trade. Another article establishes the amendment process:

The Congress . . . shall propose Amendments to this Constitution, or, on the Application of the Legislatures of two thirds of the several States, shall call a Convention for proposing Amendments.
—Article V

The amendment process is an example of concurrent powers. The federal government and the states share the power to amend the Constitution. Other powers are reserved to the states, however:

The powers not delegated to the United States by the Constitution, nor prohibited to it by the States, are reserved to the States respectively, or to the people.
—Tenth Amendment

This amendment reserves for the states or the people any powers that are not given to the federal government.

An Independent Judiciary

The fifth guiding principle, an independent judiciary, was considered essential by the framers to support the rule of law and preserve limited government. In *The Federalist* No. 78, Alexander Hamilton wrote, "The independence of the judges may be an essential safeguard against the effects of occasional ill humors in society." In other words, an **independent judiciary** would protect against abuses of the system by self-interested parties. This principle is found in Article III, which establishes the judicial branch.

The judicial Power of the United States, shall be vested in one supreme Court, and in such inferior Courts as the Congress may from time to time ordain and establish. The Judges, both of the supreme and inferior Courts, shall hold their Offices during good Behaviour, and shall, at stated Times, receive for their Services a Compensation, which shall not be diminished during their Continuance in Office.
—Article III, Section 1

As this section makes clear, judicial authority rests with the Supreme Court and other federal courts. Where the article says that judges shall serve "during good Behaviour," it essentially means "for life," unless there is just cause to remove them.

In addition, the salaries of judges may not be reduced while in office. These two provisions—lifetime tenure and a secure salary—help to insulate federal judges from political pressure and influence, and thus preserve their independence.

Individual Rights

The sixth guiding principle, individual rights, played a major role in the struggle to ratify the Constitution. The Anti-Federalists argued that the Constitution did not offer adequate protection for individual rights. The Bill of Rights was added to address their concerns.

Individual rights receive their broadest protection under the First Amendment, which says,

> *Congress shall make no law respecting an establishment of religion, or prohibiting the free exercise thereof; or abridging the freedom of speech, or of the press, or the right of the people peaceably to assemble, and to petition the Government for a redress of grievances.*
> —First Amendment

This amendment protects the rights of individuals to speak their minds and act on their beliefs without fear of arrest or persecution by the government.

In addition, the original text of the Constitution contains references to basic rights, such as trial by jury:

> *The Trial of all Crimes, except in Cases of Impeachment, shall be by Jury.*
> —Article III, Section 2, Clause 3

Trial by jury is a fundamental right guaranteed to all Americans. Another clause in the Constitution defines treason:

> *Treason against the United States, shall consist only in levying War against them, or in adhering to their Enemies, giving them Aid and Comfort. No Person shall be convicted of Treason unless on the Testimony of two Witnesses to the same overt Act, or on Confession in open Court.*
> —Article III, Section 3, Clause 1

This provision defines the crime of treason in a way that protects the rights of free speech and free expression. Under this definition, no American can be charged with treason for simply criticizing the government. Nor can such charges result in conviction without substantial evidence.

The First Amendment of the Bill of Rights guarantees Americans the freedom of speech and the right to assemble. In 2011, Americans exercised these rights by launching the movement known as Occupy Wall Street. Demonstrators carried protest signs that expressed their grievances toward the 1 percent of Americans who owned more than 30 percent of the nation's wealth.

■ 4.5 Interpreting the Constitution

Although the Constitution provided a firm foundation for a new national government, it left much to be decided by those who put this plan into practice. Some provisions that did not work as hoped were later changed by the formal amendment process. Other features of the government were established by actions of Congress, the executive branch, and the courts. These changes did not alter the wording of the Constitution, but they did clarify its provisions.

The Supreme Court plays an especially important role in our political system because it has the ultimate power to interpret, or establish the meaning of, the Constitution. Through its decisions, the Court helps to define the limits of constitutional rights and powers. Its decisions can affect your rights as a citizen.

The Process of Judicial Interpretation

When judges are asked to apply the Constitution to a legal issue, they look to five sources of information:

1. The text, or exact wording, of the Constitution itself
2. The **original intent** of the framers—what they meant or were trying to achieve—when they debated and wrote the Constitution
3. Court **precedent,** or the past decisions of the Supreme Court
4. The practical consequences for society of a particular interpretation
5. Basic moral and ethical values

Of these five, the most important are the text of the Constitution, original intent, and precedent.

Not surprisingly, judges and legal scholars do not always agree on how to interpret the Constitution. Some rely more on the original text or intent of the framers, while others give considerable weight to precedent, consequences, and values. These differences have given rise to debate over the degree to which the Constitution is a "living document" that should change with the times.

Strict Construction: Looking at the Text

On one side of this debate are those who favor **strict construction,** or a literal reading of the Constitution. Legal scholars often call this approach **originalism.** It holds that the original language of the Constitution and the intent of the framers must serve as primary guides to judicial interpretation.

One of the leading advocates of originalism is Justice Antonin Scalia. In 2005, Scalia observed that "the Constitution is not a living organism . . . it's a legal document and like all legal documents, it says some things and doesn't say others." Scalia accepts that the Constitution should be interpreted in a reasonable manner. However, he argues that judges should not try to make it conform to modern values. "I do believe you [should] give it the meaning it had when it was adopted," he said.

Loose Construction: Adapting the Constitution to Today

On the other side of the debate are those who favor **loose construction,** or a flexible reading of the Constitution. Legal scholars often call this approach **interpretivism.** It holds that modern values and social consequences must be taken into account in interpreting the Constitution.

Schools of Constitutional Interpretation

Today, as in the past, both judges and the general public are divided on how the Constitution should be interpreted. Some favor a strict interpretation, while others favor a loose interpretation. That debate is likely to continue as long as the Constitution remains the foundation of our system of government.

©TCI/Scott Willis

One of the chief advocates of interpretivism was the late Supreme Court justice William J. Brennan Jr. In a speech delivered in 1985, Brennan explained,

We current Justices read the Constitution in the only way we can: as Twentieth Century Americans. We look to the history of the time of framing and to the intervening history of interpretation. But the ultimate question must be, what do the words of the text mean in our time? For the genius of the Constitution rests not in any static meaning it might have had in a world that is dead and gone, but in the adaptability of its great principles to cope with current problems and current needs.

—Justice William J. Brennan Jr., speech at Georgetown University, 1985

Over the years, Court decisions reflecting both sides of this debate have helped to define the Constitution. Four cases that illustrate the Court's interpretive role are *Marbury v. Madison, McCulloch v. Maryland, United States v. Nixon,* and *Goss v. Lopez.*

Marbury v. Madison: Establishing Judicial Review

This case, which dates back to the early days of the republic, established the key principle of **judicial review**. This principle grants the Supreme Court the power to declare acts of Congress, the executive branch, and the states unconstitutional. In other words, the Court can overturn laws or government actions that do not comply with the Constitution. This principle is not stated directly in the Constitution, though it is implied in Article III, which outlines the Court's judicial powers. It would take the *Marbury* case to make judicial review an accepted principle.

The case had its origins in the election of 1800. That year John Adams, the incumbent president and candidate of the Federalist Party, lost to Thomas Jefferson. Just before leaving office, Adams created dozens of new federal judgeships and appointed Federalists to fill these posts. Since federal judges serve for life, this action would ensure the continued influence of the Federalist Party in the federal government. However, Adams was not able to get all the commissions, or appointments, delivered by the time he left office.

Angered by Adams's "court packing" scheme, President Jefferson instructed his new secretary of state, James Madison, not to deliver the remaining commissions. William Marbury was one of those who failed to receive his commission. Marbury took his case to the Supreme Court. He based his argument on Section 13 of the Judiciary Act of 1789. This section empowered the Supreme Court to issue a "writ of mandamus" to force an official, in this case Madison, to perform a duty for which he was legally responsible.

Chief Justice John Marshall, a firm Federalist who was himself one of Adams's last-minute appointments, faced a delicate dilemma. If he issued the writ, Jefferson and Madison might simply ignore it, thus weakening the Court's authority. If he refused to issue the writ, however, it might imply that the Court had no power to judge the actions of the executive branch. Instead, Marshall did neither.

On February 24, 1803, the Supreme Court issued its decision. Writing for the majority, Marshall said that Marbury deserved his commission and that Madison should have delivered it.

But then Marshall added an unexpected twist. He wrote that Section 13 of the Judiciary Act violated the Constitution. Article III, which established the Judicial Branch, did not, he argued, give the courts power to issue a writ of mandamus. Declaring that a law "repugnant to the constitution is void," the Supreme Court struck down Section 13 of the Judiciary Act as unconstitutional and decided against Marbury.

It was a brilliant decision, both legally and politically. Although Jefferson did not support judicial review, he could do nothing to oppose it because the Court did not ask him to enforce the writ. Marshall had thus preserved the Court's authority and also given it the power to review the constitutionality of acts of Congress and the executive branch.

Judicial review has played a key role in Court decisions since *Marbury.* One of its main consequences has been to allow citizens to challenge in court any law or government action that they believe violates the Constitution. A case such as *Goss v. Lopez* would never have come before the Supreme Court without the establishment of judicial review.

The headquarters of the First Bank of the United States was completed in Philadelphia in 1797. The creation of the national bank proved controversial because the Constitution did not expressly give Congress the power to establish a bank. In *McCulloch v. Maryland* (1819), the Supreme Court upheld the constitutionality of this use of congressional power.

McCulloch v. Maryland: Making the Constitution the Supreme Law of the Land

A second landmark case, *McCulloch v. Maryland,* also came before the Marshall Court in the early 1800s. This case affirmed the supremacy of the national government over the states and upheld the implied powers of Congress under the Constitution.

The case revolved around disputes over the creation of a national bank. In 1791, Congress chartered the First Bank of the United States, even though some national leaders, including Thomas Jefferson, argued that such a bank was not authorized by the Constitution. The bank's charter ran out in 1811 and was not renewed.

In 1816, Congress decided to charter the Second Bank of the United States. Many states opposed the creation of this new national bank, and a number of them—including Maryland—passed laws to tax its branches. The cashier of the Maryland branch, James McCulloch, refused to pay the tax. When Maryland courts ordered him to pay, he appealed his case to the Supreme Court.

On March 6, 1819, the Court issued a unanimous decision in favor of the bank and McCulloch. In his written opinion, Marshall first argued that the federal government's power to establish a bank, though not specifically cited in the Constitution, was supported by the Elastic Clause in Article I, Section 8. That clause allows Congress to make all laws that are "necessary and proper" to carry out its duties. Marshall asserted that the power to establish a national bank was implied in the enumerated powers of Congress, including the powers to lay and collect taxes, to borrow money, and to regulate commerce. A national bank, he said, would conceivably be useful for carrying out those powers and was therefore constitutional.

Marshall went on to say that no state has the power to tax the national bank or any other arm of the federal government. Such power would make state law superior to federal law, since, as he put it, "the power to tax involves the power to destroy." The people, he added, "did not deign to make their government dependent on the states." In fact, they declared just the opposite when they ratified the Constitution as "the supreme Law of the Land."

The decision in *McCulloch v. Maryland* had far-reaching consequences. By confirming the Elastic Clause, the Court supported a broad expansion of congressional power. It also sent a clear message that in conflicts between federal and state law, federal law would prevail. In both regards, the Court's decision helped to strengthen the national government.

United States v. Nixon: Reaffirming the Rule of Law

A third key case, *United States v. Nixon,* is more recent. This case reaffirmed the rule of law as a key principle of American government.

In 1974, the Supreme Court ruled that the president, like all other citizens, is subject to the rule of law. During the Senate investigation of the Watergate scandal, President Nixon claimed executive privilege and refused to release tapes of his Oval Office conversations. When ordered to do so by the Supreme Court, the White House handed over the tapes but admitted that two conversations had not been recorded and that 18 and a half minutes were missing. This cartoon reflects public suspicion about President Nixon's involvement in the scandal.

The origins of the case lie in the Watergate scandal of the early 1970s. During the 1972 presidential campaign, burglars broke into the Democratic national campaign headquarters, located in the Watergate complex in Washington, D.C. When evidence tied the break-in to President Richard Nixon, the Senate formed a special committee to investigate the incident. Under mounting pressure, Nixon and his attorney general, Elliot Richardson, also set up a special prosecutor's office to look into the matter. Richardson appointed Harvard law professor Archibald Cox as special prosecutor.

In the course of its investigation, the Senate discovered that Nixon had made secret tape recordings of his conversations in the Oval Office. Both the

Senate and the special prosecutor asked the president to hand over the tapes. Nixon refused. As justification, he claimed **executive privilege**. This is the right to keep internal discussions and documents of the White House private. Although executive privilege is not mentioned in the Constitution, various presidents throughout the country's history have claimed this right on the basis of separation of powers and national security.

After Cox demanded the tapes, Nixon had him fired. The public outcry was so great, however, that the president soon agreed to the appointment of a new special prosecutor. Cox's successor, Leon Jaworski, took Nixon to court to force him to release the tapes.

In 1974, the Supreme Court decided unanimously in the case *United States v. Nixon* that the president had to surrender the Watergate tapes. Chief Justice Warren Burger acknowledged that presidents have a legitimate claim to executive privilege. However, this claim, he said, "must be considered in light of our historic commitment to the rule of law." In cases of criminal prosecution, Burger said, executive privilege must give way to the "fundamental demands of due process."

Nixon complied with the decision and handed over the tapes. One of them proved to be a "smoking gun" that implicated the president in efforts to cover up the Watergate crimes. Faced with the prospect of impeachment, Nixon resigned. The Watergate scandal and the Court's decision demonstrated that no one, not even the president, is above the law.

Goss v. Lopez: Extending the Individual Rights of Students to Include Due Process

The case *Goss v. Lopez* involved the constitutional rights of Dwight Lopez and eight other students in Columbus, Ohio. The students, with the help of their parents, brought a lawsuit against school officials. The suit accused school officials of violating the students' constitutional right to due process by suspending them from school without a hearing. It also asked the schools to remove references to the suspension from the students' school records.

The students' suit eventually made its way to the Supreme Court. In making their decision, the justices focused on an Ohio law that allowed public school principals to suspend a student for misconduct for up to ten days without a hearing. The law did require that the student's parents be notified of the suspension and the reasons for it. The school officials being sued argued that they had acted properly under Ohio law.

On January 22, 1975, a closely divided Supreme Court delivered its decision in a 5-4 vote. Writing for the majority, Justice Byron White acknowledged that schools must sometimes use discipline to maintain an orderly learning environment.

> *The difficulty is that our schools are vast and complex. Some modicum of discipline and order is essential if the educational function is to be performed. Events calling for discipline are frequent occurrences and sometimes require immediate, effective action.*
> —Justice Byron White, *Goss v. Lopez*, 1975

White went on to argue that the legitimate need for order in a school did not justify the violation of students' due process rights. Before being suspended or expelled, students should know the charges against them and have a chance to tell their side of the story.

As a result of the *Goss v. Lopez* decision, school districts across the United States established new procedures to protect the due process rights of students like you. Should you be facing an expulsion, you have the right to be notified of the charges against you. You also have the right to a prompt disciplinary hearing. During that hearing, you must have an opportunity to hear the evidence that led to the charges. You must also be allowed to present your side of the story before an impartial person or group of people. Anything less is a violation of your due process rights under the Constitution.

Summary

For more than 200 years, the Constitution has served as a blueprint for republican government and a guarantor of basic rights and freedoms for the American people. It has endured because of its flexibility and the strength of its underlying principles.

Elements of the Constitution The Constitution is structured in three parts: Preamble, articles, and amendments. The Preamble sets the purpose of government, the articles establish the governing framework, and the amendments make formal changes.

Amending the Constitution The amendment process requires the participation of both Congress and the states. Just 27 amendments have been ratified over the years. The first ten constitute the Bill of Rights. The other 17 cover a range of issues, including voting rights and the powers of government.

Guiding principles of the Constitution The limited government envisioned in the Constitution is based on six principles: (1) popular sovereignty, (2) the rule of law, (3) separation of powers and checks and balances, (4) federalism, (5) an independent judiciary, and (6) individual rights. The principles underlie many features of our government.

Interpreting the Constitution The three branches of government all play a role in working out the details of governing under the Constitution. The courts interpret the Constitution and decide whether laws and government actions are constitutional, a power known as judicial review.

Do zero-tolerance policies violate the due process rights of students?

During the 1990s, concern about drug use and violence in schools prompted a new approach to enforcing school rules. This approach, known as zero tolerance, calls for automatic punishment for violating a rule. Schools with zero-tolerance policies immediately suspend students accused of breaking certain rules. These rules generally include possessing drugs, carrying weapons, or starting fights. Students are not given a disciplinary hearing before being expelled.

The news story here describes a zero-tolerance incident that took place in January 2005 at a school in Haverford, Pennsylvania. As you read it, ask yourself, Was the student involved deprived of her due process rights? Or did she knowingly violate a reasonable policy designed to maintain a safe and drug-free school?

Zero Tolerance: Student Suspended for Taking Medicine

by Lois Puglionesi

HAVERFORD—A Haverford High School honor roll student, known to all as a conscientious, high achiever, was suspended from school last week for taking what might be considered the equivalent of an aspirin. The suspension was based on a zero tolerance drug and alcohol policy, which expressly forbids any form of self-medicating— including use of over-the-counter products—without proper authorization. The incident sparked an outraged response from parents, and raised questions about school policy.

It began innocently enough when a senior female student experiencing menstrual cramps asked a friend for a Tylenol or Advil. The classmate had none, but in an effort to be helpful, asked a third student, who supplied a generic form of Aleve. Aleve is a non-prescription strength form of Anaprox, sold over the counter as a fever reducer, and for temporary relief of minor aches and pains.

The young woman took the Aleve, but continued experiencing discomfort and went to the nurse. When questioned, the student told the truth and admitted obtaining Aleve from another student. An assistant principal was summoned to the scene.

Although these young women may not have viewed the incident as a serious offense, officials did. School policy prohibits students "from carrying on their person any medication that is prescribed or purchased over the counter." (This includes eye drops, Tylenol, nasal sprays.) If it's necessary to take medication during school hours, the medicine must be accompanied by a written order from a physician and administered through the nurse, policy states.

The Aleve affair was deemed a level 5 violation, subject to a maximum three-day suspension prior to a hearing with the principal. Both girls were sent home. Based on findings, initial suspensions may be extended, with possible referral to an assessment team, or the police when appropriate. Disciplinary actions are recorded on school records.

A call from irate parents expedited a hearing with Haverford Principal Nicholas Rotoli.

Parents felt the punishment was inappropriate. A level 5 violation is applicable in cases where a student "possesses drug-related paraphernalia and/or possesses, uses or is under the influence of drugs, alcohol, or mood-altering substances," according to school district policy.

The student's mother argued, "There has to be a distinction between someone who takes a cough drop or a Midol, opposed to a kid who's smoking [marijuana]. It's like throwing a hand grenade on an anthill. The world isn't black and white. The school didn't look at who this child is. They didn't delve into history or character. This is a kid who wants to be in school, loves to be in school, and gives back to the community."

The mother also questioned whether students were adequately informed about the rules.

Rotoli allowed the young woman to return to school after one day, but stood by the school's response and the need for a zero tolerance policy on self-medicating.

"These policies are not put in place to be unreasonable. It's for the protection of all the kids," Rotoli said. Contrary to the family's perceptions, Rotoli insisted there was a sliding scale, that adjustments are made to individual cases pursuant to an investigation.

©TCI/Scott Willis

"We don't expel a kid for 10 days for using eye drops," he said. While distributing marijuana falls at the highest end of the drug and alcohol policy, taking pain relievers falls at the lowest, said Rotoli. But "a suspension of some extent is warranted. It's more of an educational thing—don't come to school and self-medicate. Don't take meds from others."

Rotoli emphasized the need for safety precautions in a drug-oriented society where people "believe you swallow a pill and it will take care of problems. Kids will ingest anything. People want immediate relief and don't think about possible side effects and allergic reactions," he said.

"Kids have to realize these are medicines," said 12th-grade assistant Principal Richard Kline. He expressed concerns about the theft and sale of OTCs by students, and warned of "look-alike" drugs, or illegal substances in disguise. The nurse called the Poison Control Center, in fact, because the pills in question were marked only with a code number and brought to school in a jewelry-type pillbox.

And despite the student's good credentials, Rotoli maintained, "We can't have individual policies—one for the 'better' kids and one for the others. They're all great kids. They all make mistakes."

While those "mistakes" are recorded on school records, the information is purged annually and never released, Rotoli said.

Lois Puglionesi is a reporter for the Delaware County Daily Times, *a newspaper published in Pennsylvania, near the city of Philadelphia.*

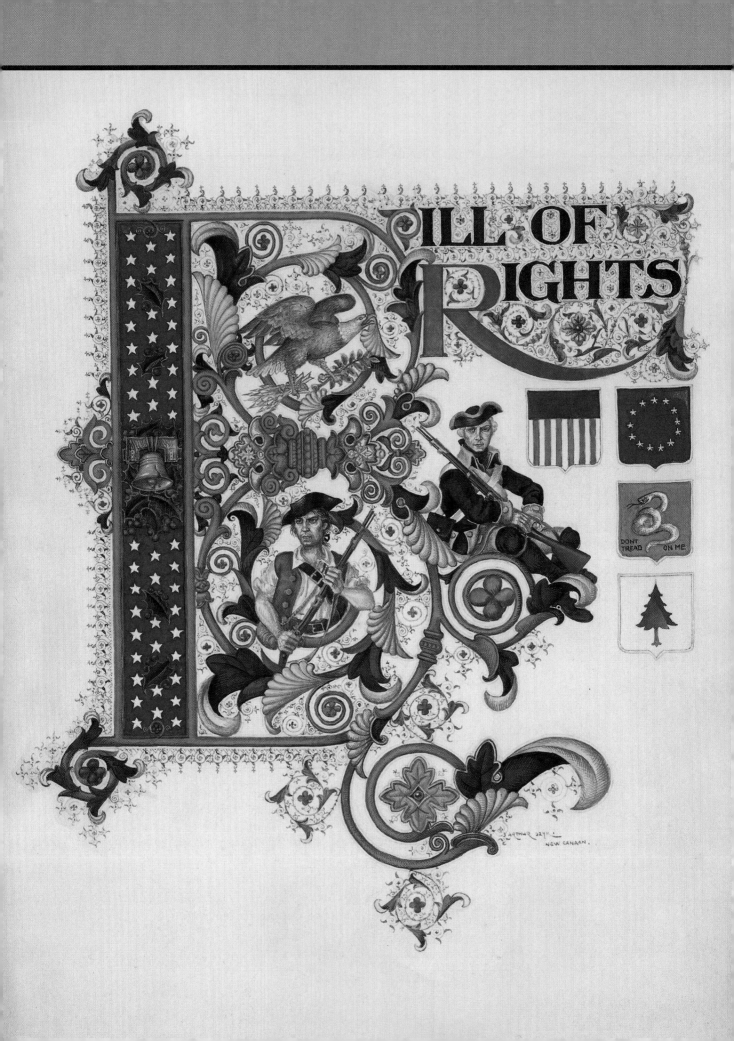

Chapter 5

The Bill of Rights and Civil Liberties

How are your rights defined and protected under the Constitution?

■ 5.1 Introduction

In the summer of 1917, the United States was desperately trying to mobilize its army to fight in World War I. The government instituted a military draft to raise enough troops to go to war. It also launched a campaign to increase public support for the war effort. To limit dissent, Congress passed the Espionage Act. Among other things, this law stated that any effort to undermine the war effort would be considered a criminal act.

Many Americans were opposed to the war and the draft. One of the most outspoken opponents was Charles Schenck, the general secretary of the American Socialist Party. Schenck and his fellow socialists took a strong stand against the draft, which they regarded as an unconstitutional violation of individual rights. They believed that Americans should not be forced to serve in the military against their will.

To promote this view, Schenck organized a mass mailing of antidraft leaflets to young men in the Philadelphia area. These flyers called the draft "involuntary servitude" and urged draftees to call for its repeal.

Some recipients found the leaflets offensive and complained to authorities. Schenck was arrested and charged under the Espionage Act. At his trial, he was declared guilty of violating the law by conspiring to undermine the war effort. Schenck appealed to the Supreme Court, arguing that the Espionage Act violated his right to free speech.

This 1949 painting by Arthur Szyk celebrates the Bill of Rights

Speaking of Politics

civil liberties
Basic freedoms that are guaranteed under the Constitution, such as freedom of speech and freedom of religion. These rights are protections from governmental intrusion or abuse.

civil rights
Guarantees of equal rights and equal treatment under the law. Unlike civil liberties, civil rights are not protections from government abuse, but rights that government must provide to its citizens, such as trial by jury and voting rights.

incorporation
The process by which the Supreme Court applies the Bill of Rights to the states through the Due Process Clause of the Fourteenth Amendment.

libel
Publishing false information about someone with intent to cause harm.

slander
Orally spreading false information about someone with intent to cause harm.

prior restraint
An attempt by government to prevent the publication or broadcast of material considered harmful.

self-incrimination
Statements, usually made under oath, suggesting that the person speaking is guilty of a crime.

double jeopardy
The prosecution of a person a second time for a crime for which the defendant has already been tried once and found not guilty. Double jeopardy is prohibited under the Fifth Amendment.

In a unanimous opinion, written by Justice Oliver Wendell Holmes Jr., the Court held that Schenck's conviction was constitutional. "The most stringent protection of free speech would not protect a man in falsely shouting fire in a theatre and causing a panic," Holmes wrote. In the Court's view, Schenck's publications created "a clear and present danger" to a nation engaged in war. "When a nation is at war," wrote Holmes, "many things that might be said in time of peace . . . will not be endured so long as men fight." In such cases, the Court said, public safety should prevail over individual rights.

Schenck spent six months in prison for his crime. Ironically, by the time the Supreme Court decided the case, in March 1919, the war was over and the draft had been suspended. The *Schenck v. United States* decision did set a larger precedent, however. It allowed the courts to apply a "balancing test" in free speech cases, weighing the rights of individuals against the broader needs of society.

Key Rights and Liberties

Civil Liberties	Civil Rights
Freedom of speech	Right to due process
Freedom of religion	Right to trial by jury
Freedom of the press	Right to legal counsel
Freedom of assembly	Right to vote
Freedom from unreasonable search and seizure	Right to petition the government for a redress of grievances

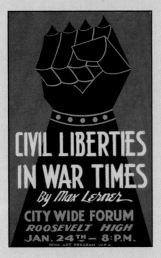

When the nation is engaged in war, limitations on civil liberties become more stringent. This poster advertises a forum on how civil liberties change during wartime.

◼ 5.2 Defining and Protecting Your Rights and Liberties

The *Schenck* case illustrates the role played by the Supreme Court in defining constitutional rights. When the framers wrote the Constitution, they said almost nothing about the protection of individual rights and liberties from government abuses. They spelled out many things the government *could* do but said very little about what it could not do. That omission was rectified by the Bill of Rights, the first ten amendments to the Constitution. These amendments guarantee two types of rights: **civil liberties** and **civil rights**.

Defining Civil Liberties and Civil Rights

Civil liberties are basic freedoms that are considered to be the birthright of all individuals. Thomas Jefferson and his fellow authors of the Declaration of Independence would have called them natural rights, or unalienable rights. In addition to the Declaration's "Life, Liberty and the pursuit of Happiness," these liberties include such rights as freedom of speech, freedom of religion, and freedom of assembly. Because civil liberties are regarded as a person's birthright, they are not something that the government can legitimately take away or infringe on.

Civil rights, on the other hand, are rights that come with being a member of society. They are not protections *from* government. Instead, they are guarantees *by* government of equal rights and fair treatment under the law. Included in this group are the right to trial by jury, the right to legal counsel, and the right to vote. These rights were among the main goals of the civil rights movement that began in the mid-1950s.

With the Bill of Rights added to the Constitution, Americans were guaranteed a broad range of civil rights and civil liberties. But these were only formal guarantees. The enforcement of these rights was another matter. In fact, James Madison worried that the Bill of Rights might serve as little more than a "parchment barrier" against government abuses. These rights and freedoms would be safeguarded only when protections were built into the structure of government. That is where the role of the Supreme Court and other federal courts has come into play.

Some judges have argued that the Supreme Court may use judicial review only to enforce rights and provisions that are specifically mentioned in the Constitution. Early on, that strict view meant that the Court did little to enforce constitutional rights in the states. Eventually, however, the Court adopted a looser view and began to apply the Bill of Rights more broadly under the terms of the Fourteenth Amendment.

Early Challenges in Enforcing the Bill of Rights

The Bill of Rights defines rights and liberties in sweeping terms. For example, the First Amendment says, "Congress shall make no law . . . abridging the freedom of speech." Does that mean government cannot limit speech in any way?

Before free speech and other rights on paper could be safeguarded, the language of the Bill of Rights had to be interpreted and applied under actual circumstances. That task would fall to the Supreme Court under its power of judicial review, a power established in the case of *Marbury v. Madison*.

Marbury laid the foundation for the Supreme Court's enforcement of the Bill of Rights, but it was only the first step. Next the Court had to decide whether the Bill of Rights applied to actions by state governments. Its first answer to this question was no. In 1833, the Court concluded in *Barron v. Baltimore* that the Bill of Rights applied only to actions of the federal government. As a result, the Court could do little to prevent states from infringing on basic rights and liberties.

After the Civil War, some people hoped that the Court's limited enforcement of the Bill of Rights would change. For support, they looked to the Fourteenth Amendment, which was ratified in 1868. The amendment states,

> *No State shall make or enforce any law which shall abridge the privileges or immunities of citizens of the United States; nor shall any State deprive any person of life, liberty, or property, without due process of law; nor deny*

to any person within its jurisdiction the equal protection of the laws.

At first, the Supreme Court interpreted the amendment very narrowly. For example, in the case of *Plessy v. Ferguson* (1896), the Court declared that racial segregation in the South did not violate the Fourteenth Amendment's **Equal Protection Clause** as long as "separate but equal" facilities were provided for all races.

The Supreme Court's reluctance to make the Bill of Rights binding on the states meant that very few cases involving civil rights or liberties came before it in the 1800s. As a leading rights organization later observed, "The Bill of Rights was like an engine no one knew how to start."

New Hope in a New Century

In the early 1900s, however, two newly formed groups began to have some success in broadening the Court's application of the Fourteenth Amendment. These groups were the National Association for the Advancement of Colored People and the American Civil Liberties Union.

The two groups had different goals. The NAACP fought for civil rights, initially by challenging segregation laws in court. The ACLU, in contrast, focused its attention on cases involving civil liberties, such as freedom of speech. However, both groups sought to give voice to citizens who felt their rights were being violated.

In 1919, not long after the decision in the *Schenck* case, free speech advocates suffered another Court loss, this time in the case of *Abrams v. United States.* This case involved a group of Russian-born political activists who were arrested for handing out leaflets critical of U.S. actions against Russia's new revolutionary government. Using the same argument applied in *Schenck,* the Supreme Court agreed that the language in the leaflets posed a "clear and present danger" to American society.

Although the *Abrams* decision represented another defeat for free speech, this time Justice Holmes voiced an important dissent to the Court's majority opinion. He said that the "clear and present danger" argument should be applied only in cases where public safety was actually at risk. Only an emergency, he wrote, "warrants making any exception to the sweeping command, 'Congress shall make no law abridging the freedom of speech.'" Holmes's dissent would later influence the Court to take a more protective stance on free speech.

Incorporation: Applying the Bill of Rights to the States

Not long after the *Abrams* case, the Court handed down a crucial decision that would expand the reach of the Bill of Rights. The case in question, *Gitlow v. New York,* involved another group of activists. This group also was arrested for handing out leaflets, this time calling for an uprising to create a socialist government. The members of the group were prosecuted and convicted in 1919 under a New York law forbidding "dangerous" speech.

Benjamin Gitlow appealed his conviction to the Supreme Court, claiming that the New York law violated his First Amendment right to free speech. Lawyers for the state argued that the Bill of Rights did not apply to state laws and that the Court did not have jurisdiction to decide the case.

The Court disagreed. In a groundbreaking decision handed down in 1925, the Court reversed its previous position and said that the Due Process Clause of the Fourteenth Amendment did extend the First Amendment to the states. This process of applying the Bill of Rights to the states through Supreme Court decisions is known as **incorporation**.

On the free speech issue, however, the Court held that the New York law did not violate the Constitution. Gitlow's conviction was upheld, though he was later pardoned by the governor of New York.

Incorporation of the Bill of Rights

First Amendment Freedom of speech, press, religion, and assembly	Fully incorporated
Second Amendment Right to bear arms	Fully incorporated
Third Amendment No quartering of soldiers	Not incorporated
Fourth Amendment Protection from unreasonable search and seizure	Fully incorporated
Fifth Amendment Rights of the accused	Mostly incorporated
Sixth Amendment Right to a fair trial	Fully incorporated
Seventh Amendment Right to a jury trial in civil cases	Not incorporated
Eighth Amendment Protection from excessive bail and punishments	Mostly incorporated

Supreme Court decisions have extended most of the rights and liberties in the Bill of Rights to the states. Exceptions, such as the Second and Third amendments, have either been rejected for incorporation or not yet been tested in Court cases. The Ninth and Tenth amendments are not listed because they do not safeguard specific rights and thus are not subject to incorporation.

The *Gitlow* case focused on freedom of speech. Subsequent cases have extended other rights protected in the Bill of Rights to the states. This table shows which amendments have been similarly incorporated.

The Role of the Supreme Court Today

Every year, thousands of people petition to appeal legal cases to the Supreme Court. Most of these cases involve a constitutional issue. They often involve a conflict over rights and liberties guaranteed in the Bill of Rights. Sometimes the conflict is between an individual or a group and the government. Other times, it is between one individual or group and another.

The role of the Supreme Court is not to retry the original case, but rather to review the legal decisions made by the lower courts. In the *Gitlow* case, for example, the Court considered whether Gitlow's earlier conviction under a New York law violated the First Amendment. After reviewing the court record and hearing the arguments, the Court upheld Gitlow's conviction.

What would have happened if the Supreme Court had sided with Gitlow? When the Supreme Court finds that a lower court's decision is unconstitutional, it may decide to reverse the decision. Often, however, it returns the case to a lower appeals court. That lower court may alter its original decision to conform to the Court's opinion, dismiss the case, or order a new trial.

When the Supreme Court makes a decision on an issue, that decision becomes a precedent, or example, for all courts to follow in similar cases in the future. Occasionally the Court overturns its own precedents. This happened in 1954, when the Court rejected its "separate but equal" decision on segregation that had been made in *Plessy v. Ferguson*. The Court found in *Brown v. Board of Education* that "separate educational facilities are inherently unequal." Segregated schools were, therefore, a violation of the Fourteenth Amendment's guarantee of equal protection of the laws.

■ 5.3 Your First Amendment Rights

Many people regard the First Amendment as the most important amendment in the Bill of Rights. It guarantees various rights, including the freedoms of religion, speech, the press, and assembly. These rights are critical to life in a democratic society.

Freedom of Religion: The Establishment Clause

The First Amendment begins with freedom of religion. It reads, "Congress shall make no law respecting an establishment of religion, or prohibiting the free exercise thereof." This statement can be divided into two parts: the Establishment Clause and the Free Exercise Clause.

The Establishment Clause guarantees the separation of church and state. Influenced by European tradition, most places in colonial America had an official church. In the colonies, everyone had to pay taxes to support the church, and in some places, only church members could vote. Some communities even made church attendance mandatory. These practices discriminated against people who did not follow the established religion.

The founders of this country believed that having a state-sponsored church was incompatible with freedom of religion. Thomas Jefferson later wrote that a "wall of separation" should exist between church and state.

By permission of Chuck Asay and Creators Syndicate, Inc.

NEWS ITEM: HIGH COURT CRACKS DOWN ON PRAYERS BEFORE FOOTBALL GAMES!

REMEMBER, BOYS, IF ANYONE ASKS, WE'RE LOOKING FOR A CONTACT LENS!

In 2000, the Supreme Court concluded that pregame prayers at public school football games violated the separation of church and state, as established under the First Amendment. Critics have challenged the decision, arguing that it represents an infringement of religious freedom.

Still, religious references do exist in government. For example, politicians say "so help me God" when taking the oath of office. The phrase "In God We Trust" appears on currency. And Congress opens its daily sessions with prayer. Some critics say that these practices violate the founding ideals. Others argue that the founders never meant to deny religion a place in public life. The issue of church-state separation has provoked heated battles over the years.

One battle took place in 1875. In response to a growing number of Catholic schools, Congressman James Blaine proposed a constitutional amendment to deny public funding to religiously affiliated schools. The Blaine Amendment failed on the national stage, but many states adopted similar laws. Today, more than 35 state constitutions have a version of the law.

Still, until the early 20th century, most students were educated in church-sponsored schools. Even as public education expanded, prayers and Bible readings continued in many schools. In general, the courts considered such practices acceptable.

In the landmark case *Engel v. Vitale* (1962), the Court changed course and struck down a New York law that provided a daily prayer for students to recite. Although the Establishment Clause had previously been interpreted to mean Congress could not create a national church, the Court ruled that it also banned state-sponsored prayer, even if voluntary and nondenominational, in public schools.

The Court's decision on the Engel case remains unpopular with many Americans, but it has led to a greater division between religious teaching and public education. Since school attendance is mandatory, the Court has argued that religious teachings in public schools would amount to forced teaching of religion by government.

In 1971, the Supreme Court decided in *Lemon v. Kurtzman* that the practice of using public funds to support private religious schools was unconstitutional. This case established a three-point "Lemon test" to determine if and when a government action violates the Establishment Clause. To be constitutional, a government action must

- have a **secular,** or nonreligious, purpose.
- neither help nor hurt religion.
- not result in an "excessive entanglement" of the government and religion.

Freedom of Religion: The Free Exercise Clause

The Free Exercise Clause establishes that all people are free to follow the religious practices of their choice. They are also free to follow no religion. If a person's religious faith conflicts with the law of the land, however, the law must prevail. This principle was established as a legal precedent in 1879 in the case of *Reynolds v. United States.*

George Reynolds was a member of the Mormon Church who followed the practice of polygamy, or having more than one spouse at a time. This practice violated a federal law, leading to Reynolds's arrest and conviction in a Utah court. He appealed his conviction on the grounds that the law against polygamy violated his free exercise of his religion.

In deciding against Reynolds, the Court drew a distinction between religious beliefs and religious practices. It pointed out that although the law may not interfere with beliefs, it may interfere with practices. The Court argued that if people were able to disregard any law because it violated their religious beliefs, the effect would be "to permit every citizen to become a law unto himself. Government could exist only in name under such circumstances."

The Court continued that line of reasoning in the 1940 case of *Minersville School District v. Gobitis.* In that case, the Court decided against two children who were suspended from school for refusing to say the Pledge of Allegiance. As Jehovah's Witnesses, they viewed pledging allegiance to the flag as a form of idolatry prohibited by the Bible. Many supporters of religious freedom condemned the decision.

Just three years later, however, the Court reversed itself. In *West Virginia State Board of Education v. Barnette,* the Court said that Jehovah's Witnesses could refuse to salute the flag. Their right to do so was protected under their First Amendment rights to religious freedom and free speech. In later cases, the Court has held that the government must show a compelling interest in forcing people to obey a law that violates their religious convictions.

Freedom of Speech

Freedom of speech is the second right listed in the First Amendment. It acts like an anchor for all the other rights in the amendment, because they are all linked in one way or another to free expression.

After its decisions in *Schenck, Abrams,* and *Gitlow,* the Supreme Court has generally supported freedom of speech. It has taken exception, however, to forms of speech that are harmful to others. Two clear examples of this are **libel** and **slander**—forms of speech, either written or spoken, that make false statements with intent to harm. Another form of speech not protected under the First Amendment is **obscenity,** or speech offensive to conventional standards of decency.

The issue of public safety was the key factor in the Court's early decisions limiting free speech. In 1969, however, the Court took a closer look at the "clear and present danger" test as advised by Justice Holmes in his *Abrams* dissent. The opportunity to do so came in the case of *Brandenburg v. Ohio,* which centered on a Ku Klux Klan leader who was arrested for giving a speech advocating illegal activities.

In its decision, the Court offered a two-part test to determine whether a "clear and present danger" exists that might justify suppressing free speech. First, such speech has to be "directed to inciting or producing imminent lawless action." Second, the speech must be "likely to incite or produce such action." The Court found that the Klan leader's speech, though containing hateful statements, was unlikely to produce any unlawful actions. Thus, the *Brandenburg* case did not pass the "clear and present danger" test.

In 1989, the Court extended this protection to include **symbolic speech,** or conduct that conveys a message without spoken words. Five years earlier, Gregory Lee Johnson had been arrested in Texas for burning a flag to protest government policies. His actions violated a state law against "flag desecration."

In *Texas v. Johnson,* the Court concluded that flag burning as an expression of opinion was protected symbolic speech. It said that a state could not prohibit such actions, even if it found them offensive. The Court struck down the Texas law as a violation of the First Amendment right to free speech.

The Court has also held that some forms of pornography are protected speech, although the government may restrict children's access to sexually graphic materials. In 1996, Congress tried to do just that by passing the Communications Decency Act. The act was designed to regulate pornography on the Internet. The Court struck it down a year later in *Reno v. American Civil Liberties Union.* The Court found that the law was so vague that it could have limited most speech on the Internet.

In this decision, as in its flag-burning decision, the Court has made it clear that to protect all speech, some offensive speech must be allowed to exist. That trade-off is one of the cornerstones of a free society.

The Supreme Court determined that the First Amendment protects the right to symbolic free speech. These demonstrators are exercising this right by dressing as prisoners to protest the operation of the Guantánamo Bay Detention Camp.

Freedom of the Press

Free speech can be interpreted to include most forms of expression. Nevertheless, freedom of the press was listed separately in the First Amendment to underscore its importance in a free society. "Were it left to me to decide whether we should have a government without newspapers or newspapers without government," wrote Thomas Jefferson, "I should not hesitate a moment to prefer the latter."

By specifically protecting the press, the First Amendment makes it clear that free speech covers the media as well as individuals. However, this has not stopped government officials from trying to stop the publication of material they dislike. In *Near v. Minnesota* (1931), the Court declared such attempts at **prior restraint** to be unconstitutional.

The *Near* case involved a newspaper that Minnesota officials wanted to shut down. The paper had published articles exposing political corruption. The Court declared that a government had no right to call for prior restraint. Keeping information from being published could be allowed only under very special circumstances, such as protecting national security. If officials were worried about possibly libelous articles, they could sue the publisher after the materials were in print.

In 1971, during the Vietnam War, the federal government did invoke "national security" as grounds for prior restraint. It did so after a former government employee, Daniel Ellsberg, leaked classified documents to the *New York Times*. He leaked this information to show that officials had been lying about the war's progress. After the *Times* published excerpts of the so-called Pentagon Papers, authorities sought to halt any further publication of the information.

In *New York Times Co. v. United States,* the Supreme Court decided against the government. The release of the papers, it said, had no notable impact on national security. This decision helped limit future efforts to use national security as a pretext for censoring the press.

The reporting on the Pentagon Papers was accurate. But what about news reports that are false? The First Amendment does not protect against libel. The fact is, however, that journalists sometimes make mistakes. Unless it can be shown that their errors were intentional and were meant to do harm, journalists are not guilty of libel.

Freedom of Assembly and the Right to Petition

Finally, the First Amendment protects "the right of the people peaceably to assemble, and to petition the Government for a redress of grievances." The right to petition the government to solve problems was

The right to peaceful assembly is an important guarantee of the First Amendment. It allows people to gather and express their views in public, either through speech or through symbolic actions, such as marches and protests. In 2011, demonstrators gathered at the Texas State Capitol to protest against proposed budget cuts to education.

originally considered the more important of the two. But over time, the right to assemble has taken on a larger role and has been the issue in many cases.

In keeping with the principle of peaceable assembly, many communities require groups that want to gather in public places to apply for permits and to follow certain rules. Some officials have used these requirements to limit the activities of groups they dislike. In 1937, for example, Frank Hague, the mayor of Jersey City, New Jersey, refused to grant the Committee of Industrial Organization (CIO) a permit to assemble simply because he disliked labor unions. The union took Hague to court.

In *Hague v. CIO,* the Court decided in favor of the labor union. It found that Mayor Hague had applied the permit law unfairly to limit the CIO's freedom of assembly. Although the Court acknowledged a city's right to set rules for the use of public spaces, it said that such rules must be enforced equally for all groups. Such rules should also be limited to "neutral" issues, such as the time, place, and nature of the meetings.

The right to petition has been the subject of only a few Court cases. One key case, however, arose during the civil rights movement. This case concerned the NAACP's efforts to encourage African Americans who had suffered from discrimination to take their cases to court. The state of Virginia accused the NAACP of breaking a state law by seeking out legal business. The purpose of such laws is usually to prevent unethical lawyers from launching lawsuits for their own gain.

In *NAACP v. Button* (1963), however, the Court concluded that the civil rights group was not seeking financial gain. It was, instead, helping people petition the government for their lawful rights. On that basis, the NAACP's efforts were protected under the First Amendment.

■ 5.4 Protections Against Abuses of Government Power

More than any other amendments in the Bill of Rights, the Second, Third, and Fourth were a response to the suppression of rights under British colonial rule. In the years leading up to the American Revolution, Britain often used its military authority to infringe on the liberties of colonists. These three amendments

"Darn it, there's only one burglar, and all he's got is a handgun."

In this cartoon, this man is excessively armed to defend himself against a burglar. The Second Amendment protects an individual's right to bear arms for self-defense, but some states still require gun owners to register their firearms and impose regulations on how and where firearms may be used.

were designed to ensure that such abuses would not take place under the new American government.

The Second Amendment and the Right to Bear Arms

The Second Amendment says, "A well regulated Militia, being necessary to the security of a free State, the right of the people to keep and bear Arms, shall not be infringed." In colonial times, people relied on local militias to provide security for their communities. The militias went on to play a key role in the revolution. After the war, British philosopher Richard Price praised these militias as model security forces for a democratic nation:

> *Free states ought to be bodies of armed citizens, well regulated and well disciplined, and always ready to turn out, when properly called upon, to execute the laws, to quell riots, and to keep the peace. Such, if I am rightly informed, are the citizens of America.*

Although the Constitution allowed Congress to create a national army and navy, the framers were wary of standing armies. They feared that the central government might use a powerful army to suppress citizens' rights. Militias, in their view, provided a better guarantee of freedom and security. They also knew that militia members usually supplied their own weapons. So they worded the Second Amendment to ensure that the government would not be able to take away people's weapons, thereby weakening the militias.

Interpretations of the Second Amendment have varied over the years. Although it was eventually incorporated in 2010, most regulation of firearms had been in the hands of state and local governments.

The federal government made no attempt to regulate weapons until the early 20th century. In 1934, however, an increase in violent, gang-related shootings and an attempt on President Franklin Roosevelt's life led to the passage of the first federal gun control law. This law placed a tax on certain powerful firearms and required background checks on buyers in order to limit the sale of such guns. In some cases, gun owners also had to register their weapons.

The Supreme Court upheld limitations on firearms in *United States v. Miller* (1939). In that case, the Court supported the conviction of two men who had failed to register a sawed-off shotgun, a particularly deadly weapon. Because militias never used sawed-off shotguns for common defense, the Court determined that government had the right to regulate such weapons.

Justice James Clark McReynolds declared, "We cannot say that the Second Amendment guarantees the right to keep and bear such an instrument."

Almost 70 years later, however, in *District of Columbia v. Heller* (2008), the Court struck down a law that banned the possession and registration of handguns in Washington, D.C. Justice Antonin Scalia maintained that the Second Amendment guarantees "the individual right to possess and carry weapons in case of confrontation." However, those who support and those who oppose gun control continue to dispute over the meaning of the Second Amendment and an individual's right to bear arms.

The Third and Fourth Amendments: Protecting Your Home and Person

The Third and Fourth amendments are designed to protect the privacy and property rights of citizens from abuses by law enforcement authorities or the military.

The Third Amendment prohibits citizens from being forced to take soldiers into their homes. Under British rule, colonists had sometimes been required to quarter, or feed and house, British soldiers. Many colonists saw this quartering law as another tool British authorities used to intimidate them.

Although the Third Amendment has had little direct application since colonial times, it offers a general guarantee for the privacy and sanctity of people's homes. As Justice Joseph Story once wrote, the purpose of the Third Amendment is "to secure the perfect enjoyment of that great right of the common law, that a man's house shall be his own castle, privileged against all civil and military intrusion."

The idea that people have a right to a certain amount of privacy also influenced the Fourth Amendment. This amendment forbids "unreasonable searches and seizures" of individuals or their property without a properly executed **warrant,** or written approval from a judge. This means that law enforcement officials may not search a person's home or property without prior consent or a legal order. A warrant must be based on **probable cause,** or reasonable suspicion of criminal behavior. It must also be very specific in describing the place to be searched and the persons or things to be seized.

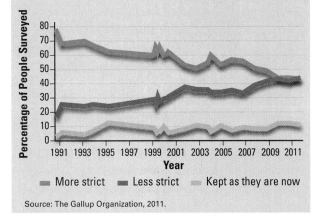

American Attitudes Toward Gun Control, 1991–2011

Between 1990 and 2011, public opinion on laws restricting the sale of firearms has varied. In a survey conducted by the Gallup Organization during these years, Americans responded to the following question: In general, do you feel that the laws covering the sale of firearms should be made more strict, less strict, or kept as they are now?

Source: The Gallup Organization, 2011.

Under certain circumstances, law enforcement officials may carry out blanket searches to protect public safety. Here, police in New York City, New York, search a vehicle at a checkpoint during a counter-terrorism inspection in 2011. The place that the police set up their checkpoint was at a bustling street near the New York Stock Exchange.

In some cases, however, the police do not need a warrant for a legal search. For example, they may search a person or property if they see criminal evidence in plain view or have probable cause to believe that a suspect is trying to destroy such evidence. Also, the Court has held that searches of students and their possessions by school officials do not require warrants.

The Supreme Court has heard numerous cases involving search and seizure. One case, *Katz v. United States* (1967), hinged on recordings of a suspect's conversation made from a public phone booth. Because the recording device was placed outside the booth and recorded only the suspect's voice, the police believed they did not need a warrant. But the Court disagreed. It concluded that a warrant was required, because the suspect had a "reasonable expectation of privacy" in a phone booth.

A year later, however, another Court decision gave law enforcement officials greater latitude to search individuals. The case, *Terry v. Ohio* (1968), involved three men whose behavior caused a police officer to suspect that they were about to rob a store. After questioning the men, the officer frisked them by patting down the outside of their clothing. Two of the suspects had guns, and they were later convicted for carrying concealed weapons. The men appealed their conviction, however, claiming that the officer did not have probable cause to frisk them. They argued that he had no evidence, other than his "hunch" that they were about to commit a crime.

The Court decided that the officer's observations provided adequate cause for the search. It said that his actions and suspicions were reasonable given the behavior of the suspects. This "stop and frisk" rule has given the police more power to try to prevent serious crimes before they happen.

■ 5.5 Your Rights in the Legal System

The next four amendments—the Fifth, Sixth, Seventh, and Eighth—concern the protection of rights in the judicial process. These amendments were designed to ensure that the justice system neither abused fundamental liberties nor punished innocent people under the pretext of preserving law and order.

The Fifth Amendment protects individuals from self-incrimination. The police are required to follow a procedure to ensure that suspects are aware of their rights.

The Fifth Amendment:
Your Rights When Accused of a Crime

If you have ever seen an arrest depicted on television, you have probably heard the words, "You have the right to remain silent." These words are based on the Fifth Amendment, which protects individuals from **self-incrimination,** or saying anything that might imply their own guilt.

This ban on self-incrimination was meant to prevent law enforcement officials from pressuring suspects into admitting guilt for a crime they did not commit. In *Miranda v. Arizona* (1966), the Court set forth a procedure for ensuring that suspects know their rights. Chief Justice Earl Warren described this procedure in his written opinion:

> *Prior to any questioning, the person must be warned that he has a right to remain silent, that any statement he does make may be used as evidence against him, and that he has a right to the presence of an attorney.*

These rights of the accused became known as Miranda rights.

The Fifth Amendment protects other rights as well. It says that no one shall be subjected to **double jeopardy.** This means that if a person is tried for a crime and found not guilty, prosecutors cannot try that person again for the same crime. It also states that no one may be "deprived of life, liberty, or property, without due process of law." This protec-

tion, known as the Due Process Clause, also appears in the Fourteenth Amendment.

The Fifth Amendment also contains the **Takings Clause**. It says that the government may not take private property for public use "without just compensation." Government may exercise a power known as eminent domain to secure private property for a public purpose, such as the construction of a road. But it must pay a fair price for the property.

The Sixth and Seventh Amendments:
Your Right to a Fair Trial

The Sixth Amendment explains how criminal trials should be conducted to protect the rights of the accused. The Seventh Amendment guarantees trial by jury in most civil lawsuits. Civil cases are those that do not involve criminal matters.

The Sixth Amendment says that criminal trials must be carried out quickly, publicly, and in front of an impartial jury. The defendant has the right to legal counsel and to see all the evidence used in the trial.

The right to legal counsel was the focus of the 1963 Court case of *Gideon v. Wainwright.* Clarence Earl Gideon was a poor, uneducated ex-convict who was arrested for theft in Florida. Unable to afford an attorney, he asked the court to provide him free legal counsel. Because Florida courts provided such services only in death penalty cases, the judge turned him down. Gideon was found guilty and sentenced to five years in prison.

While in prison, Gideon educated himself on his legal rights and filed an appeal that eventually made its way to the Supreme Court. There the justices sided with Gideon, arguing that the Sixth Amendment guarantee of legal counsel should not depend on the defendant's ability to pay. Gideon was appointed a lawyer and had his case retried. This time, he was found not guilty. Today anyone facing charges who cannot afford an attorney can have one appointed at the government's expense.

At times, a defendant's Sixth Amendment rights may come into conflict with other rights and liberties. For example, freedom of the press is a key civil liberty, and the news media have a right to cover public trials. But if this coverage affects a trial's outcome, the accused may be denied due process of law. This was the issue before the Court in the case of *Sheppard v. Maxwell.*

On July 4, 1954, Sam Sheppard's wife was murdered at the couple's home near Cleveland, Ohio. Sheppard claimed that an armed intruder had knocked him unconscious and then killed his wife. Nonetheless, he was charged with the crime and found guilty. Throughout the trial, the Cleveland press covered the story relentlessly, often in a manner that implied Sheppard's guilt.

Media coverage on a court case may influence trial results and deny due process rights to defendants. In this picture, the media are ready to cover the court hearing of football star O.J. Simpson, who was on trial for the murder of his wife. Because of the far-reaching coverage of this trial, people across the United States had formed opinions on the innocence of Simpson before the jury had reached a verdict.

Sheppard appealed his conviction while in prison, arguing that biased press coverage had prevented him from getting a fair trial. After hearing the case in 1966, the Court overturned the murder conviction, agreeing that coverage of the trial had "inflamed and prejudiced the public." Sheppard was retried in the lower court and found not guilty.

Although the Court acknowledged the media's First Amendment rights in *Sheppard v. Maxwell,* it said that press coverage should not be allowed to interfere with a defendant's right to due process. In cases where intense media coverage might unfairly influence a trial, the trial should be moved to another location or the jury should be isolated from all news coverage.

The Eighth Amendment: Your Protection from Excessive Bail and Punishments

The Eighth Amendment protects people in the criminal justice system from excessive **bail,** fines, or cruel and unusual punishments. Bail is money given over to the court in exchange for a suspect's release until his or her trial begins.

Most of the legal challenges to this amendment have involved the prohibition of cruel and unusual punishment. The Supreme Court has acknowledged that beliefs of what is "cruel and unusual" may change over time. For example, when the amendment was written, public whipping was a common punishment. Today such a punishment would be considered cruel and unusual.

Some Americans today hold that **capital punishment,** or the death penalty, is also a cruel and unusual punishment. However, most death penalty cases have focused on the method of execution, such as hanging, not on the death sentence itself. In the 1890 case of *In re Kemmler,* the Court said that any method of execution is acceptable, as long as it does not involve "torture or lingering death."

In the 1972 case of *Furman v. Georgia,* however, the Court focused on the death penalty itself. It concluded that capital punishment was cruel and unusual when it was inconsistently and unequally applied from one case to another. The Court observed that all too often, two people convicted of a capital crime received very different penalties. One might be sentenced to life in prison while the other was condemned to death.

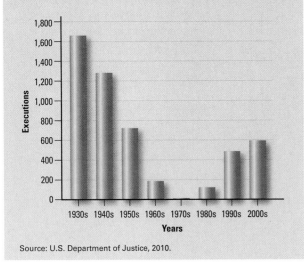

Legal Executions in the United States, 1930–2009

Legal executions in the United States steadily declined from the 1930s through the 1970s. In 1972, the Supreme Court imposed a ban on capital punishment. A Court decision reinstated the death penalty in 1976, however, and the number of executions has risen since then.

Source: U.S. Department of Justice, 2010.

The Court's decision in *Furman v. Georgia* halted all executions in the United States. Convicts on death row received reprieves. In most cases, their death sentences were converted to life in prison.

By 1976, many states had altered their laws so that capital punishment was applied more consistently. That year, in *Gregg v. Georgia*, the Court concluded that the death penalty was constitutional under the new laws. Most states reinstated capital punishment as a sentencing option. Still, limits on capital punishment exist. Juveniles and mentally retarded persons, for example, may not be executed.

5.6 Rights and Powers of the States and the People

The last two amendments, the Ninth and Tenth, are the most general amendments in the Bill of Rights. The Ninth Amendment is designed to offer protection for rights and liberties not specifically mentioned in the other amendments. The Tenth Amendment is meant to preserve the balance of power between the federal and state governments.

The Ninth Amendment: Your Rights Beyond Those Listed in the Constitution

The Ninth Amendment is the Bill of Rights' "safety net." It states that other rights and liberties may exist beyond those listed in the Constitution, and it offers protection for those **unenumerated rights**. Some of these unlisted rights were later protected under other amendments and laws. For more than 150 years, however, the Supreme Court rarely cited the Ninth Amendment and never clearly defined what rights it might include.

In 1965, in the case of *Griswold v. Connecticut,* some justices on the Court declared that the Ninth Amendment includes the right to privacy. Estelle Griswold, an official with the Planned Parenthood League of Connecticut, had been arrested for providing medical advice to married couples on how to prevent pregnancy. Her actions violated a Connecticut law that prohibited the use of contraceptives. In its decision, the Court declared that the law violated marital privacy rights. Eight years later, in *Roe v. Wade* (1973), the Court extended the right to privacy to include a woman's right to have an abortion.

Although the Constitution does not specifically mention privacy, the Court said that it was an implied right in the First, Third, and Fourth amendments. The Ninth Amendment provides further support, the Court said, by stating that a right need not be cited in the Constitution to be valid. The scope of the right to privacy remains a contested issue, however, and has not been fully resolved by the Court.

The Tenth Amendment: Powers Reserved for the States and the People

The Tenth Amendment is concerned more with federalism, or the balance of federal and state powers, than with individual rights. It limits the powers of the federal government to those granted under the Constitution, reserving other powers for the states and the people.

Under our federal system of government, the states must uphold laws enacted by Congress. When state laws clash with federal laws, federal law takes precedence under the Supremacy Clause of Article VI.

Many areas of the law, however, are not mentioned in the Constitution or granted to the federal government. Laws governing marriage and divorce are just one example. The power to regulate these

In this photograph, Estelle Griswold (left) and Cornelia Jahncke celebrate the legal victory in the 1965 case of *Griswold v. Connecticut.* Both were working with the Planned Parenthood League of Connecticut when Griswold was arrested for providing contraceptive information to married couples. The Supreme Court struck down a state law banning the use of contraceptives. At the same time, the Court introduced the idea that the right to privacy is supported by the Bill of Rights.

and many other matters that shape our daily lives is reserved for the states.

At times, the Supreme Court has struck down federal laws that overstepped the government's constitutional authority. One example was the decision in the case of *United States v. Morrison* (2000). This case focused on a law, the Violence Against Women Act, that allowed victims of domestic violence to sue their attackers in federal court. The Court struck down this law, saying that violent crime between individuals was an issue for the states, not the federal government.

Summary

The first ten amendments were added to the Constitution to safeguard civil liberties and civil rights. However, it took many years for the Supreme Court to apply the Bill of Rights to the actions of state and local governments.

The role of the judiciary The Bill of Rights defines rights and liberties in broad, abstract terms. The judicial branch interprets the first ten amendments and applies them to actual circumstances.

Protecting basic civil liberties The First Amendment protects the freedoms of religion, speech, the press, and assembly. It also guarantees the right to petition the government.

Preventing abuses of power The Second, Third, and Fourth amendments are designed to protect the rights of citizens from government abuses of power.

Safeguards under the legal system The Fifth, Sixth, Seventh, and Eighth amendments define and protect rights under the judicial system.

Powers of the states and the people The Ninth Amendment protects other, unnamed rights not specified in the Bill of Rights. The Tenth Amendment reserves powers not granted to the federal government to the states or the people.

Do you support the First Amendment?

Since 1997, the First Amendment Center has conducted an annual survey on the state of the First Amendment. One thousand Americans are randomly contacted by telephone and asked if they can name their First Amendment rights. They are then read the text of the amendment and asked questions that probe their feelings about the rights it protects.

Do you support the First Amendment, or do you think it goes too far in some cases? Find out by taking the "State of the First Amendment" survey for yourself. Record your answers on a sheet of paper. Then compare your views with those who participated in the 2012 survey.

State of the First Amendment, 2012

1. As you may know, the First Amendment is a part of the U.S. Constitution. Can you name any of the specific rights that are guaranteed by the First Amendment?

2. The First Amendment became part of the U.S. Constitution more than 200 years ago. This is what it says:

   'Congress shall make no law respecting an establishment of religion or prohibiting the free exercise thereof, or abridging the freedom of speech or of the press, or the right of the people peaceably to assemble, and to petition the government for a redress of grievances.'

   Based on your own feelings about the First Amendment, please tell me whether you agree or disagree with the following statement: The First Amendment goes too far in the rights it guarantees.

   Agree
   Disagree

   Now please tell me whether you agree or disagree with the following statements:

3. Musicians should be allowed to sing songs with lyrics that others might find offensive.

   Agree
   Disagree

4. Overall, the news media try to report the news without bias.

   Agree
   Disagree

5. It is important for our democracy that the news media act as a watchdog on government.

   Agree
   Disagree

6. Public schools should be allowed to discipline students who use their own personal computers at home to post material that school officials say is offensive.

   Agree
   Disagree

7. In the event of a national emergency, the government should be allowed to take control of the Internet and limit access to social media and to Web outlets such as AOL and Yahoo.

   Strongly agree
   Mildly agree
   Mildly disagree
   Strongly disagree

8. The government should be allowed to prosecute Internet users who illegally distribute copyrighted music and movies online.

   Strongly agree
   Mildly agree
   Mildly disagree
   Strongly disagree

9. People should be allowed to record or photograph the activities of the police in public as long as they do not interfere with what the police are doing.

   Strongly agree
   Mildly agree
   Mildly disagree
   Strongly disagree

10. As long as no money is being made, someone should be able to post copyrighted material online or on social media without paying rights fees.

    Strongly agree
    Mildly agree
    Mildly disagree
    Strongly disagree

11. Even if the money is being made, someone should be able to post copyrighted material online or on social media without paying rights fees.

    Strongly agree
    Mildly agree
    Mildly disagree
    Strongly disagree

Results of the 2012 "State of the First Amendment" Survey
Answers chosen most are shown in red.

1. First Amendment Rights Americans are able to identify:
   Freedom of the press: 13%
   Freedom of speech: 65%
   Freedom of religion: 28%
   Right to petition: 4%
   Right of assembly: 13%

2. The First Amendment goes too far in the rights it guarantees.
   Agree: 13%
   Disagree: 81%

3. Musicians should be allowed to sing songs with lyrics that others might find offensive.
   Agree: 69%
   Disagree: 27%

4. Overall, the news media try to report the news without bias.
   Agree: 33%
   Disagree: 62%

5. It is important for our democracy that the news media act as a watchdog on government.
   Agree: 75%
   Disagree: 20%

6. Public schools should be allowed to discipline students who use their personal computers at home to post material that school officials say is offensive.
   Agree: 34%
   Disagree: 57%

7. In the event of a national emergency, the government should be allowed to take control of the Internet and limit access to social media and to Web outlets such as AOL and Yahoo.
   Strongly agree: 17%
   Mildly agree: 16%
   Mildly disagree: 15%
   Strongly disagree: 44%

8. The government should be allowed to prosecute Internet users who illegally distribute copyrighted music and movies online.
   Strongly agree: 32%
   Mildly agree: 27%
   Mildly disagree 15%
   Strongly disagree: 18%

9. People should be allowed to record or photograph the activities of the police in public as long as they do not interfere with what the police are doing.
   Strongly agree: 66%
   Mildly agree: 19%
   Mildly disagree: 7%
   Strongly disagree: 5%

10. As long as no money is being made, someone should be able to post copyrighted material online or on social media without paying rights fees.
    Strongly agree: 24%
    Mildly agree: 22%
    Mildly disagree: 19%
    Strongly disagree: 23%

11. Even if money is being made, someone should be able to post copyrighted material online or on social media without paying rights fees.
    Strongly agree: 10%
    Mildly agree: 13%
    Mildly disagree: 23%
    Strongly disagree: 41%

Chapter 6

Federalism: National, State, and Local Powers

How does power flow through our federal system of government?

■ 6.1 Introduction

You might not expect the gray wolf to be involved in a power struggle between the national government and state wildlife agencies. Under our federal system of government, states traditionally exercised control over wildlife within their borders. Wolves were universally viewed as threats to people and livestock. In fact, many states paid residents a bounty, or reward, for every wolf they killed. As a result, by the mid-1900s, wolves had all but disappeared from every state except Alaska.

Concern over the dwindling population of once-common animals such as the gray wolf led Congress to pass the Endangered Species Act in 1973. This law gave control of endangered animals to the U.S. Fish and Wildlife Service. Once the gray wolf came under federal protection, state bounties were banned and the hunting of wolves was outlawed in most areas. A person found guilty of killing a wolf could be punished with a fine of $100,000 and a year in jail.

The Fish and Wildlife Service also worked to restore endangered species to habitats where they had once flourished. As part of this effort, federal officials reintroduced gray wolves to Yellowstone National Park in 1995. No wolves had been seen in the park, which includes parts of Idaho, Montana, and Wyoming, since 1939.

State flags wave beneath the Star-Spangled Banner

The reintroduction of the gray wolf in Idaho, Montana, and Wyoming caused tension among ranchers, state officials, and the U.S. Fish and Wildlife Service. At the same time, the wolves boosted tourism in the region. These vacationers are hoping to spot wolves in Yellowstone National Park.

The return of wolves to Yellowstone Park triggered a storm of protest from nearby sheep and cattle ranchers. Fearing wolf raids on their livestock, they urged state officials to wrest control of the growing wolf population away from the federal government. Fish and Wildlife Service officials resisted these efforts, fearing that handing over wolf management to the states could lead to overhunting and even extinction.

By 2007, Idaho and Montana's wolf population had grown to the point at which the Fish and Wildlife Service agreed to return management of wolves to state agencies. However, environmentalists contested this decision. After much debate, Idaho and Montana regained management of wolves in 2011. In 2012, Wyoming also regained this authority.

This long and often heated debate over who should manage the gray wolf is an example of the kinds of conflicts that can arise in a federal system of government. This chapter will trace the evolution of federalism in the United States over the past two centuries, including the important role of state and local governments within our federal system of government.

■ 6.2 The Establishment of a Federal System

The United States was the first nation-state founded with a federalist system of government. This system contributes to both a national and federal identity, making Americans proud of both their country and their state.

The framers of the Constitution formed a federalist system of government out of necessity. The delegates attending the Constitutional Convention in 1787 knew that the 13 states would be reluctant to give up any real power to a national government. As a result, the framers carefully configured how power should be divided among the national government and state governments.

The Constitutional Division of Powers

The U.S. Constitution divides powers into three categories: expressed, concurrent, and reserved. The diagram "The Federal System" shows how these powers are distributed between the national and state governments.

Expressed powers are powers specifically granted to the national government. The Constitution lists only 17 of these specific powers. Some, such as the power to coin money or to make treaties with other countries, are delegated exclusively to the national government. Others, such as the power to levy taxes, are concurrent powers shared by the national and state governments.

The Constitution says little about the powers reserved by states. But it does place some requirements on state governments. The Full Faith and Credit Clause, for example, insists that states recognize, honor, and enforce one another's public actions. Because of this clause, a driver's license issued by your home state is recognized as legal in any other state.

In addition, the Privileges and Immunities Clause says a state cannot discriminate against residents of other states or give its own residents special privileges. This means that if you move to a new state, you will enjoy all of the rights given to any other citizen of that state.

The Tenth Amendment further clarifies the constitutional division of powers by declaring that powers not specifically delegated to the national government are reserved for the states. These reserved powers include overseeing public schools, regulating businesses, and protecting state resources. The states also reserve the power to establish and regulate local governments.

The Benefits of a Federal System

While the framers had little choice but to create a federal system of government, they could see several benefits of federalism. Four of the most important are listed below.

Federalism protects against tyranny of the majority.

By dividing power among several units of government, federalism makes it difficult for a misguided majority to trample the rights of a minority. If a minority group feels abused in one state, its members can move to a state where their rights are more likely to be respected.

Jonah Goldberg, an editor with the *National Review,* compared the states to housing dorms on a hypothetical college campus to describe how this protection benefits a diverse population. On this campus, roughly half of the students like to have loud parties every night, while the other half like to have peace and quiet for studying. He wrote,

A purely democratic system where all students get to decide dorm policy could result in the tyranny of 51 percent of the students over 49 percent of the students. The party-hardy crowd could pass a policy permitting loud music and . . . parties at all hours of the night. Or if the more academically rigorous coalition won, they could ban "fun" of any kind, ever . . .

But, if you allowed each individual dorm to vote for its own policies, you could have a system where some dorms operate like scholarly monasteries and other dorms are more fun than a pool party . . . Theoretically, 100 percent of the students could live the way they want. Maximized human happiness!

—Jonah Goldberg, "United States of Happiness," *National Review Online,* 2004

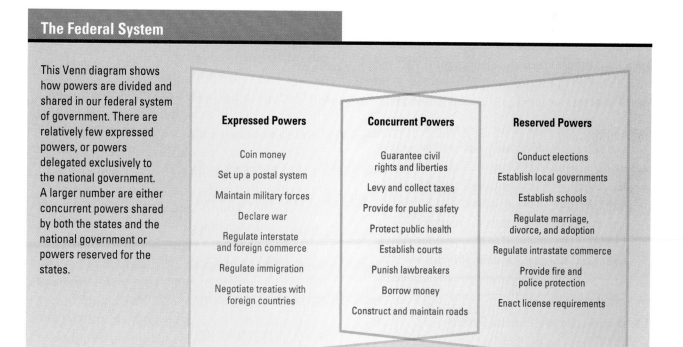

The Federal System

This Venn diagram shows how powers are divided and shared in our federal system of government. There are relatively few expressed powers, or powers delegated exclusively to the national government. A larger number are either concurrent powers shared by both the states and the national government or powers reserved for the states.

Expressed Powers

Coin money

Set up a postal system

Maintain military forces

Declare war

Regulate interstate and foreign commerce

Regulate immigration

Negotiate treaties with foreign countries

Concurrent Powers

Guarantee civil rights and liberties

Levy and collect taxes

Provide for public safety

Protect public health

Establish courts

Punish lawbreakers

Borrow money

Construct and maintain roads

Reserved Powers

Conduct elections

Establish local governments

Establish schools

Regulate marriage, divorce, and adoption

Regulate intrastate commerce

Provide fire and police protection

Enact license requirements

Federalism promotes unity without imposing uniformity. As Goldberg's example suggests, federalism allows groups with different values and different ways of life to live together in peace. Likewise, federalism allows states to pass laws that reflect the needs and goals of their citizens while still remaining part of the union of states. All states, for example, support public education for young people. But how schools are funded and regulated differs from state to state, depending on local preferences.

Federalism creates "laboratories" for policy experiments. The flexibility of federalism allows states to act as testing grounds for innovative solutions to common problems. U.S. Supreme Court Justice Louis Brandeis once noted,

> *It is one of the happy incidents of the federal system that a single courageous State may, if its citizens choose, serve as a laboratory and try novel social and economic experiments without risk to the rest of the country.*
> —Justice Louis Brandeis, dissent in
> *New State Ice Co. v. Liebermann,* 1932

If a state tries a new idea and succeeds, other states will follow suit. On the other hand, if an experimental policy fails, the problems that result are limited to one state. In some cases, a failure may provide lessons to others about better ways to implement policies.

Federalism encourages political participation. Finally, federalism provides an opportunity for people to be involved in the political process closer to home than the nation's capital. As Goldberg observed,

> *The more you push . . . decisions down to the level where people actually have to live with their consequences, the more likely it is they [the people] will be a) involved and interested in the decision-making process, and b) happy with the result. Federalism . . . requires the consent of the governed at the most basic level. Sure, your side can lose an argument, but it's easier to change things locally than nationally.*

The Drawbacks of a Federal System

For all of the benefits, there are drawbacks to a federal system. One is the lack of consistency of laws and policies from state to state. This can create problems when people move from state to state. Drivers who cross state lines, for example, may not be aware that the speed limits and traffic laws of one state may not apply to the next. Teachers and other professionals often face hurdles when they move from state to state. A teaching credential valid in one state may not allow a teacher to teach in another state without additional testing or coursework.

Another drawback of our federal system is the tension it sometimes creates between state and federal officials. The Constitution does not always draw a clear dividing line between national and state powers. For example, it does not specify whether control of wildlife should be a federal or a state responsibility. The same can be said for other issues, such as regulating air quality and providing health care to the poor. When questions arise over who is in charge, it is often left to the Supreme Court to draw the line between the state and federal authority.

■ 6.3 The Evolution of Federalism

There are approximately 88,000 national, state, and local units of government in the United States. This diagram shows how that total breaks down into a pyramid of governments. Not surprisingly, with so many different units of government at work in this country, relations among the different levels have evolved and changed over time.

Dual Federalism: A Layer Cake of Divided Powers

The framers of the Constitution disagreed among themselves about the ideal balance of power among the different levels of government. But they did agree, as James Madison wrote in *The Federalist* No. 45, that the powers of the national government were "few and defined" and the powers of the states "numerous and indefinite."

From 1790 to 1933, national and state governments maintained a fairly strict division of powers. Political scientists sometimes refer to this system as **dual federalism,** or "layer cake" federalism. In such a system, the two levels of government are part of the whole, but each has its own clearly delineated responsibilities.

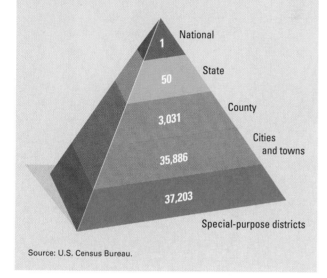
During the era of dual federalism, the Supreme Court sometimes played the role of referee between the states and the national government. For example, in *McCulloch v. Maryland* (1819), a case involving the creation of a national bank, the Court made it clear that federal laws took precedent over state laws when the two came into conflict.

A few years later, the Court further clarified the roles of the state and national governments, this time in the regulation of commerce. The case of *Gibbons v. Ogden* (1824) arose when the New York State legislature granted Aaron Ogden a monopoly on steamboat operations between New York and New Jersey. Ogden went to court in New York to force a rival steamboat operator, Thomas Gibbons, off the river. When the state court ruled in Ogden's favor, Gibbons appealed the decision to the Supreme Court.

Lawyers for Gibbons argued that New York had no authority to limit commerce on waterways between states. The Supreme Court agreed. Chief Justice John Marshall concluded that the Constitution clearly gives control of trade among the states to the national government. As a result, New York's grant of a monopoly to Ogden was unconstitutional.

The Gibbons decision drew a sharp line between state and federal power. The national government controls **interstate commerce,** or trade among the states. The states control **intrastate commerce,** or trade within their borders. This clear division of power was typical of how federalism worked during the dual federalism era.

Cooperative Federalism: A Marble Cake of Mixed Powers

The Great Depression of the 1930s led to a very different conception of federalism. As the Depression deepened, the efforts of state governments to feed the hungry and revive the economy proved inadequate. In desperation, Americans turned to the national government for help.

On taking office in 1933, President Franklin Roosevelt launched a flurry of legislation known as the New Deal. These New Deal programs ushered in a new era of shared power among national, state, and local governments. Unlike in the past, when officials at different levels had viewed each other with suspicion, they now worked together as allies to ease human suffering.

Political scientists refer to this new era as one of **cooperative federalism,** or "marble cake" federalism. Political scientist Morton Grodzins wrote of the federalist system during this period,

> *When you slice through it you reveal an inseparable mixture of differently colored ingredients . . . so that it is difficult to tell where one ends and the other begins. So it is with the federal, state, and local responsibilities in the chaotic marble cake of American government.*
> —"The Federal System," 1960

The diagram "Dual Versus Cooperative Federalism" illustrates the differences between dual (layer cake) and cooperative (marble cake) federalism.

A key ingredient in marble cake federalism was a mix of federal **grants-in-aid** programs. Grants-in-aid are funds given by the federal government to state and local governments for specific programs, such as aid to the unemployed. Such grants had long been used by the national government, but only for very narrow purposes. Roosevelt greatly expanded

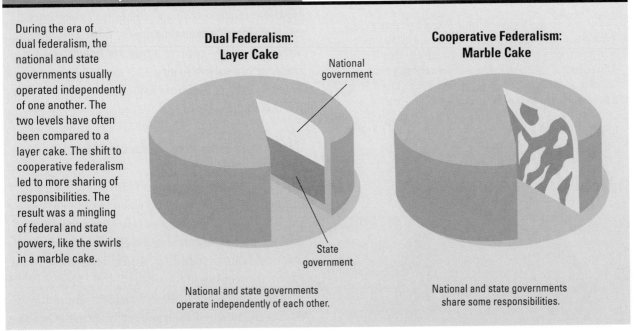

During the era of dual federalism, the national and state governments usually operated independently of one another. The two levels have often been compared to a layer cake. The shift to cooperative federalism led to more sharing of responsibilities. The result was a mingling of federal and state powers, like the swirls in a marble cake.

Dual Federalism: Layer Cake

National government

State government

National and state governments operate independently of each other.

Cooperative Federalism: Marble Cake

National and state governments share some responsibilities.

the use of grants-in-aid to get help to the needy. In 1927, shortly before the Depression began, federal funds made up less than 2 percent of state and local government revenues. This figure jumped to just over 13 percent early in the New Deal and remained near there until 1960.

Regulated Federalism: More Money with More Strings Attached

A generation later, President Lyndon Johnson set out to expand on the New Deal by creating what he called the Great Society. The Great Society was a set of programs designed to end poverty, eliminate racial injustice, and improve the environment.

Like Roosevelt, Johnson looked to state and local governments to carry out many of his new programs. As during the New Deal, the federal government provided funding in the form of grants. But unlike earlier grants-in-aid, Great Society grants often came with strict regulations as to how the money could be spent. Johnson called his partnership with state and local governments creative federalism. Political scientists, however, prefer the more descriptive term **regulated federalism**.

Johnson's Great Society legislation led to a huge increase in federal involvement in state and local

governments. Political scientist Timothy Conlan observed that by the end of the 1960s,

The federal government became more involved in virtually all existing fields of governmental activity—including many that had been highly local in character (for example, elementary and secondary education, local law enforcement, libraries, and fire protection). In addition, new public functions were established, such as adult employment training, air pollution control, health planning, and community antipoverty programs.
—Timothy Conlan, *From New Federalism to Devolution: Twenty-Five Years of Intergovernmental Reform,* 1998

Although state and local governments welcomed the new influx of federal funds, they were not happy about the federal regulations that came with the money. They were even less happy about the rapid growth of **unfunded mandates** that began in the 1960s. These are programs and regulations imposed on state and local governments by Congress without adequate funding, if any, attached to them.

Unfunded mandates were attractive to members of Congress, since members could declare that they were solving problems without having to raise taxes to fund the solutions. Instead, the mandates put the burden of paying for those solutions on state and local governments. In effect, Congress provided the recipe for solving problems but required state and local governments to provide the ingredients—both money and people—to make those solutions work.

New Federalism: Returning Power to the States

The rapid expansion of federal power in the 1960s alarmed people who valued state and local control. While running for president in 1968, Richard Nixon promised voters that he would restore "true" federalism by reigning in federal power. Nixon called his pledge to return power to the states the **new federalism**. Political scientists call these more recent efforts to return power to the states **devolution**.

Devolution began slowly in the 1970s and 1980s, first under President Nixon and later under President Ronald Reagan. Both presidents tried to shift power back to the states by encouraging them to write their own "recipes" for solving problems. The national government's role was reduced to providing ingredients, mostly in the form of federal funds.

Devolution picked up speed in 1994, when Republicans gained control of Congress for the first time in 40 years. Once in power, the new Republican majority enacted the Unfunded Mandates Reform Act. The purpose of this 1995 law was to stop Congress from burdening states with responsibilities without providing adequate funding.

A year later, Congress pushed devolution still further when it overhauled the nation's welfare system. In the past, federal officials had closely regulated how states gave out welfare payments to needy families. The 1996 Personal Responsibility and Work Opportunity Reconciliation Act, more commonly known as the Welfare Reform Act, returned control of welfare systems to state governments.

Regulated Versus New Federalism

Over the years, the national government has devised different "recipes" for federalism. During the period of regulated federalism, the national government greatly expanded its power over the states. Congress often mandated programs for state and local governments with strict regulations but inadequate funding. Supporters of new federalism sought to restore the balance between the two levels of government. This was done by returning control over many programs to the states.

Recipe for Regulated Federalism

Ingredients

| Federal programs and unfunded mandates | Federal grants-in-aid, state and local tax dollars | State and local officials |

Directions
Mix together as required by federal rules and regulations.

Recipe for the New Federalism

Ingredients

| State programs and policies | Federal block grants, state and local tax dollars | State and local officials |

Directions
Mix together as directed by state laws and policies.

The federal government continued to provide "ingredients" in the form of **block grants** to the states. But unlike the highly regulated grants-in-aid that funded Great Society programs, block grants left states free to decide how best to spend the money they received. One of the requirements imposed on state welfare programs was that they limit the time a person could receive federally funded welfare payments to five years.

The Impact of the Supreme Court on Devolution

Since power began shifting back to the states in the late 20th century, the Supreme Court has made a series of decisions that contributed to devolution. One of the first involved the Gun-Free School Zones Act of 1990, a law passed by Congress that banned firearm possession around public schools. In 1992, Alfonso Lopez, Jr., a high school student in Texas, was convicted of violating the law after taking a gun to school. Lopez appealed his conviction on the grounds that Congress lacked the power to regulate gun possession in schools.

In *United States v. Lopez* (1995), the Supreme Court agreed with Lopez and voted 5–4 to strike down the 1990 act as an unconstitutional expansion of federal power. Speaking for the Court, Chief Justice William Rehnquist reasoned that upholding this law would "convert congressional authority under the Commerce Clause to a general police power of the sort retained by the States."

The Supreme Court also limited federal power in *United States v. Morrison* (2000), a case involving a federal law that gave victims of gender-motivated crimes the right to sue in federal courts. In another split decision, the Court ruled that Congress did not have the authority to enact this law.

However, if the past is any guide, federalism will continue to evolve. In recent years, federal power has expanded in some areas. For example, President Bush signed the No Child Left Behind Act of 2001 into law. Under this act, states must provide students with qualified teachers and administer annual standardized tests in federally funded schools. Furthermore, in 2005 the Court upheld a federal law that limited marijuana usage in *Gonzales v. Raich*. In 2012, this federal law was challenged again when two states legalized recreational marijuana.

In some cases, the Court helped define what the national government can and cannot do. For instance, Congress passed the Affordable Care Act of 2010, which required Americans to buy health insurance. Those who refused would have to pay a penalty. The Supreme Court upheld most provisions of the act in *National Federation of Independent Business v. Sebelius* (2012), but declared the act "constitutional in part and unconstitutional in part." Chief Justice John Roberts, the deciding vote in this case, found that the federal mandate was constitutional because of Congress's power to impose taxes, not because of the Commerce Clause, as the government argued. The Court's decision to reject the government's argument may limit federal power in the long run, and power will continue to shift between the states and the national government.

◼ 6.4 State Governments in a Federal System

Strange things were going on in Texas in 2003. State troopers were scouring the state looking for lost legislators. The missing lawmakers were not in any danger. Instead, they were hiding out in Ardmore, Oklahoma, and later in Albuquerque, New Mexico, in an effort to stall a vote in their state legislature. The activities of state governments do not usually get much coverage in the news. But the case of the runaway Texas lawmakers made headlines across the nation.

State Constitutions: Long and Much Amended

The missing Texas lawmakers were using a provision in their state constitution to keep the legislature from voting on a bill they opposed. The constitution of Texas, like that of most states, requires a **quorum** to be present for the legislature to vote on bills. A quorum is a fixed number of people, often a majority, who must be present for an organization to conduct business. The purpose of a quorum is to prevent an unrepresentative minority from taking action in the name of the full organization.

The U.S. Constitution requires every state constitution to support "a republican form of government." Beyond that stipulation, each state is free to organize its government as its citizens choose. Nebraska, for instance, is the only state with

Nineteen states today are still governed by their original constitutions. In contrast, Louisiana holds the record for change, with 11 constitutions. Vermont has the shortest constitution with around 8,500 words. Alabama's constitution, on the other hand, has more than 350,000 words.

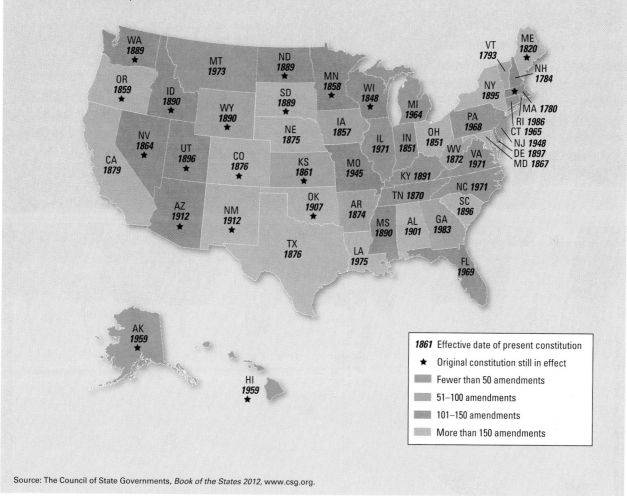

1861 Effective date of present constitution

★ Original constitution still in effect

Fewer than 50 amendments

51–100 amendments

101–150 amendments

More than 150 amendments

Source: The Council of State Governments, *Book of the States 2012*, www.csg.org.

a unicameral state legislature. Alabama, unlike other states, allows for "local amendments" to its constitution. These amendments apply only to the local areas that approve them.

In contrast to the U.S. Constitution, state constitutions tend to change frequently. Most states have adopted entirely new constitutions at least once, if not several times. Today, only five states still rely on constitutions written before 1850. This map shows when each state adopted its present-day constitution.

The map also shows that states tend to amend their constitutions relatively often. A majority of states have amended their constitutions at least 100 times. In Texas, voters were asked to approve 19

constitutional amendments during a single election. One of the amendments simply allowed towns to donate old firefighting equipment to charities. At the national level, such an issue would have been settled by an act of Congress.

Because of their many amendments, state constitutions tend to be much longer than the U.S. Constitution. The U.S. Constitution has only about 7,400 words, compared with an average of around 36,000 for state constitutions. Alabama boasts the longest constitution of all—with more than 760 amendments.

State constitutions are usually amended in one of two ways. The legislature may propose an amendment, which is then submitted to voters for approval.

About three-fourths of amendments proposed by legislatures win voter approval. Or citizens can petition for a public vote on a proposed amendment through the initiative process. About half of the amendments proposed by citizen initiatives are enacted by voters.

The Role of State Legislatures: Laws, Budgets, and Redistricting

Like the U.S. Congress, state legislatures are responsible for enacting laws, levying taxes, and creating budgets. In all states, lawmakers are elected by popular vote. Some states elect citizen legislatures, whose members meet only a few weeks per year.

Other states elect professional legislatures, whose members meet almost year-round.

State lawmakers act on a wide range of issues. For example, they enact laws that create state parks, establish graduation requirements for high school students, and regulate business activities within the state. They also pass tax laws and draw up budgets to fund everything from state prisons to community colleges.

State lawmakers are also responsible for **apportionment,** or the distribution of seats in the U.S. House of Representatives and in state legislatures. The U.S. Constitution apportions seats in the House of Representatives to the states based on population.

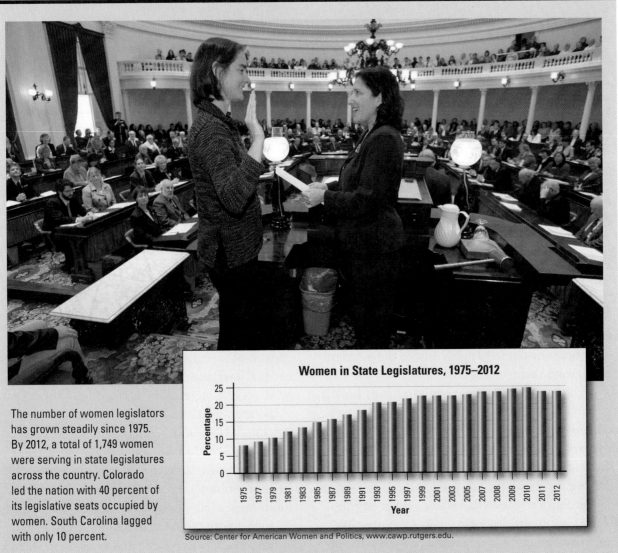

The Rise of Women in State Legislatures

The number of women legislators has grown steadily since 1975. By 2012, a total of 1,749 women were serving in state legislatures across the country. Colorado led the nation with 40 percent of its legislative seats occupied by women. South Carolina lagged with only 10 percent.

Women in State Legislatures, 1975–2012

Source: Center for American Women and Politics, www.cawp.rutgers.edu.

But Congress does not have the power to say how those seats should be distributed within a state. That decision is left up to each state.

For much of our history, state legislatures varied in how they approached apportionment. Often, lawmakers tried to draw district boundaries to benefit themselves or other members of their party, a practice known as **gerrymandering**. The term gerrymander was coined in 1811 to describe a salamander-shaped legislative district in Massachusetts. Elbridge Gerry, the governor of Massachusetts, had created the oddly shaped district to help members of his party.

In addition to gerrymandering, some state legislatures favored voters in small towns and rural areas by basing legislative districts on factors other than population. People in cities complained that legislatures dominated by rural lawmakers failed to deal with urban problems. But there was little they could do to force state legislations to apportion seats differently.

Frustration with this situation prompted a group of citizens, led by Charles Baker, to sue Tennessee's secretary of state, Joe Carr, in 1959. At issue was the failure of the Tennessee legislature to adjust the state's legislative districts since 1901. During that time, many rural families had migrated to cities.

As a result of the legislature's inaction, Baker's urban district had ten times as many residents as some rural districts had. Baker claimed that this imbalance violated his Fourteenth Amendment right to "equal protection under the laws." He asked the court to prevent Carr and other state officials from holding elections in Tennessee until district lines were redrawn.

Baker v. Carr reached the Supreme Court in 1961. In the past, the Court had treated **redistricting,** or the redrawing of voting districts to reflect population changes, as a political question. As such, it was up to state legislatures, not federal courts, to decide when and how redistricting should take place. After months of deliberation, however, the Court rejected this position. In 1962, it decided that legislative apportionment was a question for state and federal courts to consider.

The impact of this decision was immediate and far-reaching. Within a year, 36 states were involved in lawsuits over their apportionment of legislative seats. A number of these cases, including *Reynolds v. Sims,*

This 1812 cartoon shows the salamander-like shape of a Massachusetts legislative district created by Governor Elbridge Gerry. Since then, the term gerrymandering has come to mean the drawing of district boundaries in a way that favors one political party or elected official over another.

came before the Supreme Court in 1964. Speaking for the Court, Chief Justice Earl Warren wrote,

> *Legislators represent people, not trees or acres. Legislators are elected by voters, not farms or cities or economic interests . . . A citizen, a qualified voter, is no more nor no less so because he lives in the city or on the farm. This is the clear and strong command of our Constitution's Equal Protection Clause. This is an essential part of the concept of a government of laws and not men.*

As a result of this decision, state legislatures across the country were forced to redraw their legislative districts following the principle of "one person, one vote."

Today, redistricting is done every ten years after the Census Bureau reports the results of the national census. A few states have turned over the task of redrawing district lines based on census data to an independent commission. In most states, however, redistricting is still done by lawmakers.

The redistricting process is often divisive. The Texas lawmakers who fled the state in 2003 did so to block action on a redistricting bill they saw as unfair to their party. They did not have enough votes to defeat the bill. Instead, they tried to keep the legislature from voting at all by preventing a quorum from appearing at the statehouse. Redistricting continues to be a concern in Texas. When district lines were redrawn after the 2010 census, the issue was brought to the Supreme Court. In some states, however, arguments of redistricting can get even more intense.

> When fists flew in the Illinois legislature in 1981, it was not over policy. It was about politics: the politics of redistricting.
>
> That's no surprise. Redistricting is the political equivalent of moving the left field fence for a right-handed hitter. By changing the boundaries, redistricting helps some, hurts others—and leaves just about everyone else scrambling.
>
> —Jack Quinn, Donald J. Simon, and Jonathan B. Sallet, "Redrawing the Districts, Changing the Rules," *Washington Post National Weekly Edition*, April 1, 1991

The Role of State Governors: Managing the Executive Branch

State governors are usually the best-known public officials in their state. In all states, governors are elected by popular vote. Almost all serve four-year terms. In many states, they are limited to just two terms. After serving as governor, the majority return to private life. But some view the governorship as a training ground for higher office. About half of all U.S. presidents were governors first.

The most important task of a state governor is to manage the executive branch of his or her state government. In addition, most governors have the power to

- help establish the legislature's agenda.
- prepare the state budget.
- veto bills and budgets approved by the legislature.
- appoint state officials.
- grant pardons or reduce a criminal's sentence.
- command the state National Guard.
- issue executive orders.

Arizona Governor Jan Brewer

Jan Brewer became Arizona's governor in 2009. Her legislative agenda has pushed to increase the state's economic competitiveness, reform education, improve government efficiency, and challenge the authority of the federal government.

Governor Brewer's 2012 Agenda

Economic Development
- simplify tax code to aid small businesses
- promote tourism and trade by building interstate highway from Phoenix to Las Vegas
- support unemployed and underemployed adults transitioning into new careers

Education
- implement rigorous school standards
- increase parent involvement in K–12 education
- administer performance-based funding for higher education institutions

Effective State Government
- modernize State personnel system
- create a Government Transformation Office to improve government efficiency

Public Safety
- provide health services for mentally ill individuals
- improve training of child protection service officials
- improve efficiency of abuse hotline

Federalism
- support immigration reform bill Arizona SB 1070 in Supreme Court case
- oppose federal health care law
- push the federal government to restore forests in Arizona

There are many types of courts. Municipal courts deal with issues such as divorce and adoptions. County courts deal with criminal trials and lawsuits. They may also handle legal documents such as marriage licenses.

An executive order is an order issued to a government agency to accomplish a specific task or carry out a specific policy. Governors differ in how they use their power. For example, as governor of Arizona, Jan Brewer issued executive orders that called for the creation of task forces to study problems such as the economy and education.

At times, governors take actions that put them at odds with the federal government. In 2010, for instance, Brewer authorized the training of law enforcers to carry out Arizona S.B. 1070, a controversial bill that allowed police to arrest people suspected of being illegal aliens without a warrant if they do not carry proof of legal residency. However, in *Arizona v. United States* (2012), the Court determined that states do not have the authority to arrest illegal aliens.

Governors may also serve as ambassadors for their state and play a major role in promoting its economic development. As governor of Washington, Chris Gregoire led trade missions to countries in Europe and Asia. When announcing a trade mission to India in 2012, Gregoire explained, "This is our opportunity to get out in front, and make sure that consumers and businesses in India are aware of the quality items produced in Washington state."

The Role of State Court Systems: Settling Legal Disputes

If you ever have a reason to go to court, you will probably deal with your state court system. The vast majority of legal cases in the United States are handled at the state and local level. Only cases that have a bearing on federal law are heard in federal courts.

There are two main kinds of courts in state judicial systems: trial courts and appeals courts. Trial courts handle most cases that affect the daily lives of citizens. Appeals courts handle cases that are appealed, or requested to be reviewed in order to reverse the decision of a trial court. In general, appeals center on questions involving interpretation of the law.

In most states, there are two levels of trial courts. At the lower level, municipal courts deal with traffic tickets, adoptions, divorces, and minor violations of the law. Small claims courts settle disputes involving small amounts of money—usually less than $5,000. Most participants in small claims cases act as their own attorneys.

At the higher level, trial courts—with names such as superior court, county court, and district court—deal with major criminal cases and lawsuits. These are the trials usually shown in movies and television dramas.

Law enforcement at the county level is led by the county sheriff, who is usually an elected official. The sheriff department may work with the police in a city, but it also enforces laws in unincorporated areas under the county's jurisdiction.

■ 6.5 Local Governments

A savvy Massachusetts politician named Thomas "Tip" O'Neill once declared, "All politics is local." While O'Neill spent much of his career in Washington, D.C., in the House of Representatives, he realized that most of the decisions that directly affect our daily lives are made close to home. Local governments provide such basic services as drinking water, police protection, garbage collection, public schools, and libraries. Despite their importance, local governments are not mentioned in the U.S. Constitution. It is left up to each state to establish local units of government for its citizens.

Counties, Parishes, and Boroughs

Following British tradition, 48 of the 50 states divide their territory into districts called counties. Louisiana is divided into parishes. Alaska, with its large landmass and small, scattered population, divides its land into large boroughs.

The original purpose of counties was to provide government services to rural residents. Initially, these services included law enforcement, courts, road construction and maintenance, public assistance to the poor, and the recording of legal documents. Over time, some county governments expanded to provide health protection, hospitals, libraries, parks, fire protection, and agricultural aid.

Traditionally, county governments were headquartered in the **county seat**. This was often the largest or most centrally located town in the county. Ideally, the county seat was no more than a day's wagon journey from any county resident. This made it easier for people to participate in local politics.

With the rise of urban areas, towns and cities have taken over many of the functions that were once county responsibilities. In some areas, the duties of city and county governments overlap. For example, most towns and cities today have their own police forces, but the county may maintain a sheriff's office to enforce laws in areas outside city limits.

Most county governments are headed by an elected board of commissioners or board of supervisors. The board's duties vary depending on the powers granted to the county by the state. Other elected officials typically include the county sheriff, treasurer, tax assessor, and judges. The board may appoint other officials, such as the fire marshal and county coroner.

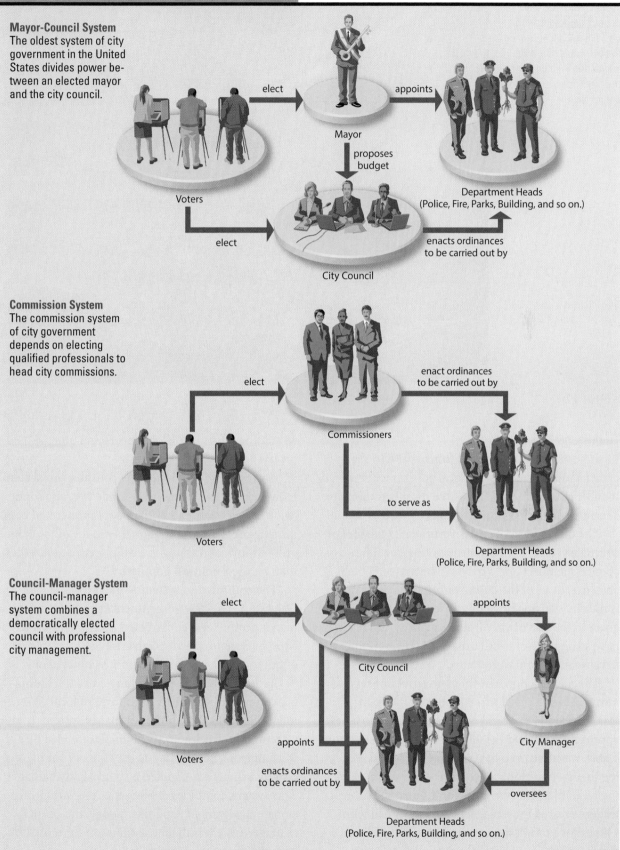

Mayor-Council System
The oldest system of city government in the United States divides power between an elected mayor and the city council.

Voters

elect

Mayor

appoints

proposes budget

Department Heads
(Police, Fire, Parks, Building, and so on.)

elect

City Council

enacts ordinances to be carried out by

Commission System
The commission system of city government depends on electing qualified professionals to head city commissions.

elect

Commissioners

enact ordinances to be carried out by

Voters

to serve as

Department Heads
(Police, Fire, Parks, Building, and so on.)

Council-Manager System
The council-manager system combines a democratically elected council with professional city management.

elect

City Council

appoints

appoints

City Manager

enacts ordinances to be carried out by

Voters

Department Heads
(Police, Fire, Parks, Building, and so on.)

oversees

New York City operates under a mayor-council system. Here the city council gathers to vote on a bill in 2008. If passed, the bill would allow the mayor and members of the city council to run for a third term.

Towns and Cities

As the United States changed from a rural to a largely urban nation, new forms of local government evolved to meet citizens' needs. The three most common are illustrated on the diagram "Forms of City Government."

The oldest form of city government is the **mayor-council system**. In this system, voters elect both city council members and a mayor. The mayor is the chief executive of the city government. The council is the city's lawmaking body. The duties and powers given to the mayor vary from city to city. Some cities have strong mayors with expansive powers. Others have weak mayors with limited powers.

The mayor-council form of government served most cities fairly well throughout the 1800s. In 1900, however, a natural disaster gave birth to a new approach. That year the Gulf Coast city of Galveston, Texas, was destroyed by a massive hurricane. Believing that its traditional government could not manage the rebuilding effort, a group of influential business leaders pressed for replacing the city council with a board of commissioners appointed by the Texas governor. The board's goal was to turn over the rebuilding effort to civil engineers and other skilled professionals.

Galveston adopted this new **commission system**. However, criticism that it was undemocratic soon led to the election, rather than appointment, of commissioners. Still, commissioners ran for office based on their formal training in civil management rather than on their political popularity.

The commission system worked wonders for Galveston. The new government rebuilt the city on higher ground and constructed a seawall to protect it from hurricanes. Seeing Galveston's success, dozens of other cities adopted the commission system.

In the 1950s and 1960s, many cities (including Galveston) switched to a third form of local government known as the **council-manager system**. In this system, citizens elect a city council (often led by a weak mayor), but the day-to-day job of running the city government is handled by a hired city manager. This system combines democratic rule with professional management expertise. Today, the council-manager system is the most common form of city government in the United States.

Special-Purpose Districts

Some functions of government are so specialized that citizens create separate units of government to deal with them. These **special-purpose districts** may overlap the geographic boundaries of counties and cities, but they operate independently from those other local units of government.

Special-purpose districts have their own elected leaders and taxing authority. Most carry out just one function, such as running a hospital or a park. Your local school board is an example of a special-purpose district. Elected school boards hire school officials, approve school budgets, and establish school policies. Some of the most common functions of special purpose districts include regulating natural resources and providing fire protection.

The Challenges Facing Local Governments

Local city and county governments and special-purpose districts face serious challenges. Because they provide so many vital services, local governments are usually more closely watched by citizens than are the more distant state and national governments. Yet local governments often lack the resources they need to meet everyone's expectations.

More than other levels of government, local governments depend on citizens who are willing to volunteer their time. People who serve on city councils or sit on boards of special-purpose districts get paid very little, if anything at all. The same is true for people who serve on city or county advisory boards, commissions, and task forces. Finding willing and able volunteers to fill these and other positions can be difficult.

To meet these challenges, local governments must be in close touch with the people they serve. This is good news for you and your family. Local officials usually welcome and listen to input from people in their community. By doing something as simple as writing a letter to your local newspaper or speaking up at a local city council or school board meeting, you can affect how decisions are made. And who knows, you might decide to get involved in local government yourself.

Summary

Our federal system divides powers among the national, state, and local governments. The U.S. Constitution gives considerable freedom to states to set up the kind of state and local governments that work best for their citizens.

Benefits of federalism Federalism promotes national unity while allowing for diversity among the states. Federalism also allows states to operate as laboratories for public policy experiments.

Evolution of federalism The way federalism works has evolved over time. During the era of dual federalism, national and state governments operated independently of one another. More recently, the federal government has become increasingly involved in state and local affairs. Federalism will continue to evolve in the future.

State governments Each state government has a legislative, executive, and judicial branch. One of the most important jobs of state legislatures is the apportionment of legislative districts.

Local governments County and city governments provide such basic services as water and fire protection. One of the challenges facing local governments is meeting citizen demands for services with limited funds.

Does federalism work in the face of natural disasters?

In August 2005, Hurricane Katrina barreled toward Louisiana and Mississippi through the Gulf of Mexico. In the aftermath, New Orleans— a populated city in Louisiana that stood below sea level— was terribly flooded. By the end of August, 80 percent of the city was underwater. Hurricane Katrina became one of the most destructive and costliest storms to hit the United States.

Government agencies such as FEMA, the National Guard, and the U.S. Army provided relief. However, many critics cite the aftermath of Katrina as a failure of federalism, stating that aid from the federal, state, and local governments was slow and ineffective. As you read this article, consider these questions: Is federalism unreliable in the face of natural disasters? Or was the ineffectiveness of government response during Hurricane Katrina an isolated incident?

Why Federalism Works (More or Less)

by David L. Paletz, Diana Owen, and Timothy E. Cook

When Hurricane Katrina hit New Orleans and the surrounding areas on August 29, 2005, it exposed federalism's frailties. The state and local government were overwhelmed, yet there was uncertainty over which level of government should be in charge of rescue attempts. Louisiana governor Kathleen Blanco refused to sign an order turning over the disaster response to federal authorities. She did not want to cede control of the National Guard and did not believe signing the order would hasten the arrival of the troops she had requested. President Bush failed to realize the magnitude of the disaster, then believed that the federal response was effective. In fact, as was obvious to anyone watching television, it was slow and ineffective. New Orleans mayor C. Ray Nagin and state officials accused the Federal Emergency Management Agency (FEMA) of failing to deliver urgently needed help and of thwarting other efforts through red tape.

Hurricane Katrina was an exceptional challenge to federalism. Normally, competition between levels of government does not careen out of control, and federalism works, more or less. We have already discussed one reason: a legal hierarchy— in which national law is superior to state law, which in turn dominates local law—dictates who wins in clashes in domains where each may constitutionally act.

There are three other reasons. First, state and local governments provide crucial assistance to the national government. Second, national, state, and local levels have complementary capacities, providing distinct services and resources. Third, the fragmentation of the system is bridged by interest groups, notably the intergovernmental lobby that provides voices for state and local governments . . .

Applying Policies Close to Home

State and local governments are essential parts of federalism because the federal government routinely needs them to execute national policy. State and local governments adjust the policies as best they can to meet their political preferences and their residents' needs. Policies and the funds expended on them thus vary dramatically from one state to the next, even in national programs such as unemployment benefits.

Levees and floodwalls were meant to protect New Orleans from rising water levels. However, after Hurricane Katrina, these barriers broke, flooding the city and submerging homes, buildings, and cars.

This division of labor, through which the national government sets goals and states and localities administer policies, makes for incomplete coverage in the news. National news watches the national government, covering more the political games and high-minded intentions of policies then the nitty-gritty of implementation. Local news, stressing the local angle on national news, focuses on the local impact of decisions in distant Washington.

Complementary Capacities

The second reason federalism often works is because national, state, and local governments specialize in different policy domains. The main focus of local and state government policy is economic development, broadly defined to include all policies that attract or keep businesses and enhance property values. States have traditionally taken the lead in highways, welfare, health, natural resources, and prisons. Local governments dominate in education, fire protection, sewerage, sanitation, airports, and parking.

The national government is central in policies to serve low-income and other needy persons. In these redistributive policies, those paying for a service in taxes are not usually those receiving the service. These programs rarely get positive coverage in the local news, which often shows them as "something-for-noth-ing" benefits that undeserving individuals receive, not as ways to address national problems.

States cannot effectively provide redistributive benefits. It is impossible to stop people from moving away because they think they are paying too much in taxes for services. Nor can states with generous benefits stop outsiders from moving there . . .

The Intergovernmental Lobby

A third reason federalism often works is because interest groups and professional associations focus simultaneously on a variety of governments at the national, state, and local levels. With multiple points of entry, policy changes can occur in many ways . . .

Policy diffusion is a horizontal form of change. State and local officials watch what other state and local governments are doing. States can be "laboratories of democracy," experimenting with innovative programs that spread to other states.

David L. Paletz is a Professor of Political Science at Duke University, Diana Owen is an Associate Professor of Political Science at Georgetown University, and Timothy E. Cook held the Kevin P. Reilly, Sr. Chair of Political Communication at Louisiana State University.

Chapter 7

Citizen Participation in a Democracy

How can you make a difference in a democracy?

■ 7.1 Introduction

In 1831, a young French aristocrat, Alexis de Tocqueville, began a nine-month tour of the United States. He wanted to learn about American democracy. As he toured the country, he was struck by the vitality of the American people and their engagement in public life.

When he returned home, Tocqueville published a book about American political life called *Democracy in America*. In this book, he wrote that "Americans . . . constantly form associations" to get things done. They formed groups to build hospitals, schools, and churches and to carry out many other civic projects. He argued that this collective action taught Americans political skills and helped to strengthen democracy.

Many years later, in the 1990s, political scientist Robert D. Putnam looked at the role of associations in modern American life. He described quite a different country from the one Tocqueville had visited a century and a half earlier. Far fewer Americans, he found, were taking part in the kind of cooperative efforts that Tocqueville had admired.

Although Americans still joined organizations, they did so mainly as "checkbook" participants. They gave money, but not time or energy, to civic causes. "We remain . . . reasonably well-informed spectators of public affairs," Putnam wrote, "but many fewer of us actually partake in the game."

A group of volunteers participating in civic engagement

Speaking of Politics

citizenship
The status of being a citizen, a person who by birth or naturalization enjoys certain rights and has certain duties in a nation-state.

lawful permanent resident
An immigrant who is legally authorized to live and work in the United States permanently, but is not a U.S. citizen. Also known as a resident alien.

undocumented immigrant
A person who has come to the United States to live and work without the required legal papers.

naturalization
A legal process through which a person not granted citizenship by birth can become a citizen of a country. A naturalized citizen enjoys most or all of the rights of native-born citizens.

ideology
A basic set of political beliefs about the roles of government and the individual in society.

liberalism
An ideology favoring an active role for government in efforts to solve society's problems.

conservatism
An ideology favoring a limited role for government and more private initiative by nongovernmental groups in efforts to solve society's problems.

civil society
Associations and other voluntary groups that form a middle layer in society between government and individual families. Civil society includes groups that people join because of family, faith, interests, or ideology.

In 2000, Putnam summarized his findings in the book *Bowling Alone: The Collapse and Revival of American Community.* The title underscored his concern that the United States was becoming a nation of disengaged citizens. He pointed to a sharp decline in bowling-league membership as a symbol of this change. Increasingly, Americans were choosing not to join bowling leagues, or any other group, but instead went "bowling alone." Putnam feared the impact this lack of social engagement might have on democracy and civic life.

Are Putnam's fears justified? Are we becoming spectators rather than players in public affairs? Keep these questions in mind as you read about the rights and responsibilities of **citizenship** and the ways that Americans today engage in the civic and political life of their communities.

7.2 Citizenship, Civic Rights, and Civic Responsibilities

The U.S. Constitution, as originally written, did not define citizenship. It made reference to citizens and listed some of their rights, particularly in the Bill of Rights. But it did not say how citizenship was to be determined. At the time the Constitution was adopted, it was generally assumed that state citizens would become U.S. citizens. It was also assumed that a person born in the United States was a citizen.

In 1857, however, the Supreme Court handed down a decision that shook up these assumptions. In the case of *Dred Scott v. Sandford,* the Court held that Dred Scott, an enslaved African American born in Virginia, was not a citizen and therefore could not sue for his freedom in federal court. Chief Justice Roger Taney argued that the framers never meant to include slaves under the protections of the Constitution. But if Dred Scott was not a citizen, what was he? And what did this decision mean for other African Americans? What rights could they claim under U.S. law?

The Fourteenth Amendment Defines Citizenship
The Fourteenth Amendment was adopted in part to address these issues and reverse the Dred Scott decision. Ratified in 1868, just three years after the Civil War, this amendment clarified who was a citizen under the Constitution. It begins with these words:

All persons born or naturalized in the United States, and subject to the jurisdiction thereof, are citizens of the United States and of the state wherein they reside.

—Fourteenth Amendment, 1868

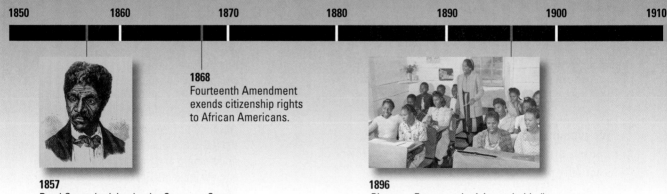

The Struggle for Civil Rights, 1857–1964

African Americans' struggle for civil rights began long before the Civil War and continued through the passage of the Civil Rights Act of 1964 and beyond. This landmark legislation opened doors not only for African Americans, but also for women and members of other minority groups.

| 1850 | 1860 | 1870 | 1880 | 1890 | 1900 | 1910 |

1868
Fourteenth Amendment extends citizenship rights to African Americans.

1857
Dred Scott decision by the Supreme Court denies citizenship to African Americans.

1896
Plessy v. Ferguson decision upholds "separate but equal" laws allowing segregation.

The purpose of the Fourteenth Amendment was to extend the rights of citizenship to former slaves. At the same time, it clearly states that all persons born on American soil are to be considered U.S. citizens, no matter where their parents were born. It also says that states cannot discriminate against citizens or deprive them of their rights without due process of law.

African Americans' Long Struggle for Civil Rights

Although the Fourteenth Amendment was designed to extend the rights of citizenship to African Americans, its immediate effects were limited. In the late 1800s, southern states passed laws, known as **Jim Crow laws,** that enforced segregation and denied legal equality to blacks. It would take many decades for the courts and Congress to overturn these laws and protect the civil rights of African Americans. The timeline below shows several key events in this long struggle.

An early setback in the struggle for equal rights occurred when the Supreme Court heard *Plessy v. Ferguson* in 1896. The case centered on Homer Plessy, a black man who had been arrested in Louisiana for sitting in a whites-only railroad car. Plessy challenged his arrest in court. He argued that Jim Crow laws that segregated blacks from whites violated the Equal Protection Clause of the Fourteenth Amendment.

The decision went against *Plessy*. The Court held that separate facilities for blacks and whites were legal as long as they were equal. This "separate but equal" doctrine was soon applied to almost every aspect of life in southern states. In most cases, however, the facilities provided for black Americans were far inferior to those enjoyed by whites.

Despite this decision, African Americans continued to fight for equal rights. They formed organizations such as the National Association for the Advancement of Colored People (NAACP), the National Urban League, and the Congress of Racial Equality (CORE) to protest racial discrimination in its many forms.

In 1954, the NAACP won a major victory in the case of *Brown v. Board of Education of Topeka*. The case focused on the rights of a young African American, Linda Brown, who was prohibited from attending a white school near her home in Topeka, Kansas. In its decision, the Supreme Court concluded that "separate but equal" facilities were by their very nature unequal. This decision paved the way for the desegregation of public schools and the launching of the modern civil rights movement.

During the 1950s and 1960s, the civil rights struggle touched all aspects of American life. The most prominent leader of the movement, Martin Luther King Jr., helped to make Americans aware of the great

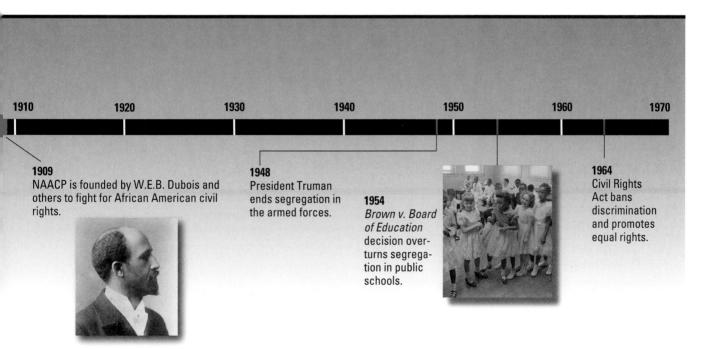

1910　　　　　1920　　　　　1930　　　　　1940　　　　　1950　　　　　1960　　　　　1970

1909
NAACP is founded by W.E.B. Dubois and others to fight for African American civil rights.

1948
President Truman ends segregation in the armed forces.

1954
Brown v. Board of Education decision overturns segregation in public schools.

1964
Civil Rights Act bans discrimination and promotes equal rights.

Migration The Civil Rights Act forced southern states to dismantle their segregation laws. The result has been a dramatic shift in black migration patterns. For most of the 20th century, blacks migrated out of the South in search of better lives. In recent years, that pattern has been reversed.

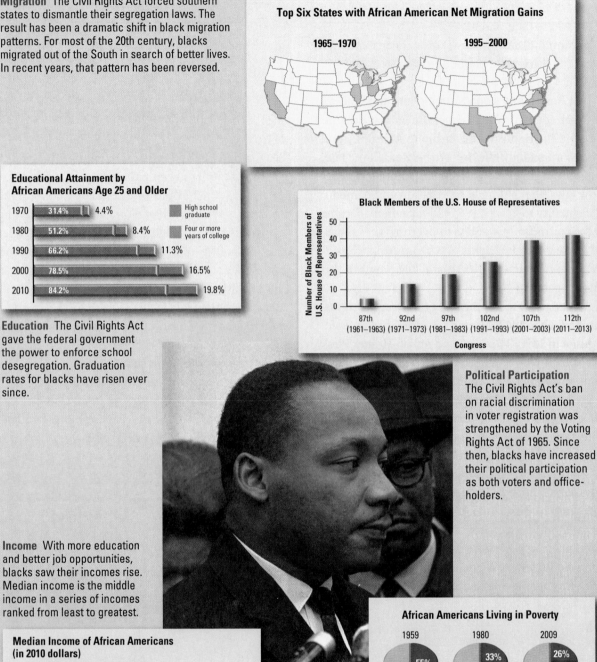

Top Six States with African American Net Migration Gains

1965–1970

1995–2000

Educational Attainment by African Americans Age 25 and Older

Year	High school graduate	Four or more years of college
1970	31.4%	4.4%
1980	51.2%	8.4%
1990	66.2%	11.3%
2000	78.5%	16.5%
2010	84.2%	19.8%

Education The Civil Rights Act gave the federal government the power to enforce school desegregation. Graduation rates for blacks have risen ever since.

Black Members of the U.S. House of Representatives

Number of Black Members of U.S. House of Representatives

Congress	
87th (1961–1963)	
92nd (1971–1973)	
97th (1981–1983)	
102nd (1991–1993)	
107th (2001–2003)	
112th (2011–2013)	

Political Participation The Civil Rights Act's ban on racial discrimination in voter registration was strengthened by the Voting Rights Act of 1965. Since then, blacks have increased their political participation as both voters and office-holders.

Income With more education and better job opportunities, blacks saw their incomes rise. Median income is the middle income in a series of incomes ranked from least to greatest.

Median Income of African Americans (in 2010 dollars)

Year	Income
1970	$31,464
1975	$32,348
1980	$31,929
1985	$32,437
1990	$34,645
2000	$42,638
2005	$39,753
2010	$38,550

African Americans Living in Poverty

1959 — 55%
1980 — 33%
2009 — 26%

Poverty By banning racial discrimination in labor unions and employment, the Civil Rights Act helped pull many black families out of poverty.

Sources: U.S. Census Bureau. William H. Frey, *The New Great Migration: Black Americans' Return to the South, 1965–2000*, Washington, DC: Brookings Inst., 2004. Harold W. Stanley and Richard G. Niemi, *Vital Statistics on American Politics 2011–2012*, Los Angeles: CQ Press, 2011.

injustices imposed on people of color. In 1963, King responded to those who argued that blacks should be more patient in their demand for equal rights by writing his famous "Letter from a Birmingham Jail."

Just over a year later, on July 2, 1964, President Johnson signed the Civil Rights Act of 1964 into law. This landmark legislation banned discrimination in most areas of American life on the basis of race, sex, religion, or national origin. It also committed the U.S. government to protecting the rights of all Americans, regardless of skin color or country of birth. The improvements in the economic, political, and social aspects of African Americans' lives show the far-reaching effects of this law.

Rights and Responsibilities

Since the passage of the Civil Rights Act of 1964, the United States has experienced a huge increase in immigration, both legal and illegal. Once in this country, most **lawful permanent residents** enjoy most of the same rights as native-born Americans. These include the rights listed in the Bill of Rights, from freedom of speech to freedom from cruel and unusual punishment.

American citizens, whether native born or naturalized, enjoy additional rights. The most important are the right to vote, to hold public office, and to claim certain social and economic benefits. Some forms of welfare payments, for example, are available only to citizens. Most jobs in the federal government are limited to citizens only.

Similarly, all people living in the United States have certain legal responsibilities. They are required to obey laws, pay taxes, and cooperate with public officials. All males who are 18, whether they are citizens, lawful permanent residents, or **undocumented immigrants,** must register for military service. This is true even though the United States currently has an all-volunteer army.

Everyone has personal responsibilities, or duties that relate to an individual's private life, such as taking care of one's own health. Personal responsibilities apply to helping one's family and friends, too. Comforting an upset friend and caring for a sick parent are examples of personal responsibility.

Citizens also have civic responsibilities. They are expected to be informed about and participate in public affairs. Volunteering to serve the public good is

Personal responsibilities and civic responsibilities are not mutually exclusive. Some actions, such as cooperating with classmates on a project, are classified in both categories because they benefit both a person individually and their community or government.

another civic responsibility. Sometimes the obligation of citizenship requires that personal desires be subordinated to the public good. For example, a woman might have to miss work to attend jury duty or a man might feel obligated to research candidates in an election even though he would prefer to play soccer.

Political engagement is a choice, not a legal requirement. However, democracies function best when citizens choose good leaders and pay close attention to what those leaders do once elected. As Tocqueville observed almost two centuries ago, "The greatness of America lies not in being more enlightened than any other nation, but rather in her ability to repair her faults." It is up to all of us as citizens to make sure such repairs are made when needed.

■ 7.3 Becoming an American Citizen

By 2010, nearly 40 million Americans, or about 13 percent of the U.S. population, were foreign born. Every year, hundreds of thousands of immigrants become U.S. citizens. They usually receive their citizenship at a large ceremony, along with many other new citizens. For most, the occasion is filled with emotion.

For Alberto Olivarez, the citizenship ceremony was a bit different, though no less emotional. In 2006, Olivarez, a Mexican-born teacher at an elementary school in Brighton, Colorado, took his oath of citizenship alone, standing before an audience of students and their parents in his school gymnasium. Like Olivarez, many in the audience were immigrants or children of immigrants.

Olivarez's wife and three children sat on the stage with him as he pledged to "support and defend the Constitution of the United States." With this oath, Olivarez became a U.S. citizen, just as he had expected. What came next, however, surprised him. The school principal explained to the audience that Olivarez's citizenship automatically made his three young sons American citizens as well. Upon hearing this news, Olivarez burst into tears. It was a benefit of citizenship he had never imagined.

American Citizens: Native Born and Naturalized

There are two ways to become a U.S. citizen. The most common way is by birth. Most Americans are born in the United States, though some are born in another country to parents who are U.S. citizens. Either way, citizens by birth automatically enjoy all the rights, privileges, and protections of citizenship.

The other way to become a citizen is through **naturalization**. This is the path that Alberto Olivarez and other naturalized citizens have taken. Naturalization is a multistep legal process that, when completed, gives the applicant virtually all the rights and responsibilities of a native-born citizen.

In 2011, nearly 700,000 people became U.S. citizens through naturalization. The largest group of new citizens came from Mexico, but tens of thousands also came from India, the Philippines, China, Columbia, Cuba, and other countries.

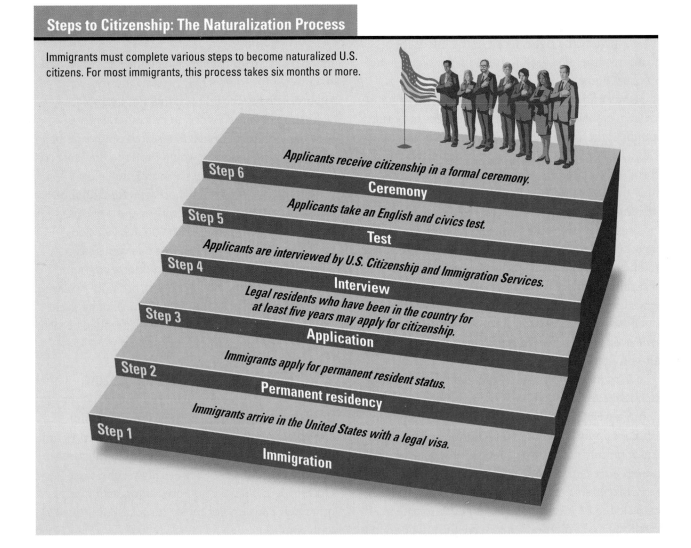

Steps to Citizenship: The Naturalization Process

Immigrants must complete various steps to become naturalized U.S. citizens. For most immigrants, this process takes six months or more.

Step 6 — Applicants receive citizenship in a formal ceremony.
Ceremony

Step 5 — Applicants take an English and civics test.
Test

Step 4 — Applicants are interviewed by U.S. Citizenship and Immigration Services.
Interview

Step 3 — Legal residents who have been in the country for at least five years may apply for citizenship.
Application

Step 2 — Immigrants apply for permanent resident status.
Permanent residency

Step 1 — Immigrants arrive in the United States with a legal visa.
Immigration

Immigrants must meet several requirements to be eligible for naturalization. They must be at least 18 years old and lawful permanent residents of the United States. In most cases, such immigrants, also known as **resident aliens,** must have lived in this country for at least five years to be eligible for naturalization.

After meeting those requirements, the next step is to complete an application for naturalization. If the application is approved, the applicant has an interview with an immigration official. At this meeting, applicants are tested on their ability to speak, read, and write English. They also take a civics test to show basic knowledge of American history and government. Sample questions from the test appear at the end of this chapter.

The final step in the naturalization process is the citizenship ceremony. Here, applicants answer a few more questions. Then they take the oath of allegiance to the United States and receive a certificate of naturalization.

Naturalization gives new citizens the right to vote and run for any public office except that of vice president or president. The Constitution says that only native-born citizens can hold these offices. Critics of this rule argue that it is no longer necessary or fair because it excludes qualified foreign-born officials. However, supporters of the clause highlight its importance in preventing foreign influence over the U.S. government.

The Status of Lawful Permanent Residents

Immigrants do not need to become citizens to stay in the United States legally, however. They may remain here indefinitely as lawful permanent residents. In 2011, the U.S. government granted permanent residency to more than 1 million people.

Immigrants seeking permanent resident status also go through an application process with the Bureau of Citizenship and Immigration Services. Preference is given to immigrants whose job skills are needed by U.S. businesses or who are related by birth or marriage to a U.S. citizen. Those who successfully complete the application process receive an identification card known as a **green card**. A green card provides proof that its holder has a legal right to live and work in the United States.

Resident aliens enjoy most of the rights of citizens. These include the right to travel freely outside the country. However, if resident aliens plan to be away for more than a year, they must apply for a reentry permit. Without this permit, they may be refused reentry to the United States. Resident aliens may also lose their permanent resident status and be deported if they are convicted of criminal activity.

■ 7.4 Political Culture in the United States

Citizens and residents of the United States operate within a **political culture**. This is a society's framework of shared values, beliefs, and attitudes concerning politics and government. It is the political environment in which Americans exercise their rights and responsibilities.

Political culture can take many forms and be expressed in many ways. The strong surge of patriotism after the 9/11 terrorist attacks of 2001 was an expression of American political culture. At the time, many Americans flew the flag to show their love of country. In quite a different way, the civil rights protests of the 1950s and 1960s were also an expression of American political culture. The millions of Americans who supported the civil rights movement shared the belief that all citizens should enjoy equal rights and opportunities.

Americans' Shared Political Values

Although Americans often disagree on specific issues, they share a number of core beliefs and values. These beliefs, some of which are listed below, shape our political culture. Keep in mind that individuals may vary in terms of their attachment to these core values.

Liberty. Americans believe that they are entitled to the greatest amount of liberty possible as long as they do no harm to others. They firmly believe that citizens should be able to express their views openly, without fear of punishment by the government.

Equality. Americans embrace equality of opportunity, without regard to race, religion, or gender. They believe that all citizens should enjoy the right to vote, to receive an education, to have a job, and to succeed in life.

Democracy. Americans support a democratic system of government. They believe that political authority comes from the people and that public officials should be accountable to the voters. The importance of majority rule and the protection of minority rights are important related beliefs.

Individualism. Americans believe in personal freedom and personal responsibility. As a general rule, they believe that every citizen is responsible for his or her own actions and well-being. This contrasts with the more collective view in some countries, where greater emphasis is placed on the government's role in meeting people's needs.

Free enterprise. Americans support capitalism and a free-market economy in which private businesses compete with relatively limited regulation by government. They accept the fact that such a system creates winners and losers in terms of wealth and economic status.

Justice and the rule of law. Americans believe that society should be governed by a system of laws that are fairly and equally applied. They believe that the rights of ordinary citizens should not be arbitrarily restricted or infringed on by government.

Patriotism. Americans feel great pride and loyalty toward their country. Many believe that the United States is the greatest nation in the world. They also take pride in the values of American democracy.

Optimism. In general, Americans are upbeat and optimistic. They see themselves as "can-do" people. They tend to believe that their lives and life in general will be better in the future.

Civic duty. Americans believe that for democracy to flourish, citizens should vote and participate in civic and political affairs. Many also see volunteering for military service or giving back to their communities through volunteer activities as an aspect of civic duty.

Two Widely Held Ideologies: Liberalism and Conservatism

Although Americans share a common political culture, they do not all hold to the same **ideology,** or basic political beliefs. For example, they often disagree on the role government should play with respect to economic policy and moral values. The most widely held ideologies in U.S. politics today are held by Americans who define themselves as liberals or conservatives.

Liberalism is an ideology that favors an active role for the government in solving society's problems. Liberals generally support government efforts to regulate business and the economy. They support policies designed to reduce economic inequality and to help the poor. They also favor the use of government regulation to protect the environment and improve the health care system.

As their name suggests, liberals strongly defend liberty and resist government efforts to interfere in people's personal lives. On a political spectrum, with

Despite their many differences, most Americans share some basic political values, including a love of country.

The political spectrum runs from the liberal left to the conservative right. This graph shows the percentages of Americans who identified themselves as liberal, conservative, or moderate in 2011. A majority of Americans put themselves somewhere in the moderate middle.

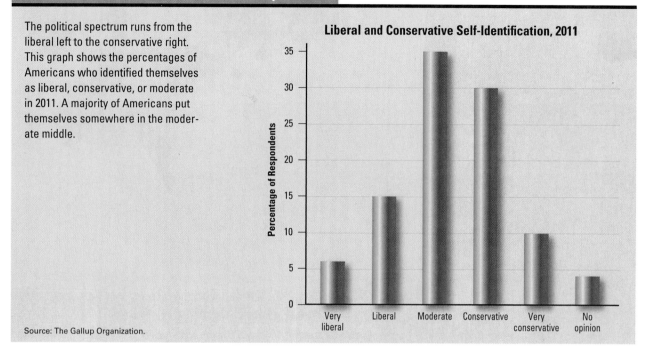

Liberal and Conservative Self-Identification, 2011

Source: The Gallup Organization.

moderates in the middle, liberals are said to be "left of center." They tend to associate themselves with the Democratic Party.

Conservatism, on the other hand, is an ideology that calls for a limited role for government in economic affairs. Conservatives generally oppose government regulation of business. Most want to limit the size of government, reduce taxes, and cut back on government programs. Instead, they look to private initiative, or efforts by nongovernmental groups such as religious congregations, charities, service organizations, and businesses, to deal with many of society's problems.

In contrast to liberals, conservatives are more likely to support government action on moral issues. Conservatives are said to be "right of center" on the political spectrum. They generally associate themselves with the Republican Party.

Over the past few decades, more Americans have identified themselves as conservatives than as liberals. Since the late 1960s, the percentage of self-identified conservatives has varied from 30 to 40 percent. The percentage of people calling themselves liberal has remained more constant, at around 20 percent. This graph compares the percentages of liberals, conservatives, and moderates in 2011.

Three Other Ideologies: Socialism, Libertarianism, and Environmentalism

Three other ideologies—socialism, **libertarianism,** and **environmentalism**—also play a role in American politics. Although these ideologies have fewer followers than liberalism and conservatism, they have inspired and motivated many people over the years.

Socialism. The oldest of these ideologies is socialism. The main goal of socialism is to limit economic inequality by ensuring a fair distribution of wealth. In a socialist system, the government owns or controls most of the economic resources needed for the production of goods and services. In theory, a socialist government manages the economy in a way that benefits the majority of citizens.

In 1901, reformers and workers who believed in socialism formed the Socialist Party of America. The party's greatest electoral success came in 1912 when its presidential candidate, Eugene Debs, won nearly a million votes. That was just 6 percent of the total votes cast, but it was a substantial showing for a socialist candidate. After World War I, however, membership in the Socialist Party declined.

Socialism never became as popular in the United States as it did in other countries, in part because it

Liberalism and conservatism are the dominant political ideologies in the United States. The significance of the two-party system has created factions within the Democratic and Republican parties. For example, politician Ron Paul ran for U.S. president in 1988 as Libertarian. He joined the Republican Party before running for president in 2008 and 2012, but maintained his libertarian views as a Republican.

conflicted with America's political culture. A strong faith in capitalism and the free enterprise system made most Americans leery of socialists' call for government control of economic resources.

Most American socialists today support what is known as **democratic socialism**. This is an ideology that advocates socialism as a basis for the economy and democracy as a governing principle. In countries that have adopted this ideology, elected leaders supervise a "mixed economy" of public and private industry.

Libertarianism. Modern libertarianism is an ideology based on a strong belief in personal freedom. A 2012 statement of libertarian principles began with these words:

> As Libertarians, we seek a world of liberty; a world in which all individuals are sovereign over their own lives and no one is forced to sacrifice his or her values for the benefit of others.
> —National Platform of the Libertarian Party, 2012

Libertarians tend to be conservative on economic issues and liberal on social issues. For example, they favor lower taxes and a free-market economy, while opposing bans on abortion or gay marriage. Libertarians want a small government and resist government regulation of any kind.

Formed in 1971, the Libertarian Party has attracted a small but loyal following. According to

Pew Research Center, 9 percent of Americans had libertarian beliefs in 2011. Libertarian candidates regularly run for office in local, state, and national elections. So far their success has been limited to the local level, where they have won election to such positions as mayor, city council member, and sheriff.

Environmentalism. This last ideology, environmentalism, unites Americans who are deeply concerned about conservation and protection of the environment. Environmentalists advocate policies designed to reduce pollution and preserve natural resources. In contrast to libertarians, they support government regulation of industry and the economy to achieve those ends.

Many members of conservation organizations such as the Sierra Club and Friends of the Earth identify themselves as environmentalists. So do members of the Green Party of the United States. "Greens" are committed to what they call "ecological and economic sustainability." By this they mean meeting the needs of the world's people today without damaging the ability of future generations to provide for themselves. As their party platform states,

> We support a sustainable society which utilizes resources in such a way that future generations will benefit and not suffer from the practices of our generation. To this end we must practice agriculture which replenishes the soil; move to

an energy efficient economy; and live in ways that respect the integrity of natural systems.
—Green Party of the United States
Platform, 2012

Like the Libertarian Party, the Green Party has been most successful in electing candidates at the local level. The party is stronger in Europe, however, and has won national offices in a number of countries.

The Moderates in the Middle: Centrism

Most Americans don't fit neatly into any ideological camp. They consider themselves moderates, or middle-of-the-road voters. These are people who sit at the center of the political spectrum, between the ideologies of left and right.

In recent years, U.S. politics have become more polarized, meaning that political parties have adopted more extreme policies. The Republican Party has grown more conservative, and the Democratic Party more liberal. This polarization is especially evident in the current Congress, which remains divided on a number of issues.

"Harold, would you say you are left of center, right of center, center, left of left, right of left, left of right, or right of right, or what?"

Liberals are considered left of center, while conservatives are on the right. But there are other positions along the political spectrum, and many Americans are not quite sure where they fit.

These strong divisions often push voters to be drawn to **centrism**. Many surveys show that moderates, along with people who describe themselves as slightly conservative or slightly liberal, make up the largest group of U.S. voters.

In contrast to people with a strong ideological point of view, centrists may hold a mix of liberal, conservative, and perhaps environmental views. Centrism is not an ideology with its own political party. As a result, during election time, centrists often cross party lines, depending on the candidates and issues of the day.

◼ 7.5 How Americans Engage in Civic Life

For most Americans, voting is the first thing that comes to mind when they hear the words "civic duty." In a democracy, voting is one of the most basic and important ways to engage in civic life.

There are many other ways to be an active citizen, however. You can read newspapers or watch the news on television to stay informed about current events. You can talk to friends about political issues or put a political bumper sticker on your car to demonstrate your support. You can become a volunteer with a community group or follow a political figure using social media. By doing any of these things, you are engaging in civic life.

Civil Society: The "Social Capital" of Democracy

At the start of this chapter, you read about Robert D. Putnam's work on civic engagement. Putnam concluded that Americans today are less likely to participate in civic associations than they were in the past. He further believes that such participation is crucial to democracy.

Putnam argues that social clubs and civic organizations are building blocks of what political scientists call **civil society**. This term refers to a middle layer of voluntary associations and institutions that exists between government on the one hand and individuals and families on the other.

Many political scientists argue that a strong civil society is essential in a democracy. The organizations that make up civil society, they point out, are nourished by citizen involvement. This involvement helps to expand a society's **social capital**. Putnam

Americans who volunteer their time do so in various types of activities. Just over a third volunteer mainly through religious organizations. Over 30 percent of volunteers devote 100 hours or more a year to volunteer activities.

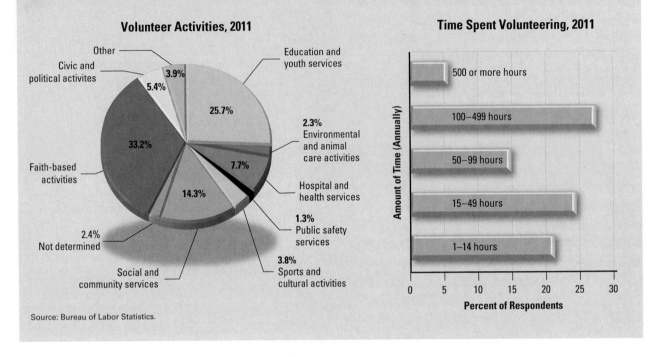

Volunteer Activities, 2011

Other — 3.9%
Civic and political activites 5.4%
Education and youth services 25.7%
2.3% Environmental and animal care activities
7.7%
Hospital and health services
Faith-based activities 33.2%
14.3%
1.3% Public safety services
2.4% Not determined
Social and community services
3.8% Sports and cultural activities

Source: Bureau of Labor Statistics.

Time Spent Volunteering, 2011

Amount of Time (Annually)

500 or more hours
100–499 hours
50–99 hours
15–49 hours
1–14 hours

0 5 10 15 20 25 30
Percent of Respondents

defines social capital as "connections among individuals" that are forged through their participation in voluntary associations.

To understand how social capital works, consider this simple example. In many communities, parents of school-age children join the local Parent Teacher Association. Through their PTA, parents work together to improve their children's schools.

While working on PTA projects, parents form new social networks and exchange information about their community. Through these networks, they may create new groups to work on other local issues. In this way, the connections forged within the PTA help to generate new energy and ideas that benefit the larger community. This is social capital in action.

Of course, the PTA is only one of thousands of volunteer organizations that one might choose to join. As the graphs above show, Americans get involved in many types of volunteer activities and for varying amounts of time. All of these efforts help to strengthen civil society and build social capital.

Putting Social Capital to Work in Texas

Social capital promotes civic engagement not only in local communities, but also in state and national affairs. Such was the case in Texas in 2006 when various citizen groups rose up to oppose the construction of new coal-fired power plants across the state. Coal is a fossil fuel that produces large amounts of air pollution and greenhouse gases. The power company that planned to build these plants assured the public that they would not pollute the air. But many Texans believed otherwise.

The first protests against the power company's plan were organized by citizens living in communities where the new plants were to be built. They argued that the coal-burning plants would harm air quality and give rise to health problems.

As opposition grew, local business leaders began to get involved in the issue. They feared that increased pollution from the plants would harm local economies by discouraging tourism and other business activity. Local public officials—including the mayors of Dallas, Houston, and other cities— began to voice their concerns.

Forms of Civic Engagement

Civic engagement takes many forms, from writing letters to organizing protests. These photographs illustrate just some of the ways citizens can make their voices heard.

Attend a Public Meeting
Find out what's going on in your community by attending a public meeting. You might be surprised to discover how many decisions affecting your life are made close to home.

Volunteer in a Political Campaign
Get involved in a political campaign. Share the excitement of election night as volunteers wait for the votes to be counted.

Circulate a Petition
Take part in a petition drive for a cause you care about. Often you can even sign a petition online.

Organize a Fundraiser
Raise money for a worthy cause. The challenge is to help people feel good about both asking for donations and giving them.

Organize a Demonstration
Put your passion to work by organizing a demonstration. Sometimes actions really do speak louder than words.

Get Involved in a Service Project
Find a way to give back to your community. You will feel good about yourself while making a difference.

In 2006 and 2007, Texas citizens fought to prevent new power plants from being built around the state. They feared that emissions from coal-fired plants, like the one shown here, would harm the environment.

In time, local protest groups banded together to form larger organizations with names like Stop the Coal Rush, the Texas Clean Sky Coalition, and Texas Business for Clean Air. Civic activists sent e-mails and letters to newspapers and public officials. They attended hearings to oppose the power company's application for building permits. They also created Web sites and held fundraisers to raise money and get their message out.

These efforts peaked in February 2007 with a large rally at the state capitol in Austin. The next day, activists met with their state representatives and other public

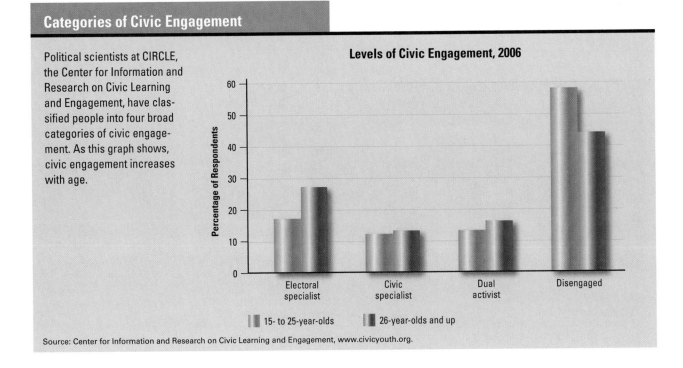

Categories of Civic Engagement

Political scientists at CIRCLE, the Center for Information and Research on Civic Learning and Engagement, have classified people into four broad categories of civic engagement. As this graph shows, civic engagement increases with age.

Levels of Civic Engagement, 2006

Percentage of Respondents

15- to 25-year-olds   26-year-olds and up

Source: Center for Information and Research on Civic Learning and Engagement, www.civicyouth.org.

officials to argue their case. Before lawmakers could act, however, the company that was planning to build the power plants announced that it was being sold.

The organized efforts of Texans to stop the new power plants from being built were nonetheless effective. The new buyers of the power company immediately announced their intention to scale back the project and explore alternatives to building more coal-fired power plants.

Four Categories of Civic Engagement: Which One Fits You?

As the Texas story illustrates, civic engagement can have a real impact, especially when people work together toward common goals. But just how engaged are most Americans?

To answer that question, political scientists survey Americans about their civic and political activities. Using those data, scholars at the Center for Information and Research on Civic Learning and Engagement (CIRCLE) have determined that most people fall into one of four broad categories of civic engagement.

Electoral specialists. This category includes those whose main engagement is through the election process. People in this group vote, volunteer in political campaigns, and try to persuade others to vote as well.

Civic specialists. People in this group focus on improving their communities and helping others. They join local civic groups, support nonprofit organizations, and take part in fundraising activities for worthy causes.

Dual activists. This category is made up of people who engage in both electoral and civic activities. They may be found passing out leaflets in a political campaign one day and volunteering in a homeless shelter the next.

The disengaged. This group is made up of people who are not significantly engaged in civic life. They don't vote or pay attention to civic affairs.

The graph shows that Americans young and old fall into all four groups. What about you? Which category best matches your level of civic engagement? And are you satisfied with your answer?

Summary

Civic participation is essential in a democracy. Citizens who get involved in civic and community groups help to strengthen civil society. At the same time, they tend to become more engaged in the political process.

Rights and responsibilities of Americans U.S. citizens have many rights. Over time, many of these rights have been extended to lawful permanent residents. Both groups also share many responsibilities, including obeying the law, paying taxes, and, for males, registering for military service.

Becoming a citizen There are two types of U.S. citizens: native born and naturalized. Naturalization is a process that takes many months. Naturalized citizens receive most of the benefits enjoyed by native-born citizens.

Political culture Most Americans share a common set of beliefs and values about politics and government. This political culture helps to unite Americans, even when they differ over ideology. The two most prominent political ideologies in this country are liberalism and conservatism.

Civic engagement Citizens can engage in civic life in many ways. When they do so, they help to build a stronger civil society.

Could you pass the citizenship test?

To become citizens of the United States, immigrants must take a civics test to show their knowledge of American history and government. An official asks them ten questions from a list of 100 possible test items. Applicants must answer six of the questions correctly to pass the test. But what do they need to know? The questions on these pages come from a sample test issued by the U.S. Citizenship and Immigration Services (USCIS). How many questions can you answer correctly?

Naturalization Test

The questions below were taken from a test used by the U.S. Citizenship and Immigration Services, or USCIS.

American Government

Principles of American Democracy

1. What is the supreme law of the land?
2. What do we call the first ten amendments to the Constitution?
3. What is one right or freedom from the First Amendment?
4. How many amendments does the Constitution have?
5. What is the economic system in the United States?

System of Government

6. Name one branch or part of the government.
7. The House of Representatives has how many voting members?
8. What stops one branch of government from becoming too powerful?
9. Under our Constitution, some powers belong to the federal government. What is one power of the federal government?

10. Under our Constitution, some powers belong to the states. What is one power of the states?
11. Who makes federal laws?
12. What is the highest court in the United States?

Rights and Responsibilities

13. What is one responsibility that is only for United States citizens?
14. Name one right only for United States citizens.
15. What do we show loyalty to when we say the Pledge of Allegiance?

American History

Colonial Period and Independence

16. What is one reason colonists came to America?
17. Why did the colonists fight the British?

Citizenship ceremonies are often large events. This photograph shows a ceremony that occurred in Idaho in 2009. That year, over 740,000 people were naturalized in the United States.

18. There were 13 original states. Name three.
19. What happened at the Constitutional Convention?

1800s

20. Name one war fought by the United States in the 1800s.
21. Name one problem that led to the Civil War.
22. What did the Emancipation Proclamation do?
23. What did Susan B. Anthony do?

Recent American History and Other Important Historical Information

24. Who did the United States fight in World War II?
25. During the Cold War, what was the main concern of the United States?
26. Who was President during the Great Depression and World War II?
27. What did Martin Luther King, Jr. do?

Geography

28. Name one of the two longest rivers in the United States.
29. Name one state that borders Canada.
30. Name one U.S. territory.
31. Name one state that borders on Mexico.

Symbols

32. Why does the flag have 13 stripes?
33. Why does the flag have 50 stars?

Holidays

34. When do we celebrate Independence Day?
35. Name two national U.S. holidays.

Answer Key

1. the Constitution
2. the Bill of Rights
3. speech, religion, assembly, press, petition the government
4. 27
5. capitalist economy; market economy
6. Congress, legislative, President, executive, the courts, judicial
7. 435
8. checks and balances; separation of powers
9. print money; declare war; create an army; make treaties
10. provide schooling and education; provide protection (police); provide safety (fire departments); give a driver's license; approve zoning and land use
11. Congress, Senate and House (of Representatives), (U.S. or national) legislature
12. the Supreme Court
13. serve on a jury; vote in federal election
14. vote in a federal election; run for federal office
15. the United States, the flag
16. freedom; political liberty; religious freedom; economic opportunity; practice their religion; escape persecution
17. because of high taxes (taxation without representation); because the British army stayed in their houses (boarding, quartering); because they didn't have self-government
18. New Hampshire, Massachusetts, Rhode Island, Connecticut, New York, New Jersey, Pennsylvania, Delaware, Maryland, Virginia, North Carolina, South Carolina, Georgia

19. The Constitution was written; The Founding Fathers wrote the Constitution
20. War of 1812; Mexican-American War; Civil War; Spanish-American War
21. slavery; economic reasons; states' rights
22. freed the slaves, freed slaves in the Confederacy; freed slaves in the Confederate states; freed slaves in most Southern states
23. She fought for women's rights, fought for civil rights
24. Japan, Germany, and Italy
25. Communism
26. (Franklin) Roosevelt
27. fought for civil rights; worked for equality of all Americans
28. Missouri (River); Mississippi (River)
29. Maine, New Hampshire, Vermont, New York, Pennsylvania, Ohio, Michigan, Minnesota, North Dakota, Montana, Idaho, Washington, Alaska
30. Puerto Rico, U.S. Virgin Islands, American Samoa, Northern Mariana Islands, Guam
31. California, Arizona, New Mexico, Texas
32. because there were 13 original colonies; because the stripes represent the original colonies
33. because there is one star for each state; because each star represents a state; because there are 50 states
34. July 4
35. New Year's Day, Martin Luther King Day, Presidents' Day, Memorial Day, Independence Day, Labor Day, Columbus Day, Veterans Day, Thanksgiving, Christmas

POLITICAL CHART.

PRESIDENTIAL CAMPAIGN, 1860

Chapter 8

Parties, Interest Groups, and Public Policy

Political parties and interest groups: How do they influence our political decisions?

■ 8.1 Introduction

In October 2012, the United States prepared for the approaching presidential election. As the race for president heated up, political ads appeared on television screens across the country. Many of these ads featured the leading candidates of the two major parties, Republican Mitt Romney and Democrat Barack Obama.

One ad shows a young, middle-class couple. The somber woman holds her child closely while her husband has his arm around her. "My name is Wayne," the man begins, "and I'm an unemployed coal miner." As his wife rocks the sleeping child, he explains that Obama's policies have severely affected the working class. "President Obama just needs to stand with hardworking American families."

In another ad, a young couple also appears on the screen with their children. Like the above ad, the man identifies himself as a recent lay-off. "I got laid off because Mitt Romney and his friends in Congress want to eliminate tax credits for the wind industry," he explains. "I think Mitt Romney is not in touch with the little guy."

Most people watching these advertisements probably assumed that they came from the **political parties** that sponsored the candidates or from the candidates themselves. Only those paying close attention to the credits knew otherwise.

A poster advertising the presidential election of 1860

Speaking of Politics

political party
An organization that seeks to achieve power by electing its members to public office.

interest group
Any organized group whose members share a common goal and try to promote their interests by influencing government policymaking and decision making.

platform
A political party's statement of principles and objectives. The specific objectives or legislative proposals in a platform are known as planks.

two-party system
A political system in which two parties dominate the electoral process and control the government.

pluralism
The idea that political power should be distributed and shared among various groups in a society.

political action committee (PAC)
An organization that raises and distributes funds to candidates running for office. Corporations, labor unions, and interest groups form PACs to channel donations from their employees or members into political campaigns.

lobbying
An organized effort to influence the policy process by persuading officials to favor or oppose action on a specific issue.

public policy
A plan or course of action initiated by government to achieve a stated goal.

In this image, Bill Clinton, a Democrat and former U.S. President, campaigns for Democratic candidate Barack Obama during the 2012 presidential election. Clinton's participation in the campaign is an example of how loyal political party members are to their party.

In fact, a conservative **interest group** called Americans for Prosperity funded the pro-Romney ad. The Obama ad was paid for by the liberal interest group the League of Conservation Voters. Although neither ad specifically asked viewers to vote for a particular candidate, the sponsors of these commercials clearly hoped to influence the 2012 election.

Increasingly, interest groups have joined political parties as key players in the American political process. Both types of organizations are actively engaged in politics, providing information to officials and the public and seeking to affect the outcome of elections. This chapter examines parties and interest groups and considers their influence on our political system today.

■ 8.2 Political Parties in the United States

Political parties have played an important role in American politics since the early years of the Republic. Yet many of the nation's founders did not approve of parties. In his Farewell Address of 1796, George Washington warned against "the baneful effects of the spirit of party." He believed that parties would divide the American people and have a negative influence on government.

John Adams and Thomas Jefferson shared Washington's concern. Adams said, "There is nothing which I dread so much as the division of the Republic into two great parties . . . in opposition to each other." Jefferson claimed, "If I could not go to heaven but with a party, I would not go there at all." Nevertheless, both men eventually became leaders of political parties, and the party system itself became entrenched in American politics.

What Do Political Parties Do in a Democracy?
The primary goal of parties is to get their candidates elected to office. However, they also have a number of other functions, some of which are listed below.

Parties recruit candidates and support campaigns. Each year, political parties seek out and enlist candidates to run for thousands of local, state, and national offices. They look for people with the skills to run a successful electoral campaign and to be effective in office. Political parties also provide some funding for candidates.

Parties help organize elections and inform voters. Although state and local governments run elections, political parties help by promoting voter interest and participation. They register voters and monitor the polls on Election Day. They also help inform voters on political issues.

Parties organize the government. Congress and most state legislatures are organized along party lines. After congressional elections, members of the majority party in Congress choose one of their members to be speaker of the house or Senate majority leader. Committee chairpersons in Congress also come from the majority party.

Parties unite diverse interests and make collective action possible. Parties bring diverse groups together by building coalitions based on shared beliefs and common goals. Delegates attending national party conventions create **platforms** that outline the party's position on important issues. In that process, they seek to balance the interests and concerns of members from across the country. Their goal is to produce a document that all party members can unite behind to achieve their shared political objectives.

Parties serve as a loyal opposition to the political party in power. The goal of a political party is to win control of the government so that it can translate its objectives into laws and policies. The party not in power, or the minority, serves as a "loyal opposition" to the majority party. Minority party members act as critics of the majority party's proposals. They also serve as government watchdogs, always on the lookout for corruption or abuses of power.

The Structure of Political Parties: Local, State, and National

Both major political parties in the United States are organized at the local, state, and national level. Committees manage the affairs of the party at each level. This diagram shows the basic organization of a major political party.

The national committee is made up of delegates from each state. A national chairperson oversees the day-to-day operations of the committee. The chairperson also makes public appearances to raise support for the party and improve its chances in upcoming elections.

The organization of state and local committees mirrors the structure of the national committee.

Each state has a central committee with a chairperson. Beneath the state committee are various county committees. Some states also have committees at the city, town, or **precinct** level. A precinct is a local voting district.

Political parties offer various ways for citizens to get involved in politics. The most common way is through voter registration. Most Americans identify with one party or the other, and they register to vote as a member of that party. Citizens can also donate money to a political party or its candidates, show their support using social media, and attend party rallies or meetings. In addition, some citizens volunteer to work on party committees or individual campaigns.

The Evolution of the Two-Party System

In 1787, when the Constitution was written, no political parties existed in the United States. Perhaps this is why the Constitution makes no mention of parties. Before long, however, the nation's leaders had begun to divide into factions, or groups with differing views. These factions soon gave rise to the nation's first political parties. By the early 1800s, a political system based on two major parties was beginning to emerge. This **two-party system** has endured to the present day.

The first parties formed around two powerful figures in President Washington's administration. Alexander Hamilton and his followers became known as Federalists. They favored a strong national government and drew their support largely from commercial and industrial interests in northern

Political Party Organization

Political parties are organized on three levels: national, state, and local. These three levels usually work independently of one another. The national party rarely gets involved in issues at the state or local level.

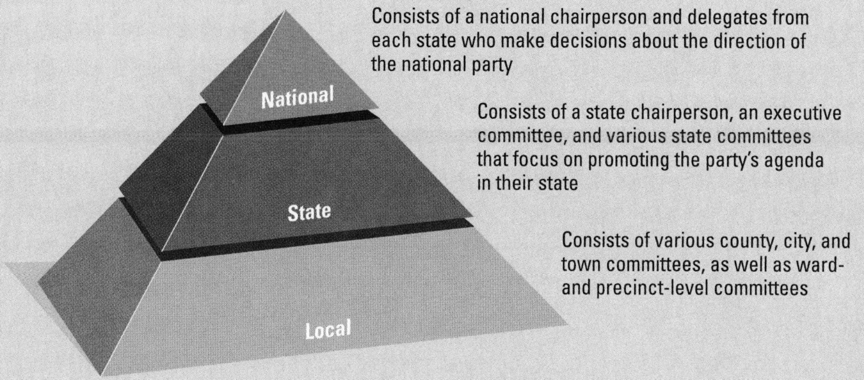

Consists of a national chairperson and delegates from each state who make decisions about the direction of the national party

Consists of a state chairperson, an executive committee, and various state committees that focus on promoting the party's agenda in their state

Consists of various county, city, and town committees, as well as ward- and precinct-level committees

National

State

Local

The tradition of two major parties in U.S. politics goes back to the 1790s. The two-party system has evolved and changed since then. By the late 1800s, Democrats and Republicans were firmly established as the two main parties.

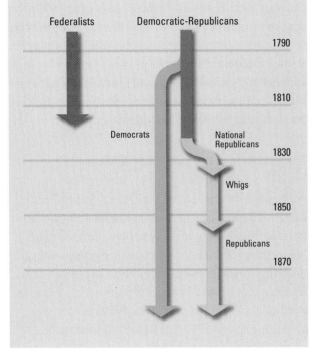

Federalists   Democratic-Republicans

1790

1810

Democrats   National Republicans

1830

Whigs

1850

Republicans

1870

of former Whigs joined with antislavery activists to form the Republican Party in 1854. During the Civil War and the presidency of Abraham Lincoln, the Republicans established themselves as the nation's second major party. The Democratic and Republican parties have dominated American politics ever since.

The Two-Party System Today

Over the years, the two parties have evolved and changed, and so have their bases of support. For example, the Democrats were once the strongest party in the South. Today the Republicans generally enjoy more support among southern voters.

In 2000, political analysts began to speak of a regional divide in American politics. The 2012 presidential election results also showed clearly defined "red states" and "blue states." The red states—mainly in the southern and central parts of the country—were those in which the majority of people voted Republican. The blue states—mainly in the Northeast and far West—were those in which the majority voted Democratic. The distribution of red and blue states led many political observers to conclude that the United States had become deeply divided along political lines. This map shows the results of the 2012 presidential election.

This red-state, blue-state political divide is probably not as sharp or as deep as the map suggests. In many states, the number of Republicans and Democrats is roughly equal. Moreover, people who call themselves Republicans or Democrats do not all agree on what their party stands for. Nevertheless, the two parties and their supporters do differ in some important ways.

Republicans and Democrats in the Twenty-first Century

While all kinds of Americans support either party, a Republican is more likely to be white, male, and relatively affluent. A Democrat is more likely to be a member of a minority group, female, and less affluent. This graph shows other differences between the Republicans and Democrats.

In general, Republicans hold more conservative views, and Democrats more liberal views, on the issues that follow.

cities. Thomas Jefferson and his supporters, known as Democratic-Republicans, favored a much weaker national government and strong state governments. They gained the backing of farmers and rural interests in southern states.

In 1796, John Adams, a Federalist, succeeded Washington in office. Four years later, however, Adams lost the election to Jefferson. After that defeat, the Federalist Party declined and, within a few years, disappeared altogether.

For a brief time, one party—the Democratic-Republicans—dominated U.S. politics. In the 1820s, however, disgruntled members broke away and formed a new political faction. First called National Republicans, the new faction later became known as the Whig Party. Around the same time, the remaining Democratic-Republicans became known simply as Democrats.

In the 1850s, the issue of slavery deeply divided the Whigs, and their party soon fell apart. A number

Size of the national government. In general, Democrats support a strong federal government and look to it to solve a wide variety of problems. Most Republicans favor limiting the size of the national government and giving more power to the states to solve problems at a local level.

Taxes. Republicans favor broad-based tax cuts to encourage economic growth and to allow people to keep what they earn. Although Democrats favor tax cuts for the poor, they are more willing to raise taxes on affluent Americans in order to support programs that they see as beneficial to society.

Regulation of business. Democrats generally support government regulation of business as a way to protect consumers, workers, or the environment.

Most Republicans oppose what they see as excessive business regulation by the government believing that too much regulation prevents economic growth.

Social issues. Republicans tend to oppose legalizing same-sex marriage, abortion, and gun control laws. Democrats are more likely to support same-sex marriage rights, abortion, and gun control laws.

Environment. Most Democrats favor strict environmental regulations. Republicans tend to oppose such regulations because they believe it hurts businesses and the economy.

While these generalities hold for the two political parties, individual Democrats or Republicans may not share the same views on every issue. Republicans who call themselves Log Cabin Republicans, for

Red and Blue America

This 2012 election map shows a country geographically divided between "red states" and "blue states." The graph shows other differences between Republicans and Democrats. For example, White evangelical Protestants are more likely to vote Republican. Jewish voters, on the other hand, are more likely to vote Democratic.

2012 Presidential Election Results

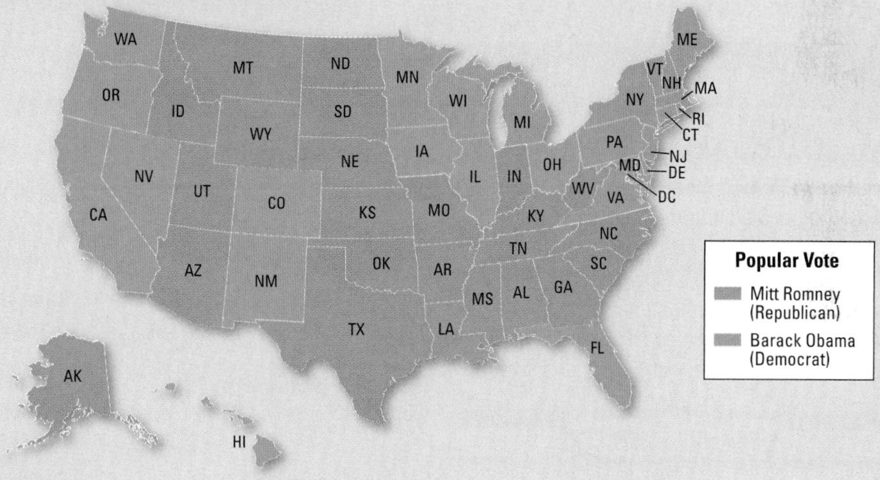

Popular Vote
Mitt Romney (Republican)
Barack Obama (Democrat)

How Americans Vote, 2012

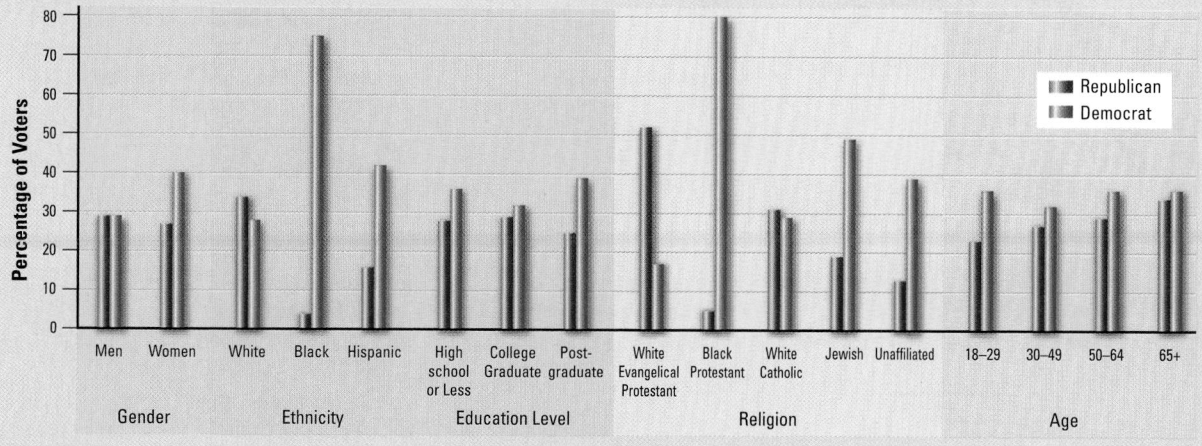

Source: AP Results, as reported by *The Washington Post*. The Pew Research Center for the People and the Press.

example, strongly support equal rights for gay and lesbian Americans. At the same time, many traditional Republicans are just as strongly opposed to granting certain rights, such as the right to marry, to gay and lesbian couples.

Nevertheless, for most Americans, identifying with one party or the other provides a useful way to make sense of the candidates at election time. In effect, party labels tell voters what the candidates stand for and help them make choices when they vote.

Third Parties: Single-Issue, Economic Protest, Ideological, and Splinter Groups

Not all Americans identify with the two major parties. Throughout our country's history, people frustrated with the status quo have formed third parties to express their opinions in constructive ways.

There are four main types of third parties in the United States. Single-issue parties tend to focus on one issue, such as taxes or immigration. Economic protest parties unite opponents of particular economic policies or conditions. Ideological parties view politics and society through the lens of a distinct ideology, such as socialism. And splinter parties develop as offshoots of the major parties. The table below lists an example of each type of third party.

Third parties have had some electoral successes. The Socialist Party gained a substantial following in the early 1900s. More recently, Independent Party candidate Lincoln Chafee won election as governor of Rhode Island in 2010. That same year, the Tea Party movement was also successful when members obtained seats in both the Senate and House. Although the Tea Party is not officially recognized as a political party, it is considered a third party by some. The Green Party has also enjoyed some success in elections, particularly at the local level.

Third parties have also advocated reforms that have eventually been adopted by the major parties.

Third Parties in the United States

Third parties have been formed for many reasons. In 1912, former Republican president Theodore Roosevelt formed the Progressive, or Bull Moose, Party. This cartoon portrays Roosevelt as Humpty Dumpty to parody the fact that his party split the Republican vote in the 1912 election, which helped ensure victory for Democrat Woodrow Wilson.

Types of Third Parties

Type	Examples from U.S. History
Single-issue party Formed to oppose or promote one issue	**National Woman's Party (1913–1920)** Promoted voting rights for women
	Right to Life Party (1970–present) Opposes legalized abortion
Economic protest party Formed to promote "better times"	**Greenback Party (1874–1884)** Promoted use of paper money, silver coinage, and the eight-hour workday
	Populist Party (1892–1908) Protested economic conditions and government policies that hurt farmers
Ideological party Formed by people committed to a set of beliefs	**Socialist Party of America (1901–1973)** Promoted government ownership of basic industries
	Libertarian Party (1971–present) Favors reducing the role of government in citizens' lives
Splinter party Formed by people unhappy with a major party	**Progressive "Bull Moose" Party (1912–1952)** Separated from the Republican Party to promote progressive reforms
	States' Rights "Dixiecrat" Party (1948) Separated from the Democratic Party to oppose desegregation

In the 1990s, for example, the Green Party helped raise awareness of environmental issues. Today "green" positions on the environment can be found in the platforms of the two main parties.

In general, however, third parties face an uphill battle given the strength of the two-party system. Smaller parties find it hard to raise money and get the media coverage they need to challenge the two major parties.

The Moderate Middle: Centrist and Independent Voters

In recent years, a growing number of Americans have identified themselves as political independents. As such, they are not aligned with any political party. According to some political analysts, the rise of independent voters represents a turn away from the more liberal or conservative views of the two major parties toward a centrist, or middle-of-the-road, position.

Nevertheless, political scientists note that many people who embrace the "independent" label still tend to lean toward one or the other major party at election time. In other words, although these voters call themselves independent, they still vote like either Democrats or Republicans. The proportion of voters who are truly independent of either party has hovered around 10 percent since the 1950s.

■ 8.3 Interest Groups in America

Americans join all kinds of groups that reflect their interests, from garden clubs and hiking groups to civic organizations. When such groups seek to influence government, at any level, they are called special-interest groups or **special interests**. The term *special interest* refers to a particular goal or set of goals that unites the members of a group. In the case of the National Rifle Association (NRA), for example, that goal is protecting the rights of gun owners. For the Wilderness Society, it is preserving wild lands.

Are Interest Groups Good or Bad for Democracy?

Many Americans distrust special interests. They believe that these groups seek to achieve their goals at the expense of society as a whole. According to this view, interest groups represent a selfish, corrupt-

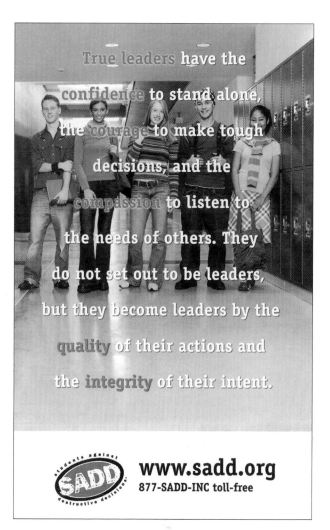

SADD (Students Against Destructive Decisions) was founded to counsel teenagers against drunk driving. It has since expanded its mission to caution against other destructive behaviors among young people.

ing force in U.S. politics. Is this a valid criticism or an unjust accusation?

More than two centuries ago, James Madison addressed this question in *The Federalist Papers*. In *The Federalist* #10, he wrote that "factions"—his term for interest groups—posed a threat to democratic government if their power went unchecked. At the same time, he believed that the growth of interest groups was inevitable, and even a good thing, in a society that prized freedom. The key issue was how to contain the threat while preserving liberty.

Madison believed that **pluralism** held the answer. Pluralism is the idea that political power should be distributed and shared among various groups in society. In theory, competition between these groups, along with an effective system of checks and balances, will prevent any one group from gaining too much power. According to Madison, interest groups competing in a pluralistic society should act as a check on tyranny and make government more representative.

Today, interest groups offer Americans a way to participate in the political process. Interest groups speak out on issues of concern to their members and the public at large. They present specialized information to government officials. They also monitor government actions to ensure that the rights and interests of their members are protected. In the process, interest groups help keep people informed about their government. Even though special interests occasionally influence the political system in negative ways, they play a critical role in the democratic process.

What Kinds of Interest Groups Do Americans Join?

There are thousands of interest groups in the United States. Although they differ in many respects, their basic goal is the same: they all try to persuade elected officials to take actions to support their interests. Special-interest groups fall into several categories, depending on their membership and goals. This table highlights four such groups.

One of the largest categories consists of economic interest groups. This category includes business groups, trade organizations, professional associations, and labor unions. Examples include the Business Roundtable, the American Medical Association, and the United Farm Workers of America.

Another broad category consists of citizen groups, many of which claim to promote the public interest. Some of these groups may also be motivated by a

Groups for Every Interest

Interest groups bring together a wide variety of people under a single cause. One of the largest and most influential interest groups is the Sierra Club. Members of the Sierra Club are dedicated to protecting wild places and promoting responsible use of Earth's ecosystem.

Four Representative Interest Groups

Group	Membership	Mission	Activities
Business Roundtable	Heads of major U.S. corporations	To ensure economic growth and a productive U.S. work-force	Research and position papers Policy formulation Lobbying
United Farm Workers of America	27,000 farm workers	To provide farm workers with the inspiration and tools to improve their lives	Labor organizing Contract negotiations Lobbying
League of United Latin American Citizens	135,000 community volunteers	To improve the living conditions and educational attainment of the U.S. Hispanic population	Lobbying Conduct leadership programs Workshops and training
National Education Association	3,200,000 public schoolteachers	To create great public schools for every student	Workshops and training Lobbying Legal actions

particular ideology or set of issues. Environmental groups, such as the Sierra Club, belong in this category, as does the American Civil Liberties Union (ACLU). Some single-issue groups, such as Students Against Destructive Decisions (SADD), also fit in this category.

Government interest groups exist at every level of government. They include groups like the National Governors Association and groups that represent mayors or city managers. Public employee unions, like the National Education Association (NEA), also belong in this group.

There are other categories, as well, such as foreign policy interest groups, nationality groups, and religious organizations. At the same time, many special interests, such as the American Legion and the Veterans of Foreign Wars (VFW), do not fall neatly into any particular category. Nonetheless, such groups may be large and highly influential.

Why Do People Join Interest Groups?

Americans join interest groups for various reasons. Some join for the information and benefits the groups offer. Many interest groups publish newsletters and host workshops and conferences for members. Some offer training that helps members qualify for higher-paying jobs. AARP, formerly the American Association of Retired Persons, an interest group for older Americans, provides information on federal health insurance benefits and prescription drug programs. The American Automobile Association (AAA) offers benefits in the form of emergency towing service and discounts on insurance and travel.

Americans also join interest groups because they agree with the group's goals and want to be part of a larger community of shared interests. The World Wildlife Fund (WWF), for example, attracts people who want to protect animal habitats. Members of the Christian Coalition of America share religious and political beliefs.

How Are Interest Groups Organized and Funded?

In an essay on democracy, policy analyst Archon Fung called "organized money and organized people" the sources of power in American politics. All interest groups need both money and people, but they are organized and financed in many ways.

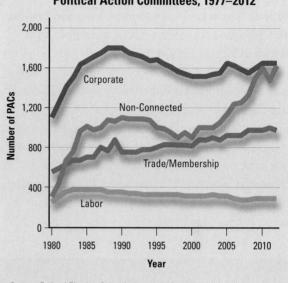

PAC Sponsors

Corporations sponsor the greatest number of political action committees. However, other types of organizations—such as labor unions and trade groups—also establish PACs.

Political Action Committees, 1977–2012

Source: Federal Election Commission, www.fec.gov.

Most interest groups have an elected board of directors or trustees who set policy and decide how the group's resources will be used. Many groups have both national and state chapters, each led by their own boards or trustees.

Funding methods vary among interest groups. Many economic and single-issue groups get most of their operating expenses from dues, membership fees, and direct mail fundraising campaigns. Some public interest groups get their primary funding from foundations or government grants.

The Rise of Political Action Committees

One way that interest groups try to influence government is by contributing money to political parties and candidates during election campaigns. Campaign finance laws passed by Congress in the early 1970s placed limits on some types of campaign contributions. But these laws allowed the creation of new funding organizations called **political action committees (PACs)**.

PACs are private groups sponsored by corporations, trade associations, unions, or other interest groups. By law, PACs are allowed to collect donations and funnel that money into political campaigns. Most of these donations come from the employees or members of the group that formed the PAC.

Over the past decades, the amount of money raised and spent by PACs has grown. In 1980, PACs contributed about $131 million to candidates. By 2012, the figure had risen to more than $560 million. Even adjusting for inflation, that is a substantial increase. Corporations were by far the top contributors to PACs, though many public interest groups, trade associations, and labor unions also make large donations.

Many Americans believe that PAC campaign contributions give interest groups too much influence over elected officials. Nevertheless, most research shows that PAC money does not buy votes in Congress. It does, however, give contributors greater access to lawmakers.

Grassroots mobilization is an important way for interest groups to influence government policy. One form of mobilization is public protest. Here, members of PETA, an animal rights' organization, call for a taxation on meat products during a protest.

How Do Interest Groups Influence Policy?

Campaign contributions are one way interest groups try to influence government policy. But they have other, more powerful methods as well, such as **lobbying**, research, litigation, and grassroots mobilization.

Lobbying. Many interest groups rely heavily on lobbying to advance their interests. Lobbying is an attempt to influence the policy process by persuading public officials to favor or oppose action on a specific issue. Lobbyists speak to members of Congress and their staffs, testify before congressional committees, and offer comments at hearings held by executive agencies. Often they provide useful information that helps officials create policies that serve the public interest.

Senator Edward Kennedy of Massachusetts noted that lobbyists play a useful role in the political process. "Without lobbying, government could not function," he said. "The flow of information [from lobbyists] to Congress and to every federal agency is a vital part of our democratic system."

Research and policy proposals. Some interest groups carry out research and write policy proposals that support their goals. In some cases, they work with **think tanks** to carry out this research. A think tank is an organization of scholars and policy experts who study public issues and write articles and books that summarize their research. Interest groups use these expert findings to influence government officials.

Litigation. Interest groups may also try **litigation,** or the bringing of lawsuits, to influence policy. One interest group that has used litigation effectively is the National Association for the Advancement of Colored People. Lawyers for the NAACP have brought numerous lawsuits to court to advance the cause of civil rights. The NAACP's most famous victory came in the 1954 Supreme Court case of *Brown v. Board of Education,* which helped bring an end to segregation in public schools.

Grassroots mobilization. Another way interest groups try to influence policy is through **grassroots mobilization**. This means rallying strong and vocal support from a large group of people at the local level.

Grassroots mobilization often takes the form of public demonstrations, such as antiwar protests or

Lobbying is one way that interest groups attempt to influence policy. Here, the president of the United Auto Workers, a major interest group, participates in a 2007 congressional hearing on the automobile industry. The testimony focused on global warming and fuel efficiency.

antiabortion rallies. Increasingly, however, it is carried out by mail or over the Internet. Interest groups call on members to write cards or flood the e-mail inboxes of public officials with messages urging a particular course of action. Interest groups have also begun using social media to raise awareness on specific issues. Web sites such as Facebook and Twitter allow these groups to easily spread their ideas and engage supporters.

What Makes an Interest Group Powerful?

Several factors help interest groups become successful. Size and money are key factors, but other criteria can also play a role.

Size and money. Interest groups often succeed when they have a large membership and substantial resources. Interest groups with millions of members can gain the attention of government officials through sheer force of numbers. With ample funds, they can afford to maintain offices around the country, hire a large staff, and pay travel and lobbying expenses. They can also produce expensive media ads to raise their public profile.

Unity of purpose. Size and resources matter, but so does the commitment of members to the group's goals. Small, single-issue, or ideological groups may demonstrate this unity most effectively because their members tend to be motivated and focused. But even a large, diverse group like AARP can show great unity of purpose. When the members of an interest group voice unified, forceful views on an issue, government leaders tend to listen.

Effective leadership. Strong leadership is another critical factor in an interest group's success. Effective leaders can clearly express the group's message and win support from others. Without effective leadership, even a group with a powerful message may fail to achieve its goals.

Information and expertise. Successful interest groups know how to gather and analyze information and deliver it to decision makers. For example, in the 1970s, Ralph Nader's interest group Public Citizen used careful research and analysis to convince Congress to pass consumer protection laws that improved car safety.

Not surprisingly, large, well-funded groups have a clear advantage in efforts to influence government policy. Nevertheless, many small but dedicated interest groups have also had a notable impact, despite their limited resources.

■ 8.4 Making Public Policy

For decades, U.S. officials have considered ways to reduce the nation's dependence on foreign oil as part of a broad-based energy policy. Should the government permit oil drilling in waters off the nation's coasts? Should drilling be allowed in national parks and wildlife refuges? Should public money be used to develop other energy sources, such as solar, wind, and nuclear power? The answers to such questions have shaped our nation's **public policy** on energy.

Public policy refers to government actions or programs designed to achieve certain goals. Creating public policy is a multistep process. Government officials, policy experts, political parties, interest groups, and concerned citizens all take part in such policymaking. This diagram outlines how the policymaking process works.

Seeing What Needs Attention: Issue Identification

The first step in policymaking is identifying problems and issues that need to be addressed. Sometimes a crisis brings an issue to public attention. This happened when Middle East oil producers blocked sales to the United States for a few months in 1973

and 1974. The resulting energy crisis forced Americans to begin thinking of ways to reduce this nation's dependence on foreign oil.

Public officials can also raise awareness of issues. Until 1964, for instance, most Americans viewed smoking as a matter of personal choice. That year, the surgeon general of the United States issued a report linking cigarette smoking to lung cancer. His report raised the issue of whether smoking should be discouraged as a matter of public policy.

Choosing Issues to Address: Agenda Setting

Government officials cannot address all the problems facing the nation at any one time. They have to make choices, selecting the issues that seem most critical and setting others aside. Agenda setting requires officials to decide which issues should be part of the **public agenda,** or set of public priorities.

Some issues pop onto the public agenda as a result of a disaster. The 9/11 terrorist attacks on the World Trade Center and the Pentagon put fighting terrorism high on the nation's public agenda. Similarly, after Hurricane Katrina devastated New Orleans in 2005, repairing damaged levees around the city shot to the top of that area's public agenda.

The Dynamics of Policymaking

Policymaking is a complicated, multistep process that involves many different actors. It begins with the identification of an issue and ends with implementation and evaluation.

Issue Identification
Officials or the general public identify important issues or problems.

Agenda Setting
Key issues become part of the public agenda, making them priorities for public policy.

Policy Formulation
Policymakers consider options and formulate policies to address the issues.

Other issues take a long time to become part of the public agenda. One example is global warming. For years, scientists have been warning about the effects of greenhouse gas emissions on Earth's climate. But for the most part, their concerns were ignored. As scientific knowledge and evidence of climate change have mounted, however, global warming has found its way onto the public agenda of many public officials and lawmakers.

Political parties and interest groups often play a role in setting the public agenda. Parties help by placing issues on their platforms, thus making those items a priority for the candidates they elect. Interest groups do the same by lobbying for certain issues.

Deciding What to Do: Policy Formulation

Once an issue is on the public agenda, government officials work on formulating a policy to address it. This step may take place within any branch of government. It can also happen at the local, state, or national level. Legislatures or city councils make policy by passing laws or statutes. Executive officials or agencies make policy by setting new rules and regulations. The judicial system can influence policy, too, through court decisions and rulings.

When officials begin to formulate a policy, they ask some basic questions: Is this a problem government should address? If so, what options should be considered? Should government pass a new law, create a new or expanded program, or offer a new benefit? What are the costs and benefits of each option?

In response to the surgeon general's report on smoking, for example, officials considered a number of policies. These ranged from warning labels on cigarette packages to regulating cigarettes as drugs. When considering such varied options, officials may ask experts to offer their opinions. They may also invite interest groups to present their views. This helps ensure that the policy they finally adopt takes various perspectives and interests into account.

Putting Proposals into Action: Policy Adoption

Many policies are formulated as legislation. These bills must first pass through Congress, state legislatures, or city councils to become law. This legislative process often results in substantial revisions. A policy proposal may be changed to gain the support of a majority of legislators. Or it may be modified to avoid legal challenges or a threatened veto by a governor or president.

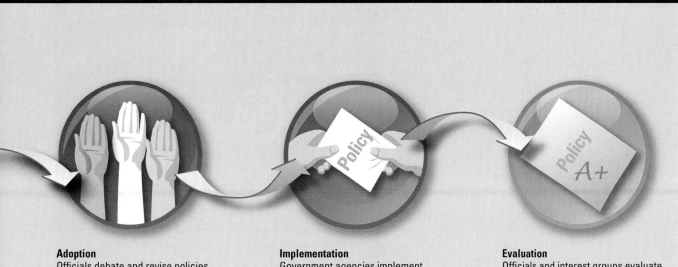

Adoption
Officials debate and revise policies before they are adopted.

Implementation
Government agencies implement and enforce the adopted policies.

Evaluation
Officials and interest groups evaluate policy results and consider any necessary changes.

Sometimes the president works with members of Congress and key interest groups to get policies adopted. President Lyndon Johnson, for instance, worked closely with Congress and civil rights leaders to win passage of the landmark Civil Rights Act of 1964. In 1990, President George H. W. Bush joined with lawmakers and disability activists to pass the Americans with Disabilities Act. This law helped make public facilities more accessible to people with disabilities.

In other cases, interest groups take the lead in getting new policies adopted. The American Cancer Society and the American Lung Association, for example, have taken the lead in promoting laws banning smoking in public places. By 2010, 25 states had enacted comprehensive smoking laws that banned smoking inside of worksites, bars, and restaurants.

Making a Policy Work: Implementation

After a policy is adopted, it must be implemented. Usually, implementation is assigned to a specific government agency. That agency then becomes responsible for making the new policy work.

After the 9/11 terrorist attacks, for example, Congress enacted a number of antiterrorism policies. The job of implementing these policies was given to the newly created Department of Homeland Security. DHS took on a host of responsibilities, from intelligence gathering to border security. To accomplish its goals, DHS officials worked closely with state and local governments.

Assessing the Effectiveness of a Policy: Evaluation

The final step in the policy process is evaluation. Government officials and concerned interest groups assess whether implemented policies have met their goals. If changes need to be made, the policymaking process begins again.

After New York City outlawed smoking in bars and restaurants in 2003, the city's Department of Health carried out a study to assess the results. Its researchers found that air pollution levels had decreased sixfold in bars and restaurants after the ban went into effect. The study also found that contrary to predictions, business remained good despite the smoking ban. A 2006 study by the state of New York found similar results.

Based on evidence of links between smoking and cancer, many cities and states have adopted antismoking policies.

Not all policies that show positive results manage to survive, however. For example, studies show that a policy of requiring motorcycle riders to wear helmets reduces the likelihood of dying in a crash by about one-third. Nonetheless, faced with stiff opposition from motorcycle riders, some states have not passed mandatory helmet laws. Moreover, a few states with such laws have repealed or are considering repealing them. For a policy like this one to be successful, it must achieve its goals and win public approval.

The Department of Homeland Security plays a leading role in implementing anti-terrorism policies. Here, a DHS helicopter patrols New York Harbor as part of heightened security measures.

Summary

Political parties and interest groups play an important part in American politics. They exert a strong influence on government and offer ways for Americans to participate in the political process.

Political parties Political parties perform various functions. They run candidates in elections and help inform voters about political issues. They also organize the government. The United States has a two-party system, dominated by the Democratic and Republican parties. Nonetheless, third parties and independent voters have an impact on elections and issues as well.

Interest groups Many Americans distrust interest groups. Nevertheless, these groups play a vital role in our political system. Interest groups provide information that helps public officials do their jobs. They also help inform Americans about the actions of their government.

Public policy The creation of public policy is a multistep process. It begins with the identification of issues. If an issue is considered important, it becomes part of the public agenda. Officials then address the issue by formulating a policy. After the policy is adopted and implemented, officials and other interested parties evaluate its results. If the policy has failed to meet its goals, the process may begin all over again.

What color are you: red, blue, purple, or none of the above?

This map of the 2012 election results shows a nation divided between "red states" and "blue states." Many Americans are convinced that the country was split by a "continental divide" between red conservative values and blue liberal values. A closer reading of the results shows, however, that this division may be more apparent than real. What do you think? How divided are we?

Americans' Political Divisions Not Necessarily Bad, Experts Say

by Michelle Austein

Today, the division among Americans is often depicted in the colors red and blue. During the contested 2000 election between George W. Bush and then-Vice President Al Gore, Americans spent weeks looking at maps depicting in red the states that voted Republican and in blue the states that voted Democrat. Since then, defining political views as "red" (Republican) or "blue" (Democratic) is a regular occurrence.

American history has shown that there are periods of polarization and periods of consensus in the political landscape. This current era of polarization is seen by many as beginning in the years following the end of the Cold War.

"There's no question that the partisan polarity between the Democrats and Republicans these days . . . runs deeper, certainly, than it did a generation ago," said Pietro Nivola, director of the Governance Studies Program at the Brookings Institution in Washington.

A number of factors influence today's divide. One is that the characteristics of parties' supporters have changed in recent decades. At one time, the Democratic Party base was in the South, and Southerners tended to hold conservative views similar to many in the

Republican Party. Today, those Southerners predominately support Republicans. Additionally, religious voters have moved more into the Republican camp, making the party more conservative and the Democrats more liberal, Nivola said.

An increase in the number of "safe seats" in Congress, seats typically held by the same political party from one election to the next, has furthered this polarization, according to Nivola. Because a congressman knows his district will support his party, he has no incentive to work with his opponents, Nivola said.

The media also has had an impact. The rise of Internet blogs, talk radio and cable news has created outlets that cater to certain political viewpoints, allowing Americans to choose to watch sources they find agreeable, Nivola said.

There are many problems with having such a polarized electorate, but there are some advantages as well, according to William Galston, senior fellow at the Brookings Institution.

"Passion, conflict and a measure of divisiveness are to be expected and, within limits, are not to be deplored," he said.

A divided government may have difficulties solving long-term domestic policy problems because it is difficult to reach compromises, Galston said. Polarization also "makes sustainable foreign policy much harder to put into place," he said, and when parties disagree, it is difficult to send a clear international message.

Additionally, "high degrees of polarization are not good for public trust and confidence," he said. "That does not mean . . . that the public is driven out of the political arena—in fact you can see high levels of political participation coinciding with very high levels of political mistrust." This is likely one of the reasons why voter turnout has been higher in recent elections.

Having distinct alternatives is one of several advantages of having a divided electorate, Galston said.

"When there is greater polarization between the parties, the electorate is offered clearer choices."

In a period of polarization, Americans realize that if they vote for a Republican, they are going to get a different type of foreign policy and a different focus on social issues than if they vote for a Democrat, Galston said. They may doubt what the differences will be when the candidates are more alike.

"Because the choices are clearer, politics are more intelligible to average citizens," he said, citing studies conducted over the past 10 years that show that Americans are improving their understanding of politics.

During a time of political consensus, those who do not

share the majority's views may not be heard. When these eras end, there is an opportunity for new political views to be represented, Galston said.

Nivola and Galston suggested some potential ways of decreasing polarization. These include setting term limits for judges so there are less contentious battles over lifetime appointments, using election run-off voting so candidates have to appeal to a wider base to gain a majority of votes rather than a plurality and establishing bipartisan commissions to oversee redistricting to reduce the number of safe congressional seats.

Michelle Austein is a staff writer for USINFO.

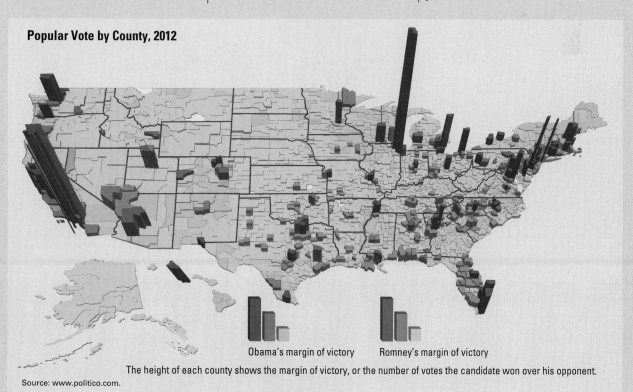

Popular Vote by County, 2012

Obama's margin of victory   Romney's margin of victory

The height of each county shows the margin of victory, or the number of votes the candidate won over his opponent.

Source: www.politico.com.

Chapter 9

Public Opinion and the Media

To what extent do the media influence your political views?

■ 9.1 Introduction

Every four years, Americans express their views on how this country should be led when they cast their ballots for president. In the months leading up to the election, voters are bombarded with television ads aimed at influencing **public opinion** about the candidates. Vast sums of money are spent on these campaign ads in the hope of persuading voters to support one candidate over another.

Is this the way to choose the leader of the free world? Adlai Stevenson, the Democratic candidate for president in 1952, didn't think so. When asked about running ads on television, Stevenson said, "I think the American people will be shocked by such contempt for their intelligence. This isn't Ivory Soap versus Palmolive."

The 1952 presidential campaign was the first to use the new medium of television extensively to reach voters. Rather than try to sell himself like soap, Stevenson opted to buy time for 18 half-hour speeches airing from 10:30 to 11:00 two nights a week. Stevenson hoped this use of television would help him build a national following. However, both the lateness of the hour and the dull "talking head" format of his speeches limited the audience. Most of those who tuned in were already Stevenson supporters.

A 1952 campaign poster for Democratic presidential candidate Adlai Stevenson

Speaking of Politics

public opinion
The sum of many individual opinions, beliefs, or attitudes about a public person or issue.

political socialization
The process by which people form their political values and attitudes. This process starts in childhood and continues through adulthood.

opinion poll
A method of measuring public opinion. This is done by asking questions of a random sample of people and using their answers to represent the views of the broader population.

margin of error
A measure of the accuracy of an opinion poll. The smaller the margin of error, the more confidence one can have in the results of a poll. The margin of error usually decreases as the number of people surveyed increases.

mass media
Means of communication that reach a large audience. Today the mass media include newspapers, magazines, radio, television, and the Internet.

spin
The deliberate shading of information about a person or an event in an attempt to influence public opinion.

media bias
Real or imagined prejudice that is thought to affect what stories journalists cover and how they report those stories.

negative campaigning
Trying to win an advantage in a campaign by emphasizing negative aspects of an opponent or policy. In the past, this type of campaigning was called mudslinging.

The power of television in politics first became evident in the 1952 presidential election. Dwight Eisenhower used television ads to promote his candidacy. His opponent, Adlai Stevenson, did not. Eisenhower won a decisive victory with more than 55 percent of the vote.

In contrast, Dwight Eisenhower, Stevenson's Republican opponent, embraced the use of 20- to 30-second "spot" ads in 1952. The idea came from advertising executive Rosser Reeves. Reeves convinced Eisenhower that he could reach more viewers with less money by running short ads during popular prime time programs. Titled "Eisenhower Answers America," each spot featured the candidate answering a question posed by an ordinary citizen. The ads showed "Ike" as a plain speaker responding to real people's concerns. Not only did more viewers see Ike's ads; they also seemed to like what they saw. Eisenhower swept to victory with more than 55 percent of the votes cast.

Stevenson's loss in 1952 didn't change his low opinion of television advertising. But when he ran against Eisenhower again in 1956, Stevenson agreed to replace his speeches with five-minute spots. The power of television to shape public opinion was just too hard, even for Stevenson, to resist.

■ 9.2 The Formation of Public Opinion

Adlai Stevenson had a low opinion of political advertising on television. But did Stevenson's personal views about TV ads match public opinion as a whole? The answer, seemingly, is no, since Eisenhower's advertising strategy apparently worked so well. From the election results, one might conclude that the public's view of using televised ads to

"sell" candidates was generally positive in 1952. In reality, however, figuring out just what "the public" thinks is not so easy. The American public today consists of more than 300 million individuals, each with his or her own personal beliefs, values, attitudes, and opinions.

How Do Individuals Form Their Political Opinions?

The opinions you may have on political issues tend to be shaped by deeply held political beliefs and values. The formation of these beliefs and values begins early in life and continues throughout adulthood. Political scientists call this process **political socialization**. To "socialize" an individual means to teach that person to be a fit member of society. Political socialization involves learning about the values, beliefs, and processes that underlie a political system in order to participate in it effectively.

The process of political socialization is important. No democracy could survive if its citizens did not share some fundamental beliefs about how their government should operate. However, this process does not produce 300 million people who think exactly alike. Political socialization involves all of the experiences that lead us to view political issues the way we do. And those experiences are never the same from one person to the next.

Many agents, or forces, play a part in political socialization. They include family, schools, religion, friends, and the mass media. This diagram illustrates these **agents of socialization**.

Political socialization is the process by which we gain our political identity. It begins early in childhood and continues throughout our lives. This diagram shows some of the forces that help shape our political values and beliefs as we grow and mature.

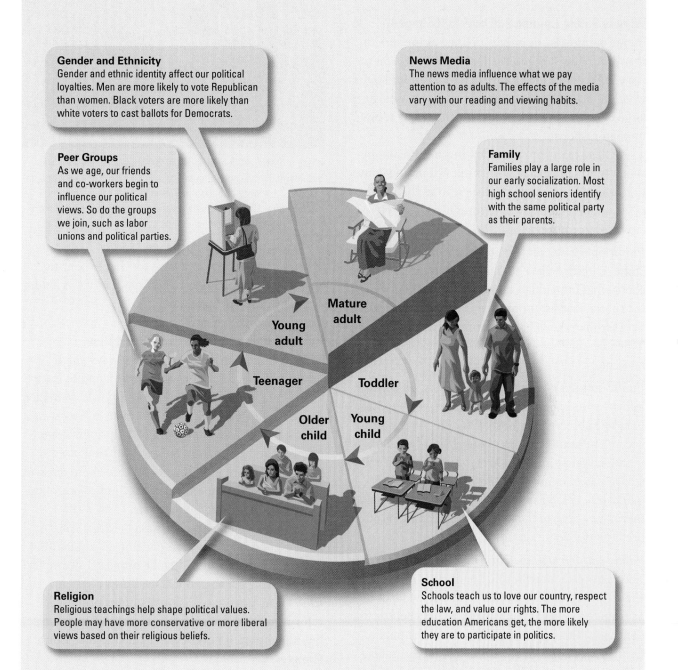

Gender and Ethnicity
Gender and ethnic identity affect our political loyalties. Men are more likely to vote Republican than women. Black voters are more likely than white voters to cast ballots for Democrats.

News Media
The news media influence what we pay attention to as adults. The effects of the media vary with our reading and viewing habits.

Peer Groups
As we age, our friends and co-workers begin to influence our political views. So do the groups we join, such as labor unions and political parties.

Family
Families play a large role in our early socialization. Most high school seniors identify with the same political party as their parents.

Religion
Religious teachings help shape political values. People may have more conservative or more liberal views based on their religious beliefs.

School
Schools teach us to love our country, respect the law, and value our rights. The more education Americans get, the more likely they are to participate in politics.

Young adult

Mature adult

Teenager

Toddler

Older child

Young child

Historical events are another important factor. Children growing up in the affluent 1950s, for example, tended to have a positive view of government. Those growing up in the 1960s—a time marked by political assassinations, urban riots, and the Vietnam War—were more likely to view government with considerable distrust.

What Is Public Opinion and How Is It Shaped?

Public opinion is commonly defined as the sum of many individual opinions about a public person or issue. This definition assumes that we can find out what public opinion on a given issue is by asking a large number of people what they think and adding up their responses.

With so many opinions floating around among so many Americans, how does public opinion come to be shaped? Political scientists who study this question have come up with several answers. Here are three to consider.

Public opinion is shaped by special interest groups. Some scholars believe that public opinion is less about what individuals think and more about what the special interest groups they belong to advocate. Because many such groups represent large numbers of people, they are listened to when they speak out on issues.

Public opinion is shaped by journalists, politicians, and other opinion makers. Scholars who support this view observe that most of us don't have time to become informed on every issue. Instead we look to influential **opinion makers** for information and advice. These opinion makers may be journalists, public officials, business leaders, or activists. Because they have access to the media, "their" opinions often become "our" opinions.

Public opinion is shaped by what politicians say it is. This last view recognizes that politicians often talk about "what the people think" without evidence to back up their claims. They may sincerely believe that they have their fingers on "the pulse of the public." Or they may hope that by claiming that the public agrees with them loudly enough, they will convince the American people that it must be true.

However public opinion takes shape, it is seldom a single view held by all Americans. Our country

Mass protests, such as this one in 2009 opposing the Iraq war, both demonstrate and influence public opinion. The more people involved, the more attention a protest is likely to get from the news media. The more media coverage a protest gets, the more influence it may have on politicians and the general public.

is simply too large and diverse for that to be true. Instead, it is more likely to be a range of views held by many different "publics."

Public Opinion as Guide, Guard, and Glue

Public opinion serves our democratic system of government in three key ways. First, it guides leaders as they make decisions about public policy. Whether conveyed through opinion polls, town hall meetings, letters, or e-mails, public opinion helps politicians know what their constituents are thinking. Politicians who ignore what the people care about do so at their own peril. When the next election rolls around, they risk being voted out of office.

Public opinion also serves as guard against hasty or poorly understood decisions. President Bill Clinton found this out when he proposed a complex restructuring of the national health care system in 1993. As public confusion about his proposed reforms mounted, the plan lost steam. Without public support, it never even made it to the floor of Congress for debate.

Lastly, public opinion serves as a kind of glue in a diverse society like ours. Widespread agreement on basic political beliefs holds our society together, even in times of intense partisan conflict.

9.3 Measuring Public Opinion

In 1936, in the depths of the Great Depression, *Literary Digest* announced that Alfred Landon would decisively defeat Franklin Roosevelt in the upcoming presidential election. Based on his own surveys, a young pollster named George Gallup disagreed with that prediction. Not only did Gallup choose Roosevelt as the winner, he publicly challenged newspapers and magazines to show the two polls side by side. The result was a triumph for Gallup, with Roosevelt winning by a landslide. For *Literary Digest,* the most widely circulated magazine in the country, the embarrassment of wrongly calling the election proved disastrous. Its credibility destroyed, the magazine soon slid into bankruptcy.

From Straw Polls to Scientific Sampling: The Evolution of Opinion Polling

After the 1936 election, many wondered how *Literary Digest* had blundered so badly. The magazine had a record of predicting presidential elections accurately since 1916 using **straw polls**. A straw poll is an informal survey of opinion con-ducted by a show of hands or some other means of counting preferences. So confident was the *Digest* of this method of predicting elections that it boasted of its "uncanny accuracy."

The magazine conducted its 1936 straw poll by mailing out more than 10 million ballots for people to mark with their choices for president. It predicted the winner based on the over 2 million ballots that were returned. What the *Digest* editors did not take into account was that their sample was biased. Most of the ballots went to people with telephones or registered automobiles. During the depths of the Depression, people wealthy enough to have phones and cars tended to be Republicans who favored Landon.

The secret of Gallup's success was his careful use of **scientific sampling**. Sampling is the process of selecting a small group of people who are representative of the whole population. Rather than mailing out surveys blindly, Gallup interviewed a sample of voters selected to mirror the entire electorate. His survey results underestimated Roosevelt's popularity on Election Day, but he did predict the winner correctly. His success marked the birth of the modern **opinion poll**.

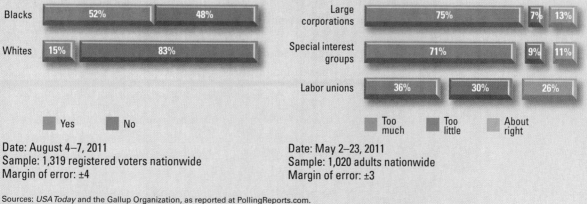

Two Typical Opinion Polls

The basic elements of an opinion poll include (1) the name of the polling organization or sponsor, (2) the question asked, (3) an analysis of the data gathered, (4) the date of the poll, (5) the sample size, and (6) the margin of error. Note that the percentages on the graphs below do not all equal 100 percent. That is because they do not show the small percentage of people who answered "unsure."

USA Today/Gallup Poll

Do you think new civil rights laws are needed to reduce discrimination against blacks, or not?

	Yes	No
Blacks	52%	48%
Whites	15%	83%

Date: August 4–7, 2011
Sample: 1,319 registered voters nationwide
Margin of error: ±4

CBS News Poll

Do you think [large corporations, special interest groups, and labor unions] has/have too much influence, too little influence, or about the right amount of influence on American life and politics today?

	Too much	Too little	About right
Large corporations	75%	7%	13%
Special interest groups	71%	9%	11%
Labor unions	36%	30%	26%

Date: May 2–23, 2011
Sample: 1,020 adults nationwide
Margin of error: ±3

Sources: *USA Today* and the Gallup Organization, as reported at PollingReports.com.
CBS News, as reported at PollingReports.com.

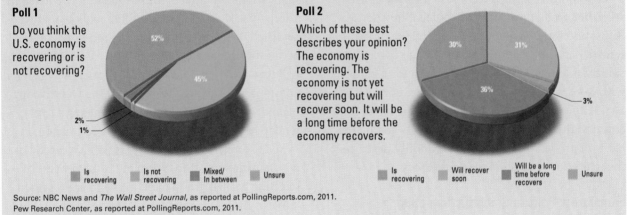

The Answer Depends on the Question

How you ask a polling question can make a big difference in the answers people give. The impact of wording was demonstrated in two polls conducted on the outlook of the U.S. economy in 2011. In the first poll, the question offered poll takers only two options for their answer. In the second, the question asked poll takers to consider both the present and future state of the U.S. economy, and to provide a more specific answer. As the results show, asking the question in this way made a considerable difference in how people responded.

Poll 1

Do you think the U.S. economy is recovering or is not recovering?

52%
45%
2%
1%

Is recovering   Is not recovering   Mixed/In between   Unsure

Poll 2

Which of these best describes your opinion? The economy is recovering. The economy is not yet recovering but will recover soon. It will be a long time before the economy recovers.

30%   31%
36%
3%

Is recovering   Will recover soon   Will be a long time before recovers   Unsure

Source: NBC News and *The Wall Street Journal*, as reported at PollingReports.com, 2011.
Pew Research Center, as reported at PollingReports.com, 2011.

The Polling Process: Sample, Survey, and Sum Up

Professional polling organizations today follow much the same methods pioneered by Gallup and other early pollsters, though with a few improvements. The first step is to identify the population to be surveyed. The target population might be all adults, members of a political party, a specific age group, or people living in one community.

Most polling today is done by telephone. Phoning people randomly ensures that pollsters interview a representative sample of people. In most **random samples,** every individual has a chance of being selected. The number of people surveyed usually ranges from 500 to 1,500. Internet surveys are also widely used.

The opinions gathered in the survey are summed up and reported in terms of the percent choosing each response. Most polls also report a margin of error stated as plus or minus (±) some number of percentage points. The **margin of error** indicates how accurately the sample surveyed reflects the views of the target population. If the margin of error is small, you can assume that the results reported are close to the opinions of the population as a whole.

The Use of Polling to Measure Public Sentiment

George Gallup saw public opinion polls as the modern equivalent of the old-fashioned New England town meeting. Politicians, he said, should view poll results as a mandate from the people. No longer could public officials ignore voter sentiment, he argued, by claiming that public opinion was unknowable.

Today, opinion polls are widely used as means of gathering information about public sentiment. Businesses use polls to measure consumers' attitudes about their products. Groups of all sorts use polls to find out what their members are concerned about.

News organizations commission polls to measure the views of the American people on major issues of the day. One regularly repeated opinion poll, for example, asks people to respond to this open-ended question: *What do you think is the most important problem facing this country today?*

As you might expect, the results change over time as new issues arise and capture the interest of the public.

Other news media polls ask very specific public policy questions. The Gallup Organization, for example, conducted a poll in 2012 to gauge public opinion on a variety of proposals related to U.S. energy and the environment. One question asked those surveyed whether, in general, they opposed or favored "imposing mandatory controls on carbon dioxide emissions [and] other greenhouse gases."

Seventy percent of the 1,024 adults surveyed answered that they did support these mandatory controls. Whether such a result would change the mind of a lawmaker opposed to added restrictions is hard to know. But a legislator who agreed with the majority view might have been encouraged by this poll to press harder for new emission controls.

Presidents and other public officials use polls to measure how well they are doing in the eyes of the voters. They use the results to help them develop policies that they hope the public will support. In addition, the news media report regularly on the rise and fall of presidential approval ratings. During the 1980s, Ronald Reagan came to be known as the "Teflon president" because bad news never seemed to stick long enough to diminish his popularity.

The Use of Polling in Political Campaigns

Three special kinds of polls are widely used during elections. A long and detailed **benchmark poll** is often used by prospective candidates to "test the waters" before beginning a campaign. Candidates use information from such polls to identify which messages to emphasize in their campaigns and which to avoid.

Tracking polls are conducted during a campaign to measure support for a candidate on a day-by-day basis. Pollsters survey groups of likely voters each night to find out how their views have been affected by the political events of that day. While each day's poll is just a snapshot of the electorate's views, taken together, tracking polls can reveal trends and shifts in attitudes over time.

Exit polls are used by campaigns and the news media to predict the winners on Election Day long before the polls close. An exit poll is a survey of voters taken at polling places just after they have cast their ballots. Because ballots are cast in secret, exit polling is the only way we have of finding out how different age or ethnic groups of people voted and why.

The use of exit polls by television networks led to controversy in 1980 when newscasters predicted that Ronald Reagan had won the presidency long before polls closed in the West. Critics charged that announcing the winner so early discouraged western voters from going to the polls. As a result, television networks are more careful now not to predict the winner in the presidential race until the polls have closed everywhere in the country.

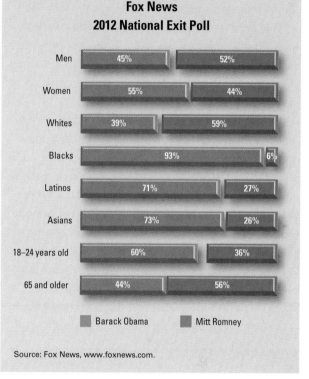

Polling of Voters on Election Day

This poll was conducted with 26,565 voters as they exited polling places across the country on November 6, 2012. Each voter surveyed filled out a questionnaire asking how he or she had voted in the presidential election. The actual vote count showed that Barack Obama won 51.1 percent of the votes cast and Mitt Romney 47.2 percent. How do these numbers compare with the exit poll results?

Fox News
2012 National Exit Poll

Group	Barack Obama	Mitt Romney
Men	45%	52%
Women	55%	44%
Whites	39%	59%
Blacks	93%	6%
Latinos	71%	27%
Asians	73%	26%
18–24 years old	60%	36%
65 and older	44%	56%

Source: Fox News, www.foxnews.com.

In 2004, an exit poll based on interviews with voters in 49 states appeared on the Internet early on Election Day. The poll showed John Kerry leading George W. Bush, prompting Kerry's aides to start polishing his victory speech. This false prediction raised serious questions about the accuracy of exit polls. "They are not perfect and they have never been perfect and we have never taken them to be perfect," says a CBS News senior vice president, Linda Mason.

The Misuse of Polling to Influence Public Opinion

At times polls are used more to shape than to measure public opinion. Elected officials and special interest groups sometimes claim to be assessing public opinion by sending out mail surveys. The questions in these surveys are often rigged to generate highly favorable results for the sponsor of the poll. Former congressman John Dowdy of Texas, for example, once sent a newsletter survey to his constituents with this question: *A drive has recently been announced to destroy the independence of Congress by purging Congressmen who refuse to be rubber stamps for the executive arm of government. Would you want your representative in Congress to surrender to the purge threat and become a rubber-stamped Congressman?*

It is hard to imagine anyone answering yes to such a highly charged question. Thus, not only are mail-in straw polls highly unreliable, as the *Literary Digest* editors discovered, but the results can also easily be skewed.

Television and radio shows also use call-in, text message, and Internet straw polls to report public opinion. In 1992, news anchor Connie Chung reported on the basis of a call-in poll that 53 percent of Americans reported being "worse off than four years ago." She went on to say, "This does not bode well for President Bush." A scientific poll conducted at the same time, but not released until later, showed that only 32 percent of the population felt "worse off" than four years before. By then, however, it was too late to repair whatever damage might have

been done to George H. W. Bush's approval rating. Despite criticism from scientific pollsters, some TV shows continue to promote call-in or Internet polls and report the results.

Polling done through social media is another method that is gaining popularity. But since these polls only survey those with social media accounts, most do not consider them scientific or accurate.

The 1990s saw the appearance of a highly suspect form of polling called the **push poll**. These polls are phone surveys, usually made close to Election Day, on behalf of a candidate. When the pollsters call, they sound like they want your views on the election. But their real purpose is to "push" you away from voting for their candidate's opponent by spreading damaging information.

A typical push poll begins by asking for whom you plan to vote on Election Day. Should you answer that you plan to vote for the opposing candidate, the next question might be, Would you support that candidate if you knew that she wants to cut spending for schools? The purpose of the question is not to give you useful information, but rather to raise last-minute doubts. The American Association for Public Opinion Research has declared push polls to be "an unethical campaign practice."

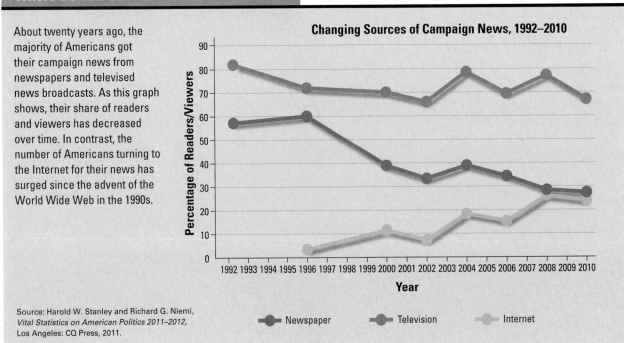

Where Do You Get Your News?

About twenty years ago, the majority of Americans got their campaign news from newspapers and televised news broadcasts. As this graph shows, their share of readers and viewers has decreased over time. In contrast, the number of Americans turning to the Internet for their news has surged since the advent of the World Wide Web in the 1990s.

Changing Sources of Campaign News, 1992–2010

Source: Harold W. Stanley and Richard G. Niemi, *Vital Statistics on American Politics 2011–2012,* Los Angeles: CQ Press, 2011.

Newspaper ● Television ● Internet

▦ 9.4 The Impact of the Mass Media on Public Opinion

Our opinions are shaped, in part, by the information we receive about the world. And never before in human history has so much information been made available to us through the **mass media**. By 2009, Americans were buying over 46 million copies of daily newspapers, the lowest number since the 1940s. However, other sources of media have grown more popular. In 2009, Americans listened to over 14,000 radio stations, and each household watched an average of 8.3 hours of television a day. Add to that the wealth of information made available through the Internet and you can begin to see why many people complained of information overload.

Where Do Americans Get Their News?

A century ago, this would have been an easy question to answer. Americans got their news from the **print media**—mainly newspapers and magazines.

A half-century ago, the answer would have been less simple. By the 1950s, the **broadcast media**—mainly radio and television—had become major sources of news. Where once the broadcast media limited their news offerings to short news summaries and nightly newscasts, we now have 24-hour news programming available on both radio and cable television stations.

To make matters still more complex, a growing number of people now get instant news on demand using the **electronic media**—computers, cell phones, and other communication devices that connect via the Internet to the **World Wide Web**. The Web makes billions of documents stored in computers all over the world accessible to anyone with an Internet connection. The rise of each new medium has changed the public's news-consumption habits.

The News Versus the "New" Media

A generation ago, most Americans looked to trusted **news media**—newspapers, news magazines, and broadcast news shows—for information on politics and public affairs. The news media rely on a small army of reporters, fact-checkers, and editors to research and report stories in an accurate, unbiased manner.

Beginning in the late 1980s, new ways to communicate with the public about politics began to appear.

News organizations have taken advantage of new media. By posting articles on social media Web sites and on smartphone applications, these organizations attract viewers who are not drawn to traditional news sources.

These "new" media include online communities, RSS feeds, online encyclopedias, internet videos, podcasts, and social media Web sites.

While running for president in 1992, Bill Clinton became a master at using the new media to talk directly to voters. He even appeared on MTV, playing his saxophone and fielding questions from young people.

In the 2008 presidential election, Republican candidate John McCain and Democratic candidate Barack Obama also utilized this new media. McCain showed off his wit and mocked his opponent on *Saturday Night Live*. Obama posted campaign advertisements on YouTube, making his campaign accessible to anyone.

Social media has also become a platform for politicians to express their views and gain followers. During the 2012 presidential election, candidates Barack Obama and Mitt Romney both used Facebook and Twitter to reach out to voters.

Late night shows, such as *The Daily Show with Jon Stewart*, weave comedy with serious political issues and have become sources of news for many viewers. Because late night shows reach viewers who may not watch traditional networks, many politicians are eager to appear on them as guests.

News-oriented Web logs, or **blogs**, have emerged as another new medium. A blog is a journal or newsletter posted on the World Wide Web. Because the Web is essentially free, anyone can create a blog to distribute his or her opinions.

More and more, readers are turning to blogs as primary sources of news. At times, blogs report stories before the news media. The scandal that eventually led to President Bill Clinton's impeachment was first reported in 1998 in Matt Drudge's blog, *The Drudge Report*. Another news blog is *The Huffington Post*, founded in 2005, which provides readers with current information on topics such as politics, business, technology, and entertainment.

While blogs are often written by specialists, in many cases these writers are not accredited. Some of what passes for news on blogs may be gossip, false rumor, or opinion. Because bloggers are not required to follow the same standards for accuracy as professional journalists, their reports should be read with caution.

The Role of a Free Press in a Democracy

The news media—old and new—have three essential roles in a democracy. The first is serving as a "watch-dog" over the government. The second is setting the public agenda. The third is supporting the free exchange of ideas, information, and opinions.

Although media has changed forms over time, the roles of media have remained constant. This photograph from 1963 shows news anchor Walter Cronkite reporting a story. Like news anchors today, Cronkite's job was to inform the public about current issues and stories.

One of the greatest concerns of our nation's founders was the potential for government officials to abuse their power. They saw a free press as a guard against corruption and the misuse of power. For more than two centuries, the media have fulfilled this watch-dog role by exposing everything from the corruption of the Grant administration to the efforts of President Nixon to cover up the Watergate scandal.

Far too much happens in the world for the press to report on everything, however. News editors and producers have to choose what to cover and what to leave out. These decisions help determine what issues get placed on the public agenda. Politicians and activists try to harness this **agenda-setting power** of the media to focus attention on issues they care about.

Finally, the news media serve as a marketplace of ideas and opinions. The airwaves today are filled with **opinion journalism**—the chatter of "talking heads" eager to share their views with the world. Most people who tune into these electronic debates do so not to receive objective analysis, but rather because they share the talk show host's political point of view.

Influencing the Media: Staging, Spinning, and Leaking

Public officials at all levels of government work hard to both attract and shape media coverage. The most common way to do this is by staging an event and inviting the press. Presidential press conferences are an example of **staged events**.

In 2007, Senator Barack Obama launched his presidential campaign by staging an event at Illinois' Old State Capitol, the place where Abraham Lincoln delivered his famous "House divided" speech against slavery in 1858. As hoped, the event attracted thousands of supporters and widespread press coverage.

Politicians also try to influence the press by granting interviews to reporters. Often they set ground rules that indicate what information reporters can use and how they can identify their source. If it is an **on-the-record conversation,** the report can quote the public official by name. If it is an **off-the-record conversation,** the reporter can use the information but may not reveal the source.

When speaking on the record, politicians usually put their own **spin** on issues. Their goal is to con-

How What We Believe Influences What We Watch

People are selective when it comes to getting the news. They pay attention to media that support their views and screen out those that do not. In 2010, people identifying themselves as conservative, for example, were more likely to tune into conservative Fox News than more liberal CNN for their news. The opposite was true for self-described moderates. This selectivity limits the impact of the news media on public opinion.

Viewers of Fox News

26%
60%
9%
5%

Viewers of CNN News

26%
45%
6%
23%

Source: Pew Research Center for the People and the Press, "Audience Profiles: Party and Ideology," June 8–28, 2010.

Conservative   Moderate   Liberal   Other/ No Response

---

vince both reporters and the public that their view of events is the correct one. They also try to include colorful **sound bites** that capture their main points in just a few words. They know that short sound bites are more likely to be run in news stories than are long speeches.

Public officials sometimes use off-the-record conversations to float **trial balloons**. A trial balloon is a proposal that is shared with the press to test public reaction to it. If the reaction is negative, the official can let the proposal die without ever having his or her name attached to it.

Off-the-record conversations are also used to **leak** information to the press. A leak is the unofficial release of confidential information to the media. Public officials leak information for many reasons. They may want to expose wrongdoing, stir up support for or opposition to a proposal, spin the way an event is covered, or curry favor with reporters. In 2000, President Clinton vetoed a bill that would have made it easier to prosecute government officials for leaking secret information to the press. Former Justice Department official John L. Martin said of the antileak bill:

The biggest leakers are White House aides, Cabinet secretaries, generals and admirals, and members of Congress. If this were enacted, enforced and upheld by the courts, you could relocate the capital from Washington to [the federal penitentiary at] Lewisburg, PA.

Are the Media Biased?

Many Americans believe that the media have a liberal or conservative bias. Nevertheless, most professional journalists strive to be fair and unbiased in their reporting. In its code of ethics, the Society of Professional Journalists calls on its members to be "honest, fair and courageous." It cautions that "deliberate distortion is never permissible."

What critics see as **media bias** may, in reality, be a reflection of how news organizations work. Most news media outlets are businesses. They need to attract readers, listeners, or viewers to survive. With limited space or time to fill, their reporters, editors, and producers have to make choices about what stories to cover. These decisions are less likely to be motivated by political ideology than by what they think will attract and hold an audience.

Journalists look at many factors in choosing what stories to cover. One is impact. Will the story touch people in some way, even if only to make them mad or sad? A second is conflict, preferably mixed with violence. Does the story involve a crime, a fight, a scandal, or a disaster? A third factor is novelty. Is the story about a "hot topic" or a breaking news event? A fourth is familiarity. Does the story involve people we all know and find interesting?

These factors influence what you see and hear as news. Because reporters like novelty, you won't see many stories about ongoing issues or social problems. Because they want conflict, you won't see much coverage of compromise in the making of public policy. And because they are looking for impact, bad news almost always wins out over good. As an old saying in journalism goes, "If it bleeds, it leads."

9.5 The Influence of the Media in Political Campaigns

In 1960, Richard Nixon and John Kennedy participated in the first televised debate between two presidential candidates. Nixon, weakened by a bout of the flu, appeared nervous, awkward, and uneasy. His face looked pale and sweaty, all the more so because he did not allow the television producers to improve his appearance with makeup. Kennedy, in contrast, appeared confident, relaxed, and appealing.

Those who watched the debate on television concluded that Kennedy had "won." Those who listened on the radio considered Nixon the winner. The difference reflected not what the two candidates said about the issues, but rather the images they projected. This outcome underscored the growing importance of image over issues in political campaigns.

Image Making and the Role of Media Consultants

Kennedy's television triumph in 1960 contributed to the rise of new players in political campaigns: media consultants. Their job is to advise candidates on how to present a positive image to voters. They make sure, for example, that their candidates wear flattering colors that will show up well on television. They coach candidates on how to speak to the press and how to respond to voters' questions.

Media consultants also help candidates plan their media campaigns. They work with the news media to get free coverage of the campaign in newspapers and newscasts. However, most media coverage comes from paid political advertising. Media consultants help decide what ads should say and where and when they should appear.

Advertising is expensive. Candidates may spend up to 80 percent of their "war chests," or campaign funds, on paid ads. Media consultants use opinion polls to make sure that money is spent effectively. They also work with **focus groups** to test the appeal

Common Persuasive Techniques Used in Political Advertising

Political campaigns use a number of persuasive techniques in an attempt to influence the opinions of voters. The more you know about these techniques, the better you will be at analyzing political advertising.

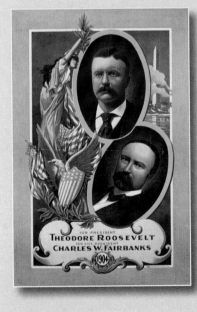

Name-Calling
Using personal attacks on an opponent to distract voters from the real issues of the campaign. The goal is to inspire doubts about the opponent's fitness for office by appealing to people's fears or prejudices. This 1964 ad uses name-calling to link presidential candidate Barry Goldwater to "right-wing extremists."

Transfer
Using symbols or images that evoke emotion to something unrelated, such as a candidate or proposition. This 1904 campaign poster links presidential candidate Theodore Roosevelt and his running mate Charles W. Fairbanks to beloved patriotic symbols such as Liberty, the American flag, and a bald eagle.

Bandwagon

Creating the impression that "everyone" supports a cause or candidate. This technique plays on people's desire to conform, or "climb on the bandwagon," rather than be left behind. This 1972 ad suggests that Americans from all walks of life are backing presidential candidate George McGovern.

The Granger Collection, New York

Together with McGovern

Testimonial

Having a well-known celebrity or personality endorse a candidate or proposal. The hope is that you will follow the person's example without questioning his or her qualifications to make such a judgment. In this 1928 ad, famous sports figures endorse Democratic nominee Al Smith for president.

The Granger Collection, New York

Card-Stacking

Presenting facts, statistics, and other evidence that support only one side of an argument. This ad begins with the fact that as governor of Massachusetts, Democratic presidential candidate Michael Dukakis supported a plan that allowed murderers to take weekend leaves from prison. It concludes that "Mike Dukakis is the killer's best friend, and the decent, honest citizen's worst enemy."

Plain Folks

The use of folksy or everyday images and language to show that the candidate is a regular person who understands the needs and concerns of the common people. In this 1872 poster, President Grant and his running mate appear as common working people.

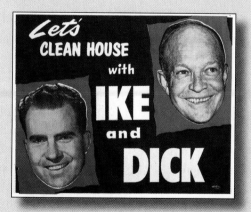

Glittering Generalities

Using vague, sweeping statements that appeal to voters emotionally, but don't actually say much of anything specific. Candidates or proposals are often described in lofty terms. This 1952 ad for presidential candidate Dwight Eisenhower and his running mate Richard Nixon urges "Let's clean house" without defining what that might mean.

of campaign messages. A focus group is a small group of people who are brought together to discuss their opinions on a topic of concern. Before the public sees a campaign ad, it has probably been discussed and tweaked by a focus group.

Types of Campaign Ads: Issue Versus Image

Political advertisements usually fall into two broad groups. The first group deals with issues, the second with images. Ads in either group can be positive or negative. Positive ads are aimed at making you like or respect a candidate, while negative ads are designed to make you dislike or fear his or her opponent. Both types of ads use persuasive techniques well known to advertisers. Some of those techniques are explained on the previous two pages.

Positive issue ads promote a candidate's position on topics calculated to appeal to voters. A positive issue ad might highlight the candidate's determination to improve funding for schools or to hold the line on taxes. Negative issue ads, on the other hand, criticize the opponent's stand on issues of importance to voters. An opponent who opposes the death penalty, for example, might be criticized in a negative issue ad for being "soft on crime."

A positive image ad might show the candidate as a selfless public servant, a strong leader, or someone who cares about ordinary people. The candidate might be portrayed as a hero or as just "plain folk." In contrast, a negative image ad might portray the opponent as weak, inexperienced, or lacking in integrity. Often negative ads include unflattering photographs of the opposition candidate. The desired effect is to convince voters that this person is somehow unfit for public office.

Attracting Media Coverage: Photo Ops and Streamlined Conventions

For all they spend on advertising, candidates and their media consultants work hard to attract news coverage as well. Almost all aspects of a campaign are designed to generate as much free publicity as possible. Often this is done by creating a **photo op**—short for photo opportunity—for the candidate. A photo op is a carefully staged event designed to produce memorable photographs and video images.

One of the most famous photo ops in recent years occurred in 2003 when President Bush, wear-

Not all photo ops work out as planned. Democratic presidential hopeful Michael Dukakis learned this the hard way in 1988. Wanting to show that he was strong on defense, Dukakis had himself photographed riding in a tank. Wearing an oversized helmet, he looked more comical than presidential.

ing a flight suit, landed on the deck of the aircraft carrier USS *Lincoln* to announce the end of "major combat operations" in Iraq. Clearly visible in the background was a banner stating "Mission Accomplished." Images of President Bush being cheered by the *Lincoln*'s crew appeared in newscasts and newspapers across the nation.

National nominating conventions are also staged to attract maximum media coverage. In the past, conventions were dominated by long-winded speeches and debates over the nominees and platform that bored television viewers. As a result, the broadcast media drastically cut their coverage of these events. In response, parties have streamlined their conventions. Most serious business is completed off camera. Prime time speeches and events are designed mainly to promote the party's ideas and candidates to the viewing public.

Media Coverage of Elections: Horse Races and Soap Operas

Studies of election news coverage show that most reporting falls into two distinct patterns. The first pattern, **horse race coverage,** treats an election as a sporting event. Horse race stories focus on who is winning and why. Issues are discussed only in terms of whether they will help or hurt the candidate's chances. Opinion polls, often sponsored by a news organization, are used to track who is ahead or behind. The results of the polls are then covered by the media as campaign news.

The second pattern of coverage, **soap opera stories,** focuses on the ups and downs of candidates and their campaigns. Soap opera stories thrive on gossip, scandals, and personality. Questions of "character" are more important than issues. During the 2004 election, for example, stories about Democratic presidential nominee John Kerry often dealt more with his "flip-flops" on issues than with the issues themselves.

In their hunger for soap opera stories, reporters sometimes practice what has become known as **"gotcha" journalism**. The aim of gotcha journalism is to catch the candidate making a mistake or looking foolish. In 2008, vice presidential nominee Sarah Palin claimed to be the victim of gotcha journalism during an interview with CBS News anchor Katie Couric. When Palin was unable to list specific newspapers and magazines she reads to keep up with world news, reporters released stories ridiculing her lack of response.

Why Campaigns "Go Negative"

At some point during a campaign, media consultants may advise a candidate to "go negative." This means switching from a positive, upbeat campaign to **negative campaigning,** also known as **mudslinging**.

The decision to go negative is not taken lightly. Polls show that the public dislikes attack ads. Going negative also leaves the candidate open to criticism for running a mean-spirited campaign. As Adlai Stevenson warned in 1954, "He who slings mud generally loses ground."

Why then take the risk? Cathy Allen, an experienced media consultant, advises clients to consider negative campaigning only when the candidate has absolute proof that the opponent has done something wrong or when the candidate is facing an uphill battle and has little to lose.

In the end, campaigns go negative because it works. Some scholars argue that negative ads work by discouraging voters who might have supported a candidate under attack from going to the polls. Others contend, however, that negative campaigning actually stimulates voter interest. They argue that going negative works not by discouraging voting, but instead by causing more voters to go to the polls and choose a different candidate on Election Day.

Like it or hate it, negative campaigning is part of our political tradition. How well it works depends on how you and voters like you react to what you see and hear during each election season.

Summary

In a democracy, public opinion serves as a guide to elected officials, a guard against costly mistakes, and a kind of glue that holds us together despite our differences. While the mass media may help shape public opinion, they are also shaped by it.

Public opinion Public opinion is the sum of a large number of individual opinions. Our basic views about politics are formed early in life through political socialization. Agents of socialization include family, schools, religion, friends, and the news media.

Opinion polling Public opinion is best measured by scientific opinion polling. Accurate results depend on surveying a random but representative sample of the target population.

Mass media Americans today receive information from print, broadcast, and electronic media. The news media serve as government watchdogs, agenda setters, and forums for an exchange of views.

Political campaigns Politicians depend on both the free and paid media to reach voters during campaigns. Today, image seems as important as issues in both campaign advertising and media coverage of candidates.

Was the 2012 Presidential Election the "Social Media Election"?

Social media played an important role in the 2012 presidential election. Candidates used social media as a campaign tool and as a method to reach out to voters.

In this article, Laurence Cruz examines how exactly social media was used in this election, focusing primarily on its significance in the candidates' campaign. However, as you read, think about these questions: What are the limitations of using social media in elections? Are there any disadvantages of social media in political campaigns for candidates? For voters?

2012—The Social Media Election?

by Laurence Cruz

After it was over, the 2008 U.S. presidential election came to be known as "the social media election"—a nod to the Obama team's tech-savvy use of the Internet to raise money and build its grassroots network. But today, with the current presidential election campaigns going into overdrive, few would dispute that 2012 is the year social media in politics has truly come of age.

Since 2008, the variety and reach of the digital tools available to supporters, campaigns and the candidates themselves have exploded, providing powerful new ways to persuade and register voters, raise money and turn people out. Republican and Democratic campaigns alike are duking it out in real time in a rapidly expanding Twitterverse and on Facebook, as well as using data-mining tools to dig into voters' online habits in order to tailor "microtargeted" messages to voters . . .

Twitter Grows Up Twitter in particular is emerging as the real-time tool of choice for campaigns, though its agility is a two-edged sword. When Clint Eastwood addressed an empty chair purported to seat Obama at last week's Republican National Convention, the crowd wasn't the only thing that went wild. Within minutes of the actor leaving the stage, "Invisible Obama" was a Twitter account with 6,000 followers and the hash-tag #Eastwooding flooded the Twitter feed. By 9:30 p.m., Obama himself tweeted a response—a photo of him in a White House chair captioned, "This seat's taken."

By one estimate, some 90 percent of senators and House members now have Twitter accounts, as do 42 governors and more than 35 world leaders. President Obama has hosted online Twitter town hall meetings on topics such as student loan interest rates, and Twitter has its own government liaison in Washington, D.C . . .

GOP presidential nominee Mitt Romney's digital director, Zac Moffatt, told *The Washington Post* that a few hours after a topic gathers steam on Twitter, the campaign turns to Facebook to see how it is resonating in the larger universe of public opinion, and by the next day, Google search provides a retrospective of how the whole issue played . . .

Dueling Social Media Campaigns
The Obama team appears to have the edge over Romney's campaign in exploiting social media tools and the Internet. According to a new study by the Pew Research Center's Project for Excellence in Journalism, the Obama campaign is using digital tools to reach voters at almost four times the rate of the Romney campaign . . .

But there were signs the Romney campaign was taking steps to close the gap. Its official website and mobile app empower voters to volunteer, donate and fundraise, as well as stay up to date with and share campaign news with friends. Clearly, both sides are leaving nothing to chance in such a hotly contested race, and both are spending heavily on digital consulting.

A Strategic Approach "[In the 2012 election], we are much more strategic integrators of technology," [Michael] Slaby, [an officer for the Obama campaign,] said. "We spend a lot more time thinking about the problems that aren't working and trying to build solutions."

The result of such "strategic integration" is tools like Dashboard, an online field office that enables organizers and volunteers to collect data about voters both online and in person and

Smartphone applications make social media accessible from almost any location, one benefit of using these platforms in political campaigns.

deliver it back to a centralized campaign database; a mobile app that supports mobile canvassing, helps supporters find campaign events nearby and share breaking news, among other things; and a new Facebook app that lets voters check their registration status and encourage their friends to register . . ."

Big Data Could Make a Big Difference It's not just social networking tools that the campaigns are exploiting. ...Big Data—a movement that's making inroads into industries as diverse as banking, retail and international shipping—is also shaping the 2012 presidential race.

Big Data typically involves data-mining tools sifting through mountains of information—in this case, voters' online habits—to find gems of actionable insight. For instance, a person who

does an Internet search for Mitt Romney or his running mate, Paul Ryan, may notice a strategically placed ad or video from the Romney campaign next time they log on, urging them to donate or persuading them to vote. Such "microtargeted" ads—already a staple of product marketing—are relatively surgical in their precision compared with the blunt-instrument effect of a TV ad.

Strategists say the 2012 election could be decided by which campaign does a better job of exploiting this breakthrough approach. But, as with social media tools, it will all come down to whether voters are moved to take action.

Laurence Cruz is a contributing writer to The Network. *Before, he has also reported stories for* The Associated Press.

Chapter 10

Political Campaigns and Elections

Elections and voting:
Why should they matter to you?

■ 10.1 Introduction

Does any one person's vote really matter? Some people do not think so. They contend that a single vote can hardly make a difference in an election that involves millions of voters. Even at the local level, a single vote is unlikely to have much impact.

In the presidential election of 2000, however, a relatively small number of votes did matter. That year, Democratic nominee Al Gore ran against Republican candidate George W. Bush. More than 100 million people voted in that election. When the votes were tallied, Gore had won the popular vote by a little more than 500,000 votes. Although a margin of half a million votes sounds like a lot, it represented only about one-half of 1 percent of the total.

Despite Gore's slim lead, Bush became president by winning the Electoral College vote. This was only the third time in U.S. history that a candidate had won in the Electoral College without receiving a **plurality** of the popular vote.

Not surprisingly, Bush's victory in 2000 was controversial. The election was so close that, in the end, it came down to a few contested votes in a single state—Florida. There, George Bush won by a mere 537 votes. Under our **winner-take-all system,** that slim margin of victory gave Bush all, rather than half, of the state's 25 electoral votes—and the presidency.

Voters waiting in line on election day

Of course, 537 votes, the number that effectively put Bush in the White House, is more than 1 vote. If just 269 more Gore supporters had gone to the polls that day, and the same number of Bush supporters had stayed home instead of voting, the result might have been very different.

The Florida tally was not the only close count in the 2000 elections. In New Mexico, Gore beat Bush by just 366 votes. An even tighter race unfolded in Michigan, where congressional candidate Mike Rogers won a seat in the House by a mere 88 votes.

The 2000 elections show that a few votes can, and often do, matter. The importance of voting, however, goes well beyond the vote tally in any one election. Voting is one of the main ways that Americans take part in the political process. An informed voter is likely to be an engaged citizen, and an active citizenry is essential to a healthy democracy. In that sense, every American who votes is helping to keep our democratic system alive and well.

10.2 The Right to Vote

Elections are a regular feature of this nation's political system. In fact, Americans hold more elections to elect more officeholders than any other nation in the world. This emphasis on elections stems from the constitutional principle of popular sovereignty. If political authority comes from the people, what better way to exercise that authority than by voting? In a 2012 opinion survey, the majority felt that voting in an election was crucial.

Yet despite this widespread view, a sizable percentage of Americans do not vote regularly. Furthermore, throughout our history, many Americans have been denied voting rights. In many cases, the right to vote has been won only after years of struggle.

Who Voted Then: The Gradual Expansion of Suffrage
When the U.S. Constitution was written in 1787, it said very little about elections. The Constitution did establish a procedure for electing the president and vice president. But it left most other details about elections and voting rights to the states.

At that time, **suffrage,** or the right to vote, was limited in the United States. In 1789, only about 6 percent of the population was allowed to vote. Most states restricted suffrage to white males who owned substantial property. John Jay, one of the authors of *The Federalist Papers,* expressed a view common to many of the nation's founders when he said, "those who own the country ought to govern it."

Over time, however, suffrage was gradually extended. During the 1820s, a political movement to eliminate property qualifications for voting swept the country. Propelled by Andrew Jackson, the first

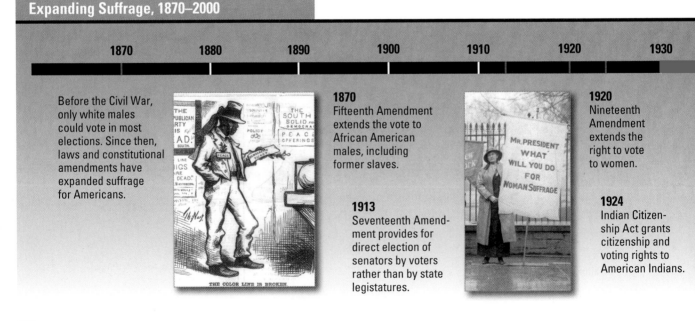

Expanding Suffrage, 1870–2000

| 1870 | 1880 | 1890 | 1900 | 1910 | 1920 | 1930 |

Before the Civil War, only white males could vote in most elections. Since then, laws and constitutional amendments have expanded suffrage for Americans.

THE COLOR LINE IS BROKEN

1870
Fifteenth Amendment extends the vote to African American males, including former slaves.

1913
Seventeenth Amendment provides for direct election of senators by voters rather than by state legislatures.

MR. PRESIDENT WHAT WILL YOU DO FOR WOMAN SUFFRAGE

1920
Nineteenth Amendment extends the right to vote to women.

1924
Indian Citizenship Act grants citizenship and voting rights to American Indians.

"common man" to become president, states opened their voting rolls to all white males. This political movement also pioneered the use of political parties to mobilize voters and get them to the polls.

After the Civil War, the adoption of the Fifteenth Amendment advanced the principle of universal male suffrage. This amendment, ratified in 1870, granted voting rights to all male citizens, including African Americans.

Early in the 20th century, other measures expanded voting rights even more. The Seventeenth Amendment, ratified in 1913, provided for the direct election of senators. Previously, senators had been elected by state legislatures. The Nineteenth Amendment, approved in 1920, gave women in all states the right to vote. The Indian Citizenship Act of 1924 helped extend suffrage to American Indians by granting them citizenship.

The Civil Rights Movement and Suffrage

For some African Americans, the expansion of suffrage after the Civil War proved short-lived. For nearly a century after the war, many states—especially in the South—found ways to deny suffrage to blacks, despite the Fifteenth Amendment. They erected legal barriers, such as literacy tests and poll taxes, to keep African Americans from the polls.

In the 1950s and 1960s, leaders of the civil rights movement made expansion of voting rights one of their key goals. They organized mass protests, calling on the federal government to ensure that African Americans could exercise their voting rights, no matter where they lived. They achieved their first victory with the ratification of the Twenty-fourth Amendment in 1964. This amendment banned poll taxes, which had kept many poor African Americans from voting.

A second major advance came with the passage of the Voting Rights Act of 1965, which banned literacy tests. In some parts of the South, this law placed **voter registration,** or the process of signing up to vote, under federal authority. In the past, local election officials in these areas had prevented African Americans from registering to vote. As a result of the Voting Rights Act, the number of African American voters increased dramatically in the South.

Voting Today: Easy Registration and Low Turnout

The next major expansion of suffrage occurred with ratification of the Twenty-sixth Amendment in 1971. This amendment lowered the voting age to 18. Previously, most states had required voters to be at least 21 years old. This amendment was adopted during national debates over the Vietnam War. At the time, many people argued that if 18-year-olds were old enough to be drafted and sent into battle, then they were old enough to vote.

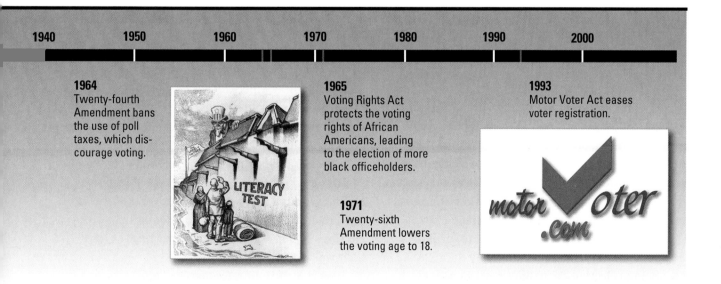

1940 1950 1960 1970 1980 1990 2000

1964
Twenty-fourth Amendment bans the use of poll taxes, which discourage voting.

1965
Voting Rights Act protects the voting rights of African Americans, leading to the election of more black officeholders.

1971
Twenty-sixth Amendment lowers the voting age to 18.

1993
Motor Voter Act eases voter registration.

LITERACY TEST

motor Voter .com

Many voters believe that their vote does not matter. However, the cumulative effect of non-voting can be substantial. If most Americans fail to vote, then election results do not represent the will of the majority.

Today, there are four basic requirements to be eligible to vote in the United States. In most states, you must be

- a U.S. citizen.
- at least 18 years old.
- a resident of the state.
- a legally registered voter.

To register to vote, you must fill out a form that asks for such basic information as your address and date of birth. You may also be required to provide the registrar of voters with proof of your identity. In general, voter registration closes a month or so before an election. However, North Dakota does not require residents to register before voting. A few other states allow voters to register at their polling place on Election Day.

To encourage more people to vote, Congress has tried to make the voter-registration process easier. In 1993, for example, it passed the National Voter Registration Act, better known as the Motor Voter Act. This law requires that states allow residents to register to vote while applying for a driver's license. It also requires states to provide voter-registration forms at social service offices and by mail.

The Motor Voter Act has been quite successful in promoting voter registration. By the 1996 presidential election, 18 million new voters had registered. Since the act was passed, there has been some increase in registration among voting-age Americans.

Increased voter registration, however, has not translated into high **voter turnout** on Election Day. Voter turnout is the proportion of the voting-age population that actually votes. Today, the United States has one of the lowest voter turnouts among the world's established democracies. Between 50 and 60 percent of American voters turn out to vote in presidential elections. In contrast, figures for many European democracies exceed 70 percent.

Political scientists point to a number of factors that might explain this difference in voter turnout. For example, ballots in some countries may be simpler, with fewer candidates and issues to vote on than in a typical American election. U.S. elections take place on workdays, which means that many voters must take time off from their jobs to go to the polls. In many other countries, elections are held on weekends or official Election Day holidays.

In some European countries, such as Belgium and Italy, voting is compulsory, not voluntary as in the United States. Voters who do not participate in elections in those countries may face fines or have their right to vote revoked.

Low U.S. turnout rates may also reflect the fact

that a majority of states deny convicted felons voting rights while in jail, on parole, or on probation. Such restrictions deny about 1 adult in 50 the right to vote.

Low voter-turnout rates have fueled concern that Americans are becoming less connected to their communities and see less reason to get involved in politics. Experts say that the 2012 presidential election showed a decrease in voter turnout compared with both the 2004 and 2008 elections.

■ 10.3 Choosing Candidates for Public Office: The Nomination Process

Approximately half a million people hold elective office in the United States. Candidates for nonpartisan offices, such as county sheriff, typically face one another in a single election. The candidate with the highest vote totals wins. For most national or state offices, however, candidates must compete for their party's nomination in a **primary election**. If they win this election, they go on to face the nominees of other parties in the **general election,** held later that year.

Primary Elections: Closed, Open, Blanket, and Nonpartisan

Primary elections, though common in the United States, are rare in the rest of the world. The idea of holding elections to choose a party's nominees was popularized during the Progressive Era in the early 1900s. Before then, nominees were often selected by party leaders who met behind closed doors. Primary elections brought the selection process out into the open and allowed party members to participate. Today, primary elections take several forms.

Closed primaries. States with a **closed primary** limit voting to registered party members. Independents are not allowed to participate. In some states, voters may declare their party affiliation on Election Day and vote in that party's primary. In general, party leaders prefer a closed primary because it limits voting to the party faithful.

Open primaries. States with an **open primary** allow all voters to vote in primary elections. In this system, also known as pick-a-party primaries, voters decide which party primary to vote in on Election Day. Independent voters like this system because it allows them to participate in the primary of their choice.

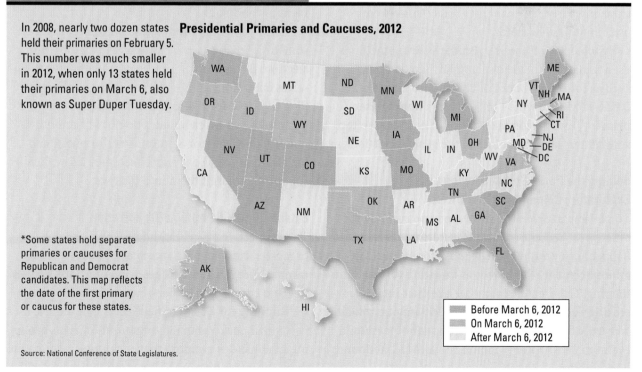

The Incredible Shrinking Primary Season

In 2008, nearly two dozen states held their primaries on February 5. This number was much smaller in 2012, when only 13 states held their primaries on March 6, also known as Super Duper Tuesday.

Presidential Primaries and Caucuses, 2012

*Some states hold separate primaries or caucuses for Republican and Democrat candidates. This map reflects the date of the first primary or caucus for these states.

Before March 6, 2012
On March 6, 2012
After March 6, 2012

Source: National Conference of State Legislatures.

In April 2011, Barack Obama declared his candidacy by posting a video that asked: "Are you in?" Obama both e-mailed supporters and "tweeted" a link to the video on Twitter, marking the beginning of a social media-centered election. Republican hopeful, Mitt Romney, announced his candidacy in New Hampshire. Later that day he posted a photograph of himself delivering this speech on Facebook with the words "Presidential Announcement" boldly written above it.

However, party leaders worry about "raiding" in open primaries. Raiding occurs when voters cross party lines to vote in the other party's primary. Usually their purpose is to help nominate a weak candidate that their own party nominee can then easily defeat in the general election.

Blanket primaries. In a **blanket primary,** voters can pick and choose one candidate for each office from any party's primary list. Today this system is used in only a few states.

Nonpartisan primaries. Primaries are sometimes used to narrow the field in nonpartisan contests, such as for school board or city council elections. If one candidate wins a majority in a **nonpartisan primary,** that person takes office. If not, the two top vote-getters face each other in the general election.

Joining the Race: Self-Announcement, Exploratory Committees, and Drafts

To participate in a primary, the person running for office must become a declared candidate. This can happen in several ways. The most common is **self-announcement,** also known as throwing your hat into the ring. Candidates simply declare their interest in seeking election to a public office. Self-announcement is usually done at a press conference or other public event. In 2007, Hillary Clinton chose to self-announce her candidacy for president on her Web site.

Before making a formal announcement, however, the candidate may form an **exploratory committee**. This is a group of advisers who evaluate the candidate's chances for election. Exploratory committees often take several weeks to test the waters and determine the level of public support for their candidate. If the committee decides that circumstances are favorable, the candidate makes a formal announcement of candidacy.

For presidential candidates, announcements are sometimes made as early as two years before the election. By announcing early, candidates give themselves extra time to raise the funds and the support they will need for the hard primary campaign ahead.

In some cases, candidates do not self-announce. Instead, they wait for a groundswell of public support for their candidacy. In effect, they allow their supporters to draft them into the race.

Establishing a Campaign Organization

To win elective office, candidates must run a well-organized campaign. In most cases, this requires a campaign organization. These organizations vary in size and complexity, depending on the race.

Running for a city council seat might require a very small, local campaign organization. This group might consist of no more than a volunteer campaign manager and a treasurer. The candidate works with this small team to write speeches, print posters and flyers, and manage other details of the campaign.

Running for president, on the other hand, demands a large, complex organization. A presidential race requires the services of hundreds of people, from unpaid volunteers to highly paid campaign professionals. Included in this staff would be a campaign manager, a public opinion pollster, a media consultant, a fundraising specialist, accountants, lawyers, and a press secretary. A presidential campaign organization would also have offices in every state. Of course, to set up and run such an organization requires money.

Building a War Chest by Dialing for Dollars

Jesse Unruh, a California politician, once observed, "Money is the mother's milk of politics." Without money, a political campaign cannot survive for long. This is true at all levels, whether a candidate is running for a local office or for president of the United States.

At the start of a campaign, candidates typically spend a great deal of time and energy raising money the old-fashioned way. They "dial for dollars," getting on the phone to ask associates and supporters for money. They hold fundraisers, such as $1,000-a-plate dinners, to solicit contributions from major donors. They also organize direct-mail campaigns and set up Web sites designed to attract funds from large numbers of small donors. If a candidate's fundraising efforts are successful, the campaign will build up a **war chest,** or funds that can be used to move the campaign forward.

During presidential primary campaigns, the candidate with the largest war chest is often hailed as the front-runner. During the 2000 election, for example, George W. Bush raised a record amount of money early in the campaign and became the leading Republican candidate. A year before the first presidential primaries in 2008, Hillary Clinton and Barack Obama were declared front-runners in the race for the Democratic nomination, based on their early success at raising record amounts of campaign funds.

Developing Campaign Strategies and Themes

In most states, the road to nomination in partisan races is the primary election. But some states use a different method: the party **caucus**. A caucus is a closed meeting of people from one political party who will select candidates or delegates.

In a caucus state, small groups of party members meet in their communities to discuss the various candidates. Each caucus then chooses delegates to represent its views at the party's state convention. Approximately a dozen states hold caucuses. The best known are the Iowa caucuses, which take place early in presidential election years. The Iowa caucuses are watched closely, because they provide the

Permission of Harley Schwadron

"15% like you as a conservative, 15% like you liberal, and 70% don't care . . . So my advice is to reinvent yourself as the 'I don't care' candidate."

In choosing a campaign theme and message, candidates often consult polls and pollsters. This cartoon takes aim at the kind of advice pollsters may give.

first indications of how well each candidate is doing at winning the support of average voters.

To prepare for caucuses and primaries, candidates must develop a campaign strategy. If this plan of action works well and the candidate wins the nomination, some of that strategy may carry over to the general election. Key elements of a strategy include tone, theme, and targeting.

Tone. Candidates must decide whether to adopt a positive or a negative tone for their campaigns. This means determining how much time and money to spend stressing the positive things about their candidacy and how much to spend criticizing their opponents.

Theme. Every candidate needs a theme—a simple, appealing idea that gets repeated over and over. A theme helps distinguish a candidate from his or her opponents in the primaries. It is also critical in the general election, when candidates from different parties compete. When running for reelection in 1984, Ronald Reagan emphasized optimism, as expressed in his slogan, "It's morning again in America." For the 2008 election, Barack Obama organized his campaign around the theme of change with the slogan "Yes we can." Obama continued with this theme for the 2012 presidential election. The slogan for this campaign was "Forward."

Targeting. Candidates must also decide whether to target specific groups of voters. Is there any group—blue-collar workers, women, the middle class, the elderly—that is particularly unhappy with the status quo? If so, that group is a likely target for specially designed appeals from candidates.

The Route to Nomination

To win elective office, candidates must first win their party's nomination. The process is similar for both congressional and presidential candidates. Presidential nominees, however, have the added step of the national convention.

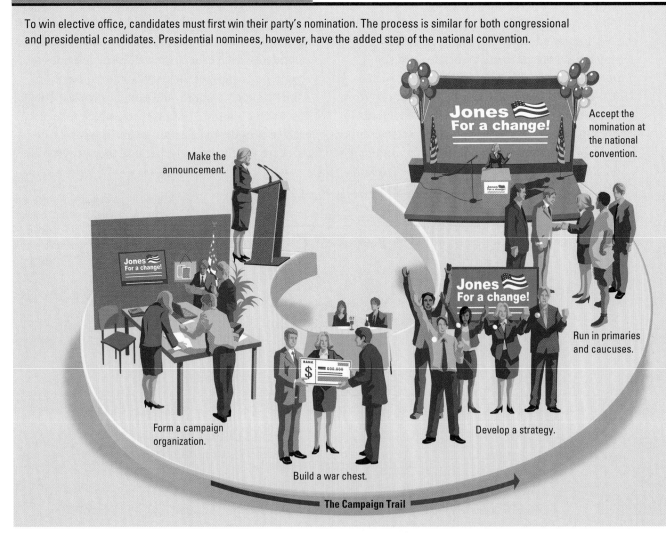

Make the announcement.

Accept the nomination at the national convention.

Form a campaign organization.

Run in primaries and caucuses.

Build a war chest.

Develop a strategy.

The Campaign Trail

Early in the primary season, presidential candidates, like Democratic hopeful Barack Obama, have time to meet and greet voters individually. As the season wears on, retail politics gives way to wholesale methods, designed to reach large numbers of voters. One popular forum is the televised debate. Here, Republican candidates for president debate during the 2011–2012 primary season.

Another aspect of campaign strategy is how to present the candidate's political views during the primaries as opposed to during the general election. For the primaries, candidates tend to couch their message in terms that will appeal to the **party base**. The party base consists of party activists who are more likely to vote in primary elections than less-committed centrists. This base also holds more extreme views than the average middle-of-the-road voter. As a result, candidates often emphasize more liberal or conservative views in the primaries than they would in a general election campaign.

Reaching the Voters: Retail Politics, Wholesale Politics, and Microtargeting

Candidates for public office try to reach voters in various ways, both during the primaries and in the run-up to the general election. Political scientists have identified three general approaches: **retail politics, wholesale politics,** and **microtargeting**.

Retail politics. This meet-and-greet style of campaigning relies on direct, personal contact with voters. Candidates take part in parades, dinners, and other local events. They stand outside factories and shopping malls to shake hands and kiss babies. During these face-to-face encounters with voters,

candidates try to present themselves as leaders who are in touch with ordinary people.

Wholesale politics. Many voters can be reached only by large-scale mail or media campaigns. Candidates may develop direct-mail campaigns, in which thousands of letters are sent to voters asking for their support. Even more common is the use of both paid and free media. Candidates and their staff prepare television ads and take part in televised town hall meetings and debates. These broadcasts can reach millions of people at a time. The Internet is also being used to reach voters on a large scale. Most candidates have a professional Web site that has an archive of campaign ads and a link that allows voters to directly donate to a campaign. Social media sites such as Twitter, Facebook, and Pinterest are also used to reach out to voters.

Microtargeting. This campaign approach uses databases to target narrow groups of voters and then reach them with carefully crafted messages. According to the *Washington Post*, candidates who adopt this technique "use the latest data-mining technology to vacuum every last scrap of information about voters." Armed with that data, they "churn out custom-tailored messages designed to herd their supporters to the polls." These messages present

National conventions are held after the primary season ends. They used to be part of the nominating process. Today, party gatherings are occasions for raising party spirit and cheering the party's nominee.

the candidate's position on issues of importance to each targeted group. For example, a candidate might target a message on social security to senior citizens.

Locking Up the Nomination

A few months before the presidential election, the Democratic and Republican parties each hold a national convention in a major American city. In the past, party conventions were a critical step in the nomination process. Party delegates would argue over the candidates, sometimes going through several ballots before picking a nominee. On occasion, an underdog would emerge from the pack to challenge, and even overtake, the leading candidate.

Today, however, presidential nominees are chosen through the primary and caucus process. The winner then announces his or her choice for vice president. The national convention has, as a result, evolved into a ritual to formally announce the party nominees and present them to the nation. The nominees also work with party leaders to frame a platform, laying out the party's position on major issues. In addition, the convention helps unite the party and excite the party base.

The Other Way to Run for Office: Nomination by Petition

Not all candidates for public office go through the usual nomination process. For independent or third-party candidates, there is another way to get on the ballot: by petition. The petition process involves collecting signatures of a specific number of qualified voters in support of one's candidacy. The number of signatures needed depends on the office being sought.

The laws governing nomination by petition differ from state to state. In 2008, a candidate running for president needed 1,000 valid signatures to be put on the ballot in Washington state. In contrast, North Carolina required a candidate to gather the number of signatures equal to 2 percent of the votes cast in the previous presidential election, or approximately 70,000 signatures.

These variations can make it difficult for independent and third-party candidates to get on the ballot in all 50 states. In 2000, for example, Ralph Nader, the presidential nominee for the Green Party, appeared on the ballot in 43 states. Four years later, Nader was able to qualify for the ballot in only 34 states.

■ 10.4 Campaigning in General Elections

Once the primary season ends, the candidates who have won their party's nomination shift gears to campaign in the general election. Although the Constitution calls for regularly scheduled elections, it does not specify when they should be held. Congress has set the date for presidential and midterm elections as the first Tuesday after the first Monday in November of even-numbered years. This is different from parliamentary systems, in which the prime minister can call a national election at any time.

Presidential, Midterm, and Off-Year Elections

There are three types of general elections in the United States: presidential, midterm, and off-year. **Presidential elections** are held every four years on even-numbered years. **Midterm elections** occur in the even-numbered years between presidential elections. **Off-year elections** are held in odd-numbered years.

Elected officials in the United States hold office for fixed terms. The Constitution sets the terms of the president and members of Congress. The only federal official affected by **term limits** is the president. The Twenty-second Amendment, ratified in 1951, limits the president to two terms in office. The terms for state officeholders are set by state constitutions.

Building a Winning Coalition: Motivating the Base While Moving Toward the Middle

Candidates gearing up for a general election must make a number of changes in their campaign strategy. One is to shift their attention from winning over fellow party members to taking on the nominee of the other major party.

To appeal to a larger cross-section of voters, many candidates also decide to modify their political message. In the primaries, the ideas and promises that appealed to the party base, with its more extreme views, may need to be moderated to attract centrists and independents. Ideally, however, this move to the middle should be done in a way that does not upset or alienate the party base.

Democrat John Kerry faced this delicate balancing act during the 2004 election. During the primary season, Kerry presented himself to party voters as an ardent critic of the war in Iraq. He did this, in part, to drain support away from his Democratic opponent, Howard Dean. Dean's strong antiwar views had fired up the party base.

The Three Types of General Elections

Type of Election	Who Gets Elected
Presidential Election Occurs every four years in even-numbered years	President and vice president One-third of the Senate All members of the House Some state and local officials
Midterm Election Occurs in even-numbered years between presidential elections	One-third of the Senate All members of the House Most state governors Some state and local officials
Off-Year Election Occurs in odd-numbered years	County supervisors City mayors City councils Most boards of special districts

Voting in General Elections

Voter turnout tends to be lower in midterm elections than in presidential elections, as the graph below indicates. Turnout in off-year elections is usually lower still.

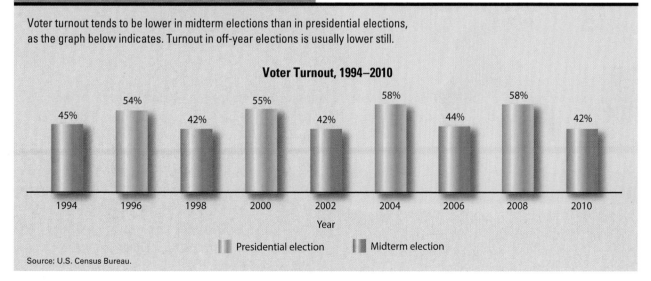

Voter Turnout, 1994–2010

1994: 45%
1996: 54%
1998: 42%
2000: 55%
2002: 42%
2004: 58%
2006: 44%
2008: 58%
2010: 42%

Year

Presidential election   Midterm election

Source: U.S. Census Bureau.

Once Kerry had won the nomination, however, he began moving to the middle. In the run-up to the general election, he tried to soften his antiwar message to win more support from moderate and independent voters. However, his efforts backfired when his Republican opponent, George W. Bush, accused him of being a "flip-flopper" on the war issue. Kerry stuck to his more centrist position for the rest of the campaign, but he lost the election to Bush.

Issues Versus Image: Stump Speeches, Photo Ops, and Televised Debates

In the weeks leading up to the general election, candidates continue to hone their message and polish their image for voters. They spend increased time on the campaign trail, making public appearances and giving variations of their standard **stump speech**. This term harkens back to the days when candidates would stand on a tree stump to deliver their speeches.

During these final weeks, candidates make every effort to remain in the public eye. One way to do this is to stage photo opportunities, or photo ops, for the media. The hope is that pictures of the event will appear on the nightly news and in the next morning's newspaper.

Politicians often use photo ops to portray themselves in a positive light. Here, Republican candidate Rick Perry poses with a young boy while campaigning for the Iowa caucus in 2012. Photographs like this one depict candidates as friendly, family-oriented people.

For congressional candidates, a favorite photo op involves joint appearances with the president or with their party's presidential nominee. The candidate hopes that being seen in public with such a powerful figure will give his or her campaign an extra boost. This boost, known as the **coattail effect,** may help a struggling candidate ride into office on the "coattails" of the next president.

The coattail effect does not always work as hoped. In 1992, Democrat Bill Clinton won the presidential election, but his coattails were too short to help fellow party members. The Democrats lost ten seats in Congress that year. Four years later, however, Clinton won reelection with longer coattails. In the 1996 election, the Democrats won eight seats in Congress. The coattail effect remains unpredictable, working for some candidates in some campaigns while having little effect in others.

Another way for candidates to boost their exposure is to take part in televised debates. In presidential elections, these debates offer many voters their first opportunity to see and hear the candidates discuss the issues in any depth. However, the image that candidates project in debates may be just as important as what they have to say. A candidate who is attractive, well-spoken, and relaxed during a debate will probably fare better than one who appears stiff and ill at ease on screen.

The impact of televised debates on voters is hard to assess. What candidates do in debates may sway some voters, while simply confirming for others the choice they have already made. Nonetheless, candidates prepare carefully for these televised events, knowing that even though a good performance may not win them that many votes, a poor showing could lose them the election.

Getting Out the Vote

In the last days before the election, campaign workers focus on getting out the vote. This means making sure that all voters who are likely to support their candidate actually cast their ballots.

In the past, almost all votes were cast at a designated **polling place** within each precinct. Today, the majority of Americans still go to the polls to vote on Election Day. However, a growing number of voters now cast **absentee ballots,** or mail-in ballots that voters can use instead of going to the polls. Since 2000, for example, the state of Oregon has conducted all of its elections by mail. A few states also allow early voting at designated voting places in the month before Election Day.

Campaign organizations use various tactics to get out the vote before and on Election Day. Before the election, volunteers talk with voters by phone or by walking through precincts and ringing doorbells to find out who is likely to support their candidate. On Election Day, they set up phone banks staffed by volunteers who call supporters and urge them to vote. The organizations may also offer free rides to voters who have no other way of getting to the polls.

Campaigns may also send **poll watchers** to polling places on Election Day. Poll watchers are volunteers who monitor the voting process. Their main job is to prevent voter fraud or efforts to intimidate voters. Poll watchers may also observe the tallying of ballots to ensure that all votes are properly counted.

Because most voting regulations are set by states and counties, voting methods and types of ballots have varied from one community to the next. In the past, most voters used some form of paper ballots or lever-controlled voting machines. Some paper ballots are relatively easy to use and count, while others are not. The infamous butterfly ballot used in Florida in the 2000 general election confused many voters. As a result, many voted for the wrong candidate by mistake.

Florida also had trouble with punch-card ballots in the 2000 election. Voters mark these ballots by punching out small bits of paper, called chads, beside their choices. Sometimes, however, the chad does not fully detach from the ballot. These "hanging chads" make it almost impossible for the machines used to count ballots to complete an accurate tally. Every time such ballots are fed through the vote-counting machine, it comes up with a different count.

Florida was not alone in having problems. Across the country in the 2000 elections, almost 2 million votes were not properly counted by vote-counting machines. To solve this problem, Congress enacted the Help America Vote Act of 2002. The goal of this act is to help states replace their old voting machines and punch-card ballots with more accurate voting technology, such as optical scanners and touch-screen machines. Progress, however, has been slow, in part because of questions raised about the accuracy and reliability of the newer electronic voting systems.

In Columbus, Ohio, these voters are using an electronic voting machine during an election. However, each voting method has some risk involved. Electronic voting, for example, is susceptible to technological "glitches" or malfunctions.

Who Wins?

Once the votes are counted, the winners are declared. In most presidential elections, the winner receives a majority of the popular vote. That was the case in 2004, when George W. Bush received 51 percent of the votes cast.

When three or more candidates are competing, the winner sometimes receives less than 50 percent of the vote. This occurred in both the 1992 and the 1996 elections, when Bill Clinton won the presidency with 43 percent and 49 percent of the popular vote, respectively. In both cases, a third-party candidate, Ross Perot, captured enough votes to prevent either of the major party candidates from winning a majority.

Our nation's winner-take-all system has a major effect on presidential elections. In most states, the candidate winning the popular vote captures all of that state's Electoral College votes. Nebraska and Maine, however, use a different system. They allot Electoral College votes based on the popular vote in each of the states' congressional districts.

Critics point out that the Electoral College system encourages candidates to focus on populous states with the largest number of electors. In theory, a candidate can win the presidency by capturing the 11 largest states and losing the other 39.

In general, candidates pay the most attention to a few **battleground states,** where the vote is likely to be close, and ignore states where the outcome is more predictable. For example, a Republican presidential candidate can expect to win Texas and other conservative southern states. Similarly, a Democratic candidate can expect to win Massachusetts and other liberal New England states. For that reason, both sides target states such as Ohio, Florida, and New Mexico, which can be won by either candidate.

Our winner-take-all-system tends to reinforce the nation's two-party system. Most public offices go to candidates of the two major parties because one or the other is likely to win the popular vote. Third parties, which usually have a narrower appeal, have much less hope of winning seats in Congress or state legislatures. Although the winner-take-all system promotes stability in government, it tends to exclude less-mainstream candidates from public office.

In contrast, many European democracies have adopted a **proportional representation** system. In these countries, citizens usually vote for parties rather than for individual candidates. A party wins seats in parliament based on its proportion of the popular vote. For example, if a party wins one-third of the vote in an election, it is awarded approximately one-third of the seats in parliament. Proportional representation thus gives smaller parties a chance to take part in government.

The Electoral College Debate

As important as the popular vote may seem, it is the Electoral College vote that decides presidential elections. The framers of the Constitution devised the Electoral College system because they did not trust voters who were spread out over 13 states to choose the head of the executive branch. Instead, they gave that responsibility to a group of electors who might better know who was best suited for that job.

At first, each state legislature chose its own electors. In 1789, all 69 electors who had been chosen this way cast their ballots for George Washington as president. A majority cast their votes for John Adams as vice president. After 1800, states began allowing voters to choose electors. When you vote for president in the next election, you will actually be voting for electors who have promised to support your candidate.

The number of electors from each state equals the number of that state's representatives in Congress. For example, Virginia has 2 senators and 11 House members, giving it a total of 13 electoral votes. Washington, D.C., has 3 electoral votes. There are 538 electors in all, which means that a candidate must win at least 270 electoral votes to become president. If no candidate wins a majority of elec-

States Up for Grabs

This map highlights the nine battleground states targeted by both major candidates in the 2012 presidential election. These states are so evenly divided between Democratic and Republican voters that they could swing either way, thereby adding crucial electoral votes to the winner's tally. Presidential campaigns spend far more time and money in battleground states than in states that already appear committed to one candidate or the other.

Battleground States, 2012

Source: CNN News, as of November 2012.

toral votes, the House of Representatives selects the president, with each state casting one vote.

Not surprisingly, the Electoral College system has provoked controversy over the years. The chief criticism is that it is undemocratic. Critics point to three elections in U.S. history—in 1876, 1888, and 2000—in which the candidate who won the popular vote failed to win the Electoral College. The most recent example was Al Gore's loss to George W. Bush in 2000.

For years, critics have called for a reform of the Electoral College. Most advocate electing the president by direct popular vote. This change would require a constitutional amendment.

However, many Americans also support the Electoral College system. Some states, especially smaller ones, fear that a reform would reduce their influence in presidential elections. Under the popular vote system, candidates might be motivated to only campaign in large states.

An alternative option is the congressional district method. Under this method, now used in Maine and Nebraska, the candidate who wins the popular vote in each congressional district gets that district's electoral vote. The overall winner in the state receives the two additional electoral votes that represent the state's senators. The consequence of this method is that if it was widespread, candidates might only focus on campaigning in specific districts rather than in entire states.

Another option is the national popular vote. Under this plan, states would cast their electoral votes for the winner of the national popular vote. This change can be implemented by state legislatures, thereby avoiding the need for a constitutional amendment. In 2007, Maryland became the first state to adopt this Electoral College reform. The reform will not go into effect, however, unless approved by enough states to constitute a majority of the Electoral College vote. Critics claim that there is little benefit to this method and argue that it diminishes federalism since it reduces the states' role in elections.

▮ 10.5 Financing Election Campaigns

In the United States today, elections are centered more on candidates than on political parties. This

Many Americans find the Electoral College system confusing at best—and at worst, undemocratic. Some would like to replace it with a system based on the popular vote. However, many highlight the benefits of this system, such as protecting the interests of smaller states and less populated areas.

was not always the case. At one time, candidates relied heavily on their parties to help them win elections. Today, however, candidates behave more like independent political actors than party representatives. They depend mainly on their own political skills and the efforts of their campaign organizations to get elected.

The High Cost of Running for Office

Money has played a large part in this shift from party-centered to candidate-centered elections. As campaigns have grown more expensive, candidates have come to rely increasingly on their own fundraising abilities or personal fortunes to win public office. For example, about $6 billion was spent on the 2012 presidential election campaigns. On average, winning candidates for a seat in the House of Representatives spent $1.5 million each. Winners of each Senate seat spent an average of $9.7 million. In future elections, the cost will likely be even higher.

The high cost of running for office is a concern for various reasons. Candidates with limited resources

American election campaigns center on candidates rather than on parties. Note the absence of party names on these campaign posters. In many other countries, the party affiliations of candidates play a much larger role in campaigns.

may find it hard to compete with those who are well funded. This lack of a level playing field inevitably excludes some people from running for office. In addition, officeholders must spend considerable time and energy building up their war chests for the next race, rather than focusing on the work of governing.

The main issue, however, is whether campaign contributions corrupt elected officials. When candidates win public office, do they use their positions to benefit big campaign donors? In other words, do politicians always "dance with the ones who brung them," as the old saying goes? Lawmakers generally say no, but the public is not so sure.

Two Strategies Guide Campaign Donations

Political scientists have observed that individuals and groups donating to campaigns choose from two basic strategies. The first is the electoral strategy. Donors that follow this strategy use their money to help elect candidates who support their views and to defeat those who do not. The goal is to increase the likelihood that Congress, their state legislature, or their city council will vote as the donor wishes it would vote.

The second is the access strategy. Donors following this approach give money to the most likely winner in a race, regardless of party. If the race looks close, the donor might even contribute to both campaigns. The goal is to gain access to whichever party wins the election. Donors using this strategy expect to be able to meet with the official they supported and present their views on issues of interest to them.

Political scientist Michael Smith points out that neither strategy involves trading money for a prom-

ise to vote a certain way on a piece of legislation. Indeed, offering money for votes is considered bribery and is clearly illegal. Donors found guilty of offering bribes—and lawmakers found guilty of accepting them—face prison sentences, not to mention ruined careers.

There have been well-publicized examples of such corruption. Nonetheless, political scientists find that most elected officials act according to their political principles, no matter who donates to their campaigns. Donors who make large contributions to campaigns might enjoy greater access to officeholders. But that access may or may not translate into influence over the actions of those officials.

Where Campaign Money Comes From

Almost all of the money used to fund election campaigns comes from private sources. A few wealthy candidates have been able to fund some or all of their campaigns from their own assets. In 2010, for example, Linda McMahon of Connecticut spent $50 million of her own money on an unsuccessful bid for a seat in the U.S. Senate. The great majority of candidates, however, must reach out to their supporters for funding.

Most campaign funds come from individual citizens. These donations are often raised through direct-mail or Internet fundraising campaigns. And they are typically fairly small, in the $25 to $100 range. Candidates also host fundraisers to raise money from large donors. In 2011–2012, the amount of money an individual could donate to a single candidate was limited by law to $2,500 for the primary campaign and another $2,500 for the general election. These figures are periodically adjusted for inflation.

In recent years, political action committees have become an important source of campaign funds. PACs are organizations formed by corporations, labor unions, or interest groups to channel funds into political campaigns. Similar to individual donations, PAC contributions to a single candidate are limited to $5,000 for the primary campaign and another $5,000 for the general election.

Public Funding of Campaigns

Another source of money for some candidates is public funds. A few states, such as Arizona and New Hampshire, use public money to finance campaigns for governor and state lawmakers. At the federal level, only presidential candidates receive public funding. This money comes from taxpayers who check a $3 donation box on their income tax forms. The money accumulates between elections and is made available for both primary and general election campaigns.

To qualify for public funds, a candidate must raise at least $5,000 in each of 20 states in small contributions of $250 or less. Once qualified, candidates can receive federal matching funds of up to $250 for each additional contribution they receive. The purpose of these provisions is to encourage candidates to rely mainly on small contributions from average voters.

Where Campaign Money Comes From

Candidates running for federal office raise funds in various ways. Donors in some parts of the country contribute far more to campaigns than do others. In 2012, California topped the nation in terms of total contributions, with New York and Texas in second and third place, respectively.

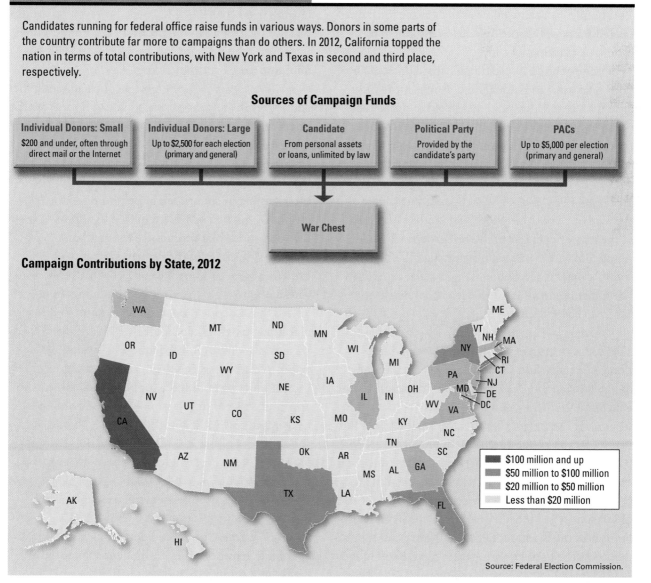

Sources of Campaign Funds

Individual Donors: Small	Individual Donors: Large	Candidate	Political Party	PACs
$200 and under, often through direct mail or the Internet	Up to $2,500 for each election (primary and general)	From personal assets or loans, unlimited by law	Provided by the candidate's party	Up to $5,000 per election (primary and general)

War Chest

Campaign Contributions by State, 2012

$100 million and up
$50 million to $100 million
$20 million to $50 million
Less than $20 million

Source: Federal Election Commission.

Public funds come with a catch. Candidates who receive public money must agree to limit their campaign spending. As a result, politicians are often hesitant about accepting public funds.

The future of public funding for presidential elections looks uncertain for two reasons. One is a drop-off in taxpayer donations for this purpose. The other is a growing reluctance among presidential hopefuls to accept public funds and to limit their campaign spending.

Reining in Soft Money and Issue Ads

In 1974, Congress created the Federal Election Commission to enforce laws that limit campaign contributions. The FEC requires candidates to keep accurate records of donations to their campaigns and to make those records available to the public. This public disclosure allows voters to see the names of all donors who contribute $200 or more to any candidate running for office.

Some Americans question if campaign contributions give some individuals and groups more influence than others. Research has failed to prove that members of Congress sell their votes in exchange for campaign contributions. However, despite this lack of evidence, the potential influence of campaign contributions has led to some regulation.

Despite FEC oversight, campaign spending spiraled upward during the 1980s and 1990s. Much of the money came from interest groups who had found loop-holes in existing campaign finance laws. Calls for reform led to the passage of the Bipartisan Campaign Reform Act in 2002, also known as the McCain-Feingold Act.

The new law attempted to solve two problems. The first was the use of **soft money** to fund election campaigns. Soft money is unregulated money donated to a political party for such purposes as voter education. In theory, soft money was not to be used to support campaigns. For this reason, it was not limited by campaign funding laws. In practice, however, parties used soft money to help candidates fund their election bids, thus boosting campaign spending.

The Bipartisan Campaign Reform Act bans the use of soft money in individual election campaigns. It also limits how much soft money an individual can contribute to a party. Furthermore, parties can use soft money only to encourage voter registration and voter turnout.

The second problem was the use of **issue ads** in campaigns. Issue ads are political ads that are funded and produced by interest groups rather than by election campaigns. In theory, these ads focus on issues rather than on candidates. Thus, like soft money, they were not regulated by campaign finance laws. In practice, however, many issue ads were barely disguised campaign ads. For example, such an ad might discuss a pollution problem and then suggest that "Bill Jones," a lawmaker up for reelection, is "a friend of polluters." Even though the ad did not say, "Vote against Bill Jones," its intention would be to influence how voters viewed the lawmaker.

The Bipartisan Campaign Reform Act bans the broadcast of such thinly disguised campaign ads in the 60 days leading up to an election. This part of the law has been challenged in court, however, by groups that see the ban as an unconstitutional limit on their First Amendment right to free speech. In 2007, the Supreme Court ruled in *Federal Election Commission v. Wisconsin Right to Life* that such ads could be banned "only if the ad is susceptible of no reasonable interpretation other than as an appeal to vote for or against a specific candidate."

Finally, the act contains a "stand by your ad" rule that requires candidates to take responsibility for their campaign commercials. Beginning in the 2004 elections, candidates were required to appear in their own ads and explicitly endorse the content.

One side effect of the reform act has been the growth of groups known as **527 committees**. These organizations are formed under Section 527 of the tax code. Because they are not tied to a political party or candidate, they are allowed to raise and spend unlimited amounts to support or oppose candidates. In effect, 527 committees and their donors have found a loophole that allows the continued use of unregulated soft money in political campaigns. As Senator John McCain, one of the sponsors of the 2002 reform law, pointed out, "Money, like water, will look for ways to leak back into the system."

Super PACs have also emerged as significant backers of political candidates. Unlike PACs, Super PACs may accept unlimited donations for political spending. However, they cannot coordinate with candidates or directly fund campaigns.

In 2010, two federal court cases paved the way for Super PACs. The first was *Citizens United v. Federal Election Commission*. In 2008, Citizens United, a conservative group, created a documentary of democratic candidate Hillary Clinton after FEC advertised a documentary that criticized the Bush Administration. FEC prevented Citizens United from running ads promoting the film in 2009. The case came to the Supreme Court that same year. In 2010, the Court held that under the First Amendment, the Government cannot limit corporate political spending in candidate elections.

The second case is *Speechnow.org v. FEC*. The 527 committee Speechnow gathered funds from individuals, not corporations, to endorse the election or defeat of federal candidates. In 2007, FEC informed Speechnow that it must register as a PAC if within one year it raised or spent over $1,000 for federal elections. As a result, Speechnow and other individuals disputed the constitutionality of the FEC Act. They argued that by requiring a group to register as a PAC and limiting the amount an individual could donate to a PAC, it violated a person's freedom of speech. The case reached the U.S. Court of Appeals. In 2010, the court ruled that the government cannot limit contributions of groups that do not directly contribute to candidates.

■ 10.6 Voter Behavior

Elections are important in a democracy. They allow citizens to participate in government. They also serve to check the power of elected officials. When voters go to the polls, they hold officials accountable for their actions. In *The Federalist Papers,* James Madison observed that elections compel leaders

> *to anticipate the moment when their power is to cease, when their exercise of it is to be reviewed, and when they must descend to the level from which they were raised; there forever to remain unless a faithful discharge of their trust shall have established their title to a renewal of it.*

> —James Madison,
> *The Federalist* No. 57, 1788

Many people believe that major donors to campaigns have too much influence in U.S. politics. Campaign finance laws have had some success in limiting special interest donations to candidates. In addition, Americans can still vote leaders out of office if the leaders do a poor job.

Elections are one of the things that distinguish a democracy from a dictatorship. Nevertheless, many Americans do not vote.

Who Does and Does Not Vote

In any given election, as many as two-thirds of all Americans who could vote do not do so. When asked, nonvoters offer a number of reasons for not going to the polls. Many say they are just too busy. Others cite illness or lack of interest. Political scientists who study voting point to three differences between voters and nonvoters: age, education, and income.

Age. The percentage of people voting varies among different age groups. Most voters are over the age of 30, and voting tends to increase with age. Once voters reach 75, however, turnout begins to decline, mostly due to ill health. The younger a person is, the less likely he or she is to vote. In the 2008 presidential election, slightly under half of all those in the 18 to 24 age group went to the polls. In contrast, over 72 percent of those in the 64 to 75 age group voted that year.

Education. Voting also varies by level of education. Americans with college educations vote in much higher numbers than do high school dropouts. Over three-fourths of all eligible voters with Bachelor's degrees voted in 2008. Less than one-third of

Young adults do not vote at the rate that older Americans do. The result may be an age bias among lawmakers, who are more responsive to the voters who elected them.

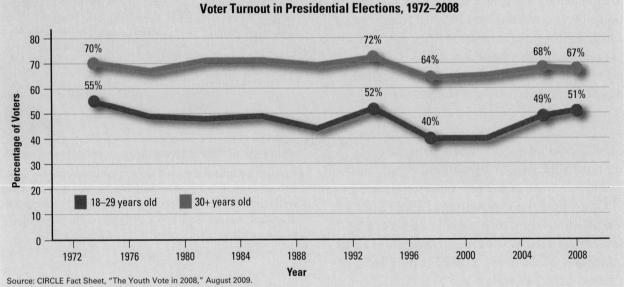

Voter Turnout in Presidential Elections, 1972–2008

Source: CIRCLE Fact Sheet, "The Youth Vote in 2008," August 2009.

those who left high school without graduating cast ballots.

Income. Voting also varies with income group. Middle-class and wealthy Americans are much more likely to vote than are those living in poverty. This difference may, in part, reflect the fact that income and education are closely intertwined. However, there may be other barriers to voting among the poor. People working at low-wage jobs, for example, may find it difficult to get time off work or to find transportation to the polls on Election Day.

How Voters Choose Among Candidates

When deciding how to vote, Americans tend to look at three things: the candidate's party affiliation, the candidate's position on issues raised in the campaign, and the candidate's characteristics.

Party affiliation. The party a candidate belongs to is the most critical factor that voters consider when choosing who to vote for. Most Americans still align themselves with a party and vote for its candidates. This is particularly true when voters are not familiar with the candidates' views or experience.

Issues. The issues raised in a campaign are a second factor that voters consider when evaluating candidates. This is particularly true of independent or **swing voters,** who do not have a strong party affiliation. These voters tend to look for candidates who hold positions on the issues that are similar to their own positions.

Candidate characteristics. Voters also choose candidates based on the candidate's personal characteristics. These characteristics can be superficial, such as the candidate's image or appearance. Voters may be drawn to candidates who seem friendly, trustworthy, or "presidential." A candidate's characteristics also include his or her skills and experience. For example, a candidate might have a long record of public service that gives voters confidence in that person's ability to govern.

This last point touches on another important factor for many voters: whether a candidate is an **incumbent** already holding office. Unless incumbents have performed poorly, voters tend to regard them as more reliable and experienced than their opponents. As a result, voters are much more likely to vote for an incumbent over an untested challenger.

Is Nonvoting a Serious Problem?

Obviously, it is desirable for citizens in a democracy to participate in elections. But how serious a problem is nonvoting? Does nonvoting behavior mean that people have lost hope in their ability to make a difference? Political scientists present two opposing views on these questions.

One view is that nonvoting has negative effects on American society. When groups, such as poorer or younger Americans, do not vote, they are effectively denied representation in government. This situation can set up a vicious cycle in which certain people do not vote because government does not serve their needs, and government does not serve their needs because those people do not vote.

Another, more positive view is that nonvoting represents a basic level of satisfaction among the population. According to this theory, many people do not vote because they are happy with the way things are. If they were not, they would make the effort to vote.

The U.S. Census Bureau surveys nonvoters after each election to find out why they did not vote. This table shows some of the reasons offered for not voting in the 2008 election.

Summary

Elections play a major role in American politics. We have more elections and elected officials than most other democracies. At the same time, the electoral process is complicated and expensive, and many voters do not participate.

Suffrage Early in our nation's history, suffrage was limited to white males. As a result of laws and constitutional amendments, almost all citizens 18 and older now enjoy the right to vote.

Primaries and caucuses Most candidates for public office must first win the nomination of their party. To do so, they compete in primary elections and caucuses for the support of party members.

General elections The nominees of each party face each other in general elections. There are three types of general elections: presidential, midterm, and off-year.

Campaign finance Money is a key factor in elections. Congress set up the Federal Election Commission to regulate fundraising and spending by candidates in federal elections. Nonetheless, the amount of money raised for and spent on elections continues to rise.

Voter behavior Voting varies with age, education, and income. Voters make choices based on party, issues, and candidate characteristics. Experts differ on whether nonvoting represents a serious problem or reflects a level of satisfaction with U.S. politics.

Should voting be voluntary?

Whether or not you agree that low voter turnout is a serious problem, it seems clear that our government would be more representative if more people voted. Low turnout is especially common among younger voters. Would you be more likely to turn out to vote if voting were no longer voluntary? Or if you might be fined or even jailed for not voting? Think about this as you read about other countries that have transformed voting from a civic responsibility to a legal duty.

Compulsory Voting

by the International Institute for Democracy and Electoral Assistance

Most democratic governments consider participating in national elections a right of citizenship. Some consider that participation at elections is also a citizen's civic responsibility. In some countries, where voting is considered a duty, voting at elections has been made compulsory and has been regulated in the national constitutions and electoral laws. Some countries go as far as to impose sanctions on nonvoters.

Compulsory voting is not a new concept. Some of the first countries that introduced mandatory voting laws were Belgium in 1892, Argentina in 1914, and Australia in 1924. There are also examples of countries such as Venezuela and the Netherlands, which at one time in their history practiced compulsory voting but have since abolished it.

Arguments for Compulsory Voting

Advocates of compulsory voting argue that decisions made by democratically elected governments are more legitimate when higher proportions of the population participate. They argue further that voting, voluntarily or otherwise, has an educational effect upon the citizens. Political parties can derive financial benefits from compulsory voting, since they do not have to spend resources convincing the electorate that it should in general turn out to vote. Lastly, if democracy is government by the people, presumably this includes all people. Then it is every citizen's responsibility to elect their representatives.

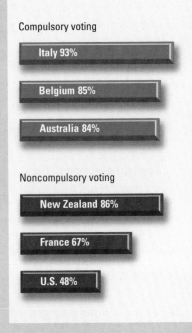

Average Voter Turnout in Selected Countries

Compulsory voting

Italy 93%

Belgium 85%

Australia 84%

Noncompulsory voting

New Zealand 86%

France 67%

U.S. 48%

Views on Compulsory Voting

Support for compulsory voting varies from country to country. It is high in Australia, where voting has been compulsory for almost a century. It is lower in other democracies where voting has always been voluntary. When asked in 2004 whether they would support a law requiring citizens to vote in national elections, only about one American in five answered yes. When compulsory voting was discussed at the National Commission on Federal Election Reform, former U.S. attorney general Griffin Bell summed up the sentiment of many Americans when he said, "This is not a free country when you are doing things like that."

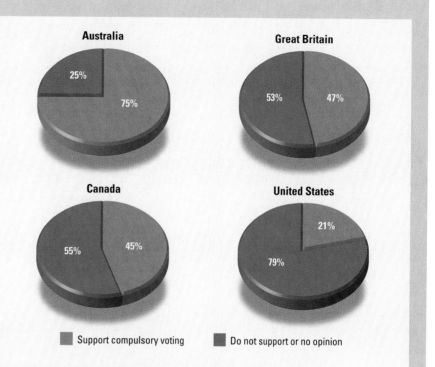

Australia
25%
75%

Great Britain
53% 47%

Canada
55% 45%

United States
21%
79%

■ Support compulsory voting   ■ Do not support or no opinion

Source: Martin P. Wattenberg, *Is Voting for Young People?*, New York: Pearson Education, 2007. Attributed to 2004 Australian Election Study, 2001 MORI survey for UK Electoral Commission, Elections Canada 2002 survey, and June 2004 ABC News survey.

Arguments Against Compulsory Voting

The leading argument against compulsory voting is that it is not consistent with the freedom associated with democracy. Voting is not an intrinsic obligation, and the enforcement of the law would be an infringement of the citizens' freedom ... [Compulsory voting] may discourage the political education of the electorate because people forced to participate will react against the perceived source of oppression.

Is a government really more legitimate if the high voter turnout is against the will of the voters? Many countries with limited financial capacity may not be able to justify the expenditures of maintaining and enforcing compulsory voting laws. It has been proved that forcing the population to vote results in an increased number of invalid and blank votes compared to countries that have no compulsory voting laws.

Another consequence of mandatory voting is the possible high number of "random votes." Voters who are voting against their free will may check off a candidate at random, particularly the top candidate on the ballot. The voter does not care whom they vote for as long as the government is satisfied that they fulfilled their civic duty. What effect does this unmeasureable category of random votes have on the legitimacy of the democratically elected government? ...

The International Institute for Democracy and Electoral Assistance is an intergovernmental organization based in Sweden. Its objective is to strengthen democratic institutions and processes around the world.

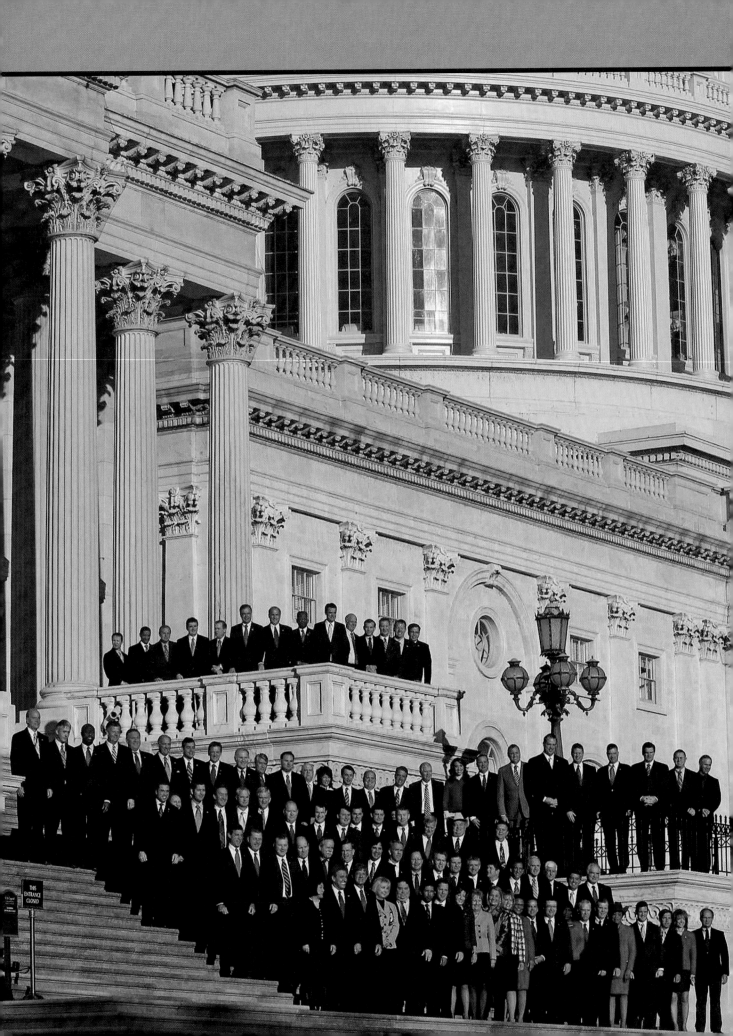

Chapter 11

Lawmakers and Legislatures

What makes an effective legislator?

■ 11.1 Introduction

Do you have what it takes to be a successful legislator? Consider these questions:

- Do you have a burning desire to serve the people and a willingness to work long hours doing the public's business?
- Are you prepared to apply common sense and sound moral judgment to the issues of the day?
- Do you possess the fortitude to read and digest documents that may be hundreds or even thousands of pages long?
- Do you value compromise?
- Are you brave enough to vote your conscience, even if it means going against the wishes of your party or the voters who elected you?

Even if you answered yes to these questions, lawmaking still may not be the career for you. As with most people who enjoy their work, one of the main goals of lawmakers is to keep their jobs. This means that along with other duties, they must always be thinking about how to stay in office. Political scientist David Mayhew makes this point in *Congress: The Electoral Connection,* his 1974 study of members of Congress:

> *It seems fair to characterize the modern Congress as an assembly of professional politicians spinning out political careers. The jobs offer good pay and high prestige. There is no want of applicants for them. Successful pursuit of a career requires continual reelection.*

Members of Congress gather before the Capitol

Speaking of Politics

constituent
A person who lives in an electoral district and is represented by an elected official.

pork
Publicly funded projects secured by legislators to benefit their home districts or states. The funds for such projects are said to come from the "pork barrel"—the state or national treasury.

standing committee
A permanent committee of legislators from either the House or Senate responsible for specific policy areas, such as foreign affairs or agriculture.

joint committee
A permanent committee of legislators from both the House and Senate that deals with matters of common interest, such as economic policy.

conference committee
A temporary committee of legislators from both the House and Senate created to work out differences in bills passed by both houses of Congress.

appropriations
Funds allocated by a legislature for a stated purpose as part of a budget or spending bill.

joint resolution
An official statement issued by both houses of Congress. Once signed by the president, a joint resolution has the force of law.

casework
Personal services provided by members of Congress to their constituents, often to help their constituents with problems they are having with the federal bureaucracy.

With Mayhew's observation in mind, think again about what you would need to be a successful legislator.

- You must be "electable"—charming, at ease speaking to crowds, and willing to tailor your views to match the results of public opinion polls.
- You must be able to raise money, and lots of it, to finance your election campaign.
- Once elected, you must become skilled at playing political games.
- When seeking reelection, you must show that you were able to bring taxpayer-funded projects back to your home district or state.

None of this means that you should abandon your idealism. Most politicians seek public office to pursue worthy goals, including making good public policy. Nonetheless, to be a first-rate legislator, you must learn how to enter and survive the rough-and-tumble world of politics.

Paul Ryan (R-WI) was elected to the House in 1998. He became the chair of the House Budget Committee in 2011. In 2012, Ryan was the Republican Vice President nominee in the presidential election. Although he was not elected to that position, he kept the support of his constituents and won an eighth term as a representative.

■ 11.2 Legislators and Their Constituents

Most legislators start out in local politics. They may have won election to the city council and then moved from there to the state legislature. Once they have gathered experience, they may try for a seat in the House of Representatives or the Senate. As lawmakers move upward on the legislative path, they serve an ever-widening group of **constituents,** or people in their home districts and states. To attain any of these positions, however, an individual must first meet certain qualifications.

Formal Qualifications: Age and Citizenship Requirements

The Constitution establishes formal qualifications for members of Congress. Members of both the House and the Senate must be residents of the state in which they are elected. They also need to meet minimum age and citizenship requirements. House members must be at least 25 years old and U.S. citizens for at least seven years. Senators must be at least 30 years old and U.S. citizens for at least nine years.

The formal qualifications for lawmakers at the state and local level are often less stringent. Young adults not long out of high school may qualify for election to school boards, town councils, or even state legislatures. In 2012, 21-year-old Justin Chenette of Maine became the youngest state legislator in the country. Chenette believes in the importance of youth involvement in politics. "It is important to get involved in the process," he told a reporter. "I want to reaffirm to young people why voting is important."

Informal Qualifications: Race, Gender, Education, and Occupation

In addition to the formal requirements for office, lawmakers may also need to meet certain informal, or unstated, qualifications. These are essentially the qualities and characteristics that people look for in their public officials.

These informal qualifications have changed somewhat over the years. James Madison and the other framers of the Constitution had in mind a certain set of high-minded and highly educated people to lead the country. Madison described them this way:

A chosen body of citizens, whose wisdom may best discern the true interest of their country, and whose patriotism and love of justice will be least likely to sacrifice it to temporary or partial considerations.

—James Madison, *The Federalist* No. 10, 1787

For some 200 years, that "chosen body of citizens" was largely made up of lawmakers who were white, male, and middle to upper class.

In the 1960s and 1970s, women and members of minority groups began to challenge the idea that all lawmakers should be successful white men. By the late 1960s, a few hundred women had won election to state legislatures and Congress. By 2012, that number had swelled to about 1,840 women serving as state or national lawmakers.

African Americans, Latinos, and members of other ethnic groups also were elected to legislatures in growing numbers. In 1971, for example, a combined total of 21 African Americans and Latinos held seats in Congress. By 2011, that number had risen to 68.

Beyond race and gender, however, at least two other informal qualifications still exist: education and occupation. Most legislators today have a college degree, and many have advanced degrees. The majority also have a background in business or law.

The Changing Composition of Congress

In the past, Congress was mostly made up of well-educated white males who worked in law or business. Since the 1970s, however, Congress has become more diverse. Moreover, a growing number of representatives and senators now see public service and politics as their occupation.

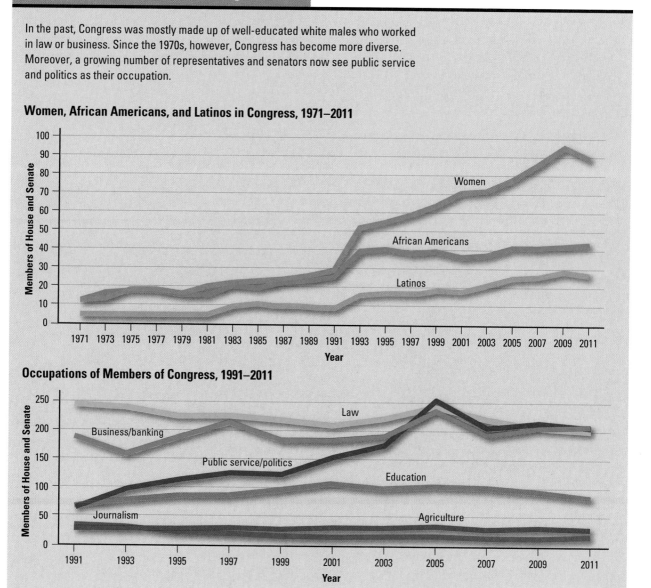

Women, African Americans, and Latinos in Congress, 1971–2011

Occupations of Members of Congress, 1991–2011

Source: Harold W. Stanley and Richard G. Niemi, *Vital Statistics on American Politics 2011–2012*, Los Angeles: CQ Press, 2011.

Apportionment: Achieving Equal Representation

The U.S. Senate has a total of 100 seats, two for each state. The House of Representatives has 435 seats, with each seat representing one congressional district. The number of seats in the House was fixed by law in 1911 and can be changed by Congress at any time.

House seats are apportioned, or divided, among the states according to each state's population. Here is how apportionment works: Every ten years, the U.S. Census Bureau conducts a census to count the nation's population. The results are used to calculate how House seats should be distributed among the states. If a state's population has boomed, it may gain one or more additional seats. If its population has dropped or stayed the same, it may lose one or more seats. Each state, however, is guaranteed at least one seat in the House. This map shows how the states fared in the apportionment following the 2010 census.

The constitutional principle behind apportionment is equal representation, also referred to as "one person, one vote." In practice, this means that each congressional district should have about the same number of people. As of the 2010 census, the number of people represented by each member of the House averaged about 710,700.

The principle of "one person, one vote" also applies to the apportionment of seats in state legislatures and even local governments. The principle does not apply to the U.S. Senate, however, where each state has an equal voice, regardless of its population. As a result, the nation's least populous state, Wyoming, has as much clout in the Senate as does the most populous state, California. However, the two senators from Wyoming represent just over half a million people, while the two from California represent more than 37 million people.

Congressional Apportionment and Representation

The map shows how the 435 House seats were apportioned after the 2010 census. Changes in population meant that some states gained seats while others lost seats. The apportionment based on the 2010 census took effect in 2013.

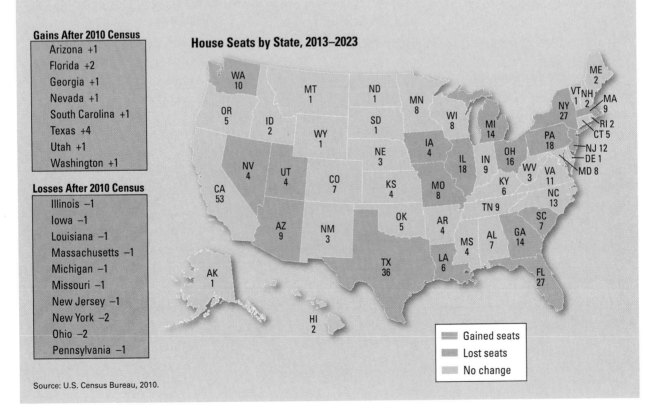

Gains After 2010 Census

Arizona	+1
Florida	+2
Georgia	+1
Nevada	+1
South Carolina	+1
Texas	+4
Utah	+1
Washington	+1

Losses After 2010 Census

Illinois	−1
Iowa	−1
Louisiana	−1
Massachusetts	−1
Michigan	−1
Missouri	−1
New Jersey	−1
New York	−2
Ohio	−2
Pennsylvania	−1

House Seats by State, 2013–2023

Gained seats
Lost seats
No change

Source: U.S. Census Bureau, 2010.

How Legislators See Their Jobs: Delegates Versus Trustees

Legislators often see themselves as fulfilling one of two distinct roles: that of a delegate or that of a trustee. Lawmakers who view themselves as delegates seek to represent their districts by responding directly to the wishes or needs of their constituents. In effect, they act as they think the people who voted them into office want them to act. This role is often embraced most enthusiastically by first-time lawmakers who are fairly new to the legislative process.

Lawmakers who see themselves as trustees, on the other hand, try to represent their districts by exercising their best independent judgment. Often, these are more experienced lawmakers who recognize that their constituents have conflicting needs that cannot always be met. In making decisions, these lawmakers try to serve the larger interests of their districts, assuming that their constituents trust them to do the right thing.

Most legislators combine these two roles. They may act as a delegate on issues clearly linked to the needs of their home districts. But on more general issues, or on issues over which there is much disagreement, they may take on the role of trustee.

Getting Elected: Turnover and the Power of Incumbency

Once elected, many legislators stay in office as long as voters keep reelecting them. Other legislators would like to serve longer, but term limits force them to leave office after a certain number of years. Term limits affect only state legislators, however. In 1995, the Supreme Court ruled that the terms of members of Congress cannot be limited except by a constitutional amendment.

Lawmakers who run for office term after term stand a very good chance of being reelected. Since 1945, representatives running for another term in the House have won reelection approximately 90 percent of the time. Around 80 percent of incumbent senators have won their reelection bids. Clearly, incumbents have a number of advantages over their challengers, including the four listed below.

Name recognition. Voters are familiar with incumbents. They see incumbents in news coverage, looking authoritative and effective. Voters tend to trust them more than unfamiliar challengers.

A NEW NATIONAL ICON – HEARTLAND CITY, USA

Members of Congress try to "bring home the bacon" to their districts by securing federal funding for local projects. Critics often label such projects as wasteful "pork." Constituents generally welcome the benefits these federally funded projects provide. But as this cartoon implies, such "pork barrel" projects can also be a waste of taxpayer money.

Office resources. Incumbents can use the benefits of their office—staff, stationery, mailing privileges, and travel allowances—to keep in touch with voters in their districts.

Campaign funds. Individuals and organizations give money in larger amounts to incumbents than to challengers. In the 2012 elections for the House and Senate, for example, incumbents raised roughly $971 million, while their challengers raised about $398 million.

Bragging rights. Incumbents can point to federally funded projects—from roads and bridges to defense contracts—that they have won for their districts. Such projects are known as **pork,** because the money for them comes from the federal "pork barrel," or treasury. Legislators who secure large amounts of pork for their home districts are admired for "bringing home the bacon." Challengers typically lack such bragging rights.

These advantages do not mean that incumbents always win. If voters think that Congress has failed to deal effectively with important issues, they may respond by voting incumbents out of office at the next election.

11.3 The Organization of Congress

The framers of the Constitution viewed Congress as "the first branch of government." In *The Federalist* No. 51, James Madison wrote, "In republican government, the legislative authority necessarily predominates." For that reason, the Constitution addresses the structure and powers of Congress first, ahead of the other two branches.

A Bicameral Legislature: The House and Senate

The Constitution establishes Congress as a bicameral legislature, consisting of the House of Representatives and the Senate. Although both chambers serve as lawmaking bodies, they are different in many respects. The lists at the bottom of this diagram highlight some of those differences.

The framers expected the House, with its larger size and more frequent elections, to act as the "people's body." It was meant to reflect the more volatile, democratic tendencies in American society. The Senate, whose members serve longer terms and were originally chosen by state legislatures, was meant to be a more elite chamber that would act as a steadying influence on Congress.

George Washington aptly described the Senate's role while dining with Thomas Jefferson. Jefferson wondered why the framers had added a second house. Washington asked him, "Why did you pour that coffee into your saucer?"

"To cool it," Jefferson replied.

"Even so," Washington said, "we pour legislation into the senatorial saucer to cool it."

In 1913, with the ratification of the Seventeenth Amendment, the Senate became elected directly by voters instead of by state legislatures. Today, unlike the bicameral legislatures in most countries, the two houses of Congress are equal in power. Even so, the houses are clearly different, and the Senate still serves to "cool" legislation coming from the House.

The Two Chambers of Congress

The Capitol building in Washington, D.C., houses the U.S. Congress. Construction on the Capitol began in 1793, but the building has been substantially remodeled and expanded since then. New wings for the House and Senate were completed in 1868, after the Civil War.

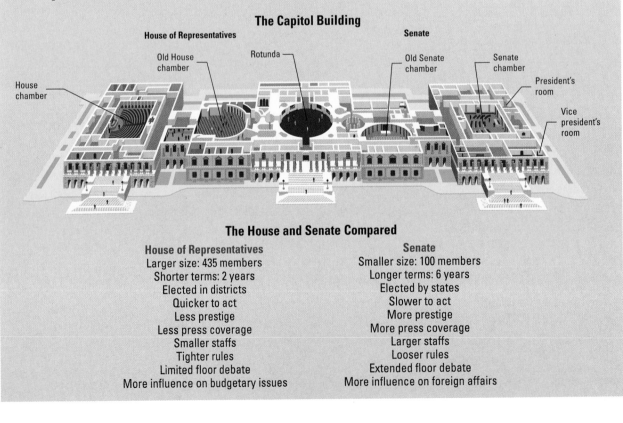

The Capitol Building

The House and Senate Compared

House of Representatives	Senate
Larger size: 435 members	Smaller size: 100 members
Shorter terms: 2 years	Longer terms: 6 years
Elected in districts	Elected by states
Quicker to act	Slower to act
Less prestige	More prestige
Less press coverage	More press coverage
Smaller staffs	Larger staffs
Tighter rules	Looser rules
Limited floor debate	Extended floor debate
More influence on budgetary issues	More influence on foreign affairs

Congressional Leadership

In 2007, Nancy Pelosi (D-CA) became the first woman to serve as speaker of the House, making her the highest ranking female politician of all time. However, when the Republicans gained control of the House in 2011, John Boehner (R-OH) took over that position and Pelosi became the minority leader.

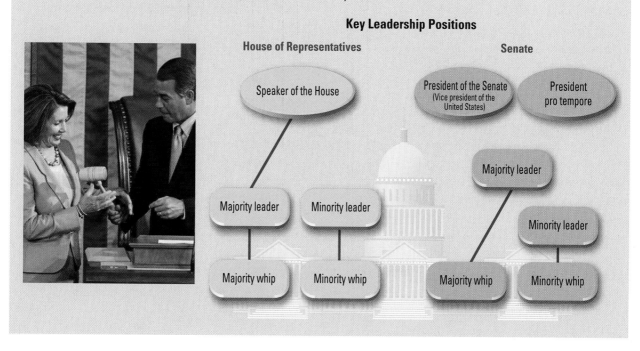

Key Leadership Positions

Leadership Roles in the House

Since the mid-1800s, Congress has based its organization on the two major political parties. In each house, the majority party—the one with the most seats—controls the agenda. Its members take the top leadership positions. The minority party, however, can have a significant impact in Congress, in part by choosing able leaders.

There are three leadership roles in the House: the speaker, the majority and minority leaders, and the whips.

Speaker of the House. The House speaker has more power and prestige than any other leader in Congress. The speaker is nominated by the majority party but wins the position through a vote of the entire House. The speaker presides over the House, assigns bills to committees, and appoints members to special committees and commissions. The speaker's most important function, however, may be deciding what bills will be debated by the full House and when. As former speaker Thomas P. (Tip) O'Neill said, "The power of the speaker of the House is the power of scheduling."

Majority and minority leaders. In the House, the majority and minority leaders are elected by their respective parties. Their duty is to manage legislation on the House floor, the large chamber in the Capitol where House members debate and vote on bills. The majority leader is the majority party's second in command. The minority leader is the minority party's overall leader and main strategist.

Majority and minority whips. These assistant floor leaders are responsible for keeping the leadership informed and persuading party members to vote along party lines. The term whip was first used in the British Parliament. In England, a whip is the person who keeps the dogs under control during a fox hunt.

Leadership Roles in the Senate

Leaders in the Senate have similar roles to those in the House. They are responsible for the functioning of their chamber. They also work to build support for legislation that advances their party's core policies. The leadership positions in the Senate are the president, majority and minority leaders, and whips.

President of the Senate. The president of the Senate is the official presiding officer of this body. The Constitution assigns this position to the vice president of the United States. In general, however, the vice president appears on the Senate floor only for ceremonies or to break a tie vote.

President of the Senate pro tempore. The president of the Senate pro tempore is the senior senator of the majority party and may preside over Senate sessions when the vice president is not there. The term pro tempore means "for the time being." Normally, however, neither the vice president nor the president pro tempore presides. Most often, other members of the majority party take turns presiding as the Senate conducts its day-to-day business.

Majority leader. The majority leader serves as the spokesperson for the party that holds the most seats in the Senate. This leader, however, lacks the speaker of the House's ability to single-handedly make things happen on the floor. The Senate majority leader must work with party members and the minority leader to move legislation to a vote.

Minority leader. This leader helps shape minority party policy and devise strategies for stopping majority-sponsored bills opposed by the minority party. The minority leader also works with the Senate majority leader to schedule business on the Senate floor.

Majority and minority whips. The main duty of these assistant floor leaders is to stand in for the majority and minority leaders. Their other duties vary, depending on the needs of their party leaders.

The Congressional Committee System

Individual legislators do not have the time or expertise to thoroughly understand all the bills that come before Congress. Instead, they rely on a division of labor, entrusting most of the work of lawmaking to various committees. Congress has five kinds of committees, some permanent and others temporary.

Standing committees. House and Senate **standing committees** are permanent committees that handle most legislative business. Each standing committee has its own broad area of responsibility, such as homeland security or foreign affairs. In addition to

---

Permanent Congressional Committees

Standing committees and their subcommittees do much of the legislative work of Congress. Joint committees oversee the operations of the Library of Congress and the Government Printing Office, as well as researching economic and tax policies.

House Standing Committees

Agriculture
Appropriations
Armed Services
Budget
Education and the Workforce
Energy and Commerce
Ethics
Financial Services
Foreign Affairs
Homeland Security
House Administration
Judiciary
Natural Resources
Oversight and Government Reform
Rules
Science, Space, and Technology
Small Business
Transportation and Infrastructure
Veterans' Affairs
Ways and Means

Joint Committees

Joint Economic Committee
Joint Committee on the Library
Joint Committee on Printing
Joint Committee on Taxation

Senator Jeff Sessions (R-AL), shown right, talks with Senate Judiciary Committee chair Patrick Leahy (D-VT), shown left, during a committee hearing.

Senate Standing Committees

Agriculture, Nutrition, and Forestry
Appropriations
Armed Services
Banking, Housing, and Urban Affairs
Budget
Commerce, Science, and Transportation
Energy and Natural Resources
Environment and Public Works
Finance
Foreign Relations
Health, Education, Labor, and Pensions
Homeland Security and Governmental
  Affairs
Judiciary
Rules and Administration
Small Business and Entrepreneurship
Veterans' Affairs

Sources: www.senate.gov and www.house.gov.

studying legislation, standing committees have another key duty: they gather information through hearings and investigations. Committee hearings are one way for Congress to monitor the policies of government agencies. Committee members can ask officials, face to face, to explain their agency's actions.

Subcommittees. Most standing committees also have several smaller **subcommittees**. The subcommittees do most of the work of reviewing proposed legislation. The vast majority of bills introduced in Congress each year "die" in committee.

Select or special committees. Both the House and the Senate sometimes form a **select committee** or **special committee** to investigate specific problems. These committees are usually temporary. Although they do not review legislation, special and select committees may make recommendations to Congress based on their investigations.

Joint committees. Congress has a small number of permanent **joint committees** made up of members of both the House and the Senate. Joint committees deal with issues of interest to both chambers. The Joint Committee on the Library, for example, oversees the operations of the Library of Congress. The Library of Congress is the research arm of Congress and is home to the world's largest library. Its collections include millions of books, photographs, documents, recordings, maps, and manuscripts.

Conference committees. A **conference committee** is a temporary kind of joint committee. It is formed to iron out differences between two versions of a bill passed by the House and Senate. Both chambers must pass identical versions of a bill for it to become law.

Staff and Support Agencies

Members of Congress do not face the rigors of committee work alone. If you have ever seen a congressional committee in action, you may have noticed the people sitting behind the committee members. You may have seen them hand a document to a member or whisper in a member's ear. These people are employed as congressional staffers, or staff members. Some work for the committee at large. Others belong to a member's personal staff.

The House and Senate each employ around 1,000 committee staffers to support the work of their various committees. This staff includes clerical workers as well as experts in the subject area of a particular

committee. The number of personal staff a Congress member has varies. Representatives average about 16 staffers apiece, while senators average about 40 staff members each. Personal staff members perform a variety of tasks, from answering constituents' questions to writing speeches and drafting bills.

The Growth of Congressional Staffs

The number of people working on personal and committee staffs has grown over time. Members of Congress rely on staffers to help them do their jobs. But as the cartoon suggests, some critics believe that staffs have grown too large.

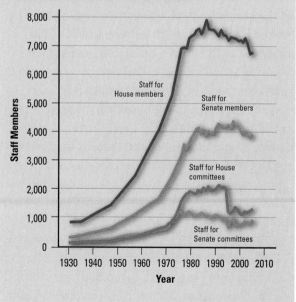

©TCI/Scott Willis

House and Senate Staff, 1930–2005

Source: Norman J. Orstein, Thomas E. Mann, and Michael J. Malbin, *Vital Statistics on Congress, 2008,* Washington, D.C.: Brookings Institution, 2008.

Founded in 1994, the Congressional Asian Pacific American Caucus (CAPAC) is open to both House and Senate members. CAPAC focuses on helping the Asian American and Pacific Islander community. Here, the members of CAPAC meet with President Obama to discuss ways they can collaborate to move their agenda forward.

In addition to staff, several support agencies provide Congress with the information it needs to do its job. The Congressional Research Service helps by researching policy questions. The General Accountability Office checks the financial accounts of government programs. The Congressional Budget Office provides House and Senate budget committees with data and analyses that aid the budget process. It also provides other committees with cost estimates related to proposed legislation.

Caucuses and Coalitions

Members of Congress have also formed a number of unofficial groups to pursue particular goals and interests. For example, there are more than 300 informal caucuses in Congress. Often, members of a caucus need not belong to the same party or even the same chamber. The National Women's Political Caucus, for example, is a bipartisan group of women in Congress. Likewise, the Congressional Black Caucus is open to all African American members of Congress. Groups like the Climate Change Caucus and the Congressional Nanotechnology Caucus attract lawmakers who have an interest in specific subjects.

Other unofficial groups have formed within one political party or chamber of Congress. The Blue Dog Coalition, for example, is a group of conservative and moderate House Democrats. The House Tea Party Caucus brings together House Republicans dedicated to advancing a conservative agenda.

◼ 11.4 The Work of Congress

Members of Congress have two distinct but interrelated jobs. They must represent their constituents in their districts or states, and they must perform their constitutional duties as national legislators. In other words, they must try to serve the voters back home while making laws for the nation as a whole.

The Powers of Congress

Article I of the Constitution states that Congress shall have "all legislative Powers." The specific powers given to Congress include the authority to

- levy and collect taxes.
- borrow money.
- regulate interstate and foreign commerce.
- coin money.
- declare war.

The Constitution also authorizes Congress to "make all Laws which shall be necessary and proper" for carrying out those powers. Through this open-ended Elastic Clause, the framers gave Congress the ability to stretch its listed powers to deal with future needs that could not be anticipated when the Constitution was written.

The only catch is that these implied powers must be linked to enumerated powers. Sometimes that link is weak. For example, Congress has enacted laws designed to limit air and water pollution based on its power to regulate interstate commerce.

Occasionally, the Supreme Court has held that Congress has stretched the Elastic Clause beyond the breaking point. This happened in the 2000 case *United States v. Morrison*. At issue was whether Congress had exceeded its authority to control interstate commerce when it passed the Violence Against Women Act in 1994. The act gave women who had been abused the right to sue their attackers in federal court.

The Court struck down the act as unconstitutional. Writing for the majority, Chief Justice William Rehnquist argued, "Every law enacted by Congress must be based on one or more of its powers enumerated in the Constitution." In this case, he continued,

> *Gender-motivated crimes of violence are not, in any sense of the phrase, economic activity . . . Indeed, if Congress may regulate gender-motivated violence, it would be able to regulate murder or any other type of violence . . . We accordingly reject the argument that Congress may regulate noneconomic, violent criminal conduct based solely on that conduct's . . . effect on interstate commerce.*
>
> —William Rehnquist, *United States v. Morrison*, 2000

How Congress Checks the Other Branches

Congress was also given powers to check the other two branches of government. These checking powers include the following:

Oversight. Congress oversees executive agencies to make sure they carry out the laws it has passed.

Confirmation. The Senate must confirm, or approve, key officials appointed to office by the president.

Impeachment. The House of Representatives can impeach a federal official, including the president, by voting to accept a formal accusation of wrongdoing against that person. The Senate then conducts a trial of the impeached official and votes on whether to remove him or her from office.

Ratification. The Senate must ratify, or approve, all treaties negotiated by the president before they can become law.

Override. Congress can vote to override, or reverse, a president's veto of legislation.

Amendment. Congress, through a vote of both houses, can propose an amendment to the Constitution. It can use this power to change the Constitution, even if this means reversing a ruling of the Supreme Court.

The Checking Powers of Congress

Congress has a number of powers that enable it to check the other two branches of government. This is part of the framers' plan for keeping any one branch from becoming too powerful.

Legislative Checks on Executive Branch

Legislative Checks on Judicial Branch

Legislative

Can override presidential vetoes, approve or reject presidential appointments and treaties, and impeach and try the president.

Can approve or reject nominations of federal judges, create lower courts, and remove judges through impeachment.

Executive

Judicial

Enacting Laws

The checking powers of Congress also apply within the legislative branch. Both houses of Congress must agree on a bill before it can become law. That means that either house can amend or reject a bill offered by the other house.

The process of crafting bills that both chambers can agree on is complex and time-consuming. The diagram "How a Bill Becomes a Law" shows the basic steps involved in turning a bill into law.

Bills may be introduced in either house of Congress. Upon introduction, they are labeled with initials: H.R. for the House or S. for the Senate. They also receive a number, which represents the order in which the bill was introduced in that chamber. So, for example, the first bill introduced in the House during the 113th Congress in early 2013 was labeled H.R.1. The first bill in the Senate was S.1.

Most new bills are sent to a committee, where they are studied and revised. If the bill survives in committee, it is sent back to the House or Senate floor for debate and a vote. Bills that pass one chamber are sent to the other house to go through the process again.

Often a bill gets amended further when it passes through the other chamber. In that case, the two versions of the bill—the House version and the Senate version—may go to a conference committee to have their differences reconciled. The House and Senate then vote on the final version of the bill. If it passes, it goes to the president for approval. If the president signs the bill, it becomes law.

This process may seem relatively simple and straightforward, but it is not. Turning a bill into law requires hard work, patience, and compromise. Most bills do not survive. For example, in 2011, more than 5,700 bills were introduced in Congress. Only 90 went on to become law.

Levying Taxes

Some of the bills that go through Congress are tax bills. The power to tax is one of the most important powers of Congress. Unlike other legislation, however, tax bills can only originate in the House. Article I, Section 7 of the Constitution says that "all Bills for raising Revenue shall originate in the House of Representatives."

Originally, government revenue—the money coming into the treasury—came mainly from taxes on goods, such as imported products. Today, the federal government relies largely on income taxes, which are collected by the Internal Revenue Service. Congress makes tax policy and oversees the work of the IRS.

Although taxes may seem a burden, they finance many of the government programs and services that Americans depend on. For example, without federal taxes, there would be no national highway system, no national system of law enforcement, no national funding for public education, and no national defense system.

The Power of the Purse

In addition to taxation, Congress has another important financial power: the power to spend. Article 1, Section 9 of the Constitution says, "No Money shall be drawn from the Treasury, but in Consequence of Appropriations made by Law."

Appropriations are public funds allocated for a particular purpose by a legislature. To fund any federal project, the government needs money, and Congress must appropriate this money. Acting in this capacity, Congress is said to have the "power of the purse."

After Congress passes a bill, one way for the bill to become law is for the president to sign it. For example, in 2008, members of Congress witnessed President George W. Bush sign a bill that regulated emerging and new Internet technologies.

Getting a bill through Congress is a complicated and lengthy process. If the bill survives and is passed by both houses, it goes to the president, who may sign it into law or veto it and return it to Congress.

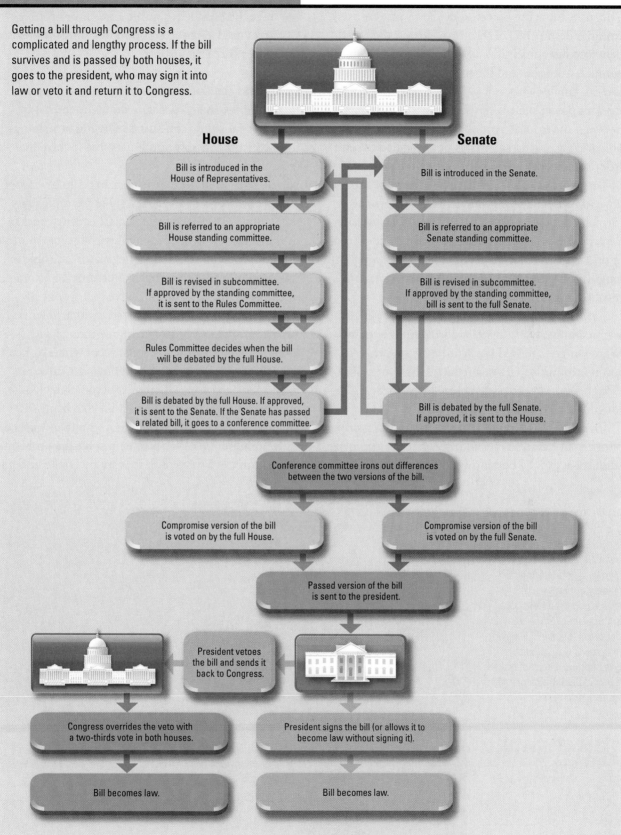

House

Senate

Bill is introduced in the House of Representatives.

Bill is introduced in the Senate.

Bill is referred to an appropriate House standing committee.

Bill is referred to an appropriate Senate standing committee.

Bill is revised in subcommittee. If approved by the standing committee, it is sent to the Rules Committee.

Bill is revised in subcommittee. If approved by the standing committee, bill is sent to the full Senate.

Rules Committee decides when the bill will be debated by the full House.

Bill is debated by the full House. If approved, it is sent to the Senate. If the Senate has passed a related bill, it goes to a conference committee.

Bill is debated by the full Senate. If approved, it is sent to the House.

Conference committee irons out differences between the two versions of the bill.

Compromise version of the bill is voted on by the full House.

Compromise version of the bill is voted on by the full Senate.

Passed version of the bill is sent to the president.

President vetoes the bill and sends it back to Congress.

Congress overrides the veto with a two-thirds vote in both houses.

President signs the bill (or allows it to become law without signing it).

Bill becomes law.

Bill becomes law.

Declaring War

Another key power of Congress granted under the Constitution is the power to declare war. But as commander in chief of the armed forces, the president also has constitutional duties related to military conflict. Congress and the president thus share war-making powers.

This power sharing has sometimes caused tension between the legislative and executive branches. Historically, the president has not hesitated to send troops into combat before obtaining the permission of Congress. U.S. soldiers have been sent into action abroad more than 200 times. Yet Congress has formally declared war only five times. The last such declaration, in 1941, brought the United States into World War II. Since then, Americans have fought in lengthy, undeclared wars in Korea, Vietnam, and, most recently, Iraq.

Congress has sometimes resisted the president's war-making efforts. In 1973, during the Vietnam War, Congress passed the War Powers Act to reassert its authority. This law requires the approval of Congress for any overseas troop deployment lasting longer than 90 days.

In such cases, Congress can stop short of issuing a formal declaration of war. Instead, it can authorize military action by passing a **joint resolution,** an official statement from both houses of Congress. Like a regular bill, a joint resolution has the power of law once the president signs it. In October 2002, Congress used a joint resolution to authorize the use of military force against Iraq.

Casework: The Care and Feeding of Constituents

In addition to their legislative duties, members of Congress must find time for **casework,** or helping their constituents solve problems that involve the federal government.

Citizens often need assistance in dealing with the complexities of federal agencies. For example, they may not have received their Social Security checks, or they may be having problems getting a passport in time for foreign travel. Often, legislators are able to use their authority to connect constituents to someone in government who can solve their problems.

Casework involves a great variety of problems. In one example, California congressman David Dreier was asked to help a constituent with a difficult adoption case. The woman had flown to Taiwan to adopt a baby. Once there, she became tangled in bureaucratic red tape and was unable to bring the child home. She contacted Dreier, who then worked with immigration officials to help solve the problem. After nearly two years of hard work by Dreier and his

In late 2002, Congress passed a joint resolution authorizing the invasion of Iraq, which began in March 2003. After nine years of American military operations, U.S. troops departed from Iraq in December 2011. Although Congress has the sole power to declare war under the Constitution, it has not issued a formal declaration of war since World War II.

In addition to their legislative duties, members of Congress must also perform casework. They try to use their positions as legislators to help their constituents solve problems. The flow-chart shows the various ways in which members of Congress work to help people in their districts.

How Members of Congress Serve Their Districts

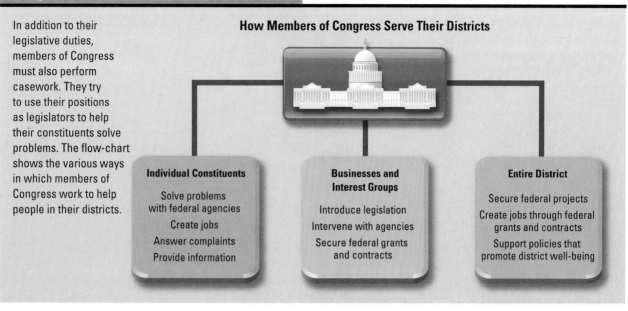

Individual Constituents

Solve problems with federal agencies

Create jobs

Answer complaints

Provide information

Businesses and Interest Groups

Introduce legislation

Intervene with agencies

Secure federal grants and contracts

Entire District

Secure federal projects

Create jobs through federal grants and contracts

Support policies that promote district well-being

staff, his constituent was able to finalize her adoption. "If it weren't for Congressman Dreier," the woman later said, "I wouldn't be a mother today."

Casework is a burden for many legislators, but it is a key part of representative government. Helping constituents is also good politics. Voters often reelect legislators who have paid attention to their needs. Members of Congress know this and have found ways to do casework while fulfilling their legislative duties. They open offices in their districts, for example, and hire staff to answer constituents' questions. They also work on other levels to help their districts. The flowchart above shows some of the ways members of Congress try to serve their districts.

◼ 11.5 How State Legislatures Compare with Congress

State legislatures have much in common with the U.S. Congress. Like Congress, they make laws and represent the voters in each state. With the exception of Nebraska, all states have bicameral legislatures, made up of an upper and a lower house. These houses are organized along party lines and do much of their business through committees, just like Congress. Nevertheless, state legislatures differ from Congress in a number of ways.

Shorter Sessions, Smaller Staff, and Lower Pay

In general, state legislators meet for less time, have smaller staffs, and receive lower salaries than members of Congress. State legislatures can be divided into three types: citizen, professional, and hybrid. These types are based mainly on the amount of time their members spend on the job.

Citizen legislatures. In citizen legislatures, members spend about half of their time as lawmakers. Citizen legislatures are commonly found in states with small populations.

Professional legislatures. As the name suggests, these are legislatures whose members are full-time lawmakers. Professional legislatures are more common in states with larger populations.

Hybrid legislatures. These legislatures fall between the previous two types. Their members spend about two-thirds of their time on legislative business.

Of these three types, professional legislatures are the most like Congress. Even so, the workload of lawmakers in professional legislatures pales in comparison with that of members of Congress. Most sessions of Congress run from January into December. Members of Congress spend well more than 300 days a year performing legislative duties. State legislators, even professional ones, work much less. For instance, in New York, legislators meet several times a week from January into June. For the

State legislatures are divided into three types, based primarily on how much time legislators spend on the job. State legislatures meet at the state capitol in chambers like the one shown here.

Types of State Legislature, 2008

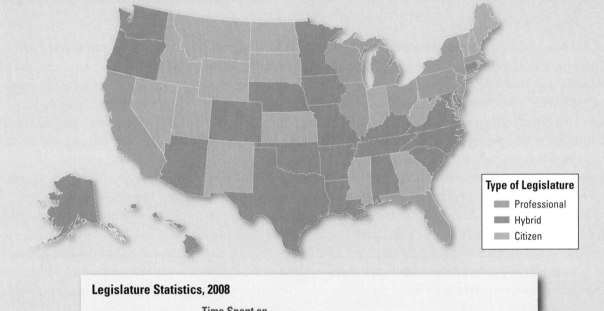

Type of Legislature
- Professional
- Hybrid
- Citizen

Legislature Statistics, 2008

Type of Legislature	Time Spent on Legislative Activity	Average Salary	Average Staff Size
Professional	80%	$68,599	9
Hybrid	70%	$35,326	3
Citizen	54%	$15, 984	1

Source: National Conference of State Legislatures, www.ncsl.org.

rest of the year, they are "on call," coming together only when necessary.

Staff size is another difference. Professional state legislators average around 9 staff assistants each, compared with 16 in the House and 40 in the Senate. Citizen legislators may have just one assistant.

Compensation is also much lower at the state level. In 2012, members of Congress earned $174,000 annually. Among the states, California paid the highest legislative salary that year, at a little more than $95,000. But most states paid far less. New Hampshire offered the lowest salary, paying its lawmakers just $100 per year. As a result, most state legislators must have other means of support. As one Massachusetts state senator put it, "No one goes into politics to get rich."

Turnover and Term Limits

Another key difference between many state legislatures and Congress is the presence of term limits. Unlike Congress, where legislators may serve an unlimited number of terms, many states limit the number of years legislators can remain in office.

The idea of imposing term limits on state officials goes back to the early days of the nation. In 1776, the constitution of Delaware set term limits for the state's governor. Many other states followed that practice.

The movement to limit state legislators' time in office came much later. As of 2012, voters in 15 states had imposed term limits of various kinds on their lawmakers. For example, in Arizona, lawmakers are limited to 8 years in each house of the legislature. In Nevada, the limit is 12 years. As a result of term limits, a total of 380 legislators in 14 states were prevented from running for reelection in 2010.

Advocates of term limits say that turnover in a legislature is beneficial. It eliminates career politicians who, they argue, lose touch with their constituency. New faces, they say, bring new ideas. In Michigan, for instance, about half of the lawmakers elected in 2010 were newcomers. Without term limits, most of them would have had a tough time getting elected.

Critics of term limits argue that such limits are undemocratic. By preventing some incumbents from running for reelection, term limits restrict the choices available to voters. They also remove experienced lawmakers from office, which may reduce a legislature's effectiveness. For example, in 2012, Missouri's state legislature experienced a high turnover of lawmakers. Many of these lawmakers were "termed out," including the speaker of the House and others who held leadership positions.

Opponents of term limits claim that such a loss of experience can devastate a legislature. Supporters argue that new legislators bring new energy to government and are more responsive to the will of the people.

Summary

Congress is the legislative branch of the national government. Its structure and powers are largely defined by the Constitution. As with all legislatures in a representative democracy, Congress is responsible for making laws and serving the people's needs.

Legislators and constituents Most legislators seek to represent the interests of their constituents while also relying on their own independent judgment. In Congress, two senators represent every state. The number of representatives depends on a state's population.

Organization of Congress The House and the Senate are organized by political parties. Much of the work of turning a bill into law takes place in standing committees and subcommittees. Members of Congress rely on staff to help with their lawmaking and constituent duties.

Powers of Congress The Constitution gives Congress specific powers, which, over time, have been stretched under the Elastic Clause. In addition, members of Congress use their office to help constituents solve problems involving federal government agencies.

State legislators As a rule, state legislators spend less time on the job, receive lower pay, and have fewer staff than their counterparts in Congress. Unlike members of Congress, some state legislators are subject to term limits.

What makes a state legislature good?

In the United States, voters elect representatives to Congress and their state legislature. For both the federal and state government, representatives act in the interest of their constituents. State legislators make decisions that influence policy within their state.

This article developed for the National Conference of State Legislatures discusses what functions your state legislature is expected to perform. How well your state legislature succeeds at these tasks is subjective and difficult to evaluate. However, you can still try to assess how good your legislature is. After you read this article, answer the questions in "Grade Your Legislature." How does your state measure up?

The Good Legislature

by Alan Rosenthal

For legislatures to be good, they must carry out the functions we expect of them in our system of representative democracy. The principal ones are balancing power, representing constituencies and making laws. In considering whether legislatures are doing their job . . . we have to examine how well they are performing these three functions.

Balancing Power

Constitutionally, legislatures are separate, co-equal branches (indeed, the legislature is the first branch of government and the executive the second) that share governmental power. So it follows that legislatures must balance the power of governors and the executive branch. A good legislature, accordingly, has to be relatively independent of the governor. It must insist on participating in the initiation of policy and refuse to rubber-stamp executive proposals . . .

Legislative power may be requisite, but that does not mean that the greater the power imbalance in favor of the legislature, the better that legislature is. More power for the legislature is not necessarily better once an appropriate balance is achieved. In other words, an imbalance in favor of the legislature is no better than an imbalance in favor of the governor. The legislature must truly be a co-equal branch of government.

Although we can measure the constitutional powers of governors and legislatures, their real power hinges as much on political factors and traditions as on constitutional and statutory ones. If we examine who initiates and enacts legislation and budgets, we should see in a general way how well the legislature is fulfilling its power balancing function.

Representing Constituencies

One of the major roles of a legislature is representation—representing various constituencies, mainly people in each lawmaker's electoral district, but also organized groups and individuals elsewhere in the state. The question is, how well does the legislature perform its representational tasks?

First, the constitutional system and the legislature ought to provide for substantial political equality, that is, "one person, one vote." This standard, enforced by state and federal courts, is generally met, although the political gerrymandering that accompanies redistricting is often used to benefit one party and incumbents in their re-election efforts.

Grade Your Legislature

Balancing Power
1. Does your legislature effectively share power with the governor?
2. Does your legislature initiate and enact its own legislation and make independent decisions about the state budget?

Representing Constituents
3. Are the numbers of women, African Americans and Hispanics in your legislature reasonably reflective of the population of your state?
4. Do the members of your legislature provide effective constituent service including responses to requests for information, casework, local projects and public expenditures?
5. Do citizens and groups in your state have ready access to information on agendas and proceedings of the legislature?
6. Does your legislature provide effective civic education for the public (of all age levels) about representative democracy, the legislative institution and the lawmaking process?
7. Is your legislature responsive to public demands and needs?

Making Law
8. Does your legislature allow effective participation and input from citizens and organized groups in lawmaking decisions?
9. Do you have effective legislative leaders who have strategic, problem-solving and consensus-building abilities?
10. Does your legislature address and solve the most important problems in your state?

Second, a variety of groups who previously lacked membership should be present in the ranks of legislators today. Women, African Americans and Hispanics most notably need opportunities to serve as well as to be represented . . .

Third, as part of its representational function, the legislature must provide service to constituencies and constituents. Constituent service is normally the job of individual members who appreciate the importance of doing a good job in this area if they hope to be re-elected . . .

Fourth, the legislature has to ensure that citizens, as well as groups, have access to members, to committees, and to the general process. The legislature must be open and provide information on agendas and proceedings . . .

Fifth, the legislature also has responsibility for civic education, especially on representative democracy, the legislative institution and the legislative process . . .

Sixth, the legislature has to be responsive, at least to some degree, to what citizens want, as well as to what the legislature determines they need. [We] have to figure out how legislative enactments—at least on major issues—square with public demands and with public needs.

Making Law
Although representing others deals with the relations between the legislature and the public, lawmaking is internally focused. It relates to the processes by which laws (and policies) are fashioned.

Lawmaking includes several related legislative activities. The legislative role in formulating, reviewing and adopting a state budget has special significance. The budget is probably the most important bill that a legislature passes. A legislature that performs poorly on the budget is likely to be an ineffective legislature overall.

The legislature's oversight role is also worth considering; that is, how and to what extent does the legislature monitor the application and effect of the laws it has enacted. Finally, we should pay some attention to legislative foresight; that is, how and to what extent the legislature looks ahead in order to develop policies to meet the future needs of the state.

Alan Rosenthal, a renowned expert on state legislatures, is a professor at Rutgers University.

Chapter 12

Congressional Lawmaking

How do laws really get made?

■ 12.1 Introduction

Some people have compared the making of laws to the making of sausage. It is a messy process that calls for mixing together many ingredients—some rather unpleasant—and stuffing them into one package. Some diagrams can explain the lawmaking process in a straightforward manner. However, because lawmaking is so complex and chaotic in real life, any diagram of this process is far too neat, as one former member of the House of Representatives made clear:

> [A] diagram can't possibly convey the challenges, the hard work, the obstacles to be overcome, the defeats suffered, the victories achieved, and the sheer excitement that attend the legislative process. It gives a woefully incomplete picture of how complicated and untidy that process can be, and barely hints at the difficulties facing any member of Congress who wants to shepherd an idea into law.
>
> You don't just have an idea, draft it in bill form, and drop it in the House hopper or file it at the Senate desk. Developing the idea is very much a political process—listening to the needs and desires of people and then trying to translate that into a specific legislative proposal.
>
> —Lee H. Hamilton, *How Congress Works and Why You Should Care*, 2004

The start of the 112th session of Congress

"Excuse me, sir, it seems the voters have a few opinions about this bill . . ."

Lawmakers have to consider many different factors as they compose a bill. Party leaders, lobbyists, and personal values all contribute to constructing legislation. Another factor, as this cartoon suggests, is the legislator's constituents, who may ask their representative to influence policy changes.

Once a bill is introduced in the House or Senate, the business of lawmaking begins. In theory, a proposed law first goes to a committee. If approved there, the bill goes to the floor of the chamber in which it was introduced for a vote. If it passes there, it goes to the other chamber of Congress for a second vote. After being approved by both the House and Senate, the bill goes to the president.

In reality, as Representative Hamilton observed, the legislative process is far more complex and filled with hazards. During the months it takes to move a bill through Congress, lawmakers can be pulled in several directions. Party leaders insist on loyalty to the party's position. Constituents may demand attention to local concerns. Lobbyists may clamor for consideration of their particular interests. And all the while, the news media watch and report lawmakers' every move.

In addition to these outside pressures, many lawmakers feel an inner pressure to make decisions based on their own principles. As one political scientist put it, "Members of Congress are inevitably caught in a crossfire of competing expectations."

■ 12.2 Convening a New Congress

Congressional elections are held every two years on the first Tuesday in November. Incumbents and challengers vie for all the seats in the House. In the Senate, one-third of the seats are up for election every two years. Most elections bring new faces to Congress. On occasion, an election creates a new majority party in the House, Senate, or both. In January, federal lawmakers, old and new, travel to Washington, D.C., to convene, or organize, the next Congress.

Meeting to Choose Congressional Leaders

Before the new Congress holds its first formal meeting, lawmakers from each chamber meet with fellow party members in what is known as either a party caucus or a party conference. Four meetings are held in all, one each for the majority and minority parties of the House and of the Senate. Party members meet often during each two-year session of Congress. But the opening meeting is the most important.

At the first party caucus or conference, members begin to organize the new Congress. Their primary task is to elect their congressional leaders: the speaker of the House, majority and minority leaders, and whips. Over the next two years, these party leaders will work to achieve consensus, or agreement, on legislation, a task that will often tax their powers of persuasion.

Another vital task at this first meeting is the formation of party committees. Unlike congressional committees, these groups serve only their political party. Through their party committees, Democrats and Republicans research broad policy questions. They consider strategies for the upcoming session and determine party positions on legislation. They also nominate party members to serve on standing committees.

Making Committee Assignments

Leaders of both parties in the House and Senate work out the number of seats the two parties will have on each standing committee. As a rule, seats are assigned to Republicans and Democrats roughly in proportion to their numbers in the chamber as a whole. The majority party leaders, however, make all the final decisions. In this way, they ensure that their party maintains control of each committee.

Woodrow Wilson once observed that, "Congress in session is Congress on public exhibition, whilst Congress in its committee rooms is Congress at work." Those committee rooms are in House and Senate office buildings located on Capitol Hill, shown above. Journalists use "the Hill" as a shorthand term for the entire legislative complex.

Nearly all House members sit on at least one standing committee. Many sit on two or even three. In the smaller Senate, members must take on more committee responsibilities. Most of the 100 senators sit on three to five of the Senate's 20 committees.

A handful of these standing committees are the most sought-after by members, either because the committees control the federal purse strings or because they deal with crucial issues of public policy. The coveted assignments include the Appropriations, Budget, and Commerce committees of both chambers, as well as the Rules Committee and Ways and Means Committee in the House and the Finance Committee in the Senate.

Before a new Congress meets, newly elected members request committee seats. At the same time, returning incumbents may ask to be moved to a more prestigious committee. The party caucus or conference, as well as the full House or Senate, must approve the committee assignments.

Historically, party leaders in Congress used their power to assign committee seats as a tool to ensure party loyalty. Members who received a requested assignment understood that they "owed" party leaders a favor. The leaders would expect to collect those favors in the future as votes on key issues. Party leaders today are less controlling, but they still use committee assignments to reward members of Congress who cooperate and to punish those who do not.

For new members, assignment of committee seats can be an especially trying experience. Like incumbents, they hope to join a committee that will allow them to serve their district's needs, while also making them look good in the eyes of voters back home. A representative from a district with an air or naval base, for example, might seek a seat on the House Armed Services Committee. Rarely, however, do lawmakers start their career with such a desirable committee assignment.

In general, new members accept whatever committee assignments they receive and try to improve their position in the future. Carl Albert, who first won election to the House of Representatives in 1946, took this attitude. Though assigned to the minor Committee on the Post Office and Civil Service, Albert was determined to start his congres-

In 2011, the Republican Party became the majority party of the House of Representatives, which gives it the power to select committee chairs. For the most part, seniority rule dictates that the majority party member with the most consecutive years of service on the committee becomes committee chair. However, party leaders do consider other factors. Here, republican leaders of the House hold a press conference.

sional career on the right foot. He marched into the office of Speaker of the House Sam Rayburn to thank him for the assignment. Rayburn's secretary mistook the youthful Albert for a teenage **congressional page**. She informed Albert that the congressman did not have time to talk to pages.

The First Day of a New Congress

Albert's dream of moving up in Congress eventually came true. In the 1970s, he served with distinction as speaker of the House. But back on January 3, 1947, he was thrilled just to be sitting in the House chamber for the first time. "With befitting solemnity," he remembered years later, "the clerk of the House began calling the alphabetical roll of members. The first called, Thomas Abernathy of Mississippi, did not respond. The second was Carl Albert of Oklahoma. 'Here,' I answered. It was the sweetest word in the English language."

The first day of any new Congress opens with a series of ceremonies. Once a quorum (a simple majority) is established, the House votes for speaker. Members vote along party lines, so the majority nominee always wins. Next the dean of the House, or the member with the most years of service, administers the oath of office to the speaker. The speaker then swears in all the members of the House at once.

Similar rituals take place in the Senate. There, the vice president swears in the members of the Senate, a few at a time. The Senate majority leader, however, receives no special swearing in.

All members in the House and the Senate take the same congressional oath of office. This oath has been used by Congress since 1868:

I, [name], do solemnly swear (or affirm) that I will support and defend the Constitution of the United States against all enemies, foreign and domestic; that I will bear true faith and allegiance to the same; that I take this obligation freely, without any mental reservation or purpose of evasion; and that I will well and faithfully discharge the duties of the office on which I am about to enter. So help me God.

■ 12.3 Working in Committee

After the opening-day ceremonies, the new Congress is ready to get to work. A great deal of that work takes place in committee—so much so that some observers describe Congress as a collection of committees that come together now and then to approve each other's decisions.

Choosing Committee Chairs and Ranking Members

Committee chairs are chosen by the majority party, mainly through a vote of its party caucus. Historically, the choice of chairs was governed by **seniority rule**. This rule automatically gave the position of committee chair to the majority party member with the most consecutive years of service on the committee. Likewise, the minority party used the seniority rule to select its top committee post—that of ranking member.

Beginning in the 1970s, however, party leaders began considering other factors, such as party loyalty, political skill, and trustworthiness, in choosing committee chairs. Even so, seniority remains the best predictor of leadership in Senate committees. It is the key factor in each party's choice of chairs and ranking members. In the House, however, fewer committee leaders are chosen based only on seniority, although it remains an important factor.

Assigning Bills to Committees

Bills come to a committee from a variety of sources, including individual citizens and interest groups. A large number originate in departments and agencies of the executive branch. These bills are put forward to advance the policies advocated by the president. No matter where a bill originates, a member of Congress must introduce it. That member becomes the bill's primary sponsor.

According to the rules of the House, the speaker distributes proposed legislation to the various committees for study. In the Senate, the presiding officer handles this task. In actual practice, however, the House and Senate parliamentarians refer most bills to a committee. Each parliamentarian is an expert on the rules and procedures of either the House or the Senate.

Once a bill is sent to a committee, the chair decides what to do with it. One option is simply to ignore it. Former representative Lee H. Hamilton found this out during his first year in the House. Hamilton and a few other members decided to introduce a constitutional amendment that would increase House terms from two years to four. Hamilton later recalled how they approached the

The Senate Committee on Armed Services focuses on legislation that deals with military affairs, including the development of weapons systems, nuclear energy, petroleum reserves, and personnel. This committee also handles important oversight functions. In this photograph taken in 2010, a lieutenant general and a defense policy expert brief the committee on an operation in Afghanistan.

"awesome and fearsome" chair of the Judiciary Committee, Emanuel Celler, to ask him how he stood on the proposal. "I don't stand on it," he replied. "I'm sitting on it. It rests four-square under my fanny and will never see the light of day."

Another option is to hold hearings on the bill, either in the full committee or in one of its subcommittees. Subcommittees are smaller groups of lawmakers that focus on particular areas within the full committee's jurisdiction. The House has more than 100 subcommittees. The Senate has approximately 70. The committee chair can refer a bill either to a subcommittee that will give it a favorable reception or to one that will not. This is another source of a chair's considerable power.

The Path of a Bill Through Subcommittee

A committee's work on a proposed bill can be divided into three phases. At each point, the legislation can move forward or die.

Phase 1: Hearings. The first phase usually begins with a **legislative hearing** in front of the subcommittee to which the bill was assigned by the committee chair. The purpose of the hearing is to listen to testimonies and gather information from individuals who are interested in or have expertise to share about the proposed legislation. The people called on to testify may include the bill's sponsors, public officials, lobbyists, and private citizens. To shine the media spotlight on a bill, a chair may even invite a movie star to testify. "Quite candidly," Senator Arlen Specter admitted, "when Hollywood speaks, the world listens. Sometimes when Washington speaks, the world snoozes."

Hearings can be fairly short, or they can drag on for days. Subcommittee chairs, for the most part, control the selection and scheduling of witnesses. If they favor a bill, they can move the hearing along. If they oppose a bill, they kill it by scheduling hearings that never seem to end.

Phase 2: Markup. If a bill makes it through the hearings, subcommittee members gather to determine the bill's final language. This meeting is known as a **markup session,** because this is when members mark up, or amend, the bill. At least one-third of

On December 4, 2009, the Senate Banking, Housing, and Urban Affairs Committee held a hearing to discuss a bill that sought to bailout the automobile industry. Here, the committee chair at the time, Christopher Dodd (left), greets Richard Wagoner, the CEO of General Motors, before the hearing. The committee listened to testimonies from auto executives to assess the proposed $34 million federal bailout.

the subcommittee's members must be present at a markup session to make up a quorum.

The chair starts a markup session by noting the bill's title and opening it up to amendment. Amendment procedures vary by committee, but typically any change in a bill must be approved by a majority of those present. The committee members usually debate the merits of each proposed amendment before voting on it.

During markup, members are often torn between their roles as delegates and as trustees. As delegates, they want to address the particular interests of their home districts or states. As trustees, they want to shape a bill that will be good for the country while also attracting support from other lawmakers, the president, and the general public.

Phase 3: Report. Once subcommittee members deal with the last amendment to the bill, they vote on a motion to return the bill to the full committee. Those who do not want the bill to move on vote no at this point. However, if a bill has made it through markup, it will most likely be sent back to the full standing committee.

The standing committee can then accept the bill as is or amend it further—even holding more hearings and its own markup session. It then votes on whether to report the bill to the full House or Senate for a floor vote. If the vote is favorable, the committee staff prepares a written report explaining why the committee recommends the enactment of this bill. It is then up to the full House or Senate to agree or disagree with the committee's recommendation.

The Power of the House Rules Committee

In the Senate, a bill reported out of committee is ready to be voted on by the full chamber. But in the House, the bill's sponsors need to clear one more hurdle: the House Rules Committee. This powerful committee acts as a "traffic cop" for House legislation. It can move a bill ahead of others on the House schedule so that it can be considered quickly. Or it can delay a bill's arrival on the House floor.

The Rules Committee also sets the rules for debate on a bill. A bill's supporters usually ask for a **closed rule**. A closed rule severely limits floor debate and amendments to a bill. A closed rule makes it easier to get a bill through the House quickly, with

"The only solution I can see is to hold a series of long and costly hearings in order to put off finding a solution."

Committee hearings are used to gather information on bills submitted to Congress. However, as this cartoon suggests, hearings can also be used to delay decisions on difficult issues.

no damaging debate or changes. Opponents, in contrast, prefer an **open rule**. An open rule allows floor debate and the introduction of amendments that could cripple or kill the bill.

The Rules Committee does not act independently of the speaker of the House. The speaker often sets the guidelines for when and how a bill will be debated on the floor. Should the speaker desire changes in a bill, for example, he or she might arrange for an open rule. Former House member Porter J. Goss observed, "How much is the Rules Committee the handmaiden of the Speaker? The answer is, totally."

■ 12.4 Debating and Voting on the House and Senate Floor

Picture yourself in a room with dozens or even hundreds of other strong-minded people. Many of them disagree with your views on just about everything. And they are not shy about speaking up for their beliefs. Nonetheless, you need to work together, in a democratic fashion, to make some very complex decisions. This is the challenge facing members of the House and Senate every time they meet to debate and vote on legislation.

"Listen, pal! I didn't spend seven million bucks to get here so I could yield the floor to you."

During debate in the House or Senate, a lawmaker can ask the person recognized to speak to yield the floor. It is up to the person holding the floor to decide whether to give up speaking time to someone else. In this cartoon, the answer is clearly no.

The Majority Party Controls Floor Debate

In both chambers, the majority party controls what happens on the chamber floor. Floor time is precious, and what is said on the floor can be used to create sound bites for the news and social media. The speaker of the House and the majority leader of the Senate determine which bills will be debated and who will be allowed to speak for how long.

Once floor debate on a bill begins, the speaker and majority leader both have the **power of recognition**. No member may rise to address the chamber without first being recognized, or given permission, by the leader. The power of recognition is so important that members of Congress do all they can to stay on good terms with their House and Senate leaders.

Armed with the power of recognition, the speaker and majority leader are usually able to run an orderly legislative process. That process has three main parts: (1) general debate on the bill, (2) debate and voting on amendments to the bill, and (3) voting on final passage of the bill.

House Debate: Keeping It Short, If Not Sweet

With 435 members, the House has to put limits on floor debate. On most bills, the Rules Committee often limits general debate to one hour—30 minutes each for the majority and the minority parties. The goal of this one-hour rule, like much that takes place on the House floor, is to keep the legislative process moving.

The bill's sponsor and main opponent usually control a bill's debate time. They dole out their precious minutes to colleagues who want to speak on the bill. Typically, House members are limited to just one or two minutes at the microphone, so they learn to make their points quickly. Still, with most floor debates now being televised on C-SPAN, members appreciate even this short amount of "face time" in front of the voters back home.

Unlimited Debate in the Senate: Filibusters and Holds

The Senate prides itself on its tradition of unlimited debate. With only 100 members, it can afford to be more relaxed about time. But sometimes, this tradition can bring the legislative process to a halt.

In contrast to the speaker of the House, the Senate majority leader has limited control over the legislative agenda. To schedule a bill, the majority leader often must work closely with the minority leader. The majority leader also has less control over floor debate. Senators must consent to limit debate. If they do not, any senator—once recognized—may speak on any subject at any length.

This right comes into play most vividly when a senator starts a **filibuster**. A filibuster involves prolonged debate or other delaying tactics aimed at blocking the passage of a bill favored by a majority of lawmakers. A Senate filibuster can go on for days, with one long-winded speaker following another. In 1957, the late Strom Thurmond of South Carolina set the record for the longest single speech. He spoke for 24 hours and 18 minutes in an effort to kill a civil rights bill. At first, Thurmond talked about civil rights. But as the hours rolled by, he read some of his favorite recipes. By the end of his marathon speech, he was reading names from a phone book.

In 1917, the Senate adopted a means of closing debate known as the **cloture** rule. At that time, this

Journalists often report about battles over bills in Congress. On February 6, 1858, a battle in the House of Representatives over the issue of slavery turned physical. More than 50 members joined in the brawl on the House floor. Such physical confrontations are rare in the history of Congress, however.

rule required a **supermajority** of two-thirds of all senators to cut off debate. Today, cloture requires only three-fifths of the Senate, or 60 votes.

A filibuster is not the only delaying tactic available to senators. They can also place a **hold** on bills to delay debate. A hold signals the lawmaker's intention of launching a filibuster if the bill is sent to the Senate floor. Because the identity of the person placing the hold may be kept secret, senators use this tactic when they do not want to openly oppose a bill.

Amendments: Riders and Christmas Tree Bills

Like the rules for debate, the amendment process also differs in the two chambers. In the House, when general debate ends, the measure is opened to amendment. Under the five-minute rule, members debate each proposed change. In theory, though not often in practice, this rule limits members who support and oppose an amendment to five minutes of debate time each. Once all amendments have been voted on, the full House is ready to vote on final passage of the bill.

The Senate follows a similar procedure, with one important difference. According to House rules, an amendment is supposed to be germane, or relevant, to the content of the bill. In the Senate, however, senators can attach amendments that are totally unrelated to a bill. Known as **riders,** such amendments may be used as "sweeteners" to win more votes for a bill. Or they can serve as "poison pills" designed to make sure a bill fails. Riders are often used to get controversial legislation or bills favoring special interest groups through Congress.

Must-pass legislation, such as an emergency funding bill, tends to attract many riders because the president is unlikely to veto such a measure. The result is often described as a **Christmas tree bill**. In 1956, *Time* magazine ran an article with that title about a trade bill that had attracted more than 100 amendments. New Mexico senator Clinton Anderson said of the result, "This bill gets more and more like a Christmas tree; there's something on it for nearly everyone."

Voting on a Bill

Floor votes in the House and Senate can be taken in three ways. In a **voice vote,** supporters all together call out "aye," meaning "yes." Then opponents call out "no." The louder voices, in the judgment of the presiding officer, win the vote. In a **standing vote,** first the supporters and then the opponents stand to be counted. Neither of these two methods records how each individual lawmaker voted.

In a **roll-call vote,** each member's vote is officially recorded. In the Senate, this is done by having a clerk call each name from the roll of senators and recording each one's vote. The much larger House uses an electronic voting system. Each member inserts his or her plastic Vote-ID card into a voting station slot and punches a button for "yea" ("yes"), "nay" ("no"), or "present." A vote of "present" means the member **abstains,** or chooses not to cast a vote on this bill.

Pressures and Influences on Legislators

Before voting on any bill, most legislators consider the views of their constituents, as well as their own personal convictions. They may also feel pressures and influences from several other, often conflicting, sources.

Interest groups. Interest groups are sometimes called pressure groups—and with good reason. Their lobbyists crowd committee rooms and the halls of Congress. They confront legislators who are undecided on how to vote on a particular bill. They can also be persistent. Senator Ben Nighthorse Campbell once said that being besieged by lobbyists is "like being attacked by a plague of locusts. Now I know what a grain of wheat feels like."

Party leaders. Leaders of each political party expect their members to support the party's public policy goal. To gain that support, leaders can pass out favors, such as the promise of a plum committee assignment or help raising campaign funds. They can also use persuasion. Lyndon Johnson, who served as Senate majority leader before becoming president, was a master of persuasion. Two journalists who followed Johnson's career described what came to be known as "the treatment."

There are three ways to vote in Congress, by voice vote, standing vote, and roll-call vote. But only the roll-call method records how each individual member voted. In the Senate, roll-call votes are done verbally. In the House, they are done through an electronic voting system. Each member's desk contains a keypad that the member uses to vote. The vote then appears on a large electronic "scoreboard." Since it was first introduced in 1973, the electronic voting system has been upgraded. However, how the system is used essentially remains the same.

During the Great Recession, lawmakers in both houses worked to create legislation that would stimulate the economy. However, the Senate and the House could not agree on a version of the bill. In 2009, the Senate and House Appropriations Committees met in a joint conference to hammer out a compromise. Ultimately, the conference settled on a stimulus package that would inject over $780 billion into the economy.

The Treatment could last ten minutes or four hours . . . Its tone could be supplication, accusation, cajolery, exuberance, scorn, tears, complaint, the hint of threat. It was all of these together . . . He moved in close, his face a scant millimeter from his target, his eyes widening and narrowing, his eyebrows rising and falling. From his pockets poured clippings, memos, statistics. Mimicry, humor, and the genius of analogy made The Treatment an almost hypnotic experience and rendered the target stunned and helpless.
—Robert Evans and Robert Novak, *Lyndon B. Johnson: The Exercise of Power,* 1966

Colleagues. Members of Congress regularly yield to the pressure to trade votes. This kind of **logrolling,** or mutual support and cooperation, is a common way to get things done in Congress. Typically, two opposing groups each want a particular bill passed, so each promises to vote for the other's measure. Simon Cameron, a politician who served in President Abraham Lincoln's cabinet, aptly defined logrolling as "you scratch my back and I'll scratch yours."

■ 12.5 Final Steps in the Legislative Process

Once the House or Senate passes a bill, the bill does not go directly to the president. Both chambers of Congress must vote to approve the bill in identical form before it goes from Capitol Hill to the White House for the president's signature.

Congress Speaks As One—Eventually

A bill first passed by the House must be voted on by the Senate and vice versa. If the bill is changed in any way by the second chamber, the House and Senate will have to work out a compromise version. This often happens informally, and leaders from the two chambers iron out their differences and come to an agreement on any amendments.

About 20 percent of the time, however, especially with major or controversial legislation, House and Senate leaders cannot reach agreement informally. In such cases, the bill is sent to a joint conference committee. The task of this committee is to work out a compromise that a majority of lawmakers in both chambers can accept and that the president will sign into law.

The speaker of the House and the presiding officer of the Senate appoint members to a conference committee. These members are known as **conferees**. Typically, each chamber appoints about a half dozen conferees, mainly senior members of the committees involved with the bill. The conferees bargain face to face. To reach agreement, they may heavily revise a bill or even rewrite it completely. For this reason, conference committees are sometimes called "the third house of Congress."

An agreement reached by a conference committee must have the backing of a majority of each

The percentage of bills and joint resolutions introduced in Congress that have made it through the legislative process has dropped over time. In the first years of Congress, lawmakers had a "batting average" of nearly 100 percent. Today the average is well below 10 percent.

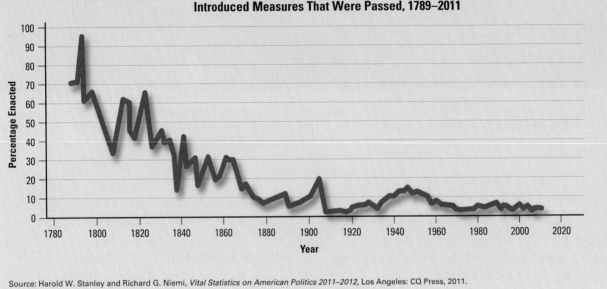

Introduced Measures That Were Passed, 1789–2011

Source: Harold W. Stanley and Richard G. Niemi, *Vital Statistics on American Politics 2011–2012*, Los Angeles: CQ Press, 2011.

chamber's conferees. That agreement, known as a conference report, goes back to the House and Senate for an **up-or-down vote**. This type of vote means that the revised bill must be adopted or rejected as is, with no further amendments, by a majority of the full House and Senate. Only if both chambers approve it can the bill be sent to the president.

The President Takes Action on a Bill—Or Not

Once the bill is delivered to the White House, the president has ten days (not counting Sundays) to do one of the following:

- Sign the bill into law.
- Veto the bill.
- Take no action on the bill. At the end of ten days, the bill becomes law without the president's signature.

A bill that has been vetoed by the president is delivered back to the first chamber that passed it. That chamber may decide that the bill cannot be saved. Or it may try to override, or cancel, the presidential veto. Historically, only a small percentage of bills approved by Congress have been vetoed.

Congress Can Try to Save Vetoed Legislation

Overriding a presidential veto is not easy. Two-thirds of the members present in each chamber must vote in favor of saving the legislation. If the first chamber fails to override the veto, the measure dies there. Otherwise, it moves on to the second chamber for a vote. If two-thirds of the lawmakers in the second chamber also approve the override, the bill becomes a law without the president's signature.

Congressional overrides are more likely when the president belongs to one party and Congress is controlled by the other, or when Congress and the president clash over a particular issue. Both conditions existed during Andrew Johnson's presidency in the 1860s. Johnson was a southern Democrat, while Congress was controlled by northern Republicans. Congress also disagreed with Johnson's plans for reconstructing the South after the Civil War.

Under these unusual circumstances, Congress was able to override 15 of Johnson's 21 vetoes. In contrast, during his four terms as president, Franklin Roosevelt vetoed a record number of 372 bills. Congress managed to override only 9 of his vetoes.

The president rarely signs a major bill without some sort of ceremony. The president often uses several pens to sign legislation and then passes those pens out to the bill's sponsors and other members. For the signing of the bill making Martin Luther King Jr.'s birthday a national holiday, President Ronald Reagan invited Coretta Scott King, the civil rights leader's widow, to the ceremony.

Summary

In theory, the lawmaking process in Congress is fairly straightforward. In reality, it is a complex struggle involving many traditions, rules, and competing interests. The rare measure that actually becomes law often bears little resemblance to the bill that was first introduced.

Convening a new Congress Before a new Congress opens, Democrats and Republicans in each chamber meet in party caucuses or conferences. There they elect party leaders, make committee assignments, and formulate strategies.

Working in committee Standing committees and their subcommittees do most of the work of Congress. Directed by powerful committee chairs, these committees study, revise, and sometimes completely rewrite bills.

Voting on bills The majority party leaders in each chamber direct the flow of bills through the process of debate, amendment, and voting. The House, because of its large size, restricts debate. The Senate allows unlimited debate.

Final steps to enactment Before a bill goes to the president, both chambers must pass it in identical form. The president can choose to sign a bill into law or veto it. To save a vetoed bill, both chambers of Congress must pass it again, but this time by a two-thirds majority of those present and voting.

Is divided government good for the nation?

The United States operates under a two-party system, which at times leads to divided government, a situation in which one party controls the White House and another party controls at least one house of Congress. Divided government forces the two branches of government to compromise, but it can also lead to gridlock.

In this article, William A. Niskanen discusses the virtues of divided government. As you read this article, ask yourself if divided government leads to balanced compromises that help the nation. Or does it create unnecessary roadblocks that impede progress in policy?

Give Divided Government a Chance

by William A. Niskanen

For those of you with a partisan bent, I have some bad news. Our federal government may work better (well, less badly) when at least one house of Congress is controlled by the opposing party. Divided government is, curiously, less divisive. It's also cheaper. The basic reason for this is simple: When one party proposes drastic or foolish measures, the other party can obstruct them. The United States prospers most when excesses are curbed, and, if the numbers from the past 50 years are any indication, divided government is what curbs them.

Let's look at some statistics. From the dawn of the Cold War until today, we've had only two periods of what could be called fiscal restraint: The last six years of the Eisenhower administration, and the last six years of the Clinton administration, both intervals in which the opposition controlled Congress. Under Clinton, the average annual increase in spending was at about 1 percent, while, under Ike, it was negative. By contrast, our unified governments have gone on fiscal benders. Harry Truman, with the help of a Democratic Congress, sent the money flying, with spending increases of as high as 10 percent a year. Lyndon Johnson was almost as profligate. And . . . unfortunately, George W. Bush, with a GOP majority, is the heir to their legacies. To put this in plain numbers, government spending has increased an average of only 1.73 percent annually during periods of divided government. This number more than triples, to 5.26 percent, for periods of unified government. That's a hefty premium to pay for a bit of unity.

Equally striking is that these spending increases have generally found the same recipient: the Pentagon. It's not that unified governments love to purchase bombers, but, rather, that they tend to draw us into war. This may sound improbable at first, but consider this: In 200 years of U.S. history, every one of our conflicts involving more than a week of ground combat has been initiated by a unified government. Each of the four major American wars during the 20th century, for example—World War I, World War II, the Korean War, and

The Pros and Cons of Divided Government

Pros

- It forces both parties to compromise. This encourages politicians to take a moderate approach to major issues and keeps extremism in check.

- It provides incentive for legislators to come up with pragmatic solutions instead of radical fixes.

- It supports the system of checks and balances because the legislative and executive branches are motivated to limit each other's power.

- It forces the executive branch to govern from the center.

Cons

- It often leads to legislative gridlock, a situation in which both parties cannot agree upon an approach to solve problems in government, making it difficult to pass laws.

- It produces obstacles when government needs to create solutions for major problems.

- It slows down the decision-making process. This causes problems when there are time-sensitive issues that need solutions.

- It increases partisanship when Congress conducts politically motivated investigations of the executive branch.

the Vietnam War—was initiated by a Democratic president with the support of a Democratic Congress. The . . . war in Iraq, initiated by a Republican president and backed by a Republican Congress, is consistent with this pattern. It also stands as the only use of military force involving more than a week of ground combat that has been initiated by a Republican president in over a century. Divided government appears to be an important constraint on American participation in war. Needless to say, this reduces outlays in both blood and treasure.

There's one more advantage to tension between our governmental branches: Major reform is more likely to last. Since passing any measure in divided government requires bipartisan support, a shift in majorities is less likely to bring on serious changes or adulterations. The Reagan tax laws of 1981 and 1986, for example, were both approved by a House of Representatives controlled by Democrats and have largely survived. The welfare reform of 1996 was approved by Clinton and a Republican Congress and also endures. By contrast, any efforts during the past several years to reform the federal tax code, Medicare, or Social Security have faltered, and any changes forced through by the GOP would almost certainly be undone as soon as Democrats returned to power. Reforms of real magnitude will almost certainly depend on preventing immoderation and securing bipartisan support, and little of that seems likely in a GOP-only government.

American voters, in their unarticulated collective wisdom, seem to grasp the benefits of divided government, and that's how they've voted for most of the past 50 years. To be sure, divided government is not the stuff of which political legends are made, but, in real life, most of us would take good legislation over good legends. As a life-long Republican and occasional federal official, I must acknowledge a hard truth: I don't much care how a divided government is next realized.

William A. Niskanen was chairman emeritus and a distinguished senior economist at the Cato Institute. He had also served as acting chairman of President Reagan's Council of Economic Advisers.

Chapter 13

Chief Executives and Bureaucracies

What qualities do modern presidents need to fulfill their many roles?

■ 13.1 Introduction

April 28, 1975, was a day like many others for President Gerald Ford. He rose early and had his breakfast. By 7:30 A.M., he was hard at work in the Oval Office. He met with advisers and other officials that morning and later gave a speech at the annual meeting of the U.S. Chamber of Commerce.

More appointments filled Ford's afternoon schedule, including a brief photo opportunity with Lisa Lyon, the Miss National Teenager of 1974–1975. Later the president attended a meeting on the economy and energy policy in the White House Cabinet Room.

But no day, however typical, is ordinary for the president of the United States. In the spring of 1975, the Vietnam War was entering its final days. The communist forces of North Vietnam were advancing on Saigon, the capital of U.S.-backed South Vietnam. It was clear that South Vietnam could fall at any moment. When that happened, the remaining Americans in Saigon would have to evacuate the city.

Just after 7:00 P.M., President Ford learned that the North Vietnamese were shelling the U.S. air base at Saigon, making evacuation by plane impossible. He convened a meeting of the National Security Council to discuss the unfolding crisis.

The White House, the home and office of the U.S. president.

During the Vietnam evacuation crisis, President Gerald Ford met repeatedly with his close advisers. Here, Ford (right) attends a cabinet meeting with Secretary of State Henry Kissinger (left).

By 11:30 P.M., the shelling had stopped. But there was another problem, as Ford later wrote about in his autobiography:

> *Refugees were streaming out onto the airport's runways, and our planes couldn't land. The situation there was clearly out of control. The only option left was to remove the remaining Americans, and as many South Vietnamese as possible, by helicopter from the roof of the U.S. embassy in Saigon. Choppers were standing by on the decks of U.S. Navy ships steaming off the coast, and just before midnight I ordered the final evacuation. Over the next sixteen hours we managed to rescue 6,500 U.S. and South Vietnamese personnel without sustaining significant casualties.*
>
> —*A Time to Heal: The Autobiography of Gerald R. Ford,* 1979

With the crisis resolved, Ford retired to his upstairs White House residence. It was 12:05 in the morning.

As this day in the life of President Ford illustrates, the job of president involves many tasks and responsibilities. Some are routine, while others are immensely challenging. All require the skills of an effective leader. This chapter examines the qualities necessary in chief executives, along with the main features of the bureaucracies they run.

13.2 Chief Executives: Mayors, Governors, and Presidents

The president is the national government's **chief executive,** the top elected official in charge of enforcing laws and carrying out government policy. State and local governments also have chief executives. In the states, this official is the governor. At the local level, it is usually a mayor.

Formal Qualifications: Age, Citizenship, and Residency

Adlai Stevenson, who ran for president twice in the 1950s, once said, "In America, anyone can become president." That is not quite true. Any candidate seeking the presidency must satisfy certain qualifications laid down in the Constitution. The president must be a native-born citizen, be at least 35 years of age, and have lived in the country for at least 14 years.

The Twenty-second Amendment, ratified in 1951, added another rule: no one who has been elected president twice or who has served one full term plus more than half of another term can seek the office again. This amendment formalized the custom of a two-term president. This custom, established by George Washington, was broken only once, by four-term president Franklin Roosevelt, prior to ratification of the amendment.

Most state and local governments set less stringent requirements for their chief executives. In Kentucky, for example, candidates for governor need only be 30 years old and must have lived in the state for 6 years. California has no minimum age or residency requirements. In that state, candidates for governor must simply be U.S. citizens and registered voters. In contrast to presidential requirements, such citizenship can be by birth or naturalization. That is why Austrian-born Arnold Schwarzenegger was able to become the governor of California but cannot be president of the United States.

Requirements for mayors are even looser. Many towns and cities require only that mayors be legal adults. Several high school seniors and college students have served as mayors. For example, in 2011, Jeremy Minnier was just 18 when he was elected mayor of Aredale, Iowa.

Informal Qualifications: Experience, Education, and Other Factors

Like lawmakers, chief executives must also satisfy certain informal qualifications for office. These are traits that voters expect in their political leaders. This graph shows the essential qualities Americans wanted their next president to have in 2007.

Typically, chief executives have backgrounds in business, law, or public service. Most are well educated. Nearly three-quarters of all presidents have earned college degrees. Most have worked their way up the political ladder by holding other elective offices.

There are exceptions, however. Abraham Lincoln, one of this country's most admired presidents, had little formal schooling. Although he had served as an Illinois legislator and a member of Congress, he had lost several political races before winning the presidency.

Historically, most chief executives have been white, male, and from the middle or upper class. In fact, all U.S. presidents were white males until 2009 when Barack Obama took office and became the first African American president. Chief executives in states and cities, however, have made even greater progress in representing a broad spectrum of the American population.

Women have made significant strides at both state and local levels. The first female governor,

Nellie Tayloe Ross, was elected in Wyoming in 1924. Since then, 35 more women had been elected governor of their states or the Commonwealth of Puerto Rico. In 2007, a record 9 of the 50 state governors were women. At the local level, female mayors led over 17 percent of American cities with populations greater than 30,000 in 2012.

Ethnic minorities have also had increasing success in gaining chief executive positions. Only two African Americans—Douglas Wilder of Virginia and Deval Patrick of Massachusetts—have been elected governor. But many blacks have been elected mayor of major cities such as New York, Philadelphia, Detroit, and Washington, D.C. In 2011, Susana Martinez assumed the gubernatorial office in New Mexico and became the first Latina governor in the United States. In 2005, Antonio Villaraigosa became the first Latino mayor of Los Angeles in more than a century. Nikki Haley, a South Asian American, was elected governor of South Carolina in 2010.

Religious affiliation can be another informal qualification, especially for presidential candidates.

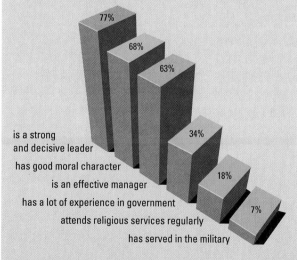

Essential Qualities of the Next President

In a survey conducted in 2007, the Gallup Organization asked Americans what qualities they were looking for in their next president. Of those surveyed, 77 percent said that it is essential that the next president is a strong and decisive leader.

Percentage who say it is essential that the next president . . .

77% is a strong and decisive leader
68% has good moral character
63% is an effective manager
34% has a lot of experience in government
18% attends religious services regularly
7% has served in the military

Source: The Gallup Organization, 2007.

Almost all U.S. presidents have been Protestant. Until John F. Kennedy's election in 1961, it was assumed that a Catholic candidate could never win the presidency. Kennedy succeeded, in part, by promising to keep his religious and political beliefs separate. "I am not the Catholic candidate for president," he declared. "I am the Democratic Party's candidate for president, who happens also to be a Catholic." Even today, a non-Protestant candidate would likely face an uphill battle in winning the presidency.

Gaining Office: Election and Succession

Most chief executives, including governors and mayors, are elected by popular vote. The president, in contrast, is chosen by the Electoral College, based on the popular vote count in each state.

In some state and local elections, the candidate who wins a plurality of the vote is declared the winner. In other states and cities, however, the candidate must receive a majority of the votes cast to win. If that does not happen, the top two candidates must compete in a **runoff election,** which is designed to produce a clear winner.

Succession rules for the presidency are spelled out in the Constitution and federal law. Should a president be unable to complete a four-year term because of death, disability, resignation, or removal from office, the law provides clear guidelines for replacing the chief executive.

The **line of succession** for the presidency begins with the vice president. If the vice president cannot serve, the next successor is the speaker of the House, followed by the president pro tempore of the Senate, and then by the secretary of state. Other cabinet members continue the line of succession in a specific order.

It is often said that the vice president is "a heartbeat away" from the presidency. Indeed, the main job of the vice president is to take over if something should happen to the president. The Constitution gives the vice president almost no formal powers other than this one.

For that reason, some politicians have shunned the chance to run for vice president. In 1848, Daniel Webster refused to become a vice presidential candidate, saying, "I do not propose to be buried until I am really dead." Nevertheless, 14 vice presidents

"It worries me that he just wants to be vice president when he grows up."

The vice president holds little formal power under the Constitution. For that reason, as this cartoon suggests, the position has often been regarded as unimportant. Nevertheless, the vice president is first in line to succeed the president, which gives holders of this office enormous responsibility.

have gone on to become chief executive. In addition, recent vice presidents have been given substantial responsibilities by the president. During George W. Bush's administration, Vice President Dick Cheney held a significant amount of power and played a key role in shaping national security policy.

In most states, a lieutenant governor holds a comparable position to that of the vice president. This official stands in for the governor when necessary but generally has few formal duties.

Staying in Office: Impeachment, Recalls, Term Limits, and Incumbency

If a president, vice president, or other official in the executive branch is suspected of wrongdoing, that person may be impeached and removed from office. The framers made the impeachment process difficult, however, to prevent it from being used for frivolous reasons. To be removed, an official must be convicted of "Treason, Bribery, or other high Crimes and Misdemeanors."

Impeachment begins in the House of Representatives. A majority of House members must vote to impeach, or formally accuse, the president or other officer of wrongdoing. The trial is then held in the Senate. Two-thirds of the senators must find the official guilty to remove that person from office.

The House has impeached only two presidents—Andrew Johnson and Bill Clinton—and the Senate found neither guilty. Richard Nixon resigned rather than face impeachment during the Watergate scandal.

But what if citizens are simply unhappy with the job their chief executive is doing? For presidents, there is no provision for midterm removal based on job performance. Many states and cities, however, do have procedures by which voters can order a recall of elected officials. The California recall took place in 2003, in which the voters chose to replace Governor Gray Davis with actor Arnold Schwarzenegger.

Almost a decade later, in 2012, Wisconsin attempted to recall a governor in a special election, but failed. As governor of Wisconsin, Scott Walker proposed a plan to help balance the state budget. This plan cut benefits for public employees and greatly limited the ability for unions to bargain. As a result,

disgruntled workers and unions organized protests. United Wisconsin, a grassroots organization, led a recall effort and petitioned for signatures, eventually gathering enough to hold a special election. Still, many Wisconsin voters supported Walker's attempts to reduce government spending. When the recall election took place on June 5, 2012, Walker won, retaining his position as governor.

Many chief executives are also subject to term limits. As noted previously, presidents are restricted to no more than two terms in office. Many states and cities also set term limits on their governors and mayors. In most cases, governors are held to two consecutive terms in office. However, in some states, they may run for reelection four years after their last term.

The power of incumbency in winning reelection is not as strong for chief executives as it is for legislators. That may be because chief executives serve as a "lightning rod" for voter discontent. When voters are dissatisfied with government, they often blame their chief executive. Since World War II, three presidents have been defeated in their run for a second term: Gerald Ford, Jimmy Carter, and George H. W. Bush.

Demonstrators protested Governor Scott Walker's budget and limitation of bargaining rights for unions. However, not all Wisconsin voters agreed with the demonstrators. Many approved of Walker's efforts to reel in government spending. Some others disliked Walker's policies but also felt wary of recalling an elected official so soon. Ultimately, voters elected to keep Walker in office.

13.3 The Growth of Presidential Power

The U.S. president today is often viewed as the most powerful national leader in the world. At one time, however, the U.S. president held far less power. During the 1800s, with a few exceptions, presidents acted mainly as "chief clerks." Other than carrying out the will of Congress, they assumed little authority other than those powers explicitly granted them by the Constitution.

Powers Granted the President Under the Constitution

The Constitution spells out the president's formal powers, which are listed in this diagram. One of the most important powers is that of commander in chief of the armed forces. The president, a civilian official, maintains control over the military and has ultimate responsibility for military decisions.

The president also has the power to grant **reprieves** and **pardons**. A reprieve is a postponement of punishment, whereas a pardon is a release from punishment. Presidents may also grant **amnesty,** or a blanket pardon, to people facing prosecution. President Jimmy Carter, for example, granted amnesty to young men who had fled the country to avoid the military draft during the Vietnam War.

The president's greatest formal power stems from Article II, Section 3 of the Constitution. This section directs the president to "take Care that the Laws be faithfully executed." Much as the Elastic Clause gives broad powers to Congress, this "Take Care" Clause grants the president flexible powers to enforce the law and fulfill other executive duties. Not surprisingly, the first president to define how the powers of the office would be used was George Washington.

George Washington (1789–1797): Establishing Precedents

As the nation's first president, Washington knew that his every action would help shape the office for future generations. "I walk on untrodden ground," he observed. "There is scarcely any part of my conduct which may not hereafter be drawn into precedent."

One precedent involved his formal title. Washington insisted on being addressed simply as "Mr. President," rather than "Your Highness" or some other majestic title. Rather than ruling like an aloof monarch, Washington traveled the country to maintain contact with citizens. He also declined to seek reelection after serving two terms in office, setting a precedent that would last until 1940.

Washington established the model for how the executive branch should be run. He appointed the

Presidential Powers

The Constitution lists various presidential powers, either exercised by the president alone or shared with Congress. The president also has many other powers that have evolved over time through custom and practice.

Powers of the President

Sole Powers
Act as commander in chief of the armed forces

Commission military officers

Grant reprieves and pardons for most federal offenses

Call Congress into special session

Receive foreign ambassadors

Ensure that laws of Congress are faithfully executed

Exercise executive power

Appoint officials to executive office

Powers Shared with the Senate
Make treaties

Appoint ambassadors, judges, and high officials

Powers Shared with Congress as a Whole
Approve legislation

George Washington's great dignity and sense of authority lent power to the office of president. He was immortalized in numerous statues and sculptures. This 1882 statue of him stands outside of Federal Hall in New York in the same spot he stood when he was inaugurated.

Andrew Jackson was a powerful president who often battled with Congress and used his veto power to block legislation. Critics called him "King Andrew." But his use of the veto to shape public policy set a precedent for future presidents.

first department heads and brought them together to create the first **cabinet**. He negotiated the new government's first treaty. He appointed its first judges. He received its first ambassadors. He signed its first laws. And he issued the first veto.

Perhaps most importantly, Washington made sure that the president would be respected as a figure of authority. He did this by projecting an air of great dignity and strength. In addition, he took tough action when necessary to ensure that acts of Congress were "faithfully executed."

Washington's determination to enforce the law was tested by the Whiskey Rebellion. In 1791, Congress passed a law that taxed sales of whiskey. Farmers in western Pennsylvania who made whiskey refused to pay the tax and even attacked federal tax collectors. Washington personally led 13,000 militia troops into western Pennsylvania to put down the rebellion. In this way, he affirmed the power of the president as the nation's chief law enforcer and commander in chief.

Andrew Jackson (1829–1837): Champion of "The People"

Like Washington, Andrew Jackson believed in using the powers given to the president to the fullest. Jackson was elected president at a time when many states had eliminated property requirements for voting. As a result, he was the first occupant of the White House who could claim to have been elected by "the people."

Once in office, Jackson saw his role as the champion of the common people. As such, he often clashed with Congress. In these power struggles, he turned to a tool seldom used by earlier presidents: the veto. Previous presidents had vetoed acts of Congress only when they viewed them as unconstitutional. Jackson vetoed legislation simply because he disagreed with it or thought it ran counter to the people's interests.

During his two terms in office, Jackson vetoed 12 bills, more than the total number of bills struck down by all of his predecessors combined. His most famous veto involved a bill renewing the charter of the National Bank of the United States. Supporters of the bank argued it was needed to stabilize the nation's economy. Jackson believed that the bank was designed to benefit the wealthy at the expense of the people. In a message explaining his veto, Jackson wrote,

> It is to be regretted that the rich and powerful too often bend the acts of government to their selfish purposes. Distinctions in society will always exist under every just government . . . But when the laws undertake to . . . make the rich richer and the potent more powerful, the humble members of society—the farmers, mechanics, and laborers—who have neither the time nor the means of securing like favors to themselves, have a right to complain of the injustice of their Government.
> —Andrew Jackson, 1832

Critics of Jackson's use of this presidential power dubbed him "King Andrew." Nevertheless, since Jackson's day, the idea that presidents can and will use their veto power to shape public policy has become an accepted feature of American politics.

Abraham Lincoln (1861–1865): Savior of the Union

Abraham Lincoln became one of the most powerful presidents in U.S. history, in large part because his election triggered a national crisis. By the time he took office in 1861, seven southern states had seceded from the United States. In his inaugural speech, Lincoln argued that no state "can lawfully get out of the Union." He went on to say,

> I therefore consider that . . . the Union is unbroken; and to the extent of my ability, I shall take care, as the Constitution itself expressly enjoins upon me, that the laws of the Union be faithfully executed in all the States. Doing this I deem to be only a simple duty on my part; and I shall perform it, so far as practicable, unless my rightful masters, the American people, shall . . . direct the contrary.
> —Abraham Lincoln,
> First Inaugural Address, 1861

Lincoln used all of his powers to carry out this duty. Once in office, he spent money. He raised an army. He ordered the navy to blockade southern ports. He declared **martial law** in Maryland and other states, placing the people there under military rule. He shut down newspapers that advocated secession. He suspended habeas corpus so that people suspected of treason could be arrested and jailed by the military without worrying about due process.

All of these actions were taken by the new president without prior approval of Congress. Moreover, when a federal court ruled in *Ex parte Merryman* (1861) that suspension of habeas corpus was unconstitutional, Lincoln ignored the ruling.

Likewise, Lincoln issued his Emancipation Proclamation without approval from Congress or even his full cabinet. When the president showed a draft of the proclamation to his cabinet members, their response was mixed. Some members supported it, while others were strongly opposed. Nevertheless, Lincoln went ahead with the plan. On January 1, 1863, he released the proclamation as an **executive order,** a rule issued by the president that has the force of law. With the order, Lincoln transformed the war for the Union into an antislavery crusade.

Lincoln's many critics argued that he had far exceeded his constitutional powers. Lincoln, however, believed that extreme measures were justified to preserve the Union and the Constitution. By his actions, he demonstrated that during a national emergency, a president might exercise almost unlimited powers.

Abraham Lincoln expanded the power of the presidency during the Civil War. Here, he meets with officers at Antietam in 1862.

Theodore Roosevelt was a powerful president who used the office as a "bully pulpit" to advance his reform agenda.

Theodore Roosevelt (1901–1909): The "Bully Pulpit"

The presidents who followed Lincoln acted more as clerks than executive officers. Then, in the early 1900s, Theodore Roosevelt breathed new life into the office. Roosevelt used the presidency as a platform from which to speak out on important public issues. "I suppose my critics will call that preaching," he said, "but I have got such a bully pulpit!"

Roosevelt was a stirring speaker who loved being seen and heard. He also knew how to work the media. He held daily press briefings. He let photographers take pictures of him at work and play. As a result, his name and smiling image were everywhere.

Roosevelt believed the president should act as a "steward of the public welfare." To fulfill that role, he took a broad view of his powers. He later wrote,

> *I did and caused to be done many things not previously done by the President . . . I did not usurp [seize] power, but I did greatly broaden the use of executive power. In other words, I acted for the public welfare, I acted for the common well-being of all our people, whenever and in whatever manner was necessary, unless prevented by direct constitutional or legislative prohibition.*
> *—Theodore Roosevelt: An Autobiography,* 1913

As the public's steward, Roosevelt created government agencies to ensure safer food and drugs. He promoted conservation of the nation's resources. He pursued an active foreign policy in the belief that the United States was destined to be a great power. The public was so impressed by his energetic leadership that he was reelected in 1904 by the greatest margin of votes in U.S. history up to that time.

Franklin D. Roosevelt (1933–1945): Maker of the Modern Presidency

Theodore Roosevelt planted the seeds that would flower during the presidency of his distant cousin, Franklin Delano Roosevelt, commonly known as FDR. More than any president before him, FDR transformed the role of chief executive from chief clerk to what we think of as the modern presidency.

Like Lincoln, FDR came into office during a time of crisis: the Great Depression. During his first 100 days in office, Roosevelt called Congress into special session and presented it with 15 major bills. Congress passed them all. Later, he won passage of such groundbreaking programs as Social Security and unemployment insurance. In promoting his New Deal reforms, he dramatically expanded the role of the president. As political scientists have put it,

> *The president's constitutional obligation to see "that the laws be faithfully executed" became, during Roosevelt's presidency, virtually a responsibility to shape the laws before executing them.*

Franklin Roosevelt's great personal charm helped win public support for expanded government power. Here, he sits by a microphone as he gives the first of his famous fireside chats.

Part of FDR's power lay in his style as president. Whereas previous presidents had used formal speeches to get their ideas across, FDR addressed the American people directly, in their own homes, through a series of radio broadcasts known as "fireside chats." In these chats, Roosevelt spoke to listeners in a warm, engaging manner, explaining his ideas and asking for their support. In this way, many Americans came to see the president not as a distant leader, but as a friend who understood their concerns.

During World War II, FDR expanded his powers still further. But rather than objecting to this growth of presidential power, most Americans applauded Roosevelt as a "savior." As one political scientist observed, "The argument was simple: The more power the executive had, the more good he could do."

Since the end of World War II, the presidency has been powerful, no matter who is in the White House. By the 1970s, some critics of presidential power voiced concerns about the rise of an "imperial presidency," meaning presidents acted more like emperors than constitutional leaders. Nonetheless, the president today is still limited in his powers to those set down in the Constitution more than two centuries ago.

■ 13.4 The Modern President's Job

President John F. Kennedy once said, "No easy problem ever comes to the President of the United States. If they are easy to solve, somebody else has solved them." Lyndon Johnson, who assumed the presidency after Kennedy's assassination, called the job an "awesome burden." After looking at the modern president's many duties, one scholar noted, "All that is missing is Mover of Mountains and Raiser of the Dead."

The Many Roles of the President

Given the complexities of the modern world, the job of president has grown more challenging. To carry out their duties as chief executive, presidents must assume many different roles. The diagram "The President's Many Roles" shows the various roles the president plays on any given day.

Chief executive. As the country's chief executive, the president acts much like the head of a large corporation. In this role, the president presides over the federal **bureaucracy,** or the various agencies and organizations that carry on the daily business of government. To keep that bureaucracy running, the president is responsible for appointing close to 2,000 federal officials. These officials, in turn, oversee the work of nearly 2 million civilian employees of the federal government.

As chief executive, the president has the power to issue executive orders. A president is most likely to use this power during an emergency or when Congress fails to take action on an important issue. For example, in 1948, Congress was divided over a bill to desegregate the armed forces. Rather than waiting for Congress to act, President Harry Truman issued an executive order abolishing segregation in the military.

Chief of state. The president also acts as chief of state, the ceremonial leader of the government. In many countries, different individuals hold the positions of chief executive and chief of state. In Great Britain, for example, the prime minister is the chief executive, while the monarch is the chief of state. In the United States, however, the president wears both hats.

As chief of state, the president represents the United States at official functions, both at home and abroad. For example, the president greets foreign leaders and hosts state dinners at the White House. Chief of state duties also include acts to promote national spirit, as when the president lights the national Christmas tree or throws out the first pitch of the major league baseball season.

Commander in chief. The job of commander in chief is one of the president's most challenging roles. As head of the armed forces, the president is responsible for the operations of the U.S. military and the overall security of the nation.

The framers believed it was important for the nation's top civilian leader to have control over the armed forces. But they also set limits on the president's control by giving Congress the power to declare war. Since World War II, however, the president has often committed troops to action without a formal declaration of war. In 1973, Congress passed the War Powers Act, which requires the president to get congressional approval to wage war.

But presidents still find ways to stretch this law. As one scholar noted, the military role of the president is "whatever Congress lets him get away with."

Chief diplomat. Another key role for the president is that of the nation's chief diplomat. In this role, the president oversees U.S. foreign policy, holds talks with foreign leaders, and negotiates treaties.

The Constitution directs the president to seek the advice and consent of the Senate in making treaties. Taking this wording literally, President Washington went to the Senate in 1789 to seek its advice on a proposed treaty with the Creek Indians. After some debate, the senators referred the matter to a committee. Washington left in disgust, preferring after that

The President's Many Roles

The president performs many roles as head of the executive branch. Here are the most important roles the president plays.

Chief citizen

Chief manager of the economy

Chief executive

Chief of state

Chief diplomat

Chief of party

Commander in chief

Chief policymaker

to communicate with the Senate in writing. All other presidents have followed his example. Presidents do consult with individual senators, however, and they must still obtain the consent of the Senate to get any treaty approved.

Chief policymaker. Since Franklin Roosevelt's administration, the president has served as chief policymaker for the nation. Although Congress makes the laws, the president has significant influence over the legislative process. The president normally sets a policy agenda for Congress in the annual State of the Union address. The president may also propose legislation or pressure members of Congress to support or oppose certain bills. Other executive powers, such as the power to call Congress into special session and to veto bills, are more key tools the president can use to shape policy.

Chief manager of the economy. The president has no formal power over the economy. However, the president does work with Congress to write a federal budget and set tax policy. The president also appoints members of the Federal Reserve Board, which works to control the money supply and keep the economy growing at a sustainable pace.

Chief of party. The president is the leader of his or her political party. Presidents tend to have deep loyalty to their party and exert great influence over party members in Congress. They typically work to ensure that their party does well in congressional elections, in hopes of gaining or strengthening a congressional majority. They may take part in campaign fundraising or other campaign events. They also typically reward loyal party members with political favors or appointments to federal office.

Chief citizen. The president is also the nation's chief citizen. In that role, the president strives to embody American ideals and to serve the nation by acting in its best interests. In times of crisis or tragedy, the president as chief citizen works to inform, inspire, and comfort the American people.

One of the president's roles is to reassure and comfort the nation at times of crisis. Barack Obama fulfilled this duty in 2012 after Superstorm Sandy hit parts of the Northeast. Here, Obama and Governor Chris Christie console residents of New Jersey.

The president's power to approve or veto legislation gives the chief executive an important role in the legislative process. As this diagram shows, a bill may pass through various steps after it is sent to the White House.

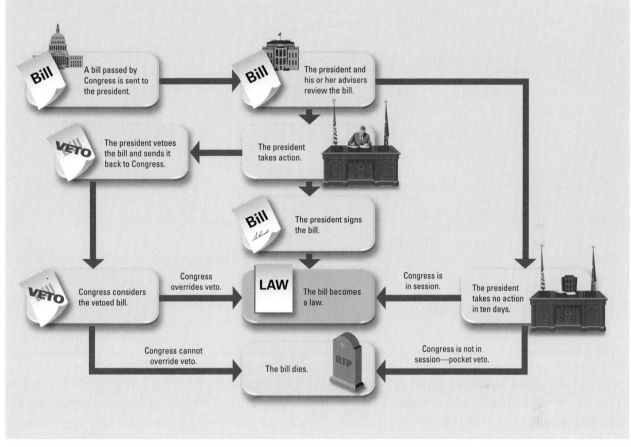

A bill passed by Congress is sent to the president.

The president and his or her advisers review the bill.

The president vetoes the bill and sends it back to Congress.

The president takes action.

The president signs the bill.

Congress considers the vetoed bill.

Congress overrides veto.

LAW The bill becomes a law.

Congress is in session.

The president takes no action in ten days.

Congress cannot override veto.

The bill dies.

Congress is not in session—pocket veto.

Presidential Checks on the Other Branches

The president also plays an important role as head of the executive branch in the federal system of checks and balances. As chief executive, the president can check the power of the legislative branch by approving or vetoing legislation passed by Congress. Likewise, the president can influence the power of the judicial branch by nominating judges to the Supreme Court and other federal courts.

The presidential veto is a powerful tool for influencing policy. The president is required to sign or veto a bill within ten days of receiving it from Congress. If the president fails to act within that time, the bill automatically becomes law. However, the president only needs to veto the bill if Congress is in session. If Congress adjourns during those ten days, the president can do nothing and simply let the bill die. This is known as a **pocket veto**.

The president can also check the power of Congress by invoking executive privilege. Although this power is not formally granted in the Constitution, it has developed over time through custom and practice. Executive privilege allows the president to deny access to White House documents, even when Congress wants to see them, on the grounds that keeping such records confidential is vital to the operations of the executive branch. The Supreme Court has recognized the right of presidents to invoke executive privilege, though not in all cases. For example, the Court refused to back President Nixon's use of executive privilege during the Watergate Scandal.

The White House complex consists of the executive residence at the center, with the West Wing and East Wing at either side. The West Wing contains the president's Oval Office, the vice president's office, and the Cabinet Room. The East Wing contains additional office space.

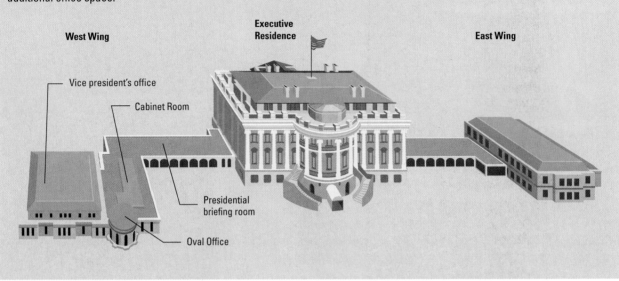

13.5 The Organization of the Executive Branch

Without help, the president could never wear so many hats, much less faithfully execute the laws of Congress. As chief executive, the president both oversees and is assisted by the vast bureaucracy that makes up and manages the executive branch. This branch consists of four main groups: the White House staff, the Executive Office of the President, the executive departments, and independent agencies. The diagram "The Executive Branch" shows how the executive branch is organized.

The White House Staff

The White House staff consists of about 400 people. It includes the president's personal lawyer, press secretary, various speechwriters, and many assistants. Many of these staffers have offices in the West Wing of the White House. The most powerful staff member is the **chief of staff,** who is considered the president's most loyal aide.

Presidents depend on the White House staff to provide them with guidance and advice on a wide range of issues. The chief of staff also serves as a "gatekeeper," controlling who gets to talk to the president and who does not.

The Executive Office of the President

The Executive Office of the President (EOP) was created in 1939 by Congress to provide support staff to the president. Today it has about 1,800 employees.

The agencies that make up the EOP perform a variety of specialized tasks for the president. The largest, the Office of Management and Budget, helps the president prepare an annual budget proposal to Congress.

Other key agencies within the EOP include the Council of Economic Advisers (CEA) and the National Security Council (NSC). The CEA provides advice on the economy. The NSC advises the president on foreign and defense policy.

Presidents can also add new agencies to the Executive Office of the President to carry out specific goals of their **administration**. For example, George W. Bush created the Office of Faith-Based and Community Initiatives, which coordinates public and private efforts to provide social services. Later, Barack Obama established the Consumer Financial Protection Bureau to educate consumers about financial products and services.

As head of the executive branch, the president oversees the work of many executive officials, staff members, and departments, some of which are listed below. There are 15 executive departments, each led by an official appointed by the president. The heads of departments make up the president's cabinet.

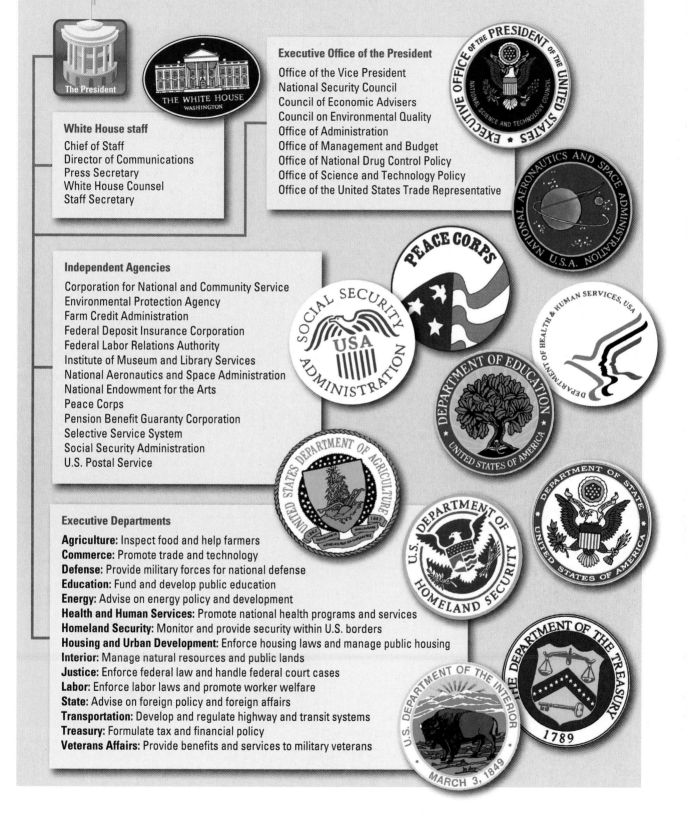

The President

THE WHITE HOUSE
WASHINGTON

White House staff

Chief of Staff
Director of Communications
Press Secretary
White House Counsel
Staff Secretary

Executive Office of the President

Office of the Vice President
National Security Council
Council of Economic Advisers
Council on Environmental Quality
Office of Administration
Office of Management and Budget
Office of National Drug Control Policy
Office of Science and Technology Policy
Office of the United States Trade Representative

Independent Agencies

Corporation for National and Community Service
Environmental Protection Agency
Farm Credit Administration
Federal Deposit Insurance Corporation
Federal Labor Relations Authority
Institute of Museum and Library Services
National Aeronautics and Space Administration
National Endowment for the Arts
Peace Corps
Pension Benefit Guaranty Corporation
Selective Service System
Social Security Administration
U.S. Postal Service

Executive Departments

Agriculture: Inspect food and help farmers
Commerce: Promote trade and technology
Defense: Provide military forces for national defense
Education: Fund and develop public education
Energy: Advise on energy policy and development
Health and Human Services: Promote national health programs and services
Homeland Security: Monitor and provide security within U.S. borders
Housing and Urban Development: Enforce housing laws and manage public housing
Interior: Manage natural resources and public lands
Justice: Enforce federal law and handle federal court cases
Labor: Enforce labor laws and promote worker welfare
State: Advise on foreign policy and foreign affairs
Transportation: Develop and regulate highway and transit systems
Treasury: Formulate tax and financial policy
Veterans Affairs: Provide benefits and services to military veterans

The Executive Departments

The **executive departments** make up a third group of organizations in the executive branch. These departments carry out the work of government in broad areas of public policy, such as agriculture, commerce, and labor.

Each department also contains federal agencies that target more specific policy areas within the department's general focus. For example, the Federal Bureau of Investigation is an agency that exists within the Justice Department, while the U.S. Mint is part of the Treasury Department.

During Washington's presidency, there were just three executive departments: War, State, and Treasury. Washington met with these departments regularly to debate issues. Today there are 15 executive departments. The newest is the Department of Homeland Security, created in 2003. All 15 department heads are members of the cabinet, which may also include the vice president and the national security adviser. As cabinets have grown in size, presidents have become less inclined to hold regular meetings. Instead, they are more likely to turn to White House staff and other personal advisers for help in crafting policy.

Independent Agencies

The executive branch also includes dozens of **independent agencies** that help implement federal policy. These groups are considered independent because they do not fall within executive departments, though they answer directly to the president. These groups go by various names, including agency, commission, administration, authority, and corporation.

One of the largest independent agencies is the National Aeronautics and Space Administration (NASA). This agency was created in 1958 to help the United States compete with the Soviet Union in the space race. Other well-known independent agencies include the Central Intelligence Agency (CIA), the Peace Corps, the Federal Communications Commission (FCC), and the Food and Drug Administration (FDA).

Some independent agencies create and enforce regulations. The FCC, for example, has jurisdiction over channels of communication, including radio and television, and the FDA was established to promote public health through regulating consumable food and pharmaceutical products.

A few federal agencies are run like businesses. They depend on revenues that they generate themselves rather than on tax dollars. The U.S. Postal Service is one such agency.

◼ 13.6 Local, State, and Federal Bureaucracies

Government at every level depends on a bureaucracy to carry out public policies. Yet bureaucracy is one aspect of government that Americans love to hate. According to critics, government bureaucracies are too large, too impersonal, and too self-serving to accomplish much. As Senator Eugene McCarthy once quipped, "The only thing that saves us from the bureaucracy is its inefficiency." But is this a fair assessment of local, state, and federal bureaucracies?

Who Are Civil Servants, and What Do They Do?

Bureaucracies are run by **civil servants,** or civilian employees working in government agencies. In popular culture, civil servants are often portrayed as mindless paper pushers who insist on following petty rules and creating mounds of paperwork, all while ignoring human needs. In reality, most government employees are hardworking, highly skilled individuals who are dedicated to their jobs.

AmeriCorps is a volunteer service organization run by a federal agency, the Corporation for National and Community Service. Here, AmeriCorps volunteers gather for a national day of service in honor of Martin Luther King Jr.

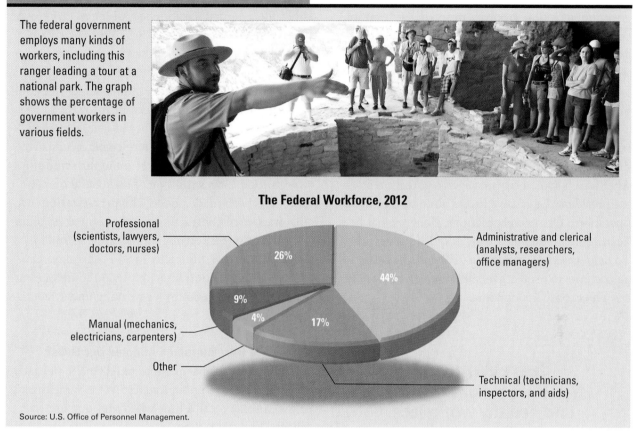

Federal Workers

The federal government employs many kinds of workers, including this ranger leading a tour at a national park. The graph shows the percentage of government workers in various fields.

The Federal Workforce, 2012

Professional (scientists, lawyers, doctors, nurses) — 26%

Administrative and clerical (analysts, researchers, office managers) — 44%

Manual (mechanics, electricians, carpenters) — 9%

Other — 4%

Technical (technicians, inspectors, and aids) — 17%

Source: U.S. Office of Personnel Management.

The work done by civil servants ranges from nursing and photography to engineering and economic analysis. Civil servants are responsible for providing many of the government services that Americans need and want. For example, public school teachers, park rangers, firefighters, and health inspectors are all government employees.

What Are the Sources of Bureaucratic Power?

For a bureaucracy to be effective, it must have the power it needs to do its job. This power stems from various sources, including those described here.

Legislative and budgetary support. A bureaucracy relies on laws and adequate funding to support its work. Without adequate funds, for example, a public school district may not be able to hire enough teachers for its students.

Interest group support. Government agencies can gain or lose power depending on the response of interest groups to their work. For example, the power of the Environmental Protection Agency may be enhanced by support from environmental groups. Or opposition from interest groups that favor fewer environmental controls may weaken it.

Expertise of bureaucrats. The ideal bureaucracy is staffed by workers who are expert at their jobs. For a bureaucracy to work well, employees must know what they are doing. For that reason, many government jobs require applicants to pass competitive exams.

Longevity or permanence. The longer a government agency exists, the more likely it is to enjoy substantial power. In the same way, seniority strengthens the hand of government workers, who tend to stay in their jobs for many years. The average federal employee has been at his or her job for around 17 years.

Effective leadership. Federal agencies typically thrive under effective leaders. Conversely, they flounder when their leadership is poor. Without effective leadership, NASA would not have been able to land a man on the moon in 1969, just eight years after President Kennedy made that achievement a national goal.

Citizen demand. Concerned citizens can help expand and strengthen bureaucracy by demanding government action to solve a problem. For example, public concerns about the safety of workers led Congress to form the Occupational Safety and Health Administration (OSHA) in the early 1970s. This federal agency enforces health and safety regulations in the workplace.

The power of bureaucracies is not unlimited, however. Ultimately, bureaucracies work under the direction of an elected or appointed chief executive, whether a mayor, a city manager, a governor, or the president. Legislative bodies also monitor their operations. On several occasions, Congress has held hearings to investigate the work of federal agencies. To help weed out corruption, Congress has also passed laws to protect **whistle-blowers,** or employees who expose wrongdoing.

Concerns about workplace safety led to the creation of the Occupational Safety and Health Administration (OSHA) during the 1970s. Today, OSHA continues to ensure safe workplaces for Americans. This poster informs teens about their rights at work.

Is the Growth of Bureaucracy Out of Control?

Bureaucracy has grown at all levels of government since this country was founded. Much of this growth has occurred since World War II, particularly since the 1960s, as government has provided more services to the American people. Although many people complain about the growth of bureaucracy, they still want the services that civil servants provide.

In recent years, the number of federal civilian government employees has leveled off. The size of the federal workforce today is about the same as it was in 1960. This shrinking of the federal bureaucracy has been made possible by **privatization,** or the practice of contracting private companies to do jobs once done by civil servants. Some 13 million people now work indirectly for the federal bureaucracy, either on contract with private companies or as state and local employees working under federal funding.

How Have Bureaucracies Affected Our Lives?

Many Americans have a story to tell about a negative experience with a public agency. At the same time, most can also recall a time when they desperately needed the services that civil servants provide. New Yorkers felt this way in 2005, when public transit workers went on strike. Some 7 million commuters suddenly lacked public transport. Many had to walk miles to get to work. When the strike ended two days later, commuters had a new appreciation for the value of public services.

On the other hand, government bureaucracy has improved the lives of many Americans. In the past few decades, it has helped achieve the following:

- fewer people living in poverty
- better air and water quality
- more rights for women and minorities
- better access to health care for the elderly
- safer food and drugs
- lower crime rates
- higher high school graduation rates
- elimination or prevention of diseases such as polio
- higher rates of home ownership
- development of the Internet
- safer highways
- more children in preschool

A century ago, many Americans lived in filthy slums that bred disease and worked in dangerous factories with few safety provisions. That has all changed for the better through the efforts of government agencies. Despite frequent complaints about bureaucratic waste and mismanagement, most Americans would be reluctant to give up the benefits that bureaucracy provides.

Presidents often talk about reducing the federal bureaucracy, but most find it difficult to cut executive staff.

Summary

The executive branch enforces the laws and carries out government policy. A chief executive leads this branch and oversees the work of the government bureaucracy.

Chief executives Mayors, governors, and presidents are all chief executives. They manage executive affairs at their level of government.

Presidential power The president has certain powers under the Constitution. Over time, however, presidential power has expanded as a result of custom and practice. Today the president enjoys powers beyond those listed in the Constitution.

Presidential roles The president plays many roles as head of the executive branch. Among these are chief executive, commander in chief, chief diplomat, and chief policymaker.

Organization of the executive branch The executive branch contains many officials, departments, and agencies. The president oversees the operations of these various groups, with assistance from advisers.

Bureaucracy Most Americans benefit from the services that local, state, and federal bureaucracies provide, despite complaints about bureaucratic inefficiency.

Do you want to be president?

It is often said that any person born in the United States can grow up to be president. This is part of the "American dream." But do young people today want the job? To answer that question, ABC News and *Weekly Reader* conducted an opinion poll of teenagers.

The following article describes the results of that survey. As you read it and look at the graphs, ask yourself, Would I want the job of president someday? If the answer is no, ask, What kind of person should be elected to that powerful office?

Run the Country? Most Teens Would Pass

by Dalia Sussman

At least one aspect of the American dream isn't quite what it's cracked up to be: While most teenagers in this country do think they could grow up to be president of the United States, the vast majority wouldn't want the job.

Fifty-four percent of 12- to 17-year-olds in this ABC News/ *Weekly Reader* poll think they could grow up to be president. That includes equal numbers of boys and girls, and more, 62 percent, of teens of color, despite a history of white male presidents.

But an overwhelming majority of teens—nearly eight in 10 —aren't interested in the job.

Why not? The top reason by far, cited by 40 percent, is either a lack of interest in politics or other career plans. An additional 20 percent say there's too much pressure or responsibility in the

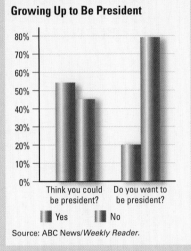

Growing Up to Be President

Source: ABC News/*Weekly Reader*.

job, 15 percent say it's too much work, and 14 percent think they wouldn't be good at it. Five percent say there's "just too much arguing" involved . . .

Younger teens are somewhat more optimistic about their prospects of getting elected president, and are twice as likely to want the job. Kids age 12–14 say they could be president by

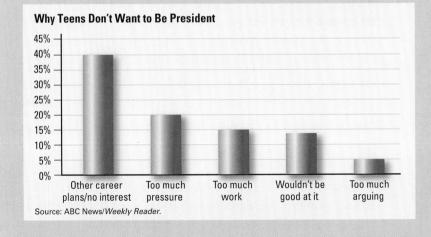

Why Teens Don't Want to Be President

Source: ABC News/*Weekly Reader*.

a 17-point margin (58–41 percent); those age 15–17 are evenly split. And 26 percent of the younger group would like to be president, compared with 13 percent of older teens.

Girls are 15 points more likely than boys to say they're not interested in the country's top job because of other career plans or a disinterest in politics. Boys are more apt than girls either to say that it's too much responsibility or too much work . . .

But lack of interest in politics does not translate into lack of interest in this year's [the 2004] presidential election.

Indeed, most teens, 57 percent, say they're at least somewhat interested in the campaign. And for good reason: seventy-two percent say that in terms of an impact on their lives, it does matter who gets elected . . .

Interest is higher among teens with college-educated parents—and it's twice as high (66 to 32 percent) among kids who think it matters in their life who's president, compared with those who don't . . .

In addition to the responses mentioned above, some respondents gave other reasons for not wanting to be president. Some

reflect the current state of the world—"I don't like war"; another, perhaps reflecting the Clinton years, was "too many scandals." One respondent cited security fears—"I don't want to get assassinated." Another critiqued the country's political structure: "I think that no one should have that much power." And one other summed it up neatly: "It doesn't sound like fun."

The poll was conducted by telephone January 7–11, 2004, among a random national sample of 505 12- to 17-year-olds. The results have a 4.5-point error margin.

Traits that Appeal to Voters—or Not

In a 2011 survey, voters indicated their degree of willingness to support presidential candidates with certain traits. Below are the results, organized by candidates' traits.

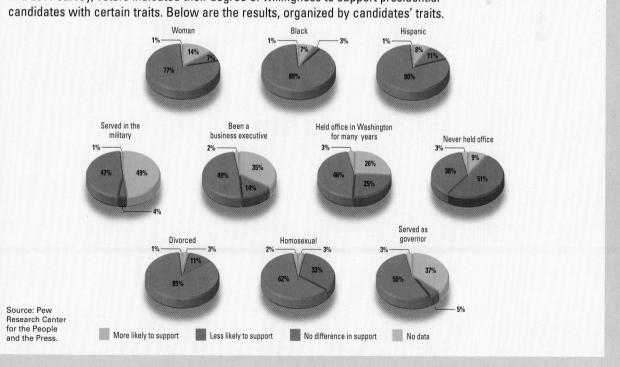

Source: Pew Research Center for the People and the Press.

More likely to support   Less likely to support   No difference in support   No data

Chapter 14

The Federal Budget

Does the federal government budget and spend your tax dollars wisely?

■ 14.1 Introduction

On January 24, 2012, the House chamber filled with representatives, senators, Supreme Court justices, cabinet heads, military leaders, and invited guests. They had gathered for the president's annual message to Congress known as the State of the Union address. The name comes from the Constitution, which says the president "shall from time to time give to the Congress Information of the State of the Union, and recommend to their Consideration such Measures as he shall judge necessary and expedient."

Just after 9:00 P.M., the Sergeant at Arms of the House called out, "Mister Speaker, the President of the United States." Barack Obama slowly made his way to the podium amid handshakes and applause. Once there, he was formally introduced to the assembled leaders and the nation by Speaker John Boehner.

In his address, Obama discussed the achievements of the U.S. military before launching into the major topic of the night: the American economy. He recalled that the Great Recession in 2008 "plunged our economy into a crisis that put millions out of work, saddled us with more debt, and left innocent hardworking Americans holding the bag." Since then, Obama said that the economy has made great strides:

President Barack Obama delivering his State of the Union address in 2012

As the cartoon suggests, presidents often use the State of the Union address to introduce proposals designed to appeal to voters, especially in election years. It remains up to Congress to decide which, if any, of these initiatives will be funded.

The state of our Union is getting stronger. And we've come too far to turn back now. As long as I'm President, I will work with anyone in this chamber to build on this momentum. . . . No, we will not go back to an economy weakened by outsourcing, bad debt, and phony financial profits. Tonight, I want to speak about how we move forward . . .

Obama went on to outline an ambitious agenda that included increasing manufacturing in the United States, building skills for American workers, reforming education and immigration policy, cutting taxes for small businesses and the middle class, removing tax cuts for the wealthy, developing clean energy, and improving infrastructure. These plans were part of Obama's vision to balance the budget and reduce the federal deficit. He continued,

When it comes to the deficit, we've already agreed to more than $2 trillion in cuts and savings. But we need to do more, and that means making choices.

The following month, on February 13, Obama presented the choices he made to reduce the deficit in the federal budget he submitted to Congress. Submitting a budget for the federal government to Congress is one of the president's most important responsibilities each year. This chapter explores how the process of creating that budget works, both before and after the president delivers the annual State of the Union address.

14.2 Who Controls the Budget Process?

"The president proposes, Congress disposes." This is how an old Washington saying sums up the process of creating a federal budget. As is true of the legislative process, however, the reality is far more complex. During some periods of our history, Congress dominated budget making. At other times, the president was clearly in charge. Today control is shared as the two branches work together to shape a budget that reflects their priorities.

Congressional Control of Federal Spending: 1789–1921

The federal budget is an estimate of the money the government will take in and spend on programs over the next **fiscal year**. A fiscal year is the period of time an organization uses for its budgeting, record keeping, and financial reporting. The U.S. government's fiscal year begins October 1 and ends September 30.

The Constitution talks about levying taxes and spending money, but it does not mention budgets. At the time the Constitution was written, the idea of trying to estimate revenues and expenditures a year in advance was new. In general, governments simply collected taxes and then spent money as needed. In times of crisis or a shortfall in income, taxes were raised to bring in extra money.

For more than a century, Congress dominated this simple method of raising and spending money.

As the Constitution requires, all proposals for the spending of federal funds originated in the House of Representatives. These requests were then combined into a single spending bill. Once the House approved the spending bill, it went to the Senate for approval. The president's role in this process was limited to signing the spending bill into law or vetoing it.

This system worked fairly well during the 1800s. Usually revenues and expenditures came out about even, creating a **balanced budget**. During some years, the country even had a small **budget surplus,** with extra funds left over. The only time the country experienced a **federal deficit,** or a shortfall of revenue, was during wartime.

In times of war, the government raised taxes and borrowed money to fund the military campaign. The money borrowed created a **national debt**. When the war ended, Congress worked to retire, or pay off, the national debt as quickly as possible.

Presidential Dominance of Budget Making: 1921–1974

The rapid growth of government spending during World War I overwhelmed Congress's old way

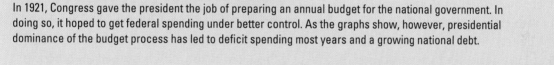

Federal Budgets, Spending, and Borrowing, 1921–1974

In 1921, Congress gave the president the job of preparing an annual budget for the national government. In doing so, it hoped to get federal spending under better control. As the graphs show, however, presidential dominance of the budget process has led to deficit spending most years and a growing national debt.

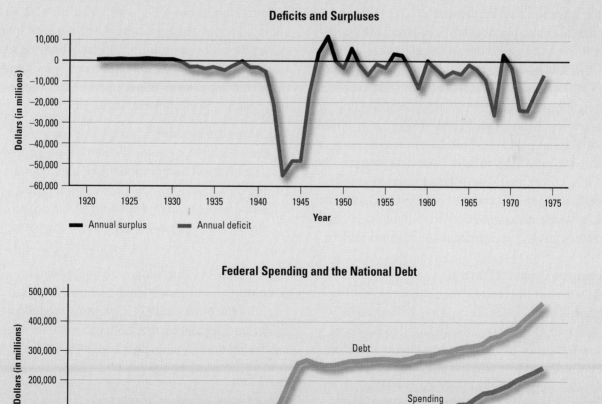

Source: Budget of the U.S. Government FY2008, Historical Tables.

of appropriating funds. By the end of 1919, federal expenditures were more than 26 times what they had been just five years earlier. Moreover, the national debt had soared to a record $26 billion.

Faced with a huge war debt and with what looked to many like runaway spending, Congress enacted the Budget and Accounting Act of 1921. This act set up the Bureau of the Budget in the executive branch to oversee a new budget-making process. The bureau was renamed the Office of Management and Budget in 1970. The act also set up the General Accounting Office to improve congressional oversight of federal spending.

Under this new budget process, the president was required to submit a proposed budget to Congress each year. The intent of this requirement was to give Congress better information with which to make spending decisions. The effect, however, was to concentrate budget power in the executive branch.

Beginning with Franklin Roosevelt, presidents used their new budget power to promote their own policy agendas. They decided which agencies and programs should be funded and which should not. Congress could override those decisions, but generally it went along with the president's budget.

By 1970, however, it was clear that the budget process put in place in 1921 had not led to a new era of balanced budgets. Year after year, presidents sent budgets to Congress that included costly new programs that lawmakers wanted to support. But few in either branch wanted to raise taxes to fund those new projects. The result was year after year of **deficit spending**—or spending financed by borrowing rather than by tax revenues. As the deficits piled up, the national debt began to rise to levels that alarmed many national leaders.

Nixon and Congress Clash

Concern over the budget process mounted during Richard Nixon's presidency. Already facing disapproval over the Watergate scandal, Nixon enraged many legislators by using the president's power of **impoundment** to nullify congressional spending decisions. Impoundment involves the refusal of a chief executive to spend funds that have been appropriated by the legislature.

Impoundment was not new. Presidents before Nixon had used this power to make small spending cuts in programs that they viewed as unwise or unnecessary. Members of Congress might grumble when their favor-

"*Don't put up any resistance! Just keep in step.*"

This cartoon captures the concern that was felt by many Americans in the early 1970s that Richard Nixon was abusing his presidential powers.

ite projects were canceled, but they did not rebel against the occasional decision to impound federal funds.

President Nixon, however, used his power to impound funds on a scale never seen before. In an effort to reduce deficit spending, he refused to spend billions of dollars already appropriated by Congress. He also used impoundment to "defund" programs he did not approve of. When asked by reporters about his use of this power, Nixon declared,

> *The constitutional right for the President of the United States to impound funds . . . is absolutely clear . . . I will not spend money if the Congress overspends, and I will not be for programs that will raise the taxes and put a bigger burden on the already overburdened American taxpayer.*
> —Richard Nixon, Jan. 31, 1973

Members of Congress saw Nixon's use of impoundment as an assault on their constitutional power of the purse. In 1974, Congress responded by enacting legislation that both increased its role in shaping the federal budget and limited the president's powers of impoundment.

Shared Control of Budget Making: 1974 to the Present

The Budget and Impoundment Control Act of 1974 created the budget process that is still in use today. This process gives the legislative and executive branches shared control over budget making.

In 1974, Congress revised the budget process to give lawmakers more control over government spending. This change has not led to an era of balanced budgets. By 1994, the national debt was ten times the size it had been in 1974. The national debt continued to increase in the years that followed.

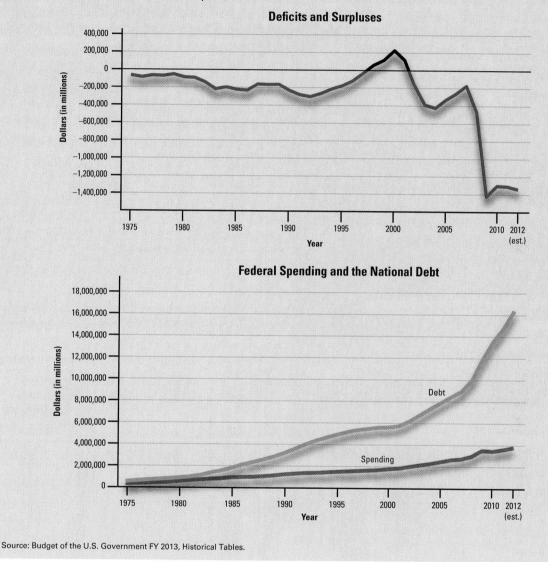

The main change brought about by this legislation was the creation of new budget committees in both the House and Senate. These committees are responsible for drafting Congress's own spending priorities, known as the **budget resolution**. The act also created the Congressional Budget Office to assist Congress in this process. The CBO provides nonpartisan estimates of revenue and spending. It also "scores" proposed tax and spending bills to indicate their impact on future budgets.

Many of the lawmakers who supported the new budget process laid out in the 1974 act hoped it would reduce conflict between the executive and legislative branches. In this they were disappointed. Even with responsibility more evenly shared, the budget process frequently leads to power struggles between the two branches. At the center of these struggles are deep disagreements over how revenue should be raised and how the tax dollars collected each year should be budgeted and spent.

■ 14.3 The Federal Budget Cycle

On February 13, 2012, President Barack Obama sent a $3.8 trillion **budget proposal** for fiscal year 2013 to Capitol Hill. The nation's economy was unsteady, but Obama believed that his proposal would help balance the budget over time. "This Budget is a step in the right direction," he wrote. "And I hope it will help serve as a roadmap for how we can grow the economy, create jobs, and give Americans everywhere the security they deserve." Republicans in the House of Representatives were not so optimistic. In response to the president's budget proposal, the chair of the House Budget Committee stated that the budget "is a recipe for a debt crisis."

From the point of view of Congress, the arrival of the president's budget proposal marks the beginning of the federal **budget cycle**. From the perspective of the executive branch, however, this is the halfway point in a process that spreads over 18 months, from initial planning to the beginning of the next fiscal year.

Phase One: The Executive Branch Prepares a Budget Proposal

Constructing a federal budget is about more than just money. It reflects the broader vision of the president and Congress about the purpose and activities of the national government. "Budgets are about setting priorities," explains economist Brian Reidl. "A rational budget process should help lawmakers set priorities and separate vital needs from unaffordable luxuries."

The task of separating "vital needs" from "unaffordable luxuries" begins in the federal bureaucracy. Months before the president submits a budget to Congress, each department and agency begins work on its own budget request for the following fiscal year.

By June, these budget requests are submitted to the Office of Management and Budget for review. The main job of the OMB, an agency within the Executive Office, is to craft a budget that reflects the policy goals and political agenda of the president.

During the summer and fall, OMB staffers review the various budget requests. They consider what is vital and affordable based on projected revenue. They also work with the president and his advisers to see how well the various requests reflect the president's priorities. Based on all of this information, the OMB prepares a budget proposal for the president to review and revise. By law, the president must submit this proposal to Congress by the first Monday in February.

Phase Two: Congress Crafts a Budget Resolution

Once the president's budget proposal reaches Congress, the House and Senate budget committees take

---

The Budget Calendar

The four phases of the budget process often overlap. During the spring and summer, federal agencies have to juggle three different budgets. They operate under their budgets for the current fiscal year. They lobby Congress for funds in next fiscal year's budget. And they work with the Office of Management and Budget to plan for the budget after that.

Phase One
Preparing the Budget Proposal

May
Departments and agencies begin planning budget requests with the help of the OMB.

June
July
August
The OMB issues detailed instructions for submitting budget requests. Planning continues.

September
Agencies and departments make budget submissions.

October
November
The OMB reviews all requests and submits a budget to the White House.

December
The OMB and the White House prepare the president's budget proposal.

January
The president signals budget priorities in the State of the Union address.

Sources: Library of Congress Congressional Research Service; House of Representatives Committee on Rules; Ethel Wood and Steven C. Sansone, *American Government: A Complete Coursebook*, Wilmington, MA: Great Source Education Group, 2000.

over. Their job is to analyze the proposed budget and to recommend changes that reflect Congress's spending priorities.

The two budget committees are assisted by the Congressional Budget Office. The CBO's main job is to compare how well the president's budget matches its own estimates of future revenues and expenses. As a nonpartisan agency, the CBO does not make policy recommendations to Congress.

During March and April, House and Senate budget committees hold hearings on the president's proposed budget. They hear testimony from OMB staffers about their analysis. They quiz agency officials about funding needs. They consult with other committees to hear their views and estimates about next year's budget.

Based on this information, each budget committee prepares its own budget resolution. A budget resolution sets guidelines for how much money Congress should spend in 20 broad categories. These categories include national defense, agriculture, and health. A budget resolution is not a detailed spending plan like the president's budget proposal. Nor does it have the force of law. But it does guide Congress over the next few months.

After each chamber passes its own budget resolution, the two versions go to a conference committee to be reconciled. The final version is supposed to be approved by the full House and Senate by April 15. That deadline is not always met, however, and some years no budget resolution has been approved.

Phase Three: Congress Enacts Appropriation Bills

Beginning as early as March, the Senate and the House Appropriations Committees start work on Congress's 13 appropriation bills. Each bill deals with one of the spending categories laid out in the budget resolution. These bills, taken together, make up the government's final budget.

Work on appropriation bills continues through the spring and summer. During this time, the president pays close attention to the budget process. If all goes well, most of the work on the 13 bills will be completed before Congress goes on vacation in August.

When Congress returns in September, it works out any differences between the appropriation bills passed by the House and Senate. The bills then go to the president for approval. The president may sign or veto some or all of the bills. In the latter case, Congress can either seek to override the veto or revise the bill to gain the president's approval. Ideally, all 13 appropriation bills are law and the budget is in place before the new fiscal year begins on October 1.

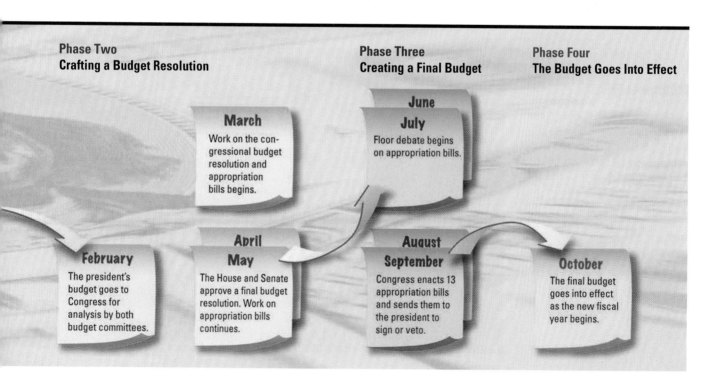

Phase Two
Crafting a Budget Resolution

March
Work on the congressional budget resolution and appropriation bills begins.

February
The president's budget goes to Congress for analysis by both budget committees.

April
May
The House and Senate approve a final budget resolution. Work on appropriation bills continues.

Phase Three
Creating a Final Budget

June
July
Floor debate begins on appropriation bills.

August
September
Congress enacts 13 appropriation bills and sends them to the president to sign or veto.

Phase Four
The Budget Goes Into Effect

October
The final budget goes into effect as the new fiscal year begins.

Phase Four: The New Fiscal Year Begins . . . Or Does It?

It sometimes happens that the president and Congress are not able to reach agreement on the budget by October 1. Usually in this situation, Congress enacts and the president signs a **continuing resolution** to keep the government working. A continuing resolution allows government programs to operate at current funding levels for a fixed period. During this time, both sides try to work out their differences on the budget.

If Congress and the president cannot reach an agreement by the time the continuing resolution ends and another one is not enacted, the result is a **budget crisis**. In extreme cases, a budget crisis can lead to a shutdown of "nonessential" government activities. Such shutdowns have occurred many times over the years, sometimes for a few hours, sometimes for several days.

One of the most serious budget crises began in 1995, when budget negotiations between President Bill Clinton and Congress broke down. A continuing resolution was passed to keep the government going for a few weeks. When that time ran out, Congress and the president could not agree on another resolution, much less a final budget. As a result, the many agencies of the federal government were shut down for weeks.

The crisis ended the following January, when the president and Congress agreed to another continu-

ing resolution. As he signed the resolution, Clinton expressed his hope that "no Congress will ever again shut the federal government down in this way."

■ 14.4 Where the Money Comes from and Where It Goes

In 1948, Florida businessman Dallas Hostetler sat down and calculated how many days he had to work each year to pay his tax bills. According to his estimate, every penny he earned from January through March went to pay taxes. Hostetler called the first day that he began earning money that he could keep for himself **Tax Freedom Day**. Over time, Tax Freedom Day has been pushed back on the calendar. Experts estimate that the average American today works four full months to fund government at the national, state, and local levels.

The Federal Government's Revenue Sources

The most important revenue source for the federal government is the **individual income tax**. This is a tax levied on an individual's or a married couple's annual income. Individual income is taxed whether it comes from wages or from earnings on investments. **Social insurance taxes** are a second major source of federal funding. You may have seen these taxes in the form of Social Security and Medicare deductions from a paycheck. These payroll taxes are used to

Most of the federal government's tax revenue comes from individual income taxes. Each year, an individual or a married couple who earns income is required to submit their taxes by mid-April. Taxes help fund the U.S. military, interest on national debt, federal agencies, and other programs.

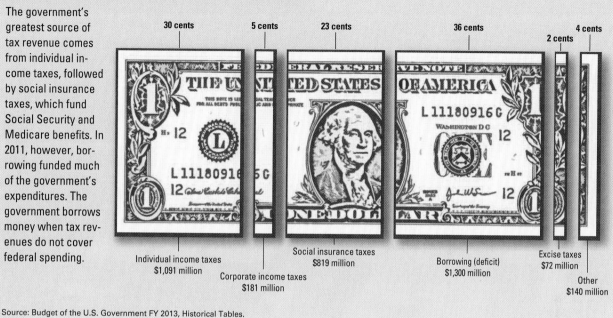

The government's greatest source of tax revenue comes from individual income taxes, followed by social insurance taxes, which fund Social Security and Medicare benefits. In 2011, however, borrowing funded much of the government's expenditures. The government borrows money when tax revenues do not cover federal spending.

30 cents

5 cents

23 cents

36 cents

2 cents

4 cents

Individual income taxes
$1,091 million

Corporate income taxes
$181 million

Social insurance taxes
$819 million

Borrowing (deficit)
$1,300 million

Excise taxes
$72 million

Other
$140 million

Source: Budget of the U.S. Government FY 2013, Historical Tables.

fund pensions and health insurance for the elderly. They also fund unemployment insurance and disability insurance for workers who are laid off or injured on the job.

The third-largest source of federal revenue is the **corporate income tax**. This is a tax paid by businesses on their profits each year. For this reason, it is sometimes called a profit tax.

The government also raises money with **excise taxes**. These are taxes levied on the sale of goods, like alcohol, and services. Your family probably pays federal excise tax on its local telephone service.

Federal taxes differ in both what they tax and whether they are progressive or regressive. A **progressive tax** is one in which the tax burden falls more heavily on wealthy than poor taxpayers. The term *progressive* refers to the way tax rates progress from low to high as one's income rises. Individual and corporate income taxes are progressive taxes.

In contrast, a **regressive tax** is one in which the tax burden, as a percentage of income, falls more heavily on poor taxpayers than on wealthy ones. Excise taxes are an example of a regressive tax. A person earning $20,000 a year pays the same excise tax on local phone service as someone earning $2 million a year. But that tax, measured as a percentage of

income, is much higher for the low-income person.

Another way for the government to fund expenditures is borrowing. When federal spending exceeds tax revenue, the government borrows from private sources and foreign countries. In 2011, the government borrowed about $1.3 trillion to fund the deficit.

Mandatory Spending: Entitlements and Interest

Only about one-third of government spending is covered by the budget hashed out each year by Congress and the president. That is because most government revenue today is already committed by law to be spent in specified ways. This **mandatory spending** can be altered only by special legislation that changes the amount to be spent.

The two main categories of mandatory spending are interest on the national debt and **entitlements**. Entitlements are programs through which individuals receive benefits based on their age, income, or some other criteria. Examples include food stamps and Social Security pensions. The amount of money spent on such programs depends on the number of people who sign up for their benefits, not on an annual appropriation. The amount of federal revenue dedicated to mandatory spending has grown significantly in recent years.

Discretionary Spending: Defense, Government Services, and Pork

The budget debated in Congress is made up of **discretionary spending**. Funding for discretionary items can be raised or lowered as Congress sees fit. By far, the biggest chunk of discretionary spending goes to the Department of Defense to support the armed forces. The rest funds the many services provided by federal agencies.

A frequent complaint about the budget process focuses on the practice of using **earmarks** to set aside funds for specific projects. The 2005 Transportation Equity Act, for instance, included more than 6,000 earmarks for home-district projects. The most notorious

How Federal Tax Dollars Are Spent

Over the years, the amount of the federal budget dedicated to mandatory spending has grown. Today about two-thirds of federal revenue is spent on interest and entitlement benefits. The remaining third makes up the discretionary budget. By far, the largest discretionary budget item is defense spending.

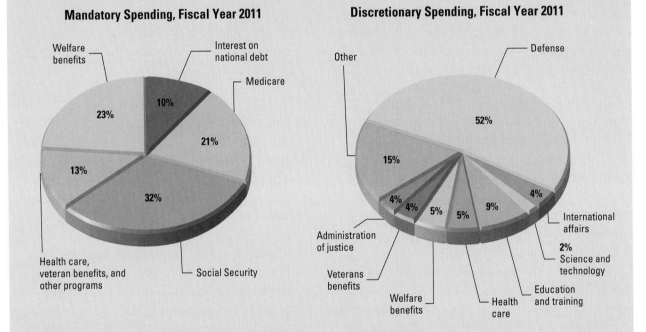

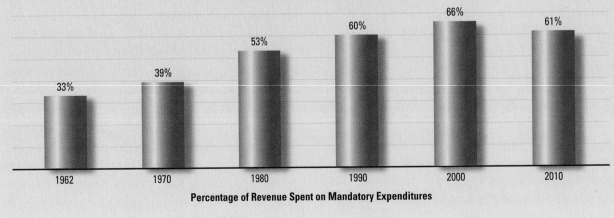

Source: Budget of the U.S. Government FY 2013, Historical Tables.

Here, California state legislators negotiate a budget to repair a growing shortfall in 2009. The state's constitution required a two-thirds vote to pass a budget, but members of Congress had difficulty agreeing on an approach on how to fix the shortfall. Eventually, the legislature approved a budget that relied on California voters to pass several propositions. When voters did not pass them, legislators returned to the capitol to negotiate a new budget.

was a $223 million set-aside to fund construction of a bridge to a sparsely populated island in Alaska. This much-criticized "bridge to nowhere" was finally removed from the bill, but not before fueling a nationwide debate over the use of earmarks to fund pork-barrel projects. In his State of the Union address in 2007, President George W. Bush called on Congress to begin earmark reform and "expose every earmark to the light of day."

Historically, lawmakers could attach earmarks to bills without identifying themselves. In response to the growing chorus of criticism, Congress has made earmarking more transparent, or open to public scrutiny. For example, sponsors of earmarks are required to make their identity public 48 hours before floor debate begins on the bill to which they have attached spending set-asides.

President Obama also supported earmark reform and called on Congress to increase transparency by publishing earmarks on a Web site open to the public. In 2009, he also asked Congress to regulate earmarks set for private businesses. Soon after, in 2010, Congress banned earmarks to for-profit companies.

▇ 14.5 Funding State and Local Government

Like the federal government, state and local governments must make decisions each year about how to collect the revenue they need and how to spend those tax dollars. The chief executive of each state, county, or city usually prepares the annual budget. The budget is then approved by the state legislature, county board, or city council. However, unlike the federal government, state and local governments often face limitations that make the creation of budgets especially difficult.

State and Local Versus Federal Budget Making

State and local governments, like the federal government, raise most of their revenue from taxes. However, they are often more limited in their power to spend money than is the federal government.

Many state constitutions, for example, require their legislatures to approve a balanced budget each year. They are not allowed, like Congress, to borrow money to fill a gap between revenue and expenses. Instead, lawmakers must either cut programs or raise taxes when revenues fall short of proposed expenditures.

Some state constitutions prohibit state lawmakers from enacting certain types of taxes. Seven states, for instance, ban the imposition of taxes on personal income. Other constitutions limit how much certain taxes can increase from year to year. In Massachusetts, for example, taxes on property cannot rise by more than 2½ percent a year. Such restrictions can be changed only if voters approve amending the state constitution.

In addition, citizens play a much larger role in tax policy at the local and state levels than at the federal level. Many states and localities require voters to approve tax hikes through referenda. Some states, such as California, require a supermajority of two-thirds of the votes cast to approve increases in many types of taxes.

Sales Tax

A tax on the sale of goods that is paid by the customer at the time of purchase. Today, 45 states and many cities have a general sales tax.

Pro: Relatively easy to collect.

Con: Regressive tax. Affects rich and poor equally.

Property Tax

A tax levied on the value of real property, such as land, homes, and buildings. Serves as the chief source of income for local governments.

Pro: Real property cannot be easily hidden from the tax collector.

Con: The tax levied on real property may not reflect the owner's ability to pay.

Individual Income Tax

A tax on the incomes of state residents. Today, 43 states and a number of cities collect income taxes.

Pro: Progressive tax. Rates vary from less than 1 percent on lower incomes to nearly 10 percent on higher incomes.

Con: High rates may drive wealthy people to states with no or low income taxes.

Excise Tax

A tax levied on the sale of certain goods or services. Also called "sin taxes" because they are often levied on tobacco, alcohol, and gambling.

Pro: Taxing "sin" is easy for politicians.

Con: If raised too high, may encourage illegal traffic in taxed goods.

Lottery

A large-scale, legal gambling game organized to raise money for a public cause.

Pro: Provides money for public services without raising taxes.

Con: Regressive tax. Low-income people buy most lottery tickets.

Bonds

Debt issued by a government to raise funds for a specific purpose. Bonds are repaid, with interest, on fixed dates.

Pro: Help governments fund large projects, such as schools, that are too costly to pay for from current tax revenues.

Con: Debt created by bond sales may be a heavy burden on future taxpayers.

Inheritance and Estate Taxes

A tax levied on some or all of the estate (property and possessions) a person leaves behind at death. Those who inherit the estate pay the tax.

Pro: Progressive tax. The larger the estate, the more taxes paid.

Con: May discourage saving if people believe their nest egg will go to the government upon their death.

User Fees

Fees charged to use public facilities and services and for permits and licenses.

Pro: Those who want public services support them with their fees.

Con: Poor people may not be able to afford fee-based services, such as trash collection

---

Faced with these limitations, state and local leaders often scramble to generate needed revenue. The list above shows eight sources of revenue commonly used to raise money for state and local government services.

How State and Local Governments Spend Their Funds

At the federal level, the bulk of spending goes to entitlements for the elderly and national defense. In contrast, state and local governments devote large shares of their budgets to services that affect young people and their families in direct ways.

The most important of those services is education. By 2012, almost 50 million children were enrolled in public elementary and secondary schools across the United States. The average amount spent on each of these students exceeded $11,400 per year. More than 85 percent of that money came from state and local governments.

Law enforcement and fire protection are also responsibilities relegated mainly to local governments. The United States did not even have a national police force until the creation of the Federal Bureau of Investigation in 1909. In many communities, police protection is the second largest public expense after education.

State and local governments also fund a variety of health and welfare services, often with assistance from the federal government. Typical examples

State and local governments rely on revenue from various sources and spend their money in multiple ways. As these graphs show, revenues in 2010 came mainly from taxes and federal funding, while around half of all expenditures went to education and to health and social services.

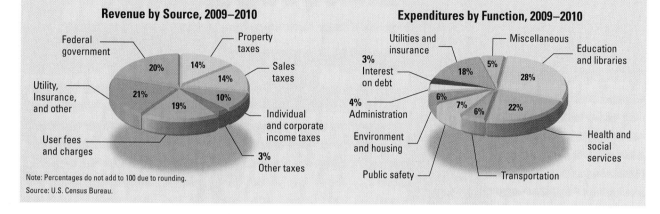

Revenue by Source, 2009–2010

Federal government 20%
Property taxes 14%
Sales taxes 14%
Individual and corporate income taxes 10%
Other taxes 3%
User fees and charges 19%
Utility, Insurance, and other 21%

Expenditures by Function, 2009–2010

Utilities and insurance 3%
Miscellaneous 5%
Education and libraries 28%
Interest on debt 18%
Administration 4%
Environment and housing 6%
Public safety 7%
Transportation 6%
Health and social services 22%

Note: Percentages do not add to 100 due to rounding.
Source: U.S. Census Bureau.

include public health clinics for low-income families, health care centers for the mentally ill, and childcare for low-income working families.

Many other services are funded at the state and local levels. For example, state and local governments spend money to build and maintain roads and bridges. They create and maintain parks and playgrounds for the public to enjoy. They fund public libraries, civic auditoriums, and museums. All of these services have been developed in response to public demand. The ever-present challenge is finding the money to pay for what the public wants.

Summary

The federal budget is an estimate of the money the government will take in and spend over a fiscal year. It is created by a long process that involves the executive and legislative branches of the government.

Control of the federal budget First Congress and then the president controlled development of the federal budget. The current budget process calls for cooperation between the executive and legislative branches.

Federal budget cycle Preparation of a federal budget is a long process that lasts almost two years. It begins with preparation of initial budget requests by federal departments and agencies and ends with a final budget approved by Congress and the president.

Revenue and expenditures Most revenue, at all levels of government, is raised through a variety of taxes. At the federal level, entitlements are the largest expenditure. At the state and local levels, education tops the expenditure list.

State and local budgets People depend on state and local governments to fund public schools, police and fire departments, roads and bridges, and health and welfare services. State and local governments pay for services through taxation, lotteries, and user fees.

What can the government do to repair the economy?

In 2008, the United States faced an economic crisis known as the Great Recession, the effects of which rolled into the next decade. When there is an economic crisis, the government can take a number of actions to improve the situation. Which action is the best to take is debatable.

Read about two different approaches that two economists argue are the best ways to deal with the U.S. economy. Which approach do you agree with?

Economists Debate Governments' Role in Repairing Economies

by Lorie Konish

Two renowned economists engaged in a fierce debate at the IMCA New York Consultants Conference on Tuesday on a question that both admitted had no concrete answer: What can the government do to repair the economy?

That question comes several years after a massive federal bailout in the U.S., and as some European nations totter on the brink of requiring rescue of their own. But the discussion titled "Keynes vs. Hayek," in honor of the famed debate between economists John Maynard Keynes and Friedrich Hayek more than 80 years ago, shows that different approaches to those problems exist just as much today.

The debate included Jared Bernstein, a senior fellow at the Center on Budget and Policy Priorities who was a member of President Barack Obama's economic team, and Russell Roberts, a professor of economics at George Mason University. Bernstein argued on behalf of Keynes' philosophies that economies sometimes require outside intervention to run smoothly. Roberts argued for Hayek's beliefs that economies should mostly have the opportunity to correct themselves.

For Bernstein, who was a newly named member of President-elect Obama's economic team in December 2008 when the U.S. economy was losing jobs at a rate of 800,000 per month, the choice was clear to create a stimulus package, he said.

Shortly after the stimulus funds were applied in 2009, the rate of GDP contraction got smaller, Bernstein said. While the unemployment rate actually increased from 7% when the stimulus was passed to 9.5% a year later, Bernstein cautioned that it's important to think about where that rate could have been, at 10% or 11%.

Bernstein argued that the opposite of Hayek's free market theory would be central planning, which has also proven it cannot work. What is needed instead is a hybrid, Bernstein said, where large government can sometimes take a lead role when necessary.

"There are times when the economy's in a bust, when there's a recession, where you need to do more stuff that looks a bit like central planning," Bernstein said.

Roberts, the professor of economics, sought to dispel the notion that government spending directly promotes economic growth.

"The New Deal didn't end the Great Depression. It was the war time spending," Roberts said. And even that injection did not benefit the economy evenly, Roberts argued. While weapons manufacturers saw a boost, the private sector did not.

Japan, which has also weathered its own prolonged downturn, has spent trillions on paving projects. The result has been good for contractors, Roberts said, yet has not resulted in a lift for the economy. The American Recovery and Rein-vestment Act may follow that same pattern.

"Did it work? The right answer is we don't know. But we don't have any evidence that it was successful," Roberts said.

That comes as the Congressional Budget Office estimates that, as of the third quarter of 2011, 400,000 to 2.4 million new jobs were created. Having a six-fold difference between those estimates—from .4 to 2.4—makes for an "imprecise world," according to Roberts.

"We should not put our children in debt . . . in the name of jump starting the economy where there's no evidence that the jumper cables are actually connected to anything," Roberts said.

Bernstein rebutted Roberts, saying he saw stimulus funding directly help job creation while he was working with Vice President Joe Biden. In an area of Florida where the unemployment rate was 20% among construction workers, one project helped put a few hundred individuals to work.

"This is what actually happened. It's not philosophy," Bernstein said. "When the government temporarily steps in and helps to replace some of the lost demand, some of the lost jobs, its helps to make people's lives a little more comfortable while the private sector is getting its act back together."

Lorie Konish is a contributor to On Wall Street, *a Web site that reports on the financial industry.*

BEN S. BERNANKE

In 2006, President George W. Bush appointed Ben Bernanke to a 14-year term in the Board of Governors of the Federal Reserve, or the Fed, the central bank of the United States. At the same time, Bush appointed him to a four-year term as chair of the Fed. President Barack Obama reappointed Bernanke for a second term as chair in 2010. The chair of the Fed plays a major role in monetary policy in the United States by having authority over the regulation of the Federal Reserve Banks, money supply, and interest rates.

Chapter 15

Courts, Judges, and the Law

How is the U.S. judicial system organized to ensure justice?

■ 15.1 Introduction

On February 2, 1790, the U.S. Supreme Court met publicly for the first time. Of the six justices that President George Washington had appointed to the Court, however, only four had managed to reach New York City, the new nation's temporary capital. The other two justices missed the Court's first term entirely.

The courtroom was crowded with onlookers as the justices arrived. Most of the observers were more impressed with the "elegance" of the justices' robes than with the judicial business at hand. In truth, there was no business. The Supreme Court's **docket,** or list of cases, was empty and would remain so for the next three years. After dealing with a few housekeeping chores, the justices ended their first session on February 10.

The Constitution, which had been ratified only two years earlier, clearly established the Supreme Court as part of a federal judiciary. Article III, Section I begins, "The judicial Power of the United States, shall be vested in one supreme Court." However, the framers of the Constitution were divided as to whether the new nation needed any inferior, or lower, courts. Some delegates to the Constitutional Convention argued that the state courts were more than able to deal with the nation's legal business. Others

The Supreme Court of the United States

Speaking of Politics

criminal law
The branch of law that regulates the conduct of individuals, defines crimes, and provides punishments for criminal acts. In criminal cases, the government is the prosecutor, because criminal acts are viewed as crimes against society.

civil law
The branch of law that concerns relationships between private parties. A civil action is usually brought by someone who claims to have suffered a loss because of another party's actions.

burden of proof
The obligation in a legal case to prove allegations by presenting strong supporting evidence. In a criminal case, this burden rests on the prosecution and in a civil case on the plaintiff.

defendant
The person or party in a criminal trial who is charged with committing a crime. Or, in a civil case, the person or party being sued.

prosecution
The attorneys representing the government and the people in a criminal case. It is the prosecution's job to show why a person accused of a crime should be found guilty as charged.

plaintiff
The person or party who brings a lawsuit, or legal action, against another party in a civil case.

writ of certiorari
An order from the Supreme Court to a lower court to provide the records of a case the Court has decided to review.

legal brief
A written document drawn up by an attorney that presents the facts and points of law in a client's case.

"And don't go whining to some higher court!"

The Judiciary Act of 1789 created a judicial system with several levels. Under certain circumstances, decisions from lower courts can be appealed to a higher court for review. There is no appeal, however, in cases decided by the Supreme Court. Decisions made there are final.

worried that a new set of federal courts would be too expensive.

In the end, the delegates compromised. The Constitution does not require the creation of inferior courts. However, it does permit "such inferior Courts as the Congress may from time to time ordain and establish."

Congress promptly moved to create these "inferior courts" by enacting the Judiciary Act of 1789. This law established a federal judicial system made up of district and circuit courts and specified the kinds of cases the courts could try. It laid out the qualifications and responsibilities of federal judges, district attorneys, and other judicial officials. It set the number of Supreme Court justices at six and established the principle that decisions of the Supreme Court are final and cannot be appealed.

With relatively minor changes, the federal judicial system created in 1789 is the same system we have today. The number and levels of courts has grown with the nation, and three more justices have been added to the Supreme Court to deal with its growing caseload. This chapter examines the federal judicial system and its relationship to state systems and to ordinary citizens seeking justice.

15.2 The Main Role of the Judicial Branch: Resolving Society's Conflicts

At the heart of every judicial proceeding is the law. And at the heart of every law is a potential conflict. Such conflicts may involve individuals, businesses, interest groups, or society at large. The judicial system's job is to resolve those conflicts peacefully, in accordance with the law, and in a manner most parties to the conflict will see as just, or fair.

Two Kinds of Legal Conflicts: Criminal and Civil

The challenge of resolving conflicts in a just manner usually begins in trial courts, which focus on sorting through the facts of a case. Cases can be categorized by whether the dispute involves criminal or civil law.

Criminal law refers to legal measures passed by a legislative body to protect the welfare of society and to provide punishments for those who fail to comply. The government, acting on society's behalf, always prosecutes criminal cases. People found guilty of violating criminal laws are punished through fines, prison sentences, probation, or similar penalties. To be convicted of a crime, a person must be found guilty **beyond a reasonable doubt,** usually by a jury. This does not mean it must be proved with absolute certainty but rather that there must be no reasonable explanation for what happened other than that the accused did it.

Civil law refers to legal measures that govern conflicts between private parties or, occasionally, between a private party and the government. Such conflicts can arise from various circumstances, including disputes over the ownership of property, injuries suffered in an accident, or questions about the terms of a contract. In most civil cases, one party sues another party for damages, or compensation of some sort.

The **burden of proof** in civil trials is lower than in criminal trials. The party bringing the lawsuit must only prove that there is a **preponderance of evidence**. This means that the party must prove that it is more likely than not that the other party is at fault and should be held liable. This decision is usually made by a jury. A jury also decides on the amount of **damages,** or money to compensate for the losses suffered, that the party found liable should pay.

The Many Players in a Court of Law

If you have ever watched a trial on television or in a movie, you have most likely seen the various players in a typical courtroom. Presiding over the courtroom is the judge. The judge controls the legal proceedings, from jury selection to sentencing. It is the judge's job to determine whether certain evidence is admissible. Before a jury decides a case, the judge instructs the jurors on how the law should guide them in making their decision.

Sitting near the judge are the people directly involved in the case being tried. In a criminal trial, the person accused of a crime is known as the **defendant**. The government lawyer or team of lawyers bringing evidence against the defendant forms the **prosecution**.

Who's Who in the Courtroom

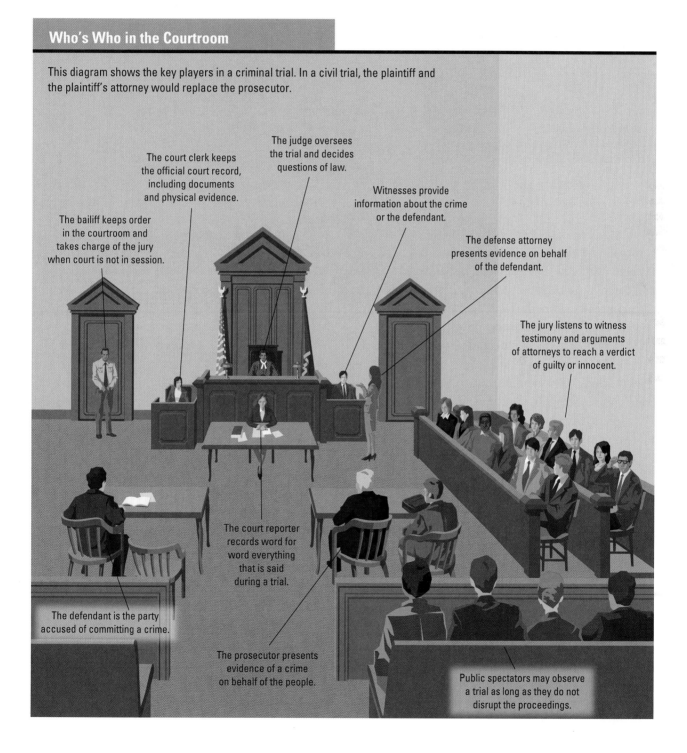

This diagram shows the key players in a criminal trial. In a civil trial, the plaintiff and the plaintiff's attorney would replace the prosecutor.

The judge oversees the trial and decides questions of law.

The court clerk keeps the official court record, including documents and physical evidence.

Witnesses provide information about the crime or the defendant.

The bailiff keeps order in the courtroom and takes charge of the jury when court is not in session.

The defense attorney presents evidence on behalf of the defendant.

The jury listens to witness testimony and arguments of attorneys to reach a verdict of guilty or innocent.

The court reporter records word for word everything that is said during a trial.

The defendant is the party accused of committing a crime.

The prosecutor presents evidence of a crime on behalf of the people.

Public spectators may observe a trial as long as they do not disrupt the proceedings.

Trial by a jury of one's peers is a right that dates back to the Magna Carta and that is guaranteed in the Constitution's Bill of Rights. A 2008 survey conducted by Harris Interactive shows that a majority of Americans believe that most juries are fair and impartial.

How often do most people who are on trial have a jury that is fair and impartial?

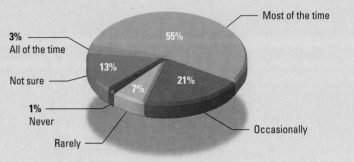

- Most of the time — 55%
- Occasionally — 21%
- Rarely — 7%
- Never — 1%
- Not sure — 13%
- All of the time — 3%

In a civil trial, the person bringing the lawsuit to court is the **plaintiff**. The person the suit has been brought against is the defendant. Usually plaintiffs and defendants are represented by attorneys who argue the case before the jury. To make a compelling case for their clients, attorneys may present both physical evidence, such as documents and objects, and the testimony of witnesses.

Additional officers of the court, such as the court clerk, the bailiff, and the court reporter, are not directly involved in a case. Instead, their job is to help with the functioning of the courtroom itself.

The Key Role of Citizens: Witnesses and Jurors

Citizens also play a key role in most trials, both as witnesses for the defense or prosecution and as jurors. Testifying in court as a witness can be an ordeal. Witnesses sometimes have to wait outside the courtroom for hours until they are called to testify. Testifying in court can be a scary experience, especially when it is the opposing attorney's turn to begin questioning. During this **cross-examination,** the witness's memory or truthfulness may be questioned. Witnesses play a crucial role in the judicial process by providing information to the jury as to who did what, when, and where.

The most important decisions in many trials are those made by the jury. A typical jury consists of 12 people, although some states allow smaller juries. To serve as a juror, a person must be a U.S. citizen, 18 years of age, able to understand English, a resident within the court's jurisdiction, and not a convicted felon. Potential jurors are usually culled from voter registration lists, Department of Motor Vehicle lists, telephone directories, and utility company lists.

For many Americans, jury duty is the only service they are directly required to perform for their government. Reporting for jury duty when summoned, however, does not guarantee that an individual will serve on a jury. Nearly four out of five prospective jurors are dismissed for a variety of reasons. Some are excused because they may have a prejudice or bias concerning the case. Others are excused if they can show that serving on a jury would create an "undue hardship."

Once selected to serve, jurors listen carefully to the evidence presented to them during a trial. When the trial ends, they deliberate with the other jurors to try to reach a unanimous verdict. The decision they reach has enormous consequences for the plaintiffs and defendants involved in criminal and civil cases. Knowing this, jurors take their responsibility seriously. More than 60 percent of those who have served on juries report that they would be willing to do so again.

15.3 America's Dual Court System

When Congress enacted the Judiciary Act of 1789, it was, in effect, creating a dual court system in the United States. The new federal judicial system was set up alongside already-existing state judicial systems. For the most part, the two systems operate independently of one another, but they can overlap. This diagram shows how that dual system looks today.

Jurisdiction Determines What Gets Tried Where

One way to sort out what gets tried where in this dual system is to look at each court's jurisdiction, or its authority to enforce laws. For example, state courts have jurisdiction over cases arising under state law. Federal courts are generally limited to cases involving federal law or the Constitution. Within each system, jurisdiction is limited by three factors:

level in the court hierarchy, geographic reach, and type of case.

Level in the court hierarchy. Each level within the hierarchy of the state or federal court system has a set of responsibilities. Trial courts, at the bottom of the hierarchy, generally have **original jurisdiction**. This means they have the authority to hear a case for the first time.

Moving up the hierarchy, appeals courts have **appellate jurisdiction**. This means they have the authority to review decisions made in lower courts. Appeals courts do not second-guess jury decisions by reviewing the facts in a case. Instead, their focus is on whether the trial in the lower court was carried out in a fair manner, with no **errors of law**. An error of law is a mistake made by a judge in applying the law to a specific case.

Geographic reach. With the exception of the Supreme Court, courts hear cases that arise within certain geographic boundaries. Within a state judicial system, the geographic jurisdiction of a trial court is

The Dual Court System

The United States has both a federal judicial system and state judicial systems. Each system has its own jurisdiction. In cases that involve both federal and state laws, however, the two may overlap. The arrows indicate the most common routes that cases take through the appeals system.

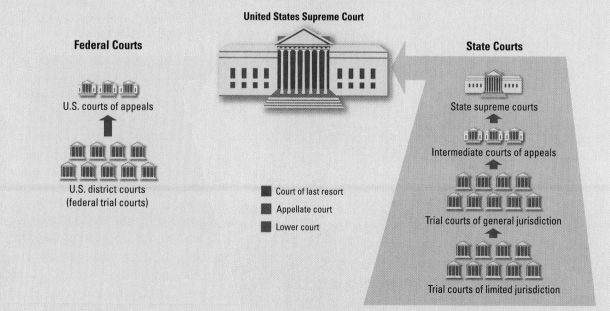

United States Supreme Court

Federal Courts

U.S. courts of appeals

U.S. district courts
(federal trial courts)

■ Court of last resort
■ Appellate court
■ Lower court

State Courts

State supreme courts

Intermediate courts of appeals

Trial courts of general jurisdiction

Trial courts of limited jurisdiction

Jurisdiction in State and Federal Courts

Cases Heard in State Courts	Cases Heard in Federal Courts	Cases Heard in Both State and Federal Courts
Crimes punishable under state law	Matters involving interstate and international commerce	Crimes punishable under both state and federal laws
Traffic violations	Disputes involving federal taxes or federal programs, such as Social Security	Environmental regulations
Divorce and child custody disputes		Certain civil rights claims
Landlord and tenant disputes	Patent and copyright issues	Civil actions involving large groups of people seeking damages (class-action suits)
Most contract disputes	Issues involving treaties and foreign countries	Issues involving the U.S. Constitution
Most personal injury lawsuits	Disputes involving citizens of other countries	
Most workers' injury claims	Bankruptcy matters	
Inheritance matters	Disputes between states	
Most issues involving regulation of trades and professions	Habeas corpus actions	

usually limited to the city or county in which that court operates. In the federal system, trial court districts are larger.

The geographic reach of appellate courts is greater than that of trial courts. Most states have regional appeals courts and a state supreme court. The federal system has 13 appellate courts. The U.S. Supreme Court accepts cases from anywhere in the United States and its territories.

Type of case. A case's subject matter also determines where it will be tried. At both the state and the federal levels, the typical trial court has **general jurisdiction**. This means the court can hear cases covering a variety of subjects.

Some courts, however, have **limited jurisdiction**. This means they specialize in certain kinds of cases. Traffic courts deal only with traffic violations. Bankruptcy courts only hear cases involving bankruptcy issues. Juvenile courts work only with young offenders.

Most Cases Are Heard in State Courts

State courts are the workhorses of the judicial system, handling several million cases a year. In 2010, the combined caseload of the 50 states and Puerto Rico totaled around 100 million cases. This equals

roughly one case for every three people. Nearly half of these cases were traffic related. In contrast, the entire federal system hears fewer cases each year than do the courts of a medium-size state.

State court systems vary in their structures. However, most states have four general levels of courts: trial courts of limited jurisdiction, trial courts of general jurisdiction, intermediate appellate courts, and courts of last resort.

Trial courts of limited jurisdiction. Local courts that specialize in relatively minor criminal offenses or civil disputes handle most of the cases filed each year. They are known as justice-of-the-peace courts, magistrate courts, municipal courts, city courts, county courts, traffic courts, or small-claims courts, depending on the state and the types of cases they hear. Their hearings are generally informal and do not involve jury trials. Cases heard in these courts may be appealed to trial courts.

Trial courts of general jurisdiction. General trial courts handle most serious criminal cases and major civil disputes. They are often called superior, district, or circuit courts. In rural areas, general trial court judges may have to travel within a large circuit to try cases. In urban areas, general trial court judges may specialize in criminal, family, juvenile, civil, or other types of cases.

Intermediate appellate courts. Intermediate courts of appeals hear appeals from general trial courts. Though the structure varies from state to state, most state appeals courts employ three-judge panels to hear and decide cases.

Courts of last resort. The name of the appeals court at the top of the state system varies from state to state. The most common name is state supreme court. Most often, these "courts of last resort" convene in the state's capital. Their jurisdiction includes all matters of state law. Once a state supreme court decides a case, the only avenue of appeal left is the U.S. Supreme Court. Such appeals are limited, however, to cases that present a constitutional issue, which is a highly unlikely occurrence.

Choosing State Judges: Election, Appointment, and Merit Selection

Each state has its own method of choosing the judges who preside over state courts. Nonetheless, there are three basic routes to a judgeship: election, appointment, or merit selection.

Judicial election. The oldest method of choosing state judges is through the election process. This method became popular during Andrew Jackson's presidency in an effort to make U.S. politics more democratic. Supporters of this method argue that judicial elections provide a public forum for debating judicial issues. They also argue that elections allow voters to remove judges who have not upheld the public trust.

This method of choosing judges is not without its pitfalls, however. First, to fund their campaigns, judicial candidates must often seek contributions from lawyers and business that may eventually appear before them in court. This may interfere with their ability to be impartial. Second, voter turnout for judicial elections is notoriously low. Most voters simply do not know enough about judgeship candidates to cast a meaningful vote.

Judicial appointment. In a handful of states, judges are appointed by the governor or state legislature. This method relieves poorly informed voters of the

responsibility of choosing judges. Nonetheless, it also has drawbacks. Governors often use their appointment power to award judgeships to those who have supported them politically. Similarly, state legislatures tend to appoint former lawmakers to be judges. Such appointees may or may not be highly qualified to serve as judges.

Merit selection and retention elections. Finally, many judges are selected through a process that combines appointments and elections. Under this system, a committee nominates candidates for judgeships based on their merits, or qualifications. The governor then appoints judges from this list.

After a fixed period, usually a year, voters are asked to confirm or reject the appointment in a **retention election**. The ballot in such an election typically reads, "Shall Judge X be retained in office?" If a majority of voters answer yes, the judge remains in office for a longer term. If a majority says no, which rarely happens, the judge is removed from office.

Supporters of this process argue that it takes the politics out of judicial appointments by focusing on candidates' qualifications rather than on their political connections or popularity with voters. At the same time, merit selection allows voters to review a judge's performance on the bench from time to time. Opponents argue that this method gives the public too little control over judges.

State courts handle most of the cases that pass through the justice system. About half of the cases handled by state courts are related to traffic.

15.4 The Federal Judiciary

At fewer than 500 words, Article III of the Constitution, which spells out the powers of the nation's judicial branch, is remarkably brief. The framers' brevity on this topic may reflect their thinking that the judiciary would be, in Alexander Hamilton's words, the "least dangerous" of the three branches. As Hamilton saw it,

> The Executive not only dispenses the honors, but holds the sword of the community. The legislature not only commands the purse, but prescribes the rules by which the duties and rights of every citizen are to be regulated. The judiciary, on the contrary, has no influence over either the sword or the purse . . . It may truly be said to have neither FORCE nor WILL, but merely judgment.
> —*The Federalist* No. 78, 1788

Over time, however, the federal judiciary has grown in both size and power in ways the framers could not have predicted.

The Constitutional Powers of the Judicial Branch

The Constitution outlines the kinds of cases to be decided by the judicial branch. Article III gives the federal courts jurisdiction in two types of cases. The first type involve the Constitution, federal laws, or disputes with foreign governments. The second are civil cases in which the plaintiff and defendant are states or are citizens of different states.

Nowhere, however, does the Constitution mention the power of judicial review. Nonetheless, in *The Federalist* No. 78, Hamilton declared that the duty of the federal courts "must be to declare all acts contrary to . . . the Constitution void."

In 1803, the Supreme Court took on that duty for the first time in *Marbury v. Madison*. In that case, the Court declared a portion of the Judiciary Act of 1789 to be unconstitutional. It thus established the power of the judiciary to review the constitutionality of legislative or executive actions.

Over time, judicial review has become the judicial branch's most important check on the other two branches. In 1886, in *Norton v. Shelby County*, the Court summed up what it means to declare an act of Congress or the president unconstitutional:

> An unconstitutional act is not a law; it confers no rights; it imposes no duties; it affords no protection; it creates no office; it is, in legal contemplation, as inoperative as though it had never been passed.

U.S. District Courts: Where Federal Cases Begin

Ninety-four district courts occupy the lowest level in the federal judiciary. These 94 courts include 89 federal

The Checking Powers of the Federal Judiciary

The framers tried to keep the federal judiciary as independent as possible from the other two branches of government. This was done so that judges could function, in Alexander Hamilton's words, as "faithful guardians of the Constitution."

Judicial Checks on Executive Branch

Can declare treaties and executive acts unconstitutional. Appointments are for life, and judges are free from executive control.

Judicial Checks on Legislative Branch

Can declare laws unconstitutional.

Executive

Judicial

Legislative

Cases in the federal judicial system usually begin in one of the 94 district courts. Judgments from district courts can be appealed to one of 13 U.S. appeals courts. Eleven of these courts, one for each of the court circuits numbered and colored on the map, cover the 50 states and U.S. territories. Another, the court for the D.C. Circuit, deals with cases in the District of Columbia, while the thirteenth has national jurisdiction over cases involving special subjects.

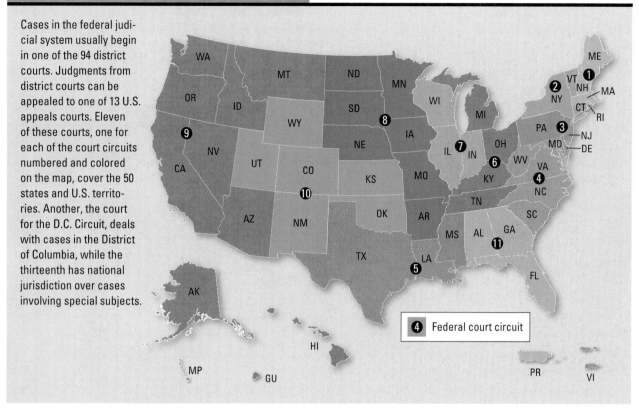

④ Federal court circuit

court districts throughout the country, with at least one district in each state. The five additional district courts are located in Washington, D.C., Puerto Rico, and three other U.S. territories. Each district court is a trial court with original jurisdiction in its region. District courts are where most cases in the federal system begin.

In the past, civil cases dominated district court caseloads. Increasingly, however, criminal cases are crowding the dockets of these courts, with drug violations leading the way. District court cases are tried before a jury, unless a defendant waives that right. In such cases, the judge decides the outcome of the case in what is known as a **bench trial**.

U.S. Appeals Courts: Where Most Appeals End

Thirteen appellate courts occupy the second level of the federal judiciary. These midlevel courts are known as U.S. courts of appeals. Only a fraction of the cases decided in district courts are reviewed by appeals courts. Of these, an even smaller number get heard by the Supreme Court.

Of the 13 appeals courts, one deals with cases arising in Washington, D.C. Another 11 review cases in circuits made up of several states. In 1982, Congress added the U.S. Court of Appeals for the Federal Circuit to the judicial system. This 13th appeals court reviews cases nationwide that involve special subjects, such as veterans' benefits, trademarks, and international trade.

The judges who staff appeals courts sit in panels of three to hear cases. Their primary job is to review district court cases to determine whether the district judge made an error in applying the law in that one trial. Sometimes, however, their decisions have a broader application than the specific case before them. This was true of the decision made by a three-judge panel in the 1996 case of *Hopwood v. Texas*.

The *Hopwood* case dealt with the University of Texas Law School's admissions policy. In an effort to enlarge its enrollment of minority students, the law school gave preference to African American and Hispanic applicants. This practice of making special efforts to admit, recruit, or hire members of disadvantaged groups is known as **affirmative action**.

An earlier legal challenge to affirmative action policies had reached the Supreme Court in 1978. In *Regents of the University of California v. Bakke,* the Court held that a university could consider race in admitting students to correct past discrimination and to achieve a more diverse student body. However, schools could not set up separate admission systems for minorities. Nor could schools reserve a quota, or fixed number, of admission slots for minority applicants.

The *Hopwood* case began in 1992, when four white students who had been denied entry to the University of Texas Law School filed a lawsuit in federal district court. The plaintiffs argued that the school's admissions policy violated their Fourteenth Amendment right to equal protection under the law. They also charged that it violated the Civil Rights Act of 1964, which prohibits discrimination based on race in any program receiving federal funding, as the school had done.

After a short trial, the court decided in favor of the university. The presiding judge said that affirmative action programs, while "regrettable," were still necessary to overcome a legacy of racism. In response, the four plaintiffs appealed their case to the U.S. Court of Appeals for the Fifth Circuit.

The appeals court reversed the lower court's decision. The judges found that the law school had created a separate admissions policy for minorities, which violated the *Bakke* rules. They declared the law school's race-based admissions policy unconstitutional.

Still, the Supreme Court can overturn decisions made in appellate courts. For example, the Supreme Court stepped in when the *Hopwood* ruling conflicted with the ruling from another appellate court case that allowed colleges to use race as a factor for admission. The Supreme Court overturned the *Hopwood* decision in *Grutter v. Bollinger* (2003). In this landmark case, a white law school applicant challenged the admissions policy of the University of Michigan Law School, which considered the race of applicants to create a diverse student body. In a 5–4 decision, the Court ruled in favor of the school, determining that although quotas are illegal because of *Bakke*, schools can still consider race during the admissions process.

Special Courts Have Specialized Jurisdictions

From time to time, Congress has established special federal courts to deal with specific categories of cases. Staffing these courts are judges expert in a particular area, such as tax or trade law. These special courts include both lower and appeals courts.

During times of war, the United States has also set up **military tribunals** to try members of enemy forces. A military tribunal is a court in which officers from the armed forces serve as both judge and jury. During the American Revolution, George Washington set up military tribunals to try spies. Abraham Lincoln used military tribunals during the Civil War to try Northerners who aided the Confederacy. Franklin Roosevelt ordered military tribunals during World War II to try German prisoners of war in the United States accused of sabotage. In 2006, Congress authorized the creation of military tribunals to try noncitizens accused of committing acts of terrorism against the United States.

Federal Judges: Nomination, Terms, and Salaries

Despite their different levels and functions, all federal courts have one thing in common: judges. These judges oversee court proceedings, decide questions

Special Federal Courts

U.S. Court of Appeals for Veterans Claims: Reviews decisions regarding benefits due to veterans.

U.S. Court of International Trade: Hears cases involving customs, unfair import practices, and other trade issues.

U.S. Court of Federal Claims: Has jurisdiction over claims for damages made against the United States.

U.S. Tax Court: Resolves disputes between taxpayers and the Internal Revenue Service.

U.S. Alien Terrorist Removal Court: Oversees procedures for deporting suspected foreign terrorists.

U.S. Foreign Intelligence Surveillance Court: Approves requests for **surveillance warrants** by federal police agencies investigating foreign spying or terrorism.

Military courts: Try cases that involve potential violations of military law.

U.S. Court of Appeals for the Armed Forces: Reviews convictions by the lower military courts.

of law, and, where no jury is present, determine the outcome of the cases before them.

The Constitution gives the president the power to appoint federal judges with the "Advice and Consent of the Senate." But it says nothing about the qualifications of judges. In general, presidents look for candidates who have distinguished themselves as attorneys in the state where an opening exists. They also tend to look for candidates who share their political ideology.

In theory, the confirmation process looks simple enough. The president submits a nomination to the Senate. The nomination goes to the Senate Judiciary Committee for study. If approved by the committee, the nomination is submitted to the full Senate for a confirmation vote. The reality, however, is more complex, mainly because of an unwritten rule known as **senatorial courtesy**. This rule allows a senator to block a nomination to a federal court in his or her home state.

Nominations are blocked through a process known as the **blue-slip policy**. When the Senate Judiciary Committee receives a nomination, it notifies the senators from the nominee's state by sending them an approval form on a blue sheet of paper. If a senator fails to return the blue slip, this indicates his or her opposition to the appointment. As a courtesy to the senator, the Judiciary Committee then kills the nomination by refusing to act on it.

Nominees who make it through the confirmation process remain in office, as Article III states, "during good Behaviour." In practical terms, this means they are judges for life or until they choose to retire.

The only federal judges not appointed to life tenures, or terms of service, are those serving in most of the special courts. With the exception of the Court of International Trade, the creation of these special courts was not expressly authorized under Article III. Instead, Congress created them using its legislative authority. As a result, Congress has the power to fix terms of service for special court judges.

The only way to remove a federal judge with lifetime tenure from office is by impeachment. Over the past two centuries, the House of Representatives has impeached 13 federal judges. Of that number, only seven were convicted of wrongdoing in the Senate and removed from office.

Article III also states that the salaries of judges with lifetime tenure "shall not be diminished during their Continuance in Office." This means that judges cannot be penalized for making unpopular decisions by cutting their pay. The purpose of these protections was, in Hamilton's words, to ensure "the independence of the judges . . . against the effects of occasional ill humors in the society."

After the president nominates a candidate for judgeship in a federal court, the Senate Judiciary Committee holds extensive hearings in which testimony is given by the nominee and witnesses who support and oppose the candidate. After the hearing, the committee gathers to vote whether to confirm or reject the nomination.

15.5 The Supreme Court

The Supreme Court is the court of last resort in the federal judicial system. William Rehnquist, who served as chief justice of that court, attended his first session in 1952 while working as an assistant to Justice Robert Jackson. Rehnquist later recalled,

> *The marshal of the Court, who was sitting at a desk to the right of the bench, rose, pounded his gavel, and called out, "All rise!" Simultaneously, three groups of three justices each came on the bench . . . When each was standing by his chair, the marshal intoned his familiar words: "Oyez, oyez, oyez . . . " This ceremony moved me deeply. It was a ritual that had been used to open Anglo-Saxon courts for many centuries.*
> —William Rehnquist, *The Supreme Court: How It Was, How It Is,* 1987

As of 2012, 108 male and four female Supreme Court justices have heard those opening words and proceeded to decide some of the nation's most contentious legal issues.

The Selection Process for Supreme Court Justices

Supreme Court justices are selected through the same process used for all federal judges. However, their appointments generally attract a great deal more attention.

When a vacancy occurs on the Court, the president pulls together a list of possible candidates to consider. The Department of Justice conducts background checks on the candidates to verify that their character, experience, and judicial philosophy meet the general criteria set by the president. This process often involves lengthy interviews with the candidates.

In the past, the American Bar Association, a voluntary association of lawyers, prescreened judicial appointments based on a candidate's experience, professional competence, integrity, and **judicial temperament**. The ABA's role in the selection process was controversial. Some critics argued that a nongovernmental organization should not have so much power in judicial appointments. Others raised concerns about political bias on the part of ABA committee members. The ABA's formal involvement in the selection process ended in 2001.

Once a candidate has been selected, the nomination goes to the Senate Judiciary Committee for review. The committee holds public hearings, during which it takes testimony from the nominee and from witnesses who support or oppose the appointment. The Judiciary Committee then recommends, by majority vote, whether the full Senate should confirm or reject the nomination.

Finally, the full Senate votes on the nomination. In the case of district and appellate court appointments, the Senate usually confirms the president's nominee. When the nomination is for a Supreme

President Obama appointed two justices to the Supreme Court. Sonia Sotomayor (left) testified before the Senate Judiciary Committee in 2009. After the committee approved her with a 13–6 vote, the full Senate confirmed her nomination, making Sotomayor the first Latina Supreme Court justice. In 2010, Elena Kagan (right) underwent the same process. For both Sotomayor and Kagan, the committee and full Senate voted along party lines with a few senators of the opposing party approving their nominations.

This illustration shows an attorney presenting a case before the Supreme Court in 2012. Cameras are not allowed in the courtroom during the oral arguments, so the news media rely on sketches, like this one made by a professional court artist. Legislation has been introduced to televise Supreme Court sessions. Although Supreme Court Justice Elena Kagan stated that "it would be terrific to have cameras in the courtroom," Supreme Court Justice Antonin Scalia expressed his concern that televised snippets from their arguments would "miseducate the American people."

Court justice, however, the stakes are higher and confirmation is less sure. In the past, the Senate has rejected around one in five nominations to the Court.

The Judiciary Committee's recommendation to confirm or reject a nomination is often affected by partisanship and the opinions of interest groups. In 1987, for example, President Reagan nominated Robert Bork for the Supreme Court. However, outcry from Democrats and interest groups, such as the ACLU, over Bork's conservative views led the committee, and ultimately the full Senate, to reject the nomination. In order to avoid this fate, presidents are careful to select candidates whose views fit theirs but are not so extreme that the Senate rejects them.

The Supreme Court Chooses Its Cases

More than one attorney, dismayed by a jury's verdict, has vowed, "We'll appeal this case all the way to the Supreme Court!" However, given the fact that the Court is asked to review several thousand cases each year but will only hear between 100 and 150, this is not a realistic promise.

The Supreme Court has both original and appellate jurisdiction. However, only a handful of original jurisdiction cases are filed each term. Overwhelmingly, the cases reaching the Supreme Court are appeals from cases that began in lower courts.

The most common way that a case comes to the Supreme Court is through a petition for a **writ of certiorari**. A writ is a legal document. A writ of certiorari is a document issued by the Supreme Court ordering that a case from a lower court be brought before it. When petitioning for a writ of certiorari, the party that lost an appeal in lower court explains why the Supreme Court should review the case.

For a writ of certiorari to be granted, four of the nine Supreme Court justices must agree to hear the case. If a writ is granted, the case is added to the Court's docket. If a petition is denied, the decision of the lower court stands.

Written Briefs and Oral Arguments

Once the Court decides to hear a case, the attorneys for both sides prepare **legal briefs**. These are written documents, sometimes hundreds of pages long, that present the legal arguments for each side in the case.

Sympathetic interest groups may also choose to file an **amicus curiae brief**. *Amicus curiae* is a Latin term meaning "friend of the court." Interest groups use amicus briefs to let the Court know that the issue at hand is important to far more people than just the plaintiffs and defendants in the case.

Eventually, attorneys from both sides appear before the Court to present their case. This phase is known as **oral argument**. In general, attorneys are

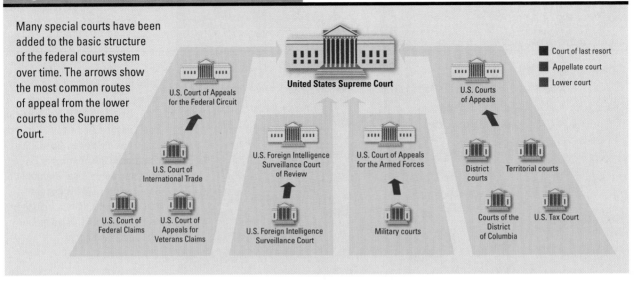

Many special courts have been added to the basic structure of the federal court system over time. The arrows show the most common routes of appeal from the lower courts to the Supreme Court.

United States Supreme Court

U.S. Court of Appeals for the Federal Circuit

U.S. Court of International Trade

U.S. Court of Federal Claims

U.S. Court of Appeals for Veterans Claims

U.S. Foreign Intelligence Surveillance Court of Review

U.S. Foreign Intelligence Surveillance Court

U.S. Court of Appeals for the Armed Forces

Military courts

U.S. Courts of Appeals

District courts

Territorial courts

Courts of the District of Columbia

U.S. Tax Court

Court of last resort
Appellate court
Lower court

allotted only 30 minutes to explain why the Court should decide in favor of their client. The Court encourages attorneys to use this time to discuss the case, not deliver a formal lecture. During oral argument, the justices often interrupt to ask questions of the attorneys. The justices may even use their questions as a way of debating one another.

As interesting as oral arguments are to the public, the real work of the Court is done in conference. When the Court is in session, the justices meet twice a week in conference to discuss cases. No one other than the nine justices may attend. The chief justice presides and is the first to offer an opinion regarding a case. The other justices follow in order of seniority. Cases are decided by majority vote. But votes in conference are not final. As Justice John Harlan observed, "The books on voting are never closed until the decision actually comes down."

Decision Options: To Uphold or Overrule

Most Supreme Court decisions either uphold or overturn a decision made by a lower court. If the lower court's decision is upheld, the case ends at this point. There is no further appeal for the losing party to pursue.

If the Supreme Court overturns a lower court's decision, it may send the case back to the lower court for further action. For example, should the Court decide that a criminal defendant was denied a fair trial, the case will be sent back to a lower court to be either dismissed or tried again.

Every decision serves as a precedent for future cases with similar circumstances. Under the doctrine known as *stare decisis* lower courts must honor decisions made by higher courts. The term *stare decisis* is Latin for "to stand by things decided." This practice brings consistency to legal decisions from court to court.

Occasionally, the Court reverses a previous decision, thereby setting a new precedent. But this is not done lightly. "I do think that it is a jolt to the legal system when you overrule a precedent," said Supreme Court nominee and future chief justice John Roberts during his confirmation hearings in 2005. A reversal may happen when the views of society have changed and when the Supreme Court reflects those changes. It may also occur when justices who voted one way leave the Court and new ones with different views take their place.

Majority, Dissenting, and Concurring Opinions

Once the Court as a whole decides a case, one justice will be assigned to write the **majority opinion**. An opinion is a legal document stating the reasons for a judicial decision. It often begins by laying out the facts of the case. Then it explains the legal issues involved, including past precedents, and the reasoning behind the Court's decision. The chief justice writes this opinion if he or she sided with the majority. If not, the most senior justice in the majority camp writes the opinion.

Justices who disagree with the majority opinion may choose to write a **dissenting opinion**. In it, they lay out their reasons for disagreeing with the majority. Some justices who sided with the majority, but for different reasons than stated in the majority opinion, may write a **concurring opinion**. In it, they explain how their reasoning differs from the majority's. Because few decisions are unanimous, these additional opinions often accompany a majority opinion.

Judicial Activism Versus Judicial Restraint

The most controversial cases decided by the Supreme Court are often those that involve judicial review. More than two centuries after the Court assumed this power, Americans are still divided about its proper use. On one side are supporters of judicial activism, and on the other are advocates of judicial restraint.

Judicial activism is based on the belief that the Court has both the right and the obligation to use its power of judicial review to overturn bad precedents and promote socially desirable goals. Liberals tend to be more supportive of judicial activism than are conservatives. They look to the Court to defend the rights of women and minorities, for example, when legislatures fail to act.

Advocates of **judicial restraint** hold that judicial review should be used sparingly, especially in dealing with controversial issues. Conservatives tend to be more supportive of judicial restraint than are liberals. In their view, elected representatives, not unelected judges, should make policy decisions on such issues as abortion rights and gay marriage.

Recent appointments to the Supreme Court have been more inclined toward judicial restraint than to activism. During Senate Judiciary Committee hearings on his nomination to the Supreme Court, John Roberts described his view of a judge's role:

> *Judges are like umpires. Umpires don't make the rules, they apply them. The role of an umpire and a judge is critical. They make sure everybody plays by the rules. But it is a limited role. Nobody ever went to a ballgame to see the umpire.*
>
> —John Roberts, 2005

Summary

The U.S. judicial system has evolved over more than two centuries to meet the needs of a changing society. Today's federal and state courts not only resolve conflicts, but also shape public policy through the judicial review process.

Dual court system The United States has two separate but related court systems: one federal and one state. The two systems maintain exclusive jurisdiction in some areas but overlap when cases involve both state and federal laws.

State judicial systems Each state has its own hierarchy of courts. Trial courts of limited and general jurisdiction handle most cases. Intermediate appeals courts and state courts of last resort review cases appealed from the lower courts.

Federal judicial system Most cases involving federal law and the Constitution are tried in U.S. district courts. Decisions made there can be appealed to higher courts, including the Supreme Court. The federal judicial system also includes special courts with very specific jurisdictions.

State and federal judges Many state judges are elected or appointed by the governor or legislature. In states using merit selection, judges are appointed and then confirmed by voters in a retention election. Federal judges are appointed by the president and confirmed by the Senate.

How did the Supreme Court rule on the Affordable Care Act?

In 2012, the Supreme Court ruled on *National Federation of Independent Business v. Sebelius*, a landmark case that challenged the constitutionality of the Affordable Care Act. Although the Court upheld most of the act, the Supreme Court justices disagreed on two important parts: the expansion of Medicaid and the individual mandate.

In its decision, the Court struck down the expansion of Medicaid and upheld the individual mandate, with Chief Justice John Roberts casting the deciding vote. As you read this article, think about how the Court's decision affected Congress's powers. Do you agree with this decision?

Obamacare Upheld: How and Why Did Justice Roberts Do It?

by David Cole

The Supreme Court closed out its 2011–12 term . . . in dramatic fashion, upholding the Affordable Care Act by a sharply divided vote. The Court's bottom line, reasoning and lineup of justices all came as a shock to many . . . I don't think anyone predicted that the law would be upheld *without* the support of Justice Anthony Kennedy, almost always the Court's crucial swing vote. And while most of the legal debate focused on Congress's power under the Commerce Clause, the Court ultimately upheld the law as an exercise of the taxing power— even though President Obama famously claimed that the law was not a tax. The most surprising thing of all, though, is that in the end, this ultraconservative Court decided the case, much as it did in many other cases this term, by siding with the liberals.

Justice Kennedy, on whom virtually all hope for a decision upholding the law rested, voted with Antonin Scalia, Samuel Alito and Clarence Thomas. They would have invalidated all 900 pages of the law—even though the challengers had directly attacked only two of the law's hundreds of provisions.

But Chief Justice John Roberts sided with Justices Ruth Bader Ginsburg, Sonia Sotomayor, Stephen Breyer and Elena Kagan to uphold the law as a valid exercise of Congress's power to tax.

What led Roberts to cast his lot with the law's supporters? The argument that the taxing power supported the individual mandate was a strong one. The mandate provides that those who can afford to buy healthcare insurance must do so, but the only consequence of not doing so is the payment of a tax penalty. The Constitution gives Congress broad power to raise taxes "for the general welfare," which means Congress need not point to some other enumerated power to justify a tax. (By contrast, if Congress seeks to regulate conduct by imposing criminal or civil sanctions, it must point to one of the Constitution's affirmative grants of power—such as the Commerce Clause, the immigration power, or the power to raise and regulate the military.)

The law's challengers—and the Court's dissenters—rejected the characterization of the law as a tax. They noted that it was labeled a "penalty," not a tax; that it was designed to encourage people to buy health insur-

Because Supreme Court justices serve for life, they are somewhat isolated from political pressures. However, they do not operate in a vacuum. When the Supreme Court makes decisions, it pays attention to public opinion. Here, demonstrators on both sides of the issue voice their thoughts about health care reform. To what extent do you think the Supreme Court should take public opinion into account?

ance, not to raise revenue; and that Obama himself had rejected claims that the law was a tax when it was being considered by Congress. But Roberts said the question is a functional one, not a matter of labels. Because the law in fact would raise revenue, imposed no sanction other than a tax and was calculated and collected by the IRS as part of the income tax, the Court treated it as a tax and upheld the law.

Chief Justice Roberts did go on to say (for himself, but not for the Court's majority) that he thought the law was not justified by the Commerce Clause or the Necessary and Proper Clause, because rather than regulating

existing economic activity it compelled people to enter into commerce . . .

The other provision challenged conditioned state's receipt of Medicaid funding on their implementation of the Act's greatly expanded Medicaid coverage. Where Medicaid initially covered only several discrete categories of persons, under the ACA it extends to all adults earning less than 133 percent of the poverty level. The states argued that threatening them with loss of all their Medicaid funding was a coercive condition on the funding. Seven members of the Court agreed that if the law were enforced to take away state's *existing* Medicaid funds it

would be unconstitutional, but the majority upheld the provision as a condition only on the funds provided for the expanded Medicaid program . . .

As Roberts put it, "We do not consider whether the Act embodies sound policies. That judgment is entrusted to the Nation's elected leaders. We ask only whether Congress has the power under the Constitution to enact the challenged provisions."

So why did Roberts do it? In part, the outcome reflects the fact that the truly radical position in this dispute was that of the challengers. Even very conservative lower court judges, including Jeffrey Sutton of the Sixth Circuit and Laurence Silberman of the DC Circuit, had concluded that the law was valid (although on Commerce Clause, not taxing power, grounds). But in addition, I cannot but think that at the back of Roberts's mind was the Court's institutional standing. Had the law been struck down on "party lines," the Court's reputation would be seriously undermined . . . and ultimately, its legitimacy is the source of the Court's power.

David Cole is a blogger and legal affairs correspondent for The Nation.

Reprinted with permission from the June 28, 2012 issue of The Nation. For subscription information call 1-800-333-8536. Portions of each week's Nation magazine can be accessed at http://www.thenation.com.

"DUE PROCESS OF LAW."

Chapter 16

The Criminal Justice System

From doing the crime to doing time: How just is our criminal justice system?

■ 16.1 Introduction

Place yourself in the following situation: You have been stopped by the police, who suspect you of committing a crime. One officer begins to read you your rights:

You have the right to remain silent. Anything you say can and will be used against you in a court of law.

You have most likely heard those words on television shows and in movies, but they have never been directed at you before. The officer continues:

You have the right to speak to an attorney.

You are struggling to make sense of what is happening. Minutes ago, you and two friends were strolling through the mall. One friend was carrying a shopping bag stuffed with new purchases from a clothing store. As you made your way across the parking lot, a police car raced up. Two officers jumped out and said you were under arrest. When you asked why, they said that you were suspected of shoplifting. They said that you had been observed taking items from a store without paying for them.

Now, as you are pressed into the backseat of the patrol car, you wonder how you got into this mess. You know you did not steal anything, but what about

Cartoon showing the long road to justice

your friends? Other questions begin to trouble you. What will happen when you get to the police station? How will you be treated? What can you expect from the police and the justice system?

The first thing to remember as you enter this system is that you are presumed innocent. If you are charged with a crime, you will have the opportunity to assert your innocence before a judge and, if tried, a jury. Throughout this process, you will also be guaranteed certain rights under the Constitution, including the right to a fair trial.

This chapter examines the workings of the criminal justice system. It follows a hypothetical case through the various stages of the criminal process, from the commission of a crime to the dispensing of justice. Along the way, it lays out the procedures used to judge criminal acts and to protect the rights of the accused.

Every year, police in the United States make roughly 14 million arrests. Juveniles, or persons under the age of 18, account for about 14 percent of those arrests. Not all of those arrested are charged with crimes, however.

■ 16.2 The Crime

In the squad car, the officers who arrested you tell you that a security camera in the mall caught you and your friends shoplifting goods from a store. They tell you that your arrest is based on probable cause, or a reasonable suspicion that you have committed a crime. As far as you know, you did nothing wrong. Is it possible to commit a crime without knowing it? The answer to that question depends on a number of factors.

Elements of a Crime: A Wrongful Act with Intent

A crime is the intentional commission of an act that violates the law. To qualify as a crime, an act must consist of two basic elements. It must be wrongful, and it must be carried out with intent. To be wrongful, an act must do harm to other individuals or to society.

A crime must always be defined through a law that specifies a particular act as illegal. People commit many wrongful acts every day in our society, but not all of these acts are crimes. For a person's bad behavior to qualify as a crime, it must have been described and prohibited by law before the act was committed.

Furthermore, a behavior can be labeled "criminal" only if an illegal act was committed with intent. In other words, the act of wrongdoing must be accompanied by the conscious intention to carry out that act. Such behavior is considered criminal, even if the suspect is ignorant of the law.

Types of Crimes: Misdemeanors and Felonies

Crimes in the United States are usually categorized as either misdemeanors or felonies. A **misdemeanor** is a criminal offense that is generally less serious than a felony. Misdemeanors are mostly punishable by fines or short jail sentences, usually of less than one year. A **felony** is a more serious crime. A conviction for a felony offense can result in extended prison time or, in extreme cases, even a death sentence. Felonies that are punishable by death are called **capital crimes**.

The circumstances or effects of a crime may help determine whether it is classified as a misdemeanor or a felony. For example, shoplifting may be classed as a misdemeanor, or petty theft, if the dollar value

Types of Felonies

Category of Crime	Examples
Violent crimes	Murder, assault and battery, kidnapping
Property crimes	Theft, burglary, shoplifting, robbery, arson
Crimes against public order	Threats to public peace and safety, environmental pollution
Crimes against government	Treason, jury tampering, perjury, tax fraud, bribery of a public official
Drug crimes	Possession, manufacture, and distribution of drugs
White-collar crimes	Counterfeiting, blackmail, bank fraud, credit card fraud, investment fraud
Victimless crimes	Gambling, prostitution
Privacy and technology crimes	Wiretapping, computer fraud, hacking, cyberstalking

of the goods stolen is less than a certain amount. This amount varies by state. In California, for example, the amount is $950. On the other hand, shoplifting may be classed as a felony, or grand theft, if the dollar value is greater than a certain amount. The value of the stolen goods thus helps define the seriousness of the crime.

The effects of an illegal act can also help define its seriousness. In the case of a violent assault, such as a stabbing, whether the victim lives or dies may influence how authorities define the crime and determine a punishment.

The Due Process Rights of Suspects in a Crime

Any person suspected of committing a crime has a number of due process rights. The words "due process" show up twice in the Constitution: in the Fifth and Fourteenth amendments. Each of these amendments prohibits the government from depriving any person of "life, liberty, or property" without "due process of law."

Basically, due process means the government cannot act unfairly, arbitrarily, or unreasonably in its treatment of criminal suspects. Observing due process means that suspects must always be told of the charges against them. It also guarantees them the opportunity to defend themselves in court.

The Constitution guarantees two types of due process: procedural and substantive. **Procedural due process** refers to the procedures, or the "how," of law enforcement. This means that if the government sets out to deprive someone of life, liberty, or property, it must do so through a fair and reasonable legal process.

The Supreme Court upheld the principle of procedural due process in the 1970 case of *Goldberg v. Kelly*. In this case, the plaintiff, John Kelly, had accused the state of New York of terminating welfare payments to recipients without giving them a fair chance to defend their rights. New York allowed residents to respond in writing to notice of such termination, but it did not give them the opportunity to appear in person to state their case. The Court determined that the failure to provide a public hearing in advance of termination violated procedural due process.

Substantive due process, on the other hand, relates to the substance of a law rather than the way it is enforced. In such cases, the Court looks at the content of the law to see how it affects due process rights. In the 1923 case of *Meyer v. Nebraska*, for example, the Court overturned a Nebraska law that forbade the teaching of foreign languages to students in grades lower than ninth grade. The case involved a teacher who taught schoolchildren to read in German.

There are seven basic events, or stages, in the criminal justice process, beginning with a crime and ending with corrections. In the case of some crimes, the stages of investigation and arrest may be reversed. Not all suspects go through all seven stages of the process.

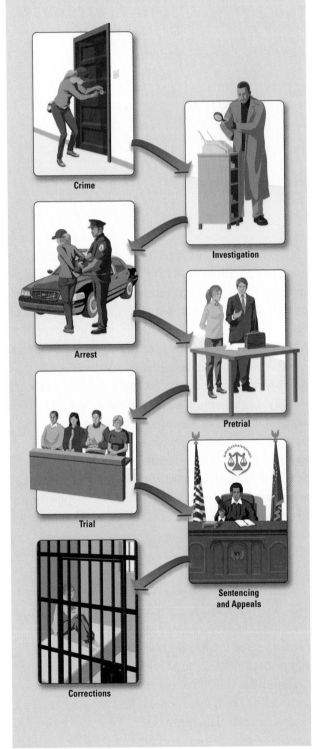

Crime

Investigation

Arrest

Pretrial

Trial

Sentencing and Appeals

Corrections

In its decision, the Court held that the Nebraska law violated intellectual liberty as guaranteed under the Due Process Clause of the Fourteenth Amendment. Writing for the majority, Justice James C. McReynolds noted that many liberties are protected under due process, including the freedom to "acquire useful knowledge." This was one of the first cases in which the Court applied substantive due process to the protection of civil liberties.

Limitations on the Due Process Rights of Juveniles

Due process rights for juveniles—persons under the age of 18—are somewhat different from those for adults. These differences stem from reform laws of the early 1900s, which sought to separate juveniles from adults in the criminal justice system. As a result of these laws, juvenile offenders were tried in special courts and housed in reform schools rather than in prisons.

The new juvenile courts created by these reforms sought to take the circumstances of young offenders into account when handing down sentences. However, the proceedings of these courts were held without juries and sometimes without attorneys. This meant that they typically failed to grant due process rights to juvenile suspects.

In 1967, the Supreme Court handed down a decision in the case of *In re Gault* that expanded the rights of juvenile suspects. Gerald Gault, age 15, had been accused of making an obscene phone call to a neighbor. At his court hearing, Gault admitted to taking part in the call. He testified that he had dialed the number but that a friend had done all of the talking.

No eyewitness testified against Gault, because the neighbor who made the complaint did not show up in court. Nevertheless, the judge concluded that Gault was guilty and sentenced him to six years in a state reform school. An adult convicted of the same crime would have served no more than 60 days in a county jail.

In reviewing the case, the Supreme Court said that juveniles should receive many of the same due process rights as adults. These include the right to be notified of the charges against them, the right to an attorney, the right to confront witnesses, and the right to remain silent. Gault had been given none of these rights. As a result of the Court's decision, Gault was released and a new hearing was held under different conditions.

Today, juveniles enjoy many, but not all, of the due process rights guaranteed to adults. For example, in *McKeiver v. Pennsylvania* (1971), the Supreme Court concluded that juries are not mandatory in juvenile cases.

In recent years, there have been growing calls for states to "get tough" on juvenile crime. In some cases, juveniles accused of serious crimes have been tried as adults. This adult status gives juveniles more due process rights, but it also means they face stiffer penalties if convicted.

■ 16.3 The Investigation

In the story at the beginning of this chapter, police officers took you and your friends into custody shortly after a crime took place. In many criminal cases, however, the arrest would take place later, after a police investigation.

When police learn of a crime, typically the first thing they do is gather evidence and talk to witnesses to identify likely suspects. They then present this information to a government prosecutor, who decides whether a suspect should be arrested and charged with a crime. For serious or complicated crimes, a criminal investigation can take weeks, months, or even years.

The Fourth Amendment Offers Protection from Unreasonable Searches and Seizures

After stopping you and your friends outside the mall, the police officers searched the shopping bag your friend was carrying to look for evidence. They found clothing and some jewelry, which your friend insisted had all been paid for with a credit card.

The officers had a right to search the bag based on probable cause. In other cases, however, suspects may have a legal right to refuse a police search. That right is based on the Fourth Amendment, which says that Americans have the right to be "secure in their persons, houses, papers, and effects." The Fourth Amendment also prohibits "unreasonable searches and seizures."

This Search and Seizure Clause means police officers must have good reason to arrest a suspect or to seize a suspect's property. They also must have a strong legal basis for carrying out a search

The Constitution and federal and state laws offer guarantees against illegal search and seizure. But citizens must remain vigilant to make sure their rights are protected.

of someone's property or possessions. In most cases, this means police must obtain a **search warrant** from a judge to carry out a legal search.

Gathering Evidence

Before prosecutors file a criminal charge, they try to make sure they have a viable case against the suspect. To do this, they must try to get as clear a picture as possible of what happened before, during, and after the crime. This requires an examination of both direct and circumstantial evidence.

Direct evidence is information provided either by a witness who saw the crime occur or by a video or audio recording of the crime. **Circumstantial evidence** is information that can be inferred from other facts. For example, if a suspect's fingerprints are found on the steering wheel of a car, police can infer that the suspect was present in that car at some point. The fingerprints thus become circumstantial evidence. If a neighbor actually saw the suspect in the car, however, that is direct evidence. For law enforcement officers to gather these kinds of evidence, they must conduct searches.

Although the Fourth Amendment is meant to protect citizens from unreasonable searches and seizures, it also implicitly allows for "reasonable"

To investigate crimes, law enforcement officials must gather and analyze evidence. Here, a forensic scientist at a crime lab examines bullet holes in a window.

police actions. But how do law enforcement officers know when a search is reasonable?

Several Supreme Court decisions in the past few decades have helped law enforcement officials answer this question. Two cases that helped officials determine when searches are reasonable include *Katz v. United States* (1967) and *Terry v. Ohio* (1968). In *Katz*, the Court determined that a search was not permitted under the Fourth Amendment whenever a person had a "reasonable expectation of privacy." In *Terry*, however, the Court held that a "stop and frisk" search was reasonable when police had cause to be suspicious of a suspect's behavior.

The Court has found other searches and seizures without warrants to be reasonable when the invasion of privacy is minimal or when special circumstances apply. Here are some examples:

- *Sobriety checkpoints.* Because the intrusion is slight, stopping motorists at roadblocks to search for drunk drivers is considered reasonable.
- *Airport searches.* Searching carry-on luggage is considered permissible to lessen the danger of airline hijacking.
- *Student searches.* In *New Jersey v. T.L.O.* (1985), the Supreme Court held that school officials can search students on school grounds without probable cause.
- *Consent searches.* Police are legally allowed to search a person's property if the person provides voluntary consent and is not coerced.

How Search Warrants Work

The Fourth Amendment sets out certain conditions under which warrants can be issued. This portion of the amendment is known as the **Warrant Clause**.

The Warrant Clause first states that any search warrant issued must be based on probable cause. Probable cause is more than just a gut feeling or suspicion. In the case of *Brinegar v. United States* (1949), the Supreme Court noted,

In dealing with probable cause . . . we deal with probabilities. These are not technical; they are the factual and practical considerations of everyday life on which reasonable and prudent men . . . act.

To obtain a search warrant, law enforcement officials must present evidence of probable cause to a judge. If the evidence is convincing, the judge will issue a warrant. The warrant describes the exact place to be searched and the items or persons to be seized. This exactness keeps officers from carrying out generalized searches without a clear idea of what they are looking for.

It is not always feasible for police to obtain a warrant before performing a search, however. In certain situations, searches may be made without a warrant. Here are some examples:

- *During a lawful arrest.* The Supreme Court has determined that police can search an arrested suspect and the immediate area of the arrest for weapons or evidence that could be destroyed.

- *When evidence is in plain view.* If evidence is plainly visible to an officer and the officer is legally entitled to be in that location, the evidence can be seized without a warrant.
- *When in hot pursuit.* If police are chasing a suspect, they can follow that suspect into a building and seize any evidence found there.
- *Automobile searches.* Police can make warrantless searches of automobiles under certain circumstances, since a vehicle might be moved before a warrant is obtained.

Illegally Gained Evidence: The Exclusionary Rule

During an investigation, police officers must be careful to obtain all evidence legally. In the 1914 case of *Weeks v. United States*, the Supreme Court held that the seizing of evidence illegally would result in the exclusion of that evidence during trial. This **exclusionary rule** has been tested many times since then. One notable instance was the 1961 case of *Mapp v. Ohio*.

The *Mapp* case began when police in Cleveland, Ohio, arrested Dollree Mapp after a search of her home turned up books and photographs judged to

Trained search dogs can provide police with the probable cause they need to carry out legal searches. The dog in this photograph is searching for hidden explosives.

be obscene. Although the police did not have a valid search warrant, Mapp was convicted for possession of obscene materials. On appeal, the Ohio Supreme Court upheld Mapp's conviction on the grounds that the Fourth Amendment's protections did not apply to state law enforcement.

The Supreme Court disagreed with the lower court's decision. A Court majority concluded that "all evidence obtained by searches and seizures in violation of the Constitution is . . . inadmissible in a state court." This meant that all levels of the criminal justice system—local, state, and federal—had to enforce rules against the use of evidence that was illegally obtained.

■ 16.4 The Arrest

In the hypothetical shoplifting case, your arrest at the mall occurred at the scene of the crime. Under such circumstances, the police do not need to get an arrest warrant. Like a search warrant, an **arrest warrant** must be issued by a judge and be based on probable cause. When officers find a likely suspect at the scene of a crime, however, they can make a **warrantless arrest**.

Law enforcement officers must follow very specific steps when making an arrest. From the moment a suspect is placed in handcuffs until the time the suspect is jailed or released, police officers are required to follow proper procedures to ensure that the suspect's rights are protected.

Due Process During an Arrest: Miranda Rights

A landmark Supreme Court decision in the 1966 case of *Miranda v. Arizona* helped ensure that police officers observe due process when taking suspects into custody. This decision requires officers to inform suspects of their rights as they are being arrested.

The *Miranda* case began in Phoenix, Arizona, in 1963, when Ernesto Miranda was arrested for rape and kidnapping after a victim identified him in a police lineup. During questioning by police, Miranda confessed in writing to both crimes. The police later admitted that they did not inform Miranda of his Fifth Amendment right against self-incrimination or of his Sixth Amendment right to have an attorney present during questioning. They argued, however, that Miranda had been arrested before and therefore must have been aware of his rights. At his trial, Miranda was convicted and given a sentence of 20 to 30 years in prison for each crime.

Miranda's attorney appealed to the Arizona Supreme Court, arguing that the confession was not admissible evidence because Miranda had been denied his legal rights. The state court denied Miranda's appeal and upheld his conviction. In 1966, the U.S. Supreme Court agreed to hear *Miranda v. Arizona*, along with three similar cases in other states.

Noting that the interrogation of Miranda was done in an "atmosphere . . . of intimidation," the Court concluded that for a confession to be valid, a suspect must be informed of his or her rights. The Court said that a confession could not be admitted as evidence unless a suspect had been told the following:

- You have the right to remain silent.
- Anything you say can be used against you in court.
- You have the right to an attorney and to have that attorney present while you are being questioned.
- If you cannot afford an attorney, one will be appointed for you before questioning begins.

JUVENILE MIRANDA/McMILLAN WARNING

1. I am a police officer, your adversary, and not your friend.
2. You have the right to remain silent.
3. Anything you say can and will be used against you in a court of law.
4. You have the right to talk to a lawyer and have him present with you while you are being questioned.
5. If you cannot afford to hire a lawyer, one will be appointed to represent you before any questioning, if you wish.
6. You have the right to have a parent, guardian, or custodian present, during questioning.
7. Any statement you make can be used against you if you are certified for trial in adult court.

Volunteered utterances or admissions, given by a juvenile following his apprehension and instruction of his constitutional rights, are admissible provided they are unsolicited.

Form 72 P.D. (Rev. 8-89)

In some places, police officers read juveniles an alternative version of the Miranda warning known as the McMillan warning. Law enforcers in Missouri, for example, may read arrested suspects the text on this card.

These **Miranda warnings** have become a cornerstone of the procedures that officers follow when making an arrest. Any statements offered by a suspect before Miranda warnings are given cannot be offered as evidence in a trial. In addition, any evidence that officers might uncover as result of an illegal confession is also inadmissible in court.

The Court has noted exceptions to its decision in the *Miranda* case, however. One is the "public safety" exception. Police can question suspects before giving the Miranda warnings if they believe public safety is at risk. For example, in 1984, New York City police chased an armed suspect into a grocery store. When they asked him where his gun was, he showed it to them. In this case, the gun was admitted as evidence, because locating the gun quickly was critical to public safety.

"Book 'Em": Processing Suspects After an Arrest

When criminal suspects arrive at the police station after their arrest, they are "booked," or processed. They are asked to give their name, date of birth, and other personal information. They are informed of the charges against them, though these charges will later be stated more formally in a courtroom. They are also fingerprinted, photographed, and searched. In some cases, suspects are required to stand in a police lineup to be viewed by witnesses.

During booking, an officer confiscates a suspect's personal property. The officer makes a list of everything taken and has the suspect sign the list.

The suspect has the right to make a phone call during booking. Most suspects call family members, friends, or a lawyer. In some cases, a lawyer may be able to get the charges dropped. Otherwise, the suspect has to remain in jail, awaiting the next stage in the criminal justice process.

■ 16.5 Pretrial Activity

The shoplifting story that began this chapter has a happy ending—at least for you. When you arrive at the police station, a detective reviews the videotape from the mall and concludes, to your great relief, that you played no direct role in the shoplifting incident. Instead of being booked, you are released without charges. It has been a difficult experience, but justice has been served and you are free to go.

It is a different story for your friends, however. The videotape provides sufficient evidence to hold them on suspicion of shoplifting. Over the next few days, they will go through various pretrial activities. During this pretrial stage, they are assumed to be innocent until proven guilty. This means the police and prosecution must show enough evidence to support the criminal charges against them.

The Initial Appearance: The Pretrial Process Begins

The Sixth Amendment requires that criminal prosecutions move forward quickly. Within 48 hours of their arrest, suspects must have the opportunity to appear in court. At this first pretrial appearance, they are reminded of their rights and of the charges against them. They are also told that if they cannot afford an attorney, one will be appointed for them at public expense.

A suspect's initial appearance in court also offers the possibility of release from jail. A judge will decide whether the defendant should be released from custody and under what conditions.

One way a defendant can be released from custody is through the posting of bail. Bail is money that a defendant hands over to the court as a guarantee that he or she will return for trial. The amount of bail is set by the judge in each particular case. Once bail has been posted, the defendant is released from jail until the trial.

A judge may decide not to set bail, depending on the circumstances of a case. For example, a judge may conclude that a defendant is a "flight risk," meaning he or she might not return for trial despite posting bail. Or a judge may decide that the defendant would pose a possible danger to others if released.

The issue of risk to others was at the heart of the Supreme Court's decision in the 1987 case of *United States v. Salerno*. The defendant in the case argued that denying bail to suspects who were considered dangerous violated their constitutional rights. The Court concluded, however, that judges could deny bail based on public safety.

At the initial pretrial hearing, defendants facing

After an arrest, a suspect is booked at the police station. As part of this process, the suspect is fingerprinted and asked to supply information to be recorded in a booking report. This information becomes part of the legal record in a criminal case.

a misdemeanor charge are required to enter a plea of guilty or not guilty. Defendants in felony cases, however, do not enter a plea until a later court appearance.

The Preliminary Hearing: Will There Be a Trial?

The next pretrial step in most felony cases is the preliminary hearing. The purpose of this hearing is to determine whether there is enough evidence to take a case to trial. The prosecutor must prove that there is probable cause that a crime was committed and that the suspect committed it.

During the preliminary hearing, the prosecutor calls witnesses whose testimony will support the prosecution's case. In some states, the courts also allow cross-examination of witnesses by the defense

Court-appointed lawyers, known as public defenders, play a crucial role in our justice system. They provide legal counsel to defendants who cannot afford a lawyer.

attorney. Preliminary hearings tend to be brief, however, as the main goal is to determine whether there is sufficient evidence to justify a trial.

Grand Juries Also Weigh Evidence

In some felony cases, a grand jury takes the place of a preliminary hearing. A **grand jury** is a type of jury that weighs evidence and determines whether a trial is warranted.

Grand juries are quite different from trial juries. They are larger, consisting of 16 to 23 jurors. These jurors serve for a set period of time—often for a month or more. They consider a number of cases rather than just one as a trial jury would. Grand juries meet in secret to protect the reputation of those under investigation.

Grand juries also differ from trial juries in that they do not hear both sides of a case. They only hear the prosecution's version of events. Jurors must consider this question: Did a crime take place, and did this defendant commit it? If they believe the answer to both parts of the question is yes, they will return an **indictment,** or formal accusation, against the suspect.

Under the terms of the Fifth Amendment, any serious violation of federal law must be brought before a federal grand jury. At the state level, however, grand juries are less common. Some states do not use either grand juries or preliminary hearings. In those states, a defendant may have to stand trial based solely on a prosecutor's formal statement of evidence to the court.

The Arraignment: Entering a Plea

Assuming there is enough evidence to go to trial, the next step in the pretrial process is the **arraignment**. This is a court appearance in which the suspect must enter a plea. If the plea is guilty, the judge will set a date to announce punishment. If the plea is not guilty, the judge will set a trial date.

Before the arraignment, a defendant may arrange a **plea bargain**. This is an agreement in which the defendant pleads guilty in exchange for a lighter sentence. Although a plea bargain may result in jail time, some defendants choose this option to avoid a longer sentence or to spare them the time and expense of a trial.

Critics of plea bargaining argue that it sometimes lets dangerous criminals get out of jail too soon. Other critics worry that it allows the government to pressure innocent people into pleading guilty for fear of a heavy sentence should they lose in court. Supporters, however, argue that plea bargaining helps keep the court system from clogging up with too many cases.

16.6 The Trial

Several weeks have passed since your friends were arrested and booked on suspicion of shoplifting. With the help of a lawyer, they secured bail and spent only one night in jail. During the pretrial phase, however, a judge determined that there was enough evidence to put them on trial. Because the value of the shoplifted goods exceeded $950, they have been charged with grand theft. Now the day has arrived when they must appear in court to defend themselves before a judge and jury.

The Right to a Speedy and Public Trial

The Sixth Amendment forms the basis of a suspect's constitutional right to a fair and impartial trial. The first phrase of this amendment says that the "accused shall enjoy the right to a speedy and public trial." But what do these words mean in practice? For example, what constitutes a "speedy trial"?

The Supreme Court has shed some light on this question. In 1972, the Court reviewed a case in which a suspect's trial was delayed 16 times before he was finally tried and convicted. Because the defendant had not objected to the first 11 delays, the Supreme Court upheld his conviction. However, the Court listed the following four factors to consider in deciding whether a trial has been "speedy":

- the length of the delay
- the prosecutor's reasons for the delay
- the defendant's views on the delay
- potential harm to the defendant caused by the delay

Congress has set a limit of 100 days after an arrest for a federal case to be brought to trial. If this time limit is not met, a case may be dismissed. Defendants have been known to waive this right, however, to give their attorneys more time to prepare or to accommodate the needs of key witnesses. Some states have followed federal guidelines and set their own limits under which a case must be tried.

The "public" part of the "speedy and public" clause has also been subject to interpretation. The framers of the Sixth Amendment believed that it was important to keep trials public in order to ensure a fair judgment for the defendant. They also assumed that society would benefit from seeing justice served.

But what happens when holding a public trial might actually hurt the defendant? In certain cases, for example, the presence of the news media at a trial could affect public opinion and influence the jury. In such cases, judges may decide to change the location of a trial or to isolate the jury.

Although television cameras are now allowed at many trials, judges have been known to ban cameras from the courtroom on the grounds that they could distort the justice process. The Supreme Court has determined that such bans do not violate the Sixth Amendment.

Inevitably, the defendant's right to a fair trial sometimes conflicts with the public's desire for access to trial proceedings. In 1979, the Supreme Court concluded in the case of *Gannett Co. v. DePasquale* that the public does not necessarily have the right to attend all trials. However, a year later, in *Richmond Newspapers Inc. v. Virginia*, the Court decided that, with the exception of cases involving national security, the public's right to view trials should be maintained if at all possible.

The Right to Be Judged by an Impartial Jury of One's Peers

Trial by jury is one of the fundamental rights guaranteed under the Constitution. In fact, it is the only right that is specified both in the main body of the Constitution and in the Bill of Rights. The Sixth Amendment, however, goes beyond simply guaranteeing the right to a trial by jury. It also mandates that the jury be impartial, or unbiased, and made up of members of the local community.

Traditionally, juries have consisted of 12 jurors who must reach a unanimous verdict for a case to be decided. Federal courts still uphold those standards. The Supreme Court has held, however, that 12 jurors are not essential to decide a case, as long as there are enough members to facilitate group deliberation.

The need for a unanimous verdict has also come into question. In the 1972 case of *Apodaca v. Oregon*,

"I am inclined to dismiss this juror."

Lawyers may choose to dismiss jurors through peremptory challenges. As this cartoon suggests, peremptory challenges can be used to remove jurors who appear to have a bias in the case. However, lawyers cannot exclude jurors based only on race or gender.

stating a specific objection. For example, a prosecutor might challenge a juror on a murder case if that person is opposed to the death penalty. If the judge approves the challenge, the juror is disqualified.

Lawyers may also exclude jurors based on a **peremptory challenge**. This is a challenge that is given without reason but that is usually based on a perceived bias in the jury candidate. Lawyers are generally granted a limited number of peremptory challenges in each case.

Until the 1980s, lawyers could use peremptory challenges whenever they chose, with no restrictions. In the 1986 case of *Batson v. Kentucky*, however, the Supreme Court concluded that this unrestricted process violated the Constitution. The case involved a black defendant who had been convicted of burglary. In the original trial, the prosecuting attorney used his peremptory challenges to exclude four black jurors, leaving an all-white jury to decide the case.

The Court held that the prosecutor's actions violated the Sixth and Fourteenth amendments. The Court said that if prosecutors try to exclude jurors based solely on race, they may be asked to explain their reasons. They may even be challenged by the defendant and ordered to change their approach. In 1992, the Court later extended these rules to defense attorneys. Two years later, it prohibited peremptory challenges based on gender.

The Right to an Adequate Defense

The last right guaranteed by the Sixth Amendment, the right to an attorney, is also essential to the judicial process. In fact, the Supreme Court has noted that the right to legal counsel is the most pervasive of a defendant's rights, because it "affects his ability to assert any other rights."

Because defendants must have access to legal counsel, the Supreme Court has said that they have the right to a free, court-appointed lawyer if they cannot afford to hire one. That right was upheld in the 1963 case of *Gideon v. Wainwright*.

A year later, the Supreme Court reinforced the legal right to an attorney in *Escobedo v. Illinois*. Danny Escobedo, the defendant in the original case, had been arrested and questioned by police in connection with a murder. During this questioning, police repeatedly denied Escobedo's requests to speak to a lawyer. He later confessed to the murder and was convicted.

the Court held that verdicts in non–death penalty cases do not need to be unanimous. However, a Court decision in 1979 made it a requirement for smaller, six-member juries to reach a unanimous verdict.

Most important, the Sixth Amendment requires that juries be impartial. This requirement mainly affects the way in which potential jurors are chosen. Possible jurors are usually selected from a master list compiled from various sources. The idea is to draw from a pool of people who represent a cross-section of the community. In *Hernandez v. Texas* (1953), the Supreme Court also required that racial groups cannot be excluded from jury selection in order to be consistent with the Equal Protection Clause in the Fourteenth Amendment. Names are then drawn at random from the master list, and those selected receive a jury summons.

During a process known as **voir dire,** the lawyers and judge in a case question potential jurors to determine whether there is any reason to disqualify them. A lawyer may challenge a juror "for cause" by

Clarence Gideon's case before the Supreme Court in 1963 helped secure every defendant's Sixth Amendment right to a lawyer. Gideon's case made it to the Court on the strength of his handwritten petition, which was filed from his prison cell.

In its decision, the Supreme Court found that the police had violated Escobedo's Sixth Amendment right to an attorney. This right applies, said the Court, when "a police investigation is no longer a general inquiry into an unsolved crime but has begun to focus on a particular suspect in police custody." This case produced the "Escobedo rule," an application of the exclusionary rule that disallows evidence gained from a confession made without an attorney present.

In 1984, the Court considered the question of what constitutes effective legal counsel in the case of *Strickland v. Washington*. This case centered on a defendant who had been sentenced to death in a murder case. The defendant had confessed to the crime but charged that his lawyer had violated his rights by not providing enough evidence in his case to avoid the death sentence.

In its decision, the Court agreed that defendants are entitled to "reasonably effective assistance" of counsel. To claim ineffective counsel, defendants must show that errors made by the attorney were sufficient to prevent a fair trial. In effect, defendants must prove that more competent counsel could have produced a different outcome. In this particular case, however, the Court upheld the man's conviction on the grounds that additional evidence would not have affected the outcome.

The Rules of Evidence in Criminal Trials

The burden of proof in a trial rests with the prosecution. It is the government's job to prove beyond a reasonable doubt that the defendant is guilty. Prosecutors seek to do this by presenting both direct and circumstantial evidence. In addition, prosecutors must obey the rules of evidence when presenting their case.

In general, evidence must satisfy two main rules to be admissible. First, it must be relevant. This means there must be a valid reason to introduce it. If a defendant is accused of murder, evidence that he is diabetic is probably not relevant. Second, evidence must be competent. In other words, it must meet certain standards of reliability. The testimony of a very young child might not be considered competent, for example, because the child might not be a reliable eyewitness.

The judge in a case has the final say on whether evidence is admissible. The judge's role is to make sure that both the defense and the prosecution follow the law and that justice is served. Either side can appeal a judge's decision, however, if they believe the judge made legal errors.

The Constitutional Protection from Self-Incrimination

One of the biggest decisions a defense attorney must make is whether to have the defendant testify. The Fifth Amendment protects a defendant's right not to testify. This is to protect the accused from self-incrimination. Still, jurors are often curious about a defendant's side of the story and may wonder why someone would choose not to take the witness stand.

The Fifth Amendment's protection against self-incrimination, however, does not prohibit the state from requiring a defendant to submit evidence such as fingerprints, handwriting samples, and DNA samples. This type of evidence is called **physical evidence**. The Court has said that the use of physical evidence is permissible to obtain a conviction.

Jury Deliberations: Beyond a Reasonable Doubt

After both the prosecution and the defense attorney have presented their final arguments, the case is handed over to the jury. The jury then retires to the jury room to deliberate behind closed doors.

The first thing members of a jury typically do is choose a foreman to act as chairperson. They then discuss all aspects of the case, including court procedures, testimony, and evidence. Jurors may also request additional information from the judge if they are uncertain about anything. Following these procedures, most juries are able to reach a verdict quickly, often in less than two hours.

Physical evidence, such as fingerprints or DNA samples, can play an important role in a criminal trial. Physical evidence also includes real items that were found at a crime scene. Here, a police officer testifies about a weapon involved in the case.

To reach a guilty verdict, jurors must agree that the defendant is guilty, beyond a reasonable doubt, of the crime in question. Depending on the laws involved, the jury may have the option of choosing to convict the accused of a lesser offense. Once the jurors have agreed on a verdict, they inform the judge and return to the courtroom. The jury foreman then announces the verdict in court.

If judged guilty, the defendant is usually taken into custody to await punishment. Following an **acquittal,** or "not guilty" verdict, however, the defendant leaves the courtroom a free person and the case is officially over. The protection of double jeopardy afforded by the Fifth Amendment prevents a person from being tried again for the same crime.

As mentioned previously, juries are usually required to reach a unanimous verdict. If they fail to do so, the result is a **hung jury**. In such cases, the judge dismisses the jurors. The prosecutor then has the option of retrying the case with a new jury.

■ 16.7 Sentencing and Appeals

Your friends' trial for shoplifting was relatively short, lasting just two days. The prosecution relied heavily on evidence from the videotape, which clearly showed them stuffing merchandise into a bag. A store clerk also testified that your friends left the store carrying the bag without paying for anything. Your friends' attorney argued that they meant to pay for the goods but simply forgot. The jury found this argument unconvincing and returned a verdict of guilty on the charge of grand theft.

After the verdict, your friends were taken to a nearby detention facility to await **sentencing**. This is the moment when the judge announces the punishment for a crime. After the sentence is announced, your friends may have the opportunity to file an appeal.

Making the Punishment Fit the Crime and the Criminal

In some trials, the jury may recommend a particular sentence as punishment for a crime. Ultimately, though, it is the judge's responsibility to assign a sentence. Judges try to make the punishment fit the crime and the criminal, assigning tougher penalties

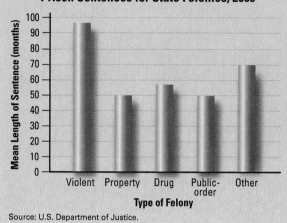
for more serious crimes or repeat offenders. However, that task is not always clear-cut.

Judges consider many factors before handing down a sentence. Often, they will request a presentence report, prepared by the court staff. This report provides details about the crime and the sentence report, prepared by the court staff. This report provides details about the crime and the surrounding circumstances. It supplies background on the defendant, including any criminal record the defendant may have. It also offers a recommendation on sentencing.

If the recommendation is imprisonment, judges can choose to apply either indeterminate or determinate sentencing. **Indeterminate sentencing** means assigning the criminal a variable term in prison, ranging from a minimum sentence to a maximum sentence. A review board may examine the case every few years to decide whether the inmate should be eligible for **parole,** or an early release from prison. For example, a judge might hand down a sentence of 10 to 15 years for a robbery conviction. A parole board might decide, however, that the prisoner is eligible for release after seven years in prison. Factors involved in that decision might include the inmate's behavior and his or her chances of staying out of trouble after returning to society.

Determinate sentencing, on the other hand, means that the judge sets a specific amount of time that a criminal must serve in prison. This option often rules out any possibility of parole, and the criminal is given a fixed date for his or her release.

In some cases, a defendant is convicted of multiple crimes and therefore given multiple sentences. In such cases, the judge may prescribe a concurrent sentence, in which the defendant serves each sentence at the same time. For example, if a person convicted on two charges received a sentence of ten years and another of five years, a concurrent sentence would release the inmate in no more than ten years.

On the other hand, the judge might prescribe a consecutive sentence. In that case, the same criminal would serve the two sentences back to back, for a total of 15 years, with little chance of parole.

Other Sentencing Options

In addition to imprisonment, a judge may choose from among other sentencing options, including those listed below. These options may be assigned on their own or in combination with others.

- *A suspended sentence.* The defendant does not have to serve time in prison immediately, but may have to serve time later if he or she is rearrested or violates a condition of parole.
- *Probation.* The defendant must report to a probation officer, who ensures that the defendant is following certain conditions set down by the judge.
- *Home confinement.* Rather than a prison sentence, the defendant serves time at home and can leave only for preapproved reasons, such as work, appointments, or school.
- *A fine.* The defendant may be required to pay a certain sum of money to the government.
- *Restitution.* **Restitution** means that the defendant must pay back or make up for whatever losses the victim has sustained.
- *Work release.* The defendant is imprisoned but is allowed to work in the community during workdays.

One goal of sentencing criminals is to help rehabilitate them so that they can live productive, crime-free lives when they are released from prison. This group of inmates received their GEDs after successfully completing an education program in jail.

The goal of sentencing is usually one of three outcomes, or a combination of all three: deterrence, rehabilitation, and incapacitation. The idea of deterrence is to assign a harsh enough sentence to discourage criminals from committing another crime. Rehabilitation is the process of helping criminals change so that they can live productive lives and be less likely to resort to crime in the future. Incapacitation ensures that criminals are locked up so that they can no longer pose a threat to society.

The most extreme form of punishment, the death penalty, has long been controversial. Some critics of capital punishment claim that it violates the Eighth Amendment, which forbids "cruel and unusual punishment." In 1976, however, the Supreme Court determined that capital punishment was permitted under the Constitution.

Nevertheless, the Supreme Court has decided against capital punishment in certain cases. In 1986, for example, it concluded that executing a prisoner who has been diagnosed as insane is unconstitutional. In 2002, it came to the same conclusion about the execution of mentally retarded persons. Three years later, in the case of *Roper v. Simmons*, the Court considered the question of capital punishment for juveniles. At the age of 17, Christopher Simmons had been sentenced to death by a state court. In its

decision, the Court said that executing minors is prohibited by the Eighth Amendment.

Raising Legal Questions During Appeals

Defendants who believe that they were wrongfully convicted have the right to appeal to a higher court. Their appeal will be heard, however, only if they can reasonably argue that the judge in their case committed an error of law. Though many appeals are filed every year, only a few are actually reviewed by appeals courts. From that handful of cases, even fewer have their original conviction overturned.

Reasons for requesting an appeal vary, depending on the case. Defendants may appeal because they believe the jury selection was flawed, their lawyer was ineffective, or the law was not interpreted correctly. They may also appeal because they feel their due process rights were denied, which was the issue in the 1963 case of *Brady v. Maryland*.

In the *Brady* case, the defendant appealed his conviction for murder on the grounds that the prosecution concealed evidence that might have influenced the death sentence he received. This evidence showed that although the defendant had been involved in the crime, another person had actually committed the murder.

The Maryland Court of Appeals, the state's supreme court, upheld Brady's conviction but said a lower court should review his death sentence. The Supreme Court agreed, arguing that withholding evidence violates due process "where the evidence is material either to guilt or to punishment."

On average, criminal defendants win on appeal only about one in eight times. In those cases, the appeals court sends instructions to a lower court to retry the case under different conditions. In about half of these cases, however, the defendants are found guilty a second time.

◼ 16.8 The Corrections System

After your friends' conviction for shoplifting, the judge handed them a relatively tough sentence as a form of deterrence. She sentenced them to 90 days of **incarceration**, or jail time, in a county correctional facility, followed by six months of probation. During their probation, they will be required to report regularly to a probation officer and to remain within the county. The judge also sentenced them to restitution, requiring them to return the stolen goods and make an oral and written apology to the store manager.

Apprehensive about serving time in jail, your friends asked their attorney whether they should appeal their sentence. The lawyer said they had no grounds for appeal, because the judge followed proper legal procedures during the trial. Instead, their attorney urged them to accept the terms of punishment.

Prisons, Parole, and Pardons

Serving time in the corrections system is a tough punishment for anyone. Inmates lose many of the rights and privileges they enjoyed in society, most notably the freedom to live their lives as they see fit.

Not all prisons are alike. White-collar or petty criminals normally end up in minimum-security prisons, where conditions are relatively lenient. Violent criminals, on the other hand, are sent to maximum-security prisons, where conditions are quite harsh.

No matter what their crime, however, all prisoners are guaranteed certain fundamental rights under the Constitution and state and federal law.

Supporters and opponents of capital punishment often hold demonstrations outside statehouses and prisons where executions are held. Opponents, like the one shown here, argue that the death penalty is a cruel and unusual punishment. Supporters of capital punishment believe that it is a fair form of justice.

The Eighth Amendment's protection against "cruel and unusual punishment" ensures that prisoners are provided a basic standard of living. Due process rights require that they be granted access to the parole process. The Fourteenth Amendment's Equal Protection Clause protects them from discrimination on the basis of race, gender, or religion.

In addition, the Supreme Court has determined that all prisoners have certain specific rights, including the right to receive mail, to get adequate medical care, and to practice their religion. In *Cutter v. Wilkinson* (2005), the Court said that prisoners cannot be denied the exercise of their religious beliefs, even if those beliefs are outside the mainstream of established religions. In most states, however, prisoners are still denied the right to vote.

After a certain amount of time, most inmates are eligible for release. Some are released because they

The United States has the largest prison population in the world. As the line graph shows, the number of inmates under the supervision of adult correctional systems has mostly grown over the past decade. The circle graph indicates the main types of crimes for which prisoners are incarcerated in state prisons.

Crimes Committed by State Prisoners, 2009

Public-order 1%
Other
Drug 18%
Property 19%
Violent 53%
9%

State and Federal Prison Populations, 2000–2010

Prisoners (in thousands)

Year

Source: U.S. Department of Justice.

have served their full sentence. Others leave prison because they have been granted parole.

The parole process varies from state to state. In some states, prisoners must apply for parole by submitting a request to the parole board. In others, the parole board automatically considers parole when prisoners have served a certain amount of their sentence. The prisoner may then be asked to appear at a parole hearing. At this hearing, the parole board hears testimony and examines evidence to determine whether parole should be granted.

Many released prisoners find that their return to society is not smooth. For one thing, the released prisoner now has a criminal record, which can make it difficult to find a job or a place to live. In some cases, former prisoners may decide to apply for a pardon. A pardon is a formal document stating that the person has paid his or her debt to society and has become a productive member of the community.

Pardons can be granted only by the president, in the case of a federal crime, or by governors, in the

"Bad news. The mailman is going to attend the parole-board hearing."

Prisoners must pass their parole board hearing to be eligible for parole. As this cartoon suggests, any negative testimony about the inmate presented at this hearing may ruin his or her chances for parole.

case of state crimes. Pardons are rarely granted, however. When they are, they restore all of the rights that were lost by offenders when they were convicted.

Summary

The criminal justice system is designed to prosecute criminals while protecting the rights of the accused. Criminal suspects enjoy certain constitutional protections as they move through each stage of the system.

Due process rights Every suspect has the right to due process of law. This means the government must act under established legal guidelines rather than in an arbitrary or random fashion. Law enforcement officers are required to follow certain procedures during the arrest of a suspect and the investigation of a crime.

Rights in the courtroom Rights granted under the Fifth, Sixth, and Eighth amendments are meant to ensure that criminal suspects enjoy fair treatment in a court of law. Defendants are protected from self-incrimination. They are also guaranteed legal counsel and a speedy, public trial by an impartial jury.

Post-trial protections A person convicted of a crime still enjoys a protective shield of rights. The Eighth Amendment requires that criminal sentences be appropriate to the crime and not "cruel" or "unusual." Convicted defendants also have the right to appeal their conviction if they believe their due process rights were denied.

Serving time Criminals sentenced to jail or prison lose many of their rights and privileges when they enter the corrections system. Supreme Court decisions, however, have guaranteed certain basic rights to prisoners.

Why is jury duty important?

Trial by jury is one of the rights guaranteed to you in the Bill of Rights. However, although Americans may hold this right sacred, they are too often no-shows when it comes to answering a summons to jury service.

As you read this article on jury duty, ask yourself these questions. First, if everyone is too busy for jury duty, who will be there to judge you? Second, what might be done to reduce no-shows to jury summonses? And third, what will you do when you receive your first summons to jury duty?

The Importance of Jury Duty

by Christina Habas, as heard on
The Bob Edwards Show

When my father was in his 20s, he was called to be a juror in a homicide case. He had two jobs, and three children under eight at home. The jury was sequestered, locked up. My father was one of only two jurors voting to acquit at the start of deliberations, and after hours of deliberation, the defendant was ultimately acquitted. My father saved the newspaper clippings from that trial for the next 49 years, sharing that experience with us many times. He relished his experience.

Now I am a trial judge in the Denver District Court, and I believe in jury duty. More precisely, I believe in the duty of the jury. Every day, citizens of every state receive a summons ordering them to appear for jury duty. Each day, I swear I can actually hear their groans. Each day as potential jurors arrive in my courthouse, their unhappiness hangs thick in the air.

This attitude is perplexing to me. I teach visiting students that jurors hold the highest position

This photograph shows summons for federal jury service. Individuals must meet certain requirements in order to serve on a jury. A few qualifications include U.S. citizenship, proficiency in English, and residence in the judicial district for a minimum of one year. In addition, those who have been convicted of a felony may not serve on a jury.

"I see jury selection has begun."

of power in a courtroom. Jurors, not judges, determine whether the government has proven its charge against a defendant; jurors, not judges, determine whether a party seeking damages deserves an award. Yet every week, I see people strive by any means necessary to be excused from exercising this authority.

Still others appear for jury service, but do not perform a juror's duty. These people declare that they will make a decision based upon the evidence and the law, yet once deliberations begin, they reject those promises in favor of advancing their own personal beliefs. Astonishingly, some of these same jurors loudly denounce "activist judges"

because of decisions that those judges make upon their own personal beliefs.

The symptoms of chronic ambivalence in this country are numerous: in community service, voting, politics. Avoiding jury duty is an acute and severe symptom. It undermines the ability of the courts to ensure that only the guilty are convicted, and that only the deserving receive compensation from those who truly caused injury. It directly causes injustice.

Many who avoid jury duty do so with no firsthand knowledge of the nature of jury service, or listen to others who are equally misinformed. In Colorado, judges meet privately with

jurors after trial to listen to their concerns and suggestions for the future. With the exception of one juror, all of my jurors have been unanimous in finding the experience to be both interesting and rewarding, just as my father had 49 years ago.

My father's participation in that trial was critical, but so was the participation of every other juror. Juries constituted of diverse members of our community are essential to ensure that verdicts represent the considered judgment of that community. Any failure of a large number of citizens to fulfill their jury duty corrupts the ability of the judicial system to fulfill its purpose of delivering justice. Because I believe in government of the people, by the people, and for the people, I believe in jury duty.

Christina Habas is a judge for the Criminal Division of Denver District Court in Colorado. She previously worked in private practice focusing on employment law, civil rights issues, insurance cases and personal injury. Habas has taught at the University of Denver and is a member of the American Board of Trial Advocates.

Chapter 17

Creating American Foreign Policy

How should the United States conduct foreign policy?

■ 17.1 Introduction

Michael and Ande McCarthy are health care workers living in Michigan. Motivated by their religious convictions, they flew to Cuba in 2001 to deliver medical supplies to a Catholic charity group. Because federal law bans travel to Cuba from the United States, they flew in and out of Toronto, Canada.

When the couple drove back to Michigan from Canada, U.S. border authorities asked where they had been. Instead of saying Toronto, the couple answered, "Cuba." A few weeks later, they received a letter saying they had violated the Trading with the Enemy Act of 1917 by spending about $750 for a Cuba vacation package and buying some souvenirs while in Cuba. The letter ordered them to appear before a federal judge and to pay a fine of $7,500 each.

The Trading with the Enemy Act is an element of U.S. **foreign policy,** or how our government deals with other nations. The U.S. government has not always viewed Cuba as an enemy. Lying 90 miles off the coast of Florida, Cuba is one of our closest neighbors. In the early 1900s, the United States and Cuba developed close economic and political ties. For the next half century, Americans invested heavily in Cuba, buying up most of the country's best farmland for sugar plantations. In addition, American tourists vacationed on Cuba's beaches.

The 1967 American chiefs of state summit meeting

U.S.-Cuban relations changed abruptly after communist revolutionaries, led by Fidel Castro, seized control of the island in 1959. A year later, Castro nationalized most of Cuba's private property. **Nationalization** is the transfer of private property to government ownership. Both Americans and Cubans who owned property in Cuba lost everything when the Cuban government seized their land and businesses.

The United States responded by placing an **embargo,** or ban, on most U.S. trade with Cuba. When Castro signed trade deals with the Soviet Union to make up for the loss of U.S. trade, the United States broke off diplomatic relations with Cuba. After the Cuban missile crisis in 1962, President John F. Kennedy imposed restrictions on travel to Cuba. In recent years, the United States has loosened its sanctions against Cuba. As of 2012, it is not illegal to travel to Cuba, and Americans may engage in basic travel transactions, such as transportation and food. However, travelers are subject to strict regulations on most other purchases.

A growing number of Americans have proposed changing U.S. foreign policy toward Cuba. Others feel just as strongly that the trade and travel bans should remain in place. This chapter explores how foreign policy decisions such as this one are made and why they are important—not only to governments, but also to ordinary people like Michael and Ande McCarthy.

■ 17.2 The Basic Goals of U.S. Foreign Policy

Over the past two centuries, U.S. foreign policy has undergone many shifts. Early presidents, starting with George Washington, embraced a policy of neutrality. They refused to take sides in the disputes and conflicts of other nations. Later presidents pursued a policy of imperialism, seeking to extend American power over other countries. Although specific policies have changed over the years, the basic goals of U.S. foreign policy have remained constant. These goals are based on what Americans see as our nation's vital interests: protecting security, preserving peace, promoting prosperity, and pursuing humanitarian ideals.

Protecting the Nation's Security

Ensuring national security is central to the foreign policy of every nation. The most important job of any national government is to protect its people from attack. This may be done both by creating armed forces and by forming military alliances with other nations. Without such protection, a country's physical survival could be at risk.

National security is not limited to defending the nation from attacks by other countries. Americans

Americans are not the only ones with strong opinions about the relationship between the United States and Cuba. For many years, a number of countries have pushed for the termination of the U.S. embargo. Here, Felipe Perez Rogue, Cuban's Foreign Minister, argues against the embargo at the United Nations General Assembly in 2008.

were reminded of this on September 11, 2001, when two airplanes, hijacked by terrorists, slammed into the World Trade Center in New York City. A third hijacked plane hit the Pentagon, the Defense Department's headquarters just outside Washington, D.C. A fourth plane crashed into a field in Pennsylvania before reaching its target. As the nation mourned its dead, it faced the fact that threats to national security can come from any group—in this instance, a terrorist network called al Qaeda that is hostile to the United States.

Since 9/11, the United States has prioritized protecting its citizens from terrorism. In a speech to Congress, President George W. Bush declared,

Our war on terror begins with al Qaeda, but it does not end there. It will not end until every terrorist group of global reach has been found, stopped, and defeated . . . Americans should not expect one battle, but a lengthy campaign, unlike any other we have ever seen.
—George W. Bush, Address to a Joint Session of Congress and the American People, 2001

As part of this campaign, the United States has worked to make it more difficult for terrorists to enter the country. Travelers crossing U.S. borders with Canada and Mexico are now screened far more carefully than they were in the past. Visitors seeking **visas** to enter the United States are now interviewed and checked against terrorist watch lists. A visa is an official document issued by a country's government that allows a foreigner to enter and travel in that country.

Preserving World Peace

A second goal of U.S. foreign policy is the preservation of peace around the world. A peaceful world is both more secure from a military point of view and better for U.S. economic interests. Trade and tourism tend to thrive in peaceful regions and dry up in conflict zones. The United States seeks peace by supporting the peacekeeping work of the United Nations. U.S. officials also work to **mediate** disputes that might lead, or have led, to armed conflict. To mediate means to attempt to solve a dispute by working with both sides to reach an agreement.

Theodore Roosevelt was one of the first presidents to try his hand at peacekeeping on the

This cartoon depicts Theodore Roosevelt as an "Angel of Peace," dragging Russia and Japan into peace talks. Roosevelt won the Nobel Peace Prize for his efforts to end a war between the two nations. In his acceptance speech, he said, "Peace is generally good in itself, but it is never the highest good unless it comes as the handmaid of righteousness."

international stage. When war broke out between Russia and Japan in 1904, Roosevelt offered to mediate. He invited representatives from both sides to meet with him in Portsmouth, New Hampshire, in 1905. Under the president's watchful eye, the warring parties worked out a peace agreement. The following year, Roosevelt became the first American to be awarded the Nobel Peace Prize for his successful mediation of this conflict.

Promoting Economic Prosperity

Most governments use foreign policy to promote the economic prosperity of their people. The United States is no exception. Since the founding of the United States, the government has sought to protect the right of Americans to buy and sell goods to and from other countries. It has also sought to increase Americans' access to raw materials and resources found in other parts of the world.

Since World War II, the United States has become a leading force in **globalization,** or the trend toward more open, less-restricted trade and communication among the world's nations. Globalization promotes the free movement of goods, money, people, information, and culture across national borders. This free movement of goods allows U.S. companies to compete for customers on a worldwide scale. At the same time, however, it has introduced new threats to U.S. economic interests.

One such threat is illegal foreign production of goods that are protected by U.S. patents or copyrights. **Patents** give an inventor the exclusive right to make or sell an invention. Similarly, a **copyright** gives developers of original works, such as music, art, books, and software, the right to control their intellectual property. Patents and copyrights ensure that the people and companies who create new products and intellectual property can benefit from their investments of time and money.

Those benefits are lost, however, when foreign producers ignore patent and copyright protections. Some of these producers make money by **counterfeiting**. This means they make and sell copies of patented products without permission from or payment to the patent holders. Others make money by modern **piracy,** or the illegal use of copyrighted intellectual property such as movies and software.

Stopping counterfeiting and piracy has become an important focus of U.S. foreign policy. Trade in counterfeit and pirated goods leads to lower sales and profits for U.S. companies. Moreover, some copycat products, such as counterfeit drugs, may be harmful to people's health.

Pursuing Humanitarian Ideals

U.S. foreign policy has also been driven by the goal of advancing humanitarian ideals around the world. Some of these ideals involve promoting freedom, democracy, and the rule of law. Others involve ending poverty and promoting human rights. Americans do this by sending foreign aid to other countries to improve the standard of living. U.S. officials also help countries move toward democracy by assisting them with elections and by monitoring elections to ensure that votes are counted fairly.

Woodrow Wilson based his decision to enter World War I as much on ideals as on national security interests. In his speech calling on Congress to declare war, he said,

The world must be made safe for democracy. Its peace must be planted upon the tested foundations of political liberty . . . It is a fearful thing to lead this great peaceful people into war . . . But the right is more precious than peace, and we shall fight for the things which we have always carried nearest our hearts—for democracy, for the right of those who submit to authority to have a voice in their own Governments, for the rights and liberties of small nations, for a universal dominion of right . . . as shall bring peace and safety to all nations and make the world itself at last free.

Global Theft

Counterfeiting and piracy pose a major threat to U.S. economic interests abroad. Drug companies and software makers are hit particularly hard by the illegal trade in counterfeit goods.

Large Industries Hurt By Counterfeit Goods

Software

Pharmaceutical

Footwear and apparel

Auto

Motion picture

Artistic recordings

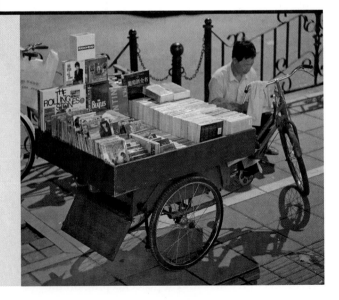

Humanitarian aid is a large part of the United States's foreign policy and is often used to improve the living conditions for people in developing countries. These U.S. Navy soldiers are loading and delivering humanitarian supplies to help foreign nations in need.

Similarly, President Kennedy's creation of the Peace Corps was based as much on ideals as on Cold War security concerns. As Kennedy put it,

> To those peoples in the huts and villages across the globe struggling to break the bonds of mass misery, we pledge our best efforts to help them help themselves, for whatever period is required—not because the Communists may be doing it, not because we seek their votes, but because it is right.
> —John F. Kennedy, Inaugural Address, 1961

17.3 The "Soft Power" Tools of Foreign Policy

Much of foreign policy involves trying to get other countries to do what you want. There are many ways to achieve this goal. Some involve "hard power," or force. Others involve "soft power," or persuasion. Political scientist Joseph S. Nye Jr. defined soft power as

> the ability to get what you want through attraction rather than coercion or payments. It arises from the attractiveness of a country's culture, political ideals, and policies. When our policies are seen as legitimate in the eyes of others, our soft power is enhanced.
> —Joseph S. Nye Jr., Soft Power: The Means to Success in World Politics, 2004

Soft power can take many forms, from diplomacy to exchanges of rock bands and artists.

Diplomacy: The Art of Conducting Negotiations

Diplomacy is the art and practice of conducting negotiations between countries. Most diplomacy is carried out by government officials called diplomats. The highest-ranking diplomat sent by one country to another is the **ambassador**. The ambassador and his staff work out of an **embassy**. The embassy's job is to represent the interests of the home country while developing friendly relations with the host country.

Under international law, ambassadors and their staff enjoy **diplomatic immunity**. This means they are exempt from the host country's laws. The purpose of diplomatic immunity is to protect diplomats from being falsely arrested or otherwise abused by their host country, especially during times of war or conflict. If a diplomat does commit a crime while in another country, it is up to the home country to bring that person to justice.

Diplomatic relations begin when a country grants **diplomatic recognition** to another country's government. Such recognition acknowledges that the government is the legitimate representative of its people. Countries use diplomatic recognition to express approval or disapproval of a government. When communists took over China in 1949, for example, the United States refused to recognize the new government. The two countries did not exchange ambassadors and establish embassies in one another's capitals until 1979.

Summits: Meetings of Heads of States

Most negotiations between countries are carried out by diplomats. From time to time, however, national leaders come together for face-to-face talks. These very high-level meetings are called **summits**.

Summits are used to address problems of mutual concern. For instance, leaders from eight industrialized countries meet annually at the G8 summit to discuss topics such as the global economy. Summits are also used to improve general relations. The United States and China used to be bitter enemies, which began with the establishment of a communist government in China in 1949. In 1972, President Richard Nixon traveled to China for a weeklong summit with Chinese leader Mao Zedong. Their talks laid the groundwork for the establishment of formal diplomatic relations between the two nations a few years later.

Treaties: Agreements to Solve Problems Peacefully

When conflicts arise between nations, diplomats try to settle them through peaceful negotiations. The solutions they negotiate are usually spelled out in treaties to which all parties agree. Treaties may be **bilateral,** which means they relate to two countries. Or they may be **multilateral** agreements that involve three or more countries.

Treaties can cover a variety of issues, from ending wars to protecting the environment. Whatever their content, treaties work much like contracts among countries. Like contracts, treaties are entered into willingly by all parties. In addition, under international law, all parties are expected to fulfill their treaty obligations.

Trade Relations: Managing Cross-Border Commerce

With the rise of globalization, cross-border trade relations have become an important soft power tool.

Countries use trade relations to show their approval or disapproval of a government. In 1975, for example, the United States cut off trade with Vietnam after it was taken over by a communist government.

By establishing trade relations, nations signal their desire for more contacts between their peoples. This was President Bill Clinton's intention when he lifted the trade embargo on Vietnam in 1994. In 2001, the former enemies signed a trade agreement that spelled out the rules of commerce between them. As a result, two-way trade between the United States and Vietnam grew from $1.5 billion a year to over $21 billion by 2011.

Most trade agreements made by the United States with other countries include a **most-favored-nation clause**. This clause means that the other country will be granted all trade advantages, such as low tariffs, that any other trading partner receives from the United States. For example, the United States heavily relies on imported mineral fuel from Canada and Saudi Arabia. Because of their natural resources, the two countries enjoy the same trade benefits so that the United States can maintain good trade relations with both nations. The effect is to put all countries with most-favored-nation status on an equal footing with one another in terms of trade with the United States.

Foreign Aid: Assisting Less Wealthy Countries

Wealthy nations often provide aid to other countries. Foreign aid can come in various forms, including cash, equipment, and personnel. In 2010, the United States provided foreign aid to over 180 countries.

In 1972, President Richard Nixon visited China for a summit meeting with Mao Zedong. While there, he and his wife, Pat, visited the Great Wall of China. "I think that you would have to conclude that this is a great wall," Nixon noted diplomatically, "and it had to be built by a great people." To his annoyance, many U.S. press reports left out the second part of his quote.

U.S. spending on foreign assistance reached nearly $35 billion by 2010. The graphs show how this aid is spent and which nations receive the most aid. In the photograph, workers in Haiti unload cooking oil sent by the United States to assist those affected by the Tropical Storm Hanna and Hurricane Ike.

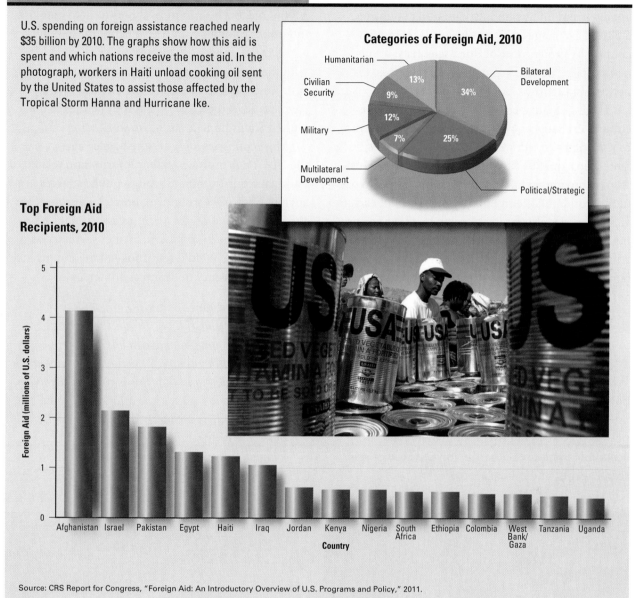

Categories of Foreign Aid, 2010

- Humanitarian — 13%
- Civilian Security — 9%
- Military — 12%
- Multilateral Development — 7%
- Political/Strategic — 25%
- Bilateral Development — 34%

Top Foreign Aid Recipients, 2010

Foreign Aid (millions of U.S. dollars) vs. Country

Afghanistan, Israel, Pakistan, Egypt, Haiti, Iraq, Jordan, Kenya, Nigeria, South Africa, Ethiopia, Colombia, West Bank/Gaza, Tanzania, Uganda

Source: CRS Report for Congress, "Foreign Aid: An Introductory Overview of U.S. Programs and Policy," 2011.

U.S. assistance programs can be divided into five major categories.

- *Bilateral development assistance.* These types of programs are designed to help with the long-term development of poor countries. They focus on economic reforms, promotion of democracy, environmental protection, and health.
- *Security assistance.* Programs in this category are aimed at protecting U.S. political, economic, and national security interests. Since the 9/11 attacks, much of this aid has gone to countries of importance in the war on terrorism.
- *Humanitarian assistance.* These programs are devoted to helping victims of human-made and natural disasters. Most of this aid goes to refugees from conflicts, floods, droughts, and other immediate threats to life.
- *Multilateral assistance.* This is aid that consists of donations from multiple countries. It is used to fund international organizations such as the United Nations Development Programme and the World Bank.
- *Military assistance.* This type of aid helps U.S. allies acquire military equipment. It also supports training for military officers and peacekeeping forces from other countries.

Cultural Exchanges: People-to-People Contacts

Many countries use cultural exchanges to increase goodwill and understanding with other countries. Cultural exchanges may involve visits to another country by groups of educators, scientists, or businesspeople. They may also involve exchanges of performing artists.

The U.S. State Department actively promotes cultural exchanges as a way to "communicate America's strengths, freedoms, hopes, and challenges." The State Department's Rhythm Road: American Music Abroad program sends jazz and hip-hop artists to parts of the world not often visited by American musicians. U.S. embassies also arrange foreign tours for performing arts groups. In addition to performing live, these American artists participate in workshops, classes, jam sessions, and radio and television appearances.

■ 17.4 The "Hard Power" Tools of Foreign Policy

Whereas soft power tools aim to persuade, hard power tools are designed to coerce another country into adopting a desired course of action. Some hard power tools, such as boycotts and **sanctions,** are economic in nature. Others involve the use of spies, secret agents, and military force.

Intelligence Gathering: Assessing Foreign Threats

Making good foreign policy decisions depends on having reliable information about the activities and intentions of other countries. Such information is called **intelligence**. "By definition, intelligence deals with the unclear, the unknown, the deliberately hidden," says George Tenet, former Central Intelligence Agency (CIA) director. "What the enemies of the United States hope to deny, we work to reveal."

Most countries have an intelligence agency like the CIA. Such agencies gather information related to national security, either through public sources or by spying. They use this information to assess possible threats to the nation. In an interview conducted shortly after the 9/11 attacks, former secretary of defense Casper Weinberger spoke of the importance of good intelligence in dealing with terrorists:

It's the importance of finding out what they're planning ahead of time. That is the task of intelligence, and you have to have a very special kind of intelligence to do that; and you have to understand that this is going to involve spying. And it's going to be attacked by some people as a dirty business. What it is actually [doing] is giving a democracy eyes. And without eyes, the democracy's not going to remain a democracy very long.

Modern technology makes spying much easier than in the past. This satellite image shows an al Qaeda training camp hidden in the mountains of Afghanistan. The camp was later destroyed by U.S. air strikes.

The United States imposes unilateral, or one-sided, sanctions on countries for many reasons. Some sanctions are broad-based, effectively cutting off trade with the other country. More often, sanctions are targeted at specific goods, such as weapons or nuclear materials, or at U.S. funds going to the target country.

Recipients of U.S.-Imposed Unilateral Sanctions, 2012

Countries subject to U.S.-imposed sanctions

Source: U.S. Department of the Treasury.

Covert Action: Influencing Events in Other Countries

Intelligence agencies also carry out **covert actions** in other countries. A covert action is a secret operation that supports the country's foreign policy. The agents who carry out such operations try to influence what goes on in another country while hiding their role in those events.

During the Cold War, the United States used covert actions to overthrow unfriendly governments. After 9/11, the Bush administration authorized a large covert action program aimed at al Qaeda. CIA agents were authorized to capture or kill al Qaeda leaders wherever those leaders are found. The CIA teamed with U.S. forces to locate and kill al Qaeda's leader Osama bin Laden in 2011. Critics charge that such actions violate human rights. Defenders answer that such tactics are needed to protect Americans from future terrorist attacks.

In recent years, remotely piloted aircrafts called drones have emerged as common tools in covert actions. Drones are used for surveillance, military operations, and other similar activities.

Boycotts and Sanctions: Applying Economic Pressure

Boycotts and sanctions use economic pressure to punish a country for its actions or policies. These hard power tools can be used by countries that act alone or in concert with other nations.

A **boycott** usually involves a refusal to buy goods from a country as a form of protest against its policies. Boycotts can also involve a refusal to take part in an international event. In 1980, President Jimmy Carter called on U.S. athletes to boycott the Moscow Olympic games. The Olympic boycott was a protest against the Soviet Union's decision to invade its neighbor Afghanistan.

A sanction is an action taken against one or more countries to force a government to change its policies. The most common sanctions are designed to punish the offending nation's economy. Economic sanctions may involve tariffs, trade barriers, and other penalties.

Sanctions have a mixed record of success. One of the most effective uses of sanctions was against South Africa's racial policies. Until 1991, the South

As this map shows, U.S. troops are deployed across the globe. These troops are stationed in almost 150 countries, a majority of which harbor less than 1,000 deployed troops.

Deployed U.S. Military Personnel Worldwide, 2011

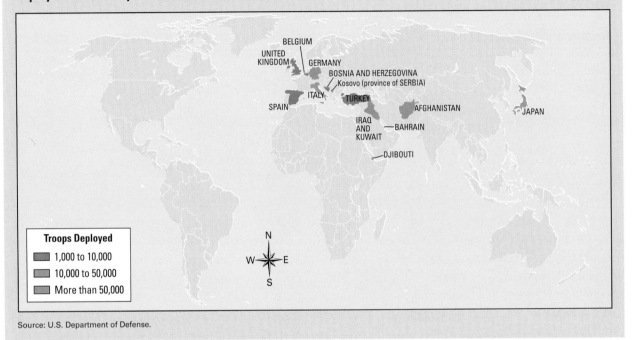

Source: U.S. Department of Defense.

African government treated black South Africans as second-class citizens. They had few political or legal rights. Economic sanctions, combined with anti-apartheid protests in South Africa, finally forced the government to abandon its racist policies. In 1994, Nelson Mandela took office as South Africa's first black president.

Military Alliances: Defending Against Attacks

Military alliances are agreements made by countries to defend one another in case of an attack. Countries join military alliances for mutual protection. Military alliances are particularly important for small countries that lack the resources to defend themselves without the help from allies.

The largest military alliance today is the North Atlantic Treaty Organization (NATO). The United States, Canada, Iceland, and nine Western European countries formed NATO in 1949. NATO's primary purpose was to guard against the threat posed by the Soviet Union and its communist allies in Eastern Europe. By 2012, NATO had expanded to 28 nations, including many former Soviet nations.

NATO members agree to consider "an armed attack against one or more of them . . . an attack against them all."

Armed Force: The Tool of Last Resort

When all other tools fail, countries may resort to war as their foreign policy tool of last resort. As British politician Tony Benn once observed, "All war represents a failure of diplomacy."

Sometimes full-scale war is not necessary to achieve the desired result. Such was the hope of President Clinton when he called for NATO air strikes against Serbia, a country in Eastern Europe, in 1999. Clinton resorted to armed force only after diplomatic efforts had failed to end Serbia's **ethnic cleansing** campaign in the province of Kosovo. Ethnic cleansing involves the mass removal and killing of an ethnic group in an area—in this case the ethnic Albanians of Kosovo.

Over the course of three months, NATO aircrafts flew 38,000 combat missions over Serbia. The conflict ended when Slobodan Milosevic, the president of Serbia, finally agreed to pull his troops out of

Kosovo. Within only three weeks, more than half a million refugees had returned to the province.

▨ 17.5 The Makers and Shapers of Foreign Policy

What do the four items listed below have in common?
- Monroe Doctrine
- Roosevelt Corollary
- Truman Doctrine
- Nixon Doctrine

If you said that they are all foreign policy statements named after presidents, you would be right. Throughout our history, presidents have played a large role in setting the direction of U.S. foreign policy. Their power to do so is rooted in the Constitution.

What the Constitution Says About Foreign Policy

The Constitution divides responsibility for developing foreign policy between Congress and the president. The president has the power to negotiate treaties. But these treaties do not go into effect unless approved by the Senate. Likewise, the president appoints ambassadors to other countries. But the Senate must approve those appointments. The president serves as commander in chief of the military. But Congress alone can declare war and controls the funds needed to fight a war.

This division of responsibilities creates what constitutional scholar Edward S. Corwin described as "an invitation to struggle for the privilege of directing American foreign policy." At times, Congress has seemed to have the upper hand in this struggle. More often, however, the president seems to have the initiative. But as the framers surely intended, neither branch can act effectively in foreign affairs without the other.

The Foreign Policy Bureaucracy

The president directs the administration of foreign policy as the head of a large foreign policy bureaucracy. This bureaucracy consists of four main sections, or areas of responsibility.

Diplomacy. This section includes the Department of State, which is responsible for managing day-to-day relations with foreign countries. It also includes the U.S. Foreign Service, or the corps of men and women who staff U.S. embassies and consulates around the world. A consulate is the part of an embassy that deals mainly with passport, visa, and trade issues.

Intelligence. This section includes the Central Intelligence Agency and the National Security Agency (NSA). Both the CIA and the NSA work to provide Congress and the executive branch with reliable information about other countries and possible threats to vital U.S. interests.

Hillary Clinton served as U.S. Secretary of State from 2009–2013. During her term she visited over 100 countries to carry out duties such as negotiating treaties. Here, Clinton visits with South Korean Foreign Minister Yu Myung-hwan in February 2010.

The Foreign Policy Bureaucracy

The foreign policy bureaucracy has four main areas of responsibility. Various departments, agencies, and offices work to devise and carry out policy in these areas.

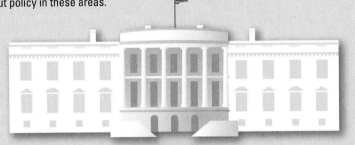

The White House

Diplomacy

Department of State

Implements the president's foreign policy.

Manages relations with foreign governments and international organizations.

Employs thousands of Americans worldwide, including many who work in the department's 265 embassies and consulates.

Assists U.S. citizens and businesses abroad.

Issues visas to foreign citizens wishing to enter the United States.

Intelligence

Central Intelligence Agency

Obtains and analyzes information about foreign governments, businesses, and persons.

National Security Agency

Obtains intelligence by monitoring communications signals.

Detects and responds to threats to computer systems.

Guards the security of U.S. information systems.

National Security

Department of Defense

Oversees all military activities.

Coordinates and supervises the U.S. Air Force, Marines, Army, and Navy.

National Security Council

Advises the president on foreign policy matters.

Regular attendees include the national security adviser, vice president, chair of the joint chiefs of staff, director of national intelligence, and secretaries of state, treasury, and defense.

Department of Homeland Security

Polices U.S. borders.

Works to keep foreign terrorists from entering the United States.

Economy

National Economic Council

Advises the president on global economic policy.

Implements the president's economic policies.

Office of the U.S. Trade Representative

Develops and coordinates U.S. international trade policy.

Works to expand market access for U.S. goods and services.

Works to uphold trade agreements.

National security. This section includes the Department of Defense and the National Security Council. The NSC serves directly under the president and includes cabinet members and agency heads. The NSC advises the president on foreign policy issues and coordinates the implementation of policies among various departments and agencies. The Department of Defense carries out foreign policy initiatives that involve military action.

Economy. This section includes the National Economic Council and the Office of the U.S. Trade Representative. The NEC advises the president on international and domestic trade issues. The Office of the U.S. Trade Representative oversees trade relations with other countries.

Congressional Influence Over Foreign Policy

Although the president directs the foreign policy bureaucracy, Congress also has considerable influence in this area. Its most important tool for influencing policy is its power of the purse. The president cannot carry out policies that Congress is unwilling to fund.

Congress can also pass laws that affect U.S. relations with other countries. The Foreign Operations, Export Financing, and Related Programs Appropriations Act of 2006 restricted foreign assistance to many countries unless certain conditions were met. For example, no funds could be sent to Kazakhstan unless the secretary of state determined that the country had improved its human rights record. The

same act also funded programs aimed at promoting democracy in countries like Iran and Syria.

In addition, Congress has the power to conduct oversight hearings and investigations into foreign policy issues. The Senate Foreign Relations Committee and the House Committee on Foreign Affairs regularly hold such hearings to shape legislation and advise the president. After the 9/11 attacks, for example, Congress held extensive hearings to determine how the hijackings were carried out, who was behind the attacks, and what the government could do to prevent future acts of terrorism.

The Power of Public Opinion Over Foreign Policy

What *you* think also influences foreign policy. Whether public concerns are expressed in messages, street protests, or opinion polls, Congress and the president pay attention. In polls taken shortly after the 9/11 attacks, the majority of Americans supported the use of military force to prevent terrorism. President Bush was aware of this sentiment when he authorized military action in Afghanistan in 2001 and in Iraq in 2003.

In times of war, Americans tend to "rally round the flag" and their fighting men and women. However, support for the troops may not extend to the policies that led the nation into war. Such had been the case in Iraq, as U.S. casualties mounted month by month. A CNN/ORC Poll completed in December 2011 revealed that 66 percent of Americans opposed the war in Iraq. This number was an increase from

This photograph shows Andrew Bacevich, a retired army colonel, testifying before the Senate Foreign Relations Committee in April 2009. He and other veterans of the Afghan War testified together to offer advice to policymakers.

the 54 percent who opposed the war when polled in 2006. This growing disapproval inspired renewed calls by opponents to bring the troops home.

President Barack Obama answered these calls in 2010 when he announced that all U.S. troops would leave Iraq by the end of the following year. While some soldiers stayed as transitional forces, the war was officially declared over in December 2011.

■ 17.6 How Worldviews Shape Foreign Policy

The way Americans think about foreign policy is strongly affected by their view of the world and its impact on their lives. Our foreign policy worldviews are influenced by the times in which we live. In turn, these worldviews shape how we view our relations with other countries. In the 1900s, four worldviews dominated debates about foreign policy. Since September 11, 2001, a fifth worldview has emerged that may affect U.S. foreign policy for many years to come.

Isolationism: Withdrawing from World Affairs
The view that the United States should withdraw from world affairs is called **isolationism**. People who hold this view do not favor helping other nations with foreign aid. Most of all, they believe that the United States should stay out of the conflicts of other countries.

This worldview gained a wider following after World War I. Americans entered that war with idealistic hopes of "making the world safe for democracy." They ended it deeply disillusioned. Thousands of U.S. troops had died while fighting in Europe, but little else had been accomplished. Certainly, the world seemed no safer for democracy when the war ended than when it began. For most Americans, the lesson of the war was this: stay out of other nations' affairs.

Containment: Controlling Aggressive Nations
The view that the United States should contain, or control, aggressive nations that threaten world peace is called **containment**. This view came out of World War II. Looking back, many Americans came to believe that this war could have been avoided, but only if the world's democracies had stood fast against the aggression that first erupted in Germany, Italy, and Japan. Instead, the democracies tried to appease the aggressors, opting for peace at any price. This only encouraged Germany, Italy, and Japan to act even more aggressively, plunging the world into a global war.

After World War II, Americans became alarmed by the Soviet Union's aggressive efforts to spread communism around the world. For the next 45 years in a period known as the Cold War, U.S. foreign policy was directed at containing communism. During that time, the United States went to war in Korea and later in Vietnam to halt what it saw as communist aggression.

Disengagement: Avoiding Military Involvements
The view that the United States should avoid military actions in other parts of the world is called **disengagement**. This worldview has been called the "new isolationism." However, although the people who believe in disengagement want to avoid military actions, they may not be against foreign aid or trade relations.

The disengagement worldview reflects the experience of Americans during the Vietnam War. When that war began, most people supported U.S. involvement in Vietnam as part of containment. But as the struggle dragged on, attitudes changed, especially among young people. Many rejected containment as a reason for going to war. Some even came to see the war as immoral. As they moved into adulthood, their motto was "no more Vietnams."

Human Rights: Using U.S. Power to Protect Others
By 1991, the Cold War was over and the Soviet Union had collapsed. With that change, containment gave way to a new worldview that was based on protecting human rights. Those who adopted this view held that the United States should use its power to protect the rights and well-being of people around the world.

President George H. W. Bush's decision to send U.S. troops to Somalia in 1992 was a response to this worldview. So was President Clinton's call for NATO air strikes in 1999 to protect ethnic Albanians in Kosovo.

Antiterrorism: Protecting the Homeland
The terrorist attacks of September 11, 2001, brought a new worldview to the forefront of foreign policy: **antiterrorism**. People holding this worldview believe that the greatest threat to the United States comes

from terrorist groups such as al Qaeda. In their view, U.S. power should be used to seek out and destroy terrorist networks. It should also be used to keep **weapons of mass destruction,** particularly nuclear weapons, out of the hands of terrorists.

This worldview shaped the Bush administration's foreign policy. In his first State of the Union address after the 9/11 attacks, President Bush singled out Iran, Iraq, and North Korea as particular threats:

States like these, and their terrorist allies, constitute an axis of evil, arming to threaten the peace of the world. By seeking weapons of mass destruction, these regimes pose a grave and growing danger. They could provide these arms to terrorists, giving them the means to match their hatred.

—George W. Bush, 2002

Americans who hold different foreign policy worldviews often disagree on how best to protect our nation's vital interests. At any point in time, one worldview may dominate over the others. But as conditions in the world change, new foreign policy worldviews may emerge and shape how the United States interacts with the rest of the world.

This cartoon was drawn in response to the terrorist attacks of September 11, 2001. That event shifted the country's foreign policy from a focus on human rights to a war on terrorism. In preparation for that long struggle, the American eagle is seen here sharpening its claws.

Summary

Foreign policy determines how the United States interacts with the rest of the world. Foreign policy decisions are based on what Americans and their leaders see as the nation's vital interests.

Foreign policy goals The most important goals of U.S. foreign policy are to protect national security, promote U.S. economic interests, preserve global peace, and pursue American ideals.

"Soft power" tools Soft power involves the use of persuasion to achieve foreign policy goals. Soft power tools include diplomacy, summits, trade relations, foreign aid, and cultural exchanges.

"Hard power" tools Hard power involves the threat or use of more forceful measures to achieve foreign policy goals. Hard power tools include covert action, boycotts, sanctions, military alliances, and armed force.

Foreign policymakers The president, Congress, the foreign policy bureaucracy, and public opinion all play a role in shaping foreign policy.

Foreign policy worldviews Five major American worldviews—isolationism, containment, disengagement, human rights, and antiterrorism—also influence American foreign policy.

Is globalization good, bad, or just inevitable?

Globalization has brought the world closer together in many ways over the past few decades. But not everyone is cheering the change. Opponents of this trend charge that globalization is harmful to the environment, workers, and national sovereignty. Another significant worry is that the spread of U.S. companies and products around the world is destroying local cultures.

Is globalization leading us to a bland McWorld? Read this article and then decide for yourself whether globalization is good, bad, or simply an unstoppable force.

A World Together

by Erla Zwingle

"Globalization"—lots of people seem to think it means that the world is turning into some consumer colony of America. Coke, CNN, McDonald's, Levi's, Nikes—if they haven't taken over the world yet, the feeling goes, they will soon . . .

Yet the globalization phenomenon is more than the mere transfer of goods, the fact that, for instance, you can buy French mineral water and Danish beer in the Shanghai airport . . . It's the advent of cheap and ubiquitous information technologies that is dissolving our sense of boundaries. More and more television channels and the Internet have contributed to what expert Daniel Yergin calls a "woven world."

When we talk about "globality" (a new buzzword), we're trying to define a world in which cultures meet and, rather than fight, they blend . . . When cultures receive outside influences, they ignore some and adopt others, and then almost immediately start to transform them . . .

Big Bird in China

For the past year and a half in Shanghai, for example, Chinese children have been tuning in to that American children's classic TV show *Sesame Street*. But here it's called *Zhima Jie,* and when you look closer, it's not simply the American show. The show's team of actors and educators has been collaborating to produce a program that promotes Chinese, rather than American, values. The kids are loving it . . .

Da Niao, Big Bird's Chinese cousin, is played here by a gentle young man who still works as a truck mechanic. The other characters are all Chinese: a lively three-year-old red monster called Little Plum; a furry blue pig, a kindly grand-father, a very sweet mother, and a little boy, An An, who is so funny and cute and smart that when I met him I could scarcely believe how perfect he was for the part.

This group does many of the usual *Sesame Street* activities—teaching numbers, for instance—but instead of the alphabet they teach the origin and meaning of Chinese characters. They explain the history and customs of certain festivals. They describe certain ancient art forms. And they also teach sharing and cooperation . . .

"We want to concentrate on reflecting Chinese families," explained Professor Li Ji Mei, who designed part of the show's curriculum, "such as what children could do to show their respect for the family. Another important part of the program is to make children realize how much their parents do for their well-being. In reflecting Chinese society," she concluded, "we reflect how people should help each other and how to share the joy in sharing"...

By now, 19 countries around the world are producing their own versions of *Sesame Street,* using television to interpret their unique cultures. It seems to be working. Does Big Bird feel he's promoting America to his tiny viewers? "I don't think so," Ye Chao [the show's Chinese producer] said. "We just borrowed an American box and put Chinese content into it"...

How Many Americas?

"Culture," anthropologist James Watson has commented, "is not something that people inherit as an undifferentiated bloc of knowledge from their ancestors. Culture is a set of ideas, reactions, and expectations that is constantly changing as people and groups themselves change."

Which brings us around to the subject of America. Where does the U.S. really fit into the big global picture? After all, America isn't the only purveyor of global goodies—it absorbs more foreign customs and objects than most Americans are probably aware of ...

Those who are quick to criticize America often seem unaware that America is not some monolithic one-size-fits-all culture, but arguably the most multicultural society on Earth. Thousands of things that we think of as American came from somewhere else: Christmas trees, hot dogs and beer, denim ... Americans are so quick to adopt foreign food, phrases, clothing, that it may be hard to see them as foreign for long ...

In other words, people forget where certain things came from, and they don't care. Americans say "ciao" and "glitch," dance to salsa (and eat it too) ... and on and on, but don't think this makes them Italian, Jewish, Hispanic, Russian, or whatever. We adopt elements of myriad immigrant cultures because they help us express ourselves better. This, I think, is the essence of cultural interchange: not adopting foreign things wholesale, but choosing them according to the values and ideas of your own culture ...

You can love your own country without having to reject all the others. I am convinced that globalization will give us new ways not only to appreciate other cultures more, but to look on our own with fresh wonder and surprise.

Globalization comes in many different forms. This photo depicts KFC, a U.S. fast-food chain, in Chengdu, China.

Erla Zwingle is a feature writer for National Geographic *magazine.*

Chapter 18

Confronting Global Issues

How effectively do international organizations respond to global issues?

■ 18.1 Introduction

On January 12, 2010, a disastrous earthquake hit Haiti, toppling major towns and triggering a series of aftershocks. Homes, hospitals, commercial buildings, power lines, and roads were destroyed. Tens of thousands died, and millions were left injured and homeless. As one of the most impoverished nations in the Western Hemisphere, Haiti did not have enough resources to deal with this emergency alone. Fortunately, help was soon on the way from all parts of the globe.

Governments and organizations around the world pledged around $4 billion to aid earthquake survivors and rebuild Haiti. Some of this money supported relief efforts organized by **intergovernmental organizations (IGOs)**. These are organizations formed by the governments of many countries. The largest IGO is the United Nations (UN). Within hours of the tragedy, workers with UNICEF, the UN Children's Fund, shipped emergency supplies to devastated areas. "The devastation is staggering," reported Léo Mérorès, the Ambassador of Haiti to the UN. "UNICEF teams are working assiduously in the country."

Private donors large and small also contributed to the relief efforts. American businesses donated everything from drinking water and medical supplies to clothing and cash. Much of the money was funneled through humanitarian groups that work

Foreign nations distribute aid to Haiti following the 2010 earthquake independently of governments. **Nongovernmental organizations (NGOs)** receiving funds included the Red Cross, CARE, and Oxfam.

On March 11, 2011, another powerful earthquake struck halfway around the world. This time a magnitude 9.0 undersea earthquake shook Tohoku, Japan. The earthquake set off a series of massive tsunamis. Waves over 100 feet tall rolled inland, washed away buildings and vehicles, and caused one of the greatest nuclear disasters in history. One of the waves flooded the Fukushima Daiichi Nuclear Power Plant and disabled the power supply, leading nuclear reactors in the power plant to melt down. In the aftermath of an earthquake, tsunamis, and a nuclear disaster, Japan was in dire need of aid. Once again, IGOs and NGOs stepped in to provide relief.

When faced with the consequences of these disasters, the world has shown its willingness to assist countries during times of emergency. But what about long-term problems like poverty, disease, and climate change? This chapter explores how international organizations are attempting to deal with these and other difficult global issues.

Groups around the world offered their assistance to Japan after the 2011 catastrophe. Here, U.S. Navy crews inspect and load relief supplies following the Fukushima nuclear power plant disaster.

18.2 The United Nations

With a membership of 193 nations, the United Nations represents almost every nation in the world. Since it was founded in 1945, it has become the forum for debating every major issue facing humankind. UN agencies like UNICEF coordinate efforts to deal with short-term crises, like the 2010 Haiti earthquake. The UN also focuses attention on tougher, longer-term issues ranging from peacekeeping to poverty.

The Founding of the United Nations

Much of world history can be boiled down to a seemingly endless series of bloody conflicts. By the 20th century, it was clear that the world would never be at peace so long as countries chose to resolve their disputes on the battlefield. The League of Nations was formed after World War I to serve as an international peacekeeper. But the League dissolved when it failed to prevent World War II. As that conflict came to a close, 50 countries joined together to form a more robust intergovernmental organization, the United Nations.

The founding countries adopted a constitution for the new IGO known as the United Nations Charter. The Preamble to the UN Charter identifies four main goals for the UN:

- *to save succeeding generations from the scourge of war, which twice in our lifetime has brought untold sorrow to mankind, and*

- *to reaffirm faith in fundamental human rights, in the dignity and worth of the human person, in the equal rights of men and women and of nations large and small, and*

- *to establish conditions under which justice and respect for the obligations arising from treaties and other sources of international law can be maintained, and*

- *to promote social progress and better standards of life in larger freedom.*

The UN Charter established several organs, or bodies, to accomplish its goals. The General Assembly is the most democratic UN organ. It is made up of representatives from all member states, each of which has one vote. Problems that arise anywhere in the world can be brought to this body. The General

A meeting of the UN General Assembly brings together representatives from almost every country on Earth. The assembly meets in regular session from September to December each year. Representatives wear headphones that allow them to hear simultaneous translations of the speaker's words into their own language.

Assembly responds by passing resolutions that are taken seriously by member states.

The Security Council is the most powerful UN organ. The council is made up of five permanent members—the United States, Russia, Great Britain, China, and France—and ten members elected by the General Assembly for two-year terms. This body is responsible for maintaining international peace.

The UN's Main Activity: Keeping the World at Peace

The most important activity of the UN is peacekeeping. In 2012, some 115,000 UN peacekeepers were carrying out missions in about 15 countries.

The UN has no permanent peacekeeping force—no standing army of its own. It depends on member states to provide troops if called upon. This system is based on the principle of **collective security**. This principle calls for the uniting of individual countries against an aggressor in order to, as the UN Charter says, "maintain international peace and security."

Typically, peacekeeping involves sending lightly armed soldiers to the site of a conflict—but only after the two sides have formally agreed to stop fighting. UN peacekeepers, easily identified by their blue helmets, often position themselves between hostile forces. By providing a buffer zone, or neutral area, the peacekeepers help the two sides maintain their peace agreement. UN peacekeepers work under orders not to fire their weapons except in self-defense. On missions to dangerous hotspots, however, they may use their weapons to defend civilians and UN personnel.

On rare occasions, the Security Council has authorized the use of armed force against a country that has broken the peace. In 1950, for example, a UN force made up of troops from 16 nations helped South Korea push back an invading army from North Korea. The UN took a similar action in 1991 after Iraq invaded its neighbor Kuwait.

The United Nations is also a key player in efforts to halt the spread of nuclear weapons. Nearly all UN members are party to the 1968 Nuclear Non-Proliferation Treaty. Only four member states are not: India, Pakistan, Israel, and North Korea.

The UN's International Atomic Energy Agency conducts inspections to verify that countries are complying with the nonproliferation treaty. In July 2006, the UN Security Council took steps to discourage Iran from producing nuclear weapons and thus violating the treaty. The council imposed sanctions on Iran that banned the shipment of nuclear materials or technology to that country.

The United Nations consists of various organs and special agencies. Some of the most important are described below, with the UN emblem in the middle. The emblem is a world map centered on the North Pole and surrounded by olive branches, a symbol of peace.

Security Council

The Security Council is responsible for maintaining international peace and security. It has 15 members. Five are permanent, including the United States, while ten fill two-year terms. Permanent members can veto any council resolution.

General Assembly

All 193 members of the UN sit in the General Assembly, the chief policymaking body of the UN. Here member states, each with one vote, debate issues and recommend action on matters covered by the UN Charter.

Secretariat

The Secretariat carries out the day-to-day operations of the UN. It has nearly 9,000 staff members located around the world. The head of the Secretariat, the secretary general, serves a five-year, renewable term.

Economic and Social Council

The Economic and Social Council is a forum for discussing international economic and social issues. It seeks to promote higher standards of living, cultural cooperation, and respect for human rights.

International Court of Justice

The International Court of Justice (ICJ), also known as the World Court, settles legal disputes brought by one nation against another. It also advises the UN's other organs on legal issues. The United States takes part in ICJ proceedings but has been unwilling to accept its authority.

International Monetary Fund and World Bank

The International Monetary Fund (IMF) and World Bank are special agencies of the UN. The IMF offers nations economic advice and serves as a "lender of last resort." The World Bank's mission is to reduce global poverty. It funds projects that build schools and health centers, provide water and electricity, and create jobs.

Other UN Activities: Improving People's Lives

Besides peacekeeping, the UN works to improve the lives of people around the world. UN agencies and programs have, for many years, devoted their resources toward issues of poverty, education, health, and human rights. The UN has also been a champion of **sustainable development**. This approach to economic development focuses on ways to meet the needs of the world's people today without exhausting the resources that will be needed to sustain future generations. Even so, as the 20th century drew to an end, more than a billion people worldwide were living on less than $1 a day.

In 2000, the UN hosted the largest gathering of world leaders in history to discuss the role of the United Nations in the 21st century. At that summit, the leaders of 150 countries ratified an agreement known as the Millennium Declaration. This document committed members of the UN to "free our fellow men, women, and children from the abject and dehumanizing conditions of extreme poverty." To reach this objective, the Millennium Declaration laid out a list of goals to be reached by the year 2015, including the following:

- *Eradicate extreme hunger and poverty.* Reduce by half the number of people living on less than $1 per day.
- *Achieve universal primary school education.*
- *Promote gender equality and empower women.* Eliminate barriers that keep women from receiving an education.
- *Reduce child mortality.* Cut the death rate among children under five by two-thirds.
- *Improve maternal health.* Reduce the death rate of mothers by three-fourths.
- *Combat HIV/AIDS, malaria, and other diseases.*
- *Ensure environmental sustainability.* Reverse the loss of environmental resources, and cut by half the number of people without safe drinking water.
- *Develop a global partnership for development.* Address poor countries' need for good government, debt relief, economic growth, and jobs for young people.

Since 2000, the UN has launched a number of projects to achieve these ambitious goals. Projects in places such as India and Ethiopia contributed to the 2015 target of halving hunger and poverty rates. The Ethiopian Commodity Exchange, for example, arranged ways for farmers and exporters to trade. By 2005, the poverty rate in developing regions was 27 percent, a decline from 46 percent in 1990.

There has also been progress made toward gender equality in classrooms. For instance, more girls in Bangladesh enrolled in schools with the Female Secondary School Stipend, which helps families pay for tuition. In secondary schools where this program was available, females made up 56 percent of the student body in 2005. Still, few females were able to attend college in developing regions worldwide.

Although HIV/AIDs and malaria are still serious threats around the globe, there have been significant efforts to stop them from spreading. Those infected with HIV in Botswana, for example, have free universal access to antiretroviral treatment. In Botswana, from 1999 to 2007, the number of children contracting HIV in Botswana decreased by about 80 percent.

The global community made great progress toward its target of cutting the number of people without safe drinking water in half as 2015 approached. Programs, such as the UN Economic and Social Commission for Western Asia, helped monitor water supply and sanitation in developing regions. North Africa, East Asia, Southeast Asia, Latin America, and the Caribbean had already met the goal by 2010.

The Millennium Development Goals have not been fully reached. However, efforts by organizations around the world helped developing countries make great strides toward meeting the 2015 targets. The UN continues to pursue its goals to create "a more peaceful, prosperous, and just world."

The Limitations of the UN

The United Nations has helped to make the world a safer, more livable place. Yet critics often point out that the UN has not fully resolved many of the issues that it has tackled. Poverty, human rights abuses, war, and environmental destruction still persist, they say, in spite of decades of attention from the UN. One reason for this is the sheer size and complexity of these problems. They are the most difficult issues facing the global community. However, there are other factors that limit what the UN can accomplish.

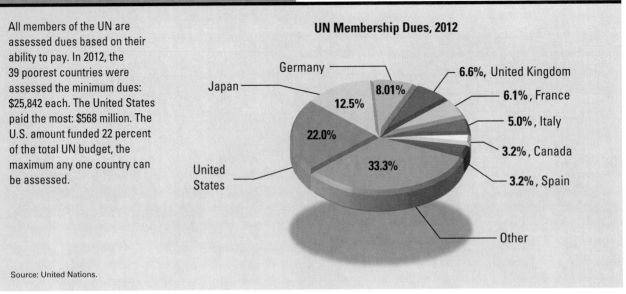

All members of the UN are assessed dues based on their ability to pay. In 2012, the 39 poorest countries were assessed the minimum dues: $25,842 each. The United States paid the most: $568 million. The U.S. amount funded 22 percent of the total UN budget, the maximum any one country can be assessed.

UN Membership Dues, 2012

Germany — 8.01%
Japan — 12.5%
United States — 22.0%
33.3%
6.6%, United Kingdom
6.1%, France
5.0%, Italy
3.2%, Canada
3.2%, Spain
Other

Source: United Nations.

One is the reluctance of the world's nations to cede any of their national sovereignty to the UN. Most resolutions approved by the General Assembly or Security Council lack enforcement. In general, only decisions related to collective security are legally binding on all members. Moreover, the UN's lack of a standing army means it must rely on member states to carry out peacekeeping missions.

Another factor is the structure of the Security Council. The five permanent members have the power to veto any action by the council. As these nations often have different foreign policy agendas, it is sometimes difficult for the UN to react effectively to problems.

In recent years, the UN has been rocked with corruption scandals and charges of mismanagement and waste. This has led many to question whether the UN can be trusted to deal with important global issues. Reform efforts are underway, but change is slow.

Despite these limitations, the UN has made progress in many areas. Because of the UN's world health programs, diseases that once plagued the world, such as smallpox and polio, have been eliminated or greatly reduced. Every year, the UN World Food Programme helps feed tens of millions of people in countries around the world. As Kofi Annan, who served as secretary general of the United Nations from 1997 to 2007, has observed, "More than ever before in human history, we share a common destiny. We can master it only if we face it together. And that, my friends, is why we have the United Nations."

■ 18.3 Intergovernmental Organizations

You have probably heard it said that there is strength in numbers. What an individual country cannot do alone, it might be able to do with the help of other countries. The United States understood this well when it joined the Allies in their struggle to defeat the Axis powers in World War II. An intergovernmental organization (IGO) is a type of alliance, though it need not be military in nature.

Promoting International Cooperation Through IGOs

Through IGOs, groups of nations cooperate to achieve common objectives. Those objectives vary from one organization to another, ranging from mutual defense to free trade.

Some IGOs share economic interests. For example, the Organization of the Petroleum Exporting Countries (OPEC) is made up of 12 oil-producing countries. They have joined together to create a stable market for oil at the best possible price for OPEC members. Trade promotion is the objective of other economic IGOs. The North American Free Trade Agreement (NAFTA), for instance, has removed trade barriers among Canada, the United States, and Mexico creating a large free-trade zone.

Other IGOs are formed to serve the security interests of their members. The countries in the North Atlantic Treaty Organization (NATO) share military resources and strategies for protecting their region. ANZUS is another IGO that creates military ties among the countries of Australia, New Zealand, and the United States.

Still other IGOs focus on political as well as economic issues. The African Union (AU) promotes democracy and sustainable development among its members. The AU has also taken on peacekeeping duties in Africa. Similarly, the Association of Southeast Asian Nations (ASEAN) promotes regional peace and stability while encouraging economic, social, and cultural development.

The UN has formed its own specialized agencies and programs that are considered IGOs. The World Bank, the International Atomic Energy Agency, and the World Health Organization are all IGOs with links to the UN.

IGOs Have Strengths and Limitations

Intergovernmental organizations would not exist if they did not provide definite benefits to their member countries. IGOs make it easier for nations to share resources, expand trade, and increase

national security. They can be helpful in coordinating responses to natural disasters.

However, membership in an IGO can have its downsides. The need to get a majority of members to support a decision may slow an IGO's response to pressing problems. Once a decision is made, each member is expected to abide by it. At times, those decisions may conflict with one nation's foreign policy or national interests. Going along with the majority may mean surrendering a bit of national sovereignty or the power to act independently.

The question of how much power to give up to an IGO has become an issue in debates over the International Criminal Court (ICC). The ICC is an independent court presently headquartered in The Hague, Netherlands. Its purpose is to prosecute individuals accused of crimes against humanity, such as genocide, ethnic cleansing, and aggression. The ICC can exercise its jurisdiction only when national courts are unwilling or unable to prosecute such crimes. Founded in 2002, the ICC conducted investigations in seven African nations in 2012.

By the end of 2012, 121 countries had joined the ICC. Several other countries, however—including China, India, and the United States—had not joined. Opposition in the United States centered on fears that the ICC might be misused to bring politically motivated charges against U.S. leaders and

The 12 oil-producing countries in the Organization for the Petroleum Exporting Countries (OPEC) determine what prices would best stabilize the oil market. Members of OPEC often work together to make decisions about the oil industry.

troops serving in other countries. One U.S. senator summed up his concerns in these words:

> It is no secret that the majority of UN peacekeeping operations are conducted in countries that are non-democratic and whose leaders are hostile to U.S. policies. Leaving our leaders, troops, and personnel vulnerable to arrest and use as political pawns would be a colossal mistake.
> —Jon Kyl. (R-AZ), 2004

U.S. supporters of the ICC, however, dismiss such fears. As one editorial put it,

> This scenario is far-fetched for several reasons. The court has no jurisdiction over an alleged war criminal if the suspect's home country conducts a genuine investigation into the allegations. U.S. peace-keepers have been accused of war crimes in the past, but never prosecuted . . . In addition, prosecutors would have to obtain the permission of a three-judge court to even initiate an investigation of U.S. forces.
> —St. Louis Post-Dispatch, July 2, 2002

■ 18.4 Nongovernmental Organizations

Another important player on the international scene is the nongovernmental organization (NGO). Generally, NGOs tackle problems that governments, through foreign aid or IGOs, cannot deal with as effectively. For this reason, governments and IGOs often look to NGOs for assistance in dealing with everything from health care to economic development.

NGOs Tackle a Host of Global Problems

Since 1970, the number of international NGOs has more than doubled to around 6,000. Most NGOs are nonprofit organizations whose funding comes from several sources. Private donors include individuals as well as corporations and foundations. Funding also comes from official sources: governments and IGOs. All these funders believe in the ability of NGOs to help solve global problems.

NGOs vary greatly in size and purpose. The largest of these organizations deal with a single issue. Amnesty International, for example, focuses on abuses of human rights and the plight of political prisoners. Save the Children is dedicated to making a difference in the lives of poor children and their families worldwide.

Many NGOs see their purpose as helping people in the world's **least developed countries (LDCs)**. These are the 50 or so countries with the lowest per capita incomes and living standards. NGO staff members in these countries make connections with local leaders and educate themselves about the needs of the people. They often take a hands-on approach to delivering assistance, whether that involves teaching, providing medical care, or caring for victims of a natural disaster.

Many NGOs focus on helping people in developing countries. In this photo, students in Kenya study at school with the support of WEMA, an NGO that helps vulnerable children. WEMA provided this school with uniforms, books, and solar lamps to improve the students' schoolwork.

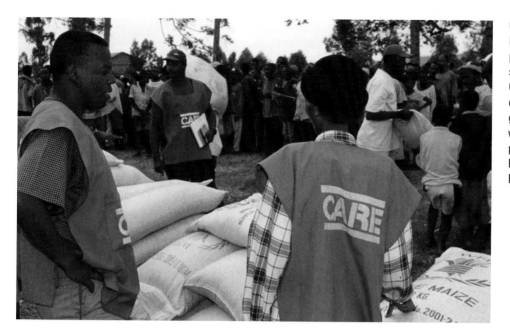

CARE is one of the many NGOs providing relief to people living in poverty-stricken countries. At times, CARE works with other organizations to address global issues. Here, CARE workers distribute food aid provided by the World Food Programme to the people of Burundi.

Disaster relief is the purpose of other NGOs like the International Committee of the Red Cross. When the earthquake struck Haiti in 2010, some NGOs were already "on the ground" in the affected areas. They were able to act as a bridge, linking victims with outside sources of relief. They helped pinpoint the worst-hit areas and direct the distribution of supplies.

NGOs serve another purpose. They provide valuable information and analyses to governments about global issues. Like other interest groups, they may lobby government officials to influence decisions on global issues that matter to them, such as foreign aid and sustainable development.

Some NGOs define their purpose as **advocacy,** or speaking out on their areas of concern. The International Campaign to Ban Landmines is an advocacy network of more than 1,400 NGOs in 90 countries. These groups are working to end the production and use of land mines. United Families International is an advocacy group that promotes pro-family policies and programs at the local, national, and international levels.

How One NGO Has Evolved: CARE

CARE was founded in 1945 as a humanitarian relief agency to help survivors of World War II. The new NGO sent millions of CARE packages containing food, supplies, and medicine to war-ravaged Europe. Since then, CARE has evolved into one of the world's largest NGOs. Its mission also changed from helping

victims of war to assisting people in need anywhere in the world. "Every CARE Package is a personal contribution to the world peace our nation seeks," said President John F. Kennedy in 1962. "It expresses America's concern and friendship in a language all peoples understand."

Today CARE is engaged in long-term projects aimed at reducing global poverty. These projects include efforts to improve basic education, prevent HIV/AIDS, increase access to clean water, boost economic opportunity, and promote environmental awareness. In 2011, CARE's work affected the lives of some 122 million people in 84 countries.

CARE continues to provide emergency aid to victims of war, famine, and natural disasters. After conflict erupted in the Darfur region of Sudan in 2003, for example, CARE supplied humanitarian aid. By 2012, CARE was providing food, water, and medical care to nearly half a million refugees from the Darfur conflict.

In addition, CARE worked to end the conflict in Sudan. It met with government leaders in the United States and Europe to suggest ways their governments might promote peace and stability in this region. It also brought representatives of different ethnic groups together in "peace committees" to help rebuild trust among them. "A sustainable solution will have to involve ordinary people at the community level," observed a CARE official, "living together and sharing limited resources."

What NGOs Do Well and Not So Well

NGOs like CARE take a hands-on approach to problems. They understand the needs of the people "at the grass roots." With that kind of relationship, they can effectively make the case to governments and donors that their concerns deserve attention and funding.

NGOs are also flexible. This makes them natural "first responders" to natural disasters, such as the 2010 earthquake. Often NGOs are able to bring help to survivors much faster than government relief agencies or IGOs. At the same time, NGOs often lack the personnel and resources to carry out large-scale, long-term relief efforts. Governments and large IGOs like the UN are better organized and funded for rebuilding efforts.

When a number of NGOs respond to an emergency, they may have issues coordinating their efforts. Each group may try to attack a problem from a different angle, depending on its resources and expertise. Without an overarching plan, they may find themselves duplicating efforts or getting in each other's way. This is where the UN can help. The UN is large enough to provide an effective plan of action and coordinate the work of a number of NGOs.

Individual NGOs working in foreign countries face other obstacles to their effectiveness. One is corruption. Throughout the world, many public officials will not provide needed documents or take official action without a bribe. Another obstacle is civil unrest. In some LDCs, the government may not be able to maintain law and order. Working in an area of civil unrest is dangerous. Warring factions may make conflicting demands of NGO staff members. In such situations, staff members must be skilled at negotiation to keep their projects going—and sometimes simply to stay alive.

■ 18.5 Protecting Human Rights

In 2006, Zmitser Dashkevich and some friends took part in a peaceful protest against the government. No big deal, right? Except that the protest occurred in Belarus, a former republic of the Soviet Union that has resisted democratic reform. Police arrested Dashkevich and charged him with "organizing or participating in an activity of an unregistered nongovernmental organization." After a closed-door trial, Dashkevich was sentenced to 18 months in prison. Where could he turn for help? The answer was one of the NGOs that focus on **human rights**.

An NGO for Every Purpose

NGOs have been established to serve a variety of goals and purposes. The three featured here are a tiny sample of the NGOs at work on projects around the globe.

The Global Fund for Women provides grants to promote the health, education, and economic security of women in poor countries. One of its recipients is the 3 Sisters Adventure Trekking agency in Nepal. Even though Nepal has a thriving tourist industry, women are often relegated to farmwork for little pay. The 3 Sisters agency trains local women as trekking guides, where they can earn good wages while developing leadership and business skills.

Doctors Without Borders/Médecins Sans Frontières (MSF) provides medical care to people affected by armed conflict, epidemics, and natural or human-made disasters. MSF is often one of the first NGOs to arrive at the scene of an emergency. Its teams arrive with specialized medical kits that may include a complete operating room or supplies to control outbreaks of such diseases as cholera or measles.

The World Wildlife Fund (WWF) works to protect endangered species including pandas, elephants, tigers, whales, sea turtles, and great apes. Staff members conduct conservation research in the field. They lobby for antipoaching laws. They also help governments establish wildlife conservation areas. One of the WWF's success stories is the preservation of the giant panda in China.

Defining the Basic Rights of All Human Beings

The basic rights that all human beings should enjoy are defined in a landmark UN document known as the Universal Declaration of Human Rights. The declaration includes many rights and freedoms that are familiar to any student of the U.S. Constitution. These include the rights to life, liberty, and equal protection under the law. They also include social and economic rights, including the right to work, own property, get an education, and enjoy a decent standard of living.

Adopted by the General Assembly in 1948, the Universal Declaration of Human Rights is nonbinding. Such is not the case with two related documents, the International Covenant on Civil and Political Rights and the International Covenant on Economic, Social and Cultural Rights. A **covenant** is a legally binding agreement. Together with the Universal Declaration, the covenants form what the UN calls the International Bill of Human Rights.

Defending Civil and Political Rights

The vast majority of UN members have ratified both the International Covenant on Civil and Political Rights and the International Covenant on Economic,

Social and Cultural Rights. A number of NGOs are working to see that they keep their word.

One of them, Amnesty International, took up Zmitser Dashkevich's cause. Arguing that the young man's rights to free assembly and speech had been violated, the NGO started a campaign to free him from prison. Members of Amnesty International around the world flooded the Belarus government with letters demanding Dashkevich's release. In the past, such letter-writing campaigns have shortened the sentences of many "prisoners of conscience."

The letters on behalf of Dashkevich were part of Amnesty's "Make Some Noise" campaign. The purpose of the campaign is to show human rights violators that the world is watching and that further abuses will also be exposed. Probably due to international pressure, Dashkevich was released early in 2008. However, he was arrested again in 2011 for alleged assault. Many say that he is innocent, arguing that his arrest was used to prevent him from protesting the reelection of Belarus's president. These claims, in addition to the fact that he was mistreated in prison, inspired Amnesty International to carry out another campaign. The organization again asked people to write appeal letters calling for Dashkevich's release.

These teenagers are protesting the arrest of Chinese artist and civil rights activist, Ai Weiwei. Ai, a vocal critic of China's government, was arrested in 2011 for alleged "economic crimes." Upon his arrest, NGOs such as the International Council of Museums petitioned for his release.

Defining the Rights of Children

In addition to the International Bill of Human Rights, the UN has created agreements called **conventions** aimed at protecting the rights of specific groups. There are conventions dealing with the rights of women, minorities, disabled persons, and other vulnerable groups, including children.

The UN Convention on the Rights of the Child spells out the basic human rights that children everywhere have. Among these rights are the right to life, survival, and protection from abuse and exploitation. The convention addresses child labor, saying,

> *Parties recognize the right of the child to be protected from economic exploitation and from performing any work that is likely to be hazardous or to interfere with the child's education, or to be harmful to the child's health or physical, mental, spiritual, moral or social development.*
>
> —UN Convention on the Rights of the Child, adopted Nov. 20, 1989

Enforcing this right, however, has been difficult. In many countries, children are employed in mines, in factories, and on farms at a young age. Families send their children to work because they need the money to survive. Employers hire children because they can pay them less than adult workers and because children may be easier to control.

Some countries have been slow to enact or enforce laws protecting child workers for fear of hurting their economies. As a result, many of the estimated 215 million child laborers worldwide work full time, often in unhealthy conditions. Most get no schooling.

Ending Child Labor Abuses

The UN is working with NGOs to encourage governments to pass stricter laws against employing children, to investigate employers who exploit children, and to improve access to education for children who do work. One such NGO is Human Rights Watch, an organization that investigates human rights abuses around the world.

In 2007, Human Rights Watch shone its spotlight on child labor abuses in the African nation of Guinea. It reported that thousands of girls as young as eight worked in near-slave conditions as household servants. Many were forced to labor up to 18 hours a day, often without pay. This and other similar reports by Human Rights Watch influenced the International Labor Organization to adopt a treaty in 2011 geared towards improving domestic and child labor laws.

Free the Children, the world's largest NGO of children helping children, takes a different approach. Free the Children fights child labor by giving parents the farm animals, tools, and machinery they need to support their families while sending their children to school. Free the Children also helps poor villages build schools and meet their basic health care needs. By 2012, this NGO had built more than 650 schools around the world, providing education to more than 55,000 poor children.

An estimated 215 million children worldwide work to support themselves and their families. This girl is working at a brickyard in Peru. Although laws in Peru and many other countries prohibit child labor, these laws are often poorly enforced.

■ 18.6 Tackling Environmental Issues: A Focus on Climate Change

For many years, the UN and a variety of NGOs have worked to bring environmental issues to the world's attention. They have often expressed their position in dramatic terms. In the 1990s, a group of scientists issued this alarming warning of trouble ahead:

Human beings and the natural world are on a collision course. Human activities inflict harsh and often irreversible damage on the environment and on critical resources. If not checked, many of our current practices put at serious risk the future that we wish for human society and the plant and animal kingdoms, and may so alter the living world that it will be unable to sustain life in the manner that we know. Fundamental changes are urgent if we are to avoid the collision our present course will bring about.
—Union of Concerned Scientists, "Warning to Humanity," 1992

Some Environmental Successes and a New Challenge

The Union of Concerned Scientists is one of the many international environmental groups that have worked to reduce air and water pollution, save endangered species, preserve the world's rainforests, and protect unspoiled places. As a result of these groups' efforts, many governments have taken steps to limit damage to the environment. In addition, people worldwide are much more aware of environmental issues than they were a few decades ago.

The latest environmental challenge confronting the world is **global climate change**. This term refers to variations in Earth's overall climate over periods of time ranging from decades to millions of years. Natural processes, such as volcanic eruptions and variations in the intensity of the sunlight reaching Earth, can cause climate change.

More recently, scientists have argued that human activities, mainly the burning of fossil fuels, are causing a **global warming** of Earth's climate. They say that Earth's temperature is rising as the result of a process known as the greenhouse effect. Gases in the atmosphere, such as carbon dioxide, act like panes of glass in a greenhouse. They let energy from the sun pass through the atmosphere to warm the surface of Earth. But they do not let all of that heat radiate back through the atmosphere into space. The gases absorb some of the heat and keep it trapped in the atmosphere. Without the greenhouse effect, Earth's average temperature would be about 60 degrees Fahrenheit cooler, too cold to sustain life.

A UN report issued in 2007 predicted that temperatures would likely rise between 3.5 degrees and 8 degrees Fahrenheit by the end of this century, based on projected levels of greenhouse gases. This change could cause significant melting of mountain glaciers and the ice sheets covering polar regions. Such a meltdown would release an enormous amount of water into the oceans, causing a rise in sea levels. As seas rise, low-lying islands and coastal areas are likely to be flooded. Rising temperatures are also likely to change weather patterns. Some regions might suffer from drought and others from floods. The result could be crop failures and famine in some regions.

International Efforts to Slow Climate Change

The United Nations has responded to the challenge of global warming in two ways. The first is by sponsoring research on global warming by its Intergovernmental Panel on Climate Change (IPCC). This group, made up of leading climate experts, has been researching the issue since 1988.

The UN has also sponsored a number of conferences focused on climate change. A 1992 meeting known as the Earth Summit produced the United Nations Framework Convention on Climate Change (UNFCCC). This international environmental treaty is aimed at reducing emissions of greenhouse gases to combat global warming. It set no mandatory limits on greenhouse gas emissions and contained no enforcement provisions. But it did call for later amendments, called **protocols,** to set such limits.

A 1997 UN conference held in Kyoto, Japan, resulted in an agreement to set mandatory emission limits. This agreement, known as the Kyoto Protocol, has become much better known than the UNFCCC itself. The Kyoto Protocol committed the world's industrialized nations to making significant cuts in their greenhouse gas emissions. Thirty-seven of these nations agreed to reduce emissions to 18 percent below their 1990 levels by 2020.

No binding goals for emission cuts were set for

developing countries at the Kyoto conference. Representatives of those countries argued that most of the emissions came from countries that had already industrialized. They also claimed that limiting emissions would unfairly stunt their economic development. As a representative from China observed, "In the developed world only two people ride in a car, and yet you want us to give up riding on a bus."

By 2013, about 190 countries had ratified the Kyoto Protocol. The most notable exception is the United States, which until recently was the top emitter of greenhouse gases in the world. President George W. Bush has argued that meeting the emissions reduction target set for the United States in the protocol would hurt the U.S. economy. He has also argued that developing nations, especially China, which now ranks first in annual emissions, should also be forced to accept mandatory cuts.

U.S. Efforts to Confront Climate Change

Although the United States is not a party to the Kyoto Protocol, it is confronting the global warming challenge at many levels. At the national level, President Obama developed a standard for cars and light-trucks to reach a fuel efficiency of 54.5 miles per gallon by 2025. He has also provided funding for research on science and technologies related to renewable energy. However, Obama's stance on climate change has also raised criticism. Workers in the coal industry complain that his policies are costing them jobs because power companies now prefer to use cleaner-burning fuels. Despite these criticisms, Obama spoke about the need to continue confronting global warming in his second term.

State and local governments have also become active in efforts to slow climate change. California led the way with the California Global Warming Solutions Act of 2006, an ambitious program aimed at reducing greenhouse gas emissions to 1990 levels by 2020. New Mexico promotes wind and solar energy by providing tax incentive for businesses and individuals. Portland, Oregon, also took action. By 2012, the city had reduced emissions to 6 percent below 1990 levels.

Environmental NGOs have been active as well. The Sierra Club, through its "Cool Cities" campaign, encourages cities to take steps to reduce their carbon dioxide emissions. The Environmental Defense Fund has used "Fight Global Warming" TV ads to educate the public about the urgent nature of the problem. The Natural Resources Defense Council has launched a campaign aimed at cutting electricity use to reduce the burning of fossil fuels in power plants.

Greenhouse Gas Emissions

This map shows emissions of carbon dioxide, a major greenhouse gas, in countries around the world. The United States and China are by far the largest emitters of carbon dioxide.

Carbon Dioxide Emissions per Country

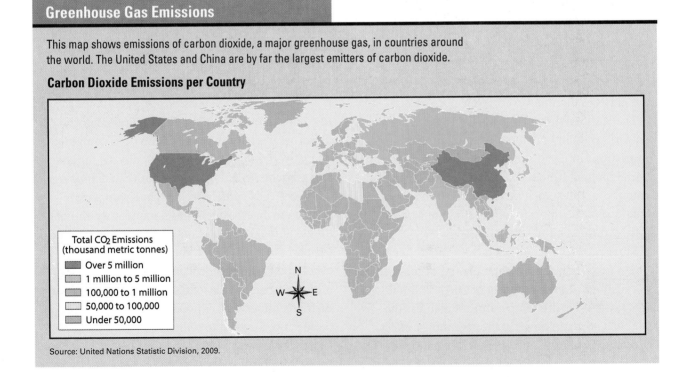

Total CO₂ Emissions (thousand metric tonnes)
- Over 5 million
- 1 million to 5 million
- 100,000 to 1 million
- 50,000 to 100,000
- Under 50,000

Source: United Nations Statistic Division, 2009.

In the private sector, some companies have made efforts to cut greenhouse gas emissions for economic reasons. For example, by replacing refrigerator lights with energy-efficient light bulbs, Wal-Mart saved $12 million a year. Similarly, IBM saved over $442 million between 1990 and 2011 by cutting back on energy usage at their data centers and making their facilities more energy efficient.

Americans are still debating how much focus should be on combating climate change. Some Americans believe that the United States should prioritize climate change in order to become less reliant on foreign oil. One benefit of energy independence is that OPEC would have less influence over the price of crude oil in the United States. However, others worry that a focus on climate change will put regulations on businesses and slow down economic growth.

Public and private groups will continue to influence policy on climate change. However, as you have learned, what position the government ulti-

Electric cars are an alternative to vehicles that run on fossil fuels. Some states provide tax incentives to individuals who purchase hybrid or electric cars.

mately takes on issues such as climate change largely depends on the actions of government officials, political parties, interest groups, and public opinion.

Summary

Over the past century, the nations of the world have learned to work together to confront global issues. Preventing violent conflict is one major concern. Other problems include extreme poverty, human rights abuses, and environmental destruction. A variety of international organizations are addressing these issues on different levels.

United Nations The UN takes on most major global issues. Its main mission has always been maintaining world peace. Working with other international organizations, the UN also pursues the goal of improving the lives of the world's people.

Intergovernmental organizations Nations form IGOs—such as the UN—to achieve common objectives. Those objectives include national security, improved trade, and political and economic cooperation.

Nongovernmental organizations NGOs are private, nonprofit groups of citizens that tackle problems through people-to-people contacts. The typical international NGO focuses on a single issue, such as poverty, disaster relief, human rights, or health concerns.

Human rights The UN made human rights a global concern when the General Assembly ratified the Universal Declaration of Human Rights in 1948. Since then, the UN and a number of NGOs have made it their mission to monitor and report human rights abuses.

Climate Change Most scientists today believe that Earth is warming rapidly because of the burning of fossil fuels. Many people believe that global climate change and the environment are issues that should be on the forefront of our nation's agenda. However, others worry that prioritizing policies related to climate change could hurt certain industries.

Can one person make a difference in the world?

It is easy to feel helpless in the face of global issues like climate change or extreme poverty. You might wonder how one person could possibly make a difference in a world of more than 7 billion people. One way an individual can make a difference is through social entrepreneurship. Read about how young adults are founding organizations that reach out to the global community. Then ask yourself, What might I do to make a difference in the world?

The Power to Lead: The Next Generation of Social Entrepreneurs

In business, social entrepreneurship is getting a lot of attention these days. While social entrepreneurs have as much creativity, passion, drive, energy and appetite for risk as traditional entrepreneurs, they are looking to solve the world's problems and maximize social value over profits—and to do so on a grand scale. Raviv Turner, cofounder and CEO of Guerillapps, a startup focused on developing social games to support real-world causes, told *Forbes* magazine this month, "The first step to becoming a social entrepreneur is identifying a social problem in need of a solution. Aspiring social entrepreneurs need not look too far to find social issues in need of solving: poverty, hunger, poor education, environmental damage, political suppression, disease and social inequality," to name a few.

A growing number of teenagers are drawn to the social entrepreneurship model—and this concept of giving back to their communities. They are defining success not only by what they can achieve for themselves, but also what they do for others. This mentality is prompting young people like Candonino Agusen, a junior at Kealakehe High School who spoke to Knowledge@Wharton High School from his home in Kailua-Kona, Hawaii, to plan a future with a social impact: "I'm interested in becoming a doctor, a general practitioner, but after I complete my residency I plan on joining Doctors without Borders and helping overseas and third-world countries," notes Agusen.

Nancy Lubin, CEO of DoSomething.org, a nonprofit that helps young people to engage in philanthropy, recently told *Crain's New York Business*, "Kids today just saw their parents go through a recession, get laid off and struggle. They look around and say: 'What's the point? I don't just want a second car in my driveway. I want a life of purpose.'" This, along with access to technology that brings the world closer than ever, is inspiring a new generation of social entrepreneurs in training.

Third-world Country Poverty
Samantha Kerker, 17, took macroeconomics as a freshman at Atlantic Community High School in Delray Beach, Fl., and fell in love with entrepreneurship. Inspired to start her own business, she invested $2,600 of her money to launch a website

selling tie-dye clothing, created from chemicals and colors that she mixed herself. Six months later, she had $7,000 and a desire to do something meaningful with her money.

When students from Lynn University in Boca Raton, where her mother works, lost their lives in the 2010 earthquake in Haiti, Kerker had her answer. Unable to travel to the disaster-stricken country, she chose the next Latin American country most in need: Nicaragua. "My mom and I packed our bags and lived, slept and breathed in third-world country poverty for a week. With the money, we built a house for a homeless family and a latrine. All the people were

incredible, humble and so happy that we were there," says Kerker.

Back home, Kerker's friends asked her if she would stay in touch with the family she helped—possibly through Facebook. "I said, 'Facebook friends? They don't even have running water or electricity!' That's when I realized that my friends didn't get it," notes Kerker.

And so was born Students for the Poor, a network of clubs operating in all 28 high schools in the Palm Beach County school district that mobilizes student participation in community service projects and global outreach. With Kerker at the helm, all the clubs held an outdoor amphitheater concert in February

to raise $30,000 to build a school in Nicaragua and to sponsor 60 students from the school district to travel to the country over spring break 2013. "I want the students to be part of the building process and experience a third-world setting," says Kerker, who this month was one of 10 high school and middle school students to win a national Prudential Spirit of Community Award for her outstanding volunteer service. "My hope is that they're going to go there and come back and be inspired like I was."

In this age of connectivity, when getting a friend's attention is one FB post away, many aspiring social entrepreneurs are rallying their classmates around

Social entrepreneurship comes in many forms. This picture depicts the players of the Milan 2009 Homeless World Cup. The Homeless World Cup is an annual event started by social entrepreneurs who sought to fight homelessness on the global level.

causes. Jordyn Schara, a junior at Reedsburg Area High School in North Freedom, Wis., runs Foundation for HOPE (Helping Our Peers Excel), a nonprofit that mentors young people to get involved in their communities. In part, says Schara, the organization is a way to "house the community service projects I do," which include a program that ships books and magazines to soldiers in Iraq, an initiative promoting reading through comic books for elementary school-aged kids, and a project to collect and dispose of unused or unwanted pharmaceuticals so that they do not end up in the water supply, while raising awareness of prescription drug abuse.

"What I've enjoyed the most is finding something in my community that isn't being addressed and jumping in to address it," says Schara, who wants to major in broadcast journalism in college and become a war correspondent. "My program is in over 18 states, and I hope to take it global. Our duty as human beings is to help each other."

Find Your Voice
With a great-grandmother who was "very close" to Ghandi, Neha Gupta says that social activism is in her DNA. Still, the sophomore at Pennsbury High School in Fairless Hills, Pa., believes that her journey starting Empowering

Orphans, an organization that has raised $500,000 in money, products and services for orphans in India and locally, has been personal as well as professional. "This process has taught me that every person has a voice," notes Gupta, who has learned to navigate the world of grant applications and organizing fundraising events. "I really didn't think that I was going to make an impact at all. I thought I could help maybe 100 kids. It's taught me that when I use my voice, it can have amazing effects."

The next generation of social entrepreneurs? Yes, if they have anything to say about it. "I've learned leadership, politics, organization, negotiations, procedures, documents, legal issues, liability issues. I would call people to set up meetings and they wouldn't call me back. I had to keep persisting," says Kerker, who intends to study social entrepreneurship in college. "I've had so many bumps in the road and so many people telling me it was impossible to do what I wanted to do. I proved them wrong. Ten years from now, I want to create my own international nonprofit business."

Knowledge@Wharton High School publishes weekly articles for high school students related to business and entrepreneurship.

Resources

TCI's online Student Subscriptions give you access to the text, reading tools, and features that help you learn vocabulary and key content.

Reading Tools

An interactive learning environment awaits you with audio tools, rich images, in-line vocabulary, Spanish, and more.

Spanish Translations

You can toggle between English and Spanish text and can have either text read to you using the text-to-audio feature. The ability to view the Spanish text is enabled by your teacher.

Reading Challenges

Take an end-of-chapter Reading Challenge to check your understanding of the content. Even though taking a Reading Challenge feels like playing a game, you're learning and discovering what you know.

Vocabulary Development Tools

Test your understanding of key terms using online flip cards.

PC, Mac, Tablet, and Smart Phone

You can use your PC, Mac, iPad, and other mobile devices to access all of these Student Subscription resources.

TCI's online Student Subscriptions give you resources to expand your learning beyond the content covered in this book.

Enrichment Essays

Each chapter of the online Student Text is enhanced with additional readings that relate to the chapter content. Full of engaging and interesting information and case studies, these essays are fun to read.

National Constitution Center Resources

Your teacher can provide links to cases and information provided by the National Constitution Center to extend your learning of the concepts in this book.

U.S. Supreme Court Cases: You Make the Call

Dive into complex and challenging Supreme Court cases in your Student Subscription. Look for the "You Make the Call" cases and grapple with issues like whether a federal law requiring licensing for firearms violates Second Amendment rights. You make the call and then read the actual Supreme Court decision.

In Congress, July 4, 1776

The unanimous Declaration of the thirteen united States of America

When in the Course of human events it becomes necessary for one people to dissolve the political bands which have connected them with another, and to assume among the powers of the earth, the separate and equal station to which the Laws of Nature and of Nature's God entitle them, a decent respect to the opinions of mankind requires that they should declare the causes which impel them to the separation.

We hold these truths to be self-evident, that all men are created equal, that they are endowed by their Creator with certain **unalienable** Rights, that among these are Life, Liberty and the pursuit of Happiness. —That to secure these rights, Governments are instituted among Men, deriving their just powers from the consent of the governed, —That whenever any Form of Government becomes destructive of these ends, it is the Right of the People to alter or to abolish it, and to institute new Government, laying its foundation on such principles and organizing its powers in such form, as to them shall seem most likely to effect their Safety and Happiness. **Prudence**, indeed, will dictate that Governments long established should not be changed for light and **transient** causes; and accordingly all experience hath shewn, that mankind are more disposed to suffer, while evils are sufferable, than to right themselves by abolishing the forms to which they are accustomed. But when a long train of abuses and **usurpations**, pursuing invariably the same Object **evinces** a design to reduce them under absolute **Despotism**, it is their right, it is their duty, to throw off such Government, and to provide new Guards for their future security. —Such has been the patient sufferance of these Colonies; and such is now the necessity which **constrains** them to alter their former Systems of Government. The history of the present King of Great Britain is a history of repeated injuries and usurpations, all having in direct object the establishment of an absolute **Tyranny** over these States. To prove this, let Facts be submitted to a **candid** world.

He has refused his **Assent** to Laws, the most wholesome and necessary for the public good.

He has forbidden his Governors to pass Laws of immediate and pressing importance, unless **suspended** in their operation till his Assent should be obtained; and when so suspended, he has utterly neglected to attend to them.

He has refused to pass other Laws for the accommodation of large districts of people, unless those people would relinquish the right of

The Declaration can be divided into four sections. The first section, the Preamble, consists of an introduction and a statement of rights. The introduction explains the document's purpose and sets a principled tone. The idea that people had the right to rebel against an oppressive government was not new. The Declaration's purpose was to show the world that Americans were justified in exercising this right.

Statement of Human Rights
The statement of rights is constructed like a logical argument. It begins with what it calls "self-evident truths" and proceeds logically to the need for revolution. Jefferson expressed this argument with such force and eloquence that his words still stand as an enduring statement of America's founding ideals.

unalienable: undeniable

prudence: common sense

transient: passing, fleeting

usurpations: unlawful power grabs

evinces: shows evidence of

despotism: rule by a dictator

constrains: forces, compels

tyranny: unjust government

candid: honest, open

Statement of Charges Against the King
The second section contains the charges against the king. Here Jefferson lists more than 20 grievances as proof of the king's unjust treatment of the colonies. This proof was needed to persuade undecided colonists to support independence.

assent: approval

suspended: temporarily stopped

Representation in the Legislature, a right **inestimable** to them and **formidable** to tyrants only.

He has called together legislative bodies at places unusual, uncomfortable, and distant from the **depository** of their Public Records, for the sole purpose of fatiguing them into compliance with his measures. He has **dissolved** Representative Houses repeatedly, for opposing with manly firmness his invasions on the rights of the people.

He has refused for a long time, after such dissolutions, to cause others to be elected, whereby the Legislative Powers, incapable of **Annihilation,** have returned to the People at large for their exercise; the State remaining in the mean time exposed to all the dangers of invasion from without, and **convulsions** within.

He has **endeavoured** to prevent the population of these States; for that purpose obstructing the Laws for **Naturalization** of Foreigners; refusing to pass others to encourage their migrations hither, and raising the conditions of new **Appropriations** of Lands.

He has **obstructed** the Administration of Justice, by refusing his Assent to Laws for establishing **Judiciary Powers**.

He has made Judges dependent on his Will alone, for the **tenure** of their **offices,** and the amount and payment of their salaries.

He has erected a multitude of New Offices, and sent hither swarms of Officers to harass our people and eat out their substance.

He has kept among us, in times of peace, Standing Armies without the Consent of our legislatures.

He has affected to render the Military independent of and superior to the Civil Power.

He has **combined with others** to subject us to a **jurisdiction** foreign to our constitution, and unacknowledged by our laws; giving his Assent to their Acts of pretended Legislation:

For **Quartering** large bodies of armed troops among us:

For protecting them, by a **mock** Trial, from punishment for any Murders which they should commit on the Inhabitants of these States:

For cutting off our Trade with all parts of the world:

For imposing Taxes on us without our Consent:

For depriving us in many cases, of the benefit of Trial by Jury:

For transporting us beyond Seas to be tried for pretended offences:

inestimable: invaluable

formidable: alarming

depository: storage site

dissolved: disbanded, broken up

annihilation: destruction

convulsions: disturbances

endeavoured: tried

naturalization: becoming a citizen

appropriations: distributions

obstructed: blocked

judiciary powers: courts of law

tenure: right to hold

offices: government jobs

combined with others: worked with Parliament

jurisdiction: authority

quartering: housing

mock: fake

For abolishing the free System of English Laws in a **neighbouring Province,** establishing therein an **Arbitrary** government, and enlarging its Boundaries so as to render it at once an example and fit instrument for introducing the same absolute rule into these Colonies:

For taking away our Charters, abolishing our most valuable Laws, and altering fundamentally the Forms of our Governments:

For suspending our own Legislatures, and declaring themselves invested with power to legislate for us in all cases whatsoever.

He has **abdicated** Government here, by declaring us out of his Protection and waging War against us.

abdicated: abandoned

He has plundered our seas, ravaged our Coasts, burnt our towns, and destroyed the lives of our people.

He is at this time transporting large Armies of foreign **Mercenaries** to compleat the works of death, desolation and tyranny, already begun with circumstances of Cruelty & **perfidy** scarcely paralleled in the most barbarous ages, and totally unworthy the Head of a civilized nation.

mercenaries: hired soldiers

perfidy: deceit, treachery

He has constrained our fellow Citizens taken Captive on the high Seas to bear Arms against their Country, to become the executioners of their friends and Brethren, or to fall themselves by their Hands.

He has excited domestic **insurrections** amongst us, and has endeavoured to bring on the inhabitants of our frontiers, the merciless Indian Savages, whose known rule of warfare, is an undistinguished destruction of all ages, sexes and conditions.

insurrections: rebellions

In every stage of these Oppressions We have **Petitioned** for **Redress** in the most humble terms: Our repeated Petitions have been answered only by repeated injury. A Prince whose character is thus marked by every act which may define a Tyrant, is unfit to be the ruler of a free people.

Nor have We been wanting in attentions to our British brethren. We have warned them from time to time of attempts by their legislature to extend an **unwarrantable** jurisdiction over us. We have reminded them of the circumstances of our emigration and settlement here. We have appealed to their native justice and **magnanimity,** and we have **conjured** them by the ties of our common **kindred,** to **disavow** these usurpations, which, would inevitably interrupt our connections and correspondence. They too have been deaf to the voice of justice and of **consanguinity.** We must, therefore, **acquiesce** in the necessity, which **denounces** our Separation, and hold them, as we hold the rest of mankind, Enemies in War, in Peace Friends.

The Government's Failure to Answer the Colonists' Complaints
The third section is a denunciation of the British people for their indifference to the colonists' plight. American leaders had petitioned the king and Parliament, but their efforts to advance their cause had met with little sympathy among their "British brethren."

petitioned: asked in writing

redress: the righting of wrongs

unwarrantable: unjustified

magnanimity: generosity

conjured: pleaded with

kindred: family relationships

disavow: publicly condemn

consanguinity: blood ties

acquiesce: agree

denounces: formally announces

We, therefore, the Representatives of the united States of America, in General Congress, Assembled, appealing to the Supreme Judge of the world for the **rectitude** of our intentions, do, in the Name, and by Authority of the good People of these Colonies, solemnly publish and declare, That these United Colonies are, and of Right ought to be Free and Independent States; that they are **Absolved** from all Allegiance to the British Crown, and that all political connection between them and the State of Great Britain, is and ought to be totally dissolved; and that as Free and Independent States, they have full Power to levy War, conclude Peace, contract Alliances, establish Commerce, and to do all other Acts and Things which Independent States may of right do. —And for the support of this Declaration, with a firm reliance on the protection of divine Providence, we mutually pledge to each other our Lives, our Fortunes and our sacred Honor.

The foregoing Declaration was, by order of Congress, **engrossed** on parchment, and signed by the 56 members.

New Hampshire
Josiah Bartlett, William Whipple, Matthew Thornton

Massachusetts
John Hancock, Samuel Adams, John Adams, Robert Treat Paine, Elbridge Gerry

Rhode Island
Stephen Hopkins, William Ellery

Connecticut
Roger Sherman, Samuel Huntington, William Williams, Oliver Wolcott

New York
William Floyd, Philip Livingston, Francis Lewis, Lewis Morris

New Jersey
Richard Stockton, John Witherspoon, Francis Hopkinson, John Hart, Abraham Clark

Pennsylvania
Robert Morris, Benjamin Rush, Benjamin Franklin, John Morton, George Clymer, James Smith, George Taylor, James Wilson, George Ross

Delaware
Caesar Rodney, George Read, Thomas McKean

Maryland
Samuel Chase, William Paca, Thomas Stone, Charles Carroll of Carrollton

Virginia
George Wythe, Richard Henry Lee, Thomas Jefferson, Benjamin Harrison, Thomas Nelson Jr., Francis Lightfoot Lee, Carter Braxton

North Carolina
William Hooper, Joseph Hewes, John Penn

South Carolina
Edward Rutledge, Thomas Heyward Jr., Thomas Lynch Jr., Arthur Middleton

Georgia
Button Gwinnett, Lyman Hall, George Walton

Statement of Independence
In the fourth section, the conclusion, Congress formally declares independence on behalf of the people of the colonies. The signers' final pledge of their "sacred Honor" was a most solemn vow at a time when honor was highly prized.

rectitude: righteousness

absolved: released

engrossed: copied in large, clear hand-writing

Delegates to the Second Continental Congress, 1776
John Hancock, a revolutionary leader from Massachusetts, was the first person to sign the engrossed Declaration of Independence. His bold signature is so widely known that when people today sign a document, they are said to be adding their "John Hancock."

This version of the Constitution retains the original text, spellings, and capitalizations. Parts of the Constitution that have been changed through amendment have been crossed out.

We the People of the United States, in Order to form a more perfect Union, establish Justice, insure domestic Tranquility, provide for the common defence, promote the general Welfare, and secure the Blessings of Liberty to ourselves and our Posterity, do ordain and establish this Constitution for the United States of America.

Article I.

Section 1.
All legislative Powers herein granted shall be vested in a Congress of the United States, which shall consist of a Senate and House of Representatives.

Section 2.
The House of Representatives shall be composed of Members chosen every second Year by the People of the several States, and the Electors in each State shall have the Qualifications requisite for Electors of the most numerous Branch of the State Legislature.

No Person shall be a Representative who shall not have attained to the Age of twenty five Years, and been seven Years a Citizen of the United States, and who shall not, when elected, be an Inhabitant of that State in which he shall be chosen.

Representatives and ~~direct Taxes~~ shall be apportioned among the several States which may be included within this Union, according to their respective Numbers, ~~which shall be determined by adding to the whole Number of free Persons, including those bound to Service for a Term of Years, and excluding Indians not taxed, three fifths of all other Persons.~~ The actual Enumeration shall be made within three Years after the first Meeting of the Congress of the United States, and within every subsequent Term of ten Years, in such Manner as they shall by Law direct. The Number of Representatives shall not exceed one for every thirty Thousand, but each State shall have at Least one Representative; and until such enumeration shall be made, the State of New Hampshire shall be entitled to chuse [choose] three, Massachusetts eight, Rhode Island and Providence Plantations one, Connecticut five, New York six, New Jersey four, Pennsylvania eight, Delaware one, Maryland six, Virginia ten, North Carolina five, South Carolina five, and Georgia three.

These annotations will help you understand the Constitution.

Preamble
The Preamble establishes that the federal government gains its power from the people, not the states. It also lists the purposes of the government: to maintain peace at home, to protect the nation from enemies, to promote the well-being of the people, and to secure the people's rights and freedoms.

Article I: Legislative Branch

Section 1: Two-Part Congress
The power to make laws is granted to Congress, which consists of the Senate and the House of Representatives.

Section 2: House of Representatives
Clause 1: Election Members of the House of Representatives are elected by the people every two years. *Electors* refers to voters.

Clause 2: Qualifications A member of the House must be at least 25 years old, must have been an American citizen for seven years, and must live in the state he or she represents.

Clause 3: Apportionment The number of Representatives from each state is based on the state's population. An *enumeration*, or census, must be taken every 10 years to determine that population. The total number of Representatives in the House is now fixed at 435. This clause contains the infamous Three-fifths Compromise, which specified that slaves ("all other Persons") were to be counted as three-fifths of a citizen when determining population. This provision was rendered meaningless by the Thirteenth Amendment (1865), which ended slavery.

When vacancies happen in the Representation from any State, the Executive Authority thereof shall issue Writs of Election to fill such Vacancies.

The House of Representatives shall chuse [choose] their Speaker and other Officers; and shall have the sole Power of Impeachment.

Section 3.

The Senate of the United States shall be composed of two Senators from each State, ~~chosen by the Legislature thereof~~, for six Years; and each Senator shall have one Vote.

Immediately after they shall be assembled in Consequence of the first Election, they shall be divided as equally as may be into three Classes. The Seats of the Senators of the first Class shall be vacated at the Expiration of the second Year, of the second Class at the Expiration of the fourth Year, and of the third Class at the Expiration of the sixth Year, so that one-third may be chosen every second Year; ~~and if Vacancies happen by Resignation, or otherwise, during the Recess of the Legislature of any State, the Executive thereof may make temporary Appointments until the next Meeting of the Legislature, which shall then fill such Vacancies.~~

No Person shall be a Senator who shall not have attained to the Age of thirty Years, and been nine Years a Citizen of the United States, and who shall not, when elected, be an Inhabitant of that State for which he shall be chosen.

The Vice President of the United States shall be President of the Senate, but shall have no Vote, unless they be equally divided.

The Senate shall chuse [choose] their other Officers, and also a President pro tempore, in the Absence of the Vice President, or when he shall exercise the Office of President of the United States.

Clause 4: Vacancies If a representative resigns or dies in office, the governor of that state can issue a "Writ of Election," calling for a special election to fill the vacancy.

Clause 5: Officers and Impeachment Power The House elects a speaker, who normally comes from the majority party. Only the House has the power to impeach, or accuse, a federal official of wrongdoing.

Section 3: Senate
Clause 1: Election Each state is represented by two senators. Senators were elected by state legislatures until 1913, when the Seventeenth Amendment was ratified. It provides for the direct election of senators by the people. Senators serve six-year terms.

Clause 2: Terms and Classification To ensure continuity in the Senate, one-third of the senators run for reelection every two years. To establish this system, the first senators, elected in 1788, were divided into three groups. One group served for two years, the second group for four years, and the third group for a full six years.

Clause 3: Qualifications A senator must be at least 30 years old, must have been an American citizen for nine years, and must live in the state he or she represents.

Clause 4: President of the Senate The vice president presides over the Senate but votes only in event of a tie.

Clause 5: Other Officers The Senate selects its other leaders and may also select a temporary ("pro tempore") president to preside if the vice president is absent.

The Senate shall have the sole Power to try all Impeachments. When sitting for that Purpose, they shall be on Oath or Affirmation. When the President of the United States is tried, the Chief Justice shall preside: And no Person shall be convicted without the Concurrence of two thirds of the Members present.

Judgment in Cases of Impeachment shall not extend further than to removal from Office, and disqualification to hold and enjoy any Office of honor, Trust or Profit under the United States: but the Party convicted shall nevertheless be liable and subject to Indictment, Trial, Judgment and Punishment, according to Law.

Section 4.
The Times, Places and Manner of holding Elections for Senators and Representatives, shall be prescribed in each State by the Legislature thereof; but the Congress may at any time by Law make or alter such Regulations, except as to the Places of chusing [choosing] Senators.

The Congress shall assemble at least once in every Year, and such Meeting shall be on the first Monday in December, unless they shall by Law appoint a different Day.

Section 5.
Each House shall be the Judge of the Elections, Returns and Qualifications of its own Members, and a Majority of each shall constitute a Quorum to do Business, but a smaller Number may adjourn from day to day, and may be authorized to compel the Attendance of absent Members, in such Manner, and under such Penalties as each House may provide.

Each House may determine the Rules of its Proceedings, punish its Members for disorderly Behaviour, and, with the Concurrence of two thirds, expel a Member.

Each House shall keep a Journal of its Proceedings, and from time to time publish the same, excepting such Parts as may in their Judgment require Secrecy; and the Yeas and Nays of the Members of either House on any question shall, at the Desire of one fifth of those Present, be entered on the Journal.

Clause 6: Impeachment Trials Only the Senate has the power to put impeached federal officials on trial. When an impeached president is tried, the chief justice of the Supreme Court acts as the trial judge. A two-thirds vote of the senators present is required to convict. Congress has used its impeachment power sparingly. Only two presidents have ever been impeached by the House and tried in the Senate. In 1868, the Senate acquitted President Andrew Johnson of charges of violating federal laws. In 1999, President Bill Clinton was acquitted of perjury charges. Facing impeachment in 1974, President Richard Nixon resigned from office.

Clause 7: Penalty Upon Conviction A federal official convicted by the Senate is removed from office. The Senate may bar him or her from future office but may not impose further punishment.

Section 4: Elections and Meetings
Clause 1: Elections States regulate their own congressional elections, but Congress may make laws changing the regulations.

Clause 2: Sessions Congress must meet at least once a year. The Twentieth Amendment (1933) moved the opening day of Congress to January 3.

Section 5: Congressional Proceedings
Clause 1: Attendance Each house judges whether its members are qualified and have been elected fairly. A majority of members of either house must be present for that house to conduct legislative business. This minimum required number is called a *quorum*.

Clause 2: Rules Each house makes its own rules of conduct for its members.

Clause 3: Records Both houses keep a journal of their proceedings. It is published as the *Congressional Record*.

Neither House, during the Session of Congress, shall, without the Consent of the other, adjourn for more than three days, nor to any other Place than that in which the two Houses shall be sitting.

Section 6.

The Senators and Representatives shall receive a Compensation for their Services, to be ascertained by Law, and paid out of the Treasury of the United States. They shall in all Cases, except Treason, Felony and Breach of the Peace, be privileged from Arrest during their Attendance at the Session of their respective Houses, and in going to and returning from the same; and for any Speech or Debate in either House, they shall not be questioned in any other Place.

No Senator or Representative shall, during the Time for which he was elected, be appointed to any civil Office under the Authority of the United States, which shall have been created, or the Emoluments whereof shall have been encreased during such time; and no Person holding any Office under the United States, shall be a Member of either House during his Continuance in Office.

Section 7.

All Bills for raising Revenue shall originate in the House of Representatives; but the Senate may propose or concur with Amendments as on other Bills.

Every Bill which shall have passed the House of Representatives and the Senate, shall, before it become a Law, be presented to the President of the United States; If he approve he shall sign it, but if not he shall return it, with his Objections to that House in which it shall have originated, who shall enter the Objections at large on their Journal, and proceed to reconsider it. If after such Reconsideration two thirds of that House shall agree to pass the Bill, it shall be sent, together with the Objections, to the other House, by which it shall likewise be reconsidered, and if approved by two thirds of that House, it shall become a Law. But in all such Cases the Votes of both Houses shall be determined by Yeas and Nays, and the Names of the Persons voting for and against the Bill shall be entered on the Journal of each House respectively. If any Bill shall not be returned by the President within ten Days (Sundays excepted) after it shall have been presented to him, the Same shall be a Law, in like Manner as if he had signed it, unless the Congress by their Adjournment prevent its Return, in which Case it shall not be a Law.

Clause 4: Adjournment During a session, neither house can close down or hold meetings elsewhere for a period of more than three days without the approval of the other house.

Section 6: Compensation, Immunity, and Restrictions
Clause 1: Salaries and Immunity
Members of Congress set their own pay and are paid out of the U.S. Treasury. Legislators may not be sued or prosecuted for their speeches and actions on the floor of Congress. This privilege protects free expression and fosters open debate.

Clause 2: Employment Restrictions
To ensure separation of powers, members of Congress may not hold any other federal office during their terms as legislators.

Section 7: Making Laws
Clause 1: Revenue Bills Only the House can propose a law raising taxes, though the Senate can offer changes. This provision ensures that people are not taxed without their consent.

Clause 2: Submitting Bills to the President A *bill* is a proposed law. A bill passed by a majority of both houses becomes law when the president signs it. If the president *vetoes*, or rejects, a bill, Congress can overrule the veto by a two-thirds vote of both houses.

Every Order, Resolution, or Vote to which the Concurrence of the Senate and House of Representatives may be necessary (except on a question of Adjournment) shall be presented to the President of the United States; and before the Same shall take Effect, shall be approved by him, or being disapproved by him, shall be repassed by two thirds of the Senate and House of Representatives, according to the Rules and Limitations prescribed in the Case of a Bill.

Section 8.

The Congress shall have Power

To lay and collect Taxes, Duties, Imposts and Excises, to pay the Debts and provide for the common Defence and general Welfare of the United States; but all Duties, Imposts and Excises shall be uniform throughout the United States;

To borrow Money on the credit of the United States;

To regulate Commerce with foreign Nations, and among the several States, and with the Indian Tribes;

To establish an uniform Rule of Naturalization, and uniform Laws on the subject of Bankruptcies throughout the United States;

To coin Money, regulate the Value thereof, and of foreign Coin, and fix the Standard of Weights and Measures;

To provide for the Punishment of counterfeiting the Securities and current Coin of the United States;

To establish Post Offices and post Roads;

To promote the Progress of Science and useful Arts, by securing for limited Times to Authors and Inventors the exclusive Right to their respective Writings and Discoveries;

Clause 3: Submitting Other Measures Other measures approved by Congress also require the president's approval or may also be passed over the president's veto.

Section 8: Powers of Congress
Congress has the specific powers listed in this section.

Clause 1: Taxation Congress has the power to levy taxes. This power was challenged early in the Republic's history by the Whiskey Rebellion. In 1797, Pennsylvania farmers attacked federal officials collecting an unpopular tax on whiskey. The government sent in the militia to arrest the rebels. This show of force demonstrated beyond a doubt the federal government's power to tax.

Clause 2: Borrowing Congress borrows money by issuing bonds, which create a debt that must be repaid.

Clause 3: Trade Regulation Congress regulates foreign trade and interstate commerce.

Clause 4: Naturalization and Bankruptcy Congress makes naturalization and bankruptcy laws. *Naturalization* is the process by which an immigrant becomes a U.S. citizen. *Bankruptcy* applies to individuals or companies that are unable to pay their debts.

Clause 5: Currency Congress establishes the national *currency*, or system of money.

Clause 6: Punishment for Counterfeiting Congress punishes counterfeiting, or the making of imitation money.

Clause 7: Postal Service Congress sets up the mail system.

Clause 8: Copyrights and Patents Congress passes copyright and patent laws to encourage creativity and invention. *Copyrights* protect authors and *patents* protect inventors so their work cannot be stolen.

To constitute Tribunals inferior to the supreme Court;

To define and punish Piracies and Felonies committed on the high Seas, and Offences against the Law of Nations;

To declare War, grant Letters of Marque and Reprisal, and make Rules concerning Captures on Land and Water;

To raise and support Armies, but no Appropriation of Money to that Use shall be for a longer Term than two Years;

To provide and maintain a Navy;

To make Rules for the Government and Regulation of the land and naval Forces;

To provide for calling forth the Militia to execute the Laws of the Union, suppress Insurrections and repel Invasions;

To provide for organizing, arming, and disciplining, the Militia, and for governing such Part of them as may be employed in the Service of the United States, reserving to the States respectively, the Appointment of the Officers, and the Authority of training the Militia according to the discipline prescribed by Congress;

Clause 9: Court System Congress has the power to create a federal court system. *Inferior* means lower.

Clause 10: Crimes at Sea Congress punishes crimes at sea. Piracy was a key concern when the Constitution was written.

Clause 11: Declaring War Congress declares war. World War II was the last time Congress formally declared war. Since then Congress has usually passed resolutions giving the president the authority to use military force where necessary. Such resolutions empowered presidents to send troops to fight the Vietnam War, the Persian Gulf War, and wars in Afghanistan and Iraq. Letters of Marque and Reprisal authorize *privateers*, or private ships, to attack and seize enemy vessels during times of war. The United States ceased issuing such letters during the Civil War.

Clause 12: Raising an Army Congress *appropriates*, or sets aside, funds for the military, usually on a yearly basis but never for more than two years. It also regulates the armed forces.

Clause 13: Maintaining a Navy

Clause 14: Regulating Armed Forces

Clause 15: Calling Up the Militia Congress has the power to call up *militias*, or armies of citizen soldiers, in times of emergency. Each state has its own militia, known today as the National Guard. Over the years, the National Guard has been called to respond to a variety of crises and natural disasters. In 2003, President Bush sent National Guard troops into combat in Iraq.

Clause 16: Regulating the Militia Congress regulates militias but leaves training to the states, under federal guidelines.

To exercise exclusive Legislation in all Cases whatsoever, over such District (not exceeding ten Miles square) as may, by Cession of particular States, and the Acceptance of Congress, become the Seat of the Government of the United States, and to exercise like Authority over all Places purchased by the Consent of the Legislature of the State in which the Same shall be, for the Erection of Forts, Magazines, Arsenals, dock-Yards and other needful Buildings;—And

To make all Laws which shall be necessary and proper for carrying into Execution the foregoing Powers, and all other Powers vested by this Constitution in the Government of the United States, or in any Department or Officer thereof.

Section 9.

~~The Migration or Importation of such Persons as any of the States now existing shall think proper to admit, shall not be prohibited by the Congress prior to the Year one thousand eight hundred and eight, but a Tax or duty may be imposed on such Importation, not exceeding ten dollars for each Person.~~

The Privilege of the Writ of Habeas Corpus shall not be suspended, unless when in Cases of Rebellion or Invasion the public Safety may require it.

No Bill of Attainder or ex post facto Law shall be passed.

~~No Capitation, or other direct, Tax shall be laid, unless in Proportion to the Census or Enumeration herein before directed to be taken.~~

No Tax or Duty shall be laid on Articles exported from any State.

Clause 17: Control of Federal Property Congress controls the District of Columbia and all other federal land. Congress governed Washington, D.C., until 1973, when an elected municipal government was established.

Clause 18: Elastic Clause This "necessary and proper" clause is known as the "elastic clause" because it gives Congress the flexibility to pass laws to carry out its functions and deal with new problems as they arise.

Section 9: Limits on the Power of Congress
Clause 1: Slave Trade This clause became obsolete after 1808, when the Constitution permitted Congress to outlaw the slave trade.

Clause 2: Writ of Habeas Corpus A writ of *habeas corpus* gives prisoners the right to challenge their imprisonment in court. Congress may not suspend this right except in extreme emergencies. Habeas corpus has been suspended only rarely in the nation's history. Since September 11, 2001, a debate has raged over whether this right applies to people detained on suspicion of terrorism. In 2004, the Supreme Court ruled that the writ must be extended to U.S. citizens imprisoned at Guantánamo, Cuba.

Clause 3: Unfair Laws This clause protects individuals from unfair laws. Congress cannot pass a law declaring a person or group guilty of a crime *(bill of attainder)*, nor can it pass a law making an act illegal after it has been committed *(ex post facto law)*.

Clause 4: Individual Taxes This clause prohibiting direct taxes on individuals was voided by the Sixteenth Amendment (1913), which permits Congress to tax individual income.

Clause 5: Taxes on Exports This clause prohibits the taxation of exported goods.

No Preference shall be given by any Regulation of Commerce or Revenue to the Ports of one State over those of another; nor shall Vessels bound to, or from, one State, be obliged to enter, clear, or pay Duties in another.

No Money shall be drawn from the Treasury, but in Consequence of Appropriations made by Law; and a regular Statement and Account of the Receipts and Expenditures of all public Money shall be published from time to time.

No Title of Nobility shall be granted by the United States: And no Person holding any Office of Profit or Trust under them, shall, without the Consent of the Congress, accept of any present, Emolument, Office, or Title, of any kind whatever, from any King, Prince, or foreign State.

Section 10.

No State shall enter into any Treaty, Alliance, or Confederation; grant Letters of Marque and Reprisal; coin Money; emit Bills of Credit; make any Thing but gold and silver Coin a Tender in Payment of Debts; pass any Bill of Attainder, ex post facto Law, or Law impairing the Obligation of Contracts, or grant any Title of Nobility.

No State shall, without the Consent of the Congress, lay any Imposts or Duties on Imports or Exports, except what may be absolutely necessary for executing its inspection Laws: and the net Produce of all Duties and Imposts, laid by any State on Imports or Exports, shall be for the Use of the Treasury of the United States; and all such Laws shall be subject to the Revision and Control of the Congress.

No State shall, without the Consent of Congress, lay any Duty of Tonnage, keep Troops, or Ships of War in time of Peace, enter into any Agreement or Compact with another State, or with a foreign Power, or engage in War, unless actually invaded, or in such imminent Danger as will not admit of delay.

Article II.

Section 1.

The executive Power shall be vested in a President of the United States of America. He shall hold his Office during the Term of four Years, and, together with the Vice President, chosen for the same Term, be elected, as follows:

Clause 6: Trade Preferences Congress may not favor one port over another and must ensure free trade between the states.

Clause 7: Spending The government cannot spend public money unless Congress has passed a law appropriating it. Congressional "power of the purse" acts as a check on the executive branch by controlling how much it can spend.

Clause 8: Titles of Nobility Congress may not establish titles of nobility, nor may federal officials accept such titles, or any gifts, from a foreign nation without congressional approval.

Section 10: Limits on the Power of the States
Clause 1: Forbidden Actions
The states cannot exercise certain powers granted to Congress or the president. These include negotiating treaties with foreign nations and creating their own money. They also may not tax imports or maintain armies without the approval of Congress.

Clause 2: Prohibition on Taxing Trade

Clause 3. Prohibition on Foreign Relations

Article II: Executive Branch

Section 1: President and Vice President
Clause 1: Term of Office The power to execute, or carry out, the laws passed by Congress rests with the president. A president and vice president are elected every four years. The Twenty-second Amendment (1951) limits the president to two terms in office.

Each State shall appoint, in such Manner as the Legislature thereof may direct, a Number of Electors, equal to the whole Number of Senators and Representatives to which the State may be entitled in the Congress: but no Senator or Representative, or Person holding an Office of Trust or Profit under the United States, shall be appointed an Elector.

The Electors shall meet in their respective States, and vote by Ballot for two Persons, of whom one at least shall not be an Inhabitant of the same State with themselves. And they shall make a List of all the Persons voted for, and of the Number of Votes for each; which List they shall sign and certify, and transmit sealed to the Seat of the Government of the United States, directed to the President of the Senate. The President of the Senate shall, in the Presence of the Senate and House of Representatives, open all the Certificates, and the Votes shall then be counted. The Person having the greatest Number of Votes shall be the President, if such Number be a Majority of the whole Number of Electors appointed; and if there be more than one who have such Majority, and have an equal Number of Votes, then the House of Representatives shall immediately chuse by Ballot one of them for President; and if no Person have a Majority, then from the five highest on the List the said House shall in like Manner chuse the President. But in chusing the President, the Votes shall be taken by States, the Representation from each State having one Vote; A quorum for this Purpose shall consist of a Member or Members from two thirds of the States, and a Majority of all the States shall be necessary to a Choice. In every Case, after the Choice of the President, the Person having the greatest Number of Votes of the Electors shall be the Vice President. But if there should remain two or more who have equal Votes, the Senate shall chuse from them by Ballot the Vice President.

The Congress may determine the Time of chusing the Electors, and the Day on which they shall give their Votes; which Day shall be the same throughout the United States.

No Person except a natural born Citizen, or a Citizen of the United States, at the time of the Adoption of this Constitution, shall be eligible to the Office of President; neither shall any person be eligible to that Office who shall not have attained to the Age of thirty five Years, and been fourteen Years a Resident within the United States.

Clause 2: Electoral College This clause establishes the Electoral College, which elects the president and vice president. The Electoral College is a group of citizens, called electors, chosen from each state to cast votes for president and vice president. Each state gets as many electors as it has members of the House and Senate combined. Before 1800, electors were usually elected by state legislatures. Today electors are chosen by the voters of each state.

Clause 3: Method of Election The original electoral method described here was modified by the Twelfth Amendment (1804). The revised method, which still operates today, calls for each elector to cast one vote for president and one vote for vice president. Most states give their entire slate of electoral votes to whichever candidate wins the most popular votes in the state. If no candidate for president gets a majority of electoral votes, then the House of Representatives chooses the president. The Electoral College is controversial because it has the potential to elect a candidate who did not win the popular vote.

Clause 4: Time of Elections Presidential elections are held on the Tuesday that follows the first Monday in November, every four years. Electors cast their votes more than a month later, on the Monday following the second Wednesday in December.

Clause 5: Qualifications The president must be an American citizen born in the United States, must be at least 35 years old, and must have resided in the United States for 14 years.

~~In Case of the Removal of the President from Office, or of his Death, Resignation, or Inability to discharge the Powers and Duties of the said Office, the Same shall devolve on the Vice President, and~~ the Congress may by Law provide for the Case of Removal, Death, Resignation or Inability, both of the President and Vice President, declaring what Officer shall then act as President, and such Officer shall act accordingly, until the Disability be removed, or a President shall be elected.

The President shall, at stated Times, receive for his Services, a Compensation, which shall neither be increased nor diminished during the Period for which he shall have been elected, and he shall not receive within that Period any other Emolument from the United States, or any of them.

Before he enter on the Execution of his Office, he shall take the following Oath or Affirmation:—"I do solemnly swear (or affirm) that I will faithfully execute the Office of President of the United States, and will to the best of my Ability, preserve, protect and defend the Constitution of the United States."

Section 2.

The President shall be Commander in Chief of the Army and Navy of the United States, and of the Militia of the several States, when called into the actual Service of the United States; he may require the Opinion, in writing, of the principal Officer in each of the executive Departments, upon any Subject relating to the Duties of their respective Offices, and he shall have Power to grant Reprieves and Pardons for Offenses against the United States, except in Cases of Impeachment.

He shall have Power, by and with the Advice and Consent of the Senate, to make Treaties, provided two thirds of the Senators present concur; and he shall nominate, and by and with the Advice and Consent of the Senate, shall appoint Ambassadors, other public Ministers and Consuls, Judges of the supreme Court, and all other Officers of the United States, whose Appointments are not herein otherwise provided for, and which shall be established by Law: but the Congress may by law vest the Appointment of such inferior Officers, as they think proper, in the President alone, in the Courts of Law, or in the Heads of Departments.

The President shall have Power to fill up all Vacancies that may happen during the Recess of the Senate, by granting Commissions which shall expire at the End of their next Session.

Clause 6: Presidential Succession
If the president dies or leaves office before the end of his or her term, the vice president becomes president. The ambiguous wording of this clause was clarified by the Twenty-fifth Amendment (1967). Congress decides who succeeds to the presidency if both the president and the vice president are incapacitated.

Clause 7: Salary Congress sets the president's salary and cannot change it during a presidential term. The president cannot accept *emoluments*, or other compensation, while in office.

Clause 8: Oath of Office The oath taken by the president is administered by a judicial officer, typically the chief justice of the Supreme Court.

Section 2: Powers of the President
Clause 1: Military and Executive Powers The president is commander-in-chief of the armed forces of the United States. This puts the military under civilian control. The president can grant pardons for federal crimes, except in cases of impeachment.

Clause 2: Treaties and Appointments The president has the power to make treaties with other nations, but the Senate must approve them by a two-thirds vote. The "advice and consent" of the Senate act as a check on presidential power. The president can name certain officials and federal judges, but a majority of the Senate must approve the president's choices.

Clause 3: Temporary Appointments
If the Senate is not in session, the president can make appointments without Senate approval. Such "recess" appointments expire at the end of the next Senate session. Presidents sometimes use recess appointments to avoid the Senate confirmation process.

Section 3.

He shall from time to time give to the Congress Information of the State of the Union, and recommend to their Consideration such Measures as he shall judge necessary and expedient; he may, on extraordinary Occasions, convene both Houses, or either of them, and in Case of Disagreement between them, with Respect to the Time of Adjournment, he may adjourn them to such Time as he shall think proper; he shall receive Ambassadors and other public Ministers; he shall take Care that the Laws be faithfully executed, and shall Commission all the Officers of the United States.

Section 4.

The President, Vice President and all civil Officers of the United States, shall be removed from Office on Impeachment for, and Conviction of, Treason, Bribery, or other high Crimes and Misdemeanors.

Article III.

Section 1.

The judicial Power of the United States, shall be vested in one supreme Court, and in such inferior Courts as the Congress may from time to time ordain and establish. The Judges, both of the supreme and inferior Courts, shall hold their Offices during good Behaviour, and shall, at stated Times, receive for their Services a Compensation, which shall not be diminished during their Continuance in Office.

Section 2

The judicial Power shall extend to all Cases, in Law and Equity, arising under this Constitution, the Laws of the United States, and Treaties made, or which shall be made, under their Authority; —to all Cases affecting Ambassadors, other public Ministers and Consuls; —to all Cases of admiralty and maritime Jurisdiction; —to Controversies to which the United States shall be a Party; —to Controversies between two or more States, —between a State and Citizens of another State; —between Citizens of different States, —between Citizens of the same State claiming Lands under Grants of different States, and between a State, or the Citizens thereof, and foreign States, Citizens or Subjects.

In all Cases affecting Ambassadors, other public Ministers and Consuls, and those in which a State shall be Party, the supreme Court shall have original Jurisdiction. In all the other Cases before mentioned, the supreme Court shall have appellate Jurisdiction, both as to Law and Fact, with such Exceptions, and under such Regulations as the Congress shall make.

Section 3: Duties of the President
The president can propose ideas for new laws. The president also reports to Congress, usually every year, on the State of the Union. In emergencies, the president can call Congress into special session.

Section 4: Impeachment
Presidents and federal officials can be removed from office if they abuse their powers or commit other "high crimes."

Article III: Judicial Branch

Section 1: Federal Courts
Judicial power is the power to decide legal cases in a court of law. This power is given to the Supreme Court and lower federal courts established by Congress. Federal judges hold office for life and their salaries cannot be reduced, thereby assuring the independence of the judiciary. Congress has set the number of Supreme Court justices at nine.

Section 2: Jurisdiction
Clause 1: Types of Cases *Jurisdiction* is the right of a court to hear a case. The federal courts have jurisdiction in cases pertaining to the Constitution, federal law, treaties, ambassadors, and maritime law. Federal courts can decide disputes between states, between states and the federal government, and between citizens of different states. In *Marbury v. Madison* (1803), the Supreme Court determined that it had the power to decide whether a law is constitutional.

Clause 2: Role of Supreme Court
The Supreme Court has "original jurisdiction"—the power to hear cases for the first time, not on appeal from a lower court—only in limited circumstances. Most of the time, the Court functions as an appeals court, deciding whether a case was properly tried in a lower court and reviewing its decision.

The Trial of all Crimes, except in Cases of Impeachment; shall be by Jury; and such Trial shall be held in the State where the said Crimes shall have been committed; but when not committed within any State, the Trial shall be at such Place or Places as the Congress may by Law have directed.

Section 3.

Treason against the United States, shall consist only in levying War against them, or in adhering to their Enemies, giving them Aid and Comfort. No Person shall be convicted of Treason unless on the Testimony of two Witnesses to the same overt Act, or on Confession in open Court.

The Congress shall have Power to declare the Punishment of Treason, but no Attainder of Treason shall work Corruption of Blood, or Forfeiture except during the Life of the Person attainted.

Article IV.

Section 1.

Full Faith and Credit shall be given in each State to the public Acts, Records, and judicial Proceedings of every other State; And the Congress may by general Laws prescribe the Manner in which such Acts, Records and Proceedings shall be proved, and the Effect thereof.

Section 2.

The Citizens of each State shall be entitled to all Privileges and Immunities of Citizens in the several States.

A Person charged in any State with Treason, Felony, or other Crime, who shall flee from Justice, and be found in another State, shall on Demand of the executive Authority of the State from which he fled, be delivered up, to be removed to the State having Jurisdiction of the Crime.

No Person held to Service or Labour in one State, under the Laws thereof, escaping into another, shall, in Consequence of any Law or Regulation therein, be discharged from such Service or Labour, but shall be delivered up on Claim of the Party to whom such Service or Labour may be due.

Section 3.

New States may be admitted by the Congress into this Union; but no new State shall be formed or erected within the Jurisdiction of any other State; nor any State be formed by the Junction of two or more States, or Parts of States, without the Consent of the Legislatures of the States concerned as well as of the Congress.

Clause 3: Trial by Jury
All defendants accused of a federal crime, except in cases of impeachment, have the right to a jury trial.

Section 3: Treason
Clause 1: Definition Treason, the only crime defined in the Constitution, is described as waging war against the United States or aiding its enemies. Criticism of the government, even in times of war, is protected by the First Amendment.

Clause 2: Punishment Congress has the power to decide how to punish convicted traitors. Punishment cannot be directed at the guilty person's relatives or friends.

Article IV: Relations Among the States

Section 1: Full Faith and Credit
Each state must honor the laws and authority of other states. For example, an adoption legally performed in one state must be recognized as legal in other states.

Section 2: Treatment of Citizens
Clause 1: Equal Privileges States may not discriminate against citizens of other states.

Clause 2: Extradition States must honor extradition orders. *Extradition* is the return of a suspected criminal or escaped convict to the state where he or she is wanted.

Clause 3: Fugitive Slaves This clause required states to return runaway slaves to their owners in other states. The Thirteenth Amendment (1965) voided this provision.

Section 3: New States and Territories
Clause 1: New States A new state cannot be carved out of an existing state or formed by the merger of existing states without the consent of the states and of Congress.

The Congress shall have Power to dispose of and make all needful Rules and Regulations respecting the Territory or other Property belonging to the United States; and nothing in this Constitution shall be construed as to Prejudice any Claims of the United States, or of any particular State.

Section 4.

The United States shall guarantee to every State in this Union a Republican Form of Government, and shall protect each of them against Invasion; and on Application of the Legislature, or of the Executive (when the Legislature cannot be convened), against domestic Violence.

Article V.

The Congress, whenever two thirds of both Houses shall deem it necessary, shall propose Amendments to this Constitution, or, on the Application of the Legislatures of two thirds of the several States, shall call a Convention for proposing Amendments, which, in either Case, shall be valid to all Intents and Purposes, as Part of this Constitution, when ratified by the Legislatures of three fourths of the several States, or by Conventions in three fourths thereof, as the one or the other Mode of Ratification may be proposed by the Congress; Provided that no Amendment which may be made prior to the Year One thousand eight hundred and eight shall in any Manner affect the first and fourth Clauses in the Ninth Section of the first Article; and that no State, without its Consent, shall be deprived of its equal Suffrage in the Senate.

Article VI.

All Debts contracted and Engagements entered into, before the Adoption of this Constitution, shall be as valid against the United States under this Constitution, as under the Confederation.

This Constitution, and the Laws of the United States which shall be made in Pursuance thereof; and all Treaties made, or which shall be made, under the Authority of the United States, shall be the supreme Law of the Land; and the Judges in every State shall be bound thereby, any Thing in the Constitution or Laws of any State to the Contrary notwithstanding.

The Senators and Representatives before mentioned, and the Members of the several State Legislatures, and all executive and judicial Officers, both of the United States and of the several States, shall be bound by Oath or Affirmation, to support this Constitution; but no religious Test shall ever be required as a Qualification to any Office or public Trust under the United States.

Clause 2: Federal Territory Congress has power over all federal territories and property. This means that it can regulate public lands, such as national parks and forests, and make laws for overseas possessions, such as Guam and Puerto Rico.

Section 4: Protection of States
Known as the "guarantee clause," this provision ensures that each state has a representative democratic government. The federal government is obliged to protect the states from invasion and from internal, or *domestic*, riots or other violence.

Article V: Amending the Constitution

The Constitution can be *amended*, or changed. Amendments must first be proposed either by a two-thirds vote of both houses of Congress or by a national convention of two-thirds of the states. A proposed amendment must then be ratified by three-quarters of the states, either in special conventions or in the state legislatures. The amendment process was made difficult so that the Constitution would not be amended too frequently or lightly. The Constitution has been amended only 27 times.

Article VI: National Supremacy

Clause 1: National Debts This clause recognizes debts incurred by the previous government under the Articles of Confederation.

Clause 2: Supremacy of National Law The so-called "supremacy clause" makes the Constitution and federal law the supreme, or highest, law of the land. If a state law and a federal law conflict, the federal law takes precedence. Federal courts can overturn state laws deemed to be unconstitutional or in conflict with federal law.

Clause 3: Oaths of Office Federal and state officials must swear allegiance to the Constitution. Public officials cannot be required to adopt or practice any particular religion.

Article VII.

The Ratification of the Conventions of nine States, shall be sufficient for the Establishment of this Constitution between the States so ratifying the Same.

Done in Convention by the Unanimous Consent of the States present the Seventeenth Day of September in the Year of our Lord one thousand seven hundred and Eighty seven and of the Independence of the United States of America the Twelfth In Witness whereof We have hereunto subscribed our Names.

Amendments

The Bill of Rights, or first 10 amendments, was passed by Congress on September 25, 1789, and ratified on December 15, 1791. Later amendments were proposed and ratified one at a time. The year of ratification appears in parentheses.

First Amendment

Congress shall make no law respecting an establishment of religion, or prohibiting the free exercise thereof; or abridging the freedom of speech, or of the press, or the right of the people peaceably to assemble, and to petition the Government for a redress of grievances.

Second Amendment

A well regulated Militia, being necessary to the security of a free State, the right of the people to keep and bear Arms, shall not be infringed.

Third Amendment

No Soldier shall, in time of peace be quartered in any house, without the consent of the Owner, nor in time of war, but in a manner to be prescribed by law.

Article VII: Ratification of the Constitution

To take effect, the Constitution had to be ratified by nine of the original 13 states. On June 21, 1788, the ninth state (New Hampshire) ratified. New York and Virginia ratified soon afterward. Rhode Island and North Carolina waited until the Bill of Rights was added to ratify. The Constitution went into effect on April 30, 1789.

First Amendment (1791)
Basic Freedoms
This amendment protects five freedoms that lie at the heart of American democracy: freedom of religion, freedom of speech, freedom of the press, freedom of assembly, and the freedom to *petition*, or ask, the government to correct wrongs.

Second Amendment (1791)
Right to Bear Arms
The right to bear arms guaranteed in this amendment is controversial. Americans are divided as to whether it applies to individuals or only to militias. The courts have ruled that individuals do have the right to bear arms, but that it is not an unlimited right. The Supreme Court has upheld some federal gun control laws, such as those requiring gun registration and waiting periods, but has ruled that other gun control measures should be left to the states.

Third Amendment (1791)
Quartering of Soldiers
In the turbulent years leading up to the American Revolution, American colonists were compelled to *quarter,* or house, British soldiers in their homes. This amendment bars the government from using private homes as military quarters, except in wartime and in a lawful way.

Fourth Amendment

The right of the people to be secure in their persons, houses, papers, and effects, against unreasonable searches and seizures, shall not be violated, and no Warrants shall issue, but upon probable cause, supported by Oath or affirmation, and particularly describing the place to be searched, and the persons or things to be seized.

Fifth Amendment

No person shall be held to answer for a capital, or otherwise infamous crime, unless on a presentment or indictment of a Grand Jury, except in cases arising in the land or naval forces, or in the Militia, when in actual service in time of War or public danger; nor shall any person be subject for the same offence to be twice put in jeopardy of life or limb; nor shall be compelled in any criminal case to be a witness against himself, nor be deprived of life, liberty, or property, without due process of law; nor shall private property be taken for public use, without just compensation.

Sixth Amendment

In all criminal prosecutions, the accused shall enjoy the right to a speedy and public trial, by an impartial jury of the State and district wherein the crime shall have been committed, which district shall have been previously ascertained by law, and to be informed of the nature and cause of the accusation; to be confronted with the witnesses against him; to have compulsory process for obtaining witnesses in his favor, and to have the Assistance of Counsel for his defence.

Seventh Amendment

In Suits at common law, where the value in controversy shall exceed twenty dollars, the right of trial by jury shall be preserved, and no fact tried by a jury shall be otherwise re-examined in any Court of the United States, than according to the rules of the common law.

Fourth Amendment (1791)
Search and Seizure

Like the Third Amendment, this amendment protects citizens against government intrusions into their property. Government officials cannot search citizens or their property, or seize citizens or their belongings, without good reason. Searches and seizures generally require a *warrant,* or written order approved by a judge. The Supreme Court has ruled that the Fourth Amendment also applies to electronic searches and wiretapping.

Fifth Amendment (1791)
Rights of the Accused

This amendment guarantees basic rights to people accused of crimes. A *capital* crime is punishable by death. *Infamous* crimes are punishable by imprisonment. A *grand jury* is a group of citizens who hear evidence of a crime and decide if the evidence warrants a trial. An *indictment* is their formal accusation. These procedures are intended to prevent the government from prosecuting people unfairly. In addition, accused persons cannot be tried twice for the same crime, known as *double jeopardy.* They cannot be forced to *testify,* or give evidence, against themselves. They cannot be jailed or have their property taken without *due process of law,* or a fair court hearing or trial. The government cannot take away private property without paying a fair price for it.

Sixth Amendment (1791)
Right to a Fair Trial

A citizen accused of a crime has the right to a jury trial that is both public and "speedy," or that takes place as quickly as circumstances allow. An *impartial* jury does not favor either side. An accused person has the right to question witnesses and has the right to a lawyer. Both federal and state courts must provide a lawyer if the accused cannot afford to hire one.

Seventh Amendment (1791)
Civil Trials

Citizens have the right to a jury trial to settle lawsuits over money or property worth more than $20. *Common law* refers to the rules of law established by previous judicial decisions.

Eighth Amendment

Excessive bail shall not be required, nor excessive fines imposed, nor cruel and unusual punishments inflicted.

Ninth Amendment

The enumeration in the Constitution, of certain rights, shall not be construed to deny or disparage others retained by the people.

Tenth Amendment

The powers not delegated to the United States by the Constitution, nor prohibited by it to the States, are reserved to the States respectively, or to the people.

Later Amendments

Eleventh Amendment

The Judicial power of the United States shall not be construed to extend to any suit in law or equity, commenced or prosecuted against one of the United States by Citizens of another State, or by Citizens or Subjects of any Foreign State.

Eighth Amendment (1791)
Bail and Punishment

Bail is money that an accused person pays in order to get out of jail while awaiting trial. The money is returned when the accused appears at trial; it is confiscated if he or she doesn't appear. Bail and fines that are set by a court must be reasonable. Punishments for crimes cannot be "cruel and unusual." The meaning of this phrase has broadened to include punishment considered too harsh for a particular crime. In 2005, the Supreme Court ruled that laws that apply the death penalty to people 17 and younger constitute "cruel and unusual" punishment and are unconstitutional.

Ninth Amendment (1791)
Rights Retained by the People

Americans have fundamental rights beyond the rights listed in the Constitution. The government cannot deny these rights just because they are not specified. This amendment was added out of fear that the Bill of Rights would be interpreted as limiting people's rights to those listed.

Tenth Amendment (1791)
States' Rights

This amendment attempts to balance power between the federal government and the states. It gives to the states and to the people any powers not specifically granted to the federal government. States' rights and the scope of federal power have been the subject of intense debate since the founding of the Republic. Slavery was perhaps the most significant issue over which this conflict played out, eventually plunging the nation into civil war.

Eleventh Amendment (1795)
Lawsuits Against States

People cannot sue a state in federal court if they are citizens of a different state or of a foreign country. The courts have interpreted this to mean that states may not be sued in federal courts without their consent.

Twelfth Amendment

The Electors shall meet in their respective states, and vote by ballot for President and Vice President, one of whom, at least, shall not be an inhabitant of the same state with themselves; they shall name in their ballots the person voted for as President, and in distinct ballots the person voted for as Vice President, and they shall make distinct lists of all persons voted for as President, and of all persons voted for as Vice President, and of the number of votes for each, which lists they shall sign and certify, and transmit sealed to the seat of the government of the United States, directed to the President of the Senate;—The President of the Senate shall, in the presence of the Senate and House of Representatives, open all the certificates and the votes shall then be counted;—The person having the greatest number of votes for President, shall be the President, if such number be a majority of the whole number of Electors appointed; and if no person have such majority, then from the persons having the highest numbers not exceeding three on the list of those voted for as President, the House of Representatives shall choose immediately, by ballot, the President. But in choosing the President, the votes shall be taken by states, the representation from each state having one vote; a quorum for this purpose shall consist of a member or members from two-thirds of the states, and a majority of all the states shall be necessary to a choice. And if the House of Representatives shall not choose a President whenever the right of choice shall devolve upon them, before the fourth day of March next following, then the Vice President shall act as President, as in the case of the death or other constitutional disability of the President. The person having the greatest number of votes as Vice President, shall be the Vice President, if such number be a majority of the whole number of Electors appointed, and if no person have a majority, then from the two highest numbers on the list, the Senate shall choose the Vice President; a quorum for the purpose shall consist of two-thirds of the whole number of Senators, and a majority of the whole number shall be necessary to a choice. But no person constitutionally ineligible to the office of President shall be eligible to that of Vice President of the United States.

Thirteenth Amendment

Section 1.

Neither slavery nor involuntary servitude, except as a punishment for crime whereof the party shall have been duly convicted, shall exist within the United States, or any place subject to their jurisdiction.

Section 2.

Congress shall have power to enforce these articles by appropriate legislation.

Twelfth Amendment (1804)
Presidential Elections

This amendment modifies the electoral process so that the president and vice president are elected separately. In the original Constitution, the candidate who finished second in the voting for president automatically became vice president. In 1800, this resulted in a tie for president between Thomas Jefferson and Aaron Burr. It took the House of Representatives 36 ballots to elect Jefferson president and Burr vice president. The Twelfth Amendment was added to prevent another tie vote.

Thirteenth Amendment (1865)
Abolition of Slavery

Section 1: Abolition
This amendment bans slavery throughout the United States. *Involuntary servitude* is work done against one's will. No person can be forced to work against his or her will except as a legal punishment for a crime.

Section 2: Enforcement

Fourteenth Amendment

Section 1.

All persons born or naturalized in the United States, and subject to the jurisdiction thereof, are citizens of the United States and of the State wherein they reside. No State shall make or enforce any law which shall abridge the privileges or immunities of citizens of the United States; nor shall any State deprive any person of life, liberty, or property, without due process of law; nor deny to any person within its jurisdiction the equal protection of the laws.

Section 2.

Representatives shall be apportioned among the several States according to their respective numbers, counting the whole number of persons in each State, excluding Indians not taxed. But when the right to vote at any election for the choice of electors for President and Vice President of the United States, Representatives in Congress, the Executive and Judicial officers of a State, or the members of the Legislature thereof, is denied to any of the male inhabitants of such State, being twenty-one years of age, and citizens of the United States, or in any way abridged, except for participation in rebellion, or other crime, the basis of representation therein shall be reduced in the proportion which the number of such male citizens shall bear to the whole number of male citizens twenty-one years of age in such State.

Section 3.

No person shall be a Senator or Representative in Congress, or elector of President and Vice President, or hold any office, civil or military, under the United States, or under any State, who, having previously taken an oath, as a member of Congress, or as an officer of the United States, or as a member of any State legislature, or as an executive or judicial officer of any State, to support the Constitution of the United States, shall have engaged in insurrection or rebellion against the same, or given aid or comfort to the enemies thereof. But Congress may by a vote of two-thirds of each House, remove such disability.

Section 4.

The validity of the public debt of the United States, authorized by law, including debts incurred for payment of pensions and bounties for services in suppressing insurrection or rebellion, shall not be questioned. But neither the United States nor any State shall assume or pay any debt or obligation incurred in aid of insurrection or rebellion against the United States, or any claim for the loss or emancipation of any slave; but all such debts, obligations and claims shall be held illegal and void.

Fourteenth Amendment (1868)
Rights of Citizens
This amendment was originally designed to resolve issues that arose after the Civil War ended and slavery was abolished.

Section 1: Citizenship
By defining as a citizen anyone born in the United States, this section extends citizenship to blacks. It prohibits the states from denying rights, due process, and equal protection of the law to their citizens. Despite these guarantees, it took nearly a century for the Supreme Court to decide that racial segregation violated the "equal protection" provision. In *Brown v. Board of Education* (1954), the Court struck down school segregation, ruling that separate schools for whites and blacks were inherently unequal.

Section 2: Representation and Voting This section nullifies the "three-fifths clause" of the original Constitution. It guarantees equal representation to all citizens. The reference to "male inhabitants" upset women's rights leaders who felt that equality for women was being pushed aside in favor of equality for blacks. In time, the "equal protection" provision would be expanded to include women, minorities, and noncitizens.

Section 3: Former Confederate Leaders Any member of government who took an oath to uphold the Constitution before the Civil War and who then joined the Confederate cause cannot be elected to any federal or state office.

Section 4: Public Debts
By voiding all Confederate debts, this section ensured that people who had lent money to Confederate states would not be paid back, nor would former slave owners be paid for the loss of their emancipated slaves.

Section 5.
The Congress shall have the power to enforce, by appropriate legislation, the provisions of this article.

Fifteenth Amendment

Section 1.
The right of citizens of the United States to vote shall not be denied or abridged by the United States or by any State on account of race, color, or previous condition of servitude

Section 2.
The Congress shall have the power to enforce this article by appropriate legislation.

Sixteenth Amendment
The Congress shall have power to lay and collect taxes on incomes, from whatever source derived, without apportionment among the several States, and without regard to any census or enumeration

Seventeenth Amendment

Section 1.
The Senate of the United States shall be composed of two Senators from each State, elected by the people thereof, for six years; and each Senator shall have one vote. The electors in each State shall have the qualifications requisite for electors of the most numerous branch of the State legislature.

Section 2.
When vacancies happen in the representation of any State in the Senate, the executive authority of such State shall issue writs of election to fill such vacancies: Provided, That the legislature of any State may empower the executive thereof to make temporary appointments until the people fill the vacancies by election as the legislature may direct.

Section 3.
This amendment shall not be so construed as to affect the election or term of any Senator chosen before it becomes valid as part of the Constitution.

Section 5: Enforcement
Congress can make laws to enforce this amendment. Beginning in the 1960s, Congress used this enforcement provision to pass new civil rights legislation, including the Civil Rights Act, the Voting Rights Act, and the Americans with Disabilities Act.

Fifteenth Amendment (1870)
Voting Rights

Section 1: The Right to Vote
States cannot deny voting rights to citizens on the basis of race, color, or previous enslavement.

Section 2: Enforcement

Sixteenth Amendment (1913)
Income Tax
The income tax amendment allows Congress to tax the earnings and income of individuals. At first only the very wealthy were taxed, but eventually the tax was extended to almost all wage earners.

Seventeenth Amendment (1913)
Election of Senators

Section 1: Elections
This amendment provides for the direct election of senators by popular vote. Previously, senators were elected by state legislatures, but deadlocked votes in state legislatures resulted in many Senate seats remaining vacant for long periods. By 1911, public demand for direct senatorial elections forced Congress to pass the Seventeenth Amendment.

Section 2: Vacancies
If a Senate seat becomes vacant, and if the legislature of that state approves, the governor of that state may appoint a replacement senator until an election can be held.

Section 3: Previously Elected Senators

Eighteenth Amendment

Section 1.
~~After one year from the ratification of this article, the manufacture, sale, or transportation of intoxicating liquors within, the importation thereof into, or the exportation thereof from the United States and all territory subject to the jurisdiction thereof for beverage purposes is hereby prohibited.~~

Section 2.
~~The Congress and the several States shall have concurrent power to enforce this article by appropriate legislation.~~

Section 3.
~~This article shall be inoperative unless it shall have been ratified as an amendment to the Constitution by the legislatures of the several States, as provided in the Constitution, within seven years from the date of the submission hereof to the States by the Congress.~~

Nineteenth Amendment

Section 1.
The right of citizens of the United States to vote shall not be denied or abridged by the United States or by any State on account of sex.

Section 2.
Congress shall have power to enforce this article by appropriate legislation.

Twentieth Amendment

Section 1.
The terms of the President and Vice President shall end at noon on the 20th day of January, and the terms of Senators and Representatives at noon on the 3d day of January, of the years in which such terms would have ended if this article had not been ratified; and the terms of their successors shall then begin.

Eighteenth Amendment (1919)
Prohibition of Liquor

Section 1: Ban on Alcohol
This amendment outlawed the production, sale, and transport of alcoholic beverages within the United States. It was the culmination of a decades-long reform effort to end the problems associated with alcohol abuse. This sweeping ban proved impossible to enforce. Prohibition led to a rise in lawlessness and organized crime as the alcohol business flourished illegally. Prohibition ended when the Twenty-first Amendment *repealed*, or canceled, this amendment.

Section 2: Enforcement

Section 3: Ratification

Nineteenth Amendment (1920)
Women's Suffrage

Section 1: Right to Vote
This amendment guaranteed women the right to vote. The women's suffrage movement had sought this right since 1848. Although some western states already allowed women to vote, activists argued that a constitutional amendment was needed to guarantee the vote to all women. The Nineteenth Amendment is sometimes called the Susan B. Anthony amendment after its most prominent and persistent advocate.

Section 2: Enforcement

Twentieth Amendment (1933)
Terms of Office

Section 1: Beginning of Terms
The president and vice president take office on January 20. Members of Congress begin their terms on January 3. Prior to this amendment, these terms of office began on March 3. These calendar changes shortened the period during which a "lame duck"—an incumbent who was not reelected or did not run for reelection—remained in office.

Section 2.

The Congress shall assemble at least once in every year, and such meeting shall begin at noon on the 3d day of January, unless they shall by law appoint a different day.

Section 3.

If, at the time fixed for the beginning of the term of the President, the President elect shall have died, the Vice President elect shall become President. If a President shall not have been chosen before the time fixed for the beginning of his term, or if the President elect shall have failed to qualify, then the Vice President elect shall act as President until a President shall have qualified; and the Congress may by law provide for the case wherein neither a President elect nor a Vice President shall have qualified, declaring who shall then act as President, or the manner in which one who is to act shall be selected, and such person shall act accordingly until a President or Vice President shall have qualified.

Section 4.

The Congress may by law provide for the case of the death of any of the persons from whom the House of Representatives may choose a President whenever the right of choice shall have devolved upon them, and for the case of the death of any of the persons from whom the Senate may choose a Vice President whenever the right of choice shall have devolved upon them.

Section 5.

Sections 1 and 2 shall take effect on the 15th day of October following the ratification of this article.

Section 6.

This article shall be inoperative unless it shall have been ratified as an amendment to the Constitution by the legislatures of three-fourths of the several States within seven years from the date of its submission.

Twenty-first Amendment

Section 1.

The eighteenth article of amendment to the Constitution of the United States is hereby repealed.

Section 2.

The transportation or importation into any State, Territory, or Possession of the United States for delivery or use therein of intoxicating liquors, in violation of the laws thereof, is hereby prohibited.

Section 3.

This article shall be inoperative unless it shall have been ratified as an amendment to the Constitution by conventions in the several States, as provided in the Constitution, within seven years from the date of the submission hereof to the States by the Congress.

Section 2: Congressional Session

Section 3: Presidential Succession
This and Section 4 provide for succession if a newly elected president should die or be unable to take office before the start of his or her term.

Section 4: Congress Decides Succession

Section 5: Date of Implementation

Section 6: Ratification

Twenty-first Amendment (1933)
End of Prohibition

Section 1: Repeal
This amendment ended national prohibition, leaving it to states to ban alcohol if they wished.

Section 2: State Laws
Alcoholic beverages may not be brought into a state where they are still banned.

Section 3: Ratification
This amendment was the only one ratified by special state conventions rather than state legislatures. Most Americans were eager to end prohibition, and this method was quicker.

Twenty-second Amendment

Section 1.
No person shall be elected to the office of the President more than twice, and no person who has held the office of President, or acted as President, for more than two years of a term to which some other person was elected President shall be elected to the office of the President more than once. But this Article shall not apply to any person holding the office of President when this Article was proposed by Congress, and shall not prevent any person who may be holding the office of President, or acting as President, during the term within which this Article becomes operative from holding the office of President or acting as President during the remainder of such term.

Section 2.
This article shall be inoperative unless it shall have been ratified as an amendment to the Constitution by the legislatures of three-fourths of the several States within seven years from the date of its submission to the States by the Congress.

Twenty-third Amendment

Section 1.
The District constituting the seat of government of the United States shall appoint in such manner as the Congress may direct:

A number of electors of President and Vice President equal to the whole number of Senators and Representatives in Congress to which the District would be entitled if it were a state, but in no event more than the least populous State; they shall be in addition to those appointed by the States, but they shall be considered, for the purposes of the election of President and Vice President, to be electors appointed by a State; and they shall meet in the District and perform such duties as provided by the twelfth article of amendment.

Section 2.
The Congress shall have power to enforce this article by appropriate legislation.

Twenty-fourth Amendment

Section 1.
The right of citizens of the United States to vote in any primary or other election for President or Vice President, for electors for President or Vice President, or for Senator or Representative in Congress, shall not be denied or abridged by the United States or any State by reason of failure to pay any poll tax or other tax.

Twenty-second Amendment (1951)
Term Limits for the Presidency

Section 1: Two-Term Limit
The Constitution did not specify how many terms a president could serve, but George Washington stepped down after two terms, and succeeding presidents followed his example. In 1940, with World War II looming, Democratic president Franklin D. Roosevelt broke precedent by running for a third term. He was elected in 1940 and again in 1944. After his death in 1945, Republicans in Congress proposed this amendment to limit future presidents to two terms.

Section 2: Ratification

Twenty-third Amendment (1961)
Electors for Washington, D.C.

Section 1: Number of Electors
This amendment gives the citizens of Washington, D.C., the right to vote in presidential elections. It allots to the District of Columbia the same number of presidential electors it would have if it were a state. Until this amendment was enacted, District of Columbia residents could not vote for president, even though they had all the obligations of citizenship, including taxation. In 1978, Congress passed a constitutional amendment that would have made the District a state, but the states failed to ratify it.

Section 2: Enforcement

Twenty-fourth Amendment (1964)
Abolition of Poll Tax

Section 1: Ban on Poll Taxes
A *poll tax* is a fee that a voter must pay in order to vote. This amendment bans poll taxes, which some states imposed to prevent African Americans from voting.

Section 2.

The Congress shall have power to enforce this article by appropriate legislation.

Twenty-fifth Amendment

Section 1.

In case of the removal of the President from office or of his death or resignation, the Vice President shall become President.

Section 2.

Whenever there is a vacancy in the office of the Vice President, the President shall nominate a Vice President who shall take office upon confirmation by a majority vote of both Houses of Congress.

Section 3.

Whenever the President transmits to the President pro tempore of the Senate and the Speaker of the House of Representatives his written declaration that he is unable to discharge the powers and duties of his office, and until he transmits to them a written declaration to the contrary, such powers and duties shall be discharged by the Vice President as Acting President.

Section 4.

Whenever the Vice President and a majority of either the principal officers of the executive departments or of such other body as Congress may by law provide, transmit to the President pro tempore of the Senate and the Speaker of the House of Representatives their written declaration that the President is unable to discharge the powers and duties of his office, the Vice President shall immediately assume the powers and duties of the office as Acting President.

Thereafter, when the President transmits to the President pro tempore of the Senate and the Speaker of the House of Representatives his written declaration that no inability exists, he shall resume the powers and duties of his office unless the Vice President and a majority of either the principal officers of the executive department or of such other body as Congress may by law provide, transmit within four days to the President pro tempore of the Senate and the Speaker of the House of Representatives their written declaration that the President is unable to discharge the powers and duties of his office. Thereupon Congress shall

Section 2: Enforcement

Twenty-fifth Amendment (1967) Presidential Succession

Section 1: President's Death or Removal
If the president dies, resigns, or is removed from office, the vice president becomes president.

Section 2: Vice Presidential Vacancy
If the vice presidency becomes vacant, the president can appoint a vice president, who must be confirmed by Congress. This amendment was first applied in 1973, when Vice President Spiro Agnew resigned in the face of bribery and corruption charges. President Nixon appointed Gerald Ford to be vice president. Within a year, Nixon himself resigned over the Watergate scandal. Ford became president and appointed Nelson Rockefeller vice president. Ford and Rockefeller became the nation's only unelected president and vice president.

Section 3: President Incapacitated
The "disability clause" provides for the vice president to act as president if the president informs Congress that he or she is too ill to perform the duties of office.

Section 4: Vice President as Acting President
This section spells out the process by which the vice president takes over as president if the president is unconscious or unable or unwilling to admit that he or she is incapacitated.

decide the issue, assembling within forty-eight hours for that purpose if not in session. If the Congress, within twenty-one days after receipt of the latter written declaration, or, if Congress is not in session, within twenty-one days after Congress is required to assemble, determines by two-thirds vote of both Houses that the President is unable to discharge the powers and duties of his office, the Vice President shall continue to discharge the same as Acting President; otherwise, the President shall resume the powers and duties of his office.

Twenty-sixth Amendment

Section 1.
The right of citizens of the United States, who are eighteen years of age or older, to vote shall not be denied or abridged by the United States or by any State on account of age.

Section 2.
The Congress shall have power to enforce this article by appropriate legislation.

Twenty-seventh Amendment
No law, varying the compensation for the services of the Senators and Representatives, shall take effect, until an election of Representatives shall have intervened.

Twenty-sixth Amendment (1971) Voting Age

Section 1: The Right to Vote
This amendment lowered the voting age to 18. Previously, the voting age was 21. The amendment was passed and ratified during the Vietnam War, when Americans questioned the fairness of drafting 18-year-olds to fight a war, but not allowing them to vote for the leaders who make decisions about war.

Section 2: Enforcement

Twenty-seventh Amendment (1992) Congressional Pay
If members of Congress vote to raise their own pay, the pay increase cannot go into effect until after the next congressional election. James Madison introduced this amendment in 1789 along with the Bill of Rights. It took over 200 years for it to be ratified by the required number of states.

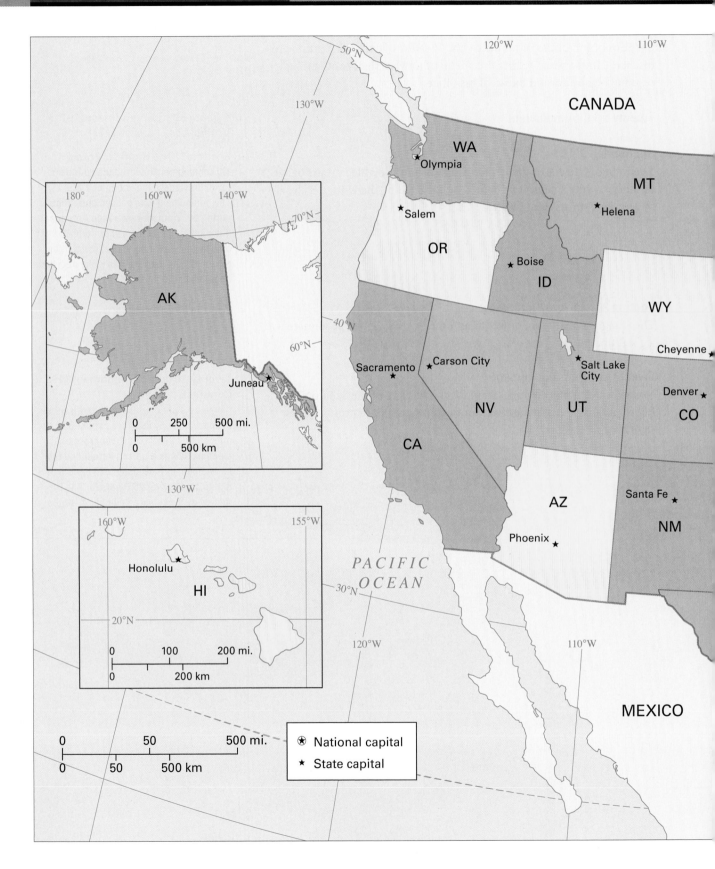

MEXICO

PACIFIC
OCEAN

CANADA

WA
★Olympia

★Salem

OR

MT
★Helena

★Boise
ID

WY
Cheyenne ★

Sacramento
★

★Carson City

NV

Salt Lake
★ City

UT

Denver ★

CO

CA

AZ

Santa Fe ★

NM

Phoenix ★

AK

Juneau ★

| 0 | 250 | 500 mi. |
| 0 | | 500 km |

HI

Honolulu ★

| 0 | 100 | 200 mi. |
| 0 | | 200 km |

| 0 | 50 | 500 mi. |
| 0 | 50 | 500 km |

⊛ National capital
★ State capital

ND
★ Bismarck

MN
St. Paul ★

SD
Pierre ★

NE
Lincoln ★

IA
Des Moines ★

WI
Madison ★

MI
Lansing ★

IL
Springfield ★

IN
Indianapolis ★

OH
Columbus ★

MO
Jefferson City ★

KS
Topeka ★

KY
Frankfort ★

TN
Nashville ★

OK
Oklahoma City ★

AR
Little Rock ★

MS
Jackson ★

AL
Montgomery ★

LA
Baton Rouge ★

TX
Austin ★

WV
Charleston ★

VA
Richmond ★

NC
Raleigh ★

SC
Columbia ★

GA
Atlanta ★

FL
Tallahassee ★

PA
Harrisburg ★

NY
Albany ★

ME
Augusta ★

VT
Montpelier ★

NH
Concord ★

MA
Boston ★
Hartford ★

RI
Providence ★

CT

NJ
Trenton ★

DE
Dover ★

MD
Annapolis ★
Washington, D.C.

ATLANTIC
OCEAN

Gulf of Mexico

N
W E
S

100°W   90°W   80°W   70°W   50°N

40°N

30°N

100°W

90°W

Tropic of Cancer

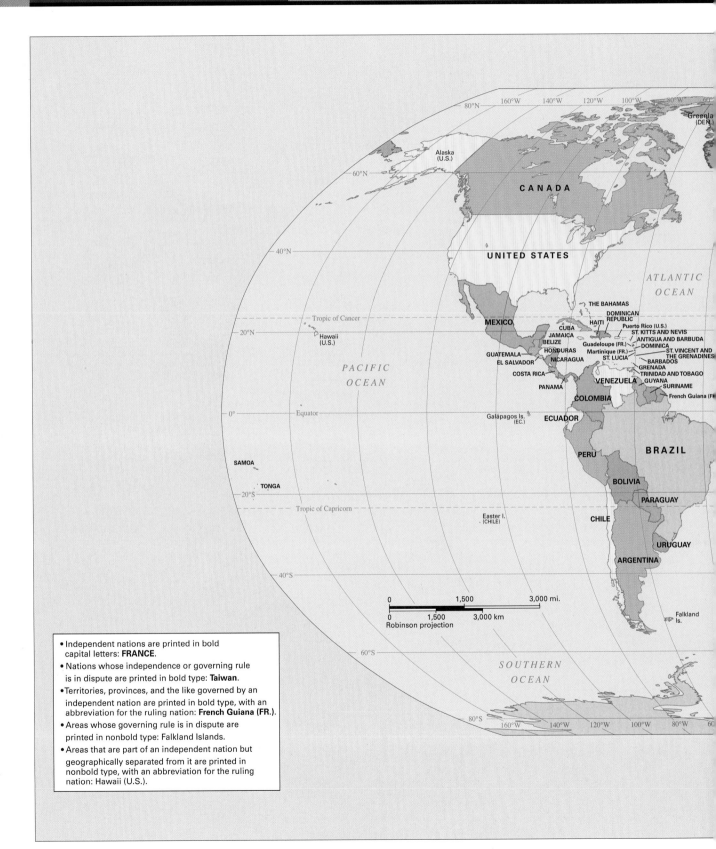

80°N 160°W 140°W 120°W 100°W 80°W 60°

Greenla
(DEN.)

Alaska
(U.S.)

60°N

CANADA

40°N

UNITED STATES

ATLANTIC
OCEAN

Tropic of Cancer

THE BAHAMAS

DOMINICAN
REPUBLIC

20°N

MEXICO

CUBA

HAITI

Puerto Rico (U.S.)

JAMAICA

ST. KITTS AND NEVIS
ANTIGUA AND BARBUDA

Hawaii
(U.S.)

BELIZE

Guadeloupe (FR.)

DOMINICA

GUATEMALA

HONDURAS

Martinique (FR.)

ST. VINCENT AND
THE GRENADINES

EL SALVADOR

NICARAGUA

ST. LUCIA

BARBADOS

PACIFIC
OCEAN

COSTA RICA

GRENADA

TRINIDAD AND TOBAGO

VENEZUELA

GUYANA

PANAMA

SURINAME

COLOMBIA

French Guiana (FR

0°

Equator

Galápagos Is.
(EC.)

ECUADOR

BRAZIL

PERU

SAMOA

BOLIVIA

TONGA

PARAGUAY

20°S

Tropic of Capricorn

Easter I.
(CHILE)

CHILE

URUGUAY

ARGENTINA

40°S

0   1,500   3,000 mi.

0   1,500   3,000 km
Robinson projection

Falkland
Is.

60°S

SOUTHERN
OCEAN

80°S

160°W 140°W 120°W 100°W 80°W 60

- Independent nations are printed in bold
  capital letters: **FRANCE**.
- Nations whose independence or governing rule
  is in dispute are printed in bold type: **Taiwan**.
- Territories, provinces, and the like governed by an
  independent nation are printed in bold type, with an
  abbreviation for the ruling nation: **French Guiana (FR.)**.
- Areas whose governing rule is in dispute are
  printed in nonbold type: Falkland Islands.
- Areas that are part of an independent nation but
  geographically separated from it are printed in
  nonbold type, with an abbreviation for the ruling
  nation: Hawaii (U.S.).

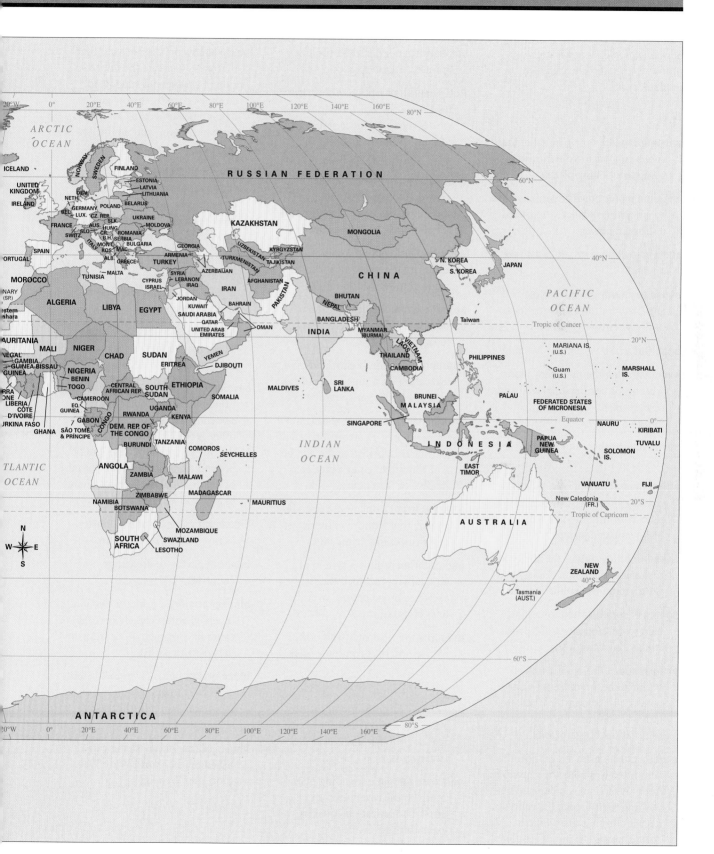

ARCTIC OCEAN

ICELAND

UNITED KINGDOM

IRELAND

NORWAY

SWEDEN

FINLAND

ESTONIA
LATVIA
LITHUANIA

DEN.

NETH.
BEL.
GERMANY POLAND BELARUS
LUX. CZ. REP.
FRANCE AUS. UKRAINE
SLO. HUNG. MOLDOVA
SWITZ. CR.
ITALY MONT. SERBIA ROMANIA
B.H. BULGARIA
ALB. KOS. MAC.
PORTUGAL SPAIN GREECE GEORGIA
MALTA TURKEY ARMENIA
TUNISIA CYPRUS SYRIA AZERBAIJAN
ISRAEL LEBANON IRAQ
MOROCCO JORDAN KUWAIT
ALGERIA LIBYA EGYPT SAUDI ARABIA
CANARY IS. (SP.) QATAR
Western Sahara UNITED ARAB
EMIRATES OMAN

RUSSIAN FEDERATION

KAZAKHSTAN

UZBEKISTAN KYRGYZSTAN
TURKMENISTAN TAJIKISTAN

AFGHANISTAN

IRAN

PAKISTAN

MONGOLIA

CHINA

N. KOREA
S. KOREA JAPAN

BHUTAN
NEPAL

PACIFIC OCEAN

Tropic of Cancer

MARIANA IS.
(U.S.)

20°N

MAURITANIA

SENEGAL
GAMBIA
GUINEA-BISSAU
GUINEA
SIERRA LEONE
LIBERIA
CÔTE D'IVOIRE
BURKINA FASO
GHANA

MALI NIGER
CHAD SUDAN

NIGERIA
BENIN
TOGO

CENTRAL
AFRICAN REP.

EQ.
GUINEA
SÃO TOMÉ
& PRÍNCIPE

GABON
CONGO

CAMEROON

SOUTH
SUDAN

DEM. REP. OF
THE CONGO

ERITREA
DJIBOUTI
ETHIOPIA
SOMALIA

YEMEN

RWANDA
BURUNDI

UGANDA
KENYA

TANZANIA

BANGLADESH
INDIA

MYANMAR
(BURMA)

MALDIVES

SRI
LANKA

LAOS
THAILAND
CAMBODIA

VIETNAM

Taiwan

PHILIPPINES

Guam
(U.S.)

MARSHALL
IS.

BRUNEI
MALAYSIA

PALAU

FEDERATED STATES
OF MICRONESIA

Equator

NAURU

KIRIBATI

ATLANTIC OCEAN

ANGOLA

COMOROS
SEYCHELLES

ZAMBIA
MALAWI

NAMIBIA
BOTSWANA
ZIMBABWE

MADAGASCAR

MAURITIUS

SINGAPORE

INDIAN OCEAN

INDONESIA

PAPUA
NEW
GUINEA

SOLOMON
IS.

TUVALU

EAST
TIMOR

VANUATU

New Caledonia
(FR.)

FIJI

20°S

AUSTRALIA

Tropic of Capricorn

SOUTH
AFRICA

MOZAMBIQUE
SWAZILAND
LESOTHO

N
W E
S

NEW
ZEALAND

40°S

Tasmania
(AUST.)

60°S

ANTARCTICA

80°S

Speaking of Politics terms are in **green** *type. Other key terms are in* **black** *type.*

A

absentee ballot a mail-in ballot that voters can use to vote instead of going to a polling place

absolute monarchy a government led by a hereditary ruler who claims unlimited powers

abstain to choose not to cast a vote on a bill

abuse of power the misuse of authority for harmful, unethical, or illegal ends

acquittal a trial verdict of "not guilty"

administration the president, along with his or her personal staff and advisers; also, a president's time in office

advocacy speaking out on issues of concern

affirmative action the practice of making special efforts to admit, recruit, or hire members of disadvantaged groups

agenda-setting power the ability to make issues a public priority and get them on the public agenda

agents of socialization forces that help to develop a person's political values and attitudes

ambassador a diplomatic official of the highest rank sent by one country as its long-term representative to another country or to an international organization

amicus curiae brief a legal document submitted to a court by a group not party to a particular case but wishing to influence the court's decision in that case; *amicus curiae* means "friend of the court"

amnesty a general pardon usually granted to a group of people

Anti-Federalists opponents of ratification of the U.S. Constitution, who favored the loose association of states established under the Articles of Confederation

antiterrorism the foreign policy view that the greatest threat to the United States comes from terrorist groups, such as al Qaeda

appellate jurisdiction a court's authority to review decisions made in lower courts

apportionment the distribution of seats in a legislature according to law

appropriations funds allocated by a legislature for a stated purpose as part of a budget or spending bill

arraignment the stage in the criminal process when a person accused of a crime is informed of the charges and allowed to enter a plea of "guilty" or "not guilty"

arrest warrant a document issued by a judge that authorizes the arrest of a suspect in a crime

authoritarian regime a system of government in which the state exercises broad control over the lives of its citizens

authority the legal right and power to give orders and enforce rules

B

bail money given over to a court in exchange for a criminal suspect's release from jail until his or her trial begins

balanced budget a spending plan in which the revenues coming into an organization equal its expenditures

bandwagon a persuasive technique that seeks to create the impression of widespread support for a cause or candidate; the goal is to convince others to "jump on the bandwagon" and not be left behind

battleground states states where the presidential vote is likely to be close; candidates often focus on these states in the hope of picking up key electoral votes

benchmark poll a long, detailed survey of voter opinion designed to help political candidates craft their campaigns

bench trial a court case in which a judge, not a jury, decides the outcome

beyond a reasonable doubt the legal principle that the evidence presented in a trial must allow for no other reasonable explanation than the one given; the phrase "guilty beyond a reasonable doubt" is part of the instruction given by a judge to a jury in a criminal case

bicameral made up of two houses, as in a bicameral legislature

bilateral having to do with two countries

blanket primary a primary election in which voters can choose one candidate for each office from any party's primary list

block grants funds given by the federal government to states without restrictions on how the money should be spent

blog a journal or newsletter published on the World Wide Web; short for "Web log"

blue-slip policy the process by which a senator can block the nomination of a federal official, such as a judge, who comes from his or her home state; the blue slip refers to a blue approval form that senators may or may not choose to sign

bond a certificate of debt owed to a lender by a government or corporation; a government issues bonds to raise money, promising to repay the value of the bonds, plus interest

boycott a refusal to buy a country's goods, or to take part in an international event involving that country, as a protest against the country's policies

broadcast media means of communication that distribute information through the airwaves to a mass audience, particularly radio and television

budget crisis a situation caused by the failure of Congress and the president to reach agreement on a new budget and that may result in the shutdown of government programs

budget cycle the various steps of the government budget process, from planning to implementation

budget proposal the president's annual budget plan as proposed to Congress

budget resolution an official statement outlining Congress's spending priorities for the annual budget

budget surplus the amount by which an organization's revenues exceed its expenditures

burden of proof the obligation in a legal case to prove allegations by presenting strong supporting evidence; in a criminal case this burden rests on the prosecution and in a civil case it rests on the plaintiff

bureaucracy a large, complex organization that functions under uniform rules and procedures

C

cabinet the heads of the executive departments of the federal government

capital crime a felony punishable by death

capitalism an economic system in which individual investors, or capitalists, privately own the means of production; also known as a free enterprise system

capital punishment the imposition of the death penalty on a person by the state

card-stacking a persuasive technique that involves the use of facts, statistics, and other evidence to support one side of an argument

casework personal services provided by members of Congress to their constituents, often to help their constituents with problems they are having with the federal bureaucracy

caucus a meeting of party members to choose party officials or nominees for elective office

centrism an ideology at the middle of the political spectrum that combines elements of both liberal and conservative thought

charter a written grant of authority

checks and balances a system in which each branch of government can limit the power of the other branches

chief executive the top elected official in charge of enforcing laws and carrying out government policy

chief of staff the head of the White House staff

Christmas tree bill a bill with so many riders attached to it that it seems to offer something for everyone

circumstantial evidence information about a crime that can be inferred from other facts

citizenship the status of being a citizen, a person who by birth or naturalization enjoys certain rights and has certain duties in a nation-state

city-state a sovereign state consisting of a city and its surrounding territory

civic virtue the ancient Roman idea that citizens should serve their country

civil having to do with citizens, as in civil rights

civil case a legal case that does not involve criminal conduct, such as a lawsuit

civil disobedience a form of protest in which people disobey a law they consider unjust

civil law the branch of law that concerns relationships between private parties

civil liberties basic freedoms guaranteed under the U.S. Constitution, such as freedom of speech and freedom of religion

civil rights guarantees of equal rights and equal treatment under the law, such as trial by jury and voting rights

civil servant a civilian employee who works in a government agency

civil society associations and other voluntary groups that form a middle layer in society between government and individual families

closed primary a primary election in which voting is restricted to party members

closed rule a condition placed on a bill by the House Rules Committee that severely limits floor debate and amendments; this allows the bill to move through the House quickly, with few changes

cloture the process used to end a filibuster in the Senate; at least 60 senators must support a cloture vote to overcome a filibuster

coattail effect the influence that a popular politician may have on voters, making them more likely to choose other candidates from his or her party

coercion the use of force or threats to make people do things against their will

collective security a system for maintaining peace based on an agreement among nations to act together to prevent or defend against aggression

command economy an economic system that relies mainly on the central government to determine what goods and services to produce and how to produce them

Commerce Clause a clause in Article 1, Section 8 of the U.S. Constitution that allows Congress to regulate trade with other nations and among the states

commission system a form of city government led by a group of professional commissioners chosen for their skills and expertise; became popular in the early 1900s

communism a system of government in which a single political party controls both the government and the economy; also, the theories developed by Karl Marx regarding the development of an ideal, classless society

compact a written agreement between two or more parties or nations to perform some action

concurrent powers powers shared by the federal and state governments under the U.S. Constitution

concurring opinion a document issued by Supreme Court justices who agree with a Court decision, but for different reasons than those expressed in the majority opinion

confederal system of government a political system in which independent states form a nation but retain their power under a weak central government

conferees the members of a congressional conference committee

conference committee a temporary committee of legislators from both the House and Senate created to work out differences in bills passed by both chambers

congressional page a high school junior who works as a messenger and errand-runner in the House or Senate

conservatism an ideology favoring a limited role for government and more private initiative by nongovernmental groups in efforts to solve society's problems

constituent a person who lives in an electoral district and is represented by an elected official

constitutional democracy a democratic government based on a written constitution

constitutionalism the belief that governments should operate according to an agreed set of principles, which are usually spelled out in a written constitution

constitutional monarchy a system of government in which the powers of a monarch are limited by a constitution, either written or unwritten

consulate a branch of an embassy that deals mainly with passport, visa, and trade issues

containment the foreign policy view that the United States should contain, or control, aggressive nations that threaten world peace

continuing resolution a joint resolution, passed by Congress and signed by the president, that allows the government to operate at current funding levels for a fixed period; required when Congress and the president cannot reach agreement on a new budget

convention an international agreement on matters of broad interest

cooperative federalism a federal system with considerable sharing of powers among national, state, and local governments; also known as "marble cake" federalism

copyright the legal right granted to creators of original works—such as books, music, art, and software—to control the production, sale, or distribution of those works

corporate income tax a tax paid by businesses on their profits each year

council-manager system a system of city government in which an elected city council makes policy decisions but leaves the daily task of running the government to a hired city manager

counterfeiting the illegal copying and sale of items protected by patents; also the forging of money

county seat the town or city in which a county government is based

coup d'etat the sudden overthrow of a government by a small group of military officers or political leaders; from a French term meaning "blow to the state"

covenant a legally binding agreement

covert action a secret operation that supports a country's foreign policy

criminal law the branch of law that regulates the conduct of individuals, defines crimes, and provides punishments for criminal acts

cross-examination the questioning of a witness in court by an attorney for the opposing side

D

damages money paid by the liable party in a lawsuit to compensate for losses suffered by the plaintiff

defendant the person or party in a criminal trial who is charged with committing a crime, or the person or party being sued in a civil case

deficit spending government expenditures financed by borrowing rather than by tax revenues

delegated powers powers granted to the national government rather than to the states under the U.S. Constitution

democracy a system of government in which citizens exercise supreme power, acting either directly on their own or through elected representatives

democratic socialism an ideology that advocates socialism as a basis for the economy and democracy as a governing principle

despot a tyrant or ruler with absolute powers

determinate sentencing the practice of assigning a convicted criminal a fixed term in prison

devolution the transfer of power from a central government to a regional or local government

dictatorship a system of government in which a single person or group exercises supreme power by controlling the military and police

diplomacy the art and practice of managing communication and relationships between nations

diplomatic immunity international law that protects diplomats and their families from being arrested or tried in countries other than their own

diplomatic recognition official acceptance of a regime as the legitimate government of its country

direct democracy a democratic form of government in which citizens make public decisions directly, either in a popular assembly or through a popular vote

direct evidence information about a crime provided by a witness who saw the crime, or by a video or audio recording of the crime

discretionary spending government expenditures that can be raised or lowered as determined by Congress

disengagement the foreign policy view that the United States should avoid military actions in other parts of the world

dissenting opinion a document issued by Supreme Court justices who disagree with a Court decision, stating the reasons for their dissent

divine right of kings the idea that European monarchs had a God-given right to rule and thus deserved absolute power

docket the list of cases on a court's schedule

double jeopardy the prosecution of a person a second time for a crime for which the defendant has already been tried once and found not guilty; prohibited under the Fifth Amendment

dual federalism a federal system with a fairly strict division of powers between the national and state governments; also called "layer cake" federalism

due process the principle that no person can be deprived of life, liberty, or property without fair legal procedures and safeguards

E

earmarks specific spending proposals that members of Congress attach to legislation, usually to benefit their home districts or states

economic system a way of organizing the production and consumption of goods and services

Elastic Clause a clause in Article 1, Section 8 of the U.S. Constitution that allows Congress to stretch its lawmaking powers to include laws that are "necessary and proper" for carrying out its duties; also known as the Necessary and Proper Clause

Electoral College a body of electors from each state who cast votes to elect the president and vice president

electronic media computers, cell phones, and other communication devices that connect via the Internet to the World Wide Web

elite a small group of people within a larger group who have more power, wealth, or talent than the others

embargo a ban on trade with another country

embassy the official headquarters of an ambassador and his or her staff

eminent domain the government's right to take private property for public use, as long as fair compensation is paid; the right to fair compensation is guaranteed under the Fifth Amendment

entitlements benefits that must be provided to all eligible people who seek them; examples include Social Security and Medicare

enumerated powers those powers of the national government that are specifically listed in the U.S. Constitution

environmentalism an ideology that emphasizes conservation and protection of the environment

Equal Protection Clause a clause in the Fourteenth Amendment declaring that no state may deny "equal protection of the laws" to any person within that state

error of law a mistake made by a judge in applying the law to a specific case

estate tax a tax placed on the value of a person's property and possessions at the time of death

ethnic cleansing the mass removal and murder of an ethnic group in a particular area

excise tax a tax levied on the sale of certain goods and services

exclusionary rule the principle that illegally seized evidence cannot be used in a court of law

executive department an organization within the executive branch that carries out the work of government in a broad area of public policy, such as agriculture or labor

executive order a rule or regulation issued by a president or governor that has the force of law

executive privilege the right to keep internal discussions and documents of the White House private

exit poll a survey of voters, taken as they leave the polling place, to predict the winners on Election Day

exploratory committee a group of advisers who evaluate a potential candidate's chances of getting elected before launching a campaign

expressed powers the powers given specifically to the national government by the U.S. Constitution; also known as enumerated or delegated powers

F

factors of production the basic resources required to produce goods and services: land, labor, and capital

fascism a totalitarian system in which businesses remain in private hands but under government control

federal deficit the amount by which the national government's annual expenditures exceed its revenues

federalism a political system in which power is divided between a central government and smaller regional governments

Federalists supporters of ratification of the U.S. Constitution, who favored the creation of a strong federal government that shared power with the states

federal system of government a type of government in which power is shared between the national government and smaller regional governments within the nation

felony a serious crime that is usually punishable by more than one year in prison

feudalism an economic and political system of the European Middle Ages in which landowners granted land to tenants in return for military assistance and other services

filibuster the tactic of using endless speeches on the Senate floor to delay or prevent passage of legislation; filibusters are not permitted in the House

fiscal year the 12-month accounting period an organization uses for budgeting, record keeping, and financial reporting

527 committees groups not tied to any political party that can raise and spend unlimited funds to support or oppose candidates; formed under section 527 of the tax code

focus group a small group of people who are brought together to share their opinions on a topic of concern

foreign policy a course of action developed by a country's leaders to pursue the nation's vital interests in its dealings with other countries

formal authority power to give orders and enforce rules that has been defined in a legal or official way

free enterprise system an economic system that relies on the profit motive, economic competition, and the forces of supply and demand to direct the production and distribution of goods and services; also known as capitalism

G

general election an election in which voters choose among candidates from different parties to fill an elective office

general jurisdiction the authority of a court to hear cases on a variety of subjects

gerrymandering drawing the boundaries of a legislative district with the intent of giving one party or group a significant advantage

glittering generalities a persuasive technique that involves the use of vague, sweeping statements that appeal to the emotions but convey little of substance

global climate change variations in Earth's overall climate over periods of time

globalization the trend toward more open, or less restricted, and free travel, trade, and communication among nations and their peoples

global warming an increase in world temperatures, believed to be caused by increased greenhouse gases in the atmosphere

"gotcha" journalism election news coverage that focuses on catching the candidates making mistakes or looking foolish

government institutions and officials organized to establish and carry out public policy

grand jury a group of citizens who examine the evidence in a serious criminal case to decide whether a person accused of a crime should be indicted, or charged

grants-in-aid funds given by the federal government to state and local governments for specific programs

grassroots mobilization the rallying of strong and vocal support from a large group of people at the local level

green card an identification card issued to immigrants who are legal residents of the United States

H

habeas corpus the right of accused persons to be brought before a judge to hear the charges against them

hold a request by a senator to delay action on a bill

horse race coverage political campaign reporting that focuses on who is winning and why

human rights rights that are regarded as belonging to all people; such as the right to life, liberty, and equality before the law, as well as freedom of religion, expression, and assembly

hung jury a jury that is deadlocked and cannot agree on a verdict

I

ideology a basic set of political beliefs about the roles of government and the individual in society

impeachment a formal charge of wrongdoing against the president or other public official; the first step in removal from office

implied powers those powers of the national government, and particularly of Congress, that are not specifically listed in the Constitution, but which the government can reasonably claim as part of its governing responsibility

impoundment the refusal by a chief executive to spend funds that have been appropriated by the legislature

incarceration imprisonment in a jail, prison, or other correctional facility as punishment for a crime

incorporation the process by which the Supreme Court applies the Bill of Rights to the states through the Due Process Clause of the Fourteenth Amendment

incumbent a public official seeking reelection to the position he or she currently occupies

independent agency an organization within the executive branch that does not belong to any executive department and answers directly to the president

independent judiciary a system of judges and courts that is separate from other branches of government

indeterminate sentencing the practice of assigning a convicted criminal a variable term in prison

indictment a formal accusation of criminal behavior handed down by a grand jury; this means that the accused person will be brought to trial

individual income tax a tax levied on the annual income of an individual or a married couple

individual rights the rights and liberties that can be claimed by individuals by virtue of being human; also called natural rights or human rights

inheritance tax a tax placed on those who inherit property and possessions after a person's death

initiative process a form of direct democracy in which citizens propose laws and submit them directly to the voters for approval

institution an established organization, especially one providing a public service, and the rules that guide it

intelligence information about the activities and intentions of other countries

interest group any organized group whose members share a common goal and try to promote their interests by influencing government policymaking and decision making

intergovernmental organization (IGO) an international group formed by nations, often with the goal of increasing trade or security

interpretivism an approach to interpreting the U.S. Constitution that takes modern values and social consequences into account; also known as loose construction

interstate commerce trade that takes place between two states or among several states

intrastate commerce trade that takes place within the borders of a state

isolationism the foreign policy view that the United States should withdraw from world affairs

issue ad a political advertisement funded and produced by an interest group rather than by an election campaign

J

Jim Crow laws laws that enforced segregation and denied legal equality to African Americans

joint committee a permanent committee of legislators from both the House and Senate that deals with matters of common interest, such as economic policy

joint resolution an official statement issued by both houses of Congress; once signed by the president, a joint resolution has the force of law

judicial activism the principle that the Supreme Court should use its power of judicial review to overturn bad precedents and promote socially desirable goals

judicial restraint the principle that judicial review should be used sparingly, especially in dealing with controversial issues

judicial review the power of the courts to declare laws and executive acts unconstitutional

judicial temperament the personal qualities considered important in a judge, such as patience, compassion, and commitment to equal justice

jurisdiction the subject matter over which a court may exercise authority; also, a court's power to hear a case

L

lawful permanent resident an immigrant who is legally authorized to live and work in the United States permanently, but is not a U.S. citizen; also known as a resident alien or legal resident

leak an unofficial release of confidential information to the news media

least developed countries (LDCs) the poorest countries in the world, numbering around 50, with the lowest per capita incomes and living standards

legal brief a written document drawn up by an attorney that presents the facts and points of law in a client's case

legislative hearing a meeting of lawmakers to hear testimony and gather information on a proposed piece of legislation

legitimacy the quality of being accepted as an authority, often applied to laws or those in power

libel publishing false information about someone with intent to cause harm

liberalism an ideology favoring an active role for government in efforts to solve society's problems

libertarianism an ideology based on a strong belief in personal freedom and a minimal role for government

limited government a political system in which the powers exercised by the government are restricted, usually by a written constitution

limited jurisdiction the right of certain courts to hear only specialized kinds of cases, such as traffic violations or bankruptcy issues

line of succession the order of successors to the presidency if the president is unable to serve as specified in the Constitution and federal law

litigation the process of bringing a lawsuit against someone

lobbying an organized effort to influence the policy process by persuading public officials to favor or oppose action on a specific issue

logrolling the trading of votes among legislators to ensure the passage of various bills in which they have a special interest

loose construction a flexible approach to interpreting the U.S. Constitution, taking into account current conditions in society

lottery a large-scale, legal gambling game organized to raise money for a public cause

M

Machiavellian characterized by cunning or ruthless methods to obtain and maintain power; associated with the political philosophy of Niccoló Machiavelli that "the end justifies the means"

majority opinion a document issued by the Supreme Court that states the reasons for its decision as determined by the majority of justices

majority rule the idea that decisions approved by more than half of the people in a group or society will be accepted and observed by all of the people

mandate of heaven an ancient Chinese doctrine that the ruler was the "son of heaven" and thus enjoyed supreme authority

mandatory spending government expenditures required by law to be allocated in specified ways

margin of error a measure of the accuracy of an opinion poll

market any place or situation in which people buy or sell goods and services

market economy an economic system that relies mainly on markets to determine what goods and services to produce and how to produce them

markup session a meeting of a legislative committee at which members amend, or "mark up," a bill before putting it to a vote

martial law military rule established over a civilian population during a time of emergency

mass media means of communication that reach a large audience

mayor-council system a system of city government in which voters elect both city council members and a mayor; the mayor may have either weak or strong executive powers

media bias real or imagined prejudice that is thought to affect what stories journalists cover and how they report those stories

mediate to attempt to solve a dispute by working with both sides to reach an agreement

microtargeting an approach to campaigning that uses databases to identify specific groups of voters who can then be targeted with campaign messages designed to appeal to their interests

midterm election an election held in the even-numbered years between presidential elections

military tribunal a court in which officers from the armed forces serve as both judge and jury

militia a reserve army made up civilians who are trained to fight and can serve full time in an emergency

ministry an executive branch department, often in a parliamentary system

Miranda warnings the list of rights that must be read to a criminal suspect at the time of his or her arrest

misdemeanor a minor crime, typically punishable by a fine or no more than one year in prison

mixed economy an economic system that combines market forces with elements of a command economy

monarchy a system of government in which a single ruler exercises supreme power based on heredity or divine right

most-favored-nation clause a clause in a U.S. trade agreement that grants trade advantages to a foreign country doing business with the United States

mudslinging emphasizing the negative aspects of an opponent or policy; a feature of negative campaigning

multilateral having to do with three or more countries

N

name-calling a persuasive technique that involves attacking a candidate's opponents to distract voters from the real issues of a campaign

national debt the amount of money a country owes to lenders

nationalization the transfer of private property to government ownership

nation-state an independent state, especially one in which the people share a common culture

naturalization a legal process through which a person not granted citizenship by birth can become a citizen of that country

natural law a universal set of moral principles believed to come from humans' basic sense of right and wrong that can be applied to any culture or system of justice

natural rights rights that all people have by virtue of being human

Nazism a form of totalitarianism and type of fascism, based in part on the myth of racial superiority; developed in Germany before World War II

Necessary and Proper Clause a clause in Article 1, Section 8 of the U.S. Constitution, which says that Congress can "make all laws which shall be necessary and proper" for carrying out its duties; also known as the Elastic Clause

negative campaigning trying to win an advantage in a campaign by emphasizing negative aspects of an opponent or policy

new federalism a federal system guided by a policy of returning power to the state and local governments; block grants are a key element of new federalism

news media newspapers, news magazines, and broadcast news shows

nongovernmental organization (NGO) an international group formed by private individuals and associations to provide a service or pursue a public policy

nonpartisan primary a primary election in which political parties do not play a role, such as a local school board election

O

obscenity speech or other forms of expression considered offensive to conventional standards of decency

off-the-record conversation a news interview held under rules that allow the reporter to reveal the content of the interview but not the source

off-year election an election held in odd-numbered years

on-the-record conversation a news interview held under rules that allow the reporter to reveal both the content of the interview and the source

open primary a primary election in which voters can choose which party primary they vote in on Election Day regardless of their party affiliation; also known as a pick-a-party primary

open rule a condition placed on a bill by the House Rules Committee that permits floor debate and amendments; this allows opponents to change the bill or even kill it

opinion journalism the expression of personal views and opinions in the news media, with little or no attempt to make that coverage objective

opinion makers people who have a strong influence on public opinion

opinion poll a method of measuring public opinion by asking questions of a random sample of people and using their answers to represent the views of the broader population

oral argument the phase in a Supreme Court case when attorneys from both sides present their views on the case

original intent what the framers of the U.S. Constitution meant or were trying to achieve when they wrote the original document

originalism an approach to interpreting the U.S. Constitution that relies primarily on the original language of the document and the perceived intent of the framers; also known as strict construction

original jurisdiction a court's authority to hear a case for the first time, before it appears in any other court

P

pardon a decree that frees a person from punishment for a crime

parliament a legislative assembly in which elected representatives debate and vote on proposed laws

parliamentary democracy a political system in which voters elect lawmakers to represent them in the nation's parliament; the elected lawmakers choose a prime minister to head the executive branch

parole an early release from prison based on good behavior

party base political activists who embrace the core values of their party and are more likely to vote in primary elections than are centrist voters

patent a grant from the government that gives an inventor the exclusive right to make or sell an invention

peremptory challenge a rejection of a prospective juror for which no specific reason need be given

photo op a carefully staged event designed to produce memorable photographs and video images

physical evidence any physical object submitted as evidence in a trial, including fingerprints and DNA samples

piracy the illegal use of copyrighted intellectual property, such as movies or software

plain folks a persuasive technique that involves the use of everyday images and language to convince voters that a candidate is a regular person who understands the needs and concerns of average people

plaintiff the person or party who brings a lawsuit, or legal action, against another party in a civil case

platform a political party's statement of principles and objectives

plea bargain an agreement whereby a defendant pleads guilty in return for a lesser charge or reduced sentence

pluralism the idea that political power should be distributed and shared among various groups in a society

plurality the largest number of votes in an election; in elections with more than two candidates, the winner by a plurality may receive fewer than 50 percent of the votes cast

pocket veto the automatic killing of a bill by refusing to either sign it or veto it; this can occur only in the final days of a congressional session

political action committee (PAC) an organization that raises and distributes funds to candidates running for office

political culture a society's framework of shared values, beliefs, and attitudes concerning politics and government

political party an organization that seeks to achieve power by electing its members to public office

political socialization the process by which people form their political values and attitudes

politics the process and method of making decisions for groups, generally applied to governments though also seen in other human interactions

polity an ancient Greek concept of representative government in which the well-intentioned many rule for the benefit of all

polling place the location in each precinct where voters cast ballots

poll watcher a volunteer who monitors the voting process at the polling place

popular sovereignty the principle that the people are the ultimate source of the authority and legitimacy of a government

pork publicly funded projects secured by legislators to benefit their home districts or states

power the ability to cause others to behave as they might not otherwise choose to do

power of recognition the power of the House speaker or Senate majority leader to grant permission to speak on the House or Senate floor; no member may address the chamber without being recognized by the leader

precedent a decision by a court that serves as an example or guide for future decisions

precinct a local voting district of a city or town

preponderance of evidence the idea that the weight of the plaintiff's evidence in a civil trial clearly points to the defendant being at fault

presidential democracy a political system in which voters chose a president to lead the government as head of the executive branch

presidential election an election held every four years on even-numbered years

primary election an election in which voters determine their party's nominee for an elective office

prime minister the chief executive in a parliamentary democracy

print media means of communication that distribute information with paper and ink to a mass audience, particularly newspapers and magazines

prior restraint an attempt by government to prevent the publication or broadcast of material considered harmful

privatization the practice of contracting private companies to do jobs once done by civil servants

probable cause reasonable suspicion of criminal behavior

procedural due process the principle that the procedures followed by the government in enforcing the law must not violate constitutional rights and liberties

progressive tax any tax in which the burden falls more heavily on the rich than the poor

property tax a tax levied on the value of real property, such as land, homes, and buildings

proportional representation an electoral system common to parliamentary democracies in which citizens vote more for parties than for individual candidates; a party wins seats in parliament based on its proportion of the popular vote

prosecution the attorneys representing the government and the people in a criminal case

protocol an amendment or addition to a treaty or convention

public agenda a set of priorities for public action

public good a product or service that is available for all people to consume, whether they pay for it or not

public opinion the sum of many individual opinions, beliefs, or attitudes about a public person or issue

public policy a plan or course of action initiated by government to achieve a stated goal

push poll a phone survey sponsored by a political candidate that provides damaging information on an opponent in order to "push" voters away from that opponent

Q

quorum a fixed number of people, often a majority, who must be present for an organization to conduct business

R

random sample a group of people selected at random from the general population; used in opinion polling

ratification formal approval of an agreement, treaty, or constitution

recall election an electoral process through which citizens can vote an elected official out of office

redistricting the process of redrawing the geographic boundaries of legislative districts after a census to reflect population changes

referendum process a form of direct democracy in which citizens vote to approve or reject laws passed by a legislature

regressive tax any tax in which the burden falls more heavily on the poor than the rich, at least as a percentage of their incomes

regulated federalism a federal system dominated by the national government; tightly controlled grants and unfunded mandates are key elements of regulated federalism

representative democracy a democratic form of government in which elected representatives make public decisions on behalf of the citizens

representative government a political system in which power is exercised by elected leaders who work in the interests of the people

reprieve a postponement of punishment for a crime

republic a nation in which supreme power rests with the citizens and is exercised by their elected representatives

republican government a representative political system in which authority comes from the people and is exercised by elected officials

republicanism the idea that people elect leaders to a governing body of citizens

reserved powers powers kept by the states under the U.S. Constitution

resident alien an immigrant who has legal status in the United States; a lawful permanent resident

restitution a repayment by an offender to a victim for losses, damages, or injuries resulting from a crime

retail politics an approach to campaigning based on direct contact with voters

retention election an election in which voters are asked to confirm or reject a judge's appointment to office

revenue government income, raised through taxes and other means, to be used for public expenses

rider an amendment attached to a bill that has little or no relation to the subject of the bill

roll-call vote a method of voting in Congress in which members register their vote individually, either by voice vote (in the Senate) or by electronic means (in the House)

rule of law the principle that government is based on clear and fairly enforced laws and that no one is above the law

runoff election a second election to determine a clear winner, following a first election in which no candidate received a majority of the votes

S

sales tax a tax on the sale of goods that is paid by the customer at the time of purchase

sanction a measure taken by one or more nations to pressure another country into changing its policies or complying with international law

scientific sampling the selection of a small group of people that is representative of the whole population; used in opinion polling

search warrant a document issued by a judge that authorizes law enforcement officers to search a person's property or possessions

secular not religious or spiritual in nature

select committee a temporary committee formed by either the House or Senate to investigate a specific problem; also called a special committee

self-announcement the action of announcing one's candidacy for public office

self-incrimination statements, usually made under oath, suggesting that the person speaking is guilty of a crime

senatorial courtesy a rule that allows a senator to block the nomination of an official to a federal position, such as a judgeship, in his or her home state

seniority rule the tradition that a congressional committee member's seniority—the number of years of unbroken service on a committee—determines that member's position on the committee

sentencing the stage of a trial when the judge announces the punishment for a crime

separation of powers the idea that the powers of a government should be split between two or more strongly independent branches to prevent any one person or group from gaining too much power

single-party state a nation-state in which only one political party is allowed to rule under the constitution

slander orally spreading false information about someone with intent to cause harm

soap opera stories election news coverage that focuses on the ups and downs of candidates and their campaigns

social capital the attitude, spirit, and willingness of people to engage together in civic activities; the connections and bonds that people can draw on to solve common problems

social contract theory the idea that the legitimacy of a government stems from an unwritten contract between the ruler and the ruled; a ruler who breaks this contract by abusing people's rights loses legitimacy and may be overthrown

social insurance tax a tax used to fund government assistance to the elderly and to unemployed or disabled workers

socialism an economic system that calls for public ownership of the means of production

soft money unregulated money donated to a political party for such purposes as voter education; by law, parties cannot use soft money to support a specific candidate or campaign

sound bite a short quote for the news media that conveys information or opinions in a catchy or memorable way

sovereignty the right to exercise supreme authority over a geographic region, a group of people, or oneself

special committee a temporary committee formed by either the House or Senate to investigate a specific problem; also called a select committee

special interest a group that seeks to influence government policy-making and decision making to further its particular goals; an interest group

special-purpose district a local government district established for a specific purpose, such as providing school or fire services; these districts operate independently of other local units of government

spin the deliberate shading of information about a person or an event in an attempt to influence public opinion

staged event a political event organized to attract and shape media coverage

standing committee a permanent committee of legislators from either the House or Senate responsible for specific policy areas, such as foreign affairs or agriculture

standing vote a method of voting in Congress in which members stand up as a group, first those who support the bill and then those who oppose it; individual votes are not recorded in a standing vote

stare decisis a legal doctrine requiring lower courts to honor rulings made by higher courts

straw poll an informal survey of opinion conducted by a show of hands or some other means of counting preferences

strict construction a literal approach to interpreting the U.S. Constitution, using the exact words of the document

stump speech a candidate's "standard" speech, which is repeated throughout his or her campaign

subcommittee a small legislative committee within a larger, standing committee; subcommittees do much of the work of reviewing legislation

substantive due process the principle that the substance of the laws enforced by the government must not violate constitutional rights and liberties

suffrage the right to vote

summit a gathering of heads of state or other high-ranking officials to discuss matters of great importance to their countries

supermajority a number of votes greater than a simple majority, sometimes required to pass a particular motion or proposal

supranational organization a world or regional organization that is not tied to any one country

Supremacy Clause a clause in Article VI of the U.S. Constitution, stating that it is the "supreme Law of the Land"; this means that federal law supersedes all state and local laws

surveillance warrant a court authorization that allows wiretaps, videotaping, property searches, and other spying on criminal suspects

sustainable development economic development that meets the needs of people today without exhausting the resources that will be needed to sustain future generations

swing voter an independent voter who does not have a strong party affiliation

symbolic speech conduct that conveys a message without spoken words

T

Takings Clause a clause in the Fifth Amendment that prohibits the government from taking private property for public use "without just compensation"

Tax Freedom Day the date, calculated each year, when the country has earned enough income to pay its annual tax burden; rising budgets have pushed this date back over time

term limits a restriction on the number of terms an elected official may serve in a given office

testimonial a persuasive technique that involves showing famous people endorsing a candidate or proposal in order to convince others to support that person or cause

theocracy a government headed by religious leaders

think tank an organization of scholars and policy experts who study public issues and write articles and books summarizing their research

totalitarianism an extreme form of authoritarian rule in which the state seeks to control every aspect of its citizens' lives

tracking poll a survey used on a daily basis during a political campaign to measure the level of support for a candidate

traditional economy an economic system in which decisions about what to produce and how are made on the basis of customs, beliefs, and tradition

transfer a persuasive technique that involves associating a candidate or idea with a positive symbol or image, such as the American flag

trial balloon an idea or proposal voiced by a public official to a reporter, off the record, to test the public's reaction; if the reaction is negative, the official can drop the idea without damaging his or her reputation

tribute payments in money or goods to ancient empires by smaller states that were under their control

two-party system a political system in which two parties dominate the electoral process and control the government

U

unalienable rights a person's basic individual rights to life, liberty, and the pursuit of happiness; Thomas Jefferson's interpretation of John Locke's natural rights

undocumented immigrant a person who has come to the United States to live and work without the required legal papers

unenumerated rights rights not specifically listed in the Bill of Rights but given general protection under the Ninth Amendment

unfunded mandate a regulation or policy imposed by the national government on state and local governments without adequate federal funds to carry out the policy

unicameral made up of one house, as in a unicameral legislature

unitary system of government a political system in which the constitution concentrates power in the national, or central, government

up-or-down vote a direct vote on a bill in the full House or Senate; the bill must be approved or rejected as is, with no further amendments or delays

user fee a fee charged to use public facilities and services and for permits and licenses

V

veto power the power of the president to reject a bill and send it back to Congress

visa an official document issued by a country's government allowing a foreigner to enter and travel in that country

voice vote a method of voting in Congress in which members call out their vote as a group, first those who support the bill (saying "aye"), followed by those who oppose it (saying "no"); individual votes are not recorded in a voice vote

voir dire the process during jury selection in which the lawyers and judge question potential jurors to determine whether there is reason to disqualify them from a trial

vote of no confidence a majority vote in parliament showing disapproval of a prime minister's performance; such a vote prompts new elections and a change of leadership

voter registration the process of signing up to vote

voter turnout the proportion of the voting-age population that actually votes

W

warrant a document issued by a judge that authorizes law enforcement officers to carry out a search, seizure of evidence, or arrest

Warrant Clause a portion of the Fourth Amendment that sets out certain conditions under which warrants can be issued

warrantless arrest an arrest of a suspect without a warrant, often at the scene of the crime

war chest funds collected by a candidate to spend on a political campaign

weapons of mass destruction weapons that can produce widespread death and destruction, such as nuclear or chemical weapons

whistle-blower an employee or former employee who exposes wrongdoing within an organization in the hope of stopping it

wholesale politics an approach to campaigning that targets large numbers of voters through direct-mail or media campaigns

winner-take-all system an electoral system that awards offices to the highest vote-getters without ensuring representation for voters in the minority; under this system, a slim majority of voters can control 100 percent of elected offices

World Wide Web an information system that makes documents stored in computers around the world accessible to users via an Internet connection

writ of certiorari an order from the Supreme Court to a lower court to provide the records of a case the Court has decided to review

Page numbers in **bold** indicate definitions.

A

AARP, 143

Abdullah, King, 22

Abrams v. United States, 82

absentee ballots, **182**

absolute monarchies, **20**

absolute monarchs, **20**

abstain, **224**

abuse of power, **3**

accused, rights of, 64, 90

acquittal, **300**

Acton, Lord, 3

Adams, John
   court-packing scheme, 72
   Declaration of Independence and, 45
   as diplomat, 49
   Electoral College and, 184
   independence speech, 37
   on political parties, 136
   presidency and, 138

Adams, Samuel, 49

administration, **231, 244**

advertising, in election campaigns, 164–166, 188

advocacy, **335**

affirmative action, **278**

Affordable Care Act of 2010, 104, 284–285

African Americans
   as chief executives, 233
   in Congress, 197
   desegregation of military by Truman and, 240
   use of federal courts to end segregation, 277–278
   voting rights, 173

African Union (AU), 333

age, and voter behavior, 189, 190

agenda-setting power, **162**

agents of socialization, **154,** 155

AIDS, 331

airport searches, 292

Albert, Carl, 217–218

alcohol, sales banned, 65, 66

Allen, Cathy, 167

al Qaeda, 316
   September 11, 2001, 311, 316

ambassadors, **309, 313**

Amendments. *See* constitutional amendments

American Association for Public Opinion Research, 160

American Automobile Association (AAA), 143

American Bar Association (ABA), 280

American Cancer Society, 148

American Civil Liberties Union (ACLU), 81, 143, 281

American democracy, roots of
   Anti-Federalists' views, 51–52
   Articles of Confederation, 47–48
   benign neglect, 43–45
   Bill of Rights, 54–55, 64
   colonial views of government, 38–42
   compromises, 49–50
   Constitutional Convention, 49
   creating a new government, 46–47
   Declaration of Independence, 45–46, 55
   English Enlightenment thinkers, 40–41
   English roots, 39–40
   executive branch, 50–51
   Federalists' views, 52–53
   foundational concepts, timeline, 38–39
   framing constitutions, 47–51
   French Enlightenment thinkers, 40–42
   introduction, 37–38
   ratifying the Constitution, 51–54
   religious and classical roots, 38–39
   Revolutionary War, 42–47
   state constitutions, 47
   summary, 55

American Legion, 143

American Lung Association, 148

American Revolution, 20

Americans for Prosperity, 136

American Socialist Party, 79

"Americans' Political Divisions Not Necessarily Bad, Experts Say" (Austein), 150–151

Americans with Disabilities Act, 148

AmeriCorps, 246

amicus curiae briefs, **281**

amnesty, **236**

Amnesty International, 334, 337

Annan, Kofi, 332

Anti-Federalists, **51–52**

antismoking laws, 148

antiterrorism, **322–323**

ANZUS, 333

Apodaca v. Oregon, 297–298

appeals (criminal trials), 300–303, 305

appearance, initial, 295

appellate courts, 275, 277–278

appellate jurisdiction, **273,** 275, 277–278

appointment, of judges, 275

apportionment, **97, 106,** 198

appropriations, **195, 206,** 259

Appropriations Committee (Senate), 225

Appropriations Committees (House of Representatives), 225

Aquinas, Thomas, 38

Arab Spring, 22, 34–35

"The Arab Uprisings and Their Global Repercussions" (Puddington), 34–35

"A Republic, If You Can Keep It" (Beeman), 56–57

aristocracy, 6

Aristotle, 6

Arizona v. United States (2012), 109

C

cabinets, **231, 236–237**
California, 233
California Global Warming Solutions Act, 340
cameras in the courtroom, 281
Cameron, Simon, 225
campaign contributions, 188
campaign finance, 188–189, 191
campaign funds, 199
campaign organizations, 176–177
Campbell, Ben Nighthorse, 224
Canada, 43
candidates
    characteristics of, and voter behavior, 190
    choosing, 136, 175–186, 190
    political party affiliations and, 186
    route to nomination, 178
capital, 30
capital crimes, **288**
capitalism, **31**
capital punishment, 91–92, 302, 303
Capitol Hill, 217
carbon dioxide emissions, 340
card-stacking, in political campaigns, 165
CARE, 335
Carr, Joe, 107
Carter, Jimmy, 235, 317
Carthage, Punic Wars, 12
casework, **195, 208–209**
Castro, Fidel, 310
caucuses, **171, 177**
    in Congress, 204, 216
    in elections, 177–178, 191
Celler, Emanuel, 220
censuses, 50
Central Intelligence Agency (CIA), 246, 319, 320
centrism, **127**
centrist voters, 141
characteristics of, and voter behavior, 190
Charles I, 39
charter, **39**
Charters of Freedom, 54
Chávez, César, 10–11

checks and balances, **59, 68**–69, 205, 243, 276. *See also* separation of powers
Chenette, Justin, 196
Cheney, Dick, 234
chief citizen, 241, 242
chief diplomat, 241–242
chief executives, **232.** *See also* president
    election of, 234
    qualifications for, 233
    removal of, 234–235
    types of, 232, 249
chief manager of the economy, 241, 242
chief of party, 241, 242
chief of staff, **244**
chief of state, 240, 241
chief policymaker, 241, 242
child labor abuses, 338
children, rights of, 290–291
China
    Communist Party, 26
    form of government, 5, 21, 33
    legitimacy of rulers, 4
    power to rule, 2
    summit between Nixon and Mao, 314
    U.S. diplomatic relations with, 314
choosing, 136, 175–180, 190
    political party affiliations and, 186
    route to nomination, 178
Christian Coalition of America, 143
Christie, Chris, 242
Christmas tree bills, **215, 223**
Chung, Connie, 160
church-state separation, 83–84
Cincinnatus, 46
circumstantial evidence, **291**
citizen demand, and bureaucracies, 247
citizen groups, 142
citizen legislatures, 209
citizenship, **117, 118**
    process of, 121–123
Citizens United v. Federal Election Commission, 189
city governments, 111, 112
city-states, **18**–19
civic duty, 124

civic engagement, 117, 127–131, 131
civic life, 127–131
civic specialists, 130, 131
civic virtue, **39**
civil, **12**
civil disobedience, **12**–13
civil law, **269, 270**
civil liberties, **79, 80,** 93
civil rights, 66, 79, **80,** 118–121, 173
Civil Rights Act (1964), 120, 121, 148
civil servants, **246–247**
civil society, **117, 127–128**
civil trials, 64, 90, 270, 271
Clay, Henry, 9
clear and present danger test, 80, 82, 85
climate change, 339–341
Climate Change Caucus, 204
Clinton, Bill, 136
    action against ethnic cleansing in Serbia, 318
    budget crisis and, 260
    on César Chávez, 10
    foreign policy of, 322
    government information given to press and, 163
    health care and, 156
    impeachment of, 236
    1992 presidential campaign, 182, 183
    1996 presidential campaign, 183
    trade with Vietnam, 314
    use of new media, 161–162
Clinton, Hillary, 319
closed primaries, **175**
closed rule, **221**
cloture, **215, 222**–223
CNN, 163
coalitions, 181–182, 204
coattail effect, **171, 182**
coercion, **2,** 3, 5, 316
Cold War, 317, 322
Cole, David, 284
collective action, 8–9
collective security, **327, 329**
colonial forms of government, 42
colonial views of government, 38–42
command economies, **17, 31**–32
commander in chief, 240–241

Notes

Chapter 1

1: Thomas Paine, *Common Sense,* 1776, at www.bartleby.com. **1–2:** CNN News/Orc International Poll, Sept. 23-25, 2011, at "Major Institutions," www.pollingreport.com. **2:** Max Weber, in John Kenneth Galbraith, *The Anatomy of Power* (Boston: Houghton Mifflin, 1983). Kenneth E. Boulding, *Three Faces of Power* (Newbury Park, CA: Sage, 1990). **3:** Paine, *Common Sense.* Lord Acton, in a letter to Mandell Creighton, Apr. 5, 1887, at www.bartleby.com. **4:** Thomas Hobbes, *Of Man, Being the First Part of Leviathan* (New York: P.F. Collier & Son, 1909–1914), at www.bartleby.com. **6:** Aristotle, *Politics,* Book IV, trans. Benjamin Jowett, at classics.mit.edu. **9:** Margaret Mead, Institute for Intercultural Studies, www.intercultural-studies.org. **10:** Bill Clinton, in "Remarks by the President in Medal of Freedom Ceremony," Aug. 8, 1994, at www.medaloffreedom.com. **11:** Niccolò Machiavelli, *The Prince,* trans. W. K. Marriott (New York: Everyman's Library, 1505/1908), at www.constitution.org. **14–15:** From POWER SHIFT by Alvin Toffler, copyright © 1990 by Alvin Toffler and Heidi Toffler. Used by permission of Bantam Books, a division of Random House, Inc.

Chapter 2

19: "Pericles' Funeral Oration," in Thucydides, *History of the Peloponnesian War,* trans. Rex Warner (New York: Penguin Classics, 1954/1986). **23:** Ayatollah Khomeini, in DK Publishing, *How Governments Work: The Inside Guide to the Politics of the World* (New York: Dorling Kindersley, 2006). **32:** Karl Marx and Friedrich Engels, *The Communist Manifesto,* trans. Samuel Moore (London: Penguin Classics, 1888/1967). **33:** Deng Xiaoping, in John Gittings, *The Changing Face of China: From Mao to Market* (New York: Oxford University Press, 2001). **34–35:** Arch Puddington, "The Arab Uprisings and Their Global Repercussions," 2012, at www.freedomhouse.org. Used by permission.

Chapter 3

37: John Adams, *Familiar Letters of John Adams and His Wife Abigail Adams, During the Revolution* (New York: Hurd and Houghton, 1876). Gerald Ford, "Remarks on the Bicentennial Celebration," July 4, 1976, at www.ford.utexas.edu. **40:** Hobbes, *Leviathan.* **41:** Hobbes, *Leviathan.* John Locke, *Two Treatises of Government,* ed. Peter Laslett (Cambridge: Cambridge University Press, 1988). Baron de Montesquieu, *The Spirit of the Laws,* trans. Thomas Nugent (London: J. Nourse, 1777). Jean-Jacques Rousseau, *The Social Contract,* 1762, at www.fordham.edu. **42:** Rousseau, *Social Contract.* **44:** George Washington, in a letter to Bryan Fairfax, Aug. 24, 1774, at gwpapers.virginia.edu. **47:** George Washington, in a letter to Lewis Nicola, May 22, 1782, at "Rediscovering George Washington," www.pbs.org. **52:** George Mason, *Objections to This Constitution of Government,* 1787, at www.gunstonhall.org. James Madison, *The Federalist* No. 10, Nov. 22, 1787, at www.ourdocuments.gov. **53:** James Madison, *The Federalist* No. 51, Feb. 6, 1788, at www.ourdocuments.gov. George Washington, "First Inaugural Address," Apr. 30, 1789, at www.archives.gov. **54:** Washington, "First Inaugural Address." Thomas Jefferson, in a letter to James Madison, Dec. 20, 1787, at "The American Presidency," www.brittanica.com. Jefferson, in a letter to James Madison, Mar. 15, 1789, at "The Founders' Constitution," press-pubs.uchicago.edu. William Blackstone, *Commentaries on the Laws of England,* 1765, at "Rights of the People: Individual Freedom and the Bill of Rights," usinfo.state.gov. **55:** James Madison, "Amendments to the Constitution, in *Annals of Congress,* Vol. 1, June 8, 1789, at "Congressional Observer Publications," www.proaxis.com. **56–57:** Robert R. Beeman, "A Republic, If You Can Keep It." Reprinted with permission of the National Constitution Center. Originally published online at www.constitutioncenter.org.

Chapter 4

64: Alexander Hamilton, speech at New York Ratifying Convention, June 28, 1788, in *Citizen Hamilton: The Wit and Wisdom of an American Founder,* eds. Donald R. Hickey and Connie D. Clark (Lanham, MD: Rowman & Littlefield, 2006). **66:** James Madison, *The Federalist* No. 51. **66–67:** James Madison, *The Federalist* No. 39, Jan. 16, 1788, at www.constitution.org. **68:** James Madison, *The Federalist* No. 47,

Jan. 30, 1788, at www.constitution. org. **69:** Alexander Hamilton, *The Federalist* No. 78, June 14, 1788, at www.constitution.org. **70:** Antonin Scalia, speech at the Woodrow Wilson Center, Mar. 14, 2005. **72:** William J. Brennan Jr., speech at Georgetown University, 1985, in *The Oxford Guide to the United States Government,* eds. John J. Patrick, Richard M. Pious, and Donald M. Ritchie (New York: Oxford University Press, 2001). **76–77:** Lois Puglionesi, "Zero Tolerance: Student Suspended for Taking Medicine," *Delaware County Daily Times,* Jan. 28, 2005. Used by permission.

Chapter 5
81: American Civil Liberties Union, "The Bill of Rights: A Brief History," Mar. 4, 2002, www.aclu.org. **86:** Thomas Jefferson, in Linda Monk, *The Bill of Rights: A User's Guide* (Alexandria, VA: Close Up Publishing, 1995). **87:** Richard Price, in Leonard W. Levy, *Origins of the Bill of Rights* (New Haven, CT: Yale University Press, 1999). **88:** Joseph Story, *Commentaries on the Constitution* (1893), at "The Founders' Constitution," press-pubs.uchicago.edu. **94–95:** "State of the First Amendment, 2012" at First Amendment Center, www. firstamendmentcenter.org. Used by permission.

Chapter 6
99: Jonah Goldberg, "United States of Happiness," *National Review Online,* Dec. 1, 2004, at www.nationalreview. com. **100:** Goldberg, "Happiness." James Madison, *The Federalist* No. 45,

Jan. 26, 1788, at www.constitution. org. **101:** Morton Grodzins, "The Federal System," *Goals of Americans* (1960). **102:** Timothy Conlan, *From New Federalism to Devolution: Twenty-five Years of Intergovernmental Reform* (Washington, DC: Brooking Institution Press, 1998). **108:** Jack Quinn, Donald J. Simon, and Jonathan B. Sallet, "Redrawing the Districts, Changing the Rules," *Washington Post National Weekly Edition,* Apr. 1, 1991. **109:** Chris Gregoire, quoted in "Gov. Gregoire to lead delegation on trade mission to India, Korea," Sep. 25, 2012, at www. governor.wa.gov. **114–115:** David L. Paletz, Diana Owen, and Timothy E. Cook, "Why Federalism Works (More or Less)," at Flat World Knowledge, www.flatworldknowledge.com.

Chapter 7
117: Alexis de Tocqueville, *Democracy in America,* ed. Richard D. Heffner (New York: Signet Classics/ Penguin, 2001). Robert D. Putnam, *Bowling Alone: The Collapse and Revival of American Community* (New York: Simon & Schuster, 2000). **121:** Tocqueville, *Democracy in America.* **126:** Libertarian Party platform, at www.lp.org. **126–127:** Green Party platform, at www. gp.org. Robert D. Putnam, Bowling Alone: The Collapse and Revival of American Community (New York: Simon & Schuster, 2000). **132–133:** U.S. Citizenship and Immigration Services, www.uscis.gov.

Chapter 8
135: League of Conservative Voters, "Romney Opposes Wind Energy Tax Credit," *YouTube* video, 0:31, October 1, 2012, at www.youtube. com. Americans for Prosperity, "We Stand with Coal," *YouTube* video, 1:05, October 24, 2012, at www.youtube.com. **136:** George Washington, "Farewell Address," 1796, at www.ourdocuments.gov. John Adams, in a letter to Jonathan Jackson, Oct. 2, 1780, in *The Works of John Adams, Second President of the United States: With a Life of the Author* (Boston: Little, Brown and Company, 1854), at books.google. com. Thomas Jefferson, in a letter to Francis Hopkinson, Mar. 13, 1789, at "The American Presidency," www.britannica.com. **143:** Archon Fung, "Can Social Movements Save Democracy?" *Boston Review,* Feb./ Mar. 2003, at bostonreview.net. **144:** Edward Kennedy, Dick Clark, and Robert Stafford, quoted in "The Swarming Lobbyists," *Time,* Aug. 7, 1978. **150–151:** Michelle Austein, "Americans' Political Divisions Not Necessarily Bad, Experts Say," Dec. 2007, at www.america.gov.

Chapter 9
153: Adlai Stevenson, 1952 presidential campaign, found in Jennifer G. Hickey, "Ads Treat Voters as Consumers—Washington Diary," Nov. 12, 2002, at findarticles.com. **158:** Gallup Poll, March 9–11, 2012, at "Full Trends: Environmental Proposals," www.gallup.com. **159:** Linda Mason, quoted in David Bauder, "News Organizations Proceeding with

Caution in Use of Exit Poll Information," Nov. 8, 2006, at Associated Press, www.associatedpress.com. **160:** John Dowdy, in Robert Erickson and Kent L. Tedin, *American Public Opinion: Its Origins, Content, and Impact* (New York: Longman Publishing Group, 2006). Connie Chung, in Erickson and Tedin, *American Public Opinion.* Erickson and Tedin, *American Public Opinion.* American Association for Public Opinion Research, "AAPOR Statement on 'Push' Polls," June 2007, at www.aapor.org. **163:** John L. Martin, quoted in Vernon Loeb, "Senate Bill Aims to Curb News Leaks," *Washington Post,* June 14, 2000. **167:** Adlai Stevenson, in William L. Safire, *Safire's Political Dictionary* (New York: Random House, 1978). **168–169:** Laurence Cruz, "2012—The Social Media Election?" Sep. 2012, at The Network from CIsco, www.newsroom.cisco.com.

Chapter 10

172: John Jay, in Carl Becker, *The United States: An Experiment in Democracy* (New Brunswick, NJ: Transaction publishers, 2001 [originally published in 1920]). **176:** Richard Adams, "Barack Obama tweets the start to his 2012 re-election campaign," *The Guardian,* April 4, 2011, at www.guardian.co.uk. Mitt Romney, Facebook profile, June 2, 2011, http://www.facebook.com/mittromney. **177:** Jesse Unruh, in Jackson K. Putnam, *Jess: The Political Career of Jesse Marvin Unruh* (Lanham, MD: University Press of America, 2005). **179:** Chris Cillizza and Jim VandeHei, "In Ohio, a Battle of Databases," *Washington Post,* Sep. 26, 2006, at www.washingtonpost.com. **188:** John McCain, in "McCain

Urges Reform of 527s," June 29, 2006, at mccain.senate.gov. **189:** James Madison, *The Federalist* No. 57, Feb. 19, 1788, at www.constitution.org. **192–193:** International Institute for Democracy and Electoral Assistance, "Compulsory Voting," Feb. 11, 2005. Reproduced by permission of International IDEA from "Compulsory Voting" © International Institute for Democracy and Electoral Assistance 2001. **193:** Griffin Bell, in Martin P. Wattenberg, *Where Have All the Voters Gone?* (Cambridge, MA: Harvard University Press, 2002).

Chapter 11

195: David Mayhew, *Congress: The Electoral Connection* (New Haven, CT: Yale University Press, 1974). **196:** Justin Chenette, quoted in "Lyndon State Senior Justin Chenette Elected State Rep. in Maine," Nov. 7, 2012, at www.lyndonstate.edu. James Madison, *The Federalist* No. 10. **200:** James Madison, *The Federalist* No. 51. George Washington and Thomas Jefferson, in Alan Gitelson, Robert Dudley, and Melvin Dubnick, *American Government* (Boston: Houghton Mifflin, 2007). **201:** Thomas P. O'Neill, Nov. 15, 1983, at www.rules.house.gov. **209:** Mary Reese, in "For Constituents, Help Is on the Hill," Feb. 22, 1999, at dreier.house.gov. **212–213:** Alan Rosenthal, for the National Conference of State Legislatures, "The Good Legislature." Used by permission.

Chapter 12

215: Lee H. Hamilton, *How Congress Works and Why You Should Care* (Bloomington: Indiana University Press, 2004). **216:** Congressional Quarterly, Guide to Congress, 5th ed., vol. 1 (Washington, DC: CQ

Press, 1999). **217:** Woodrow Wilson, *Congressional Government: A Study in American Politics* (1885), at www.wilsoncenter.org. **218:** Carl Albert, *Little Giant: The Life and Times of Speaker Carl Albert* (Norman: University Oklahoma Press, 1990). **220:** Hamilton, *How Congress Works.* Arlen Specter, in Bob Pool, "Survivors Take Stock of Gains Against Cancer," *LA Times,* May 30, 1997, at www.latimes.com. **221:** Porter J. Goss, in David E. Rosenbaum, "Big Hurdle for the Tax Bill: The 'Rule,'" *New York Times,* Apr. 2, 1995, at www.nytimes.com. **223:** Clinton Anderson, in "The Christmas Tree Bill," *Time,* Mar. 26, 1956, at www.time.com. **224:** Ben Nighthorse Campbell, in Alan F. Pater and Jason R. Pater, eds., *What They Said in 1993: The Yearbook of World Opinion* (Monitor Book Company, 1994). **225:** Robert Evans and Robert Novak, *Lyndon B. Johnson: The Exercise of Power* (New York: New American Library, 1966). **228–229:** William A. Niskanen, "Give Divided Government a Chance," Oct. 1, 2006, at the Cato Institute, www.cato.org. Used by permission.

Chapter 13

232: Gerald R. Ford, *A Time to Heal: The Autobiography of Gerald R. Ford* (New York: Harper & Row, 1979). **234:** John F. Kennedy, in a speech to the Greater Houston Ministerial Association, Sep. 12, 1960, at www.americanrhetoric.com. **236:** George Washington, in a letter to Catherine Macaulay Graham, Jan. 9, 1790, in Jared Sparks, *The Writings of George Washington* (Boston: Russell, Shattuck, and Williams, 1836). **238:** Andrew Jackson, "Veto Message Regarding the Bank of the United States," July 10,

1832, at The Avalon Project at Yale Law School, www.yale.edu. Abraham Lincoln, "First Inaugural Address," Mar. 4, 1861, in Carl Sandburg, *Abraham Lincoln: The Prairie Years* (New York: Harcourt, Brace & Co., 1928). **239:** Theodore Roosevelt, at American Experience, www.pbs.org. Theodore Roosevelt, "The New Nationalism" speech, Aug. 31, 1910, at usinfo.state.gov. Theodore Roosevelt, *Theodore Roosevelt: An Autobiography* (New York: Macmillan, 1913). Theodore J. Lowi, Benjamin Ginsberg, and Kenneth A. Shepsle, *American Government: Power and Purpose* (New York: W. W. Norton, 2005). **240:** Gitelson, Dudley, and Dubnick, *American Government.* **241:** Bruce Fein, quoted in "Wanted: One Chief Executive, No Experience Required," Jan. 10, 2001, at Leading the Nation, cnnstudentnews.cnn.com. **250–251:** ABC News/Weekly Reader Poll, "Run the Country? Most Teens Would Pass," Jan. 11, 2004. Special permission granted by Weekly Reader, published and copyrighted by Weekly Reader Corporation. All rights reserved.

Chapter 14
253–254: Barack Obama, State of the Union Address, Jan. 24, 2012, at www.whitehouse.gov. **256:** Richard Nixon, Jan. 31, 1973, at www.presidency.ucsb.edu. **258:** Barack Obama, "The Budget Message of the President," Feb. 13, 2012, at www.whitehouse.gov. Paul Ryan, quoted in "Ryan: President's Budget Ensures Debt Crisis and Decline," Feb. 13, 2012, www.budget.house.gov. Brian Reidl, "What's Wrong with the Federal Budget Process," Jan. 25, 2005, at The Heritage Foundation, www.heritage.org. **260:** Bill Clinton, quoted in "Record-breaking Federal Shutdown

Ends," Jan. 6, 1996, www.cnn.com. **263:** George W. Bush, State of the Union Address, Jan. 23, 2007, at www.whitehouse.gov. **266–267:** Lorie Konish, "Economists Debate Government's Role in Repairing Economies," Jan, 2012, www.onwallstreet.com. Reprinted by permission.

Chapter 15
276: Alexander Hamilton, *The Federalist* No. 78. **279:** Alexander Hamilton, *The Federalist* No. 78. **280:** William Rehnquist, *The Supreme Court: How It Was, How It Is* (New York: William Morrow, 1987). **281:** Elena Kagan, quoted in "Cameras in the Court," June 29, 2010, at www.c-span.org. Antonin Scalia, quoted in Alicia M. Cohn, "Justice Scalia: Cameras in Supreme Court would 'miseducate' Americans," *The Hill,* July 26, 2012, at www.thehill.com. **282:** John Harlan, in Gitelson, Dudley, and Dubnick, *American Government.* John Roberts, Supreme Court confirmation hearing, Sep. 13, 2005, at www.asksam.com. **283:** Roberts, Supreme Court confirmation hearing, Sep. 12, 2005. **284–285:** David Cole, "Obamacare Upheld: How and Why Did Justice Roberts Do It?," *The Nation,* June 28, 2012, at www.thenation.com. Used by permission.

Chapter 16
307–311: "The Importance of Jury Duty," Copyright ©2011 by Christina Habas, part of the This I Believe Essay Collection found at http://www.thisibelieve.org, Copyright ©2005–2013 by This I Believe, Inc. Reprinted with permission.

Chapter 17
311: George W. Bush, Address to a

Joint Session of Congress and the American People, Sep. 20, 2001, at www.whitehouse.gov. Theodore Roosevelt, Nobel Lecture, May 5, 1910, at nobelprize.org. **312:** Woodrow Wilson, U.S. Declaration of War with Germany, Apr. 2, 1917, at www.firstworldwar.com. **313:** John F. Kennedy, Inaugural Address, Jan. 20, 1961, at www.bartleby.com. Joseph S. Nye Jr., *Soft Power: The Means to Success in World Politics* (New York: PublicAffairs/Perseus Books Group, 2004). **314:** Richard Nixon, Feb. 1972, at "The Nixon Visit," Nixon's China Game, www.pbs.org. **316:** U.S. State Department, "Rhythm Road: American Music Abroad," at exhanges.state.gov. George Tenet, in Donna Miles, "Tenet Details Intelligence About Iraq's Weapons Program," American Forces Press Service, at www.defenselink.mil. Casper Weinberger, at "Interviews," Target America, www.pbs.org. **318:** The North Atlantic Treaty, Apr. 4, 1949, at www.nato.int. Tony Benn, at Moving Words, www.bbc.co.uk. **319:** Edward S. Corwin, *The President: Office and Powers, 1787–1984* (New York: New York University Press, 1984). **323:** George W. Bush, State of the Union Address, Jan. 29, 2002, at www.whitehouse.gov. **324–325:** Erla Zwingle, "A World Together" at Globalization, magma.nationalgeographic.com.

Chapter 18
327: Léo Mérorès, quoted in "Aid begins to arrive in Haiti for earthquake survivors in dire need," Jan. 14, 2010, at www.unicef.org. **331:** United Nations Millennium Declaration, Sep. 18, 2000, at www.un.org. **332:** Kofi Annan, "Message for the New Millennium," Dec. 30, 1999, at news.

bbc.co.uk. **334:** Jon Kyl, "Senator Calls on Congress and White House to Protect Troops from International Criminal Court," Dec. 10, 2004, at Global Policy Forum, www.global policy.org. "Rules Are Fine—For Them," *St. Louis Post-Dispatch,* July 2, 2002. **335:** John F. Kennedy, 1962, at www.care.org. Paul Barker, quoted in "CARE Stresses Long-Term Political Solution to Darfur Conflict," Aug. 1, 2007, at www.care.org. **336:** "Belarus must respect freedom of assembly, association and expression," Amnesty International, August 26, 2008, at www.amnesty.org. **337:** Edward Wong, "Chinese Defend Detention of Artist on Grounds of 'Economic Crimes,'" *The New York Times,* April 7, 2011, at www.nytimes.com. **338:** UN Convention on the Rights of the Child, Article 32, Nov. 20, 1989, at www.unhchr.ch. **339:** Union of Concerned Scientists, "World Scientists' Warning to Humanity," Apr. 1992. **340:** Joseph E. Aldy, "Per Capita Carbon Dioxide Emissions: Convergence or Divergence?" discussion paper for Resources for the Future (2005), www.rtf.org. **342-344:** From Knowledge@ Wharton, 5/21/12 Issue, © 2012 Knowledge@Wharton. All rights reserved. Used by permission and protected by the Copyright Laws of the United States. The printing, copying, redistribution, or retransmission of this Content without express written permission is prohibited.

Credits **415**

Shutterstock **144**: Frontpage/Shutterstock **145**: Ed Stock/iStockphoto **148**: JohnKwan/Shutterstock **149**: Reuters/CORBIS

Chapter 9
152: David J. & Janice L. Frent Collection/CORBIS **154**: Bettmann/CORBIS **154**: National Geographic Image Collection/Alamy **156**: Rena Schild/Shutterstock **161**: Woodooart/Dreamstime **162**: Bettmann/CORBIS **164**: David J. & Janice L. Frent Collection/Corbis **164**: Library of Congress **165**: The Granger Collection, NYC **165**: The Granger Collection, NYC **165**: The Art Archive at Art Resource, NY **165**: David J. & Janice L. Frent Collection/Corbis **165**: David J. & Janice L. Frent Collection/Corbis **166**: Associated Press **169**: winhorse/iStockphoto

Chapter 10
170: age fotostock/SuperStock **172**: Library of Congress **172**: Library of Congress **173**: Library of Congress **174**: 1999 Kevin KAL Kallaugher, The Baltimore Sun, www.kaltoons.com **176**: Giorgio Magini/iStockphoto **176**: John Tully/Corbis **177**: Permission of Harley Schwardron **179**: GYI NSEA/iStockphoto **179**: Rick Friedman/Corbis **180**: Library of Congress **182**: Bob Daemmrich/Alamy **183**: GYI NSEA/iStockphoto **185**: © 2013 Steven G. Artley-Artleytoons, Used by permission **186**: Gerard Gaal/Dreamstime **189**: Morin, The Miami Herald, Miami, USA/Cartoon International Arts www.cartoonweb.com

Chapter 11
194: GYI NSEA/iStockphoto **196**: meltechfoto/Shutterstock **199**: RJ Matson, The St. Louis Post Dispatch, and PoliticalCartoons.com **201**: GYI NSEA/iStockphoto **202**: GYI NSEA/iStockphoto **204**: White House Photo/Alamy **206**: Brooks Kraft/Corbis **208**: Jason Schulz/Dreamstime **210**: Andre Nantel/Shutterstock

Chapter 12
214: GYI NSEA/iStockphoto **216**: Cartoonresource/Shutterstock **217**: Library of Congress **218**: GYI NSEA/iStockphoto **219**: GYI NSEA/iStockphoto **220**: GYI NSEA/iStockphoto **221**: Cartoon Bank **222**: Cartoon Bank **223**: Library of Congress **224**: Bettmann/CORBIS **225**: GYI NSEA/iStockphoto **227**: Ronald Reagan Library, National Archives

Chapter 13
230: Richie Lomba/Dreamstime **232**: Library of Congress **234**: 2007 Cotham from cartoonbank.com **235**: Suzanne Tucker/Shutterstock **237**: oversnap/iStockphoto **237**: Library of Congress **238**: Library of Congress **239**: Library of Congress **239**: Franklin D. Roosevelt Library, National Archives **241**: mediaphotos/iStockphoto **241**: Rena Child/Shutterstock **241**: Richard Gunion/Dreamstime **241**: GYI NSEA/iStockphoto **241**: William J. Clinton Library, National Archives **241**: Matthias Haas/iStockphoto **241**: Leslie Banks/iStockphoto **241**: Roel Smart/iStockphoto **242**: Pablo Martinez Monsivais//AP/Corbis **246**: Corporation for National and Community Service **247**: Radekdrewek/Dreamstime **248**: O.S.H.A

Chapter 14
252: Martin H. Simon/Corbis **254**: Jeff Parker/www.caglecartoons **256**: Edmund S. Valtman, 1973, Library of Congress **260**: wonderlandstock/Alamy **263**: GYI NSEA/istockphoto

267: GYI NSEA/istockphoto

Chapter 15
268: Brandon Bourdages/Alamy **270**: The New Yorker Collection 1998 Al Ross from cartoonbank.com. All Rights Reserved **272**: Moodboard_Images/iStockphoto **275**: Corbis Premium RF/Alamy **279**: GYI NSEA/istockphoto **280**: K2 images/Shutterstock **280**: GYI NSEA/istockphoto **281**: Dana Verkouteran/AP/Corbis **285**: Cheryl Casey/Shutterstock.com **285**: Gerry Boughan/Shutterstock.com

Chapter 16
286: Library of Congress **288**: Rich Legg/iStockphoto **292**: Corbis RF Best/Alamy **293**: Navarone/Dreamstime **294**: Mikael Karlsson/Alamy **295**: Exactostock/SuperStock **296**: Steven Robertson **298**: Andrewgenn/Dreamstime **299**: Getty Images **300**: Guy Cali/Corbis **302**: Marmaduke St. John/Alamy **303**: Robert J. Daveant/Shutterstock **304**: Marmaduke St. John/Alamy **304**: Marmaduke St. John/Alamy **305**: The New Yorker Collection 1998 Leo Cullum from cartoonbank.com. **306**: Michelle Milano **307**: Tom Cheney/The New Yorker Collection/www.cartoonbank.com

Chapter 17
308: Everett Collection Inc/Alamy **310**: Ed Stock/iStockphoto **311**: Library of Congress **312**: jacus/iStockphoto **313**: SuperStock/Alamy **314**: Byron Schumaker/Alamy **315**: David Snyder/Dreamstime **316**: Getty Images **319**: Ed Stock/iStockphoto **321**: GYI NSEA/iStockphoto **323**: 2001 Steve Breen, Copley News Service **325**: Xiaofeng123/Dreamstime

Chapter 18